John Bull's
...tion and British Society,
1871–1971

JOHN BULL'S ISLAND
Immigration and British Society, 1871–1971

Colin Holmes

MACMILLAN

First published 1988 by
THE MACMILLAN PRESS LTD
Houndmills, Basingstoke, Hampshire RG21 2XS
and London
Companies and representatives
throughout the world

ISBN 0–333–28209–4 hardcover
ISBN 0–333–28210–8 paperback

A catalogue record for this book is available
from the British Library.

Printed in Hong Kong

Reprinted 1992

The Publishers wish to acknowledge the following illustration
sources:

The Manchester Jewish Museum, the Bradford Heritage Recording
Unit, the Sheffield Local History Library, the National Museum of
Wales and the BBC Hulton Picture Library.

Contents

Preface

THIS book is a survey of immigration into Britain between 1871 and 1971, or rather a consideration of a number of salient developments during the hundred years which culminated in the important Immigration Act of 1971. The three main themes which come under discussion are: which immigrant and refugee groups came to Britain during these years and why did they come? What were the major distinguishing features of the economic and social history of such groups? How were these newcomers received by British society? These themes are separated for the purpose of analysis and discussion. However, interlinkages are recognised and ideally chapters need to be read in whole rather than in part. My emphasis throughout is upon the first generation: a history of the descendants of immigrants and refugees would require another and different book.

Soon after I began the research it became clear that there were significant gaps in existing information and knowledge. I have tried to fill some of these and indicated other areas where additional work is still required. In doing so, I concluded my collection of material in February 1986. In a wide-ranging survey of this kind a clear cut-off point is particularly essential. Some unpublished work which I saw, or knew of, has been printed subsequently and this point is recognised in the notes. It is also worth emphasising at this point that my focus is that of the historian, albeit one who is prepared to search beyond conventional sources for information and illumination. No attempt is made to compete with the specialised work of migration theorists or the models of sociologists.

In producing the book I have benefited from the help and advice of a number of friends and colleagues, several of whom deserve special mention. David Mayall, whose forthcoming monograph on gypsies in Britain is awaited with interest, read some of my work. So did Kenny Lunn, who provided me with particular guidance on labour and immigration. I am also grateful to Panikos Panayi who is currently extending our knowledge of Germans in Britain during the Great War. Tony Kushner, now the Parkes Fellow at Southampton

University, who is a rich source of information on recent anti-Semitism in Britain, was particularly helpful and generous in pointing me in the direction of sources which related to the Second World War. Tom Gallagher was kind enough to loan material from his collection. Vic Gilbert, vigilant as ever, kept his eyes open for useful source material and I am also grateful to him for compiling the index. Alan Booth commented on recent aspects of British economic history. I benefited also from Michael Banton's reading of 'the post-war years' and the conclusion and from Vaughan Bevan's 'tutorials' on immigration law. Finally, I am particularly indebted to Victor Kiernan, who read the whole of the typescript and, drawing upon his wide knowledge, made a number of valuable suggestions. The full responsibility for the book, however, is mine alone.

I incurred a number of additional debts in the course of my research. In particular, I need to thank members of staff in the Bradford Heritage Recording Unit, the British Library, the British Library of Political and Economic Science, Colindale Newspaper Library, the County Library in Nottingham, Hull University Library, the Imperial War Museum, the Institute of Jewish Affairs, the Manchester Jewish Museum, the Office of Population Censuses and Surveys, the Public Record Office, Sheffield City Library, Sheffield University Library and the Wiener Library. It is also a pleasure to recall a particularly memorable visit to Southall with Manjit Dhesi and her father Sohan Dhesi. Pam Smith, who typed the whole of the manuscript, quickly and efficiently, deserves special thanks. Macmillan waited with great patience for the typescript, and I am grateful to Vanessa Couchman's understanding in this respect. The Nuffield Foundation provided the funds, without which the research could not have been completed.

Finally, my deep personal thanks go to Joyce Holmes and Rachel Holmes who lived with this book for far too long and did so with understanding, good humour and patience.

Colin Holmes

PART ONE

PART ONE

Introduction

'England with all the follies of feudalism and toryism which are peculiar to it is the only country to live in', Alexander Herzen to Karl Vogt, quoted in E. H. Carr, *The Romantic Exiles* (London, 1933), p. 135.

'"Have you ever heard", said Jonah, "of the Society for the Prevention of Cruelty to Alien Enemies?"
Adèle shook her head.
"I think you must have", said Jonah, "some people call it the British nation."', Dornford Yates, *Berry and Co* (London, 1920), p. 226.

1.

'WHEREVER homo sapiens made his first and on the whole regrettable appearance, it was not in Britain: all our ancestral stocks came from somewhere else'.[1] Indeed, 'The British are clearly among the most ethnically composite of the Europeans'.[2] Even so, there has been some reluctance to recognise this fact. The English, particularly, have long taken a deluded pride in their valorous ancestry, whose virtues were far more pleasing than those of the mongrel breed satirised in 1701 by Daniel Defoe in *The True-Born Englishman*.[3] However, it would be difficult to locate an epoch when some immigration did not take place.

But who needs to be considered when examining this process of inward movement? At the moment the term 'immigrant' has been given a precise definition in official statistics. The Office of Population Censuses and Surveys in its calculations of movement into the United Kingdom, has adopted the international statistical definition which categorises an immigrant as any person who, having resided abroad for a year, has declared an intention on entry of staying for a minimum period of one year. However, the OPCS has stressed that this categorisation does not correspond with any current legal definition.[4] Outside official sources the term has been used in a variety of ways, and, with a frightening elasticity, it has even been stretched to include those children born in Britain to immigrant parents.[5]

Viewed from an historical perspective, immigration between 1871 and 1971 involved some groups which arrived in Britain in order to find work on a temporary basis. The Irish minority contained many such sojourners into the twentieth century. Student sojourners of various nationalities also arrived. Other groups, such as the West Indians who came after the Second World War, intended a lengthier if not in every case permanent period in Britain in their search for work and subsequent self-improvement. Both groups, the sojourners of varying duration and those newcomers who settled permanently, are deserving of attention. Indeed, a wide range of people who for economic, social or cultural reasons, or a combination of these, took a decision to leave their native countries with the intention of staying temporarily or permanently in Britain require consideration. In addition, Britain witnessed over many years the arrival of refugees such as those who came in the 1930s from Nazi Germany in search of a base, temporary or permanent, from political, religious or racial persecution, or a mixture of such pressures.[6]

It should not be assumed, however, that groups were always susceptible to an easy categorisation or that a predictable future awaited them. At times, for example, governments were faced with dilemmas over what constituted a refugee.[7] Moreover, a mixture of personal and impersonal forces meant that over the course of time some sojourners became reconciled to a longer stay. Furthermore, the hopes of refugees were often dashed; there was seldom a quick return home.[8] In a neat reversal of the poet's strain it has been remarked that 'Many corners of English graveyards are for ever Poland, Italy or Spain'.[9] The graves contained in such spots are the cold, sombre reminders of a continual complex historical movement with its special mixture of human hopes, aspirations and disappointments.

2.

WHAT evidence is there of the presence of immigrants and refugees before 1871? Which groups were involved in the process of immigration? The movement of population into what is now called Britain stretched back towards the beginnings of recorded history, after the area became physically separated from the rest of Europe. In the ancient world, after this separation had occurred, the Roman invasion resulted in an army of occupation, visible signs of whose presence continue to attract interest in remote Northumbria around Hadrian's Wall, in Bath and elsewhere. But the invasion also brought in other Roman citizens even if numbers were not large. These 'heterogeneous outsiders' included traders and other colonists 'and, probably most numerous, soldiers from anywhere in the empire who settled after their years of service, with citizen status'.[10] As the wheel of history continued to turn, the later Saxon and Viking invasions introduced other cultural influences and, later still, the population which survived the Norman invasion in 1066 was soon to encounter a motley band of military and trading groups who came in the wake of the Conqueror.

Invasion was evidently a major influence in bringing about a mixture of peoples. After the Conquest in 1066, however, invaders became essentially a feature of the past. 'Immigration from now on was a matter of peaceful entry' by individuals or groups who had to find ways of fitting into a more or less orderly society under unified control.[11] In the medieval epoch newcomers arrived in the shape of Flemish clerks, Jewish financiers and traders and Lombards from Northern Italy, who also engaged in finance. Hanseatic merchants from north Germany, whose activities centred on their London depot, the so-called Steelyard near Blackfriars, constituted another powerful group of newcomers. In addition, craftsmen came from Flanders to work in the woollen industry, particularly in East Anglia; Germans, who had a reputation for mining expertise, could be found working in the silver and lead mines in the Lake District; Frenchmen worked in the early iron industry; Hollanders came to make salt, brew beer and develop the linen industry.[12]

The success of some of these groups, or individuals within their ranks, at times generated forms of xenophobia and resentment within the settled population. In 1290, for example, at a time when he was short of funds, Edward I exploited resentment against the Jewish community and proceeded to order the expulsion of Jews from his kingdom, once he had confiscated their bonds and personal possessions.[13] Much later, the Hanseatic merchants also came under attack. The association lost its special advantages in 1576 and 1579, and finally in 1589 the Steelyard came to an end.[14] The likes of George Gisze, from Danzig, captured for posterity by Hans Holbein in 'The Merchant of the Steelyard', were to be no more. Such hostility, directed against Jews and the Hanseatic merchants, constituted the tip of a more persistent friction.[15]

From the sixteenth century to the demonic changes brought about by the Industrial Revolution newcomers with diverse origins continued to arrive. Gypsies, who told enquirers that they had originated in Egypt, appeared in increasing numbers throughout the land, and although they did not pose an economic threat to the settled population they were persistently regarded with great suspicion if they showed signs of transcending their function as entertainers.[16] In addition, in the following century, there were increasing references to the presence of Africans, whose history in Britain can be traced back at least as far as the Roman occupation.[17] Although in the sixteenth century the Black population – the term is used throughout to denote only those of African or Afro-Caribbean origin – was numbered only in the hundreds, it did give rise to some official concern, which was reflected in 1596 when the government wrote to the local officials in London and other towns indicating that there were too many 'blackamoores' being introduced into the kingdom.[18] Following this, in 1601 a proclamation ordered their expulsion, although like the earlier attempt to expel the Jews in 1290, it could not be enforced absolutely.[19]

Apart from the arrival of gypsies and Africans, other groups of newcomers arrived in the early modern epoch. Italians 'first came to prominence (in Scotland) in the wake of the Renaissance in the sixteenth century' and were employed by James IV and VI to entertain the court at Holyrood House.[20] Among other groups to arrive were the Huguenots, Protestants from France, who were driven abroad after the death of Henry II in 1559 plunged France into more than 30 years of disruption and civil war. Protestants in the Spanish Netherlands also suffered at the hands of Catholic oppression and the repressive rule introduced by the Duke of Alva in 1567 produced its own flow of refugees. But the event most commonly associated with the tribulations of the Protestant minority, was the massacre in Paris on St Bartholomew's Day, on 24 August 1572, which caused a large number of refugees to scurry for shelter, some of whom fled to the eastern counties of England where their impact became particularly marked in towns such as Colchester.[21]

Many newcomers in the early modern epoch settled in the urban centres. But not all were to be found there. Germans engaged in the mining industry could still be spotted in remote parts of England. Furthermore, the influence of newcomers from the Netherlands was especially evident in the English countryside in the early years of the seventeenth century. On account of the experience they had gained in their native environment they were particularly adept in the management of water and one of their most distinctive contributions to the countryside was made by Cornelius Vermuyden who drained the Isle of Axholme in the 1620s.[22]

The seventeenth century witnessed other important developments. In 1656, after many years in exile, it was proposed that Jews should be readmitted for settlement in England and they were officially recognised as a community in 1664.[23] Shortly afterwards, Louis XIV's 'atavistic proscription of the Huguenots', through the Revocation of the Edict of Nantes in 1685, resulted in an addition to the French Protestant families who had arrived in the previous century.[24] Many of these later arrivals came from northern France, from Normandy and Brittany, and a fair proportion of the gentry among them settled down in Ireland after taking their revenge on the Catholics at the Battle of the Boyne in 1690. But others stayed in England and for them London was the great attraction, as it was for a large number of other newcomers. Once they were settled, the Huguenots developed the silk industry in Spitalfields, where names such as Fournier Street and houses on Princelet Street still bear testimony to a French presence. Apart from their skill in the silk trade they displayed a particular expertise in a number of crafts such as the making of clocks and instruments. On the whole, in fact, they were an important influence on the increasing commercialisation of society. 'Numbers of Huguenots from the middling ranks', we have been told, 'worked their way to solid professional or commercial positions and founded middle class families of good standing; in addition, not a few of them shone as merchants or financiers among the luminaries of the City'.[25] But their contribution to society went beyond the fundamental level of getting and spending. They also set up their own schools and made a distinctive impact on the world of scholarship. Within a Protestant country, in the course of building new lives, they were also able to pursue their religion without fear of reprisal.[26] A striking reminder that they did, can be found in the quiet of Winchester Cathedral in the memorial to Jean Serres, formerly of

Montauban, a man 'mourned by English friends in whose country he had taken refuge and who admired his indomitable spirit and faith in the Protestant religion'.[27]

For two centuries after the arrival of the Huguenots in the seventeenth century no major influx of immigrants or refugees took place although the flow of individuals and groups into Britain continued unabated. It was a German, George Frideric Handel, who composed the music for the Royal Fireworks in 1749 to celebrate the victory of Britain, a country ruled by German-born kings since 1714, over its major rival, France, in the War of the Austrian Succession. Handel's work was merely one reflection of the cultural talent that was imported from Europe.[28] On a less resounding note, the Palatinate refugees who arrived early in the eighteenth century were a source of public disquiet.[29]

But there were important developments during these years which involved the world beyond Europe. The so-called triangular slave trade, centred on ports such as Liverpool and Bristol, was at its peak in the eighteenth century and it guaranteed a continuing Black presence. Planters returning from the Caribbean, for example, were known to bring their Black slaves with them. Similarly, nabobs from the East sometimes imported slaves or attendants which in itself resulted in the development of a small Asian population.[30]

By the Georgian years an uncertain number of Blacks were scattered throughout British society, often in a service capacity as stable boys, grooms, valets or butlers. George I brought over two Black favourites, Mustapha and Mahomet, when he came from Hanover. Samuel Johnson had his servant Francis Barber, whose portrait was committed to canvas by Joshua Reynolds, and Reynolds himself had a Black servant in Bob White. In addition, some Blacks could be found in the armed forces; several regiments engaged Black trumpeters and drummers. Other Blacks provided various services and entertainment. Harriet, a Black whore, depicted by Hogarth in 'The Discovery', collected a distinguished clientèle, and Bill Richmond, who came to Britain from America, was a well-known figure in the boxing ring. Another familiar face was that of Black Billy Waters, a street musician, who worked a pitch outside the Adelphi Theatre in the Strand.[31]

Only a few Africans managed to transcend such roles. One who did was George Polgreen Bridgewater, a violinist, who made his reputation in London and benefited from having royalty as his patron.[32] A number of Africans in the course of receiving a European education also fared better than most.[33] Furthermore, a clutch of writers also made their mark. One of these was Ignatius Sancho. In his case he was aided by the Duke and Duchess of Montagu who provided him with books and educational opportunities as well as a degree of later financial support to offset his personal fecklessness. The result of Sancho's development was reflected in his poetry, two plays, a work on musical theory, as well as a posthumous collection of letters. Another striking example of this other Black world was Olaudah Equiano. Like Sancho he was sold into slavery, but purchased his freedom in America and succeeded in educating himself through the help of white patrons. Equiano's most notable monument was his autobiography, *The Interesting Narrative of the Life of Olaudah Equiano, or Gustavus Vassa, the African, written by himself*, which appeared in 1789 and was an immediate best seller. Although both Sancho and Equiano achieved a degree of personal success they were not blind to the less fortunate fate of their Black contemporaries. In fact, along with their contemporary, Ottobah Cugoano, who had been brought to England in 1772, and was subsequently released from slavery by his master, they became involved in the agitation to abolish the slave trade. It was individuals such as these who constituted what has been called 'The Free Black Voice'.[34]

But it is worth reiterating that unlike Sancho, Equiano and Cugoano, the majority of Blacks were not free. Reminders of this subjection came strongly off the pages of eighteenth-century publications which carried advertisements on the sale of slaves. Other notices carried a more dramatic illustration of the status of Blacks. One of these advertisements read 'Matthew Dyer intimates to the public that he makes silver padlocks for Blacks or Dogs; collars etc'.[35] In fact, the status of Blacks became the subject of protracted debate and legal argument. Did slaves retain their slave status after they were brought from the colonies? Or should they be regarded as free once they breathed the air of Britain? It has often been assumed that the Mansfield Judgement of 1772 ended slavery in England, where most of the slaves in Britain were held, and thereby satisfied a campaign waged by reformers such as Granville Sharp. But this opinion can hardly be sustained. In a legal sense slavery in Britain was abolished with the Act of Parliament of 1834 that ended the institution in the colonies. In practice, however, it can be argued that slavery disappeared in England 'sometime between the 1760s and

1790s' not so much through the processes of law but as a consequence of the resistance and escape of the slaves themselves.[36]

Another important development in the late eighteenth century came in 1786 when the Sierra Leone scheme was devised. The intention of this project was to remove Blacks from British society at a time when the Black population, which was swollen following the American War of Independence, became perceived in official circles as a major social problem. This attempt at resettlement removed about 350 Blacks but the rest stayed in Britain.[37]

In the early nineteenth century there were Blacks who played a part in radical movements. There was also evidence of political activity by Indians by the 1830s.[38] In addition, Ira Alridge, was prominent as an actor, and another Black, Tom Molineaux was busy in the boxing ring.[39] Side by side with prominence and success, however, there was continued evidence of poverty among Blacks which was most graphically demonstrated in London in the rookeries of St Giles where, since the late eighteenth century, Blacks had been joined by Lascars who had been discharged from the ships of the East India Company.[40] The distress of this Asiatic minority, in fact, gave rise to continuing public concern.[41]

It should be recognised that even at the height of colonialism in the eighteenth century non-European minorities were overshadowed in size by those diverse groups who arrived from Europe from the western, central and eastern parts of that continent.[42] Moreover, all groups of newcomers in England, Wales and Scotland came to be dominated in numerical terms from the late eighteenth century by the growing presence of the Irish. The expansion of the economy in the late eighteenth century in the course of the Industrial Revolution substantially increased the demand for workers beyond the confines of the countryside where the migrant Irish had been traditionally employed and although part of this demand was met by the internal redeployment of labour it could not be entirely satisfied through such change. In similar situations most countries have made liberal use of foreign labour. But in the case of England, Scotland and Wales a supply was nearer at hand in Ireland; Irish strength helped to hew the railway network, to load and unload cargoes in the docks and to work the factories of King Cotton.[43]

The arrival of workers from Ireland was particularly evident between 1846 and 1856.[44] In fact, the weight of Irish immigration between the 1840s and 1860s was not surpassed again in the course of the nineteenth century. Although it was propelled by a great sense of human urgency this movement in the early and mid-Victorian years was 'purposive' rather than 'blind';[45] migration to Scotland was principally from Ulster,[46] the Irish in London came from the province of Munster, particularly from Cork,[47] and a significant number of the Irish in Bradford came from Queen's County and from Mayo and Sligo.[48]

In addition to the recruitment of a sizeable amount of raw labour from Ireland, as a result of which many Irish peasants were urbanised in England, Wales and Scotland, often in an atmosphere of suspicion and hostility, which at times, as in Stockport in 1852, resulted in collective violence against the Irish,[49] industrialisation in Britain eventually attracted 'fresh groups of capitalists from the continent'.[50] There was a prominent German minority deeply involved in finance and others from that part of the world were to be found in industry. The Engels family, whose primary business interests were in the Rhineland, was not alone in building new enterprises in Britain.[51] Ludwig Mond arrived in Britain from Germany in 1863 and soon set up a chemical business in Lancashire.[52] Within ten years he had joined forces with J. T. Brunner, the son of a Swiss pastor who had settled in Liverpool, to start Brunner-Mond, which in 1926 merged with Nobel Industries, the British Dye-Stuff Corporation and United Alkali Limited, to form ICI, Britain's best-known chemical company.[53] Other lesser-known entrepreneurial skills fructified in Britain and large northern cities such as Manchester and Bradford owed a great deal in the nineteenth century to German immigrant enterprise, the visual symbols of which can still be detected by an observant and watchful eye.[54]

Other groups who arrived between the mid-eighteenth century and the mid-Victorian years, came in flight from political upheaval or to escape the terror of persecution. For example, Jews arrived from Poland and Germany in the eighteenth century as a result of persecution which coincided with a deterioration in their economic conditions.[55] But the influx that captured greatest attention was that of the émigrés who left France in the wake of the 1789 Revolution. They were drawn particularly to London, where a small colony was established near Leicester Square.[56] However, it was not only Frenchmen who were affected by developments associated with the Revolution. The events unleashed in Paris in 1789 did not end there. The message of the Revolution was carried along with the tramp of revolutionary armies and it reverberated throughout most of Europe in the first half of the nineteenth century. As a result, immigration into Britain was further increased. In some cases the newcomers were political revolutionaries who fled to Britain in order to escape harassment and arrest. Karl Marx was one who concluded his exile in Britain. So too did Antonio Panizzi, a Liberal Italian émigré. While Marx worked away, as legend would have it, at seat 07, in the British Museum, Panizzi, who became principal librarian of the BM, planned its new reading room.[57] In turn, this contemplative blue-domed retreat was to become the haunt of many later émigrés who spun out their years of exile as the Museum's regulars.[58] However, not all of the early nineteenth century émigrés were Socialist or Liberal. Some represented the reverse side of the political coin. Louis Philippe from France and Prince Metternich from Austria both found temporary refuge in Britain. Then, as now, in fact, there was more to 'Mr. Smith' than the name would reveal. Such political émigrés, with their own societies, clubs, organisations and parties, replaced the religious refugees of former days.[59]

3.

Since 1871 immigrant and refugee groups have continued to arrive. Indeed, the years between 1871 and 1971 were some of the most significant in the history of immigration into Britain. To cite two developments only, immigrants were drawn increasingly from Britain's former imperial territories and, in the wake of strong pressures, Britain's traditional open-door policy on immigration was significantly amended. The experiences of some newcomers who arrived during these years, particularly those whose presence created responses which influenced official policy, have been assiduously recorded. As a result, the Jewish minority who arrived from the Russian Empire between 1881 and 1914 and the refugees from Hitlerite Germany have both received attention. So have the recent immigrants from the Caribbean, India and Pakistan. Indeed, a whole battery of sociologists, social workers, urban geographers and political scientists, often known pejoratively as 'the race relations industry', has been busily engaged for many years in studying these recent arrivals.[60] In sharp contrast, however, the *historical* experiences of minorities from the Caribbean and the Indian sub-continent have been less well treated.[61] Other groups have had their history captured at specific times but interest in them has then ended. The impact of German clerks on the late nineteenth-century clerical labour market, for example, a matter of deep concern at the time to English clerical workers, has been discussed within the wider context of the history of clerical workers.[62] The small Chinese community in the late nineteenth, early twentieth centuries has also attracted some interest.[63] In both cases these studies are small fragments isolated in time; there is no history of these minorities. But we should be grateful for existing detail, as we should also for the work of those who have started to recover the history of the Lithuanians and Catholic Poles, groups which, along with Jews, formed the great exodus from the tsar's empire in the late nineteenth, early twentieth century.[64]

Elsewhere, however, the gaps are more pronounced. Information on the Irish falls off considerably following the mid-Victorian years and there is no satisfactory general historical survey of the Irish minority in Britain.[65] Furthermore, Italians attracted attention, some of it of a sharply hostile nature, when they increased in numbers in the late nineteenth century. However, the history of this phase of immigration from Italy to Britain has remained largely neglected. The Italian immigration that followed the Second World War has also attracted little interest.[66] The history of French immigration into Britain has suffered from similar neglect.[67] Moreover, there are significant gaps elsewhere. For example, the history of the central and east European groups such as the Poles, the Ukrainians and, later, the Hungarians, who arrived in Britain after the end of the Second World War, has only just started to attract an appropriate level of attention.[68]

Anyone who, at this point in time, attempts to write a general history of immigration soon becomes aware of these variations. At times it is like staying at an oasis but as one moves elsewhere the territory can become an unexpected barren wasteland. A pioneer can effect some improvement, but the ground that needs to be covered is enormous and the best hope is that later travellers, cultivating their own special terrain, will add, by degrees, to the richness of the landscape.

4.

NONE of the foregoing should be taken to imply that the movement of population has been exclusively one-way. There is a long history of emigration from Britain and the outward exodus of population became very significant in the early nineteenth century. Part of this movement was organised. There were government-assisted colonisation schemes and Dr Barnardo's organisation was involved in arranging the emigration of children.[69] However, the majority of those who left their roots travelled 'for the most part either alone or with members of their immediate families or with friends to face the risks and uncertainties, the dangers and strangeness of new countries'.[70] The clenched hands of Ford Madox Brown's 'The last of England' serve as a permanent visual reminder of such unknown perils.

 Apart from the pressures that built up at times in Britain and the encouragement held out to emigrants in the receiving societies, emigration like immigration was facilitated by the improvement in communications which helped to open up a knowledge of some other societies. Movement in both directions was also aided by the revolution in transportation symbolised for those who shook the dust of Europe from their feet by the dominance of steam ships on the Atlantic run by the mid-1860s.[71] Some who made that long journey to America stayed there permanently but others passed to and fro between the two countries according to existing opportunities.[72] As the nineteenth century wore on, parts of the Commonwealth also assumed an increasing importance for emigration, and movement into these countries totally dwarfed that which went into the tropical territories acquired during the Imperialist expansion of the late nineteenth and early twentieth centuries. In these tropical areas rule was exercised through financial domination, the sweat of a small number of administrators and the blood of regular soldiers, rather than through the export and settlement of a population from the metropolitan country.[73]

In the present century movement out of Britain still continued. Australia, New Zealand, South Africa and North America, all proved attractive to British emigrants.[74] Moreover, some British subjects, reluctant to contribute socially from their success, retreated into the selfish, self-inflicted loneliness of a tax-exile territory.

In other words, between 1871 and 1971 Britain exported a

population; it did not simply gather to itself newcomers from many lands. Indeed, at most times during these hundred years Britain was a net exporter of population.[75] This observation helps to provide a sense of perspective to any consideration of why immigrants and refugees came to Britain between 1871 and 1971, the lives they led in their new-found environment, and the varying responses which their arrival and presence drew from within the ranks of the settled population.

PART TWO

PART TWO

I. Immigration in the Age of Imperialism

'The mere acceptance of the Jewish race, the mere recognition of its presence, does not rid either the Jewish people or the great majority of foreign peoples among whom they find themselves of an acute problem attached to their very presence', *The Eye-Witness*, 7 September 1911.

'I'm going back to Glenties when the harvest fields are brown,
And the Autumn sunset lingers on my little Irish town,
When the gossamer is shining where the moorland blossoms blow
I'll take the road across the hills I tramped so long ago –
'Tis far I am beyond the seas, but yearning voices call
"Will you not come back to Glenties and your wave-washed Donegal?"',
P. MacGill, *Songs of a Navvy* (Windsor and Londonderry, 1911), p. 24.

1.

By 1871 anyone curious enough to travel through Britain in search of immigrants and refugees would have experienced no difficulty in locating such groups. At this time Britain, the world's major economic power, drew labour and capital from less-developed nations. Moreover, Britain was widely perceived as a centre of liberal refuge where the persecuted of other lands could take shelter. The result was that between 1871 and 1914, when the British were busy painting the map red in the course of their imperial expansion, and when economic and social problems were becoming apparent in the heart of the Empire, immigrants and refugees continued to arrive. In the course of their stay such groups exercised an influence over British society and in the process were themselves often influenced and changed by their new environment. The responses which immigrants and refugees encountered from within British society, which were a compound of past and present influences and pressures, helped to ensure changes in the lives of most immigrants and refugees. But such comment is to anticipate. It is essential first of all to determine which groups were present in Britain between 1871 and 1914.

2.

An observer of immigrant minorities in Britain, taking stock in 1871, would have discovered that the largest group came from Ireland. Immigration from this source could be traced back to medieval times and by the beginning of the nineteenth century there was a firmly established tradition of emigration across the sea to Britain.[1] Soon after the Act of Union in 1800 by which Ireland became part of the United Kingdom, the scale of emigration increased considerably. This movement, particularly evident in the 1840s and early 1850s, to which passing reference has already been made, was reflected in the growth of Irish communities in London, Lancashire and Scotland which were to be stamped for a long time as 'Irish areas'.[2]

The great immigration of the 40s and 50s can be traced in the census returns. But, taken at a specific point in time, these statistics miss intercensal changes which can be particularly important in the case of a minority such as the Irish which contained a well-recognised transient population. Even so, as a general guide the census figures remain useful, and an examination reveals the numerical impact of the immigration that occurred during the early Victorian years. In 1841 there were 289,404 Irish recorded in England and Wales (or 1.8 per cent of the total population); in 1851 the Irish numbered 519,959; by 1861 the community had increased to 601,634; by the following census in 1871 numbers had fallen to 566,540 (2.5 per cent of the total population in England and Wales).[3]

In Scotland the pattern of development was slightly different. In 1841 the Irish numbered 126,321 (or 4.8 per cent of the total population); by 1851 they were 207,367. However, at the next census the size of the community had declined slightly to 204,083. Ten years later absolute numbers of the Irish had increased to 207,770 (6.2 per cent of the total population in Scotland).[4]

In the late nineteenth century Irish immigration entered into decline. As late as 1881 the local newspaper in St Helens, Lancashire, remarked on the 'pretty constant inflow of stalwart young men from Ireland'[5] but as the century drew to its close immigration fell off quite markedly.[6] In 1901, in England and Wales, to which the majority of the newcomers were drawn, there were 426,565 Irish recorded in the census. In Scotland numbers amounted to 205,064. By 1911, the last census before the war, the number of Irish in England and Wales had fallen still further, to 375,325 (1.0 per cent of the total population) and to 174,715 in Scotland (3.7 per cent of the total population).[7] Even so, it is worth emphasising yet again that the Irish remained the largest immigrant minority in Britain. Furthermore, in the nineteenth century, as at other times, there was an additional unquantifiable number of people born in Britain to Irish parents who also regarded themselves as Irish, even though they were excluded from this category in the official returns.[8]

By 1911 this Irish population was still concentrated in the old areas of settlement that had been developed in the mid-nineteenth century. As a result, there were major concentrations in Lancashire, in London and the area in and around Glasgow. Elsewhere, the Irish could be found in garrison towns, such as York, and in a number of growing cities, such as Cardiff.[9]

Why did this movement from Ireland of mainly young and single people take place and why did it continue to occur, even if at a greatly reduced level in the nineteenth century?[10] Religious conflict between Protestants and Catholics contributed to some early emigration but in the eighteenth and nineteenth centuries it has often been suggested that the basic pressure which preconditioned Irish emigration was the economic exploitation of Ireland by the British.[11] This expropriation of the fruits of the Irish economy meant that the country was unable to sustain its population. Hence the caustic remarks in Act 4 of *Man and Superman*:

MALONE: . . . me father died of starvation in Ireland in the Black '47. Maybe you've heard of it?

VIOLET: The Famine?

MALONE (with smouldering passion): No, the starvation when a country is full of food and exporting it, there can be no famine.

In these circumstances, and also the flooding of Ireland with goods

from the more advanced economy across the water, it has been argued
that there was pressure, often of a desperate gnawing intensity, to look
outside Ireland. But 'No simple Malthusian or economic model can
account for the Irish pattern of emigration'.[12] For example,
emigration was low from those areas where pauperism was high,
because people lacked the means to leave.[13] Furthermore, the pull of
perceived opportunities in Britain assisted the process of transfer, as
did the presence of relatives and friends in Britain and it was through
such interconnections that the movement from Ireland assumed the
character of a chain migration. In the last resort, as with other groups,
the emigrants were those who had 'the resources, the will, the
information and the aspiration to move'.[14] It was through such
influences and in such fashion that labour was transferred from the
periphery to the centre of economic development in the United
Kingdom. After 1890 a slight majority of those who geared
themselves up to travel to Britain were women.[15]

In the late nineteenth century as the number of Irish entering
Britain began to decline, America, by contrast, was increasingly
within the financial reach of the emigrants.[16] To many Irish, Chinese,
Jews and others America was a golden land where fantasies could be
realised and fortunes made. It was also, significantly for the Irish, a
country that had cast off British rule.[17] America, therefore, acted as a
magnet and much of the Irish immigration to that country had a
permanent stamp to it. In Britain, by contrast, although communities
did develop, the short distance between the various parts of the
United Kingdom meant that Irish immigration continued to have its
transient, sojourning element.[18] In 1871 when the Irish constituted
the largest single immigrant minority, there were a number of other
European nationals in Britain. Even when added together, however,
they were smaller in size than the Irish.

A German presence in the British Isles had become well-
established by 1871, when indeed the Germans constituted the largest
minority from continental Europe. In the census of England and
Wales in that year they numbered 32,823 out of an overall European-
born population of 89,829; as such the Germans constituted 0.1 per
cent of the total population. Germans were also present in Scotland
where the absolute number of European immigrants was much
smaller. This predominance among European-born minorities lasted
until the 1890s when the Germans were overtaken by the weight of
immigrants who arrived from Russian Poland. In 1911, however,

they were still a relatively significant immigrant minority. The census recorded 53,324 Germans resident in England and Wales (still 0.1 per cent of the total population) and in Scotland they occupied third place in the numerical ranking of immigrants behind the Russian Poles and the Italians.[19] London was one major centre of settlement but Germans were to be found elsewhere such as in Manchester and Bradford.[20]

This German minority was made up of a number of distinct strands. By the 1850s and 1860s the presence of German clerks began to attract comment and in the 1871 census of England and Wales the number of foreign-born commercial clerks, merchants and brokers was recorded separately. On the basis of this return and the later decennial figures it is possible to trace an increase in the number of foreign-born clerical workers. In 1871 there were 2,512; in 1911 the figure had increased to 6,949. The largest single national group came from Germany, and almost all of these newcomers were men. This particular group increased in absolute terms between 1871 and 1911 from 1,262 to 2,748, but declined in relative importance within a labour force that expanded, mainly through the addition of female workers, from 91,042 in 1871 to 477,535 in 1911.[21]

Why was it that these often highly-qualified German clerks, equipped with several foreign languages, as well as a knowledge of shorthand and book-keeping, were willing to come to Britain? Various explanations have been advanced. It was claimed by contemporaries that the policy of compulsory military conscription in Germany was one powerful influence. 'With the prospect of military service before them it is useless [for German youths] to make any definite business engagement'. Consequently, they were prompted to spend a couple of valuable years away from home, perfecting their knowledge of foreign languages and business methods before returning home for a spell in the armed forces. A more widespread, and probably more accurate, explanation emphasised that German immigration was primarily a function of the higher wage levels and better working conditions that prevailed in Britain. At the same time, the Germans were gaining experience which would be invaluable to them when they decided to return to their newly-created Empire.[22]

In addition to this immigration of clerks, there was a contemporaneous influx of other Germans, often Jewish, who were anxious to deploy their commercial or professional talents in Britain. Probably no more than a few thousand of these immigrants came to

Britain during the years that passed between the young Victoria's accession to the throne in 1837 and the advent of Hitler in 1933. But importance cannot be equated automatically with numbers, and some individuals were to achieve a social prominence.[23] Men such as Sir Ernest Cassel, Sir Ernest Oppenheimer, Sir Felix Semon, Hugo Hirst and Sir George Herschel, all made important and distinctive contributions to British society and the history of the British Empire.[24]

Since more than a sprinkling of these German newcomers were endowed with considerable ability, it might be wondered why they did not exercise these talents in Germany. In answer to this, it has been emphasised that although the German economy was expanding rapidly after 1870[25] it was quite widely believed in Germany that Britain, with its more advanced economy, offered still greater opportunities for advancement. Moreover, if personal progress could be achieved within an atmosphere of toleration, so much the better. In other words, a second force which drew the newcomers to Britain was the strong national tradition of Liberalism which, it was believed, had significant implications for the treatment of newcomers.[26] One central European perception of this came from Sigmund Freud after he had visited his half-brother in Manchester in 1875. This experience left an 'ineffaceable impression' on him and he returned home to Austria envying the atmosphere in which his half-brother was able to bring up his family.[27]

There was an additional ingredient caught up in the flow of immigration from Germany which captured public attention. Included in this movement were the German gypsies. The first gypsies in Britain, who arrived in the fifteenth century, came from the Balkans which was then undergoing Turkish occupation, in the course of which gypsies were uprooted from their settled communities and sedentary occupations and pushed towards western Europe. However, they projected an image of themselves as natives of Egypt and as Christians on pilgrimage. Had it been known that they originated in India, Europeans would have been left in stunned amazement. But a prolonged debate was to take place over the origins of the gypsies before it became possible to cut through the mass of tradition, rumour and deliberate falsehood, and establish where these lay.[28]

Since its first appearance a gypsy population had been continuously present in Britain and numbers were augmented periodically through immigration. The German gypsy influx that occurred particularly between 1904 and 1906 should be regarded as one aspect of this wider process. It was also part of a more widespread gypsy movement in the early twentieth century. In 1903, for instance, 'a party of Servian Gypsies from France' were located at Esher. Comment continued to appear on the Servian gypsies as they reappeared over the next few years and then between 1911 and 1913 another group from the Balkans, the gypsy coppersmiths, attracted attention. But none of these groups caught public interest to the same degree as the German gypsies, a few hundred of whom came to Britain between 1904 and 1906.[29]

Why did they come? Theirs was essentially a forced movement. In the decade before the First World War most west European governments, drawing strength from a long-standing hostility towards gypsies, tried to impose a tighter control over gypsy life or to expel this small, powerless minority. In France discussions took place in 1912 about the possible expulsion of gypsies from the Third Republic and, in the event, it was decreed that they should carry special identification papers. In the atmosphere of strong nationalism that prevailed in Germany a similarly repressive state policy emerged. This policy resulted in the expulsion to Holland of the German gypsies, who had in fact originated in Macedonia. In turn, Holland decided to ship its unwanted cargo to Britain. It was as a result of such pressures that contingents of German gypsies arrived and travelled the length and breadth of the country between 1904 and 1906. The victims' wishes, hopes and aspirations were not of any significance in this movement; in all probability they had little knowledge of the country to which they were directed.[30]

It was through such a mixture of clerks, capitalists, professional men and gypsies, at times supplemented by musicians in German bands, a phenomenon remarked upon in a popular song, pork butchers, waiters, an uncertain number of German miners and labourers, whose history so far has not been recovered, that the German population grew in the late nineteenth, early twentieth century. Such groups added to the political refugees of earlier times.[31] If some of this German contingent attracted the attention of various sections of the British public, from the 1880s the major focus of attention in Britain shifted towards the arrival of newcomers from Russian Poland, most of whom were Jews.

These Russian Poles did not constitute the first Jewish settlers in

Britain but they did add significantly to the size of the Jewish community. By 1871 this minority, composed of Sephardic and Ashkenazic Jews, with its own forms of institutional life, had become emancipated. In other words, it had been freed from the social disabilities it had encountered *as Jews*.[32] It was also a community that had begun to diversify itself in an occupational as well as a geographical sense, although there was still a strong concentration in the commercial and services sector of the British economy and London remained a very important centre of Jewish settlement.[33] There are no absolutely satisfactory statistics on population size, but it has been estimated that in 1875 the Jewish community numbered 51,250.[34]

By 1901 the number of Russian Poles in England and Wales, where the great majority was concentrated, had reached 82,844 or 0.3 per cent of the total population. By 1911 the size of the resident Russian Polish population in England and Wales had climbed to 95,541, when it still constituted 0.3 per cent of the population. By this time the Russian Poles also constituted the largest European-born minority in Scotland.[35]

As might be expected, London was one important centre of settlement. In 1901 there were 53,537 Russian Poles living in London and by 1911 this figure had risen to 68,420.[36] Whereas the established Jewish elite could enjoy a suburban life, the newcomers congregated initially in working-class areas in the centre of the cities where they settled.[37] Within London they became concentrated in the East End, particularly in Stepney, an old immigration reservoir, so that, at the time of the 1901 census, 80 per cent of the Russian Poles living in London could be found in that particular borough.[38] A great deal of attention has been lavished on this London group, but not all the newcomers gravitated there. In Leeds the Leylands area of the city witnessed a particularly rapid rise in Russian Polish immigration from the 1880s onwards[39] and Manchester, already a cosmopolitan city, also attracted Russian Polish immigrants who settled particularly in the Redbank area of the city.[40] Smaller numbers were present in Scotland and Wales.[41]

Not all of these Russian Poles were Jews and it is necessary to exercise a degree of caution in specifying how many were, since none of the official figures was concerned with an examination of religious categories. But, even if precise figures are elusive, it is generally agreed that most of these Russian Poles were in fact Jewish.[42]

How is it possible to explain the gathering presence of these newcomers that took place from the 1880s? There were basically two developments in the tsar's empire that exercised a major impact over this. From the eighteenth century onwards, the Jewish population, which was not emancipated until 1917, was concentrated mainly on the western boundary of Russia, in an area that stretched from the Black Sea to the Baltic which was known as the Pale of Settlement. This confinement of Jews went back to the years between 1783 and 1794, when the tsarist state acquired large numbers of Jews as a result of the dismemberment of Poland. There was some relaxation in official policy in the course of the liberalisation that followed the disasters of the Crimean War. But, in the late nineteenth century, the majority of Jews were still confined to the Pale, where in 1897 they formed about 11.6 per cent of the total population.[43] And it was here that the Jews began to experience an increasing pressure on resources. The Jewish population grew rapidly in the nineteenth century, but the economy of the Pale did not grow vigorously enough to provide adequately for its inhabitants. In these circumstances labour was transferred from eastern Europe towards the more advanced economies of the West.[44]

But economic pressures alone did not constitute the force that encouraged emigration from the tsar's empire. A key influence was the unremitting persecution which prevailed between 1881 and 1914. This repressive policy was directed at all minorities in the tsar's empire but it pressed with particular severity upon the Jews.[45] This policy was a major influence behind the movement of Jews to Britain, France, Argentina, South Africa and, above all, America.[46] Why did this persecution arise? The reasons are complex but might be summarised as follows. In the late nineteenth century it was recognised in some official circles that the tsarist state had to modernise in order to survive. Yet, in the longer term, a state with its roots in the peasantry risked the prospect of being undermined by the processes that it initiated. In short, a profound contradiction existed at the heart of Russian modernisation. Against this background the Jews, who had a strong traditional involvement in commerce and trading, were closely identified with the development of capitalism. As a result, they risked the hostility of conservative sections within the Russian bureaucracy. At times of economic and social unrest and during years of political uncertainty, such as in 1881–82 and 1903–6, this hostility became strikingly apparent. On these occasions, when the state unleashed its razor-like policy of anti-Semitism, the conflict was sharpened by the support this policy received from the Orthodox Church and various social groups within Russian society, such as the peasantry, who had their own scores to settle with the Jewish minority. The involvement of the state and the weakness of any Liberal counterweight resulted in the emergence of an especially savage brand of anti-Semitism. Moreover, any attempt by Jews to fight back against the tsarist regime only exacerbated the hostility since in anti-Semitic circles it suggested that ultimately Jews were disloyal to the state. The overall result of these interacting influences was that the severest form of anti-Semitism in Europe before 1914 occurred in Russia, and with the surfacing there after 1903 of *The Protocols of the Elders of Zion*, which charged Jews with elaborate plans for undermining and ultimately controlling the world, a new and ominous dimension was added to the ideological armoury of anti-Semitism, the full significance of which was to emerge only later.[47]

The basic pressures behind the movement of Jews to the West, among whom there were both immigrants and refugees, although the categories were not always easy to disentangle, have now been identified. But what of the countries to which they travelled? There was always an element of chance in where the immigrants landed, 'whether the ship arrived in Leith, Cardiff or Liverpool'.[48] But were the newcomers completely ignorant of Britain? Or was there some traffic in information which also helped the process of immigration? It is likely that some of the 'acute refugees' who left suddenly to avoid death or persecution did not ask too many questions and had no clear idea of their ultimate destination. But the 'anticipatory' refugees who mulled over the prospects were curious about the world outside.[49] Was it possible to live in relative freedom? Was it possible to remain Jewish? These were important questions and the answers to them came in a wide variety of sources, ranging from the dependable to the dubious. As part of the emerging composite picture produced by these questions, the message was conveyed that the newcomers would reach 'a free country' and, whatever difficulties they might face, this prospect of freedom was no mean consideration after their experiences in Russia.[50]

Set against these pressures and considerations the decision to emigrate, to leave Russian Poland, even as part of a chain exodus from a village or a town, was ultimately a personal matter, 'a compound of emotions, calculations and individual circumstances'.[51]

Once the uncertainty had been resolved intending emigrants made their way first of all to the ports of Bremen, Hamburg, Rotterdam and Libau, the major points of embarkation. A short time later they would be in London, Grimsby, Harwich or Glasgow, anxious to build new lives for themselves in Britain or to rest and gather their bearings before moving even further away from the *shtetlach* of eastern Europe.

So much for the Jewish emigration from Russia. In a context where most minorities in the tsar's empire were persecuted it is hardly surprising that others decided to emigrate to breathe the freer air of western Europe.[52] The Lithuanians were one such group who came. Numbers, it is true, were quite small. By 1914 there were approximately 1,000 of them in London and 4,000 in England as a whole. But it was Scotland which became 'the chief center of Lithuanian cultural and intellectual life in Britain'.[53] Here the few hundred Lithuanians present in the late 1880s had increased to 7,000 by 1914.[54] The majority came from the countryside and had little experience of urban civilisation.

The reasons for their emigration were mixed. In part, it related to the pressure that developed on land resources in the late nineteenth century. But it was also affected by political persecution. From the late eighteenth century onwards the Lithuanian state, which had been merged into Poland in the late fourteenth century, had become absorbed into the Russian Empire and henceforth a policy of Russification was introduced. This form of repression became more pronounced in 1863 after the failure of the Polish-Lithuanian uprising which had its origins in a rejection of Russian colonial policy. 'The reprisals were harsh and swiftly implemented ... the right of assembly and association were withdrawn, all Lithuanian literature was banned, the Cyrillic replaced the Latin alphabet, attendance at Russian Orthodox services was made compulsory and, from 1874, all males between 21 and 45 years were conscripted into the tsarist army for a term of six years'.[55] It was against this background that the emigration initially took place and the Lithuanians who arrived in Scotland – where they were generally referred to as Poles – were pushed towards Britain rather than pulled by any vision of a land of peace and plenty. Many who came wanted to stay only long enough to acquire the resources that would enable them to move on to America. Others also saw their stay as temporary; these brave souls envisaged a return home once Lithuania was released from the political tyranny that was exercised from St Petersburg. Few of those who came, however, could have foreseen the 1917 Revolution that was to affect their lives so dramatically.[56]

Among other European minorities were the Italians who arrived as part of the major emigration from Italy in the late nineteenth century. Financiers from the 'geographical expression' that was later to become Italy had been prominent in the Middle Ages and other newcomers had arrived in the eighteenth century when, in the so-called 'revolution of manners', contact with Italian culture was quite fashionable.[57] But it was in the late nineteenth century that there was a noticeable acceleration in immigration from Italy. In England and Wales the 1871 census recorded an alien Italian population of 5,063, and by 1911 this number had risen to 20,389. The key decade for the increase in recorded residents – the transience of the Italians means that census returns almost certainly omit part of the picture – was between 1891 and 1901. These years were followed by a period of stagnation in the early twentieth century. In Scotland 268 Italians were counted at the 1871 census; the number had increased to 4,594 in 1911.[58] The Italians who went to Scotland came from two departure zones, 250 miles apart. Barga in the province of Lucca in the north of Italy and Picinisco in the province of Frosinone to the south of Rome, were the two starting points of what amounted to a chain migration, as pioneers helped friends and relatives to leave. In England and Wales it has been noted that most of the late nineteenth century Italian immigrants came from particular areas of northern Italy, although numbers from the south also increased.[59]

Some of this movement related to pressures within Italian society. It was not just a sense of adventure that lured men and women, but primarily men, from Italy to Britain, nor was it the improvement in communications between the two countries, although the prospect of easier travel facilitated the process. The political unification of Italy, achieved by 1870, was a necessary precondition for the development of a capitalist economy in Italy but the process of unification and the political accommodation it involved, meant that the country was divided into a semi-feudal south and a more advanced north. The south was severely affected by changes in the international economy in the late nineteenth century which resulted in the collapse of the economic system in that part of Italy. Since industry in the north was not expanding fast enough to absorb all of those displaced, the result was a period of mass emigration. Italians in the north also came to Britain. For example in the northern provinces the development of capitalism into the countryside enabled landowners to uproot some peasant families. Many Italians who came to Britain, therefore, were from the countryside although other groups such as masons and carpenters, from the north, who sought out better opportunities abroad during the summer months, mingled amongst them.[60]

In all parts of Italy emigration was aided by stories, tales and impressions emanating from those who had already ventured abroad, as well as those who came back to Italy, with coat and cigar, 'arrayed like Signori'.[61] Italian emigration was also sensitive to the economic and social changes that were taking place in the more economically complex receiving centres such as the demand for labour in the service sector in Britain. Finally, in the last resort, in Italy, as elsewhere, the strength of individual initiative was also important; immigrants needed a 'staunchness of soul' which not everyone possessed.[62]

The Italians who did arrive were drawn particularly to London; indeed, the most common route to Scotland was via London.[63] Up to 1881 the largest number was to be found in Holborn, around Hatton Garden and Saffron Hill, and Holborn remained an important place of settlement down to the Great War.[64] Between 1881 and 1891, however, an increasing number of Italians were to be found in Finsbury, King's Cross and also in Soho. Finally, from 1891 to the Great War the old centre of the Italian minority in Hatton Garden and Saffron Hill stagnated, whereas there was a noticeable increase in the number of Italians in the more recent areas of settlement.[65] Elsewhere in Britain 'sizeable communities' could be found in Glasgow and Manchester, where Ancoats became known as 'Little Italy'. There was also an Italian presence in centres such as Cardiff, Sheffield, Liverpool, Leeds, Bradford and Newcastle.[66]

It would be a mistake to assume that Europeans alone contributed to the population diversity in late nineteenth century Britain. When Dr Thorndyke, expert forensic scientist and rival of Sherlock Holmes, took a stroll in Upper Bedford Place he remarked that 'the Asiatic and African faces that one sees at the windows of these Bloomsbury boarding-houses almost suggest an overflow from the ethnographical galleries of the adjacent British Museum.'[67] But who were the Asians and the Africans, travellers from beyond the oceans?

The name of Tan Chet-Qua appears among the ranks of sculptors working in late eighteenth-century Britain. Moreover, in the same century the Sackville family employed a Chinese servant: Blacks were common by this time and a Chinese had more originality. Furthermore, the record of an affray in 1782 involving Chinese sailors in the East End of London, suggests a Chinese presence in the capital at least as early as the eighteenth century.[68] Additional evidence on the presence of Chinese sailors came a few years later in a report on Lascar and other Asiatic seamen in 1814–15; these men, transients between ships for the most part, were employees of the East India Company which until its dissolution in 1833 exercised a monopoly over British trade with the Far East. However, it was not until the late nineteenth century that the Chinese population began to show a noticeable increase. Even then it remained small in absolute terms. In 1871 the number of Chinese aliens was, at a maximum assessment, 207. By 1911 it was 1,319.[69] Such returns, however, almost certainly underestimated the size of the Chinese minority in Britain. Others, who originated in Hong Kong, would be subsumed under the undifferentiated category whose birthplace was given as the British colonies and dependencies. But, in any calculation, the number was insignificant compared with those Chinese who emigrated to America and Australia.[70]

The Chinese diaspora was fed partly by the chronic overpopulation and poverty of China but it was also influenced by developments in the countries to which the Chinese were drawn. The discovery of gold in the mid-nineteenth century and the demand for cheap 'coolie' labour were both influential in drawing the Chinese to the west coast of America, and also to Australia.[71]

In the case of Britain there were no gold mines to be worked but there was a demand for Chinese labour as trade developed with the Far East. In the course of the nineteenth century the treaties of Nanking in 1842 and Peking in 1860 opened up China to British trade – the carrying of opium and tea were important aspects of this commerce – and a major boost to Far Eastern trade came with the opening of the Suez Canal in 1869. 'British trade with the Far East expanded with great rapidity; and most of the early Chinese came as seamen on board the increasing number of cargo boats that were sailing East, mainly out of the port of Liverpool'.[72] On these new steam ships there was a demand for stokers and it was in this capacity much of the colonial and Chinese labour was employed. In addition, it was particularly in demand on tramp steamers which went from port to port according to the availability of cargo. This trade resulted in men spending longer periods away from home and Europeans shunned such employment.[73] It was in these circumstances that a Chinese population developed in Liverpool where it added to the racial cosmopolitanism of Liverpool society. Other Chinese communities were established in London, and there was also a Chinese presence in Cardiff. It is impossible to shed light on the geographical origins of all of these newcomers, but in the East End of London, at least, the majority came from Kwangtung province.[74]

Africans and Indians also added to the mosaic of minority communities in Britain. At the height of colonialism and the slave trade, the Black community, the origins of which stretched back into history, could be counted in the thousands and this was still the case in the early years of the nineteenth century.[75] At this point in time the Black population has been described as 'large' and 'prominent'[76] and it was increased periodically by the inward movement of Blacks who were fleeing from the yoke of slavery in America.[77] However, in the course of the nineteenth century the Black population entered into a numerical decline. When Henry Mayhew was working on his survey of *London Labour and the London Poor* in 1861 he drew attention to a 'few negroe beggars' in the capital but it is also possibly significant that Mayhew recorded the comment of one of the street minstrels: 'Some Niggers are Irish. There's Scotch niggers, too. I don't know a Welsh one but one of the street nigger singers is a real black – an African'.[78] This remark could imply rarity although the evidence on size is uncertain.

It has been suggested that the decline was related chiefly to changing conditions in the Caribbean. The Black population in Britain had always been unequal in a gender sense; the number of men had always predominated over that of women. This population could continue to grow and maintain its racial distinctiveness only if there was continued immigration or a levelling up of the female/male ratio. Such developments did not happen because of events in the Caribbean. By the 1840s 'the two main stimuli to black emigration, white prosperity and the related phenomenon of black slavery ceased to operate'.[79] This is not to say that the Black population in Britain disappeared, but rather that it became significantly smaller as new immigration decreased and many but not all Blacks merged into the residuum of poor Whites and other disadvantaged racial minorities.[80]

The Black population was maintained at this lower level after 1871 partly by the so-called 'Black jacks', Black sailors who still found their way to Britain or were unceremoniously dumped in British ports by shipping companies. Representatives of this group could be found particularly in London and Liverpool where they were regarded as transients, strangers who had been brought by one ship and would depart one day in another, whether to the West Indies or West Africa. In fact, however, some did not leave. They settled down and thereby helped to sustain a Black presence.[81]

Other groups helped to increase the size of the Black minority and complicate its class structure. A number of transient African businessmen who helped to grease the wheels of Imperial commerce could usually be found. Moreover, there was a student population, drawn overwhelmingly from wealthy Black families in the Caribbean and Africa. These groups were to be found particularly in London, but also in other centres such as Cambridge, Liverpool and Edinburgh. Many in official positions in the British government hoped that through their exposure to western culture they would help to guarantee the future of the 'Greater Britain'.[82]

As in the case of Blacks, part of the population deriving from the Indian sub-continent, found itself in Britain because it was dumped here. Eurasian seamen and circus performers both suffered this fate. They indeed, along with Indians mainly from Punjab and Sind, who were rendered financially impoverished in the course of pursuing litigation in Britain, became a source of public concern.[83] But the structure of the Indian population in Britain was complex rather than simple. Some wealthy Indians took up residence in the heart of the Empire.[84] The feckless Punjabi prince, Duleep Singh, was exiled to Britain and rebuilt Elveden house in Suffolk to serve as his sybaritic sanctuary.[85] The queen had her faithful Indian 'munshi'.[86] There was a small business community by the late nineteenth century.[87] And, as with the Blacks, there was a student population. Some of these, the impecunious members of the Indian student community, numbered at 1–2,000, many of them reading for the Bar, came within the focus of the parliamentary enquiry into distressed colonial subjects that reported in 1910.[88] But others were much better off. 'London in those days was exciting, the centre of empire, of course, full of its own importance, crowded with horses, buses and hansoms. You can imagine how it was for me at the age of 13', the old man, now 88 years of age, mused in Delhi when he met the Indian correspondent of *The Times*. 'I had travelled down from Rawalpindi to Bombay, took ship to Marseilles, a train to Calais and finally a bus to prep school in Notting Hill Gate. It was 1908.' For Hardit Singh Malik life proceeded smoothly. Clifton College, Bristol was followed by Eastbourne College, after which Malik went up to Balliol College, Oxford, where he read History. August 1914 saw him playing cricket for Sussex against Kent.[89] Here he was following in the steps of the renowned K. S. Ranjitsinhji, who entered the game in 1893 and enjoyed his first regular season for Sussex, the county of his choice, in 1895.[90]

A number of other students, later to become well known, also came to Britain. Between 1887 and 1890 Gandhi read for the Bar and served for some time on the board of the Vegetarian Society.[91] Another arrival who came as Gandhi departed, was Mohammed Ali Jinnah, 'the creator of Pakistan'. He also studied for the Bar before returning to India in 1896.[92] A few years later Jawaharlal Nehru arrived in England and went to Harrow School between 1905 and 1907, before proceeding to Cambridge and then reading for the Bar in London.[93] The law also attracted Mohammed Iqbal, later to become known for his poetry.[94]

The census returns between 1871 and 1911 picked up other groups whose history has been mainly neglected. There was a French population, swollen by just over 1,000 refugees from the Commune, most of whom stayed in Britain until 1879–80, when the granting of a political amnesty allowed their return to France.[95] There were Spaniards in the Merthyr Tydfil district, recruited to Dowlais when local labour was in short supply in 1899.[96] There was 'a Czech colony of a thousand or so in London in the early years of [the twentieth] century, mostly tailors and waiters, but with a school of their own and a club founded in 1909 by Count Lutzow, Bohemia's patriotic historian'.[97] In the late nineteenth century there was also an increase in the Polish population as the earlier political refugees were joined by a number of their fellow countrymen, principally from western Poland, an area that was suffering from the effects of Prussian colonisation. These newcomers were to be found in London, in Lanarkshire, where they were often confused with the Lithuanians, as well as in Lancashire and Cheshire. In London they were usually employed by Jews in Whitechapel, but they could also be found in the Beckton Gas Works in Silvertown. In Lanarkshire they worked in the traditional heavy industries and in the north of England they were to be found in the saltworks at Winsford and Nantwich. In institutional terms the Polish presence was reflected particularly in London, with the establishment of the Polish Society in 1886 and the setting-up of the Roman Catholic Mission to the Poles in 1894.[98]

From beyond Europe there were always White Americans anxious to drink in European culture, particularly in a country where they could understand the language. There was also a long tradition of American writers and artists making their home in Britain. A colony made up of these groups was to be found in London at the end of the eighteenth century,[99] and in the following century a number of well-known writers settled in England.[100] Stephen Crane enjoyed playing the country gentleman. Henry James also made his home across the Atlantic. 'My choice is the Old World', he proclaimed, 'my choice, my need, my life.'[101] The artist, James Macneill Whistler, was also attracted to England.[102] William Waldorf Astor arrived in 1890 and was followed in 1906 by another businessman, Gordon Selfridge, who opened Selfridge's in 1909. Jacob Epstein, the sculptor, came to London in 1905. The journalist, R. D. Blumenfeld, who became editor of the *Daily Express* in 1904, was another well-known trans-Atlantic pilgrim.[103]

3.

AFTER identifying the main immigrant and refugee groups between 1871 and 1914, it is possible to turn to the economic and social life of the more significant minorities, beginning once again with the Irish.

During these years some Irish immigrants were to be found within the ranks of government employees.[104] Michael Collins, later to achieve prominence as a nationalist leader, was just one of the newcomers who found employment in the Post Office.[105] Some Irish were also to be found in the police and the armed forces. It was estimated in 1891, for example, that men of Irish birth made up 14 per cent of the British army.[106] Others were to be found in the police force, where there was a noticeable presence in the Special Branch after its formation in 1887.[107] There were also Irish doctors and lawyers. Indeed, one of the latter, Charles Russell of Newry, became Lord Chief Justice, 'the only Catholic to occupy that great office since the Reformation'. This career recognition was one salient reminder that 'a talented and determined Irish Catholic could succeed in England if prepared to conform politically'.[108] But Russell's career was hardly typical.

By 1870 the Irish had developed strong links with the agrarian sector of the British economy, often taking short-term employment at busy times of the agricultural year, and this association remained evident down to 1914. However, circumstances were changing in the late nineteenth century. As mechanisation increased, the Irish played a less significant role as harvesters.[109] In Scotland they could still be seen at busy times of the year gathering in corn, working in the potato fields and singling turnips.[110] In England, however, the main body of Irish rural labourers worked in the north and no longer travelled further south than Warwickshire and north Cambridgeshire,[111] although one group, caught for posterity by the watchful, roaming eye of Richard Jefferies as they bivouacked close to London, revealed that the Irish did manage on occasions to penetrate further south.[112] Faced with a decline for their services the Irish extended the range of their activities. Furthermore, and related to this, they started to become semi-permanent rather than short-term residents.[113]

Those Irish who worked in the countryside were in many cases engaged in activity with which they were familiar on arrival. But what of those other Irish, who exchanged a life in rural Ireland for a new one in urban Britain? Although there was evidence of some upward mobility, the majority were concentrated in semi-skilled and unskilled occupations.[114] In London, for example, they were to be found in a wide range of such occupations[115] but 'For the Irish in the mass', an observer wrote in 1901, 'the docks are the happiest ground'.[116] They were also particularly well-represented in the equally onerous portering trade at Covent Garden.[117]

A similar structure was present in Scotland. Irish immigrants could be found as property landlords, publicans and pawnbrokers.[118] But the bulk of the Irish were outside these occupations. Here they found employment in the 1880s as labourers involved in the construction of railways.[119] They also laboured in the heavy industries stimulated by this railway expansion, in the early oil industry between West Lothian and Fifeshire – 'Paddy the Cope' worked at Jadeborough[120] – as well as in hawking, huckstering and the egg trades.[121]

The sizeable number of Irish women immigrants has remained particularly neglected in historical accounts. But it has been noticed that some were to be found in the textile mills of Lancashire. Others took on laundry work.[122] A large proportion were also to be found in domestic service; for example, 30 per cent of the employed Irish women recorded in the 1911 census of Scotland were engaged in this type of work.[123]

The concentration of the Irish towards the bottom end of the occupational structure resulted from a complex interaction of influences. The barrier of illiteracy confined some.[124] Furthermore, since many Irish workers were recruited into employment through contact with the Irish community, patterns of employment established earlier in the century proved tenacious;[125] hence their continued presence in the docks. The transitory nature of some of the immigration,[126] the influence of the Roman Catholic Church which, although it urged respectability, counselled against too much worldly success,[127] and a sense of alienation from their surroundings, derived from a belief that Britain was responsible for the problems of Ireland, were additional pressures which operated in varying degrees upon individuals and helped to produce the 'remarkably conservative pattern' of Irish occupational life. But, in addition, their confinement was related to the discrimination that the Irish faced from within British society. 'Nowhere else save in Orange Canada', we have been told, 'did the Irish abroad meet with such sustained antagonisms as in nineteenth century Britain'.[128]

The overall influence of Irish workers on the British economy has been the subject of an unresolved debate. It has been suggested that they were a key element in bringing about the Industrial Revolution[129] and, more generally, that they 'clearly filled a necessary role in the immense industrial expansion of Britain'.[130] More recently, however, a degree of caution has been injected into this discussion. Even if British capitalists found Irish labour a useful convenience, it was in no sense indispensable. Indeed, the argument that the Irish were essential because Britain had insufficient labour or because the native workforce was immobile, has been seriously questioned.[131]

However, this image of Irish labour as an indispensable ingredient in the process of economic growth has been argued on other grounds. It has been contended that the Irish did essential work which natives shunned as too dirty, too dangerous or too degrading. But this claim has also been rejected as 'unconvincing'. A great deal of the British infrastructure was laid before the Irish arrived in numbers. Even the railways were completed for the most part without their help. Moreover, there were always large parts of the country where they did not exert much economic influence. It has been conceded that without their input there might have been 'marginally less economic growth' but claimed at the same time that the difference 'would hardly have been substantial'.[132]

Finally, because there was a supply of alternative labour in Britain, it has been argued recently that the influence of Irish labour on wage levels was neither as severe as native workers suggested nor as favourable to the mainland capitalists as might be inferred from those who have argued that immigration was essential to economic growth. The main influence of the Irish, according to recent opinion, both as regards wages and employment, was felt in the less prosperous areas of Britain which Irish immigrants tended to avoid. If the Irish had not immigrated, the surplus labour in these parts which was able to move to the towns and cities might have fared better than it did. By contrast, in the towns where Irish workers settled, their influence was far less pronounced.[133] However, in view of the limited testing of this opinion, it should not be regarded as definitive.

Among the distinctive features of Irish social life was the degree of residential segregation and concentration in areas such as Liverpool and London, as well as some other parts of the country.[134] Within these Irish quarters, such as Scotland Road, Liverpool, there were often further subdivisions which derived from the immigrants' geographical origins in the old country. To some extent this spatial segregation also reflected a general need, shared by other immigrants, to live close to people who shared similar beliefs and values but it resulted additionally from the various economic and social constraints which the majority of the Irish encountered. Most of these Irish quarters had a depressing aspect, and although Irish immigrant life was not static, so that the second half of the nineteenth century saw some improvement in the lives of the Irish, 'Booth's description of the rat-infested Irish ghetto of dockside London at the close of the nineteenth century is as chilling as anything penned in the worst years of the famine influx'.[135] It was in these urban concentrations that evidence of social disorganisation among the Irish, involving crime and drunkenness, for example, was most clearly in evidence.[136] The transition from rural Ireland to urban Britain, in which 'clock time replaced sun time and multistory apartments supplanted thatched cottages',[137] was not without its human cost.[138]

The Irish were therefore visible in an occupational and spatial sense and their visibility was underlined by the persistence of Irish culture. In Scotland at least this persistence was revealed in the continued use of Gaelic. For many years on Sunday evenings, well into the second half of the nineteenth century, in the Calton district of Glasgow, in an area known as 'Connacht Square', 'it was customary for groups of native speakers, scattered at work over the city on weekdays to meet . . . and, stretched on the grass, gossip by the hour in their own tongue'. Further confirmation of the persistence of the past was evident in the *Catholic Directory* in 1882 which recorded the death of a priest who had laboured in the vineyard of East Lothian and whose success and popularity was related to his fluency in the Irish tongue.[139]

This sense of cultural distinctiveness was enhanced in the late nineteenth century through the Gaelic Revival. Together with the foundation of organisations such as the Gaelic League and the Ancient Order of Hibernians and other developments such as the football-cum-benefit society activities of Celtic, founded in 1887, there was ample evidence of an Irish cultural vitality.[140]

The social distinctiveness of the Irish was further enhanced by their connection with the Roman Catholic Church. The Church, through its emphasis on qualities such as self-help and temperance, played an important role in sustaining the immigrants once they were across the water and living in a complex, industrial society, even if, in other respects it held back their social progress by insisting upon a continuing degree of priestly control over their lives.[141] In turn, Roman Catholicism was influenced by the presence of the Irish.[142] The pennies of Erin's poor exiles helped to build its churches and it has been claimed that Irish immigration was 'one of the most important factors in the Catholic revival'.[143] Even so, the Irish did not capture the Church.[144] Furthermore, to underline this interacting influence from a different perspective, there was over the course of time some modification of the mysterious brand of Catholicism which the Irish carried with them on their arrival in Britain.[145]

An emotional love of Ireland and its culture as well as an attachment to the Catholic faith were distinctive features in the lives of most of the Irish in Britain. A rounded view of their social life would also need to consider their political activity, bearing in mind that their attachment to Ireland and Roman Catholicism exerted an influence over their political behaviour and, at the same time, influenced their reception in British society.[146]

Some of the political energy of the Irish was directed into nationalist politics. A number of dramatic incidents such as the Fenian bombing campaign in 1868[147] and the Phoenix Park Murders in 1882,[148] brought home to any sensitive person the message that action was needed on 'the Irish Question'. Indeed, the issue was to become a central feature of British politics.

Some of the Irish, and, more so, those of Irish-descent, had obtained the vote in 1867 or 1884 and were therefore able to exert a political influence in the ensuing debate. In 1875 the Home Rule Confederation of Great Britain helped to organise the Irish Nationalist vote and the cause was further assisted by the formation in 1882 of the Irish National League of Great Britain which had T. P. O'Connor as its first President and John Denvir as its first General Secretary. This organisation and the later United Irish League provided the institutional props beneath Irish Nationalist politics at Westminster.[149]

This political activity provided a further stimulus to the growth of an Irish consciousness. 'An almost inevitable concomitant of any nationalist movement is the heightened interest taken in all things having to do with one's cultural heritage'.[150] Furthermore, it encouraged the emergence of a press sympathetic to Irish political aspirations. The *Glasgow Observer*, founded in 1885, and the *Glasgow Examiner*, which came out in 1895, reflected the importance of Scotland as a centre of Irish nationalist activity. In England there were similar developments between 1902 and 1912. For example, T. P. O'Connor, who was returned for the Scotland division of Liverpool in 1885 as a Home Rule candidate – there were also Home Rule members of the City Council – was the driving force behind *TP's Weekly*.[151]

The Irish pursued their nationalist aspirations down to the Great War. The Liberals, the progressive party on Home Rule, Irish Nationalist candidates headed for Westminster or, in some cases, Sinn Fein, which after 1906 dangled the prospect of an independent Ireland rather than the more limited prescription of Home Rule, were all recipients of such political support.[152]

The nationalist cause could often count upon support from within the priesthood,[153] and, to a greater extent, so could the involvement of the Irish in the campaign for Catholic education, a principle that was eventually accepted in the 1918 Education Act.[154] But the immigrants and the Church did not always march in step. An involvement in the early labour and trade union movement, for example, could not count automatically on the Church's blessing. Even so, there was a discernible Irish presence in trade union organisations. In 1889 an Irish immigrant, P. J. King, started to organise the workers in the Alkali industry, among whom there were many Irish, and his successor was Patrick Healey, another Irishman.[155] James Connolly and James Larkin, born and brought up in Irish communities in Britain, were more major figures.[156] In London men with Irish names were prominent in the great dock strike in 1889 which, it has been suggested, marked a major step forward in the integration of the Irish into the London Labour movement.[157] Ben Tillett was the recognised leader and James Toomey was President of the Strike Committee,[158] and it was the Irish Catholic connection which enabled Cardinal Manning to exercise an influence over the strike.[159]

By 1914 the Irish had generally managed to effect a transition from a rural society to one of the most advanced industrial countries in the world. This transition was not a painless, effortless process but it did proceed more smoothly than at one stage seemed possible. However, it did not mean that the Irish rejected their origins altogether. The annual celebrations of 17 March, St Patrick's Day, provided one firm reminder of their roots, and, like many other groups their internal sense of cohesion was reinforced by the hostility they encountered in Britain. But generalisations need to be carefully drawn.[160] Experiences differed between regions and classes. Furthermore, there were uncertainties that still had to be resolved. Religious and class differences affected relations with the Liberals and there were other political tensions.[161] How, if at all, for instance, was it possible to reconcile 'the "Red Flag" with "Faith of Our Fathers" and "God Save Ireland" '?[162] Those Irish who had firm initial ideas on such matters did not always retain that reassuring certainty in their new environment. The process of immigration exerted its own effects upon perceptions and horizons.[163]

In considering the continental European minorities, and beginning with the Germans, it should be emphasised that the clerks from Germany were not a homogeneous group. The better connected and more skilled were concentrated as foreign correspondents; it was here that they could make profitable use of their language skills in the development of overseas business. Foreign clerks, particularly Germans, monopolised this kind of work. By contrast, head clerks such as Mr Pooter were not troubled by their competition and few Germans found employment in the lower reaches of clerical work. But wherever they were employed, the Germans were widely regarded as efficient and successful.[164]

Many of the German businessmen and financiers who arrived at the same time also carved out profitable careers in their new environment. There were success stories, for example, in electrical engineering and chemical production. Germany made great strides forward in both industries in the late nineteenth century and some of this success was transferred to Britain by the immigrants.[165] Older industries were also influenced by Germans. In the heartland of the industrial north German Jews in Bradford came to play a prominent role in the textile industry, becoming known as 'the merchant princes'.[166] There was a noticeable German influence resulting from their presence in Manchester, and elsewhere in Britain Germans were 'exceedingly prominent from 1875 onwards' in the Dundee jute trade, although their influence seems to have declined by 1914.[167] As for finance, there was a pronounced German-Jewish influence by the late nineteenth century. If the activities of Nathan Meyer Rothschild, first in Manchester and then in London, attracted interest in the late eighteenth, early nineteenth century, by the late Victorian age his place had been taken by newcomers such as Edward Cassel, who found Britain a particularly congenial home for his varied financial activities.[168]

All such activity by Germans, whether as clerks, businessmen or financiers, was quite different from the work undertaken by the German gypsies who engaged in a little horsetrading, a traditional form of gypsy activity, and also welcomed the pennies tossed to them for their acrobatic displays. The provision of entertainment had long been a licensed preserve for gypsies.[169]

Little or nothing has been unearthed so far on the social life of the German gypsies other than that part of it involving the hostility and persecution meted out to them by sections of British society. However, more information is to hand on the more settled, if in some cases still essentially transient, German population.

Most of the recorded information about German social life has been derived from the capital.[170] By the 1860s the Germans had already established two important clubs which were to remain well-known features of the immigrant community down to the Great War. The Deutsches Athenaeum was founded in 1860 and the Turnverein

(Gymnasium) was established in the following year. The former catered for the elite members of German society; the latter, a kind of Mechanics Institute, was less elitist and, in fact, had a majority of English members. With the arrival of the German clerks more clubs appeared. These various establishments fulfilled a number of functions. The clubs provided a base where Germans could become acquainted with one another, where they could eat at a reasonable cost, receive instruction in the English language, read German newspapers and hear about the latest employment prospects. There was also a clear moral intention in mind. It was hoped that the clubs would steer the newcomers away from the snares of the public house.[171]

Organisations of this kind were only the tip of German social activity in London. Socialists and Communists from Germany formed their own political clubs. In addition, there were several German schools, a German orphan asylum, a home for German governesses, another for German servants, as well as German lodging houses. There were also a few German-language newspapers, a number of churches that catered for the German population, as well as a German hospital in Dalston. The hospital, which had been founded in 1845, was reputedly one of the best managed in London in the late nineteenth century and open to all nationalities. For those who wanted social or financial help, the Germans were served by the Society of Friends of Foreigners in Distress, founded in 1806, and the German Benevolent Society, which was formed eleven years later. In other words, the Germans were generally well organised, with a number of support networks to sustain them in their new environment.[172]

It has been suggested that members of the German elite showed little interest in maintaining their German origins. 'Germany became little more than a shadow that passed in the night'.[173] In fact, however, it was not so easy to obliterate the past. Many of the newcomers, bankers such as Edgar Speyer and S. Japhet, still had family or business links with Germany.[174] Moreover, as Britain and Germany drifted towards conflict in the years before 1914, there were those in Britain who did not allow the Germans to forget their origins.[175]

Before the war, however, members of the German elite had managed to make a number of significant social contributions to British society. Apart from helping to keep Edward VII in a state of financial solvency and providing Winston Churchill with sound investment advice, Ernest Cassel gave generously to the London School of Economics.[176] Other Germans contributed directly to the world of scholarship.[177] A wider cultural influence was also evident. In late nineteenth, early twentieth century Germany and Austria, Jews were particularly prominent in the cultural life of Berlin and Vienna.[178] Indeed, the theatre and the world of music were both heavily reliant on their patronage. Once in Britain this interest did not lapse and it was particularly evident in the help that was given to music. Sir Henry Wood might not have saved the insecurely started Promenade Concerts without the generosity of Edgar Speyer.[179] And Wood's indebtedness was paralleled elsewhere. Charles Hallé, another immigrant from Germany, was deeply indebted to German-Jewish merchants in Manchester who gave the city the foundations of its music and the country a national institution.[180]

The German immigration, therefore, influenced British society in a number of important ways but these newcomers did not attract the same degree of attention as the immigrants who arrived from Russian Poland, whose numbers increased markedly from the 1880s.

The Jewish newcomers from the Russian Empire concentrated initially in a limited range of occupations. In some cases they were able to pursue the type of work they had followed in Russia. These major occupations included the ready-made clothing trade, cabinet making and bootmaking, in all of which there was a tendency for the newcomers to be employed by their coreligionists.[181]

The influence of the Jewish newcomers on employment and wages has been the subject of dispute partly because the immigration coincided with the emergence of new processes and organisation which made it difficult to unravel the specific effect of the immigrants. This complication was emphasised by the Royal Commission on Alien Immigration, which in its 1903 report drew attention to the 'great conflict of testimony' on these issues.[182] Later opinion has stressed the stimulus to the economy and thereby to job creation which resulted from the immigration and emphasised that although Jewish workers were sweated in their working conditions and hours of work, they benefited in terms of their hourly earnings.[183] But even in these later assessments, some of which, with exaggeration, have presented an image of Jewish immigrants as the personification of all economic virtues, there have been differences in emphasis. It has been suggested recently, for example, that the positive economic results of the immigration occurred later than many have imagined.[184]

These newcomers who arrived from Russia and whose occupational concentration remained evident for many years[185] spent a good part of their lives in workshops. Indeed, in view of the large number of references to the Jewish newcomers as the personification of capitalism, it might be wondered whether they had any other dimension to their lives.[186] But the recent arrivals, both men and women, exercised a social impact on Britain and in turn were influenced by the new environment.

The full immediate extent of the cultural influence of the Jewish newcomers was particularly evident in the immigration reservoirs where the bulk of the immigrants first lived, particularly in the East End and in Leeds. One prominent cry from those who opposed the immigration was that certain areas in the East End were being transformed into Jerusalem.[187] And it is possible to understand why this allegation was made.

The Russian Poles concentrated in certain well-defined areas, partly to establish close links with their fellow-immigrants in a new and strange environment and partly to secure employment, both of which needs were reinforced by the hostility and discrimination which the newcomers had to face.[188] As a result of these interacting pressures, immigrants crowded into certain properties and some entrepreneurs from within the Jewish community, as well as other landlords, exploited the situation to their own advantage. At the same time, some of the fiercest opposition which they encountered developed out of this context. Jewish newcomers, it was asserted, created the housing problems in the areas of heavy immigrant settlement.[189] In fact, however, at least as far as the East End is concerned, the Jews did not cause the housing problems; their presence *exacerbated* a situation which had complicated economic and social origins and in which the newcomers themselves featured as victims.[190]

What is clear, however, is that within the space of a short period of time the immigrants and refugees introduced a new, distinctive, immigrant cultural life into their areas of settlement. The religious needs of immigrants were catered for by the introduction of *steibels*, small house-based synagogues, where newcomers could practise the kind of religion they had known in Russia rather than what they regarded as the watered-down version of Judaism which served the needs of the Anglo-Jewish community. *Hadarim* were also established where children could be brought up in the ancient ways of Judaism.[191] At the same time shops which catered for the needs of the Russian Poles were established, much to the consternation of local traders, and Jewish restaurants sprang up where the immigrants could meet, talk and eat. Together with other developments, such as the establishment of 'Shewshiks', the famous Jewish ritual and vapour baths in Brick Lane, the result was that the East End and Stepney in particular, became an island of immigrant Jewish culture. The Yiddish-speaking newcomers who lived in such areas inhabited a different world from the more acculturated German-Jewish elite and the old-established representatives of Anglo-Jewry and this 'distance' created its own forms of conflict.[192]

It was not only over religion that a divide opened up between the old and the new Jews. Political differences also emerged. In Russia the persecution of the Jews generated some sympathy for the socialist groups opposed to the tsar. As a result, Jews, some of whom denied their Jewishness, were to be found in the Menshevik faction and in organisations such as the Jewish Bund. These individuals were moved by visions of the world far different from the predominantly Liberal outlook of the Anglo-Jewish elite.[193] In the case of some newcomers the fight against tsarism was continued from British soil. For others the context of their political lives was made up of a number of overlapping layers, which involved an interest in political developments in both Britain and Russia. The upshot of these influences was that some of the newcomers formed Jewish anarchist or socialist groups.[194] Others were attracted to socialist organisations with a wider base such as the Social Democratic Federation, founded in 1884 and, later, to the British Socialist Party. In some instances the individuals who offered this commitment had fired guns against the Russian authorities in the course of the political struggles taking place in the tsar's empire and these steel-like immigrants sharpened the temper of socialism in Britain.[195]

Some Jewish workers also involved themselves in trade union organisation. There has been a tendency to underplay this dimension of Jewish life and many have written about an inexorable transformation of Jewish workers into capitalists.[196] But, at times, in areas such as Leeds, for example, the conflict between the two sides of industry in the tailoring trade was intense.[197] In the event, Jewish trade unionism made only a limited amount of progress before 1914.

However, this was not related primarily to any disinclination on the part of the newcomers to organise themselves but principally to the structure of the trades in which the Jews found employment.[198]

Whereas the political background which had been acquired by the newcomers from Russia remained important down to the Great War and, in the short term, helped to mould the course of socialism in Britain, it has been argued that in other respects, practices from the past were significantly modified. This change was reflected in the lifestyle of some women immigrants. The immigration from eastern Europe was dominated by young men, but women were counted among the Russian Polish newcomers; in 1891–92, for example, they made up one quarter of the arrivals.[199] Like most women, these Russian Poles have been largely ignored in historical writing but the recovery of their past has shed light on changing patterns of immigrant behaviour. When one newcomer, who arrived in Manchester as a child in 1914 was asked, 'Do you know what your grandfather did for a living?' she replied, 'What my grandfather did for a living was to study and pray. I don't think he ever did anything else, but spent his life in study and prayer . . .'. In the Pale of Settlement there were religious men devoted to a life of spirituality who left the task of earning a living to their women. But, once in Britain, there is some evidence to suggest that in certain cases this pattern of life became changed, in the course of which women became supportive in a different way through their role as homemakers. But claims regarding the transformation should not be overdone and much still remains obscure; in areas such as Leeds many Jewish women continued to work.[200]

There was other, more conclusive evidence of a responsiveness to the new environment. By the 1850s Anglo-Jewry was undergoing a transition towards a pattern of lower birth and death rates. However, this modern, westernised process was challenged by the arrival of the newcomers from Russian Poland, whose culture had encouraged early marriage and a pro-natalist stance, based on the injunction: 'Be fruitful and multiply'. As a result, 'The initial effect of mass immigration was to retard completely Anglo-Jewry's advanced position in the demographic transition cycle'.[201] Yet within the space of a generation marriage among the majority of Jewish newcomers was being delayed and fertility patterns began to converge with Anglo-Jewish and national patterns. This adjustment has been explained in terms of a more general cultural change, 'the abandonment of the traditional way of life of the *Ostjuden*, symbolised by the Yiddish language, and the whole-hearted adoption of a new life-style – that of the westernized English-speaking Anglo-Jew'.[202]

Changes or modifications in life-style were assisted by education, and one major emergent emphasis involved an attempt to harmonise the new and the old, to bring about the acculturation of the young so that they would be less visible than their parents and feel less like outsiders while still remaining faithful to the tenets of Judaism. In these circumstances it has been written that '. . . Not the least striking transformation in the immigrant was the alacrity with which he turned over his children to the educational system of his new land, whether Board or Jewish denominational (voluntary) schools, which were the antithesis of all he had experienced in the *heder*. At the same time, the immigrants preserved the *heder* in spite of every effort by outsiders to root it out'. But this stereotype, with its emphasis on the moulding force of assimilatory pressures, would simplify the influences to which these Jews were exposed. Within the immigrant areas the promulgation of socialism and Zionism also exerted their respective influences and were to become woven into the history of the Jewish minority.[203]

Much less is known at present about the Lithuanians who arrived at the same time from the Russian Empire; existing knowledge of parts of their economic and social life is restricted mainly to the group that settled in Scotland.[204] Many of the men north of the border eventually found employment in the coal mines, following an earlier spell as labourers in the iron and steel industry.[205] However, there is evidence of a wider pattern of employment. In 1889 Messrs Merry and Cunningham, who employed Lithuanian labour in their iron and steek works at Glengarnock in Ayrshire and at Carnbrae in Lanarkshire, told a House of Commons select committee that some of their Lithuanians had been employed previously in the sugar works in Liverpool and salt works in Cheshire. The same firm also told the committee: 'Long before we had any of them they were employed in railways work by Mr. McDonald, the contractor for the Fairlie Tunnel on the Glasgow and South Western railway . . .'.[206] Even so, wherever they were employed, the Lithuanians seem to have been concentrated in heavy labouring activity.

Their arrival created some consternation among Scottish miners who accused the newcomers of undercutting and blacklegging.[207] But here, as elsewhere in the history of immigration, it is important to

distinguish between short-term and long-term developments. As time
progressed, Lithuanian colliers began to organise and unite with
Scottish miners in order to defend their joint interests. In one major
incident in 1905 at Loganlea, a pit at which large numbers of
immigrants were employed, a strike against low rates of pay was
successful because of the solidarity of the men and seven years later
the Scottish coalfields witnessed another united stand between
Scottish and Lithuanian workers over the question of a minimum
wage. Developments such as these were significant for changing the
perceptions that Scottish miners had of the Lithuanian
newcomers.[208]

This unionisation of Lithuanians has been related partly to the
changing nature of the miners' union, and, in particular, its shift from
a 'labour aristocratic' to an 'industrial unionist' stance and also to the
growth of socialism among Scottish miners which led to a greater
interest in unifying the workforce.[209] But a danger exists in writing the
history of minorities through the activities of the majority. In this case
it is important to recognise that important changes also occurred
within the Lithuanian community in the early twentieth century.

In the early days, there was a strong continuing interest and
involvement in Lithuania and Lithuanian culture. This was reflected
in the appearance of a number of Lithuanian-language publications
such as *Vaidelytė* (*Vestal*), which first appeared in Glasgow in 1899, and
which was followed in 1905 by *Laikas* (*Time*). A similar interest was
revealed in the establishment of the Sviesa (Enlightenment) Society,
which was concerned specifically with the propagation of Lithuanian
culture among the immigrant community. Further evidence of the
continuing influence of their Lithuanian background was evident in
the shape of a burgeoning socialism, revealed in the circulation of the
imported *Darbininkų Balsas* (*Workers' Voice*), the official organ of the
Lithuanian Social Democratic Party (LSDP). This interest in
socialism resulted in the formation of a branch of the LSDP at
Bellshill in 1903 and the start of publication four years later of
Rankpelnis (*Worker*), which continued to appear fortnightly until 1923.
This involvement in socialism helped to draw together Lithuanian
and Scottish Socialists.[210]

However, these socialist inclinations were not universally held
among the Lithuanians. The Sviesa society, for instance, held itself
aloof from any such developments. Furthermore, a deep rift
developed between the Lithuanian clergy and many other members

of the community. The priests had been keen initially to secure the unionisation of the immigrants, but once they perceived a link between Socialism and the trade unions their encouragement faltered. This was hardly surprising. Socialism was condemned in the 1891 papal encyclical, *Rerum Novarum*, and in January 1914 the clergy in Lanarkshire began to publish a weekly, *Išeivių Draugas* (*Emigrants' Friend*), which attempted to counteract the influence of the Lithuanian Socialist Federation of Great Britain (LSF) as the LSDP had become known after 1907. The publication of this clerical-backed weekly 'represented the final stage in the breakdown of the community into two main factions: those who were committed to the Catholic faith and those who adhered to some form of socialist doctrine'. The First World War was to drive them further apart.[211]

Whereas the majority of Lithuanians were engaged in labouring activity, Italian immigrants were more strongly represented in the service sector. Up to the early 1880s the Italians were closely identified as street musicians and street performers. Others were noted for making and selling plaster statuettes; newcomers from the Lucca valleys were particularly prominent in this type of work. A number of artisans also came to work in Britain.[212]

In the 1880s, however, important changes became evident in the economic life of the Italian minority. Street music activity continued in evidence and one contemporary observer commented on the city presence of 'the pretty little Italian child who came from the South . . . and [sang] happily all day'.[213] But the use of children became less evident as an Italian law of 1873 affected the employment of Italian children abroad and pressures grew to improve the condition of child labour in Britain.[214] In these years the selling of statuettes also declined, as did the number of artisans. At the same time, unskilled Italians, general labourers, appeared. There was also a marked shift towards the making and selling of ice cream. Furthermore, from the 1890s to the First World War there was a noticeable increase in the number of Italian waiters and cooks. Domestic service, an expanding market, and hairdressing also attracted Italian labour as the nineteenth century drew to its close.[215]

The most remarkable development of Italians in the ice cream trade was evident in Scotland. By 1911 it was estimated that there were one thousand shops scattered throughout the country, with a particular concentration in the Clyde and Forth districts.[216] There were 220 *gelaterie* in Greenock and Coatbridge, and discerning customers also had a reasonable choice in Edinburgh.[217] Such establishments did not always confine themselves to the sale of ice cream. Soft drinks were dispensed and, in some cases, the clientèle could enjoy a game of billiards.[218] In other words, the ice cream shops were more like cafés. In the course of this development some significant entrepreneurs emerged. One of the most successful, was Leopold Giuliani, who by 1901 owned more than 60 cafés in the Clydeside area.[219]

The Italian minority was also characterised by a close-knit social life.[220] A preference for each other's company has always been a characteristic of Italian immigrants[221] and this was reflected in the organisations and associations they created. In London St Peter's Church in Clerkenwell and the Italian Hospital, both of which had been founded before 1870, continued to flourish with the arrival of more immigrants. Furthermore, 'several Italian political, economic and leisure associations and a number of Italian language periodicals reinforced this community feeling'.[222]

This strong sense of community was reflected in and assisted by the spatial concentration of Italians. As a result, the community was made up of a number of economically interdependent households and this provided a solid base around which an equally interdependent community life could be forged and immigrants could help to sustain each other.[223] But the concentration, such as that evident in Holborn or the Finsbury and King's Cross areas, was not an undiluted benefit. Contemporary investigations stressed the degree of overcrowding among the Italians and some observers dwelt at length on the insanitary conditions of some properties.[224] It was a situation which Italians were to find turned against them.[225]

Distinctive patterns also emerged in the economic and social life of those groups who originated from beyond Europe. The Chinese, it has been observed, were employed mainly as seamen. In 1901 it was estimated that 61 per cent of the Chinese were involved in this type of work. By 1911, although the figure had fallen to 36 per cent, seafaring remained the major source of Chinese employment, with the Ocean Steam Company's Blue Funnel line, based in Liverpool being a particularly important employer.[226] Under the Merchant Shipping Act of 1906 all foreign seamen had to face a language test. However, it is unlikely that in practice this had a serious impact on the employment of Chinese sailors since British subjects were exempted from the test. As a result, the Chinese had only to state that they were from Hong Kong in order to avoid the test and 'To make this statement, only a few words of English drummed into them by the Chinese crew contractors were needed'.[227]

There was, however, a noticeable new trend in the pattern of Chinese employment. This involved the setting-up of laundries. The first Chinese laundry on Merseyside, opened in 1887, was Chin Yee's at Newington, and the number of such establishments continued to increase in the early twentieth century.[228] In London in 1901 just over 6 per cent of the Chinese were employed in laundry and washing service occupations; by 1911 this number had increased to just over 26 per cent. Before the widespread ownership of washing machines and the advent of the launderette the Chinese laundry fulfilled a useful role in the service sector.[229] However, if the merchant navy and the laundry trade absorbed the majority of the Chinese, there was a scattering in other occupations.[230] In Liverpool a small number of shops had appeared by 1914 and the first restaurant was present in Forrest Street by 1907. In London it was noticed in the 1901 census there were four teachers, eleven indoor servants, four commercial business clerks and four general shopkeepers or dealers. There was also a small number of students. But, down to the Great War, the majority of the Chinese were engaged in seafaring activity.[231]

There was also a spatial concentration of the Chinese within the cities of Liverpool, London and Cardiff. The nature of their work, their concentration in seafaring, led most Chinese to congregate in areas near the docks. Hence their presence in the Pitt Street area of Liverpool. By 1914, in fact, the largest concentration was in Liverpool[232] but any contemporary reference to 'Chinatown' would have been understood as a reference to the Chinese settlement in the East End of London. Unlike the Chinatown of San Francisco, this London settlement did not cover an extensive area. It consisted only of two streets, Pennyfields and Limehouse Causeway. In 1914 there were some 30 Chinese restaurants in this area and a Chinese population of 300–400, which fluctuated according to the number of ships that were tied up in the Thames. In other words, it was, to some extent, a transient population.[233]

Within their areas of settlement the Chinese maintained a noticeable degree of social separation. Work in the merchant navy generated its own sense of transience and, in the case of the Chinese, this social separation was reinforced by the fact that most were sojourners intent on returning home once it was financially worthwhile to do so. Moreover, the separation also reflected the Chinese view that theirs was a superior culture which they were not interested in losing. In short, there were a number of layers that separated the small, sealed Chinese community from the British.[234] It was a separation that was further reflected in a number of Chinese mutual aid organisations such as the Oi T'ung Association founded in the East End in May 1907,[235] the Chinese Seamen's Union founded in the same year, and the maintenance of political links with China in the period leading up to the end of the Manchu Dynasty in 1912.

The degree of social separation was not absolute. A community made up overwhelmingly of men, looked beyond itself for sexual contacts. 'A voluble Irishwoman' who was interviewed by George Wade in one of the many investigations undertaken of the East End, retailed that she had taken a Chinese for her second husband and much preferred him to the 'son of Erin' into whose shoes he had stepped.[236] Further complimentary evidence of this kind came from the Chief Constable of Liverpool, who told the Home Office in 1906 that the Chinese had 'no difficulty in getting English women to marry them, to cohabit with them or to act the prostitute with them'.[237] Even so, allegations relating to sexual irregularities, along with an emphasis upon their involvement in opium smoking and gambling, were among the staple fare of anti-Chinese sentiment.[238]

Finally in this survey of pre-war communities, some consideration is necessary of the small, predominantly transient groups of Blacks and Indians with their recognisable class blend of seamen, entertainers, students and businessmen, that could be found particularly in ports and university towns. Such groups had a number of distinguishing features.[239]

A contemporary investigation noticed that once Eurasians, Africans and West Indians became unemployed it was extremely difficult for them ever again to find employment.[240] Yet the hostility they encountered from White seamen alone, guaranteed that there was a persistent problem of unemployment.[241] Various charities were continually picking up the human wreckage from this situation. The Strangers' Home for Asiatics, Africans and South Sea Islanders, for example, which had opened in West India Dock Road in Limehouse in 1857, shortly after the suppression of the Mutiny in India, still continued to function. Apart from providing succour in hard times those who ran the hostel had more than half an eye on the prospect of Christian conversion.[242]

Similar evidence of distress was evident within the ranks of the students, particularly those who came from India. In one particularly tragic case it was noticed that 'an educated man, an undergraduate, acted as a showman to a tea company and stood in front of the doors as an advertisement'.[243] In other cases an unexpected law suit or the inability of Indian tenants to pay their rents, could soon bring about an adverse change in personal circumstances.[244] Together with those who had become financially impoverished through the cost of legal disputes, and the seamen of various nationalities, victims of discrimination and stranded between ships, the distressed Indian students added a distinctive but generally overlooked part of 'the condition of England question' which had developed in the heart of the Empire by the late nineteenth century. At the same time, the Singh Maliks and the Nehrus of this world were immune from such problems.[245]

By way of final emphasis, it is possible to write in more positive vein about a number of political developments. Pan-Africanism, which was 'largely created by Black people living in Britain', had its origins in the eighteenth century from which point its sense of racial solidarity, its self-awareness and campaign for Africa for the Africans, had been kept alive by a number of early pioneers. In the late nineteenth century one of these was Celestine Edwards, from Dominica, who settled in Britain sometime in the 1870s. But the fact that 'the threads of emergent Pan-Africanism were at last drawn together, and a Pan-African conference convened in London in July 1900 was due above all to the work and vision of . . . Henry Sylvester Williams', who came to London in 1896 and founded the African Association in 1897.[246]

The organisation called the Pan-African Association that derived from the 1900 Conference, and the journal, *The Pan-African*, which also emerged, were both short-lived. However, both were of symbolic significance. The emergence of a stronger strain of early twentieth century Pan-Africanism was also assisted by the work of Dusé Mohamed Ali.[247] It was Ali, together with the Sierra Leonean businessman and journalist, John Eldred Taylor, who in 1912 in the shadow of the Universal Races Congress held in London in 1911, launched the *African Times and Orient Review*, 'the first political journal produced by and for black people ever published in Britain'; this publication continued to appear until the end of 1920 and during these years gave further support to the development of Pan-

Africanism.[248] As in the case of Indian nationalism, this Black political self-awareness was to move ahead at a considerable pace in the twentieth century.[249]

In the field of Indian nationalist politics a key figure was Dadabhai Naoroji. Naoroji, a Parsee, came to Britain in 1855 as a partner in Cama and Co, the first Indian business house to be established in this country,[250] but he is better known for his social and political activities. In 1861 he formed the London Zoroastrian Association to look after the welfare of Parsees in Britain, and in 1865 helped to form the London Indian Society, which had the aim of bringing together Indians and English to exchange views on India.[251] Naoroji was also an early member of the Indian National Congress and instrumental in setting up a British Committee of the Congress in 1889.[252] There was, however, an additional related dimension to Naoroji's career. In 1892 he was returned as Liberal MP for Central Finsbury, holding the seat until 1895. This success provided him with a bigger public platform from which to advance claims for the welfare of India, a theme which attracted strong sympathy from some of the Irish Nationalists at Westminster.[253]

Naoroji was one personification of a strongly identifiable Indian nationalist movement at work in Britain, sections of which by the turn of the century had become convinced of the necessity to engage in an armed struggle against British occupation. A key figure here was S. Krishnavarma who launched the Home Rule Society – the name suggests an Irish influence – in 1905. This society stood for absolute freedom from British control, in pursuit of which it advocated both passive and active resistance. Its formation was one significant expression of the 'gradual but steady radicalization' of Indian students and intellectuals, reflected particularly in the activity of Veer Savarkar, that took place from the middle of the nineteenth century in the so-called 'junction box' of the empire as well as on the sub-continent.[254]

4.

THIS discussion still leaves the question of responses from within British society towards the various immigrant and refugee groups to be considered during a time when, down to 1905, no controls existed over the entry into Britain of any group of immigrants or refugees.

Over the course of time images or stereotypes – the terms are used throughout to denote stylised beliefs relating to immigrants or refugees – were formed in Britain, and in considering responses towards these groups both in terms of attitudes and treatment, these historical influences need to be taken into account. This process of categorisation occurs in every nation. The images that circulated in Britain therefore, promulgated with varying degrees of sophistication and emphasis in academic works, literature, the press, the pulpit and other sources that flowed into public discussion, had their parallels in other countries. In every country such images reflect specific patterns of historical development and forms of specific contact. It is not suggested that stereotypes of any immigrant or refugee group remain constant or congealed. Nor is it intended to imply that such images are of simple, one-dimensional construction. Moreover, it is not suggested that there is a clear direct link at all times between perceptions and behaviour. Finally, none of the emphasis on inherited stereotypes should be taken to mean that responses of whatever kind are shaped only by the past: more immediate influences also play their part in the process of interaction.

In more specific terms what can be said of the Irish? The long-standing Protestant hostility towards Roman Catholicism, which was often perceived as a religion which comforted the enemies of Britain, helped to heighten the visibility of the Catholic Irish. Moreover, it has been claimed that the long years of colonial rule over Ireland helped to generate an impression of Irish inferiority which was further reinforced by the ascriptive treatment accorded to Irish immigrants between the 1840s and 1860s. It has also been suggested that with the development of Anglo-Saxonism in the course of the nineteenth century this impression assumed a racial dimension. On the other hand, some observers have wished to qualify such emphases by suggesting that stereotypes of the Irish combined both negative and positive qualities and to warn at the same time of the dangers inherent in applying a late twentieth-century understanding of race and racism to earlier situations: in other words, it has been suggested that the images were complex rather than one-dimensional.[255]

In 1871 with memories of the recent history of Irish immigration in mind the Census of Scotland commented: 'It is painful to contemplate what may be the ultimate effect of this Irish immigration on the morals and habits of the people and on the future prospects of the country'. By this time the bulk of Irish immigration into nineteenth-century Scotland had already occurred, but hostility towards the Irish did not disappear even if evidence of it, in common with the general history of the Irish in Britain after 1871, remains substantially unrecovered. There is, for example, little hard evidence on Scottish-Irish relations in the labour market, although Keir Hardie's withering attack on Irish colliers in the 1880s could suggest there was still some continuation of earlier fears and antipathies. Elsewhere, however, more is known. The influence of the Kirk guaranteed that sectarian hostility towards the representatives of 'that auld chap in Rome' was still expressed from time to time. Furthermore, the nationalist struggle for an independent Ireland produced expressions of hostility from within Scottish society. On occasions, in fact, religious and political opposition combined together. Moreover, at times, it was expressed within a framework derived from a perceived racial difference.[256] Such antipathies did not always stop at the spoken or printed word. In Coatbridge, in Lanarkshire, there were a number of violent incidents relating mainly to Orange and Green disputes. Indeed, such hostility, often brought to a crescendo on 12 July, was a feature of working-class life in a number of Scottish cities. Finally, there was further evidence of opposition in the violence directed towards the Irish at Partick and Glasgow in 1875 and at Coatbridge in 1883 over the Home Rule issue.[257]

The Scots did not have a monopoly of hostility. A suspicion of Roman Catholicism was also a pronounced feature of Welsh social life and, although after 1880 there was a sympathetic symbiosis of Welsh and Irish nationalism,[258] this alignment did not result in a total evaporation of anti-Irish sentiment. On the contrary, economic and religious influences working together could become addled into a powerful anti-Irish compound. On 9 July 1882 the Home Office was informed that serious anti-Irish violence had broken out in Tredegar. As a result, the Home Secretary despatched a military force to South Wales, but before the situation was brought under control considerable damage had been done to Irish property. This violence occurred against a background of change in the iron industry which affected local employment; it was in these circumstances that long-standing religious animosities were brought to the surface. Moreover, the violence was influenced by the Phoenix Park Murders in May 1882 when Lord Frederick Cavendish, the newly appointed Secretary for Ireland, and Thomas Burke, his Permanent Under-Secretary, were knifed to death in Dublin by Irish nationalists. In short, the incident revealed the complex intertwining of economic, religious and political antagonisms that could be involved in anti-Irish hostility.[259]

In England conditions in the labour market were also important in directing hostility towards the Irish. In 1888 Ben Tillett, a man of part-Irish descent, singled out for attention the threat he perceived from the presence of the Irish in the London docks. Even an involvement by some Irish and those of Irish-descent in trade union activity did not totally diminish fears about the role of the Irish in general in the labour market.[260] Age-old echoes of the Irish as a social problem also continued to be heard in some quarters down to the Great War. Engels had referred to Ireland supplying England and America with 'pimps, thieves, swindlers, beggars and other rabble'[261] and Irish criminality continued to attract critical comment.[262] The propensity of many of the Irish to consume alcohol, evident in Ireland, but which in Britain was probably not unrelated additionally to the pressures of immigration, was also held against them; even sympathetic observers worried over this love of the bottle and priests recognised it as a major problem.[263]

Furthermore, as in Scotland and Wales, some hostility was also expressed on religious grounds. A certain degree of suspicion was exhibited towards the Irish newcomers by English Catholics.[264] Irish Catholicism, it is worth reiterating, was different from the English variety.[265] Among the Irish, it has been suggested, there was 'a greater puritanism of outlook', a greater stress on 'a naive faith and, perhaps more important, a significant fusion between religion and nationalism'.[266] But if Catholics could be suspicious of each other, hostility also erupted between Protestant organisations and the newcomers. An important influence here, as in Scotland, was the development of militant Orange Associations.[267] Such activity was prominent in the north-west, particularly in 'the Marseilles of England', Liverpool.[268] It was evident, too, in nearby Birkenhead, where an outbreak of violence occurred in 1882 after a group of Irish had insulted the Salvation Army. This religious brand of hostility had deep roots in English society but it was exacerbated by the restoration of the Catholic hierarchy in England in 1850. It might well be an exaggeration to claim that '. . . the greatest heat of anti-Irish bigotry has stemmed from religious differences',[269] but religion, singly or in combination with other fears, was an important source of friction between 1870 and 1914. This claim should hardly cause any surprise;

anti-Catholicism 'was central to Victorian culture' and, as such, had a broad measure of support.[270]

By the late nineteenth century the fight for Irish independence was also exerting an effect over responses towards the Irish in England just as it did in Wales and Scotland. This hostility, which was capable of developing a religious dimension, was particularly influenced by events in Ireland. Phoenix Park acted as a major catalyst in England just as it did elsewhere.[271] In the dark shadow of the nationalist knives, attacks on the mainland Irish occurred at Camborne, and at Brighouse in Yorkshire, whilst the Irish in Stalybridge lived anxiously under the threat of attack from Protestant Orangemen.[272]

So how is it possible to summarise the reception of the Irish? In some urban centres such as on Tyneside and in Dundee local conditions guaranteed that hostility was relatively weak.[273] Furthermore, evidence from the Oxfordshire and Lincolnshire countryside would suggest that by the late nineteenth century there was less opposition than in the past to 'they jabberin' old Irish' and their 'Paddy wagons'.[274] Indeed, it is possible that for a variety of economic, religious and political reasons, there was a general reduction in hostility and the Irish were less evidently categorised as outcasts.[275] However, a happy picture drawn on such lines needs to be qualified. In centres such as Liverpool a particularly fierce anti-Irish sentiment existed which was capable of combining various complementary strands of antipathy and susceptible to political exploitation.[276] On a personal level, if Catholics were anxious to avoid lapses from the faith through intermarriage, evidence from Salford would suggest that there was continued opposition in Protestant working-class families to intermarriage with some elements of the Catholic Irish.[277] In other parts of the country a smouldering anti-Irish tradition lurked beneath the surface ready to be triggered into social significance as it was in Tredegar in 1882.[278] Irish nationalist activity, Gladstone's conversion to Home Rule notwithstanding, exercised a detectable leverage over sentiment.[279] Furthermore, by the late nineteenth century some of this anti-Irish hostility had assumed a racial dimension, even if this had a complexity that sometimes has been imperfectly understood.[280]

Overall, however, responses to the Irish were complex. 'An English radical or Liberal repelled by an Irishman's Catholicism might well rejoice in his radicalism or Liberalism; a High Churchman repelled by an Irishman's Liberalism might well respect his Catholicism . . .':

this complexity was further underlined by the respect held out by preachers of Anglo-Saxonism for certain Celtic qualities.[281] Finally, it is revealing that in Robert Roberts' Salford opposition to a mixed marriage arose when it involved 'some *low* Mick from the Bog'.[282] This qualification is a reminder that opposition to the Irish was directed mainly at the Irish working class.[283]

The debates over the Irish presence did not mean that other groups escaped public attention. In the case of the Germans there were royal links with the House of Hanover and, more recently, the marriage of Albert and Victoria added another link to the dynastic chain. The existence of such bonds, it has been suggested, helped the image of Germans in Britain. Moreover, it might be thought that the increasing emphasis on the Germanic origins of British society and its institutions – a link assiduously fostered in Victorian Britain by a number of historians such as E. A. Freeman – would influence the reception of Germans. But, in practice, life was more complex. The behaviour of the Hanoverians was not of undiluted benefit. The opposition of William Cobbett, that sturdiest of English yeoman, to the Germanisation of the British army, an opposition brought to a head by the flogging of English soldiers by Germans at Ely in 1809, was mirrored elsewhere. Furthermore, the arrival of Albert was not regarded at the time with undisguised delight. At the same time, refugees from Central Europe were generally well-received within Britain. All told, however, a good deal remains unknown about the perceptions and treatment of Germans – and indeed other European minorities – but it would appear that these involved a degree of complexity and, as with all groups, responses were likely to be influenced by specific and changing circumstances. Would the German Jews manage to avoid the anti-Jewish antipathies that were evident in Britain in the late nineteenth and early twentieth centuries? How would all Germans fare if tension developed between Germany and Britain?[284]

Issues such as these were to be raised between 1871 and 1914, but it is possible to begin from a different vantage point. City firms might benefit from the expertise of German labour skilled in European languages. However, clerical workers perceived the situation in a different light and their mood of opposition was well caught in the 1880s in the columns of *The Clerks' Journal*. It was claimed that these Germans undercut their British contemporaries and it would indeed appear that the often highly-qualified German clerks were willing to work for the level of wages 'paid to British female shorthand typists or junior clerks at the bottom end of the labour market'. This undercutting was particularly important in one highly specialised area, the employment of foreign correspondents. Some of the more experienced German clerks in this category requested salaries of between £100–£150 a year, but most were willing to work for a sum between £60 and £90 and some for as little as £40. British clerks who applied for such posts all demanded salaries of £100 or more. A small number of foreign correspondents from Germany were prepared to work without a salary, although they were not so numerous as was sometimes imagined.[285]

However, hostility towards the German clerks was influenced by more than wage competition. It was closely related to the general commercial ambience of the last quarter of the nineteenth century. During these years there was an increase in clerical unemployment as firms failed to cut their costs in the face of increasing competition and falling profits. Consequently, there was an oversupply of low-status clerks. It is true that better-placed clerks were not seriously affected by problems of unemployment, low wages and job competition, but this group did face other difficulties. It had become a recognised practice that ultimately these workers would achieve economic independence and set up business on their own account. But the failure of firms in the Great Depression and the increase in the scale of business organisation combined to reduce such opportunities. In these circumstances the entry of German clerks into key positions and, in some instances, the capacity of the newcomers to establish their own businesses, created a seething resentment. In other words, the antipathy expressed towards 'Max von Sauerkraut' was located within a complex web of economic and social change, an 'understanding' of which was only too easily reduced to the German presence.[286]

The hostility encountered by the clerks was further exacerbated by the wider issue of Anglo-German rivalry that developed after 1870. There was a strand of admiration in Britain for German economic and social organisation; in fact, Germany and Japan were two exemplars that were placed before the British public in the years between 1870 and 1914.[287] But images of national states are never one-dimensional, and during these years a fear developed of Germany's growing economic power. E. E. Williams's paranoid *Made in Germany* was a classic example of this paranoia.[288] Following the

Franco-Prussian War of 1870–71 a simultaneous fear developed of German military strength which gathered pace from the late nineteenth century and this fear also influenced perceptions of those Germans living and working in Britain.[289]

In the case of the German-born elite, a sharp deterioration in their position, some of which reflected the growth of anti-Semitic sentiments, became evident after the death of Edward VII in 1910. Until then individuals such as Sir Ernest Cassel and Sir Felix Semon had managed to exercise their talents in Britain without encountering any remarkable hostility. But with the death of the king a powerful source of patronage was lost and the older elite in British society who were ever ready to despise the *nouveaux riches* foreigners, yet perfectly happy to profit from their connection with them, turned increasingly savage. Max Beerbohm's cartoon, 'Are we as welcome as ever?' which depicted some of the newcomers worrying about the future, caught the mood of the times.[290]

But the changed atmosphere in which the rich Germans found themselves was related to more than the death of the king. Trade rivalry and the drift towards war also created major problems for the elite just as it did for the German clerks. In these circumstances favourable images could change and an admiration of German efficiency could become translated into fear. In this changing situation some of the German-born businessmen continued to maintain close links with Germany. They were particularly anxious about the possible outbreak of hostilities and many worked hard for the cause of Anglo-German friendship. Indeed, even those Germans who had no commercial ties with Germany were disconcerted by the deteriorating political situation. But there were those in Britain who regarded any attempt to improve relations with Germany as an act of treachery. George Chesney's novel, *The Battle of Dorking Sands*, had speculated as early as 1871 about a possible German invasion of Britain and as the years rolled on, popular literature such as that written by John Buchan and William Le Queux, became stuffed with German villains.[291] These literary artefacts also reflected the 'spy fever' which gripped Britain before the war and further underlined the German menace. In these circumstances sections of the Conservative press, such as Leo Maxse's *National Review*, regarded Germany with unmitigated hatred. Maxse was deeply suspicious of all Germans and those who tried to bridge the gap between the two nations were accused of working in the interests of 'the Fatherland'.

Such tensions, which led to the Official Secrets Act in 1911, were to increase once war broke out in 1914.[292]

Some of the sharpest xenophobic hostility before 1914 was reserved not for the German clerks or businessmen but for the so-called German gypsies who first arrived from Rotterdam on 1 December 1904. Soon after they landed, the gypsies were being forcibly driven over county boundaries by police forces acting on behalf of their local authorities. In sharp contrast to such reactions, the newcomers were a source of great delight to members of the Gypsy Lore Society, which had been founded in 1888 to study gypsy culture. The sympathies of this group, however, were overshadowed by the continuing hostility the gypsies encountered.

The gypsy newcomers were never numerous, an indication that the emergence of hostility does not correlate in simple fashion with numbers, and they had not broken any law when they entered the country. They were able to support themselves and constituted no financial drain on the British. However, a number of influences combined to drive them back to the Continent. There was some concern, as there had been for centuries, about the nomadic life style of the gypsies. Furthermore, there was some disquiet in government circles that the dumping of the gypsies might be the first step in the arrival of unwanted cargoes from the Continent. There was considerable relief, therefore, in Whitehall, when two charitable organisations, the Society of Friends of Foreigners in Distress and the German Benevolent Society decided to assume responsibility for shipping the gypsies back to Germany. 'So far so good' one satisfied Home Office official noted on the official file.[293]

The first stage of the German gypsy episode was over. But soon, as further gypsies began to arrive, hostility once more developed against them. They encountered opposition from the indigenous gypsies. They were attacked by police and workmen in Lancashire in August 1906. In Leicestershire the police drove them over the county boundary into Warwickshire and, when they were in Northampton, the Chief Constable, in a communication to the Home Office written on 30 November 1906, made no attempt to disguise his own hostility. They were, he wrote, 'a most objectionable band to have roaming about the Country . . . they live by masterful begging and thieving . . .'. In short, they were 'a standing menace to law and order'.[294]

By this time tension had increased because their presence had become part of a wider issue. It had been taken up by the anti-alien lobby which had campaigned against Jewish immigration since the 1880s and now believed it had an opportunity to secure a tightening of the 1905 Aliens Act which had been passed by the time the second batch of gypsies arrived. 'How are we to get rid of these wretched people?' asked Sir Howard Vincent, the inveterate anti-immigration campaigner.[295]

For its part the Liberal government which came into power in 1905 and inherited the 1905 Aliens Act from the previous administration, expressed its willingness to take action against any shipping company which it believed was trading in gypsies between Europe and Britain. But, more decisively, the government, through the agency of the police, rounded up the gypsies who had already landed in Britain. The gypsies had not contravened the 1905 Aliens Act but, as a result of the harassment they had encountered, many of them were prepared to be transported back to an uncertain future in Europe. Consequently, behind the protective cover of the Society of Friends of Foreigners in Distress the government deported the gypsies to Germany. The government had shown a degree of resolution. It had been firm with a weak and exposed minority. It had gone part of the way down a path to placate the anti-alien lobby. It doubtless felt pleased with itself.[296]

Other gypsies continued to arrive from the Continent down to the Great War, but outside the immediate tensions generated by the 1905 Aliens Act, they did not attract the intense interest that attached itself to a few hundred earlier arrivals.

The hostile agitation surrounding the 1905 Aliens Act into which the gypsies were drawn, was directed mainly against the Jewish newcomers from Russian Poland whose numbers rose persistently after 1880. It would be a mistake to assume, however, that these Jews encountered a universal, unremitting hostility.

When the immigration from Russian Poland began, it is doubtful if much thought had been given in Britain to the Jewish community residing in such far-off parts. What is more certain is that by the time of their arrival a number of well-defined images of Jews were present in British society. By the 1880s the centuries-old image of Jews as Christ-killers, a source of much historical antipathy and discrimination, had lost much of its force, although strands of religious opposition towards Jews continued to exist. By this time, however, other impressions had assumed some significance. The

prolonged battle for Jewish Emancipation, which lasted longer than
for any other religious minority, had generated a perception in some
quarters outside Anglo-Jewry that the Jews were an awkward
minority. Moreover, the restrictions on Jewish employment before
Emancipation and the subsequent concentration of Jews in business
and finance, led to the stereotype of Jews as the personification of
capitalism; this image, in particular, was to influence divergent
responses towards the Jews. However, the degree to which such
images circulated, and the nature of their transmission, remain
uncertain. What can be suggested, however, is that the responses
towards the newcomers from Russian Poland were closely related to
specific tensions located in the economic, social and political context
of the late nineteenth and early twentieth centuries.[297]

For example, they were portrayed often in Smilesean terms as the
incarnation of self-help, hard work, self-denial and deferred
gratification.[298] Sometimes this claim was cast in a broad historical
context in which the Russian Jews were likened to the Huguenot
immigrants of the seventeenth century, from whose settlement it was
claimed, the country had derived important economic benefits.[299] It
was not uncommon to find such sentiments being supported by the
observation that emigration from Britain exceeded the weight of
immigration; a remark which carried the implication that the arrival
of the newcomers from the Russian Empire could not pose any serious
social problems. There was also a strong opposition among Liberals
to any proposal which would exclude those immigrants without
visible means of support. Moreover, although the tradition of political
asylum weakened in the late nineteenth century, Liberal voices were
still raised against any proposal to exclude those suffering
persecution, particularly when it derived from the actions of the
tsarist despotism.[300]

But it was not from the strength of Liberal ideology alone that the
immigrants received support. Their case was also argued from within
sections of the Labour movement. William Morris's Socialist League,
founded in 1894, was prominent in this respect although it was an
organisation which had disappeared before the great influx of Jews
occurred. Positive responses also emerged from within the Social
Democratic Federation at the same time as sections of the SDF were
engaged in attacks on Jewish capitalists. But such support was not
evident everywhere and at all times and the responses of socialists to
the wider 'Jewish Question' were quite complex.[301]

A degree of complexity was also evident in the responses of the established Anglo-Jewish elite, whose apex was represented by the so-called 'Cousinhood' of major families. It was feared initially within this group that the immigrants would direct attention to the Jewish community and threaten the *modus vivendi* between Jew and Gentile which had been worked out in the Victorian years. An involvement by some Jews in the White slave traffic was one avenue through which it was believed all Jews might become visible. Anxieties such as this, as well as class differences, affected the perceptions and responses of the Anglo-Jewish elite and led to its involvement in the return of some immigrants to Eastern Europe. On the other hand, some prominent members of the community assisted the settlement of the newcomers. The foundation of the Poor Jews' Temporary Shelter was one indication of such help and, on balance, the immigrants might well have suffered more than they did, had it not been for the presence and influence of the established Anglo-Jewish community.[302]

Finally, although Liberals inside and outside parliament were prominent in the defence of the immigrants, the view of Britain as a refuge and haven for the oppressed and persecuted from other lands stretched beyond the ranks of the Liberal Party. Indeed, it congealed as a widely-held tradition. It is significant that in spite of pressures from a number of their backbenchers, which could count upon a measure of public support, there was a clear reluctance among Conservative governments to interfere with the inflow of immigration whether of Jews or other aliens. The result was that even the 1905 Aliens Act, passed by a Conservative administration, was only a muted measure of control, although it is probable that its psychological impact was greater than its provisions would suggest.[303]

Even so, vociferous voices were raised against the immigration from Russian Poland and hostile pens scratched out antipathetic messages. Such opposition ranged along a number of issues. At the same time as some Liberals could write fulsomely about the Jewish immigrants as the personification of capitalist virtues, others who accepted much of this image drew different conclusions. J. A. Hobson commented in stereotyped vein that the virtues of the Jewish immigrant were his vices. It was because the immigrant was 'willing and able to work so hard for so little pay', because he was prepared to undertake any kind of work out of which he could make a living and because he surpassed the native Londoner in 'skill, industry and adaptability', that the foreign Jew was 'such a terrible competitor'.[304] To those like Hobson who rejected the philosophy of laissez-faire economics a defence of the immigrants as Ricardo's *homo oeconomicus* was not compelling. A common perception of their qualities could lead to substantially different conclusions about the desirability of the presence of these immigrant Jews.[305]

The praise that was lavished generally and generously on the immigrants on account of their putative economic virtues, also made little headway among those sections of society who perceived a threat to their employment as a result of the immigration from Russian Poland. This strand of hostility was particularly strong in the areas of immigrant settlement such as the East End. On occasions, in fact, it could be claimed that a major economic problem in this area, that of sweating, was related chiefly to the 'swarms of foreign Jews' who had 'invaded the East End' and turned it into a sweater's paradise.[306]

But it was not only allegations relating to employment, reflected at Trade Union Congresses in 1892, 1894 and 1895 that revealed the build-up of tension over immigration from the Russian Empire. In the early years of the present century, the alleged impact of immigrant Russian Poles on the housing market also became a focus of hostility. In the East End, the major area of settlement, they were accused of securing property at the expense of the local inhabitants and the activities of some Jewish landlords were called into question.[307] It was in an attempt to defuse such developments, expressed in the press, at public meetings, and outbreaks of physical violence, that organisations such as the Four Per Cent Industrial Dwellings Company were set up by wealthy representatives of Anglo-Jewry to secure the dispersal of the immigrants.[308]

Allied to such fears were those which concentrated on the striking intrusion into the East End of London of an alien culture. The *East London Advertiser* provided one indication of this fear at the turn of the century. 'People of any other nation, after being in England for only a short time, assimilate themselves with the native race and by and by lose nearly all their foreign trace. But the Jews never do. A Jew is always a Jew'.[309] This anxiety concerning the challenge to an indigenous, tenacious working-class culture, was echoed elsewhere, as when James William Johnson of the British Brothers' League gave evidence before the Royal Commission on Alien Immigration. On this occasion he took the opportunity to emphasise that the immigrants lived 'according to their traditions, usages and customs' in a way which, he asserted, was wholly deleterious to the Englishman. Indeed, in Johnson's opinion, it could be claimed that Whitechapel was becoming a New Jerusalem.[310]

Such economic and social fears provided staple elements in the opposition to the Jews from the Russian Empire. But additional fears and arguments became stitched into the response patterns. J. L. Silver, the influential editor of the *Eastern Post and City Chronicle*, hoped he would never see the day when there would 'be grafted onto the English stock and diffused into English blood, the debilitated, the sickly and the vicious products of Europe'.[311] Moreover, David Hope Kyd, a Conservative parliamentary candidate, speaking in the East End in 1903, asserted that prolonged association and intermarriage with aliens would lead only to the 'extermination of the British workingman in the East End of London'.[312] Such fears were not confined to the East End. Similar sentiments sprang with considerable viciousness from the pages of *England under the Jews*, Joseph Banister's virulent outpouring of hatred against 'the Jew's nature and race' which Banister found 'objectionable'.[313]

None of this antipathy, it should be stressed, emerged in a vacuum. It related to the debate that was taking place over the state of the nation, when Britain was no longer 'the workshop of the world', when protectionist sentiment developed against foreign goods and labour, when there was much public concern about the sweated trades and the lives of unskilled and casual workers, and when conditions in British cities gave rise to public anxiety. These developments and the associated fears that the nation was overstocked, that resources were fixed, and also that the nation had reached if not passed the zenith of its industrial development, placed the immigration of the Russian Jews, whose presence touched these issues at a number of points, in a particularly sharp focus. In the East End there were, additionally, specific local pressures, especially in the employment and housing markets, that provided a raw local context for the emergence of various local conflicts.[314]

But did the opposition amount to any more than hot air? It is theoretically possible for antipathy to exist without discrimination, the practice of differential treatment.[315] But in fact discrimination did occur. In Bethnal Green in 1901 the Liberal and Radical Club passed a resolution that in future no candidate would be accepted as a member if he were a Jew. Furthermore, in Leeds, it was not unknown for immigrant Jews in search of employment to encounter the stumbling block 'No Jews need apply', a restriction that ted in the housing market.[316] However, discrimination was ... confined to those centres with a rising immigrant population. When Lewis Namier applied for a Fellowship at All Souls in 1911, one of those present at the election meeting commented: 'The best man by far in sheer intellect was a Balliol man of Polish-Jewish origin and I did my best for him, but the Warden and the majority of Fellows shied at his race . . .'.[317] Such discrimination was a firm reminder that antipathy towards Jews could cut across the barriers of social class.

In some instances this opposition to Jews from the Russian Empire transcended the level of individuals and led to the formation of organisations. This was evident in 1901 with the founding of the British Brothers' League. The BBL, essentially an alliance of East End workers and backbench Tory MPs such as Sir Howard Vincent and Major William Eden Evans-Gordon, dominated the organised response in the East End to Jewish immigration in the early days of the century and its 'monster' meeting at the People's Palace on 14 January 1902, which resounded to the strains of 'Soldiers of the Queen', 'God Bless the Prince of Wales', 'There's no place like home' and 'Britons never shall be slaves', received particular prominence.[318] However, although the BBL continued to exist until 1905, its major thrust had gone by 1903. It had depended ultimately on the support and organisation of backbench Tory MPs and, as anti-Semitism within the movement assumed overt proportions, the MPs beat a retreat. Their new home was the more respectable Immigration Reform Association, established in February 1903, which became the key pressure group working for immigration control in the years that led up to the 1905 Aliens Act.[319]

In its most extreme form opposition to the immigrants was reflected, not in literature, speeches or pressure groups but in collective violence. In June 1903 in Bethnal Green in the area known as Jew's Island violence was directed towards Jews after a causal connection had been established in the minds of some local residents between the displacement of a number of long-established families and the presence of Jewish newcomers.[320] Violence, however, was not confined to London. In the Leylands area of Leeds running fights were a frequent occurrence, particularly on pay day, when local gangs selected Jewish newcomers for particular attention. Salford witnessed similar scenes.[321]

Violence on a more substantial scale occurred at Tredegar in South

Wales in the summer of 1911. In July of that year the Chinese community in Cardiff found itself under attack and in the following month the valleys erupted with violence against the Jews. The timing was not accidental. The year-long Cambrian coal strike had ended in August 1911 and in the same month the national rail strike began. There was, therefore, at this time considerable hardship in South Wales and it was against this background that the violence occurred. Certain Jewish middlemen were believed to have exploited the hardship for their own ends and this provided a spur to the violence, although the events can be understood only by taking into account a number of other influences, such as the alien visibility of the Jews, and, probably, the strong currents of the Baptist revival then sweeping through the valleys of South Wales, which added a strain of religious hostility to the conflict.[322]

Among the various immigrant groups that arrived in Britain after 1870, it was the Russian Jews who magnetised public attention.[323] But did their presence lead to any changes in the national policy on immigration? In 1871 there were no restrictions on entry into Britain. Legislation had been passed in 1793, following the Revolution in France, which allowed for the exclusion of aliens in wartime. However, this legislation was repealed in 1826 and the new Aliens Act of that year and the 1836 Aliens Registration Act were both concerned with the registration rather than the regulation of entry. Furthermore, even in an age obsessed with those aspects of life that could be 'measured and weighed and calculated',[324] these Acts were not vigorously enforced. A few years later in 1848, when revolution spread across Europe, and the Chartists planned their great rally on Kennington Common, new legislation allowed the Home Secretary to control the entry of aliens and provide for their deportation. This act remained on the Statute Book for two years but it was never used. Hence, by 1871, there were no restrictions on the entry of aliens.[325] Some of those who opposed the entry of the Russian Poles were concerned about this state of affairs and the majority report of the Royal Commission on Alien Immigration recommended in its 1903 report that 'undesirable' aliens should be kept out of Britain.[326]

Such were the recommendations. In fact, the 1905 Aliens Act, as it appeared on the Statute Book, bore little relationship to the recommendation of the Royal Commission. The first bill, introduced by Balfour's Conservative government in April 1904, followed closely the Commission's report of the previous year. But it encountered considerable parliamentary opposition. How was it possible to decide who fitted the category of 'persons of notoriously bad character' and 'persons likely to become a public charge', all of whom it was intended to exclude? How feasible was it, in practical policy terms, to create areas in which the settlement of immigrants would be prohibited? Faced with opposition, the government put the Bill to a Grand Committee where it was abandoned.[327]

The second bite at restriction came in 1905. The aim was still to exclude 'undesirable and destitute aliens' but these terms were now more sharply defined and there was no reference to those of 'notoriously bad character'. Controls were established over an 'immigrant ship', defined as one which carried twenty or more alien steerage passengers. Such ships were required to berth at specific immigrant ports. Immigrants could go before an Appeals Board if objections were raised to their admission and any immigrant who could prove that entry to Britain was being sought to avoid persecution for a political offence was explicitly safeguarded. The provisions relating to expulsion remained essentially the same as in the previous Bill and depended on a court order. Finally, the clause on prohibited areas disappeared in the new measure. In the committee stage further concessions were made; for example, considerable safeguards were devised for religious refugees. Furthermore, the Bill no longer concerned itself with transmigrants. It was a measure with these emphases that became the 1905 Aliens Act on 10 August 1905.[328]

Down to 1914 the Act was administered in turn by Conservative and Liberal governments and modified under both. In tune with the powers conferred upon him by the Act, the Conservative Home Secretary, A. Akers-Douglas, decided quickly that an immigrant ship should be defined as one which carried twelve alien steerage passengers rather than the twenty stipulated in the Act. In 1906, however, once the Liberals were in office, the new Home Secretary, Herbert Gladstone, raised the number to twenty.[329] Furthermore, under the Liberals the benefit of the doubt in cases involving religious and political asylum was operated generally in favour of the immigrants and the categories favoured by exemption were also widened. As a result, the anti-alien lobby began to talk about a drastic change in the nature of the Act. But it has to be recognised that the Liberals, although they were prepared to work the Act as humanely as possible, made no attempt to repeal it or to consider the fundamental issue of how the Act might be worked in the future by an anti-alien Home Secretary. In their unease, the Liberals were prepared to go so far but no further. Indeed, in the years immediately preceding the war well-publicised episodes involving alien crime and anarchism, such as the Tottenham outrages, the Hounsditch robbery and the siege of Sidney Street, made it difficult to make concessions; in fact, there was a greater prospect of the restrictive sections of the Act being strengthened.[330]

The 1905 Act was brought on to the Statute Book by the campaign that was mounted against the Jews from Russian Poland but it affected all aliens, including the Lithuanians, who like the Russian Poles were emigrants from the tsar's empire, and about whom there was little if any pre-existing knowledge in Britain.

With the immigration of the Lithuanian Catholics into Lanarkshire and other areas of Scotland, certain sections of the local workforce 'perceived a distinct threat to their way of life'. This fear was particularly evident in the coal industry where there was a sharp increase in the employment of alien labour. At first it would seem that reaction was muted, but by the late 1880s a distinct strain of hostility had surfaced which continued into the early twentieth century.[331]

In its early days the campaign against Lithuanian workers was associated particularly with Keir Hardie who 'saw their employment as a possible threat to the new Ayrshire Miners' Union . . .'.[332] Like Irish workers before them, it has been noticed that the Lithuanians were often perceived partly as undercutters of the local workforce and a source of blackleg labour. It was also urged that they were a danger to the safety of all miners since they were unskilled workers, operating in an unfamiliar working environment, with at best only a rudimentary knowledge of the English language.[333] Such responses need to be set within their appropriate context. On 18 May 1903 Robert Smillie, the president of the Lanarkshire miners, told the Royal Commission on Alien Immigration that because of unemployment in the mines of Lanarkshire Scottish miners were emigrating to the United States and Canada.[334] It was in these difficult times that some coal owners tried to reduce their costs by employing Lithuanians 'usually at lower rates'.[335] Hostility in the mining communities grew out of this particular ground.

From a different perspective, the situation was described with contrary emphases. John Ronaldson, the inspector of mines for the West of Scotland, dilated on the virtues of the Lithuanians. He told the Royal Commission on Mines in 1907 that 'they were far more amenable to discipline than our own men'. This observation, he affirmed, was 'the universal testimony of the managers'. If Lithuanians knew they had a task to do they did it and in this respect they formed 'a striking contrast' to 'a good many' Scottish workmen.[336]

It has been suggested that Lithuanian immigrants *were* used at times to undercut local labour and as strikebreakers.[337] As a result, the apprehension of British workers can be understood. However, the opposition to Lithuanians as a source of cheap labour diminished in the early twentieth century with the increasing unionisation of the Lithuanian miners and in these circumstances a major reversal of sentiment occurred.[338] It has also been suggested that there was some gradual reduction in the hostility that Lithuanians encountered outside the workplace. This was particularly evident in labour circles which had earlier castigated Lithuanians as a threat to Scottish 'health and morality' or indeed as 'a plague' that had descended on the country.[339]

However, not every strand of hostility disappeared. Some of it remained in what have been described as the 'petit bourgeois viewpoints' which appeared in local newspapers. Here the immigrants were referred to as 'a barbarous, treacherous people' and those in the Bellshill district were categorised as 'the very scum of their nation'.[340] Moreover, the progressive involvement of Lithuanians in trade union and Socialist activity not only upset the Lithuanian clergy, it also shattered their image, in the eyes of Scottish employers, as a cheap and docile labour workforce, on which grounds they had previously been tolerated.[341]

After the passing of the 1905 Aliens Act when deportation was possible on the basis of a court order, it was not uncommon for Lithuanians who transgressed the law in the course of industrial disputes to find themselves the subject of a deportation order under the 1905 Act.[342] Those with previous sentences were particularly exposed. It was also believed in the trade union movement that Lithuanians received generally harsher treatment at the hands of the local magistrates and police for their participation in industrial disputes.[343] The full weight of official hostility to Lithuanians, however, was to emerge later in the course of the First World War which was decisive in another respect for the Lithuanian community.[344]

Finally among European groups, the Italian immigrants came from a country which in view of its classical and later cultural connotations held a special place in the world of the educated Victorian elite in Britain. Moreover, there was considerable enthusiasm and practical help from mid-Victorian Britain for the cause of Italian unification. Within Britain itself, by 1871 the small number of Italians had been notable as bearers of culture, entertainers and political refugees. Although the religious among them were representatives of Catholicism in a predominantly Protestant country, in their various roles the Italians seem to have been generally tolerated, in the sense that individuals and groups positively endured or 'put up with' their presence. Nevertheless, it has been suggested that in a world where 'niggers begin at Calais' Italians in the mass were not highly esteemed by the British. But this assessment is impressionistic; it is worth reiterating that little is known about the categorisation of Europeans by the British and popular perceptions remain obstinately obscure.[345]

Between 1871 and 1914 Italians in Britain came into public focus in a number of situations. In a society where an interest in the family, children and childhood assumed an increasing significance, a strong strain of moral criticism emerged over the exploitation of children in the street trades, which was a dominant feature of Italian employment down to the 1880s. These youngsters were sold into the charge of *padroni* (masters) in Italy who then proceeded to work the children under their 'protection' in British cities. Before the introduction of tighter controls over the employment of children, both in Italy and Britain, there does seem to have been a problem here, involving a considerable degree of human exploitation which captured the caring attention of, among others, Thomas Barnardo, as well as the vigilant eye of the Charity Organisation Society. This concern over the exploitation of children overshadowed that deriving from the noise and nuisance of street music. Disquiet over this development, which reflected part of a general concern about the turmoil of urban life, drove John Leech, the *Punch* cartoonist, to distraction, and led to some sharp criticism of the Italians in the 1860s.[346]

By the late nineteenth century, however, attention was diverted away from the street musicians towards the waiters, cooks and domestic workers who arrived in increasing numbers to service the needs of the British middle class.[347] For those who employed them in their homes Italians were counted as a necessary support for a civilised life style. 'A man must have his biscuit!', an earlier Duke had exclaimed, 'when a friend hinted that four Italian confectioners in his kitchen might be superfluous',[348] and in the late nineteenth century there were those commentators who perceived the 'confectioners, cooks and waiters' as 'notable exceptions' to the majority of Italians who were considered morally contemptible.[349] Viewed from a different perspective, however, Italian service labour was greeted with less enthusiasm. In the late nineteenth century its arrival 'stiffened competition' in casual employment and it would seem that English waiters found their employment becoming more precarious.[350]

In Scotland hostility also developed towards Italians on account of the competition they generated through their considerable presence in the ice cream business. Mixed in with business jealousy was a degree of religious hostility from Protestants.[351] Furthermore, the United Free Church condemned Sunday trading by Italians and some members of the clergy lost no opportunity to emphasise that there were better uses to which the working class could put their money than handing it over to Italian businesses.[352]

In addition, some public concern was expressed about the degree of overcrowding among the Italian community. It was a concern which was related to fears of disease and moral decay, both of which were often related to urban deficiencies. These anxieties had been evident since the mid-nineteenth century and public concern showed little sign of diminution as the century wore on. Indeed, in 1879 *The Lancet* produced a specialist report on the Italians in London which concluded that their colony 'would soon become a standing menace to the public health of London'.[353] This anxiety became linked with the increasing impression made by Italians in the ice cream trade; the ice cream makers were accused of manufacturing their product in filthy conditions.[354]

The emphasis on living conditions became linked with another charge which stressed an involvement by Italians in criminal behaviour. Such activity was sometimes associated with Italian clubs which were formed in London, particularly in Soho.[355] Clubs of a different kind were also noticed; for example, it was suggested that a grave public danger arose through the attachment of Italians to the 'secret socialistic or revolutionary leagues' which some conservative souls, concerned with preserving the stability of British society, perceived as proliferating in abundance as a result of Britain's open-door policy. In the late nineteenth century London was certainly a home for a number of European anarchists, including the well-known Italian activist, Enrico Malatesta.[356] Moreover, the House of Commons, the Tower, Greenwich Observatory, London Bridge and Nelson's Column were all subjected to bomb attacks. Joseph Conrad's *The Secret Agent* caught a whiff of the ambience which provided the background to this particular segment of anti-Italian hostility and also down to the Great War led to continued rumblings against a wide range of anarchist groups.[357]

All told, responses towards the Italians were complex. The grandeur of Italy's past did not always guarantee a positive response towards the Italian minority. But among those who raised their voices against Italians it was possible to find distinctions being made between Northerners and Southerners, with hostility reserved for the latter. Furthermore, the overall tenor of comments heard by the Royal Commission on Alien Immigration in 1903 was neither damning nor damaging. Indeed, Arnold White, one of the fiercest critics of Jewish immigration, was much more positive about the Italians, particularly the second generation, who, he claimed, in contrast to the Jews 'absolutely blend with the nation'.[358] Viewed from another perspective, however, this response was an early reminder that toleration or acceptance of a group was sometimes linked to the understanding that ultimately it should lose any distinctive self-identity.

This discussion still leaves responses towards non-Europeans, the Chinese, the Blacks and the Indians to be considered. Before 1871 there were few in Britain who had any direct contact with the Chinese minority. The exception was in the ports where they had just begun to appear in larger numbers, encountering in some instances a degree of suspicion and distrust among White seamen who viewed Chinese merchant sailors as a source of cheap and docile labour. In addition, stereotyped opinions circulated on the Chinese in the shape of the reports from commentators who had visited the Far East. In this material there was some emphasis on the diligence of the Chinese. But there were also references to their depravity, and, on balance, it was the backwardness and stagnation of China which predominated in public discussion. Overall, however, perceptions were complex and this complexity continued to be evident in the images of China and the Chinese that emerged between 1871 and 1914.[359]

But what can be said of the Chinese in Britain? The diligence which the Chinese were perceived to possess was a distinctly double-edged quality. 'The women [of East London] have been fitly termed . . . Chinamen . . . they accept any work at any wage'. So wrote the young Beatrice Potter in 1888.[360] In advancing this perception of the Chinese, she was not alone. In 1873 *The Times* commented, 'In the present discontent of our coal miners it may not be inopportune to state what is the amount received by their Chinese brethren'.[361] The same paper returned to the theme four years later, emphasising that '. . . when white men make exorbitant demands for wages, when they begin striking and giving trouble in a thousand ways, the employer of labour may be glad that he is not absolutely dependent on them and that he has at hand a more docile race of beings'.[362] In the same year *The Times* carried a report from a correspondent in New South Wales which drew attention to the other side of the coin, in its remark, 'All the working classes instinctively resent the idea of a Chinese proletariat'.[363]

This fear of the Chinese as a source of cheap labour was undoubtedly present in Britain in the late nineteenth century. Publications such as *Clarion*, *Justice* and *Reynolds's Newspaper* all expressed their concern at the prospect of Chinese competition, but with the increasing recruitment of Chinese into the shipping industry, it was from among seamen that the fiercest and most persistent hostility developed.[364]

It was for Chinese seamen that J. Havelock Wilson MP, the self-styled 'Captain' Edward Tupper and sources sympathetic to the National Sailors' and Firemen's Union (NSFU), reserved their fiercest vitriol.[365] 'You know, we know and they know, that the Chinaman isn't worth a toss as a seaman', *The Maritime Review* told its readers, '. . . his only claim to indulgence is that he is cheap'.[366] This fear and the perception of Chinese as strikebreakers were constantly emphasised in campaigns mounted by the NSFU in the decade before the war which filled the pages of the Union's newspaper, *The Seaman*. It was strikebreaking activity, in fact, which triggered off attacks on Chinese property in Cardiff on 20 July 1911.[367]

But tension was not confined to the merchant marine. In Liverpool in 1890 the newly-formed Union of Laundresses and Washerwomen expressed fears about the continued employment of its members at a time when there was only one registered Chinese laundry – an indication, perhaps, that there were unlisted laundry premises.[368] In the following year the local Trades Council also became anxious about the involvement by Chinese in the laundry trade and the adverse consequences which, it was believed, this activity created for local White labour.[369] In worrying on this score, the Council had a strange ideological bedfellow in the shape of the *Daily Express* which in 1907 expressed its concern about the 'large numbers' of British workers who were driven into unemployment by the economic activities of the Chinese.[370]

This fear of Chinese workers undermining the livelihood of their White contemporaries was put on graphic display at the 1906 General Election when in constituencies such as Liverpool West and Toxteth the use of Chinese labour in the South African mines became a major issue. Some radical humanitarians were appalled by the conditions under which these Chinese had to work. Others, however, contended that employment in the mines should be preserved for Whites. The campaign aroused atavistic passions and Graham Wallas was later to remark 'Anyone . . . who saw much of politics in the winter of 1905–6 must have noticed that the pictures of Chinamen on the hoardings aroused among very many of the voters an immediate hatred of the Mongolian racial type . . .'.[371]

It is difficult to assess the effects of the employment of Chinese in the shipping trade. There is little doubt that some Chinese engaged in strikebreaking, but to what extent, if at all, did Chinese labour influence wage levels? The evidence is uncertain, but at present it would appear that, until the establishment of a standard rate in the port as a result of the 1911 Seamen's Strike, any effects were experienced chiefly among those seamen in the Cardiff tramp trade.[372]

In order to appreciate the full range of tension generated by the Chinese presence, however, it is important to look beyond the labour market. In some quarters allegations emerged regarding sexual behaviour among the Chinese. This concern was evident in Liverpool where a Commission of Inquiry set up by the City Council reported in 1906 that '. . . the Chinese appear to much prefer having intercourse with young girls, more especially those of undue precocity' and the same report alleged 'The evidence of seduction of girls by Chinamen [was] conclusive'.[373] A similar concern was evident in London a few years later. In addition, a number of commentators were anxious to draw attention to an involvement by Chinese in various forms of gambling.[374] But possibly the major expression of social opposition arose through the link that was often established between the Chinese minority and opium smoking.

Thomas de Quincey's *Confessions of an English Opium Eater* (1821) reveals that long before there was an established Chinese presence drug taking was not unknown in the literary world. Indeed, Coleridge had travelled along the road to Xanadu with such help. Opium and its preparations, in fact, were openly on sale in Victorian Britain and it was not until the 1860s that opium smoking began to capture public attention. It did not take long after that, however, through sources such as Dickens's *Mystery of Edwin Drood* (1870), Blanche Jerrold's and Gustave Doré's, *London. A Pilgrimage* (1872) and Oscar Wilde's *The Picture of Dorian Gray* (1891), for images of the opium den to take root. Those members of the public who read in lighter vein could extract references to drug taking from the adventures of Sherlock Holmes, or the Fu Manchu novels of 'Sax Rohmer' which began to appear in 1913. To some extent the concern which developed among middle-class moralists over drug use in the late nineteenth century was part of the wider condition of England question, involving as it did a fear of social degeneration, uncertainty and decay, and the issue of opium smoking in particular was sharpened by the undoubted involvement of some Chinese. It was also in part the domestic reflection of the campaign against the Indian opium trade with China which gathered pace in the late nineteenth century.[375]

Sexual contact, gambling and drug taking might be theoretically discrete, but in practice, in discussions of the Chinese, such issues often merged. Claude Blake, a reporter on the *Sunday Chronicle*, in an article called 'Chinese Vice in England. A View of Terrible Conditions at Close Range', managed to pack in references to the seduction of English girls through opium[376] and 'Captain' Edward Tupper linked the fears of sex and drugs when he gave credence to the widely circulated belief that Chinese men doped young girls with sweets in the course of converting 'these slips of growing white womanhood' into the 'body slaves of the laundry lords'.[377]

It is possible to restrict anti-Chinese hostility to such local issues, but it would be unnecessarily myopic to do so. The wider context was the Yellow Peril, the fear of future Asian dominance, which emerged in the late nineteenth century in America, Australia and Europe. In Britain a powerful impetus was given to this fear by the 1900 Boxer

Rebellion as well as the Japanese victory in the Russo-Japanese war of 1904–5. The prospect of invasion by the hordes of Asia, possibly organised by Japan, grew feverish in some quarters, particularly as the level of fertility among the Chinese was contemplated. It was quite possible to hold this fear alongside an admiration of Japanese efficiency; it could also coexist generally with an appreciation of Chinese porcelain and a passion for rhododendrons from China, both of which were much in vogue in upper-class circles in the early twentieth century.[378]

In fact, perceptions of the Chinese were generally complex. However evil and threatening they were alleged to be, Christian religious groups were still keen to possess their souls.[379] More down-to-earth ship owners with an eye fixed on profit rather than souls, persisted with their employment in defiance of the campaigns mounted by the NSFU. Indeed, Alfred Holt and Co of Liverpool, major employers of Chinese on the Blue Funnel Line, almost certainly helped alien Chinese sailors to circumvent the 1905 Aliens Act.[380] Furthermore, there was some resistance in official circles to the image of the Chinese as a social problem. In 1906 the Head Constable of Liverpool did not work himself into a state of anxiety over the question of alleged Chinese sexual behaviour, and this same lack of concern was evident in the 1910 Limehouse enquiry into the sexual life of the Chinese.[381] As for an involvement by Chinese in gambling, a Liverpool stipendiary magistrate reserved his strictures for the police rather than the defendants. 'It is a pity in the circumstances', he commented, 'that the authorities could not shut their eyes to it'.[382] The police also adopted a relaxed attitude over opium smoking. In 1906 the Head Constable of Liverpool admitted the fact of opium smoking within the Chinese community but stressed that it constituted no offence against the law and no crimes resulting from it had ever come to his attention.[383] A police report from Birkenhead written at the same time adopted a similar tone.[384] The more open-minded investigators who entered discreetly into the opium dens of the East End were also generally disabused of any view that opium smoking constituted a major social problem.[385]

In short, the Chinese were numerically insignificant in the years before the Great War, but this did not mean that they were immune from hostility even if public opinion was divided over the effects of their presence. Moreover, although they remained numerically insignificant, the Chinese were to be a focus of continuing public attention in the early twentieth century, during the Great War and afterwards.[386]

Finally, in considering the reception of Blacks, principally Africans, and Indians, it is once again necesary to recognise the history of pre-existing contact both in Britain and beyond, some of which was of long duration. By 1871 British public opinion had divided Blacks and Indians into those who were fit only to be hewers of wood and drawers of water, destined to service the British whether at home or overseas, in a variety of subordinate positions, and a small minority, particularly from well-connected backgrounds, who had received better treatment. The Mutiny in India in 1857 and the Morant Bay incident in 1865 in the Caribbean both excited adverse opinion in Britain. Impressions of Blacks were also derived from a North American context. Furthermore, information continually filtered through from military men, travellers, missionaries and traders in various parts of the British Empire, although it is far from certain who tuned in to such reports, or indeed what was extracted from such impressions. Impressions were also derived from school books and other conduits of popular indoctrination. In general, it has been suggested that Indians were ranked higher than Africans, but not all African qualities were condemned and not all the qualities of Indians were well-understood. By 1871 it has also been suggested that a crucial change was taking place in Victorian perceptions in the sense that there was an increasing tendency to racialise the two groups. At a scientific level this emphasis on race was particularly evident in the Anthropological Society of London, which was founded in 1863. But it has also been argued that increasing class pressures, the feverish quest for status, exercised a greater impact than scientific learning and helped to harden the situation in the sense that assumptions of racial superiority were compatible with existing attitudes to class differences.[387]

Against this background, how in fact, did the numerically insignificant Black and Indian minorities fare in Britain between 1871 and 1914? The seamen, of various nationalities, encountered what has been described as 'blatant discrimination'.[388] In the words of a contemporary survey, there was a 'repugnance of Masters and Engineers to mix coloured seamen and firemen with white'.[389] But it was not only masters and engineers in the merchant navy, who erected restrictions. A West Indian who secured work in Tilbury docks had to leave when White workers threatened to strike rather than work with him. It is hardly surprising that among those who experienced such responses a degree of bitter disillusionment took hold.[390] It has also been recorded that African students at Cambridge had to contend with opposition from their White contemporaries and it would seem that Indian students were even less popular.[391] The biographies of those who came as students, however, tend to gloss over these experiences. But a decision to convene a conference in London in July 1913 revealed a degree of public concern.[392]

In the late nineteenth century it was suggested that certainly down to the 1897 Jubilee eminent Blacks were particularly at risk in working-class areas.[393] But it was not only Blacks who encountered antipathy. Some prominent Indians became a particular focus of attention. When Dadabhai Naoroji announced his intention to contest the parliamentary seat at Central Finsbury Lord Salisbury was led to comment in a speech at Edinburgh on 30 November 1888: '. . . however far we have advanced in overcoming prejudices, I doubt if we have yet got to that point of view where a British constituency would elect a black man'.[394] In Salisbury's book even the Indian elite should know its place.

However, there is evidence to suggest that responses towards the Indian minority at least were more complex than has so far been suggested. One Indian visitor drew a sharp contrast between the treatment of well-connected Indians in India and England. In the former it was remarked that the Indian was 'relegated as far as the European is concerned, to complete social ostracism mitigated by the privilege of subscribing largely to official functions'. In England, however, 'he is admitted into the best English clubs, is seated under the gallery next door to a Bishop or a Judge, mixes freely with English ladies and realises he is a brother or a man'.[395] Rabindranath Tagore expressed it differently: 'Those who know the English in India do not know Englishmen'.[396]

It is difficult, if not impossible, to assess the value of these comments but one expression of the complexity of responses arose in the wake of Salisbury's denigration of Naoroji. Instead of profiting from his remark, Salisbury found himself at the sharp end of criticism from Gladstone, John Morley and the crown.[397]. And the reverse of Salisbury's outlook was revealed when William Digby commended Naoroji to the Liberal Association of Holborn. According to Mr Digby, Naoroji was 'an Englishman as well as an English subject';

furthermore, his 'long residence in this country and his thorough mastery of our tongue added to his English appearance' ruled out any objection to his not being English.[398]

The impact of Imperialism, which inculcated a perception of White supremacy and dominance, helped therefore, to restrict the lives of some Black and Indian seamen. Students and representatives of the professions, unsettling reminders that 'The Lords of Human Kind' did not possess all the talents, also encountered hostility, which was graphically revealed in 'the Edalji Case'.[399] Yet other Blacks were treated as objects of anthropological curiosity.[400] But there was another aspect to the lives of such minorities. Blacks, as well as Indians, could make an impression as sportsmen.[401] Furthermore, in the midst of strong currents of antipathy, the career of Naoroji, M. M. Bhownagree, a Parsee who sat as a Conservative MP for Bethnal Green North-East between 1895 and 1906,[402] and that of the Black Briton, J. R. Archer, who became Mayor of Battersea in 1913, revealed the complexity of responses within Britain towards Indians and Blacks, whether immigrant or British-born.[403]

5.

BETWEEN 1871 and 1914 it is possible to trace a diverse number of immigrants and refugees who came to Britain, even if in absolute terms and in relation to the total population, their numbers were small. Smallness, however, did not result in invisibility. Whatever the exceptions in the case of individuals, such groups did not wholly disappear into British society; there was no assimilation in the sense that there was a loss of cultural identity, even if there was evidence of a number of specific adjustments to the new environment. Moreover, this separateness was additionally underlined through several sharp differences of interest which were present between these small groups and sections of British society. In fact, there was little evidence between 1871 and 1914 of the much-vaunted tradition of toleration in Britain, let alone acceptance. But, at the same time, there was little indication of a blanket, unremitting hostility towards immigrants and refugees. The responses which did emerge in the process of interaction and which were moulded by the past and the immediate present, displayed a complexity masked by a concentration on such extremes. Moreover, it is necessary to guard against the blanket categorisation of hostility where it did arise, as racism, before paying careful attention to context. Those who stroll back into history and assess it from the vantage point of the 1980s illuminate nothing of the past. Against this background it is now time to consider the impact of the Great War on immigration into Britain, on the lives of existing immigrants and refugees and on those groups brought to its shores by the sound of battle which echoed in Europe and even beyond the European boundary.[404]

II. The Strains of War, 1914–19

'One refugee is a novelty, ten refugees are boring, and a hundred refugees are a menace', Donald P. Kent, *The Refugee Intellectual* (New York, 1953), p. 172.

'What do you think that the latest rumour . . . is? That Papa has turned out to be a German spy and has been discreetly marched off to the Tower, where he is guarded by Beefeaters. I got rather a rotten time of it for about three days', the future Earl Mountbatten of Burma writing to his mother from Osborne in 1914. Quoted in K. Rose, *King George V* (London, 1983), p. 171.

1.

DURING a short period of time, in the First World War and its immediate aftermath, British society witnessed a series of traumatic historical changes. An initial euphoric reaction to the war, which gripped many sections of society, was soon followed by a more sober assessment of what the war involved. Vast battles, Mons, the Somme, Passchendaele, which still remain etched in the memory, mountainous casualty lists, the need by 1916 for conscription which in turn led to the increasingly thorny issue of conscientious objection, the greater involvement of women in the labour market, the downfall of Asquith's government in 1916 and the emergence of David Lloyd George as war leader, industrial unrest as the war dragged on, and the need for greater state control over everyday life, evidenced by the introduction of food rationing in 1918, were some of the more dramatic events. Abroad there was a revolution in Russia in 1917, the collapse of other established empires in the wake of the war, and, at the same time, as British influence diminished, there was a strengthening of the international position of the United States. Mr Britling lived at a dramatic time. Moreover, in common with other wars the First World War exercised a significant impact on the lives of immigrants and refugees. Even so, historians have neglected such matters.[1] As a result, anyone asking, who were the newcomers that came to Britain during the First World War? What were the salient features of their economic and social life? What kind of responses did they encounter? would be unable, as yet, to find a comprehensive answer to these questions, all of which deserve attention.

2.

BRITAIN was brought into the First World War after German troops violated Belgian neutrality in August 1914. Following the German bombardment of Malines in September 1914 a large number of refugees began to congregate in Antwerp and it was in these circumstances that a decision was taken to bring some of the Belgians to Britain. The influx took place essentially between the autumn of 1914 and the end of 1915 and it was at its height in the period to the end of March 1915. After 1915 the traffic in Belgians moved in a reverse direction; more left than arrived. The numbers involved in this population transfer, including those Belgians recruited in clandestine fashion from the Continent, are difficult to establish. However, the names of 240,000 refugees scattered throughout Britain had been recorded on the central register of refugees by 1919; in addition, it was estimated that some 19,000 wounded Belgian soldiers came to Britain during the war.[2]

Where did the refugees come from? Which trades and occupations did they represent? A survey carried out in 1914–15 revealed that approximately ten Belgian town areas were heavily overrepresented, about twelve were proportionately represented, and the rest of the country was more or less underrepresented. Even if some slight weighting were allowed to centres such as Antwerp and Ostend in order to account for the initial movement of the refugees that took place into these cities after hostilities started, the differences were still quite striking. Antwerp, for example, contained 5.4 per cent of the Belgian population in 1914, yet it provided 26.5 per cent of the refugees. The representation between provinces was also extremely unequal. Refugees from rural areas, for example, were overshadowed by those from urban centres. Finally, the Flemish population predominated over the Walloon elements.[3]

The refugees were also unrepresentative of the Belgian working population. Compared with the occupational structure of Belgium in 1900, an analysis of the refugee population undertaken in 1914–15 revealed that the professions of law, medicine and education were significantly overrepresented among the exiled Belgians. Clerks, both men and women, were also present in significant numbers. Goldsmiths and lapidaries, whose work tended to be undertaken in Antwerp, the major embarkation port, and who had the means to pay for their escape, were also in evidence. Another overrepresented group was made up of fishermen. They constituted 0.12 per cent of the Belgian labour force in 1900 yet 1.24 per cent of the refugee population in 1915. In contrast, Belgian workers employed in agriculture, mining and textiles were not well represented.[4]

Even after the high point of entry of 1915 there was still some inward movement as wounded Belgian soldiers came to Britain to meet their families. It was out of such strands that the Belgian minority in Britain, hitherto almost totally neglected by historians, experienced a dramatic increase in numbers.[5]

By 1919 other alien groups had attached themselves to British society. Some of these newcomers put down their roots in Britain: in other cases, however, their stay was transitory. After the Bolsheviks came to power in October 1917, some of the White Russians who travelled westwards to avoid the new civilisation of the Bolsheviks found their way to Britain, although greater numbers finished up in Berlin or Paris. Anna Pavlova stayed for a time in Britain; others of lesser distinction also arrived. By 1921, in fact, it was estimated that 15,000 Russian refugees from the Revolution had arrived but this number soon dwindled through emigration.[6] In addition, a few hundred Armenians, refugees from Turkish persecution, continued to arrive, just as they had since the late nineteenth century.[7]

However, not all the arrivals during the war possessed alien status. It has also been suggested that 'World War I produced an enormous increase in Britain's Black population'.[8] Britain needed all the resources it could muster to fight the war and it was in such circumstances that colonial workers began to increase. Labour was in a sellers' market after 1916 when conscription took men away to the Front and some Black seamen left their ships to find work on land.

Others arrived by less calculated means; vessels were sometimes requisitioned by the government and their crews subsequently deposited in Britain.[9] Among those who came specifically to find work a fair proportion went into the war industries and found employment in the munitions and chemical industries in the north and Midlands.[10] Other Blacks continued with their work as seamen and, together with another minority group, the Chinese, helped to guarantee the functioning of the merchant navy and the maintenance of essential supplies.[11]

This varied Black contribution to the war effort was supplemented by a direct involvement in the hostilities through service in the British West Indies Regiment and the West India Regiment. At no point, however, were Black troops allowed to engage in front-line activity in the European theatre; any such involvement would have offended against the accepted canons of warfare.[12] Indian troops also fought in the war and, in their case, were used in the front line in Europe. Wounded Indian troops, in fact, were a common sight in Brighton, although they seem to have been segregated from the local population, and, more unusually, the smoke of funeral pyres could be witnessed swirling over the Sussex Downs as those who died were cremated according to their religion.[13]

In some of the hostile attitudes towards recent immigrants from the Caribbean and the Indian sub-continent these varied contributions to the war effort have been completely ignored. In view of the claim that a civilisation, a way of life, was preserved in 1914–18 and again in 1939–45 by Whites only, these generally neglected contributions by other British subjects deserve to be placed on record.

After the war some of the West Indian servicemen who were demobilised in Britain decided to stay in the mother country. So did a number of Indian ex-servicemen; some of the Sikh pedlars and door-to-door salesmen, a not uncommon sight in the early twentieth century, were descended from their ranks. Furthermore, 'A large number of black men who had been brought over to Manchester and other cities to work in munitions and chemical factories stayed on once the war was over'.[14]

It was through these developments that West Indians and Indians were added to the metropolitan society. Some found their way, like many earlier newcomers, to London. Liverpool, Tyneside and Cardiff, were other areas of settlement. Nevertheless, even if the process can be identified, it is difficult to return a precise figure for the

size of this increase. It has been claimed that in some areas it might
have been significant, even if absolute numbers remained small. One
suggestion, for example, is that on Tyneside, the Black population
increased fourfold. In Cardiff another source has claimed it was the
influx of newcomers in the war that 'established Loudoun Square . . .
with the adjoining streets, quite definitely as the coloured quarters of
the city'. As for the country as a whole, the increase has been
described as being in the order of 'several thousands'. Whatever the
precise number, it is generally recognised that most of these
newcomers were men.[15]

3.

WHAT were the salient features of the economic and social history of
the Belgian refugees? For some of the men any uncertainty regarding
their future was soon resolved. In accordance with a compulsory
military decree of 1 March 1915 Belgian men between the ages of 18
and 25 were obliged to enrol and appear before a Belgian recruiting
committee for enlistment or exemption from military service. Shortly
afterwards, following the introduction of conscription by the British
government in January 1916, by a decree of 21 July 1916 the Belgian
government called up for military or public service all Belgian men
between the ages of 18 and 41. Henceforth both Belgians and British
were placed under similar obligations and this helped to defuse the
antipathy which was directed towards the Belgians over the issue of
conscription early in 1916.[16]

When a sample survey was undertaken relating to civilian
employment in 1916 it transpired that 47.5 per cent of the Belgian
men were still following their original occupations. Gunsmiths and
those in war-related industries were much in demand. In addition, 70
per cent of telegraphists, 69 per cent of the clerks, 64 per cent of the
teachers and 63 per cent of tailors were able to pursue their original
occupations. Moreover, some Belgian tradesmen, pastry cooks and
butchers, for example, soon established themselves in Soho. By
contrast, in 1916 only 10 per cent of the Belgian dockers were to be
found in the docks. Furthermore, only 17 per cent of the shopkeepers
and 23 per cent of the builders were able to carry on with their
occupations. Men in these categories who found alternative
employment went mainly into the expanding munitions industry once

an amendment to the Aliens Consolidation (Restriction) Order of 1916 permitted aliens to be employed in this type of work. Transfers into other occupations would seem to have been negligible.[17]

Among women refugees changes in occupation by 1916 were relatively few; 81 per cent remained in their original occupations. This figure was significantly influenced by the fact that 95 per cent of Belgian domestic servants pursued similar employment in Britain at a time when the British upper classes were losing 'their girls', '*My* Grace', '*My* Annie', to more lucrative wartime occupations. Other refugee women were drawn into domestic service. There was also a noticeable presence of Belgian females in the munitions industry.[18]

The armaments industry, in fact, was a significant source of employment both for men and women. Of those over 15 years of age who were repatriated between December 1918 and June 1919, 66 per cent of the men and 20 per cent of the women had permits to work in this particular industry.[19] The visible symbols of this involvement were evident in the munitions complex at Birtley in County Durham, the Pelabon works at Twickenham and the Kryn and Lahy metal works at Letchworth.[20]

Wherever the refugees settled, they created small enclaves of Belgian life and culture to sustain them until their return. This was evident in the settlement at Earls Court. After paying a visit there the Belgian Minister to England remarked that the area had been 'transformé . . . en un oasis belge où nos compatriotes en exil retrouvent un coin du sol natal'.[21] Miles away from London, at Birtley in County Durham, where Belgians engaged in the production of 6 and 8-inch shells made their major contribution to the wartime munitions industry, a further re-creation of Belgium took place. Here the 4,000 Belgian workers, and full management staff, as well as 'Belgian policemen, Belgian law and even Belgian beer created the illusion of a Belgian town'.[22]

By 1919 this refugee episode had passed into history, but reminders of it existed long afterwards whether in the shape of the National Projectile Factory at Birtley, the run-down Kryn and Lahy works at Letchworth, absorbed into the George Cohen group in 1928, what are still called 'the Belgian houses' in Derby, the painting by Franzoni on the 'Landing of the Belgian Refugees August 1914', which is in Folkestone Library, and in the existence of women, now growing old in Belgium, whose name of Angele commemorates their birth in England. Such reminders of 'Europe on the move', of populations displaced by war, were to be amply increased within a short space of time.[23]

The history of Blacks and Indians during the years between 1914 and 1919 continues, in large part, to remain obscure. 'There was good money to be earned at sea during the war period and up to 1919 and the coloured men prospered'.[24] However, very little, if any, information has been recovered to add to such a bald conclusion. Moreover, the wages of Blacks in the munitions industry and their precise role within it, have so far remained obscure.[25]

On account of the weight of their involvement in the shipping industry Blacks – on whom more has been recovered than on the Indian population – remained confined for the most part to those parts of Britain which had witnessed earlier Black settlement. In other words, they were concentrated in ports, near the docks, in 'deprived and blighted urban areas'.[26] This concentration was to be important. The inadequate infrastructure and the prevailing culture of these essentially working-class enclaves, together with the hostility of the surrounding White society, helped to restrict particularly the social mobility of the Black population and that of the other racial minority groups congregated in such areas.

Cardiff, a major centre of the tramp shipping trade, was a microcosm of such problems. In the late nineteenth century there was a discernible increase in the size of its Black population. Indeed, 'By 1909 . . . Cardiff was as important a home for black sailors as London'. This importance was maintained during the First World War. Moreover, as economic prospects dimmed in some of the war industries, many of the Black unemployed turned towards Cardiff where the tramp trade recruited casual labour. Although uncertainty abounded in the shipping trade, and racial discrimination was prevalent, it was possible when work could be found to earn more in Cardiff than in Liverpool. The city, therefore, acted as a magnet.[27]

In this process 'single dwelling houses became apartment houses, and two and three persons compressed themselves into the space that before the invasion had been occupied by one'.[28] It was impossible in this area for Blacks and other racial minorities to live a life which in many respects was untouched by White society. However, the search for employment in the shipping industry established some contact with the wider world and a photograph of a mixed Black and White party on a convivial outing in Cardiff in 1919 also serves as a reminder that there were other forms of social contact.[29]

Whatever the difficulties faced by many of its members during the war, it has been emphasised that the Black community grew in self-confidence. One indication of this confidence was displayed in Pan-African activity, the origins of which preceded the war. Among the significant developments during the war was the establishment in London in 1918 by students and some business people of the African Progress Union, the overall aim of which was 'to promote the general welfare of Africans and Afro-Peoples'. Dusé Mohamed Ali was a founder member and J. R. Archer was chosen as its first President, a post he held for three years, before being succeeded by John Alcindor, a Trinidadian doctor practising in London, who had been involved in Pan-Africanism before the war. The outlook of this Black activism was revealed in a speech by Archer at the inaugural meeting of the African Progress Union, shortly after the end of the Great War:

> The people in this country are sadly ignorant with reference to the darker races and our object is to show to them that we have given up the idea of becoming hewers of wood and drawers of water, that we claim our rightful place within this Empire. That if we are good enough to be brought to fight the wars of the country we are good enough to receive the benefits of the country. One of the objects of this association is to demand – not ask, demand; I will 'demand' all the time that I am your President. I am not asking for anything, I am out demanding.[30]

Similar sentiments were present in the response of the African Races Association of Glasgow to the violence in that city in 1919 and such declarations were to become increasingly evident during the interwar years.[31]

4.

In discussing the economic and social life of minorities during the war attention has been focused upon Belgian and Black newcomers. However, in considering reactions towards minorities it is necessary to move beyond these groups. For example, the outbreak of hostilities had immediate implications for the long-established German-born minority.

Soon after the conflict began, the government introduced a tight measure of control over alien immigration and the lives of all aliens currently living in Britain. When immigrants began to arrive in large numbers from Russian Poland in the late nineteenth century, successive governments pondered a good deal before the Aliens Act was finally passed in 1905.[32] None of this equivocation was evident in 1914. Plans for a larger measure of control over aliens had been laid before the war as the international political situation grew increasingly tense. The matter was given increasing priority by the contingency planners of the Committee of Imperial Defence which was reflected in the establishment of its Aliens Sub-Committee in March 1910. It was accepted in Whitehall that 'powerful new legislation' affecting aliens would be required in the event of a future war. It was the same kind of thinking which led in 1911 to the compilation by the Military Operations Directorate of the War Office and the police of an unofficial register of aliens. The list identified those who were considered to be actual or potential spies. Finally, in August 1913, detailed recommendations which incorporated the views of various Whitehall departments were presented by the Committee of Imperial Defence to the government; these recommendations laid the framework for a firm degree of greater control should war break out.[33]

Soon after the hostilities began, the government introduced the Defence of the Realm Act, on 8 August 1914. This Act, which was modified in 1915 and 1916, became a symbol of state restriction and control during the war.[34] Even before this piece of legislation, the Home Secretary, Reginald McKenna, introduced a more specific measure of control, the Aliens Restriction Bill. After its first reading the House went immediately into Committee and by the end of a single day, on 5 August 1914, the Bill passed into law. In defending the measure, McKenna emphasised that it was possible to distinguish between 'alien friends and alien enemies' and that the object of the proposed legislation was 'to remove or restrain the movements of undesirable aliens'.[35] In fact, the distinction between friends and enemies was not always simple: the Czechs seem to have had 'least difficulty' in establishing that 'they were not hostile to the Allies', but 'the authorities were less perceptive' in their responses to Poles.[36] Moreover, in contrast to McKenna's soothing words, the Act endowed the Home Secretary with wide powers over the landing, registration, movement and deportation of all aliens. The Belgians, for example, were caught up in its provisions.[37]

There is no doubt that the Act was a decisive step in the history of control over alien immigration. '. . . It finally swept away the vestiges of the traditional laissez-faire approach which had generally prevailed during periods of peace, had flourished in the nineteenth century and was not wholly destroyed by the ill-conceived Aliens Act of 1905.'[38] Furthermore, two days after the Aliens Restriction Act was passed, the British Nationality and Status of Aliens Act received the royal asssent. Whereas the former was concerned with entry, movement and deportation, the latter, which was passing through parliament when the war began, attempted to give a clear definition of British nationality and from 1915 provided guidance to the police and local military authorities in their treatment of aliens during the war.[39]

In these circumstances the German minority, increasingly threatened as war approached, was now openly exposed.[40] Its fragile position was further emphasised when the government, in tandem with the 1914 Aliens Act, accepted the need for the internment or repatriation of enemy aliens. This decision to intern or repatriate marked a new and important departure. Indeed, 'The most fundamental and contentious questions of aliens policy which wartime governments faced were those concerned with the criteria to be applied in deciding which enemy aliens should be interned, which repatriated and which allowed to remain at liberty'.[41] It is worth pursuing this question of official policy a little further.

In the first nine months of the war, when there was a strong current of anti-German sentiment, internment was concerned with the removal of enemy aliens who were perceived as a danger to the state; there was, after all, a handful of German spies in Britain even if the public exaggerated their activity.[42] Official policy was strengthened in May 1915 when, following the sinking on 7 May of the Cunard liner, the *Lusitania*, off the coast of Ireland, with the loss of 1,201 lives, it became based broadly on the premise that an enemy alien should be interned unless he could present compelling arguments to the contrary. This second phase in the government's approach lasted between May 1915 and December 1916. At the end of 1916 when Asquith was replaced at 10 Downing Street by Lloyd George, it was expected that this change would inaugurate a harsher policy of internment and that greater concessions would be made to the Germanophobia which had surged with particular venom at various stages of the war. However, although Lloyd George was prepared to ride on this particular wave, he did not introduce any new, significant policy changes, in spite of the rising hatred of Germany and all things German that swelled up in the country, as it did in the course of 1918 at the time of the German offensive on the Western Front.[43]

During the war more than 32,000 enemy alien men were interned and when the peace was signed 24,450 were still in the camps. Women were never brought under control and most of the others who secured exemption were the young, i.e. those under military age, the infirm, those who were mentally ill, long-term residents with strong British family ties and members of friendly nations who happened to have Germany or Austria-Hungary as their birthplace.[44]

The repatriation aspect of government policy posed its own problems. On a straight exchange of personnel Germany and Austria-Hungary would have benefited. Moreover, since some enemy aliens had no wish to be repatriated, there was a further problem in any straight exchange. How then did the government proceed? In the autumn of 1914 the repatriation of women, children, elderly men, invalid men of military age, ministers of religion and medical doctors, was decided upon by the government. In May 1915 as the official policy on internment hardened, so too did the response to repatriation. Women, and men over military age, were henceforth obliged to show why they should not be expelled. In the event from the beginning of the war to mid-November 1919, when the process had been completed, 28,744 aliens were repatriated, of whom 23,571 were Germans. The majority departed voluntarily but some were compelled to leave.[45]

Those enemy aliens who were excluded from the rigours of internment or repatriation were not free to live their lives exactly as they wished; the 1914 Aliens Restriction Act, which remained 'the keystone of Britain's alien policy throughout the war' saw to that.[46] Even so, they were able to live qualitatively better lives than those who were interned, resentment against which spilled over into camp violence at Douglas on 19 November 1914.[47] Nevertheless, whatever problems internment produced, whether for the internees or for the War Office and the Home Office, the government departments charged with its administration, the policy was maintained and at one stage 500 camps were scattered throughout the country. The two major establishments were on the Isle of Man; in addition to that at Douglas there was a camp at Knockaloe near Peel. Other camps were set up in a variety of places, including London, York and

Southampton. It was an unusual spectacle to encounter such camps in Britain. It was equally rare for the country to catch sight of German prisoners of war; indeed, the presence of captured military personnel had not been witnessed since Napoleonic times.[48]

Some courageous voices were raised against the anti-German sentiment that the war unleashed. George V, mindful perhaps of his own exposed lineage, was a force for moderation.[49] Josiah Wedgwood spoke out against it in the Commons and Lord Ribblesdale adopted a similar stance in the Lords.[50] But there was little doubt that the wartime leaders had strong support for tough policies and the government's own propaganda against Germany – the exaggeration of German atrocities in Belgium for instance – reinforced popular anti-Germanism.[51]

Any previous admiration for Germany and Germans vanished like a dream: it was discovered suddenly that the Germans and their country had long been a menace to European civilisation.[52] In this atmosphere popular anti-Germanism was evident at an early stage of the war. 'There were wild stories that grocers were lacing their provisions with poison.' Rumours circulated that barbers were liable to cut their customers' throats, Sweeney-Todd style, and suspicion also fell on 'faithful and long-serving governesses'.[53]

Against this background there were attacks in 1914 on German-born citizens in Deptford, Poplar, Keighley and Crewe.[54] It was in October 1914, in this kind of atmosphere, that Prince Louis of Battenberg was hounded from his post as First Sea Lord after a campaign waged against him in *The Globe*.[55] This popular antipathy increased after the Germans sank the *Lusitania*.[56] 'Now for the Vendetta', proclaimed *John Bull*. 'I call for a Vendetta', wrote its super-patriotic editor, Horatio Bottomley, 'a vendetta against every German in Britain whether "naturalised" or not . . . you cannot naturalise an unnatural beast – a human abortion – a hellish freak. But you can exterminate it. And now the time has come'.[57] Such sentiments were not totally unwelcome in Westminster; indeed, it is worth emphasising yet again that some government sources helped to foster anti-Germanism. Exaggerated accounts of German atrocities in Belgium that were fed to the public undoubtedly helped in generating the heat of anti-Germanism and assisted the process of recruitment.[58]

In the wake of the attack on the *Lusitania* Germans were attacked in Liverpool.[59] A search was started for Germans in the East End, where

German shops were singled out, attacked and looted; in one instance at least the owner was in fact English but had a German-born wife.[60] In this atmosphere anyone with German connections was understandably terrified. This was illustrated in graphic form in the *East End News*:

> Re William Andrew Utz
> I, William Andrew Utz, butcher of 243 High Street, am a British-born subject. I was born at 42 High Street Poplar, and my mother was a Mary Ann Webster of Stepney. I have been in the business of a butcher for many years, following my father in his long-established shop at the said 42 High Street Poplar.[61]

Naturalised Germans who had changed their names were not necessarily safe in this atmosphere.[62] The fear created in these circumstances also spread to other aliens who anticipated that they might become indiscriminate targets of popular violence. A desperate and well-justified fear seized hold of the Russian Jews in the East End who dreaded that they might have to face a pogrom in Britain.[63] Moreover, although it has passed unrecognised, the xenophobia became sufficiently generalised to embrace attacks on the Chinese in Liverpool.[64]

It was after the *Lusitania* incident that German merchants were removed from the Baltic Exchange and the Stock Exchange also expelled those members who had German origins.[65] There were angry scenes, too, on the Corn Exchange and at Smithfield Market meat traders boycotted German buyers and their agents.[66] 'The German knights of the Garter were solemnly struck off the roll and their banners removed from the chapel at Windsor.'[67] It was also in 1915 that Viscount Haldane, who had close connections with Germany and German culture, was made the scapegoat for the deficiencies of the Asquith government following a hounding in the press, carried out particularly by those two veteran anti-alienists, Leo Maxse and Arnold White.[68]

But perhaps the best-known indication of popular anti-Germanism arose with the so-called Loyalty Letters. Sir Arthur Pinero, the playwright, author of *Dandy Dick* and *The Second Mrs. Tanqueray*, suggested in a letter to *The Times*, written after the sinking of the *Lusitania*, that 'Germans who are naturalized British citizens holding prominent positions in the country' should raise their voices against

Germany rather than, as he put it, 'sit on the gate'.[69] In the following issue the paper began to publish what have become known as the 'Loyalty Letters' through which prominent public figures of German or German-Jewish origin, affirmed their loyalty to their adopted land.[70] Sir Ernest Cassel, the prominent financier, and Sir Felix Semon, the well-known surgeon, were just two of those who bowed to this kind of pressure. Individuals such as Sir Edgar Speyer who refused to write, suddenly found their lives becoming less agreeable.[71] Although some of those pressurised into writing letters were Jewish, public concern did not concentrate on the issue of their Jewish origins but on their enemy alien origins. In some quarters, however, the chance to draw attention to an individual's Jewish background and elevate this into a matter of social significance was too tempting to pass over. In general, the opposition did not build up along these lines but the issue was complicated by the fact that a surface anti-German sentiment could be a disguise for an essentially anti-Jewish hostility.[72]

This intense xenophobia expressed in 1914–15 did not evaporate after the second year of the war. It was a popular move when, with the continued carnage on the Western Front, and growing uncertainty about Russia, in 1917 George V abolished German titles in his family and adopted the family name of Windsor.[73] This transformation occurred at a time when popular anti-Germanism was particularly strong.[74] In the following year the Jonas case in Sheffield, which resulted in Joseph Jonas, a German-born businessman, being put on trial for allegedly selling military secrets to the Germans before the war, served as a reminder of the continuing strength of popular wartime xenophobia towards enemy aliens.[75] The results of this popular wartime anti-Germanism which gave some clout to the activities of organisations such as the British Empire Union and the National Party persisted after the war.[76] Jonas, for example, never recovered his standing. Anti-German sentiment also hung heavily over the debate on the proposal for a new Aliens Act in 1919.[77] Moreover, the physical consequences of anti-Germanism remained. In Nottingham prewar Coburg Road had become Corby Road and Bismarck Terrace had been converted into the more innocuous Baldwin Terrace.[78] In general, therefore, a distrust of Germans lingered on long after the immediate circumstances of its creation.

In the case of the Belgians, allies in the war against 'the Hun', a well-thumbed, widely-used school textbook has informed successive generations that 'The gallant refusal of the Belgians to tolerate a

German march across their country was much admired in Britain'.[79] Before the war the Congo Reform Association had aroused liberal and humanitarian opinion against Belgian atrocities in the Congo, but in general it can be said that 'when the Belgian refugees arrived in 1914 [the British public] had only the vaguest knowledge of their country and the character of its people'. What did exist on such matters was contradictory and confused. In the event, the Belgians were regarded initially as Davids who had been overwhelmed by a brutal Goliath and this helped to influence their immediate reception.[80] F. H. Townsend's 'Bravo Belgium!' and Bernard Partridge's 'The Triumph of Culture', both of which appeared in *Punch*, caught the prevailing mood of elite public opinion and this sympathy was further indicated in the formation of the War Refugees Committee on 24 August 1914.[81] Within a fortnight the Committee, which afforded an avenue through which middle-class philanthropists could absolve their guilt at the fate of Belgium, and at the same time do their bit in the war, had at its disposal hospitality for 100,000 refugees, cheques, food and innumerable offers of personal help. Expressions of sympathy were in fact widespread. In Folkestone, where many of the refugees landed, successful appeals were made for local support.[82] Further up the country in Nottingham the Rev. J. C. Cox, the well-known antiquarian, offered his services for a lantern lecture, provided a collection of £5 was guaranteed for the Belgian Relief Fund.[83] Similar activity took place in Derby and in the north, in Sheffield, the local press informed readers in French, Flemish and English how victims of persecution in the Netherlands had sought and found refuge in Sheffield three hundred years earlier and expressed the hope that once again hospitality would be forthcoming.[84] The Reverend Andrew Clark remarked on examples of generosity in Essex.[85] There was also a strong expression of sympathy for the refugees from within Welsh society.[86]

It was not long before an interest in the refugees spread beyond the world of private charity. This was indicated on 9 September 1914 when Herbert Samuel announced in the House of Commons that the Local Government Board would assume the main responsibility for the reception and welfare of the refugees.[87] By October the Local Government Board was regulating the arrival of the refugees, a task previously undertaken by the War Refugees Committee, and allocating the newcomers to various reception camps. Camps were established at Alexandra Palace, Earls Court, Edmonton Refuge and Milfield House and managed for the Local Government Board by the Metropolitan Asylums Board.[88] In such circumstances the role of the War Refugees Committee was reduced to that of a liaison group, acting with local bodies to find secondary accommodation and providing assistance to Belgian soldiers on leave. For some time it also disbursed monies to local committees, but in 1916 the government rescinded this function. In short, although it was not disbanded until 3 December 1918, the role of the War Refugees Committee progressively diminished from 1914 onwards.[89]

Further evidence of the government's determination to exercise control over the situation was revealed by its decision to engage in the compulsory registration of refugees. This operation which began in September 1914 was particularly valuable in assisting the Belgians to trace relatives, but it served other important functions. For example, it helped to monitor the employment of the refugees, thereby minimising any conflict that might have developed with British labour.[90]

In addition, the government played a major role in winding-up the refugee episode. By August 1916 the Local Government Board had the repatriation of the refugees under consideration and at the end of the war agreement was reached between the British and Belgian governments over the next step.[91] The former agreed to meet the costs of the transfer and the task was undertaken by the Local Government Board and the local refugee committees. At the time the transfer started there were 120,000 refugees still in the country. The first party sailed at the end of November 1918 and this was followed by another departure on 15 December. This free repatriation or transfer offer remained open until 6 May 1919, by which time the majority of Belgians had left the country and the small number that remained was slowly being reduced.[92] However, some remained. In 1911 it was estimated that there were 4,794 Belgians in Britain. By 1921 there were 9,892.[93] Some of this increase derived from the refugee episode.

It has been noticed that the Great War gave an opportunity for the 'last great flowering of grand scale private charity'[94] and the early responses to the Belgians provided confirmation of this activity. However, it has also been emphasised that the war brought about a significant extension of state involvement in the management of Britain and in this respect the supersession of the War Refugees Committee and the overshadowing of the local refugee committees by the Local Government Board and the Metropolitan Asylums Board were examples of a wider process that took place in Britain during the wartime years.[95]

The intervention by the state in the refugee episode was fortunate from the point of view of the refugees. At all times public sympathy can be a fickle jade and, in the event, the enthusiastic popular responses of 1914 towards the Belgians were not always maintained. This change was remarked upon by Lady Lugard in an address to the Royal Society of Arts in March 1915. 'The movement of private hospitality . . . has . . . exhausted its first impulse', she told her audience and in the following year Ernest Hatch commented, 'It would be idle to assert . . . the flame of righteous anger is still burning with the same fierceness as . . . in the beginning of the war'.[96] As the flame died, responses to the refugees became dimmed.

In fact, although the emphasis so far has been upon the degree of public sympathy expressed towards the refugees, public opinion was never unanimous in its responses. Soon after the first refugees appeared, *The Times* complained about 'a cataract' of workers invading Britain.[97] Voices were also raised from within the ranks of organised labour. The concern from this quarter related to the possible implications for employment, which was coupled with a sturdy determination to protect the interests of the British working class. In the event, the grounds for conflict were minimised by the policies that were adopted to meet with the situation. The transfer of Belgian men into the armed forces, the priority that was accorded in employment to British workers, the initial settlement of the refugees in camps before their wide dispersal, all reduced the grounds for tension from within British society, as did the fact that the Belgians remained allies in the fight against Germany. The result was that when the war-weary British began to add up and grieve over their own losses, the Belgians encountered apathy rather than hostility.[98]

As a result, whatever problems the refugees faced, their lives bore little relationship to that of exploited oriental coolies, which was how they were depicted in German propaganda.[99] This image, made in Germany, was nowhere evident in André Cluysenaar's graphic illustration of 'La Grande Bretagne accueille les réfugiés belges' which formed the frontispiece to *A Book of Belgium's Gratitude*, published in 1916;[100] nor did it emerge in the pages of *La Renaissance*, published in Sheffield, which urged the refugees to perpetuate the memory of 'the great work done by Great Britain for our compatriots, exiled or suffering by the war'.[101]

The war and its aftermath also brought in its train serious consequences for another minority group, the friendly aliens from Russian Poland. The major issue that led to this conflict was the introduction of conscription in January 1916. The British soldiers portrayed in the early photographs of the war, those 'swimmers into cleanness leaping', marching off to the Front, confident that the war would be over by Christmas 1914, were volunteers or regular soldiers.[102] It was they who went to the defence of Belgium and discharged the hatred that swelled up against the Germans. But as the hostilities dragged on and the horrors of the Front became widely known, there were insufficient volunteers for the country's military requirements. It was against this background that the British government introduced conscription in January 1916.[103]

The introduction of this measure placed increasing pressure on the Belgian minority to engage in military service. But it was not merely Belgians that were affected.[104] At this time there was a large number of Russian Polish immigrants living in areas such as the East End of London and Leeds who had not taken out British nationality and were not in the colours. Once conscription was brought in, it could hardly be expected that these friendly aliens would be allowed to avoid what were widely perceived as their military responsibilities. However, the resistance that could arise if an attempt were made to involve these mainly Jewish aliens in the war was well appreciated by Vladimir Jabotinsky, who at this time was trying to raise his own pro-Zionist force, the Jewish Legion. In a later comment on the 'Jewish ghettos' Jabotinsky referred to the imaginary wall that separated these areas from the rest of society. The prevailing view in the 'ghetto' was 'Nobody interferes with us'.[105] In other words, whereas the position of the Anglo-Jewish establishment was that Jews should support the war – and Anglo-Jewry played its full role between 1914 and 1918 – there were those among the Russian aliens who perceived the world quite differently. Why, they asked, should they support the tsar's state which had persecuted them? Moreover, the Socialists in the ghetto declared their total opposton to any involvement in what was regarded as a capitalist war.[106]

These attitudes became increasingly unacceptable to the government, particularly after January 1916. Voluntary recruitment schemes and pressure from within Anglo-Jewry had little effect on bringing any substantial number of aliens into the war and the government's resolve to grasp the problem was strengthened by the reports it was receiving from Special Branch about the discontent over this issue in areas such as Leeds and the East End of London.[107]

There were voices outside the Russian Polish community who were prepared to defend those aliens holding out against military service. Joseph King, the Liberal MP for North Somerset, was always bobbing up with questions in the House of Commons which put the case of those who stood out against military service. However, King's was a minority view and in Leeds and the East End in the course of 1917 opposition was translated into physical violence. In these areas there were doubtless those who had old scores to pay off against the immigrants. Grievances that had built up during the years of high immigration were provided with a context in which such antipathy could be released. Evidence of this opposition was soon forthcoming in 1917.[108]

In a letter to the Home Office on 4 June 1917 the Chief Constable of Leeds wrote: 'I beg to inform you that during the past two or three days there have been disturbances between English youths of this City and those of the Hebrew persuasion'. There had been previous expressions of hostility but the events described by the Chief Constable possessed a more serious hue. Indeed, a similar degree of violence had not been witnessed in the city for many years. There were altogether 1,400 alien Jews, mainly of Russian origin, in Leeds who were eligible for military service and it was estimated that only 26 had joined the armed forces. Although 200 Russian Jews who had become naturalised British subjects had entered the ranks, attention was focused upon 'the shirkers'. The Chief Constable was in no doubt it was the conscription issue which lay at the heart of the problem.[109]

The violence which broke out in Leeds was soon repeated in London. Some sections of the East End press took a firm line over the military service question and an indication that these newspapers reflected popular opinion emerged at a meeting held in Bethnal Green Town Hall on 23 January 1917. It was emphasised on this occasion that the aliens were shirking their responsibilities: it was also alleged that when British boys were dying at the Front, Russian Polish aliens were busy consolidating their economic and social position in British society.[110]

It was not until September 1917, in other words one month after the Military Service (Allied Conventions) Act which stated that male Russians of military age should serve either in the British or Russian army, that violence occurred in London. In early September there were clashes around Euston between some of the local population and a number of Jews who were on the point of leaving for Russia. But the major incident occurred shortly afterwards on 23 and 24 September 1917. It began in Bethnal Green between 'several Englishmen and Russian Jews' in the late afternoon of 23 September, although the dispute had its origins in an incident that occurred in Bethnal Green the previous evening. It would seem that a Russian alien had told an Englishman, a wounded soldier, that the Englishman was a fool for having enlisted. When the two men met on the following day the dispute was renewed and soon triggered off a violent incident in which 5,000 people soon became involved.[111]

The conscription issue was never fully settled in a manner that suited the British government. It was suggested that exemptions from military service were granted too easily by the Russian authorities in London. Furthermore, shortly after the Military Service Convention had been signed, the Russian state fell to the Bolsheviks in the autumn of 1917. Soon after this transfer of power the Russians signed a unilateral peace treaty with the Germans at Brest-Litovsk on 3 March 1918 and duly extricated Russia from the war. In these circumstances Russian subjects in Britain were freed from the threat of conscription. The only real satisfaction the British government received was through the deportation of aliens such as G. V. Chicherin and Peter Petroff, who were in the vanguard of opposition to the war. If there was some public concern about Russian Jews as war profiteers, there is no doubt that the conscription issue raised even stronger emotions.[112]

The question of conscription also affected the small Lithuanian minority who had formerly lived in the tsar's empire. Indeed, in the case of those who had settled in Scotland, the signing of the convention 'had a dramatic impact on the . . . community'.[113] Following the 1917 Convention the majority of the men returned to Russia. Out of the 1,800 who were called up, 700 joined the British army and 1,100 went back to the tsar's empire. The decision to opt for a return to Russia reflected a widely-held belief among the Lithuanians that the British government would be unable to handle a large-scale return operation and an equally strong conviction that even if the British excelled themselves in their efficiency, the prevailing chaos in Russia and the shortcomings of the ramshackle Russian bureaucracy, meant there was a good chance that military service might be avoided altogether. In the event, however, the

Lithuanians miscalculated and fewer than 350 of the Conventionists were to return to Scotland. This small contingent was made up of those who could prove they had fought on the side of the allies once they had returned to Russia and those who had served in the Slavo-British Legion in the Allied intervention campaigns against the Bolsheviks. Those Lithuanians who had fought with the Bolsheviks or could offer no proof of their allegiance to the allied cause were refused permission to return. The dependants of these men, who were in receipt of small allowances from December 1917, also came under threat when this support was withdrawn by the Treasury from the end of March 1920. The withdrawal of such payments forced the remnant of dependants back to Russia. As a result, between February and March 1920 approximately 600 Lithuanian women and children were deported.[114] This action, together with the removal of men as a result of the Convention and the entry controls which were established afterwards in the 1919 Aliens Act and the associated Orders in Council, seriously affected the vitality of the Lithuanian community in Scotland. Those Lithuanians who did remain, became progressively invisible members of Scottish society.[115]

The commemorative pottery of the Great War provided ample evidence of European allied unity against Germany. Such brightly-coloured objects could hardly be expected to take cognisance of Russian-Polish objections to military service. Moreover, although Irish troops fought in the war – not all Irishmen regarded England's difficulty as Ireland's opportunity – their activities went mostly unsung. It was more common in England to emphasise the 'betrayal' of the 1916 Easter Rising rather than to underline the wartime support from Ireland.[116] The commemorative ware also failed to emphasise that the British – and the French – drew upon the resources of their respective empires in this struggle. Although the British were prepared to use their Imperial subjects, the restrictions placed on the use of Black troops revealed a racialist perspective reinforced through years of Imperial control.[117] Moreover, the extent to which race thinking was evident in Britain was underlined in a survey conducted in 1918 which remarked on the strength of what was called 'race prejudice' towards all Imperial groups. It was suggested that very little of this hostility was formed on the basis of personal contact; most of it was 'derived' from the process of Imperialism. This observation was another way of claiming that 'the general public [had] been subjected to the prejudices of colonial settlers, administrators, travellers etc., whose attitudes [were] more or less the result of direct contact'.[118]

An incident in 1918 at Belmont Road Military Auxiliary Hospital in Liverpool when White troops attacked fellow Black patients indicated that such hostility could be translated into action.[119] But it was in the following year that collective violence became particularly evident. In Britain in the course of the transition from war to peace, 1919 proved to be 'a troubled year'.[120] In July riots broke out among soldiers who had just been discharged or were awaiting demobilisation. In July and August running battles occurred between young Londoners and the police and in August there was mass looting in Liverpool after the Police Union strike. Above all, however, 1919 was remarkable for the so-called race riots that occurred in British ports and for the degree of social tension in the empire which provided the wider context of the events that occurred within the metropolitan society.[121]

The outbreaks of collective violence in Britain began in Glasgow in January 1919.[122] In the following month on Tyneside Arab seamen came under attack.[123] In April there was trouble in Winchester after a Black colonial and a White American had engaged in dispute over a woman.[124] In the following May and June there were a number of violent incidents in London, in Canning Town.[125] But it was the violence in Liverpool and Cardiff that captured most public attention.

In Liverpool tension was evident against a deteriorating employment situation early in 1919; with the end of the war it seemed that merchant seamen would once more be made to battle in an industrial jungle in order to find employment. In May the tension which grew out of this context was increased after the police became involved in a running battle with a group of Blacks who had been operating an illegal gaming house. These developments were a prelude to the events of the following month which began when a West Indian, John Johnson, was stabbed and severely wounded by two Scandinavian sailors after he had refused to provide them with a cigarette. A number of Johnson's friends retaliated against the Scandinavians and from this juncture the violence assumed a more serious dimension. The local police raided boarding houses used by Black sailors, and one Black sailor, Charles Wotten, was pursued by a fierce and baying crowd to Queen's Dock, torn from police hands, and thrown into the water where he drowned; the response of sections of the White population in this situation of heightened tension was such that by early June 'an anti-black reign of terror raged in Liverpool'. By 10 June 'the police held 700 Blacks for their own safety', and numbers showed signs of increasing. Furthermore, by this time the violence perpetrated by members of the White community was becoming indiscriminate; anyone with a dark skin was at risk. However, 'the active intervention' by the police was crucial and the violence eventually subsided, but not before serious injuries had occurred.[126]

In South Wales the violence started in Newport, spread to Barry and then to Cardiff, where the incidents 'found their most violent form and their most significant long-term effects'.[127] In Newport on 6 June 'a coloured man', was alleged to have made a derisive remark to a White woman and this led to attacks on Chinese, Greeks and 'coloured men'. This development set the pattern for the events throughout South Wales, in the sense that a relatively minor dispute led to a more serious situation. The peak point of all these developments occurred on 12 June but scattered incidents continued to occur for the next few days.[128]

How can the events in Liverpool and Cardiff be explained? An analysis of events in the former has drawn attention to the emergence of an international division of labour derived from the colonial-imperial connection and which was based essentially on colour. For example, Black sailors who signed on in Britain were paid a higher rate than if they had been recruited in a colonial port. In this respect there was a clear incentive for such men to pick up a ship in Britain. But the seamen were in a 'Catch 22' situation; if they tried to 'sign on' in Britain they encountered White hostility and if they picked up a ship elsewhere they had to accept reduced rates of pay. Employment became a particularly sensitive issue in Liverpool as the demobilisation of men who had served in the army and navy swelled the size of the Black population many of whom were in direct competition with recently-demobbed White workers.[129]

But the question of employment did not by itself account for all the hostility. Sexual competition was also an issue; in the words of one study, 'there was a feeling of sexual competition and the fear of miscegenation on the part of the white population'.[130]

Once hostility had developed, the targets of White hostility were exposed on account of their spatial visibility. The *Liverpool Echo*, for example, distinguished between what it called 'China town', 'dark town' and 'other alien quarters'. Such spatial separation also tended in itself to create suspicion.[131]

In the course of its development, the violence provided an opportunity for some individuals to exploit the situation for their own ends. But it would be unwise to believe, however convenient it might be for some, that hooliganism was a major influence in generating the violence; to do so would be to mistake the shadow of 1919 for the substance.[132]

But if such emphases are needed to explain the conflict in Liverpool, a wider rim needs to be placed around the picture. The incidents in the ports were also a reflection within a metropolitan context of the racialism that had developed as a result of British colonial and imperial rule. By laying claims to jobs and White women the traditionally subordinate Blacks had overstepped the mark and needed to be reminded of their place. Such assumptions were never far from the centre of the events that took place in Liverpool.[133]

It has been suggested that the violence in South Wales was also a reaction against the gains which non-Europeans had accumulated during the war. Traditional White preserves such as jobs, housing even more so, and women, all seemed under threat.[134] These developments provided the background to the Chief Constable's report to the Home Office on 13 June 1919, in which he wrote: 'There can be no doubt that the aggressors have been those belonging to the white race'.[135]

It is not without interest that almost 30 per cent of the Whites arrested during the violence had Irish names. The expansion of the Black community during the war took place primarily to the north of Butetown in an area which had been a centre of Irish settlement since the mid-nineteenth century. A fear of this incursion developed within the Irish minority, which was in the process of securing a firmer base for itself in Cardiff society, and such anxieties might have been brought to the surface under the influence of events in Liverpool.[136]

But other pressures helped to trigger off the incidents. At the end of the war demobilised White ex-servicemen in Cardiff as well as Liverpool found themselves in an overstocked labour market. This sense of being sold short in a land fit for heroes, was exacerbated by the 'severe economic depression and housing crisis' that affected South Wales at the end of the war. In other words, the conflict was 'a symptom of Cardiff's social and economic transition to the post-war world' in which Whites were determined to reassert their sense of superiority and priority.[137] The same can be said of Glasgow, 'an economic plague spot', where the difficult transition was revealed not only by the inter-racial conflict in the city but by the 40-hour strike which began in the same month.[138]

Finally, in Cardiff as in Liverpool, the events of the hot summer of 1919 cannot be disentangled from the hazy cultural stereotypes that had developed during the long years of colonialism and imperialism. These images, although more complex than is sometimes claimed, helped to focus attention on all 'coloured men', as they were described in reports in 1919, and particularly those among them who had 'uppity' ideas which challenged the status quo.[139] In this respect West Indians and West Africans were regarded by the police in Cardiff as 'less amenable to treatment' – the phrase is significant – than Arabs, Somalis and other 'kindred types'.[140]

Following the events, it has been claimed that the courts engaged in 'scandalously biased treatment' against anyone who did not have a white skin. But a more detailed investigation suggests that this verdict is too bald. In Cardiff, for example, an even-handed approach in sentencing soon replaced an early bias.[141]

What is certain is that in the aftermath of the violence there was pressure from some sections of White British society for the repatriation of 'coloured men'.[142] One difficulty here was that British subjects could not be compulsorily deported. Nevertheless, the Home Office view was that 'so far as possible all unemployed coloured men should be induced to return to their own countries as quickly as possible'.[143] Moreover, 'persuasion' was contemplated to achieve this.[144] As for those individuals who were not British subjects, it was intimated by the Home Secretary that he would be prepared to make Deportation Orders in suitable cases.[145] Eventually on 19 June 1919 a conference was held at the Colonial Office to discuss the question of repatriation and committees were established in seven port towns.[146] However, although repatriation committees were set up in Hull, South Shields, Glasgow, Cardiff, Liverpool, London and Salford, only small numbers did eventually avail themselves of the opportunity to leave.[147] For the majority who stayed, the future was to become bleak long before the onset of the world crisis and depression in 1929.[148]

In their haste to recover the history of Blacks, most historians have paid less attention to the attacks that were made on the Irish in 1919 and some have overlooked the fact that in Glasgow, Liverpool and

London violence was also carried out against the Chinese.[149] With the outbreak of war the National Sailors' and Firemen's Union had called off its campaign against Chinese seamen but its antipathy towards such labour did not die away. Moreover, a press report of 1919 which claimed that the Chinese had benefited from the war by taking the work of Englishmen fighting at the front, by overflowing from their 'original quarter', and by forming alliances 'in some cases with white women', revealed that wider hostility was present.[150]

But there was another issue which focused increasing attention on the Chinese minority during and after the war which related to the involvement by some Chinese in drug trafficking. A link between the Chinese community and opium smoking had been well-established by 1914 but a wider concern now emerged.[151] During the war there was some public anxiety about the use of other drugs such as cocaine, which resulted in 1916 in the regulation of narcotics by Regulation 40B of the Defence of the Realm Act. Some Chinese were perceived as an integral part of this wider drugs sub-culture which was evident in Britain in the early twentieth century even if, for a variety of reasons, it was on a smaller scale than in America.[152]

Specific incidents such as the death in April 1918 of a shipping merchant, William Gibson, from an overdose of morphine and that of the actress Billie Carleton from an overdose of cocaine in the following November, created widespread, often prurient interest. The fact that both individuals had established contact with Chinese drug pushers was readily seized upon and the Carleton case was sensationalised by Sax Rohmer in his novel called *Dope* which appeared in 1919. It was against this background that the Dangerous Drugs Act of 1920 was passed. Further legislation followed in 1923 after the death in March 1922 of a dancer, Freda Kempton, who had allegedly been supplied with drugs by Brilliant or Bill Chang, a well-connected restaurant owner, and the invisible Mr King of Rohmer's *The Yellow Claw*, which appeared in 1925.[153]

In fact, there was probably as much involvement by Americans as Chinese in the development of a drugs sub-culture but it was the Chinese connection during the war and afterwards which attracted public attention.[154] This connection was reflected in headlines such as 'Yellow Peril in London'[155] and 'The Lure of the Yellow Man'.[156] These sensationalist exposés built upon prewar fears as did reports on the dangers of entrapment which could result from indiscretions in games such as *pak kap piu*, and the sexual exploitation of White women by Chinese men.[157] There was often an interweaving of all these fears. Moreover, at a time when Chinese restaurants were becoming more prominent, myths about Chinese cuisine, reflected in headlines such as 'Rearing dogs to provide tasty dishes', were also stirred into the pot.[158]

The 1919 Aliens Act limited the immigration of alien Chinese and, together with the deportation of a number of drug dealers, particularly Chang, agitation over the Chinese and drugs died away shortly after the war. Even so, it never entirely evaporated.[159]

Several references have been made in passing to the 1919 Aliens Act, which serve as a reminder that the close of the war and its aftermath witnessed a continued debate about the presence of aliens. In fact, this issue was reflected in two legislative developments. In August 1918 the British Nationality and Status of Aliens Act amended the Act of the same name passed in 1914; the 1918 Act dealt with naturalisation and allowed for the revocation of the naturalisation certificates of those aliens who had displayed disaffection or disloyalty during the war. Of greater significance, the year following the war witnessed the appearance of a new Aliens Act.[160]

Whereas the 1914 Aliens Restriction Act was passed in the course of a single day, the 1919 Act emerged after a long debate. Some MPs were worried about the continuation of tight restrictions over alien immigration once hostilities had ceased. Sir Donald Maclean, father of the man who died in Moscow as 'Mark Fraser' in 1983,[161] referred to the 'great and noble traditions' of entry which, he believed, had raised Britain 'in the estimation of mankind' and contributed 'a great deal' to the country's 'material prosperity'. In his view, this heritage should not be forgotten.[162] Josiah Wedgwood was equally unhappy about the drift of restrictionist opinion and spoke out frequently in similar vein.[163]

But the stronger voices were elsewhere. In 1915, after the sinking of the *Lusitania* Horatio Bottomley had told his readers in *John Bull* that once the war was over the vendetta against Germans must be kept up. 'No shop, no factory, no office, no trade, no profession must be open to him'.[164] In 1919 Bottomley was in the House as an Independent and his theme remained 'Britain for the British socially and industrially'.[165] Ben Tillett, the man who had led the dockers in 1888, and now a super-patriot, urged the House not to forget the *Lusitania*; the country could not afford to be soft on the Germans.[166] In the course of pressing for a tight control over aliens an appeal was also made to historical precedent; attention was drawn to the fact that the controls over aliens introduced in 1793 in the wake of the French Revolution were not lifted until 1826, in other words, just over ten years after peace was restored following the long war against France.[167] But the predominant restrictionist sentiment had a blunter edge. 'We do not want German blood any more in this country' exclaimed one member, Mr Stanton, 'we have had it in high places and we want no more'[168] and this stance was echoed by Sir Ernest Wild, the MP for West Ham, who played a prominent part in the debate, and set his face firmly against any expression of 'invertebrate sentimentality'.[169] It was not only the presence of Germans that aroused Wild's antipathy. The prospect of legislation in 1919 afforded a chance to keep out the Jews, whose prewar immigration he deplored.[170] Wild's remarks were a firm reminder that the debate over the presence of Jews from Russian Poland did not end in 1914. 'Bolshevik sympathisers' started to be deported in 1919 and issues raised by the immigration from Russian Poland contributed 'in no small measure' to the pressure for tighter controls over aliens.[171] The degree of anti-Semitism that also lurked in the debate was reflected in Noel Pemberton Billing's reference to 'the mentality of the Asiatic', a remark which was described by Captain William Ormsby-Gore as 'naked antisemitism'[172] Other speakers had their own special axes to grind. J. Havelock Wilson, another old trade union leader now in the House, was particularly anxious to exclude Chinese aliens from work in the shipping industry. In short, the exclusionist case in 1919 was knitted together of many strands: an overarching emphasis on a fear of aliens as Bolsheviks following the 1917 Revolution in Russia would be wide of the mark.[173]

The fruits of such sentiment were gathered on 23 December 1919, one month after a general election campaign in which Lloyd George had channelled a strong tide of nationalism and anti-Germanism, when an act to continue and extend the provisions of the Aliens Restriction Act of 1914 was placed on the Statute Book. Whereas the 1914 Act was passed to deal with the circumstances of war and national emergency, the 1919 measure, passed initially for one year, was in fact renewed annually until 1971 and together with various Orders in Council, such as those of 1920, 1925 and 1953, formed the basis on which successive governments based their policies towards the entry, employment and removal of aliens. Entry became dependent upon the discretion of an immigration officer; there were clearly defined restrictions on the employment of aliens; the Home Secretary also possessed considerable powers regarding deportation.[174] The liberal procedures of the Victorian age and indeed of the years between 1905 and 1914 belonged to a different and vanished world.

III. 'The glass is falling hour by hour.' Immigration, 1919–39

'I always found the name false which they gave us: Emigrants
That means those who leave their country. But we
Did not leave, of our own free will
Choosing another land. Nor did we enter
Into a land, to stay there, if possible for ever.
Merely we fled. We are driven out, banned.
Not a house, but an exile, shall the land be that took us in',
B. Brecht, 'Concerning the Label Emigrant', in J. Willett and
R. Manheim (eds), *Bertolt Brecht, Poems, Part Two 1929–1938*
(London, 1976), p. 301.

'Right laws and sound morals form the strongest safeguard of every
national State but a sound racial basis is also necessary. A nation
may be enriched by the varied contributions of foreign immigration
but if the stream of immigration grows unchecked into the volume
of a great river, a nation may lose the integrity of the solid core
which is the basis of its tradition. And the nation which loses its
tradition has lost its very soul', E. Barker, *National Character*
(London, 1927), p. 47.

1.

THE interwar years have been described as ranking among the
saddest and most exciting in recent history.[1] The impact of the First

World War did not cease in 1918 but continued to reverberate until the next major outbreak of hostilities. The war triggered off the Bolshevik Revolution and henceforth, in spite of Western attempts to undermine it, Communism became a feature of European society, fracturing the old world that existed before 1914. This break-up of the old Europe was emphasised by other developments which drew strength from the First World War. The 1916 Easter uprising in Dublin received an eventual partial consummation in the establishment of the Irish Free State. The emergence of Fascism and Nazism exercised a major impact on a number of European societies, such as Germany, Italy, Portugal and Spain. Among the Liberal democracies an increasingly isolationist America emerged as the major source of power and influence.

Along with these political developments the interwar years were marked by a considerable degree of economic turbulence, some of which also grew out of the consequences of the First World War. By the early 1930s unemployment, a depressing symbol of such turbulence, was a major social feature in all the leading capitalist economies and, in turn, the problems afflicting these societies extended into primary producing countries. Such developments were not unrelated to the political changes of the interwar years.

Against this background Europe witnessed a remarkable procession of refugees attempting to escape from persecution, or governments which they found uncongenial.[2] This movement was particularly a feature of the 1930s. At this time, however, intending emigrants, disenchanted with a bleak present and uncertain future, found it difficult to find anywhere a Samarkand, a golden land where a better life could be guaranteed. In these circumstances, although some movement to new lands did continue, the process of reverse migration was evident.

Britain could not isolate itself from these political and economic developments. The First World War further reduced the strength of national confidence – the 1905 and 1919 Aliens legislation were symptoms of this sapping of strength – and although the old order and its essential institutions survived intact and exercised a distinctive influence over postwar Britain, this continuing influence occurred in a country which was nevertheless seriously affected in the 1930s by the international economic crisis. Against this gloomy background it might be asked who were the immigrants and refugees that came to Britain? what kind of lives did they lead? how were they received?

2.

As Soviet rule extended itself in Russia, Europe witnessed the continued movement to the West of anti-Bolshevik groups, and in the case of Britain this immigration was particularly evident after the fall of Archangel to the Red Army in February 1920.[3] By 1921 there were over one million Russian refugees exiled throughout the world which resulted in the League of Nations creating a High Commission in mid-1921 to deal with the refugee problem. Fridtjof Nansen who was appointed to this post also had to concern himself with other refugee groups, such as Armenians, and by 1930 some progress had been made in defining 'the legal status of these largely stateless persons . . . and in their settlement in Europe and elsewhere'.[4]

Apart from events in Russia, the consolidation of Fascist rule in Italy and the upheaval consequent upon the Spanish Civil War also succeeded in driving refugees to Britain.[5] But it was the grip of Hitlerism that served principally to swell the British refugee population. 'In successive waves they came', one commentator wrote, 'from Germany, from Austria, from Czechoslovakia, each of Hitler's advances registered by their arrival, distant ripples of a large disturbance, swallows which made a winter'.[6] From among their ranks the groups from Germany and Austria have captured most interest. A high proportion of these refugees were Jews, although many had no strong religious or cultural convictions, and it is on these particular newcomers that information is most plentiful.[7]

Within six months of Hitler becoming Chancellor of Germany on 30 January 1933 the National Socialists had succeeded in subjugating all their political opponents. Once this control had been achieved, a start was made on a policy aimed at coordinating almost every aspect of German life. It was against this background that the emigration began from Central Europe.

Jews, even if they had rejected their origins, were subjected almost immediately to a number of legal enactments designed to prevent their employment in the civil service, universities, schools and the law.[8] In addition, those Jews who had been naturalised since 1918 had their German nationality stripped from them. Then on 15 September 1935 the so-called Nuremberg Laws were adopted unanimously by the Reichstag. In essence, these laws converted the notion of 'the "purity of German blood" into a legal category. The legislation forbade marriage and extra-marital relations between Germans and Jews and disenfranchised those "subjects" or "nationals" of Germany who were not of German blood'.[9]

However, persecution did not proceed in an unbroken pattern. 'Periods of violence and draconian measures were followed by periods of relative calm'. Different groups in different areas were affected at different times. Moreover, anti-Semitism was nothing new and this encouraged the hope that it might blow itself out.[10] As a result, there was no automatic, progressive exodus of Jews.[11] However, 1938 marked a decisive turning-point. In March the Germans occupied Austria and with the *Anschluss*, the union of the two states, the process of Aryanisation was injected into Austrian life. In the spring of that year hostility was stepped up a further rung as Jewish-owned shops in the Kurfürstendamm district of Berlin were daubed with swastikas and anti-Semitic graffiti. Then in the autumn, on 9 and 10 November, the so-called *Kristallnacht* pogrom was unleashed, in the course of which 91 people were killed, a large number of synagogues were destroyed and at least 20,000 Jews were arrested and swallowed up in the concentration camps which already had been constructed for opponents of the projected thousand-year Reich. In effect, through these measures notice was being served on the Jewish community that it could expect no quarter from the National Socialists. In the next few months Jewish property was confiscated and an organised assault was made on Jewish communal life. The intention and effect of this programme was to drive an increasing number of Jews from the expanded territory of the Reich.[12]

From 1933 to 1939, in fact, the emigration of Jews was encouraged by the German government. As early as September 1933 a special arrangement enabled Jewish emigrants to Palestine to retain part of their assets. Restrictions were soon placed on these transactions, however, and by 1938 it was almost impossible for Jewish emigrants to take any of their capital abroad. But emigration as such was still encouraged. As a result, in spite of the difficulties they encountered in leaving the Greater Reich and gaining admittance to Britain and other countries, it has been estimated that 226,000 Jews left Germany between 1933 and the beginning of the war in 1939. Furthermore, 134–144,000 left Austria and the 'Protectorate of Bohemia and Moravia'. Altogether therefore, although accurate figures elude us, something like 360–370,000 Jews fled from the Greater Reich between 1933–39. Such refugees amounted to a third of the Jews who lived in the expanded Reich in the year that the Second World War began. Approximately 57,000 of those who departed went to the United States, 53,000 to Palestine and 50,000 to Britain. Others were dispersed across a number of countries including France, Belgium, Switzerland, Argentina, Brazil, Australia and Canada.[13]

The majority of the refugees, Jewish or not, were adults and for the most part professional people. Information is most plentiful on the Jews, among whom there was a heavy representation of academics, doctors, lawyers, artists and businessmen.[14] Many settled in London where a poet spotted the studious in the British Museum, that old haunt of the exiled:

Between the enormous fluted Ionic columns
There seeps from heavily jowled or hawk-like foreign faces
The gutteral sorrow of the refugees.[15]

Academics were to be found in university towns and once they had secured a permanent post they were in a position to bring over members of their family. Businessmen were often to be found in the north of England as well as London.[16] There were, additionally, scattered through the country after 1938 several thousand unaccompanied refugee children who faced a difficult future.[17]

The problems which the Jewish minority in Europe had to confront between 1933 and 1939, paled into total insignificance compared with those which European Jewry had to face during the Second World War. Few could have imagined on 1 September 1939 the nature of the anti-Semitic policies that Germany was to pursue in the Second World War.[18] Other 'enemies of the regime' who managed to escape before the war were also soon to count their blessings, whatever difficulties and uncertainties they faced in their lives outside Hitlerite Europe.

The arrival of the refugees from Nazism substantially reconstituted a German-born population which had been reduced by the repatriation that had taken place during and immediately after the First World War. Furthermore, since 90 per cent of the newcomers were Jewish, they also added to the size of Anglo-Jewry and provided a recognisable Central European dimension to that community.

Even so, the largest minority in Britain, built up over many years, remained the Irish. In 1921 the number of Irish-born counted in the census of England and Wales was 364,747 (1.0 per cent of the total population) and by the time of the 1931 return it had increased slightly to 381,089 (but still only 1.0 per cent of the overall population of England and Wales). In Scotland the figures in 1921 and 1931 were 159,020 (3.3 per cent of the total population) and 124,296 (2.6 per cent of the overall population of Scotland) respectively. In other words, in Britain as a whole, although the Irish remained the largest immigrant group, their absolute and relative size had declined between 1911 and 1931. In England and Wales the majority of the Irish came from the Irish Free State; in Scotland, by contrast, the larger number of a smaller global total had birthplaces in Northern Ireland.[19]

The continuing relative strength of the Irish minority, noticeable particularly in the north-west and south-east of England, was evident at a time when Anglo-Irish relations were undergoing a significant transformation.[20] However, the official establishment of the Irish Free State on 6 December 1922 did not result in an immediate transformation of southern Irish society which provided the majority of the Irish immigrants to Britain. Incentives to migration still existed. Unemployment remained high; the Irish Free State could not isolate and insulate itself from the problems of the world economy. The continuing demographic pressures in the Free State added to these economic difficulties. In addition, the influence exerted by the close patterns of family and community life, in which, for example, status came with age, remained strong and provided a further spur to movement.[21] Britain, on the other hand, where Irish support networks existed, held out better prospects. For example, there was the chance of picking up unskilled work, which the Irish could still obtain even in the 1930s.[22] Furthermore, certain developments in America, which had swallowed up increasing numbers of Irish since the late nineteenth century, succeeded in diverting to Britain some of those who took 'the exile's road'.[23] The noble sentiments of Emma Lazarus, offering America to the 'tired', the 'poor' and 'the huddled masses yearning to breathe free', became subject to qualifying footnotes and dependent clauses in the late nineteenth century and Irish immigration started to be controlled soon after the First World War.

In an atmosphere of intense national xenophobia in America, an emergency measure was passed in 1921 which introduced the principle of numerical restriction upon the basis of nationality. The law limited the number of immigrants of each nationality in the following year to 3 per cent of the number of persons of that nationality living in the United States at the time of the 1910 census.[24] It was an act that constituted 'the most important turning-point in American immigration policy'. It placed the first, absolute numerical restriction on immigration from Europe and its provisions guaranteed that within a generation the foreign-born population would cease to be a major factor in American history.[25] In the case of Great Britain and Ireland a quota of 77,342 was established.[26]

This legislation was extended for two more years in 1922 and was then superseded by the Johnson-Reed Act in 1924. The latter placed an upper limit on total immigration and assigned quotas to each nationality based upon numbers present at the time of the 1890 census. The Irish Free State was given a quota of 28,567, which was further reduced to 17,853 in 1929 when the 'national origins' system became fully operational. In 1930, in response to demands made in the shadow of the 1929 crash and the ensuing world economic crisis, that immigration should be further reduced, the Hoover administration ordered a more rigorous enforcement of an earlier piece of legislation, passed in 1917, which prohibited the admission of immigrants likely to become a public charge. Quotas were not affected, but the Irish, along with other immigrants, now had to stand a test of individual solvency or secure a guarantor in America.[27]

After 1914, in fact, America was gradually replaced by Britain as the main destination of the Irish. But it is doubtful if American legislation was the crucial direct influence over this development since the Irish quota was never even filled. The change in the direction of the Irish was also related to the cheaper and easier access that Britain offered – for example, there were no restrictions on Irish immigration such as affected the alien refugees – and the change in Anglo–Irish political relations after 1921. It was from an interaction of influences, therefore, that the Irish took the shorter journey, although it should be emphasised that net emigration from Ireland for a sizeable period of the interwar years, between 1926 and 1936, was at a particularly low level.[28]

Nevertheless, a number of important developments occurred in the nature of the immigration. For example, a deterioration in the economic position and social status of women in Ireland in the early twentieth century led to an increase in the already relatively large female immigrant population. Moreover, there was a substantial component of Protestant emigration from Southern Ireland to

Britain. All told however, at no time during the interwar years did the immigration take the Irish minority up to the percentage levels of the total population it had reached in England, Wales and Scotland in the mid and late nineteenth century. Furthermore, there was a time in the early 1930s that Ireland, along with other countries, witnessed the return of many of its emigrants. But in the case of the Irish Free State this reversal of the traditional traffic was short-lived, relating only to 1931 and 1932, after which there was a net movement of population out of the country which continued until the outbreak of the Second World War.[29]

The difficulties within the capitalist system during the interwar years, particularly in the 1930s, had a serious effect on the primary producing countries within the British Empire. The British West Indies was one such area. The British had been quite content to exploit the natural resources of the islands for centuries but had displayed little inclination to develop their infrastructure or the living standards of the local workers. The extent of this neglect became clear in the report of the Royal Commission which was established to enquire into the condition of the islands following a period of labour unrest between 1934 and 1938. The Commissioners' report painted a depressing picture of deficiencies in the agricultural system, inadequate housing and defective systems of health and education. Even so, such problems did not lead to any large increase in Britain of workers from the Caribbean even though all those classified as British subjects enjoyed the right of unrestricted entry. Indeed, compared with Irish and Jewish minorities the size of all the so-called 'coloured' groups, although precise figures remain hazy, was relatively small and continued to be so for some time to come. The violence of 1919 was reported in the colonies and acted as a deterrent to movement. But this information did not act in isolation. The economic problems affecting Britain, which led to the persistence of high levels of unemployment in the 1930s, also discouraged immigration. Moreover, the hostility and discrimination which had to be faced in these depressing conditions, knowledge of which was also disseminated abroad, provided further discouragement.[30]

Against this background, the existing small working-class groups of Blacks and Indians were built up in various ways. Some servicemen remained in Britain after their demobilisation following the Great War. Moreover, some of the workers imported in that conflict decided to remain. In addition, sailors appeared as they had done in the past.

Some were transient but others put down roots. Such groups were clustered particularly in London and also in port towns such as Cardiff and Liverpool where they were subjected to White violence in 1919. A small population involved in commerce and business could also be found.[31]

In addition, Black writers, students and political figures, some of whom combined a number of roles, were in evidence. Claude McKay, the Jamaican writer, arrived in 1919 via the United States, in order to see the 'factory chimneys pouring with smoke', but had become disillusioned with English society by 1920.[32] Even so, the lure of the metropolitan society was particularly evident in the 1930s. It was in this decade that 'there developed a black intellectual group which was to exercise a political influence out of all proportion to its numbers in the years after 1945'.[33] Jomo Kenyatta came first of all in 1929 and then again in 1931.[34] C. L. R. James arrived in 1932, and George Padmore in 1935 after a period as a Comintern agent in Europe.[35] Another important activist to arrive during the interwar years was Ras Makonnen.[36] Moreover, it was not only Africans who were in London during these years, mixing politics and education; the career of Krishna Menon serves as a reminder that the cause of Indian independence was also advanced in interwar Britain.[37]

Other prominent Blacks also arrived between the wars. The Guyanese actor Robert Adams was one entertainer who came to Britain.[38] Another was the American, Paul Robeson, who made London his base 'in his unique struggle for the black cause'.[39] If Robeson's hopes were to be frustrated, the aspirations of Marcus Garvey had already taken a severe battering. Garvey, who had first been in London before the Great War, played a major role in raising the level of Black consciousness in America between 1916 and the early 1920s through his Universal Negro Improvement Association. In 1927, however, he was deported from the United States and by the mid-1930s had based himself in London. 'The whole world gets its lead from London', he wrote in 1934, and 'since the Universal Negro Improvement Association is the leading Negro movement in the world, it is very appropriate that its headquarters or semi-headquarters should be in that city'.[40] It was here, at the heart of the Empire, at 2 Beaumont Crescent, in an atmosphere of increasing disillusionment, that he spent his last declining years before his death in 1940.[41]

3.

BEFORE considering the economic and social life of the mainly Jewish refugees from Nazism, there is a case for discussing the developments that were taking place amongst those Jews who had arrived at an earlier date as refugees from persecution in the tsar's empire.

By the 1930s some of the long-term economic influence of this immigration was starting to be evident, although the full consequences were not manifested until later. The development of Montague Burton, and also Marks and Spencer, which became a public company in 1926, constitute two of the better-known examples of entrepreneurship which were linked to the earlier immigration. Furthermore, these years witnessed the emergence of entrepreneurs among the children of the immigrants. It was at this time that Isaac Wolfson began to lay the foundations of Great Universal Stores, which was to become one of the largest retail groups in Britain. Moreover, immigrants, or the children of immigrants, with names such as Selig Brodetsky and Louis Golding were making a different kind of contribution to society.[42]

Other economic and social developments, some of which resulted from the First World War, were also evident. In Leeds the war had led to an increase in the number of immigrants taking out naturalisation papers. It also had other related social consequences. The young men who enlisted were taken out of their Jewish environment and put into a military regime where uniformity was of paramount importance and there was little recognition of specifically Jewish needs. 'Living at close quarters with Gentiles', it was remarked, 'often led to an adoption of Gentile ways and attitudes – from a belief in self-defence to a taste for Yorkshire pudding'. Once these young men were back home it was not easy to impose on them 'old patterns of authority and obligation'. In other words, it has been suggested that over the medium and longer term the war assisted in the 'secularisation and acculturation of the Jews'.[43]

During these years there were shifts in the residential pattern of Jewish settlement in Leeds. There was a discernible movement 'out of the Leylands towards Chapeltown and Roundhay, through the Camp Road and North Street areas'. Wealthier families, in fact, were moving further afield into non-Jewish areas such as Headingley and Harrogate and 'By 1937 the Ghetto of the Leylands was almost completely deserted. . . .'[44] It was a process evident elsewhere. The

1934 Social Survey of Merseyside noticed, for example, that the Russian Poles were no longer concentrated in Brownlow Hill near Lime Street station and remarked on 'their steady dispersal to all parts of the city, especially the new suburbs'.[45]

Similar trends also influenced the contemporaneous movement that took place out of the East End of London towards areas such as Hampstead and Golders Green. In this case the transfer was facilitated by the economic success some East Enders had enjoyed during the First World War and by the extension of the Northern Line underground. It was relatively easy by the interwar years to run an East End business and to live in north London. But it is important to guard against the assumption that all Jews deserted the East End and that the Jewish community in this part of London disappeared. There was in fact a vibrant cultural life in the old 'ghetto' during these years. The Yiddish theatre, though less evident than at the turn of the century, still continued. There was also a vigorous literary culture revealed for example, by Simon Blumenfeld's *Jew Boy*. There was, furthermore, a lively political culture and a noticeable attachment of Jews to the Communist Party of Great Britain. Most of those Jews who remained were working-class Jews and it was they, together with their children, who had to bear the brunt of the verbal and physical attacks launched by the BUF when Mosley marched his troops into the East End.[46] These Jews and the large Jewish population living in the Gorbals slumland of Glasgow, where Jews swelled the number of those who were unemployed and in receipt of state and charitable aid, constituted the often overlooked working-class component of the Jewish community.[47]

Nevertheless, it remains a fact that some of the more recent Jewish immigrants who arrived in the 1920s soon began to make a mark for themselves in the interwar years. Armin Krausz emigrated in May 1923 from Hungary and soon discovered that there was no market for cheap Hungarian wines in England but he persisted in business and established Harris Miller, which has remained an independent feature of Sheffield's cutlery trade.[48] The career of Jules Thorn unfolded on a grander scale. Thorn, who was born in Austria in 1899, first came to Britain as a young company representative and then settled to build his own business which went public in 1936. Thereafter, until his retirement in August 1976 he drove the company forward and created one of the leading firms in the United Kingdom, with a particular strength in the area of consumer electronics.[49]

Another influential newcomer from central-eastern Europe was Alexander Korda. Korda had left Hungary after the fall in August 1919 of Kun Béla's government, with which he had been in sympathy, and, after much travelling, arrived in Britain in 1931. It was not long before he was to add to the already recognisable presence of Jews at many levels in the entertainment industry.[50]

In the case of the refugees from Nazism who arrived in the 1930s there were immediate expressions of relief at being free from persecution. 'How do I explain and put into words that surging, joyful relief I felt at being finally out of Germany after so many false starts?', one refugee was later to write.[51] Entry into Britain was not an easy process and there were antipathies that had to be faced even after arrival.[52] But of the 50,000 or so who were admitted, information is once again most plentiful on the perceived success stories. All immigrant minority groups receive a psychological uplift from any success that derives from within their ranks and there is therefore a tendency to dwell on remarkable achievements. At the same time, members of the receiving society can rejoice at the foresight that allowed such newcomers to settle in their new home. But in the case of some of the refugees from Hitlerite Europe it should not be forgotten that their employment prospects were extremely precarious and slow to improve. 'The immediate and striking impression' that emerged from a recent survey was that even into the 1950s refugee life could be 'marked not only by constant moves in and out of jobs but also in and out of bedsitters, in and out of London and, last but not least, in and out of Britain'.[53]

As in the case of other refugee groups there were difficulties attendant upon their traumatic experience of upheaval that had to be transcended or accommodated before the refugees of the 1930s could build new lives outside the influence of Hitlerism. In such circumstances the refugees could not count upon much assistance from existing Austrian and German communities: these groups had been seriously reduced by the First World War.[54] In the case of the Jewish refugees, however, there was an existing, well-organised community which could offer support, but this did not always manifest itself as an unmixed blessing.[55] Faced with these problems and strains of antipathy from within British society, there was some re-emigration.[56] Furthermore, some child refugees who were put to work in agriculture in centres such as Whittinghame Farm School in East Lothian, were specifically encouraged to emigrate.[57] Among those who remained a discernible impact can be traced although it has to be recognised that 'impact' is a slippery concept, difficult to use except in a rough and ready sense and, to repeat, not everyone shared in the success stories.[58]

However, at a time when the majority of the Black minority in Britain was experiencing severe difficulties in the labour market, and at a time when workers in the north of England were often faced with the prospect of long-term unemployment, there has been an emphasis on the successful activities of Jewish refugee businessmen, particularly on those who developed their interests in the depressed areas of the north. The economic damage inflicted on these areas during the world economic crisis encouraged the introduction in 1934 of a special areas policy designed to assist in the process of economic recovery and it was to these parts of Britain that the authorities tried to direct the refugee businessmen. However, not all entrepreneurs went to these forbidding regions. London, as always, exercised its own powerful pull; indeed, it has been claimed that Leipzig declined as an international fur market as refugees set up business in London.[59]

According to a Home Office memorandum, the total number of refugee businesses established between April 1935 and July 1938 was 187. By August 1939 another source estimated the number of firms at approximately 500, of which at least 300 were in the Special Areas. This late spurt was further evidence of the gathering momentum of emigration from Austria and Germany that took place in the last year or so of the peace.[60]

One company founded by refugees was the textile firm Mansfield Hosiery, which developed into Nottingham Manufacturing Company, the founders of which, the Djanogly family, had left Russia in 1917 and settled in Chemnitz before being uprooted by Nazism.[61] Another company that developed as a result of the influx of refugees in the 30s was Marchon Products which specialised in the production of detergents. This was founded in 1939 by Franz Schon and Frederick Marzillier. The company was taken over eventually by the Albright and Wilson group.[62] Such firms were begun by adult refugees but on a more generous time-scale, some of the children who came over as refugees also exercised an influence over business life in Britain.[63] The most recent glittering example of this success is the Octopus Publishing group, a company dominated by a former child-refugee, Paul Hamlyn.[64] Such initiatives constitute only part of a much larger development originated by the refugees from Germany. Walter Fliess brought with him an expertise in vegetarian cooking and soon established himself as a restaurateur and writer.[65] Frtiz Hallgarten brought his expertise in wine; so, among others, did Otto Loeb.[66]

What, then, was the total economic result of this activity? Hard evidence does not exist; it is an area that economic historians have neglected. However, according to one estimate, made in 1947, the refugees, Jews and non-Jews, had established over 1,000 firms in Britain which employed 250,000 people. In other words, the number of new jobs created was several times greater than the total number of refugees admitted into Britain. If this piece of evidence is regarded as an acceptable yardstick, the arrival of the newcomers had a positive effect on the economy.[67]

By way of sharp contrast relatively little has emerged to shed light on those who came with backgrounds in medicine or law. It is evident, however, that both groups faced particular difficulties in their transition to British society. German medical qualifications were not recognised in Britain and the newcomers also experienced hostility from within the profession. For their part, lawyers found there was no market for German law, although international lawyers fared better. In effect, for most of those refugees who wanted to continue with a career in law a period of retraining was necessary. Artists were less affected by the upheaval in their lives although it was a decided advantage to bring a known reputation from Germany.[68]

In the case of refugee academics more is known. Success stories were evident among this group, sometimes within a short space of time. However, it is important to guard against any assumption that this was an easy and effortless transition. Universities were not expanding and the few tenured posts that did appear were zealously guarded.[69] Moreover, the academic refugees, in common with other exiled German groups, had to surmount a number of hurdles. In most cases a new language had to be learned which initially restricted their capacity to engage in teaching activity.[70] A set of cultural values had to be absorbed from scratch. Hans Krebs, a future Nobel prizewinner, who settled in what George Orwell called 'the ugliest town in the Old World', recalled his own efforts to come to terms with the change: 'I also tried to make myself familiar with the literary heritage, beginning with things like "Alice in Wonderland" and nursery rhymes. And I found a great deal of help from a book by E.

Denison Ross called "This English Language" '.[71] Furthermore, in the case of many refugee physicists, their expertise in the theoretical side of their discipline placed them outside the mainstream of research activity in Britain. The result was that a number of talented individuals were unable to secure any permanent post and had to set their sights elsewhere, in the Commonwealth, or in a number of prominent cases in North America.[72]

Some indication of the influence of those scholars who remained can be derived from an analysis of Fellows of the Royal Society which discovered that between 1848 and 1900 'only seven Jews were elected to the ordinary Fellowships as against 869 non-Jews'. This proportion was closely related to the relative size of the two communities. By 1947, however, the number of Fellows of full Jewish parentage was more than five times that which their proportion to the general population would justify; in the case of foreign-born Fellows, the percentage was even higher. In a comment on these figures in 1955 it was emphasised that 'the immigration between 1933 and 1939 [was] to a large extent responsible for the increase in the proportion of Jews [as Fellows] during the last decade'.[73] This scientific scholarly influence was to be a continuing process. Krebs, Kurti, Peierls and Perutz were a few of the jewels in the crown. This contribution was further underlined when some of those who came as children gained scientific eminence. Once again there was no easy path to success; young refugees, uprooted from their origins, had to confront a variety of difficulties and antipathies. Furthermore, success, wherever it was evident, whether in the short or long term, did not confine itself to science. The world of scholarship benefited generally and generously in both the short term and the long term. The names of Carsten, Eysenck, Gellner, Gombrich, Pevsner, Pollard, Popper and Simon speak their own testimony.[74]

Although their lives had been disrupted by political developments, the major expressions of political activity by the refugees in Britain did not emerge until the war. However, across a number of fields of interest, various refugee organisations did appear before the lights went out once again over Europe. For example, the Free German League of Culture was founded in December 1938.[75] Moreover, religious Jews established the New Liberal Jewish Congregation at Belsize Square Synagogue in the summer of 1939.[76] There were also two intellectual developments associated with the refugees. One of these, which had a political relevance, celebrated its fiftieth anniversary in 1983. In 1933 Dr Alfred Wiener, an émigré from Austria, founded the Central Information Office in Holland. But Holland was within easy reach of the Germans and with the threat of war in 1939 Wiener moved yet again. On this occasion, with the support of the British government, he transported his collection of material to London and his new home opened at 19 Manchester Square, W1, on the day that war broke out. Wiener's work in cataloguing the crimes of Nazism was useful to the British authorities and during the war the Library formed part of the Ministry of Information. The Library was returned into private hands after the war and in 1965, the year after Wiener's death, it became known as the Institute of Contemporary History. Succeeding generations have reason to be grateful for access to its treasures.[77]

Another important cultural development involved the transfer of the Warburg Institute from Hamburg to London in 1933. The negotiations to achieve this transfer began in 1928 and although there was interest among British scholars, nothing could be done until there was a guarantee of financial support. Once this assistance was secured, six staff and 60,000 books arrived in London and accommodation was found in Thames House, a large office building in Millbank. The arrival of the Institute coincided with a growing interest in the visual arts and with continuing support from the Courtauld Trust and the Warburg family the Institute began its contribution to British cultural life which was to continue long after Hitlerism was effectively dead and buried.[78]

If we now turn to the economic and social life of the Irish, traces of continuity were evident. There was a continuing concentration, as regards employment, on 'Heavy labour in the building industry, railway and road construction and maintenance, and in the heavy and more deleterious branches of metal and chemical manufacture'. These occupations have been characterised as 'the typical avenues of employment for [Irish] men – jobs which had little appeal to the British worker'.[79] As a result, Irish workers could still find employment in the bleak interwar years. However, the observant eye of George Orwell noticed them in 1931 even further down the social scale, as prominent among the down and outs, part of London's lumpenproletariat, where they would have been visible a century earlier.[80]

But a total emphasis on continuity would distort the history of the Irish in the labour market. Changes in recruitment methods for dock labour reduced employment opportunities, particularly in Liverpool. Furthermore, municipal employment tended to be restricted to local applicants and this restriction also affected prospects among the Irish of finding work.[81]

A concentration on working-class Irish, moreover, would miss other elements that made up the Irish community. There was a small, professional middle-class circle of Irish immigrants in London before 1914 and the recruitment of a professional class continued to take place. These 'better class' immigrants as they have been called, tended to segregate themselves from the majority of the Irish community although there was never a total separation. Irish doctors and Irish lawyers, for example, could still make a good living for themselves catering for the needs of the working-class Irish. But apart from links of this kind, a degree of social distance was often observed. This social isolation of different Irish groups, it has been suggested, allowed for the easier exploitation of Irish working-class immigrants by the British.[82]

But the fact remains that most of the Irish were located in the working class and within their areas of settlement were also to be found in the lowest rank of the so-called 'housing classes', confined to decaying properties in areas with a weak social infrastructure.[83] But the housing problems encountered in the cities were relatively insignificant compared with the conditions under which seasonal workers in the rural areas of Scotland had to live.

This problem in the countryside had been identified in the late nineteenth century. Soon afterwards, a Royal Commission on Housing in Scotland in 1918 had recommended that every local authority should have the power to frame bye-laws dealing with the housing of potato-diggers; it was also suggested that, where necessary, the Local Government Board should be empowered to compel a local authority to exercise that power. As so often happens, these recommendations were not put into immediate effect and it took a tragedy at Ayrshire in September 1924, when a fire broke out in a barn, killing nine people, to bring the issue back into public focus.

Following this tragedy, legislation in 1925 in the form of the Housing (Scotland) Act provided that a local authority should make bye-laws to secure the proper accommodation of seasonal workers. The Department of Health was given the power to require such changes. But additional legislation notwithstanding, problems remained. In September 1937 a fire broke out at Kirkintilloch, in which ten workers from County Mayo were trapped and died. This incident directed attention once more to the accommodation of the seasonal Irish. The upshot was the introduction of tighter controls in 1937 in the Housing (Agricultural Population, Scotland) Act. In short, there were serious deficiencies in the housing of Irish seasonal workers in Scotland throughout most of the interwar years.[84]

The struggle to overcome disadvantage as well as the fight for Irish independence helped to generate a degree of political consciousness within the Irish minority. But political responses in the early twentieth century were more complex than might have been supposed. During the First World War when the 1916 Easter Rising occurred, there were 'no recorded incidents of disaffection' among Irish troops in the British army.[85] Indeed, when Sir Roger Casement unveiled his vision of an independent Ireland to Irish POWs at Limburg, 'They hissed him into inaudibility' and 'only fifty soldiers joined his brigade in the course of the war'.[86] Casement's dreams were shattered with his capture in Ireland on 22 April 1916, two days before the Rising began, and ended with his execution in Pentonville in the following August.[87] At no time in 1916 was there any major shift of the Irish to Ireland to shoulder arms against the British. In fact, the Rising generated a considerable degree of division and disagreement. When it occurred, some of the Irish community in Glasgow perceived it as the work of pro-German forces and wanted nothing to do with it. But, at the same time, Republican units drilled in the city. The continuing tension in Ireland through the period of the 'troubles', the Anglo-Irish Treaty of 1921, the establishment of the Irish Free State in 1922 and the trauma of its aftermath, sustained such differences.[88]

By the early 1920s much of the steam had evaporated from Irish nationalist politics within Britain even though these were years of turmoil in Ireland.[89] Thousands could line the streets from Brixton prison to Southwark Cathedral in 1920 when the body of a dead hunger-striker, Terence MacSwiney, a former Lord Mayor of Cork, was carried along the route but their presence could be regarded as sympathy or curiosity rather than any overt expression of support for Irish nationalism.[90] What is more significant is that organisations such as the Irish Self-Determination League, the United Irish League and the Irish Democratic League all found themselves adversely affected by the lack of sustained momentum in the course of the 1920s. However, this flagging support did not prevent the formation in the 1930s of the Connolly Association, which attempted to win support for the ending of partition at the same time as working closely with the British Labour movement for the interests of Irish immigrants in Britain.[91]

More startling evidence to the British that they could not regard Irish nationalism as dead and buried came in the increase in IRA activity which was evident from 1936 onwards. This realisation gained a new dimension in January 1939 when, after an ultimatum to the British government, an IRA bombing campaign began which was to last for fourteen months.[92] This offensive started on 16 January with an explosion just outside the control room of the Southwark power station. Other attacks followed soon after in Birmingham, Manchester and Alnwick. These events heralded the start of a nationwide campaign which, before the war, culminated in an explosion in Broadgate, Coventry, in which five people were killed and a further sixty injured. However, it is worth noting that this campaign, which reflected tensions within Irish politics as well as an opposition to the British government, was carried out mainly by volunteers sent over from Ireland with a specific mission to accomplish.[93]

Among the Irish who put down their roots in Britain a number of other significant political developments can be detected. Down to the First World War the Irish had thrown most of their weight behind the Liberal Party. This allegiance began to change during the First World War. But it was the postwar crisis in Ireland when some Liberals supported the repressive policies of a Conservative-dominated coalition government that hastened the collapse of Irish support for the Liberal Party. In these circumstances the sympathies of an increasing number of immigrants turned towards Labour. Once the Irish Free State had been established in 1922 and the cause of Irish nationalism flowed less strongly among the immigrants, this attachment became even more pronounced. By such time the Liberal Party was seriously divided and the Labour Party seemed more in tune with the needs of the mainly working-class Irish minority.[94]

Sustenance of a different kind during the difficult interwar years still came from the Roman Catholic Church and it was through the agencies of the Church and the Labour Party that many of those Irish living permanently in Britain, old hands and recent arrivals, made their major institutional contact with British society. The Church was able to accommodate the politics of the Labour Party but some other forms of political activity carried out by the immigrants disturbed the priests. For example, the activities of the Connolly Association, which had the reputation of being a Communist front organisation, fell under clerical suspicion. There had been an early involvement of individuals of Irish descent in the development of the Communist Party of Great Britain, most notably in the persons of Tom Bell, Willie Gallacher, Arthur MacManus and J. T. Murphy, and any such activity was regarded as anathema by the representatives of the Church who believed that ultimately they alone, through the Church and its schools, had the prerogative to teach the Irish 'the way they should go'. It was not unknown for a conflict of loyalties to develop on this account.[95]

What were the salient features of the economic and social life of the Black and Indian groups in Britain? Some indication of the involvement of Indians in business activity can be gleaned from a 1933 survey of Indians overseas which drew attention to a number of firms in the import-export business based mainly in Manchester and London. In addition to these businesses, which helped to turn the wheels of Imperial commerce, there were two firms of accountants as well as one stockbroker, Gordon Ray of 27 Throgmorton Street, EC2. Altogether it was possible to identify 48 business organisations which could be designated as 'Indian'.[96]

But those covered in this survey were no more representative of Indians than the well-known Black sportsmen and entertainers[97] were typical of the Black minority. The majority among the Blacks, Indians and what contemporaries described hazily as 'coloured groups' could be firmly categorised as working class. The shipping industry continued to be a major employer, although by the mid-1930s, partly because of intense international competition, one out of every three registered seamen was unemployed.[98] In these circumstances rivalry for employment was intense and this competition spilled over into racial hatred, discrimination and collective violence which resulted in increased unemployment for Blacks as well as other racial minorities.[99]

This involvement in the shipping industry was reflected in a spatial concentration of Africans, Indians and West Indians in the ports. Those who lived in the dock areas tended to concentrate even within these localities. In Liverpool settlement occurred mainly on the south side of the city, in Liverpool 8, and in Cardiff, too, a similar concentration was apparent, in the Butetown district, which became known, disparagingly, as 'Tiger Bay'.[100] These areas contained minorities of various nationalities who concentrated there as a result of a number of interconnecting pressures. In many cases, as members of a disadvantaged working class, prospects of residential improvement were limited. Moreover, there has always been a general tendency for most minority groups to congregate, at least initially, with those who share a similar background and culture. But there can be no doubt that the concentration in Liverpool and Cardiff was significantly related to the discriminatory power wielded by the White community which was soon brought into action whenever Blacks attempted to move beyond their allotted residential base.[101]

Within their areas of settlement the Blacks and other racial minorities shared in part the social horizons and assumptions that were held by the disadvantaged White working class. In all cases aspirations were seriously affected by the economic and social conditions that prevailed in such districts; as a result, successive generations became locked into a way of life from which it was difficult to escape. Those who were not White faced a particularly difficult task. Nevertheless, there was a degree of resilience in the face of disadvantage. Some found consolation in the folds of religion. Political groups also came into being. It was noticed in Cardiff that some Africans and West Indians allied themselves to the Sons of Africa, a body which was anxious to be regarded as 'a highly respectable organization by coloured and white alike'. This particular group represented 'the more solid and accommodative part of the coloured community'. Others, however, more radical in outlook, joined the Colonial Defence League or the Colonial Defence Association as it is sometimes called, the object of which was to protect the interests and rights of the colonial minority, if necessary through militant action.[102]

Both these organisations were testimony to the growth of strands of political consciousness among the Black proletariat in Britain which should be considered as part of a wider Black awakening during the interwar years. Specific events in Britain such as the 1919 violence and, in Cardiff, the discrimination practised against what were called coloured seamen as a result of the local police's interpretation of the 1925 Special Restriction (Coloured Alien Seamen) Order, were two local influences that influenced Black consciousness. But this Black awareness was also stimulated by events in Africa, the Caribbean and the United States. Moreover, there was a growing recognition among the politically-conscious that, in order to achieve freedom, pressure had to be applied in Britain, the centre of colonial and imperial power.[103]

Whatever difficulties had to be faced, there was a greater degree of freedom in Britain than existed in the subjugated territories to mount a political campaign and such freedom was put to effective use. One of the new arrivals expressed this in his own inimitable way. 'At a stroke you got removed from a world that talks about the ju ju into one of ideas and movements'.[104] In the 1920s, at a time of developing Pan-Africanism, Black awareness in Britain was reflected in the activity of a number of organisations.[105] The African Progress Union, founded in 1918, and by 1921 under the leadership of the Trinidadian-born doctor, John Alcindor, was one of these.[106] There were also student bodies such as the Union for Students of African Descent, the origins of which stretched back to 1917, and the Gold Coast Students' Association.[107] The most significant step forward in student organisation, however, came on 7 August 1925 with the foundation by a Nigerian law student, Ladipo Solanke, of the West African Students' Union (WASU).[108]

But it could be argued that even more significant developments were to come in the following troubled decade.[109] The Scottsboro case in America, the Italian invasion of Abyssinia in 1935, the Trinidad oil fields riot of 1937 and strikes in Jamaica in 1938 all helped to fuel Black consciousness.[110] WASU became increasingly anti-imperialist in the course of the 1930s and the Italian invasion triggered new groups into existence such as the International African Friends of Abyssinia, which was later replaced by the International African Service Bureau.[111] The 30s also witnessed a growing concentration of formidable individual talent which built up Black consciousness in this decade.[112] C. L. R. James, whose classic study, *The Black Jacobins*, appeared in 1936, George Padmore, and I. T. A. Wallace-Johnson, were all involved in the International African Service Bureau. Their activities, along with that of Jomo Kenyatta and Ras Makonnen, came to overshadow the work of Marcus Garvey. There was overall a vitality about such activity which was fully reflected in the publication of books, journals and newspapers, many of which circulated throughout the Black diaspora. It has been suggested that the long-term influence of the Pan-Africanists on British society was ambiguous. However, there is no doubt that, along with their White sympathisers, they provided a significant impetus to the cause of

Black liberation outside Britain which was to bear fruit sooner than most would ever have dreamed.[113]

The political activity undertaken by Black groups and radical Black activists needs to be set alongside that of the League of Coloured Peoples (LCP) which occupied a middle role between White paternalist groups and radical Black organisations.[114] The LCP was formed in 1931 by Dr Harold Moody, a Jamaican, who had first moved to London, at the age of 22, in 1904.[115] Its fourfold aims were set out in the early issues of its journal, *The Keys*. These were: to promote the social, educational and political interests of its members; to interest members in the Welfare of Coloured Peoples in all parts of the world; to improve relations between the Races; and to cooperate and affiliate with organisations sympathetic to Coloured People.[116] Notwithstanding some accounts of its history, the LCP was from its origins a multiracial organisation and the musical allusion in the title of its journal was intended to reflect this position.[117]

The general tenor of the LCP, which was 'a social club, housing bureau, pressure group, investigative agency and employment agency', with a small membership of Blacks, Indians and Whites, was its moderation. Moody, who presided over the organisation from its inception until his death in 1947, saw to that.[118] This moderate outlook was reflected in *The Keys*, which carried articles on Booker T. Washington, the predominant and moderate voice of Black America in the years before the Great War, on the necessity for racial cooperation ('Our slogan is not "Black against White" but "Black with White" for the greater benefit of both') and on the academic attainments of 'some of our successful students'. This selection of topics provides a flavour of the atmosphere which surrounded the organisation.[119]

Activists such as Ras Makonnen were prepared to have a relationship with the League as a matter of convenience but were later critical of the LCP. 'It was involved in mild protest or, if you like, harassing the goody-goody elements in Britain'.[120] The fact that the LCP was prepared in 1934 to support the Colonial Office in the opening of a British government sponsored hostel at Aggrey House – a response which created a rift between WASU and the LCP – was one development which helped to create this moderate image.[121] Even so, the degree of radicalisation within the League brought about by the Italian invasion of Abyssinia in 1935, the challenging editorials by Peter Blackman carried in *The Keys* at a slightly later date, and the willingness of the League to cooperate with more radical Black elements suggest that such moderation was not unqualified.[122]

In their search for allies, however, the more radical Blacks came to look elsewhere. Some had a tortured and tortuous relationship with the Communist Party and the Comintern.[123] In the 1930s Black aspirations had been at a discount in the Communist book: attention was concentrated on India. But the formation in 1930 of the International Trade Union Committee of Negro Workers (ITUCNW), in which George Padmore played a leading role before his formal expulsion from the Comintern in February 1934,[124] and the increasing interest in African affairs taken by the League Against Imperialism (LAI), which within two years of its foundation in 1927 'was very much under direct Communist control', marked a shift in emphasis.[125] WASU, for example, received help from the League against Imperialism and the Negro Welfare Association was an LAI creation.[126] But the nature of the response of world Communism to the Abyssinian crisis and its increasing involvement in the 1930s with anti-Fascist struggles rather than anti-Imperialist agitation, succeeded in alienating significant sections of Black support.[127]

The political activities of the Black diaspora have been given close attention over the past few years even if there are areas that remain untouched and unknown. However, the political activity undertaken by Indians and their sympathisers on behalf of Indian independence should not be forgotten.

It has now been largely forgotten, but the return of Parsees to the House of Commons continued in the interwar years when Shapurji Saklatvala was returned for Battersea North, John Burns's old seat, in the October 1922 General Election. 'Sak', as he was widely known, had first come to Britain in 1905 for medical treatment. He possessed already an acute and sensitive social conscience and this developed further in Britain where he joined the Independent Labour Party. In 1921, however, Saklatvala entered the ranks of the Communist Party of Great Britain and it was as a Communist, supported locally by J. R. Archer, that he sat in the Commons for Battersea until 1929. He tried, without success, to re-enter the House but his lack of success did not dim his attachment to the Communist cause, for which he worked until his death in 1936. He died, we have been told, with 'his principles and personal commitment unchanged', and these guaranteed his continuing opposition to Imperialism and his support of groups who tried to free themselves from its powerful influence.[128]

Considerable work was also undertaken by others on behalf of the Indian cause. Some of the activists were Indian students studying in Britain, among whom there was a long tradition of political awareness. In 1936, the organisation of such activity was improved with the agreement between Majlis at Cambridge and similar societies in Oxford and London, to form a nationwide association, which resulted in the following year in the establishment of the Federation of Indian Students in Great Britain.[129] A key figure in this radicalisation, in which there was a pronounced Communist Party influence, was Mohan Kumaramangalam, who was later to enjoy a distinguished public career in an independent India.[130]

In addition, a number of other organisations of varying ideological outlook, were active in the interwar years. One such group owed its origins to Krishna Menon who came to Britain in 1924. The Amritsar massacre in 1919 convinced many Indians that a tougher, more radical, opposition to British rule was called for and this was reflected in the stance of the Indian National Congress, which proceeded to drop its commitment to strictly constitutional agitation. In Britain there were important developments related to this change of strategy. Menon revitalised the old Commonwealth of India League, the formerly named Home Rule for India British Auxiliary, which had been founded in 1912 by Annie Besant, and converted it into the India League, committed to *swaraj* (self-rule). In the course of time the India League was to exercise an important influence over British attitudes towards the sub-continent and was particularly influential within the Labour Party.[131]

The League marked only one dimension of Menon's life in Britain which saw him as a student at the LSE, a publisher (together with Allen Lane he started the Penguin-Pelican imprint), as well as a St Pancras borough councillor. But it was perhaps the India League, and its role in 'telling the British people of the sins [such as the Meerut conspiracy case of 1929–33] that were committed in India in their name',[132] which marked Menon's greatest achievement. As with the Pan-Africanists, the full flowering of this anti-Imperial political activity was to be seen after the Second World War.

4.

THE nationalist fervour which prevailed at the end of the First World
War had provided the necessary background for the 1919 Aliens Act.
Indeed, the difficult years of transition from war to peace kept alive
strong strains of nationalism and xenophobia. This atmosphere was
evident in a debate in February 1923 in which Conservative
spokesmen stressed the need for 'a strict control . . . over alien
immigrants'. So anxious indeed were they in their intent, that they
overlooked the fact that the 1919 Aliens Act was still in operation! In
the course of the debate it was stressed that unemployment was
running at a high level and in these circumstances a strict control
should be maintained over 'the alien revolutionary agitator' i.e. the
Jew. At the same time, the debate allowed for a continued expression
of opposition to the prewar immigration from Russian Poland and a
lamentation that the face of the East End had been drastically
changed by a Jewish presence.[133] The motion was opposed by a
young Clement Attlee and George Lansbury, both of whom allied the
Labour Party to a more liberal position, complained about an alleged
class bias that characterised legislation on immigration, attempted to
rebut any suggestion of a link between Labour and Bolshevism, and,
at the same time, complained about the deportations that were taking
place under the 1919 Act.[134] Even so, the reference from one Labour
member to 'hook nosed patriots' who sang God Save the King 'in
broken English', revealed that the Conservatives had no monopoly of
vicious stereotypes.[135]

Jews were not the only focus of attention in this parliamentary
debate in 1923 – alien seamen also featured in the discussion[136] – but
the Jewish dimension did loom large. So it did in the series of articles
called 'Alien London' which appeared in The Times in November and
December 1924.[137] Furthermore, the fear that unemployment could
allow alien agitators to stir up revolution, which was emphasised in
another debate over alien immigration in February 1925, revealed a
continuing coded concern about Jewish Bolshevism. And Labour
spokesmen were reminded that a party which was internationalist, or
preferred 'to consider the interests of aliens to the interests of our own
people', could expect to lose elections as Labour had done in the
so-called Red Letter election of October 1924. These strands of
hostility, emanating from Westminster and Printing House Square;
found echoes in other quarters.[138]

In the case of Jews, an additional, more rarified, indication of continuing concern about the presence of Russian Poles came in the form of an essay by Karl Pearson, the biometrician, based on data from the immigration of the late nineteenth century.[139] After assessing evidence drawn from the Jews' Free School in Spitalfields, which 'specialized in the Anglicisation of the young',[140] Pearson concluded: 'Taken on average and regarding both sexes, this alien Jewish population is somewhat inferior physically and mentally to the native population'. Pearson conceded that there were children of alien Jews who had distinguished themselves in British life. However, he emphasised that 'No breeder of cattle . . . would purchase an entire herd because he anticipated finding one or two fine specimens included in it; still less would he do it if his byres and pastures were already full'. The law of patriotism for a crowded country was to admit only those who provided it either physically or mentally with what it lacked or possessed only in limited quantity. In the case of the Jewish immigrants, Pearson suggested that they should be settled in Palestine or a similar area, far away from the overcrowded cities of western Europe.[141]

Before his article appeared, Pearson had given the essence of his views in a talk delivered in the University of London and his message was seized upon by The Britons, an organisation which from its origins in 1919 was deeply committed to a belief in the Jewish world conspiracy, as spelt out in *The Protocols of the Elders of Zion*, an English translation of which The Britons published in 1920 under the title *The Jewish Peril*.[142] It is hardly surprising, therefore, that the organisation gave prominence to Pearson's comments.[143] Adverse reflections on the genetic endowment of Jews written by G. P. Mudge, also received publicity from The Britons.[144] Such emphases were later welcomed by Lt. Col. A. H. Lane, and incorporated into his frequently reprinted book on *The Alien Menace*.[145]

In contrast, Pearson's work found no favour with Anglo-Jewry and the Board of Deputies sponsored a reply in the following year. The conclusion of this particular piece of research, which received help and guidance from the now notorious Professor Cyril Burt, concluded on the basis of IQ tests that, 'On an average, both in General Intelligence and in attainments in English and Arithmetic, Jewish children are definitely superior to the non-Jewish children attending the same school, the superiority being more marked with the boys than with the girls'.[146] This exercise, together with Pearson's earlier analysis, help to underline the fact that the science of race has never been value-free.[147]

When, shortly after these surveys had been completed, refugees began to arrive from Hitlerite Germany, voices were raised from the beginning in their defence and organisational support was also forthcoming. This assistance was particularly evident within the Anglo-Jewish community. An early welcoming hand was extended by the long-established Jews' Temporary Shelter in Whitechapel. This organisation, under the presidency of Otto M. Schiff, who had already gained experience in assisting the Jewish war refugees from Belgium, was particularly active in meeting the immediate needs of those refugees who had neither relations nor friends to support them.[148] The work of the Shelter was supplemented by the Central British Fund for German Jewry which was founded in 1933.[149] Following a further fund-raising exercise in 1936 this organisation became known as the Council for German Jewry. The Council was responsible for the allocation of the sums raised for the refugees among appropriate voluntary bodies. It also acted as a pressure group on the government and was particularly active in this respect in 1939 in the wake of the *Kristallnacht* pogrom.[150] Apart from his connection with the Jews' Temporary Shelter, Otto Schiff played an important role in the formation in 1933 of the Jewish Refugees Committee, later called the German-Jewish Aid Committee, an organisation which arranged for the admission of Jews, and also busied itself with their maintenance, training, employment or re-emigration.[151]

From an early date there was an understanding between the Jewish community and the British government that the Jews would look after their own without recourse to public funds, and there can be no doubt that such support and other initiatives from within the established community eased the path of many refugees who might otherwise have been excluded by the 1919 Aliens Act.[152] Indeed, such activity has attracted celebratory comment.[153] But a sense of perspective is required in any consideration of Jewish responses. In the late nineteenth century the established Anglo-Jewish community had been ambivalent in its response to the immigration from Russian Poland and its reaction to the refugees from Nazism was no less complex. There were those members of Anglo-Jewry who wished that the refugees had decided to establish themselves elsewhere.[154] Furthermore, the German-Jewish Aid Committee, whatever support it provided, was anxious to convert the Germans into English people as soon as possible and tried to insist on the refugees keeping a low profile. This policy was evident in its 1939 pamphlet *When you are in England. Helpful Information and Guidance for every Refugee*, which has been described as, 'A rather crude, if not outright offensive attempt to placate British xenophobia . . . . '.[155]

Groups outside the Jewish community also attempted to provide support for the refugees. For example, in 1933 the Society of Friends established a German Emergency Committee which opened offices in Paris and Prague as well as within Germany.[156] Furthermore, in the same year the Academic Assistance Council, later called the Society for the Protection of Science and Learning, was formed under the influence of William Beveridge, the Director of the London School of Economics. This body, the members of which were prominent in various walks of public life, was concerned with securing employment for academics and helping those scholars without private means.[157] At the same time, some student refugees of outstanding ability were helped by the International Student Service which provided grants and training facilities. The International Solidarity Fund of the Labour Party and Trades Union Council was also active in the early stages of relief activity.[158]

When, by degrees, it became apparent that the German refugees were not all Jewish, the Society of Friends was joined by other religious groups. These included committees of the Church of England, the Church of Scotland, and the Catholic Church, as well as the International Hebrew-Christian Alliance. These bodies and several other organisations pooled their efforts in the Christian Council for Refugees from Germany and Central Europe, which raised funds and also took up questions relating to the refugees with the Home Office.[159]

By 1938 it was recognised that the various refugee organisations and their provincial committees required a degree of coordination. As a result, in that year a Central Co-ordinating Committee, later called the Joint Consultative Committee on Refugees was set up in London. Following this initiative, it was decided early in 1939 to centralise the offices of the main organisations under the Committee, which led to the purchase of a hotel in Bloomsbury. Renamed Bloomsbury House the former hotel became the headquarters of the major organisations involved in working with refugees.[160]

All this activity was one side of the picture but there was another.

Some of the strongest antipathy towards the refugees came from within the medical profession. As early as 1933 when middle-class, white-collar professions faced their own uncertainties in the world depression, fears were expressed about the number of refugee doctors being admitted and there were pleas to safeguard the interests of their British counterparts. 'We have ever been the refuge of the oppressed and exiled', one letter writer to the *British Medical Journal* insisted, 'but surely as the profession is already overcrowded, charity begins among ourselves'.[161] Fears of this kind refused to die down and received some public sympathy outside the medical profession.[162] The issue came to a head with the admission of Austrian doctors who were fleeing from the expanded Reich created after the *Anschluss* in 1938. In these circumstances the British Medical Association set up its own committee to advise the Home Secretary on the conditions under which such refugees should be permitted to settle in Britain. It was reported in 1938 that the Association had secured an agreement with the Home Office for a severe limitation on the number of refugees that would be admitted. In future each application was to be carefully scrutinised and the refugees were to be required to undertake at least two years' clinical study before they were allowed to practise.[163] Opposition of a similar kind was heard from architects and also from within the academic world.[164] The success stories should not be allowed to obscure this antipathy based upon professional fears for employment in the interwar economic crisis.[165]

Anti-alien sentiment was also reflected in the House of Commons, just as it had been during the earlier arrival and settlement of the Russian Poles. One prominent voice in the 1930s was Captain Archibald Ramsay, Conservative MP for Peebles, a leading sympathiser with Germany and founder of The Right Club, who was later to be interned during the war under Regulation 18B.[166] Furthermore, it was not unknown for sentiments in the House to assume an anti-Semitic dimension. The interventions of Edward Doran, the Unionist member for Tottenham North, an early opponent of the refugees, reflected this sentiment quite openly[167] and, in more coded fashion, so did the activity of W. P. C. Greene. Greene's position, however, was interesting in another respect. On the one hand he was convinced of the need to preserve 'the purity of our race' but, on the other, he believed that capitalists, whatever their race, were of benefit. In his complex approach to immigration Greene was not alone.[168]

Expressions of opposition towards the refugees were not especially remarkable. Indeed, at this time 'Anti-semitism was in the air: an unmistakeable tang'.[169] In the general public this opposition was generally reflected not in any high-flown theory but in that kind of amorphous antipathy towards Jews which has been a persistent and widely-reflected feature of British society.[170] It was not uncommon in the popular press for example, to find the refugees, portrayed specifically as Jews, in accounts which suggested that they were busily engaged in undermining society and the British way of life.[171]

A strain of anti-Semitism was also manifest in the responses of Fascist and racial nationalist groups, such as the British Union of Fascists, the largest and most influential Fascist group which had grown up with the crisis of capitalism in the early 1930s. An early opposition, revealed in headlines such as 'Refugees to have your boys' jobs', appeared in the Blackshirt press and it was difficult, even when it was attempted, to prevent this hostility assuming an anti-Semitic dimension.[172] By the late 30s, in fact, the BUF had become more openly anti-Semitic. Indeed, from 1934 onwards, the organisation developed a growing interest in 'the Jewish Question'. This involvement was indicated in part by its hostility towards the refugees arriving from Hitlerite Europe. But, drawing upon a local tradition of hostility which stretched back to the days of the immigration from Russian Poland, the BUF also attacked the longer-established Jewish population that remained in the East End of London. It was this East End campaign, symbolised by the so-called battle of Cable Street in 1936 which led in the same year to the passing of the Public Order Act.[173]

Faced with this mixed climate of opinion how did the government respond to immigration? The 1919 Aliens Act, together with Orders in Council, such as those of 1920 and 1925, gave the Home Secretary wide powers to control the entry and deportation of aliens and, if Conservative ministers such as William Joynson-Hicks relished their powers, governments of whatever complexion remained essentially restrictionist. If Conservatives were not slow to claim that Labour's electoral defeat in 1924 related to its sympathy towards aliens, in practice, whatever opinions were expressed by the Party when in opposition, Labour's Home Office ministers in the interwar years were restrictionist in outlook. Marx was able to find refuge in England in the nineteenth century but J. R. Clynes, the Home Secretary in Ramsay MacDonald's second administration, was adamant in his refusal to accept Leon Trotsky, even for a temporary stay, in 1929.[174]

In the 1930s as refugees began to arrive from Germany and Austria, it was argued at first that the size of the British population and the substantial level of unemployment which prevailed in the country, required a cautious approach. Caution, in fact, remained the official watchword down to 1939 and entry was granted predominantly to those refugees who had the prospect of permanent immigration elsewhere; one symbol of this caution was the 'Kitchener Camp for Poor Persons' opened in January 1939 at Richborough in Kent, 'where over three thousand Jewish refugees were temporarily housed pending their re-emigration to other countries'.[175] However, against this background there were some shifts in policy both in response to political pressures and the rising number of refugees.

From January 1933 until September 1935, a time when numbers remained small, the government offered asylum to only a few refugees who were often wealthy and well-connected.[176] During these years the question of admitting refugees also extended to Palestine which had been designated as a British mandated territory in 1920. Here too, a shadow was soon to be cast over the prospect of relief for refugees. A restrictionist sentiment was present, for example, in the 1937 Peel Commission which recommended that no more than 12,000 Jewish immigrants each year should be admitted to Palestine. Fearful as it was of Arab reactions to the arrival of Jews, the report was hardly unwelcome to the British government.[177]

It was in the following year, after the *Anschluss* of March 1938, that the flight from Austria began. In these circumstances the British government decided to institute a visa system for German and Austrian refugees in order to staunch a possible flow that might overwhelm voluntary organisations and create public resentment.[178] In its administrative practice the British government had also begun by this time to distinguish between aliens and refugees, a distinction present in the 1905 Aliens Act but which had lapsed in the aliens legislation of 1914–19.[179] With its reluctance to admit a large number of refugees into Britain, and with its implementation of restrictions on immigration into Palestine, following the Peel Commission report, the British government began to look for suitable centres for settlement within the Empire – just as it had done 30 or so years earlier at the time of immigration from Russian Poland. By the summer of 1938, therefore, the refugee question had assumed an important international dimension which was signified by the calling of the Evian Conference in July 1938. The intention of this conference was to seek a coordinated international solution to the question. But any hopes held out at Evian were aborted; nothing of substance emerged from the deliberations.[180]

In late 1938 attention switched partly to Czechoslovakia with the German occupation of the Sudetenland following the Munich Agreement of September 1938 between Germany, Italy, France and Britain. This agreement led to the convergence of refugees on Prague. Eventually, some of these Czechs came to Britain and following the German seizure of Czechoslovakia in March 1939 they were joined by other refugees. In these circumstances a portion of the funds, essentially 'guilt money', which the British government had placed at the disposal of the truncated Czech government in 1939, was set aside for refugee work and in July 1939 the Czech Refugee Fund was set up to administer these resources. By the outbreak of war approximately 8,000 Czechs had found their way to Britain. The government's response to the Czech crisis marked a softening of offical policy and this was reflected in other directions. Following the *Kristallnacht* pogrom in November 1938, and as countries all over the world became more restrictive, there was a further relaxation of entry procedures for Germans and Austrians. Evidence of this change came in the summer of 1939 when the government, with some reluctance, signified its general willingness to help in defraying the costs of emigrating refugees, provided other governments also contributed to the cost of this exercise.[181]

In other words, there was some easing of entry in the course of late 1938 which continued into 1939. This relaxation was related partly to the energetic lobbying of pro-refugee groups but, in more cynical vein, it has been suggested that it was criticism of the British government's Palestine policy that 'compelled greater liberality' within Britain and the Empire.[182] In the case of Palestine, the Peel Commission was followed by a White Paper of May 1939 which recommended that during the next five years no more than 75,000 Jews should be admitted to Palestine and, at the end of that time, there should be no further immigration without the acquiescence of the Palestinian Arabs.[183] In these circumstances restrictions remained on entry into the area but from late 1938 onwards the illegal immigration of Jews into Palestine increased considerably, much to the irritation of the British authorities.[184]

In terms of an overall balance sheet, it has been suggested that, compared with other countries, British policy towards the refugees was 'comparatively compassionate, even generous'.[185] But this conclusion should be kept in perspective. For some countries one refugee was too many and the pressure from refugees to enter Shanghai, the one free port where no visa was required, testified to the international restrictions on the admittance of refugees. But if it is easy enough to score points off those officials responsible for restrictionist policies, it is important at the same time to guard against the sin of 'presentism', and not let judgement be clouded by a knowledge of what ultimately happened to those who never managed to escape Hitlerism. The full extent of this horror was not available or envisaged by 1939.[186]

There were fewer international pressures that affected the reception of the Irish. Even so, as in earlier times an understanding of reactions towards this minority requires an awareness of the impact exerted by the wider Irish Question on British political life.

In general there has been a tendency to write about the Irish in Whiggish terms, as an increasingly tolerated minority. However, this optimism needs to be qualified. For instance, tension which derived from a perception of the Irish as economic competitors still had some life left in it. Such hostility became evident as the economic problems of the interwar years began to appear. Scotland, with its involvement in the old heavy industries, was particularly affected by the world economic crisis and such circumstances provided the trigger for the continuation of old animosities.[187] But it was not only in Scotland that anti-Irish sentiment was manifested. Apart from the effects of changes in recruitment methods in the docks and in the pattern of municipal employment, in the hard times of the 1930s it was not uncommon for notices indicating 'No Irish' to be on display in the Midlands and other areas.[188] Why should we employ 'men dubious of value to any community' a correspondent ventured to ask in *The Times*, particularly when there were so many unemployed among 'our own people'. Such opposition did not have it all its own way. In reply to this question a Lincolnshire farmer praised the 'morality, industry, sobriety, thrift and good faith' of Irish agricultural workers, who, it was claimed, had never tried to undersell local labour.[189] It was a defence which was presumably shared by some other employers of Irish labour.

Apart from hostility which arose over specific issues such as employment, there were occasions when a whole range of economic and social problems was related to the continued presence of an Irish minority. In 1931 in the course of an electioneering campaign on Merseyside, where there was a long tradition of sectarian campaigning, H. D. Longbottom, the candidate for Protestant Democracy, held Irish immigration responsible for unemployment, the continued existence of slums (a reminder that many urban Irish as well as rural workers had to endure squalid conditions), and the persistence of high rates; indeed, Longbottom, the candidate for Protestant Democracy, went even further on one occasion and suggested that the Irish – essentially the Catholic component – should be required to have five years' residence before they became eligible for poor relief.[190] It was in similar vein that G. R. Gair, who possessed a philosophic racist view of society, argued in three issues of the *Liverpool Review* for the exclusion of the Southern Irish from Britain on the grounds of their racial undesirability and the related economic and social danger which he was convinced that they posed to British society.[191] According to Gair, the presence of the Southern Irish, categorised as 'a branch of the Mediterranean race', could only damage the 'Nordic' civilisation of Britain. In less extreme, but still hostile terms, J. B. Priestley, reflecting in Paddy's Market, Liverpool, associated the Irish from the Clyde to Cardiff with 'ignorance and dirt and drunkennness and disease' and was seemingly not averse to a 'grand clearance' of such an undesirable minority.[192]

In raising the responsibility of the Irish for social problems, it was always possible for politicians on Merseyside to draw support from the deep well of sectarian differences. This influence was also evident in Scotland. One of the major sources of friction here centred upon the 1918 Education Act which placed the education of Catholic children on an equal footing with those of the Protestant faith. Some Protestants were terrified of any inroads being made into their ascendancy and the anxiety created on this score was evident in 1922 in the first education authority election that followed the Act, when Glasgow resounded with Protestant cries of 'Rome on the Rates'.[193]

In all of this economic and social opposition there were elements of continuity with the past, the reiteration of themes that had been evident in the nineteenth century. In these earlier times hostility had been given an additional impetus when it fell under the influence of the Irish struggle for national independence.[194] The continuing influence of this factor was also apparent in the interwar years. On 21 November 1920 an execution squad under orders from Michael Collins shot twelve British army officers and two auxiliary officers of the Royal Irish Constabulary in Dublin, and in turn this action converted Irish people on the mainland into targets for revenge. The interiors of certain 'Irish' public houses in working-class areas of London were smashed up and there was also an attempt to damage Roman Catholic churches.[195]

A similar tension developed immediately before the outbreak of the Second World War, when the IRA began to engage in violence on the mainland. Faced with this situation, there was some pressure for the government to act. As a result in July 1939 the Prevention of Violence Act was passed. The Act compelled Irishmen in Britain to register with the police and, in appropriate cases, provided for their deportation. However, since most of those who planted the bombs came over on assignment from Ireland, and entry remained unrestricted, it was difficult to stamp out this activity. Arrests were made by Special Branch and some activists, were sent to jail. Nevertheless, the campaign still continued and following the worst explosion at Coventry in August 1939 intercommunal tension broke out in Liverpool and Glasgow and IRA prisoners languishing in Dartmoor were beaten up. Moreover, the bombings were not easily forgotten.[196]

If the political struggle for an independent Ireland created specific tensions for Irish immigrants, so did the development of Scottish nationalism. An interaction of economic and political pressures, with national and international features, gave a powerful impetus to Scottish nationalism during the interwar years, when the National Party of Scotland was formed in 1928.[197] In the 1920s and 1930s a number of publications emerging from within the ranks of the Scottish nationalists portrayed the Irish as a major social problem. Such material contained a number of frequently-repeated emphases. The Scots were perceived as in danger of eclipse. 'They were being replaced in their own country by a people alien in race, temperament and religion'.[198] Moreover, in this nationalist canon numbers were made to count. 'Today', it was asserted, 'every fifth baby born in Scotland is a little Irish Catholic'. It was further alleged that, 'most significant and sinister of all', one third of the crimes committed in Scotland were the work of Irishmen. It was fantasised that by 1981 violence between the Scots and Irish would be rampant. It was also claimed that by that date the seriousness of what was happening would be recognised in the 1981 census. As a consequence Irish immigration would be regulated.[199] Such an outpouring, if not fully representative of Scottish nationalism, was not an isolated phenomenon. It was claimed a few years later in another work that 'viewed in any light' Irish immigration was 'a national problem and a national evil of the first importance'.[200] Here again the growth of an Irish Catholic population and its association with criminal activity received a major emphasis. Within the heart of Scotland it was claimed there existed a society within a society under the control of 'obscurantist magic men'. Moreover, this state of affairs was regarded as having deep historical roots. 'The Irish Problem', it was claimed, was a monument to the state of affairs that had prevailed since the 1707 Act of Union, as a result of which no measures were passed for Scotland until they became necessary in England.[201] This alleged subjugation of Scotland and its consequences for Irish immigration into Scotland continued to be stressed in some circles of Scottish nationalism until the end of the interwar years.[202]

Such fear and hostility occurred at a time when the rate of Irish immigration was relatively weak.[203] But a close reading of the debate makes it clear that the anxiety was only in part about immigration. Another important ingredient was the high gross Catholic birth rate. The Protestant component of Irish immigration was not perceived in nationalist circles as a social problem.[204] This fact was also made quite explicit in a report, *The Menace of the Irish Race to our Scottish Nationality*, submitted in 1923 to the General Assembly of the Church of Scotland,[205] and it was underlined by the militant Protestant groups such as Alexander Ratcliffe's Scottish Protestant League and John Cormack's Protestant Action Society, both of which emerged in the interwar years.[206] However, the other side of the picture would show that in 1929 the *Glasgow Herald* ran a series of articles that was sympathetic to the Catholic Irish.[207] Furthermore, in the midst of anti-Irish sentiment from Scottish nationalist sources, there were those Scots who welcomed the Catholic Irish minority. Their presence, it was suggested on one occasion, would help in sweeping away many of the repressive inhibitions perceived as hanging over Scottish life since the Reformation.[208] Opinion in England on the Irish presence was also mixed. The accepted involvement of some Irish immigrants and people of Irish descent in the Labour movement[209] and, from the other perspective, the continuing welcome held out by some employers, were a clear indication of the other side of the coin to anti-Irish hostility.[210] Taken altogether, therefore, responses to the Irish in Britain were mixed, and further analysis would probably reveal that individuals who stood on either side of the issue did not always hold views that were one-dimensional, exclusively tolerating, accepting or rejecting the Irish.[211]

A switch of emphasis away from the popular level to the centre of British political debate reveals that some pressure was exerted for a measure of control over Irish immigration. A Committee under Sir John Anderson, formerly Governor of Bengal, who was soon to be involved in the internment of aliens, drew up special proposals for restriction in 1928 and the issue was considered by the Cabinet.[212] The fear was that the restrictions on immigration to America would lead to a flow of Irish undesirables to Britain, and it was proposed that in order to counteract this possibility a permit should be introduced with the intention of restricting entry and establishing controls over the movement of labour. Penalties for employers who evaded such controls and provision for the deportation of Irish immigrants were also advocated. Northern Ireland would have been included in this scheme and it was suggested that any objection from sources in Ulster could be countered by a threat that unemployment funds would not be renewed. Once broached, the issue of control did not easily disappear. Discussion on the restriction of immigration and the repatriation of immigrants surfaced in 1929, in 1932 and again in 1934–35. Indeed, the issue continued to persist. On 2 March 1937, in a telling sentence, Lt. Col. T. C. R. Moore asked Malcolm MacDonald, the Dominions Secretary: 'Would it not be possible to put an import duty on Southern Irish human beings as is placed on Southern Irish animals?'[213] This question was asked at a time when an Inter-Departmental Committee met to discuss and report on the issue of Irish immigration. Its conclusion, reported to the House, was that the Irish did not constitute a major economic and social problem. But pressure continued to be exerted on Westminster, particularly from areas such as Liverpool. In the event no restrictions were imposed but such pressures, discussion and enquiry, provide a salutary additional corrective to the optimistic view of the history of the Irish in Britain.[214]

A glance thrown in a certain direction towards Blacks in Britain might have given the impression of general toleration or acceptance.

Learie Constantine was charming the crowds with his cricketing elegance in the Lancashire League; indeed, in one publication, he was proclaimed 'the idol of Nelson'.[215] At the same time, Leslie Hutchinson, 'Hutch', was busily engaged entertaining high society in London's fashionable night clubs, such as the Café de Paris and Quaglino's.[216] Other Black musicians were prominent in the early development of jazz, at a time when no fashionable party was complete without a jazz band.[217] In the theatre a Black presence was evident in the presence of Paul Robeson who played opposite Peggy Ashcroft in *Othello* in 1930; between 1935 and 1939 Robeson also occupied himself with films such as *Sanders of the River*, which was released in 1935, for which he atoned in *Song of Freedom* in 1936 and *The Proud Valley* in 1939.[218] Moreover, exotic figures such as Professor Edgar B. Knight, 'the great Abyssinian herbalist who died at Wombwell in Yorkshire in the early thirties'[219] and Prince Zalemka, and Rass Prince Monolulu, the well-known racehorse tipsters, with their cry 'Ivegottanorse! Ivegottanorse!', exercised a popular appeal and fascination.[220]

But to dwell on these Black lives – there is more information about Blacks than other groups from the Empire – would be to stay on the surface of society. As entertainers, whether as boxers, musicians or prostitutes, Blacks had long been tolerated. Even here it is interesting to note that to Evelyn Waugh 'Hutch' was a 'nigger pianist',[221] that by the 1930s the British Boxing Board of Control had decided no coloured man could box for a British title,[222] and that although Robeson could play Othello there was an outcry in some sections of British society when his role led him to kiss Peggy Ashcroft.[223] Furthermore, although crowds might pay to see Robeson on the stage, the Savoy Grill could still refuse him admission to a party given in his honour.[224] Moreover, beyond this transient, mostly superficial world of glitter, entertainment and excitement, there was abundant evidence during the interwar years of Blacks being forcefully reminded of 'their proper place'.[225]

One indication of White antipathy was apparent in the difficulties encountered by Black students and professionals. It might have been true that 'African and West Indian students did not experience the harsher forms of race prejudice which were aimed at seamen and other permanent settlers'. Even so, the high hopes with which many came to England were shattered by the hostile reactions they encountered. It was not unusual to encounter this hostility at an early stage in their quest for accommodation. It was adverse experiences of this nature that encouraged Ladipo Solanke to form the West African Students' Union in 1925.[226]

But it was upon working-class groups that the heaviest burdens were to fall. Conflict was particularly evident in the shipping industry and reached its most acute form in Cardiff. Before the Great War fears about competition in the labour market were directed by British seamen mainly towards the Chinese. During the interwar years, although Chinese seamen were still the focus of some hostile attention, a wider concern developed among White British workers.[227] This postwar conflict had its roots in the severe international competition which exercised a serious adverse impact on the British merchant fleet, particularly on the tramp shipping trade for which Cardiff was well known.[228] Against this background, 'hard won gains on conditions and pay were lost in the 20s', and the National Sailors' and Firemen's Union (NSFU), closely shackled to employers after the establishment of the National Maritime Board in 1918, could do little to prevent this deterioration.[229] In these circumstances 'the most bitter economic competition between white and coloured seamen took place', with the former rationalising their difficulties as the responsibility of the latter.[230] If this conflict was particularly evident in Cardiff, it also occurred in other ports such as South Shields.[231]

In the depressing and uncertain conditions that faced men in the shipping industry, the NSFU, supported by some Labour MPs, and sections of the press mounted a fierce attack on the employment of coloured seamen, as they were generally and indiscriminately called. The entry of alien workers was restricted by the 1919 Aliens Act and the 1920 Aliens Order. Article 6 of the Act, however, provided exemptions which alien seamen could exploit. The NSFU wanted tougher controls and, following pressure by it and other interested parties, the Special Restriction (Coloured Alien Seamen) Order was published in 1925; 'briefly it brought coloured alien seamen into line with other aliens and obliged them to register in accordance with provisions made under the 1920 Order'. In practice, the entry of coloured British seamen without adequate proof of origin was threatened, and locally, 'Whereas it had once been accepted that most of the coloured population in Cardiff were British subjects, now the onus of proof was placed on the coloured man'.[232]

In fact, the 1925 Order was applied so vigorously by the police and other local officials that few seamen could satisfy the authorities as to their British nationality. In the early 1930s this policy virtually confined the majority of such men to unemployment. Soon afterwards, in 1935, a further adverse development emerged in the form of the British Shipping (Assistance) Act. This measure, which subsidised the tramp shipping industry, stipulated that first preference in the recruitment of firemen and seamen should be given to those of British nationality. But, as a result of the application of the 1925 Order, in Cardiff some British subjects, without satisfactory documentary proof of their origins, had become converted into aliens. Over the next two years, therefore, another extraordinary spectacle presented itself. Organisations such as the League Against Imperialism (LAI) which argued that labour should unite to secure equal conditions of work and wages for all seamen, irrespective of colour and country of origin, took up the case of these disadvantaged workers. So did the Seamen's Minority Movement, which like the LAI was a Comintern organisation. The League of Coloured Peoples, which dispatched P. Cecil Vincent and George Brown to Cardiff in 1935 in time to witness a violent conflict in the docks which arose over the discriminatory employment practices following the local application of the 1925 Order, and local organisations such as the South Wales Association for the Welfare of Coloured People, also took up the struggle against 'the local state'. As a result, British citizenship was restored to more than 1,600 men anxious to make a living at sea. Even so, for much of the 1930s the so-called coloured seamen, whatever their origins, were at a serious disadvantage in the labour market and some of those unable to find work had their problems exacerbated when they applied for relief to the Public Assistance Committee. Moslem sailors from Asia or the Near East, for example, who lived communally found themselves as a result in receipt of discriminatory rates of relief.[233]

Tension in the labour market was joined at times by an antipathy which expressed opposition towards any form of interracial sexual contact. The collective *frisson* generated in 1920 by E. D. Morel's pamphlet, *The Horror on the Rhine*, provided startling evidence of this fear. The furore over the Robeson-Ashcroft kiss in *Othello* in 1930 and the hostile reaction to the well-connected Nancy Cunard, compiler of the classic anthology, *Negro*, displaying her penchant for Black male company, underlined the sensitivity of interracial sexual contact particularly when it involved Black men and White women.[234] This disapproval was further revealed in 1929 when the Chief Constable of Cardiff 'argued before the local Watch Committee for legislation to prohibit interracial sexual intercourse on lines similar to the recently passed 1927 Immorality Act in South Africa'. Similar tension was evident on Merseyside where the Liverpool Association for the Welfare of Half-Caste Children, which was closely connected with the University Settlement in Liverpool, commissioned a survey of such children from Miss M. E. Fletcher, a former student of the Liverpool University School of Social Science. This report, published in 1930, portrayed these 'half-caste juveniles' as a social pathological problem who contributed to the process of moral decline. With the emphasis in Fletcher's report on the social problems resulting from the presence of 'coloured seamen', essentially West Africans, it is hardly surprising that its conclusions were welcomed by the NFSU which was not averse to a mixture of sex and economics in order to protect the interests of White seamen. By contrast, the report was widely condemned by some of the missions involved with the Black population in Liverpool and it was also attacked by the League of Coloured Peoples. The controversy surrounding the report shook the University Settlement and the Liverpool Association for the Welfare of Half-Caste Children, and it has been suggested recently that a new approach to the question of minorities on Merseyside emerged soon afterwards with the publication of the social surveys of the area undertaken for Liverpool University by D. Caradog Jones. But this work continued to regard the settlement of African sailors as a 'blot' on Merseyside society and was particularly critical of 'the serious results attendant upon their intermarriage with white women'.[235]

What is certain is that Fletcher's report did not mark the end of social concern about interracial sexual contact and the children of such relationships. The Liverpool Association for the Welfare of Half-Caste Children was revived in 1934 and it was encouraged in its work by a 1934–35 survey of social conditions in a number of ports and dockland areas compiled by Captain F. A. Richardson on behalf of the Joint Council of the British Social Hygiene Council and the British Council for the Welfare of the Mercantile Marine. This report, which was heavily influenced by the views of the Cardiff police on such matters, stressed 'the unsatisfactory conditions [of the] dockland districts' and was particularly concerned about the presence of 'coloured men' and 'their mating with our women'; prostitution, the spread of venereal disease and, above all, the development of a 'half-caste' population, were the dangers that were emphasised in this connection. It is significant that Richardson's report received considerable publicity whereas other, more measured discussions of similar issues were relatively ignored.[236]

Such surveys reflected and fuelled White antipathy. In particular the issue of interracial sexual contact was seized upon by the Anti-Slavery Society, which under the direction of John Harris turned towards a consideration of Blacks in Britain as its traditional fight against slavery was eclipsed by the involvement in this work of the League of Nations. Harris regarded the Fletcher Report as 'an extraordinarily able document' which contained 'the most impressive and authoritative detail', and in the 1930s he tried to use it and similar evidence to restrict Black immigration into British ports. But if Harris, like Fletcher, was concerned about interracial sexual contact, as a member of a formal deputation to the Home Office in July 1936, which was supported by the Liverpool Association for the Welfare of Half-Caste Children, he was also anxious to stress, with recent interracial violence in mind, that 'political dangers' were likely to result from a Black presence. The ideal solution, it was suggested to the government, would be the progressive return of Black sailors to their country of origin. As for the young population of mixed-race origins, Harris urged that 'steps might be found for raising the standard of these children nearer to that of the white races rather than to leave them to drift down to that of the black'. The response of the Home Office was muted. But Harris's activities need to be recognised. In its administration of The Welfare of Africans in Europe War Fund, the Anti-Slavery Society had displayed a marked paternalist or hostile streak towards the Black claimants and in the 1930s, from his London vantage point, Harris was able to put the Society in the forefront of 'a coherent national lobby: the first real lobby specifically opposing black immigration' to emerge in British society.[237]

In the midst of such hostility there were opposing developments. Apart from exclusively Black organisations and the LCP, dominated by Harold Moody, there should be some recognition of the stand taken by the Joint Council to Promote Understanding between White and Coloured People in Britain. Whereas the LCP was a multi-racial organisation run by a Black, Harold Moody, the Joint Council, which also had a multiracial character, owed its origins to White Quakers and other church groups and it was dominated during its brief life by

a Quaker, John Fletcher. Dr Moody served on its council, as did the
novelists, Winifred Holtby and Vera Brittain. To a great extent the
Council was modelled on the lines of the Joint Council which had
been developed by White Liberals in South Africa after the First
World War – a further indication of Southern African influence in the
early evolution of race relations in Britain.[238] The Joint Council did
not display any enthusiasm over mixed marriages. It did protest,
however, against discrimination, the so-called 'colour bar', and it was
this problem which occupied most of its time until 1932 when it began
to run out of steam 'as the more politically significant League of
Coloured Peoples was formed', a development which preceded the
increasing disorganisation of the Joint Council in the course of the
1930s.[239]

Among other groups, the League against Imperialism also deserves
more than a passing mention. Founded in 1927, in the following
decade this organisation was to the forefront in defending those
oppressed by western Imperialism. The policies of the LAI 'followed
closely the shifts of tactics within international communism' and
between May 1929 and 1932 most of the resources of the British
section were devoted to a campaign on behalf of the prisoners of the
Meerut conspiracy trial. But at all times the organisation was
involved with metropolitan developments; for example, it had
particularly close links with a number of groups designed to protect
the interests of Black workers. Wherever it turned, and whatever it
espoused, the British section was heavily influenced by Reginald
Bridgeman, 'a remarkable personality', born an aristocrat, who spent
four decades 'faithful to the policies of the Left', sustained by 'his
passionate belief that the ordinary people of the world, especially
those whose skins were brown or black, were oppressed and exploited
and ill-treated'.[240]

Bridgeman is an intriguing figure, of compulsive interest. Nancy
Cunard is also capable of magnetising attention. But their
commitments should not obscure the role of other White public
figures who stood for African freedom. Apart from Winifred Holtby
and Vera Brittain, these included Fenner Brockway, Reginald
Sorensen, Arthur Creech Jones, Isabel Ross, McGregor Ross,
Leonard Barnes and Norman Leys. And Indian Independence was a
cause well-served not only by Brockway and Sorensen but also by
Ellen Wilkinson and Reginald Reynolds. The full account of their

various activities, which were sharpened by the local and international context of the 1930s, still remains to be written.[241]

In summary, during the interwar years a small number of the population designated as 'coloured', could achieve a high degree of economic and social success. Entertainers could enrich themselves and if, like Hutch, they were so inclined, they could obtain wealthy lovers. Individuals such as Harold Moody, Saklatvala and Krishna Menon were able to exercise a degree of political influence. But beneath the surface perceived racial distinctions, symbolised by colour, were endowed with a significance in particular situations. Students seeking somewhere to live could suddenly find their racial origins thrust into their face; housing and accommodation were in fact areas of general sensitivity.[242] The greater the pity, therefore, that Jomo Kenyatta financially exploited the English family that took him into their home.[243] Race was also given a social significance and used as a device to shut men out of work and confine them to a life of loneliness in Britain's bleak docklands.[244] Women were also disadvantaged on account of their race.[245] Racial difference was used by the police in a way that abused civil rights and natural justice.[246] Deep-seated social-sexual fears were also related to perceptions of racial differences; hence there was a continuing obsession with the so-called half-caste population.[247] In all these situations there was an affirmation that Britain was a country for White people, even if this White population itself had varied and conflicting interests. There was little evidence of a pervasive scientific-based hostility – most people were content with a 'common-sense' awareness – but those who wanted sophisticated support for their view of the world could turn, if so inclined, to the findings of academic research. There was no shortage of evidence from psychologists and eugenicists to suggest that the White race was superior to all others and that interracial sexual contact was dangerous. Support for White supremacy could also be derived from the work of certain anthropologists. Moreover, some geographers advanced similar views on racial typology.[248] Academic thought, however, was not one-dimensional. The network of academic exiles from Germany contributed to a countervailing opinion and just before the war the notion of 'identifiable racial types' was rejected particularly in *We Europeans*, written by Julian Huxley and A. C. Haddon, although this work had exerted little general impact by the time the war began.[249] For those members of the public who shied away from the rigours of science, views of White supremacy could be sustained more easily by turning to popular literature and the increasingly pervasive flickering image of the cinema, whether the final production was home grown or, as was often the case, imported from Hollywood.[250]

But which aspects of this cultural tradition of White supremacy exerted a wide influence? A dissatisfaction with vague references to the influence of a static, one-dimensional cultural tradition has been replaced recently by an emphasis on specific trends such as the emergence of an ideology of racial segregation which can be traced in both elite and popular thought. But this new emphasis is only a beginning: the skein of historically derived information on race remains essentially uncoiled.[251] Whatever its form, such race thinking as existed in Britain had been strengthened during the age of Imperialism and it survived the First World War. But could it persist in a total war, fought in part against racial intolerance, in the course of which Britain once more drew upon the varied resources of its Empire and Dominions?

IV.   In a Context of Total War, 1939–45

'It is very easy in wartime to start a scare', Sir John Anderson to his father on 2 March 1940, quoted in J. W. Wheeler-Bennett, *John Anderson, Viscount Waverley* (London, 1962), p. 239.

'On the 13th March 1940 when the African crew of the M/V ACCRA, an Elder Dempster Liner, were about to sign on, they unanimously asked that their wages be increased to £9 plus the War Bonus of £5 making a grand total of £14, as against the total of £17.2.6., being paid to other seamen by other Shipping Companies – Elder Dempster Ltd refused this demand and sent a man to coerce the men to change their attitude: and when the men stuck to their demand, they were told that before they could be given that wage they [Elder's] will sooner give the money to "Dogs" – a very commendable attitude indeed. In consequence of this, the Company signed on a white crew for £17.2.6. . . . It is incredible to think that while a Nation . . . is hard engaged in fighting for freedom and liberty [this] refined serfdom should prevail', Pastor G. Daniels Ekarte of the African Churches Mission to Ronald Kidd of the National Council for Civil Liberties, 11 February 1941 [NCCL Archives].

1.

THE developing European crisis of the 1930s leapt forward a further stage with the German invasion of Poland in September 1939. During the next six years Europe was to witness the conduct of war on a previously unparalleled scale and the conflict which began in Europe was soon to spread into other parts of the world. In East and West nations became locked in fierce conflict. In order to sustain their involvement in the war nations engaged in the planned if sometimes frantic mobilisation of resources which led to a significant concentration of political and administrative power within the leading belligerent nations. In parallel with these developments there was also massive devastation resulting from the war. For the first time the world realised it possessed the potential for its self-destruction. These traumatic changes affected not merely those in uniform; the Home Front assumed greater prominence than during the First World War and civilian lives were significantly affected in a variety of ways. In some cases civilian populations were systematically exterminated; the fate of the Jews and the often overlooked gypsies provided brutal evidence of this. In other cases those who survived were cut off from their roots and sent into uncertain exile as refugees. Yet others, Ukrainians, Latvians and Estonians, for example, were removed from their homes and exploited as forced labour, only to find at the end of the war that the changing political face of Europe resulted in their classification as displaced persons. Such developments did not take place in a clearly unfolding context; the war introduced sudden shifts of policy and alignments as the interests and fortunes of the belligerent nations changed. These complex, changing and challenging events could hardly fail to exert an influence over the movement of population to Britain, the nature of the economic and social activity of immigrants and refugees and their relationships with British society; indeed, the war was to affect older-established minorities as well as recent arrivals.

2.

IN 1940, the year after the German invasion of Poland, and at a time when the German army had penetrated into western Europe, George Orwell noticed the arrival of French and Belgian refugees at Waterloo and Victoria stations. They were, he recorded, 'a mostly middling people of the shopkeeper-clerk type'.[1] However, had he visited ports in southern England he would have found whole communities of fishermen from these countries who had also fled to seek refuge in England. All these newcomers from France and Belgium, moreover, were only part of a wider national conglomeration of refugees that came to Britain during the war.[2] In 1943, for example, it was estimated that the European refugee population amounted to

114,400. The total number that came between 1939 and 1945 remains uncertain. It can be stated, however, that a small proportion of those who arrived were Jews; as a result, it has been estimated – precise figures are difficult to obtain – that there was a net addition of 'no more' than 10,000 to the Jewish refugee population in the course of the war.[3]

However, the depth of human experience cannot be revealed by crude numerical returns. The movement of European Jews, for example, was far from easy; indeed, there might be some surprise that any such movement occurred. Hitler's invasion of Poland on 1 September 1939 advanced so rapidly that Jews, a special and major target of German aggression, did not find it easy to escape. However, at this early stage of the war the Germans themselves were not opposed to Jewish emigration. 'Between 1939 and mid-1941 expulsion, in addition to expropriation, persecution and sporadic murder, was one of the central goals of Germany's Jewish policy.' The main organisation concerned with these matters was the Reich Central Bureau for Jewish Emigration, which from October 1939 onwards was under the direction of Adolf Eichmann. It was in line with this preparedness to export 'the Jewish problem' that the Germans considered in 1940 whether to send all European Jewry to Madagascar, a scheme which had been floating around anti-Semitic circles in Europe since the 1920s.[4]

In practice not all Jews were in a position to move. However, in terms of official policy, it was not until August 1941 that the emigration from German-occupied territory of Jews aged between 18 and 45 was expressly forbidden. A total prohibition on all further Jewish emigration from the Reich was issued on 23 October 1941.[5]

Nevertheless, a small number of Jewish refugees were able to leave Nazi-occupied Europe after the imposition of this restriction.[6] The fact that more did not succeed was related only in part to the difficulties they experienced under Nazi rule. It was also connected with the attitudes that existed in the potential receiving societies. Indeed, it has been suggested that the failure of Jews to emigrate 'was primarily due to the extreme reluctance of all countries to admit them'.[7] The small increase in the Jewish population in Britain as a result of refugee immigration took place against this background.

Not all newcomers to Britain came from the European continent. There was also some immigration from Ireland. When war broke out Britain could not count on Eire as an ally. Even before hostilities started there was a clear indication from Dublin that the Southern Irish had no intention of becoming embroiled in a future European conflict. Specific tensions resulted from these contrasting stances. For example, by the 1921 Anglo-Irish Treaty, Britain was guaranteed strategic naval bases on the south-west coast of the Irish Free State. However, in 1938 Eamonn de Valera, the Irish prime minister, had negotiated the return of these bases, and with Eire's neutrality in the war their loss was keenly felt. Ports such as Cobh, Lough Swilly and Berehaven would have given British ships an extra 200 miles' range in the Atlantic. The Irish refused to concede them and the resulting impasse soured Anglo-Irish relations during the war and for many years afterwards. But if the Irish maintained their neutral position, any deviation from it was usually in Britain's favour. As a result, Eire provided Britain with both food and labour almost throughout the entire war. At the same time, contrary to some British fears, Southern Ireland never became a centre of German espionage and influence. In this respect, German hopes of an Irish back door, stimulated by the IRA bombing campaign that began in 1939 and continued into the war, were disappointed.[8]

Before considering the movement of population from Southern Ireland, it might be noticed that by arrangement with the Northern Ireland Ministry of Labour some workers were transferred to Britain from Ulster. From the beginning of 1940 to the middle of 1945 approximately 60,000 men and women came to work in Britain and in mid-1945 almost 50 per cent of the transferred workers were still employed in British industry.[9]

Until the fall of France in June 1940 there were no restrictions on travel between Eire and Great Britain.[10] Even in these circumstances, moreover, seasonal agricultural workers from Southern Ireland continued to arrive without much hindrance until the spring of 1941.[11] Over the longer term, however, the British government had to balance its inclination to control the movement of citizens from a neutral country who might pose a threat to national security, and its pressing need for labour to aid the war effort. As a result, the British state became involved in the control of immigration from Southern Ireland. An arrangement between the two governments in July 1941, which was revised in September of the same year, guaranteed from this point 'a steady flow to Britain of some thousands of Irish workers every month'.[12] Although there were adjustments to this arrangement in the course of the war,[13] the only exception to it came in 1944 when preparations were under way for the Allied invasion of Europe. In these circumstances the British government imposed a ban on travel from Britain, and the Dublin government, fearing that its citizens might be drafted into military service, stopped any further recruitment of workers from Eire. For most of the war, however, workers from Southern Ireland continued to arrive in Britain, adding thereby to the largest immigrant minority in Britain. This fact can at least be confirmed, even if there are no complete records of the number of Southern Irish who were recruited for the war effort and scattered themselves through Britain.[14]

It was against this background that various government establishments partially satisfied their labour requirements. The Ministry of Supply, for example, was particularly active in recruiting workers for the munitions industry from 1941 onwards. Recruitment was also undertaken by private firms such as ICI and Austin. The Federation of Civil Engineering Contractors, the members of which had relied for many years on Irish workers, was also active in the recruitment of Southern Irish labour.[15]

The government in Dublin gave its encouragement to the traffic between the two countries. There was no magical, quick cure for Eire's economic problems once independence had been attained and the onset of the world economic crisis after 1929 made it increasingly difficult to remedy the problems which had grown through years of external domination and exploitation. In these circumstances it was recognised that the transfer of certain types of labour to Britain would ease the serious problem of unemployment in Southern Ireland.[16]

Furthermore, the immigrants had their motives for coming to Britain. In some cases the Irish welcomed the opportunity to contribute to the defeat of Hitlerism. The same commitment, and possibly the lure of military excitement, resulted in 60,000 citizens of Eire joining the British armed forces. In other cases the prospect of employment as opposed to continued unemployment in Ireland was another contributory factor which encouraged workers to move and, as at other times, some of the Irish who crossed the water were assisted in their decision by the knowledge that friends and relatives were already living in Britain.[17]

Irish workers in the war economy were supplemented by groups from further afield. Apart from drawing upon the expertise of various groups of aliens, the British government imported labour from the Dominions. In addition, the small population derived from the

Caribbean and the Indian sub-continent, witnessed a marginal increase in size during the war.[18]

When manpower shortages became acute in the course of 1940–43 as men were drawn away to serve in the armed forces, a few hundred West Indians were brought to England.[19] The purpose of this recruitment, however, was not primarily economic; after all, there was no importation of labour on a major scale. As much as anything, the Colonial Office wanted to show its best face to the world and the enlisted arrival of West Indians in Britain was a token nod in this direction. Skilled men who were not easily absorbed into the Caribbean economy, the depressed condition of which was adversely affected by the war in 1940–41, were particularly suitable clients. Welders, electricians, fitters and motor mechanics were well-represented among those who made the hazardous sea journey and they were joined by trainees who were placed in government training centres. The scheme ended in 1943, by which time workers in the islands were probably less anxious to involve themselves in Britain on account of the opportunities created in America by the expansion of the US war economy. All told, however, it has been estimated that 340 technicians and trainees were brought to Britain between 1940 and 1943.[20]

The technicians, who arrived between February and April 1941 were directed initially into the north west, particularly into Lancashire, one of the existing centres of Black population. Some workers, for example, were placed in employment at the Royal Ordnance Factories at Kirkby and Fazakerley and others were employed at the Ellesmere Port works of ICI.[21]

In addition, Britain recruited timber workers from Newfoundland and British Honduras. By the 1930s Britain was importing 95 per cent of the timber it consumed and when, in the early stages of the war, Germany overran Norway, this supply was seriously disrupted. Furthermore, when the war spread to the Atlantic, imports from Canada were also cut off. Necessity was the mother of self-reliance and groups of workers were imported with the specific aim of utilising local sources of timber. The first group to arrive, around 2,000 strong, was brought to Scotland from Newfoundland. Then the government turned to the British Hondurans.

With some degree of exaggeration it has been claimed that conditions in British Honduras in the 1930s were little better than those prevailing under slavery. But the persistent exploitation of the resources of the territory, combined with the failure of the British to build up a sound economic infrastructure, as well as the immediate impact of the interwar economic crisis on the demand for timber, united to create a depressing environment. Nevertheless, a sense of loyalty to Britain still survived, and, allied to the prospect of self-betterment, guaranteed that volunteers were available for the British war effort. From July 1941, therefore, the Ministry of Supply and the Colonial Office began recruiting the British Honduran Forestry Unit. Altogether, 1,938 men applied to come in the first batch; of these 857 were rejected on medical grounds. The remaining 541 left the Caribbean on 5 August 1941 and were joined by other workers in the following year. For most of those Hondurans who came to Scotland it was to be a depressing experience: 'suffering', 'humiliation', and 'disillusionment' still remain in the memory of one volunteer.[22]

Between 1939 and 1945 changes were also evident in the small population from the Indian sub-continent. During the war at the same time as men from this part of the world were recruited into the merchant marine, a number of seamen came ashore looking for factory work which held out the prospect of relatively well-paid regular employment rather than the casual routine with which they had to contend in the merchant navy. This internal migration was reflected in the increase of Indians in centres such as Birmingham. In 1939 there were approximately 100 Indians living in the city, including 20 doctors and students. By 1945, however, this number had increased to 1,050.[23] Furthermore, under a scheme instigated by Ernest Bevin, who became Minister of Labour in May 1940, a number of Indian trainee munitions workers arrived in order to undergo instruction at government Training Centres in Letchworth and Manchester before returning 'to increase the output of munitions in India'.[24]

Military personnel were also recruited from the colonies and India as well as from within the resident Black population. However, very little has been unearthed on this development, and the fullest account, dealing with Blacks, is lacking in coherence, context and balance. It is known, however, that complaints about a colour bar in the armed forces were being heard in 1939 after Black students from various universities and Aggrey House, the hostel for African students financed by the Colonial Office, were frustrated in their efforts to join up. A reluctance to employ Black troops in Europe was nothing new but it caused considerable resentment. In the course of the war, as the Colonial Office once again tried to show its best face to the world, only to be slapped on numerous occasions by the War Office, there was some modification of the government's original stance. Blacks did manage to enter the RAF as aircrew and groundcrew although there is no unanimity regarding the numbers involved. The army and the navy, however, proved tougher to crack. The former did recruit skilled tradesmen and members of Dr Harold Moody's family were fortunate enough to secure commissions in the British army. Whatever its scale, the military contributions of Blacks and the even more forgotten role of troops, particularly Sikhs from the Indian sub-continent, deserves to be recognised, if only because there has been much loose talk recently on the theme that 'we [the white population] did not fight the war so that Blacks could come to our country'.[25] At the same time it should not be assumed that entry into the armed forces marked an end of racial discrimination; evidence continued to accumulate on this score.[26] Nor did it end feelings of isolation and alienation. 'No friend, no girl, no-one in all England. I am alone and the only time I feel at all happy is when I am in my Spitfire alone in the clouds', wrote Jimmy Hyde, a young, much decorated Trinidadian airman.[27]

Other groups, some of them refugees in military uniform, added to the cosmopolitan texture of Britain during the war years.[28] Among these were Poles who retreated from their homeland to keep alive the Eagle's spirit in exile. The Poles were evident during the war in cities such as Edinburgh and London and during these years a community infrastructure was developed: Polish priests administered to this strongly Catholic minority and after the summer of 1940 the Polish government-in-exile became located in London. As a group, the Poles encountered mixed and changing reactions from the surrounding British population.[29]

These wartime exiles were not the first Poles to arrive in Britain. In the previous century alone, for example, there were Poles among the early and mid-nineteenth century political refugees and others arrived as part of the great exodus from the tsar's empire.[30] Following this period, emigration from Poland to Britain between the two world wars was on a small scale; in 1931, the last census before the Second World War, there were in Britain 44,462 individuals who were classified as having Poland as their birthplace. In other words this Polish-born group amounted to only a small fraction of the total population in Britain. The onset of the war, however, with Hitler's invasion of Poland in September 1939, resulted in a new phase in the history of the Polish community in Britain which was to have a continuing significance.[31]

The war was to have a traumatic impact on Polish society. Between 1939 and 1941 the country was subjected to German and Russian territorial ambitions. Some of the population was transported to Russia. Other Poles were deported as slave labour to Germany. The Jewish population was largely exterminated. Such events, which formed the larger background to the arrival of Poles in Britain, were a further, and particularly brutal, reminder of the 'bitter bread' of Polish experience.[32]

How in the circumstances of the war did Poles begin to arrive in Britain? With the invasion of their country by the German army and the collapse of Polish resistance, a number of Poles took refuge in the surrounding territories. From here, there was some movement to the focus of exiled Polish resistance in France and by June 1940 Polish forces in France numbered 84,500.[33]

When the collapse of France seemed imminent, General Wladyslaw Sikorski arranged for the transfer to Britain of his government-in-exile and a number of his troops. As a result, 30,500 men, military personnel in exile from their homeland, arrived in June 1940. In addition, approximately 3,000 Polish civilians landed later in the summer of that year.[34]

This wartime colony was expanded in size by the periodic arrival of refugees, but it was 1941 before the population was significantly increased. This increase occurred after the so-called Sikorski-Maisky agreement of 7 July 1941 by which the Soviet government proclaimed an amnesty for the 1.5 million Poles who had been deported to Russia between October 1939 and June 1941 following the Nazi-Soviet non-aggression pact of 23 August 1939. The German attack on the Soviet Union on 22 June 1941 upset this arrangement and the Poles who had been transported to Russia were amnestied in the wake of the German invasion. This amnesty resulted in the creation of an army of 108,000 men under General Wladyslaw Anders; these men were evacuated from Soviet territory so that they could join their fellow Poles in the British army.[35] The civilians held by the Russians were also released and settled initially in Palestine, Egypt, India and parts of East Africa before eventually arriving in Britain. These people, the soldiers and their families, who formed the backbone of the Polish community in Britain after the war, never forgot their experiences in the Soviet Union and most of them remained full of fiercely anti-Russian sentiment.[36] But after 1941 Russia, symbolised by Stalin, 'Uncle Joe', and effectively represented in Britain between 1939 and 1943 by Ivan Maisky, previously an exile himself from tsarism, was an ally in the fight against Nazism.[37] Wartime Polish hostility to the Soviets, therefore, resulted in little public sympathy.

Polish wartime forces were increased by deserters from the Wehrmacht and prisoners captured by the Allied troops in western Europe. Apart from these Poles who had lined up with Germany, a number of officers and men liberated from German prisoner-of-war camps also added to the wartime forces. Altogether, it was estimated that 21,750 ex-POWs were absorbed by Polish army units in Germany and Italy and later brought to England.[38]

The Poles, therefore, made an important contribution to the fight against Hitlerism. Polish airmen fought in the Battle of Britain and, although their contribution has been overlooked, Polish airborne troops fought alongside the British at Arnhem.[39] But for many the courage of the Poles was most graphically illustrated in the capture of Monte Cassino in May 1944, when the Polish Second Corps sustained heavy losses.[40] After so much heroism and suffering, however, the dream of a free Poland emerging from the ruins of Hitler's defeat, was to prove an illusion and for many Poles what began as a wartime exile became a permanent break with their homeland. Such refugees constituted the first large foreign settlement in Britain once the war had ended.[41]

Czechs, many of them in military uniform, were another exiled minority.[42] In addition, there were representatives of the Free French who rallied behind Charles de Gaulle and waited for an opportunity to repossess their *patrie* from the German yoke.[43] Less conspicuous but nevertheless important were those refugees who engaged in propaganda work against Nazi Germany: Germans and Hungarians were among those employed in such activity.[44] Furthermore, and particularly significant, there were Americans, Black and White, who with their informal and free-spending habits were the focus of much public interest after their arrival in the spring of 1942.[45] In addition, Chinese sailors appeared in larger numbers as they made an invaluable contribution to the supply lines secured by the merchant navy.[46] Indeed, with the need for seamen in the war, the restrictions imposed on coloured alien seamen in the Special Restriction

(Coloured Alien Seamen) Order of 1925, around which so much controversy developed, was duly revoked.[47] The same year witnessed amendments to the 1914 British Nationality and Status of Aliens Act to take account of the use of aliens in the British war effort.[48] Finally, in addition to the various groups of allies congregating in Britain, as the war progressed the country witnessed the rare presence of POWs, whose labour was employed on urgent and important tasks when there was a shortage of local workers.[49]

3.

In discussing the economic and social history of wartime minorities, no attempt is made to incorporate the military personnel who pullulated in Britain during the war. The focus is firmly upon the civilian population. Viewed from this dimension the Second World War witnessed a number of important developments in the economic and social life of the Jewish community. In part, it exercised a negative impact on economic activity. 'The war led to the closure of shops and factories because of bombing, the call-up of principals, the curtailment of the manufacture and sale of civilian goods, the compulsory concentration of industry to effect economies and – a special case – the internment of refugees among the "enemy aliens".'[50] But these developments provide only part of the picture. The war extended the range of Jewish employment, some of which resulted in a greater involvement with non-Jewish employers.[51] It also provided fresh opportunities for Jewish capital; Isaac Wolfson was able to buy up a number of companies and Gerson Berger, who arrived from Roumania in the 1920s, was enabled by the black-out regulations to establish a thriving torch factory in Stepney which provided some of the funds for his subsequent movement into property.[52] For other Jews, long-established in Britain, and some recent refugees, such changes in employment and economic fortune were of secondary significance in the sense that their lives were lived primarily within a military context. As in the First World War Anglo-Jewry played a full part in contributing personnel to the war effort.[53]

The social life of Jews on the Home Front was significantly influenced by the war; this was particularly true of Jews who lived in the East End.[54] The Jewish Hospital, for example, was badly damaged in the course of the aerial devastation that hit the area. In these circumstances a degree of camaraderie developed among East Enders which bridged national origins.[55] But the bombing pressures also encouraged movement away from the area. The population of Stepney declined by 60 per cent during the war, although in the case of the Jews spiritual and other links with the East End still remained.[56] Part of this dispersal arose through the evacuation of children, an exciting yet daunting prospect for the youngsters involved, and one which for Jewish children and those of mixed race origins, carried its own special challenges.[57] Together with this decline in population, there was an erosion of the cultural and institutional life which had grown up with the immigrants from Russian Poland even if in some respects – in the theatre and continuing echoes of Yiddish – a degree of resilience could also be detected.[58]

The German bombs were a new threat. But the older threat of anti-Semitism continued to press on the lives of Jews during the war and helped to influence political and institutional developments.[59] Some Jews believed that a more secure future could emerge from a Communist society, and there was a continuing and increasing involvement by Jews in the Communist politics of the East End. In other words, in the old Russian Polish 'ghetto' radical political influences proved to be tenacious. The pressures which descended on this working-class area of London as a result of the war, and the Communist Party's positive responses to such problems, were influential in bringing about the return of Phil Piratin, as MP for Stepney in 1945. Other members of the community, however, had their eyes focused elsewhere. It was the war which witnessed the emergence of a powerful Zionist ideology within the Board of Deputies. But the future of Zionism, or indeed any other form of Jewish life, depended upon the survival of Jews, and in tandem with other developments Anglo-Jewry became involved in the formation of relief agencies to help the shattered remnants of European Jewry. Moreover, those German and Austrian Jews who had managed to escape to Britain began to assume greater organisational control over their lives; this development was symbolised in the summer of 1941 with the foundation of the Association of Jewish Refugees in Great Britain which has remained the biggest and most important Jewish refugee organisation. Some Jews also helped to keep alive Social

Democratic and Communist opposition to Hitlerite Germany while spending their exile in Britain.[60]

Apart from these trends and developments, the social life of alien Jewish refugees was significantly influenced by the British government's policy of internment. During the First World War the British government had introduced a policy of internment towards enemy aliens and in 1939 this minority category came under public scrutiny yet again. Before 1914 British governments had been largely unaccustomed to dealing with the issue of a sizeable enemy alien minority in wartime, but the policy experiences of those years laid down the basis for what happened between 1939 and 1945; even so, the connection has been generally unrecognised or underemphasised.[61] The complex reasons for internment are discussed later in a consideration of official policy. Here it is sufficient to note its introduction and that, as a result, a policy of categorising and interning enemy aliens began in September 1939 and intensified in the dark spring of 1940. Although the policy was significantly softened in the course of 1940–41, it persisted into 1945. In order to accommodate the internees, camps were established in many parts of the country. Some were transit camps into which internees were herded prior to their further detention elsewhere. As in the First World War, what were intended as more permanent camps were also established, particularly on the Isle of Man, which became virtually 'a prison island'. Some internees were subsequently deported, mainly to Canada and Australia.[62]

How were the lives of those categorised as enemy aliens affected by this aspect of official policy? Life in the camps was dominated by the kind of strictly regulated routine which characterises guarded communities and most institutional life. Roll call, the strict meal schedules (lunch at 1.00, supper at 7.30 p.m.) and 'lights out' at 10.30 have a familiar ring.[63] The life of the internees was also partly affected by the attitudes and behaviour of those who guarded the camps, whether the rough, tough, Grenadier Guards at the Kempton Park camp, a collecting station for class 'C' aliens (the least dangerous category), or the more compliant men of the Lancashire Regiment who guarded the internees at Warth Mills, a transit camp near Bury, where conditions were deplorable.[64] Here, after an initial hostility, 'a brisk trade' developed between the two parties 'covering such forbidden essentials as newspapers, cigarettes and unrationed food in that order of priority'.[65] Moreover, the quality of life was also affected by the infrastructure of the camps. Some indication of this came with the report of the Home Office departmental enquiry into conditions at Huyton camp near Liverpool, the best-known house camp outside the Isle of Man.[66] The investigation conducted by Lord Snell drew attention to deficiencies in accommodation (some of the refugees had to live in tents) and the unsatisfactory sanitary arrangements. Snell's report also emphasised the inadequate degree of medical support at Huyton and the fact that the food was quite unsuitable for the infirm. Most of the camps would appear to have experienced similar problems.[67]

The quality of camp life did not depend solely on external influences; it was also affected by the inmates themselves. Apart from the tension that arose over the provision of creature comforts, and the minimum essentials of a civilised life, ideological tensions developed at times. For instance, the small number of Nazi sympathisers among the German-born population made their presence felt. This particular tension was evident on one occasion at Lingfield Park camp, one of the 'Race course camps',[68] when a poster suddenly appeared on the main tote building with the message, 'No entry for the Jews'.[69] It was to avoid such friction that the government eventually placed those sympathetic to Nazism – as defined in somewhat arbitrary terms – in a separate camp at Swanwick in Derbyshire. But complaints were still being heard in 1941 that the government had failed to cure this problem.[70]

Amid these pressures there was evidence of human adaptability. Some Jewish internees, for example, underwent an intensification of religious experience. Chaim Raphael, a young Intelligence Officer at the time, was 'deeply moved' at Lingfield Park by a small group of Orthodox Jews whom he discovered pondering over the Midrash of the Book of Lamentations. It was after all the Ninth Day of the month of Ab, the day on which in AD70 the Temple had been destroyed in Jerusalem.[71] Music also played an important part in camp life. Hans Gál composed 'The Huyton Suite' which appeared in the Hutchinson camp journal.[72] Instrumentalists were also in demand. How many listeners to the pianos of Rawicz and Landauer on the BBC Light Programme in the years after the war realised that a few years previously they had entertained the other internees at Hutchinson camp?[73] In some camps, such as Onchan, which like Hutchinson was situated on the Isle of Man, the inmates as well as producing the journal, *The Onchan Pioneer*, also organised a busy lecture programme on a wide range of topics, rather like a small-scale Open University.[74] In the women's camps, too, there was a similar bustle of activity. On the one hand, the internees tried to keep themselves busy for their own sakes and, at the same time, they were anxious to ensure the education of their children.[75]

Like Abé's woman in the dunes, therefore, some internees were able to adapt.[76] In certain cases their feelings about internment, expressed in the course of the experience, were less bitter than those of most later commentators.[77] But others could not come to terms with their situation. Those internees who had only recently been inmates of camps such as Buchenwald and Dachau projected an understandably gloomy presence which affected the state of morale.[78] Moreover, some earlier immigrants from Galicia, who had not become naturalised, found themselves citizens of the Greater German Reich after the *Anschluss* and with the outbreak of the war were interned. They, particularly, we have been told, were 'bewildered, unable to comprehend what was happening to them'.[79] Many internees who did not have this problem found life difficult in other respects; the restriction on sexual freedom, for instance, was not always easy to accommodate.[80] In contrast, some thrived in their confined environment. Karl Schwitters, the co-founder of Dadaism, was one of these. He enjoyed a fresh burst of creative activity when he had a captive audience.[81] There were other cases too where good came out of evil. The young Claus Moser, for example, developed an interest in mathematical statistics which was to take him eventually to the Wardenship of Wadham College, Oxford.[82] Furthermore, three out of four members of the Amadeus String Quartet met as a result of the British government's internment policy.[83] However, the impact that internment would have exercised over the internees if it had been of longer duration – the majority of internees were released in the course of 1941 – is open to question, even if some human beings can survive an horrendous and protracted confinement.[84]

For a variety of reasons the history of internment has captured attention.[85] But there were other dimensions to the life of enemy aliens. One way of obtaining release from the camps for category 'C' internees came to be through service in the Auxiliary Military Pioneer Corps.[86] Some men stayed in this regiment, but others transferred into combatant units and some engaged in various kinds of Intelligence work. Altogether it has been estimated that 8,000 aliens, men and women, served in the armed forces.[87]

Contributions to the war effort came in other forms. For example, the government enlisted the assistance of the scientists among the central European refugees, although not all areas of wartime work were opened to them. In order to harness this available talent Sir Henry Tizard, the scientific adviser to the Air Ministry, set up a small committee in January 1940 with Dr R. V. Jones as Liaison Officer.[88] The Committee was funded by Simon Marks of Marks and Spencer. When internment descended in the autumn of that year the Committee tried to keep the scientists out of the camps and secure the early release of those who were interned.[89] Its protests were not always successful and the deportation of some internees resulted in the loss of scientific expertise.[90] Even so, on release, refugee scientists made an important contribution to the war effort. It would seem that they were effectively excluded from working on developments in radar and partly as a result of this restriction 'they gradually found their way into the nuclear effort'.[91] In the course of the research to which they contributed, Britain learnt how to control a nuclear explosion, which was a vital step on the way to the production of the atomic bomb. However, there is more than a grain of irony in the fact that when they had helped to make this discovery 'they were still forbidden to possess bicycles and had to obtain special permission from the local police when they went to London in order to report their discovery to the Government's scientific advisers'.[92]

The economic and social history of the Southern Irish who arrived during the war was less traumatised. However, in the course of the war the activities of this group were placed under increasing control. Once the British government had accepted that its wartime needs required a flow of labour from Ireland, tight arrangements were laid down for the transfer of workers from one country to the other. Furthermore, once these Irish workers were in Britain controls were established over their employment. In addition, at all times their continued residence was dependent upon the approval of the authorities. Finally, whereas there was a historical tradition of allowing movement backwards and forwards between Ireland and Britain without any restriction, in the course of the war controls were established over passenger traffic between Eire and Britain.[93]

Control over labour was an essential feature of the wartime economy, but some of the imported Irish workers adapted to the situation only with difficulty.[94] One of the more perceptive newcomers wrote in ironical vein: 'I belonged to a big building firm, by virtue of my having been sent to them by the all-powerful Labour Exchange in Ely of the Isle. I had come across from Ireland with a label on me like a shoulder of bacon! The building firm paid my fare. The Royal Air Force gave me a camp to live in, a bed to lie on and a job to do. What more could anyone want?'[95]

Within this controlled context it would seem that at first the Irish tended to pursue the type of work they had followed for generations and in which older-established Irish immigrants were still employed. In other words, there was a concentration on the heavy, unattractive jobs where labour was difficult to recruit. As a result, many went into civil-engineering and various kinds of building work, including the construction of military installations.[96] Irish women tended to find employment in the cotton mills, in nursing and domestic service.[97] But it has been suggested that, as time went on, there was a significant change in employment patterns among the Irish minority in the sense that the scope of their work became 'increasingly wide'. Or, in the words of the same commentator, 'The war served the purpose of opening the way for greater occupational choice and mobility for the Irish immigrant to Britain and paved the way for direct Irish infiltration into almost every branch of industry in the period since the end of the war'.[98] However, this assessment was an impressionistic rather than a reasoned case based on firm evidence.

In some cases the departure to wartime Britain opened up a new and challenging environment. 'Among those who settled down in the heat and racket of the drop forging shops in the murk of the Black country', an official historian has commented, 'there were some who had rarely if ever seen a motor car until their journey to Dublin *en route* for England'.[99] But whatever degree of adjustment was needed in this situation, the workers from Eire made an important contribution to the wartime economy. In the munitions industry, for example, the input of Southern Irish labour, which amounted to 30,000 out of two million workers, was valuable 'out of all proportion to its numbers'.[100] As the war progressed, Britain's labour surplus diminished and Eire provided an important marginal labour supplement.[101] Moreover, these workers were mobile and not subject to the preference rulings under which British labour was allocated. This degree of flexibility was important in the later stages of the war when the allocation of labour assumed increasing importance.[102]

These wartime workers needed accommodation, and some of the Irish were placed in private houses. Others, however, began their lives in transit hostels that were set up in different parts of the country before they moved on to find a base for themselves elsewhere.[103] But those who worked in agriculture or on building projects were often accommodated on site where they were effectively segregated from the rest of the community. Such accommodation was often of a rough and ready variety, isolated from the surrounding world. 'There was no social life for me at Witchford', one of the workers wrote. 'Since the locals were so distant towards us we could not go into their houses and talk to them as people do in Ireland, so when I returned from work I either sat on my bed in silence, wrote letters to my friends, or tried to kill time in some other simple way'.[104]

The newcomers from Eire who arrived during the war formed only part of the Irish population living in Britain and it has been suggested that the war also exercised a noticeable influence over the development of the established community. In the case of the Irish in Cardiff, for example, it has been claimed that 'The outbreak of the Second World War contributed a great deal to the ending of the period of isolation; there were, during the ten years before 1939, signs that the Irish were beginning to filter into the general framework of [the city] but the war accelerated the process of breaking down barriers. . . .'[105] Taken in conjunction with the emphasis on widening areas of Irish employment, this evidence might suggest an amelioration in the economic and social life of the Irish minority. Furthermore, it can be readily understood how a concentration upon these developments and the limited amount of nationalist activity engaged in by the Irish in Britain during the war, has resulted in a Whiggish interpretation of Irish incorporation particularly of the relatively long-settled Irish. But it is dangerous to ignore the other side of the coin, the attested, continuing hostility to the Irish minority, which in its haziness did not automatically discriminate between the Northern and the Southern Irish. A balanced assessment of the position of the Irish minority cannot ignore such responses.[106]

How, if at all, did the Second World War influence the lives of what was generally called 'the coloured population'? What were the salient features of the economic and social history of such groups? In answering these questions it is possible to begin in Liverpool. The Liverpool Association for the Welfare of Half-Caste Children, which had sponsored the Fletcher Report in 1930, changed its name in 1937 to the Liverpool Association for the Welfare of Coloured People and in turn this organisation sponsored its own survey of the economic and social status of 'coloured families' in Liverpool.[107] This report, which was completed towards the end of 1939, appeared in 1940.

The investigation concentrated mainly on families with a West African father who was domiciled in Britain and registered for the purposes of unemployment insurance. It emphasised the strong link between such men and the shipping industry. Few of them were able to secure alternative employment. 'The men are unaccustomed to alternative trades, less skilled, and lack a knowledge of English: consequently, they cannot fit into the normal social or industrial life.' As a result, if they were unable to secure a ship, they were likely to find themselves unemployed for considerable periods of time. Sometimes this was the result not only of a lack of skill; the report also remarked on the presence of an antipathy among the White population which affected employers and workers alike. As a result, the West Africans, along with the West Indians, East Africans and other men who came within the scope of the investigation, tended not to displace White workers.[108]

In general, the report presented a gloomy picture. A more positive assessment would be difficult to sustain. A greater percentage of the men referred to in the survey were unemployed in 1939 than at the time of the Merseyside survey in 1934, although it is possible that domiciled workers, registered for unemployment insurance, were more prone to suffer this problem than the floating, transient population of 'unattached coloured men'. There was also evidence that in general the families included in the survey paid more than Whites for similar types of accommodation, even though the difference in rentals was not significant for all types of property. In general, however, the former group emerged from the survey with a greater degree of economic disadvantage. Moreover, the report emphasised the serious disadvantages endured by the children in such families when compared with their young contemporaries.[109]

In considering such gloomy evidence it should be recognised that the men encompassed in the survey were in no sense recent immigrants. Over half of the 190 included in it had been in Britain for 20 years.[110] It was this depressed population that was supplemented

by the technicians and trainees who arrived early in the war on
Merseyside.

Their arrival, along with that of the foresters from British
Honduras, formed only part of the Black contribution to the Allied
war effort. Apart from service in the armed forces where some
achieved distinction, and in the merchant navy, 'many coloured
people' shouldered the heat of civil defence work in areas such as St
Pancras.[111]

The technicians and trainees, when they arrived, expanded the
sphere of Black employment. The entry of Black workers into
factories would have been unthinkable in the interwar years. At first
the workers were placed as contingents in specific factories, but in the
course of the war their employment became more diffused.[112]

The arrival of the British Hondurans in Scotland in 1941–42 to
work in the timber industry also marked a new departure in the
employment of Blacks.[113] However, even with these changes, it has
been remarked that the largest group of Black workers, excluding
those serving in the armed forces, were to be found in the merchant
navy with which Britain's Black population had been associated for
many years.[114]

The Blacks who came over to work on Merseyside to toil in the
'Lancashire Arsenal',[115] found temporary accommodation in hostels
in Birkenhead, Wavertree, Liverpool, Manchester and Bolton.[116]
However, many of the men did not stay long in hostels but tried to find
private accommodation. Those who pursued this course of action in
Liverpool often found themselves on the south side of the city where
Blacks were familiar faces. Those West Indians who did settle there,
often did so in conditions of multi-occupation. Apart from the obvious
tensions that this situation could create, resentment was also bred by
the fact that skilled technicians found it difficult to accommodate
themselves to the continual, hovering presence and proximity of men
with whom they would not normally have associated in the West
Indies. Such concentration, multi-occupation and attendant
exploitation, were related partly to long-standing problems in the
Liverpool housing market. But the difficulties of the West Indians
were accentuated by the hostility they encountered from within the
White population, which also restricted their choice of
accommodation.[117]

For their part the British Hondurans, based in Scotland, were
accommodated chiefly in camps when they first arrived and this

arrangement persisted throughout the length of their stay. In this respect they did not encounter the rebuffs that the West Indians on Merseyside encountered. But not all the camps offered satisfactory facilities; the camp established at Duns, which was described as 'dirty and sordid . . . a sea of mud', provided little in the way of comfort and facilities.[118]

The economic and social life of those Blacks and Indians who moved during the war from old-established areas of settlement to the industrial centres of Britain has been left largely unrecorded.[119] But in older areas of settlement it showed continuing signs of an almost unremitting bleakness. Evidence on this was furnished towards the end of the war in a report on the 'coloured population' living in Stepney. At a time when the Jewish population in the area, the old centre of immigration from the tsar's empire, was diminishing, 'an increasing number of coloured seamen' came into the neighbourhood. One physical indication of their influx was the opening of a hostel, mainly for such workers, in Leman Street in the summer of 1942. Other men – the population was predominantly male – were to be found in the building trade, in Beckton gas works, in tailoring or as stokers in local factories.[120]

It was relatively easy, in fact, compared with the prewar days, to find employment. But recreational facilities were scarce and sparse; the men spent most of their time in the small cafés, in the ownership of which there was a strong Maltese involvement. It was here that they tended to form their relationships with White women, some of whom were prostitutes. The children of such unions, were of major interest to the compilers of the wartime report. The prevalence of the colour bar and the ambience in which the children had to live meant that many of them could expect an unstable, uncertain or insecure future. The report possessed its fair measure of stereotypes but it was written from a humanitarian, caring standpoint and the picture it painted was almost unremitting in its sombre tone. The impression from the Stepney report was that the Colonials, Indians and others, who constituted the population categorised as 'coloured', lived in virtual isolation from the surrounding White population.[121]

These economic and social restrictions did not go unchallenged. The League of Coloured Peoples (LCP), for example, still led by Dr Harold Moody, continued its activities throughout the war, defending the rights of Africans, Indians, West Indians and other smaller groups, emphasising their contribution to the war, and also taking a stand on the wider struggle for freedom in Africa, India and the Caribbean.[122] Among its campaigns the LCP was quick to take up the question of the colour bar in the armed forces and pressed the Colonial Office on this. The exclusion of Blacks from the Colonial Service was another issue taken up by the League. In neither case did the LCP, which could count upon the support of 'thoughtful whites', worried about Britain's future relationship with the colonies, make as much progress as it wished.[123] But the establishment by the Colonial Office of an Advisory Committee concerned with the welfare of 'Empire Colonials', which resulted in the setting-up of hostels for colonial subjects, as well as the appointment in 1943 of two commissions concerned with higher education in the colonies generally and the Caribbean specifically, resulted partly from the lobbying of the League.[124] These developments were regarded by the LCP as important steps forward, and it has been remarked that the League, which was given a fresh sense of mission by the war, 'probably saw the high water mark' of its influence in 1943.[125] There is no doubt, in fact, that Moody's later years, particularly his attempts between 1944 and 1947 to establish a Colonial Cultural Centre in London, and his calls for a Coloured People's Charter, were not marked by the same degree of success.[126]

The war also marked an important stage in the development of Pan-Africanism. With the outbreak of hostilities the leaders of Pan-Africanism who had gathered in Britain in the 1930s found themselves dispersed, within Britain and abroad. But their political activity still continued and was aided in part by the war. Surrounded by a persistent emphasis on freedom, which was loudly proclaimed in the war against Hitlerism, Pan-Africanists were able to argue that this quality was indivisible.[127] Furthermore, this raised level of consciousness was assisted by the presence in Britain of the Black Americans.[128]

In these circumstances certain important developments occurred. Ras Makonnen, for example, went up to Manchester. This enabled him to link up with his friend, Peter Milliard, who had a medical practice in the city. Once settled in the north, Makonnen enrolled for a higher degree at the university and also developed a successful restaurant business. Money from Jewish and Quaker contacts enabled him to set up the Ethiopian Teashop which was followed by similar ventures. Makonnen objected in principle to taxation levied by a bourgeois state and used his business profits for political purposes. Makonnen and Milliard were joined in Manchester by Jomo Kenyatta and this overpowering city, once 'the very symbol of industrial capitalism', was soon to become an important centre for Pan-African activity.[129]

In 1944, looking towards a new future after the war, a loose umbrella-organisation, the Pan-African Federation was formed in which Milliard and Makonnen were leading figures. This organisation had for its central concern the independence of Africa and the welfare of all African peoples.[130] It was against this background that the 1945 Pan-African Congress which has come to be regarded as a landmark in the history of decolonisation was held in Manchester.[131]

The idea of a congress to further the promotion of Pan-Africanism was floated early in 1945 by George Padmore and a preliminary meeting was held in Manchester in March 1945. The official proceedings were opened by the Lord Mayor of Manchester in Chorlton-on-Medlock Town Hall in the following October.[132] The first session, presided over by Amy Garvey, was concerned with 'The Colour Problem in Britain' but the discussion soon ranged beyond British society.[133] This wider interest was reflected in the formation soon afterwards of the West African National Secretariat which emphasised that the aim of Pan-Africanism 'was no longer to seek justice within the framework of the British and other colonial empires but to demand rapid independence for the black subject peoples of those empires'.[134] This position, after all, was consonant with a war that had been fought in the name of freedom. It is ironical that the Congress was almost entirely ignored by the British press.[135]

4.

THE responses towards immigrant and refugee minorities that emerged within wartime Britain were derived from a mixture of historical and more immediate influences. As a result, the aliens of allied nationality, the so-called friendly aliens, were not always enthusiastically received. For example, the Ministry of Information detected an early opposition to Belgian refugees, some of which was influenced by earlier experiences with Belgians in the First World War. In general, attitudes towards aliens were often mixed and liable to modification according to changing circumstances, although

Mass Observation reports would suggest that Czech nationals were consistently well-regarded.[136]

But this comment is to anticipate. In 1939 there were people in the German Reich who had aspirations to come to Britain. How did the British government respond to the prospect of their entry? With certain exceptions visas granted before the war to enemy nationals ceased to be valid from 11.00 a.m. on 3 September 1939. One consequence of the implementation of this policy was that 'the numbers of Jewish refugees entering the country declined sharply'.[137] Furthermore, those Jewish refugees who tried to gain entry to Palestine also encountered severe difficulties. The government's White Paper of May 1939 laid down that Jewish immigration into Palestine would be permitted for a further five years but that during this time no more than 75,000 immigrants would be allowed into the country. It was claimed that beyond this level 'the economic capacity' of Palestine would be placed under strain. Following the outbreak of the war, the White Paper remained 'the formal basis of British policy in Palestine and by extension of Britain's general approach to the Jewish problem throughout the war'. On 2 September 1939, in fact, the day after the German invasion of Poland, British troops fired on an illegal immigrant ship, the *Tiger Hill*, killing two people as it landed refugees from Poland, Roumania, Bulgaria and Czechoslovakia at Tel-Aviv. This action set the scene for an uncompromising British stance. Indeed, the government White Paper was pursued so rigorously that in 1939 and 1940 the number of admissions into Palestine fell below the levels permitted in the White Paper. Nevertheless, whatever the difficulties, attempts were still made by Jewish refugees to reach Palestine, notwithstanding agonising disasters such as the accidental blowing-up of the *Patria* by *Haganah* saboteurs.[138]

The search for sanctuary was soon affected by other developments. By the autumn of 1941 the Germans and their allies had succeeded in closing the escape routes from Europe.[139] Only a few determined souls could now escape.[140] In these circumstances it became clear that those who had possessed the luck or percipience to escape from Hitler's enveloping influence, like those who had escaped earlier from the sabres of the tsar's Black Hundreds, were indeed fortunate.

But what were the salient features of the responses evident in British society towards those refugees who had managed to escape from the German Reich in order to build new lives in a more liberal environment? Germanophobia, present before the Great War, stimulated by the 1914–18 hostilities, evident during the interwar years and given an additional impetus between 1939 and 1945, spilled over to affect the lives of the refugees even though they were themselves alienated from German society.[141] Consequently, although there was some relaxation of the conditions under which doctors and dentists without English qualifications could be employed,[142] some refugees continued to be denied employment on account of their origins or had problems finding work. Even those refugees who did not encounter discrimination could still be exposed to anti-German antipathies against which age was no barrier.[143]

Furthermore, at times anti-Germanism was capable of sliding into anti-Semitism; hence the rueful comment of one refugee, 'It was bad enough to be a German; even more to be Jewish; but most of all to be German-Jewish'.[144] By the Second World War those Jews who had arrived young from the tsar's empire were growing old. But side by side with them there was a second and even third generation that had been born in Britain. All these groups, along with other Jews, including the recent refugees from Nazism, had to contend with anti-Semitic sentiment during the war.[145] This hostility did not disappear by virtue of the fact that the country was engaged in a war against a country that had come to represent the full horrors of anti-Semitism. The career of Leslie Hore-Belisha, Secretary of State for War until January 1940, was affected by his Jewish origins. The Foreign Office, for example, opposed his transfer to the Ministry of Information 'not solely because of [his] flashy approach but because the man was a Jew'.[146] Furthermore, the old issue of Jewish loyalty, raised in one form or another in 1875–76, 1899–1902 and 1914–18, came to the surface yet again.[147] Allegations of sharp trading practices by Jews also continued to echo from the past and the charge of black marketeering assumed particular prominence in the circumstances of wartime scarcity.[148] In addition, there were complaints from the East End, where anti-Semitism had been fanned by the BUF in the 1930s, and from other parts of London, about the alleged overrepresentation of Jews in air-raid shelters.[149] The most celebrated attack came in 1943 after panic broke out in Bethnal Green tube station during an air raid as a result of which 173 people were killed. The atmosphere surrounding this incident was picked up by Mass Observation 'They're saying it was all the fault of the Jews. They lost their nerve. You know like they did in the blitz. They haven't got steadiness like we have. We may be slow but we are sure. But the Jews are different, they're like foreigners; in fact you might say they are foreigners'.[150]

Such hostility was not limited to the uncertain days at the beginning of the war. Indeed, there was a belief that 1943 witnessed a marked upturn in anti-Semitism.[151] Cartoons such as 'Mr. Smith, I Presume' by Moon in the *Sunday Dispatch*,[152] articles such as 'Alien in our Midst' in the *Daily Dispatch*,[153] correspondence in the *New Statesman* on 'the behaviour of foreign Jews'[154] and evidence in Home Intelligence reports in October 1943 on hostility towards refugee Jews building up businesses, underlined this impression.[155] Furthermore, the circulation of anti-Semitic material in Brighton towards the end of the war revealed that the expression of antipathy continued after 1943.[156] Indeed, early in 1945, George Orwell, aware of this sentiment, conducted an investigation into the whole question of wartime anti-Semitism.[157] The influence of such anti-Jewish opinion supplemented by a similar antipathy in Whitehall, formed an important ingredient in the evolution of the policy of internment and influenced the wider response of the British government to the fate of European Jewry.[158]

The fact of internment and its impact on the lives of those interned have already been considered, but what were the pressures which led to the introduction of this policy? At one stage before the war, the government had taken the view that there should be no general internment of aliens if hostilities broke out, although enemy aliens would be subjected to certain restrictions. However, a sub-committee of the Committee of Imperial Defence, concerned with 'Control of Aliens in War', reported on 1 April 1939 that although there would be no automatic internment of male enemy aliens on the outbreak of a war, some general internment would be inevitable 'at a very early date'. The full Committee of Imperial Defence accepted this recommendation on 6 April and approved the action of the War Office in reserving accommodation for 18,000 civilian internees.[159]

In these circumstances British Counter-Intelligence was assiduous in its collection of material on the 74,000 Austrian and German aliens living in Britain and it was on the basis of MI5 reports that 415 enemy aliens were arrested and interned during the first few days of the war.[160] Some of these people were Nazi sympathisers but others were not; MI5, under the control of the ageing Vernon Kell, was suspicious of all alien businessmen and journalists. With MI5 information and the administrative files of First World War internment to hand, the Home Secretary, Sir John Anderson, announced on 4 September 1939 'an immediate review of all Germans and Austrians' and the setting-up of tribunals to assist with this investigation.[161] Confidential instructions issued by the Home Office to the one-man tribunals indicated that the proceedings were not to be held in public, that the aliens could not employ a barrister although they might bring a friend, and that the tribunals were not to be regarded as courts but as administrative bodies. The main task of the tribunals was to divide enemy aliens into three categories: 'A' (to be interned); 'B' (exempt from internment but subject to restrictions); and 'C' (exempt from internment and restrictions). About 100 tribunals were soon established and by January 1940 there were 528 enemy aliens who had been interned, 8,356 aliens who had been subjected to restrictions and 60,000 who remained at liberty.[162]

At first there was relatively little pressure for the extension of internment to those aliens whom the tribunals had placed in the 'B' and 'C' categories.[163] Public opinion at this stage of the war was less xenophobic than it was in the early days of the 1914–18 war. But there was a noticeable hardening of anti-alien sentiment with the German invasion of Denmark and Norway in April 1940 and the push into the Low Countries and France in the following May. A Mass Observation report in April drew attention to 'a considerable increase of antagonism against recently arrived Jews and refugees in particular'. Few were worried about the politics of the newcomers or the threat of espionage; indeed there was not a single suggestion that the refugees should be imprisoned or interned; the resentment was 'more diffuse . . . only a stage beyond general resentment to the foreigner coming amongst us and *settling*, a resentment which is felt to a very large degree about for instance the Irish, and even very frequently about the Welsh'. The impression at Mass Observation was that hostility was stronger 'among the middle and upper classes' than among 'the masses'. But the survey noted that a strong press campaign was being mounted against the refugees which was capable of exerting an influence over public opinion. Even at this stage, the survey affirmed, in bold capitals, 'IT IS BECOMING THE SOCIALLY DONE THING TO BE ANTI-REFUGEE'.[164]

A Mass Observation report of the following month identified a further increase of opposition. The German attack upon Holland and an account from the British ambassador there of cooperation between

German paratroops and Germans already living in Holland added a new dimension to the situation. Anti-alien sentiment became 'the currency of respectable talk'.[165] It was expressed in parliament, particularly among Conservative back benchers. Moreover, certain government departments such as MI5 and the War Office helped to spearhead the campaign.[166] But how did the cabinet respond to this 'heightened public animosity'?[167]

The day after the Churchill coalition government had been formed on 10 May 1940, one of its first actions was to declare the establishment of a 'protected' area along the eastern and southern coasts, within which all German and Austrian men between the ages of sixteen and sixty were to be rounded up and interned.[168] It was a decision that was widely approved by the British public.[169] But these steps did not satisfy some pressures within Whitehall. On 16 May the Joint Intelligence Committee recommended, as a matter of urgency, that the limited internment measures applied to the coastal belt should be extended throughout the country to 'all enemy aliens both male and female between the ages of 16 and 70'. It was also suggested that 'special measures should be taken for the control of non-enemy aliens'. Following this development, in the second half of May all those enemy aliens, men and women, in category 'B' who hitherto had been restricted but not interned, were rounded up and put into camps.[170]

The final stage was reached in the following June when, towards the end of the month, a decision was taken to intern all 'C' category German and Austrian men. This decision followed hard on the arrest of Italians following the entry of Italy into the war on 10 June. The result of these operations was that by the end of June 1940 the only collective exceptions to the internment of enemy aliens were non-suspect German and Austrian women in category 'C' and non-suspect Italian women. The police were also under instructions not to detain the invalid and the infirm. Furthermore, the Home Secretary stated that special consideration was given to Germans and Austrians in category 'C' who had specialist knowledge useful to the war effort. In practice, however, such consideration was not always evident. How many individuals, therefore, were interned? Owing to the administrative confusion that surrounded the policy, it is difficult to provide precise figures, but it has been suggested that it involved 22,000 Germans and Austrians and 4,300 Italians. Altogether five government committees administered the internment system.[171]

The majority of the German and Austrian internees were Jews, but the *Jewish Chronicle*, the predominant voice of the community, did not at first oppose the policy of internment. On the contrary, it believed that in the circumstances the policy could not be resisted. The established Jewish community had always been anxious about the prospect of newcomers heightening the visibility of Jews and thereby encouraging anti-Semitism and this fear prevailed in the early stages of the war.[172] It was far safer to go along with government policy which, as contemporary investigations revealed, had a wide measure of public support.[173]

However, voices were raised in the spring of 1940 against government policy. George Bell, the Bishop of Chichester, a powerful and disturbing moral voice during the war, and Professor Gilbert Murray, whose sensitive liberal antennae had led him to protest against the treatment of Black workers in Britain, were two of the prominent public voices that were heard.[174] Victor Cazalet, a strong supporter of General Franco in the 1930s, Eleanor Rathbone, who had always been a patron saint to the refugees, and Colonel Wedgwood, a longstanding critic of government policy towards aliens and refugees, were just three voices that expressed disquiet in the Commons. Finally, the National Council for Civil Liberties under the energetic direction of Ronald Kidd stood firm and four square against internment.[175]

Nevertheless, the government pressed ahead and in the summer of 1940, with the internment programme firmly established, it decided to proceed a stage further. It began to engage in the large-scale deportation of aliens. In pursuit of this policy some 8,000 enemy aliens were deported, mainly to Canada and Australia. This overseas programme did not proceed smoothly; on the contrary, it 'produced a host of difficulties and some minor scandals'. Criticism of the arrangements led to an official enquiry in 1941 after which there was an improvement in the conditions under which internees were held and some of those who had been deported were allowed to return to Britain.[176]

At the same time as organised deportations were taking place, aliens were encouraged to make their own arrangements to proceed to the United States. Several thousands made this journey. But a stumbling block was the American insistence that persons admitted in such circumstances had to be provided with a guarantee by the British government that they would be permitted to return to Britain not later than six months after the end of the war. The reluctance of MI5 to agree to this American proposal, even though the Home Office was prepared to go along with it, seriously restricted those who might have been tempted to participate in this 'offer'.[177]

It took the *Arandora Star* disaster on 2 July 1940 to place government policy under increasing criticism and scrutiny although the *Jewish Chronicle* had already reversed its position of supporting internment. The luxury Blue Star liner, with a hastily assembled cargo of Germans, Austrians and Italians, classified by the authorities as dangerous aliens and therefore suitable for deportation to Canada, was hit by a torpedo off the west coast of Ireland fired from U47 which had previously destroyed the *Ark Royal* in Scapa Flow in October 1939. In this later incident U47 claimed 175 German and 486 Italian lives.[178]

Following this tragedy there was 'outspoken criticism of the Government's internment policy' since it was widely alleged that a number of the victims did not hold Nazi or Fascist sympathies and had been mistakenly selected for deportation. Victor Cazalet and Eleanor Rathbone were particularly penetrating in their comments.[179] The official enquiry which followed the disaster broadly vindicated the government but its publication in December 1940 did little to stem the tide of criticism. 'By then the public had turned irreversibly against both deportation and mass internment', even if defenders of official policy could still be found.[180]

The number of deportations was reduced drastically after the *Arandora Star* embarrassment and it was in these circumstances that the return of some internees from Canada to Britain was allowed.[181] At the same time, changes started to become evident in the government's internment policy. In fact, the speed at which these changes occurred was extremely marked. Towards the end of July 1940, a White Paper laid down that certain classes of detainees were eligible for release, although it was still possible to refuse release on grounds of national security.[182] This was only one month after the government had decided to intern category 'C' cases.[183] Under the pressure of public opinion the category of internees eligible for release was widened still further in the autumn.[184] Even so, regulations governing release were stringent. However, the terms were interpreted with more liberality than many expected and the relaxation of official policy became even more noticeable at the beginning of 1941 when Churchill became converted to a liberal position. By this time the government minister most closely associated with the introduction of internment was no longer directly involved; in October 1940 Sir John Anderson had been moved from the Home Office, where his post was assumed by Herbert Morrison, in order to replace Neville Chamberlain as Lord President of the Council.[185]

A number of developments, footprints in the sand, marked the stages by which the system of internment was finally dismantled. It was announced in March 1941 that approximately 2,500 internees had already been freed; in April this number had increased to 14,250 and by August the figure had risen to 17,745.[186] By the end of August, in fact, there were only two internment camps left on the Isle of Man whereas there had been nine in November 1940. By July 1942 the number of internees had been reduced to 300–400 and in the course of 1943–44 some internees were exchanged in transfers of personnel between Britain and Germany.[187] By the end of 1944 only the hard core remained. It is uncertain how many of those internees detained into 1945 were refugees as opposed to personnel who came into British hands during the war. What is clearer, however, is that there was a progressive relaxation of internment from the spring of 1941, after the threat of invasion was lifted but before 'the long tunnel of defeat was at an end'.[188]

It was not in Britain alone that the Allied powers pursued internment policies. In the United States, for example, American citizens of Japanese origin found themselves herded into camps.[189] In Britain it was by any standards an insensitive, as well as a badly-handled and inefficiently-organised operation, in spite of the administrative precedent that stood from the Great War.[190] But whilst recognising these features of the episode, there still remains an element of uncertainty about the pressure that led to its introduction, if only because certain government files have not yet been released.[191] The policy needs to be treated as more than an irrational episode, a touch of 'May Madness'.[192] It is important to give due weight to the social context in which the policy was introduced when an isolated and weakly-defended Britain faced a triumphant and still impressively strong Germany.[193] In these circumstances certain government departments, the War Office and MI5 for example, gained a stronger voice and were prepared to use it.[194] Moreover, after the fall of Neville Chamberlain in May 1940, such forces were aided by a political context in which an essentially Tory administration under Winston Churchill was keen to display its toughness.[195] In its pursuit of aliens as part of this policy the government could draw upon the strong strains of anti-alienism and anti-Semitism that existed within British society.[196] Indeed, the internment episode can be regarded as the culmination of the hostility which had been directed towards the alien refugees before the War.[197] Some of the strongest voices urging the government towards internment were from sections of British society, such as the Rothermere press, which had previously flirted with Mosley and the British Union of Fascists or the policy of appeasement.[198]

It was also in such circumstances that the government's attitude towards the use of Defence Regulation 18B, which after September 1939 provided the Secretary of State with powers to detain people without trial, 'took a dramatic turn'.[199] In the early stages of the war it had been used against people 'of enemy origin – although technically British subjects', and, it has been suggested, a few minor members of the BUF.[200] In the early summer of 1940, however, the detention of Fascists began to proceed apace.[201] These people were easier targets than the more influential 'Fellow Travellers of the Right' who had lent sympathy of various sorts to Hitlerite Germany in the 1930s.[202] But it was not only Fascists who were interned, even if on account of the recent campaign to rehabilitate Oswald Mosley they have received the greatest amount of publicity.[203] In the panicky, feverish atmosphere of early 1940 shop stewards in the engineering industry whose activity was regarded as 'impeding the war effort' were also at risk.[204] Indeed, critics writing in the heat of the internment episode were keen to place the issue within a context in which there was a sharp general contraction in civil liberties for British people.[205]

At this juncture more needs to be said regarding the treatment of enemy aliens. The experiences of the small number of Japanese aliens interned briefly after March 1942 have remained obscure.[206] Moreover, in contrast to the experiences of the Germans and the Austrians, relatively little account has been taken of the Italian internees. The Italian-born population which was returned at 20,771 in the 1911 Census of England and Wales had reduced slightly to 20,401 in 1921 and by the time of the next return had declined still further to 18,792. The disruption of the First World War, the introduction of aliens legislation in 1905 and 1919, as well as the restrictions on emigration applied by Mussolini, who came to power in 1922, all combined to reduce the scale of Italian emigration. In

Scotland, however, the Italian-born population increased between 1911 and 1921 from 4,696 to 5,599 after which it declined to 5,178 in 1931. Throughout the period between 1911 and 1931, therefore, the Italians in Britain amounted to only a minute proportion of the total population.[207]

By the interwar years the formerly ubiquitous Italian organ-grinder was becoming an increasingly rare sight. Ice cream sellers, however, proved to be more resilient. But the most noticeable feature of the community was the extent to which Italians 'had come to occupy a dominant position in the hotel and catering trades from the owners of such establishments down to waiters and domestic workers'.[208] They were also firmly established in other sections of the service sector. In Scotland this presence was reflected in the growth of organisations such as the *Associazione dei Gelatieri* (Association of Ice-Cream Traders), which had branches in Glasgow, Edinburgh and Dundee and the *Collegio dei Parrucchieri Italiani* (College of Italian Hairdressers).[209]

At the same time, there were a number of political developments that were to become significant. In 1923 a branch of the Italian Fascist movement was established in Glasgow, composed mainly of war veterans' associations and businessmen, and meetings throughout the 1920s attracted large audiences, although it is likely that these were as much social as political events.[210] For its part, the Italian government was prepared to exploit such sentiment, as part of a general strategy whereby 'Italians living abroad were wheedled at great cost to the exchequer into being [Mussolini's] greatest fans and propagandists'.[211] In the course of this campaign immigrants were invited to receptions at the Italian embassy in London and children were given holiday treats.[212] Such attention bought some support for Mussolini in London, Manchester and other English cities as well as in Scotland.[213]

Very little hostility was expressed towards such activity in the 1930s but this situation was to change in the summer of 1940 when Mussolini declared war on Britain. When the war against Germany had started in the previous year, those Italians who had assumed British nationality were called up for military service in the British army. Once Italy entered the hostilities the other Italians were placed in a difficult situation. Some returned to fight in the Italian armed forces. But those who did not return home soon encountered hostility. There were 'riotous demonstrations' against them in Scotland and similar attacks occurred in England.[214] 'E and I last night walked through Soho', George Orwell wrote in his wartime Diary on 12 June 1940, 'to see whether the damage to Italian shops etc. was as reported'. His conclusion was that there seemed to have been some exaggeration in the papers but examples of damage were clearly visible, as were attempts by the Italians themselves to deflect this hostility. 'The majority had hurriedly labelled themselves "British" '. Gennari's, the Italian grocers was plastered with placards carrying the message, 'This establishment is entirely British'. The Spaghetti House, Orwell noticed, had renamed itself the British Food shop.[215]

In view of the fact that Italians were now enemy aliens they were subjected to internment. On 10 June 1940 the Home Office instructed the police to detain all Italian men aged sixteen to seventy with less than twenty years' residence in Britain, as well as those Italian men and women who were regarded with suspicion by MI5.[216] 'Why should they pick me up? . . . I've been in England since 1907 and I've never been any trouble' protested P. G. Leoni, who had opened the renowned Quo Vadis restaurant in Soho in 1926.[217] For its part, however, the *Hotel Review* rejoiced at the shock that was delivered to Italian enterprises.[218] It was against this background that the 4,300 Italians were interned.[219] Some of those in the Grade A category were despatched abroad eventually to internment camps and it has been noticed that more than 400 Italians were killed when the *Arandora Star* went down. This disaster, commemorated by a monument in London's Italian Church in Clerkenwell, has assumed considerable importance in the collective remembrance of Italians in Britain.[220] Others, who were not shipped to Canada or Australia, served their period of internment alongside other enemy aliens.[221] The history of Italians in Britain after the ending of their internment remains essentially unrecovered. However, there is evidence to suggest that antipathy towards the Italian minority was not sustained; a Mass Observation survey of April 1943, before Italy had surrendered to the Allies, revealed that Italians were relatively popular with the public compared with some of Britain's allies. This finding emphasises yet again the complex and shifting nature of responses towards immigrant minorities.[222]

Unlike the Germans, Japanese and Italians, who were made enemies by the war, the Southern Irish were neutral. But this neutrality posed problems for the British government, and the presence of this minority, whether newcomers or long-established, generated specific tensions in British society.

It has been noticed that once the government had taken the decision to import labour from Eire, it threw a system of tight control over the process of movement and over the lives of Southern Irish citizens after they had landed in Britain. More needs to be said, however, on the mechanics of this arrangement, from an official British perspective, information on which was provided in a survey of 1943.[223]

After a worker had been offered employment by a British employer, whether in the public or the private sector and approval had been granted by the Dublin government, the liaison officer of the British Ministry of Labour sent prior notification of travel to the regional offices of the Ministry of Labour, to the firms where the Irish were going to work, and to the reception officer of the Ministry of Labour at Holyhead. Employers were encouraged to send representatives to meet the arrivals on their landing at the Welsh port. If workers were unable to reach their intending place of employment within the day of their arrival, they were accommodated en route at reception centres.[224]

When the Irish landed, immigration officers made it clear to them that they were obliged to take up the job specified on their visa. It was forbidden to engage in other employment without the permission of the Ministry of Labour.[225] As part of this same system of labour control, workers had to register with the police of the district in which they had their place of employment and were required to provide the police with a photograph. Finally, workers were obliged to obtain the permission of the police in order to stay longer than the date stamped on their travel permit card, which was usually six months. Workers were also obliged to leave Britain at any time when required to do so by the Home Secretary. Agricultural workers were not required to obtain permission for changes in employment or to register changes of address. However, they were expected to remain within the agricultural sector.[226]

All workers engaged in the principal war industries were eligible for certain types of allowance on the same terms as those British workers who found themselves transferred from home. This system involved a lodging allowance of 24/6d a week, payable to workers, whether married or single, who were maintaining a home in Ireland or had one or more dependants. In addition, a settling-in grant of 24/6d was paid

at the end of the first week's employment to those workers who were
not entitled to a lodging allowance. Women were entitled to an
additional grant of ten shillings.[227] In practice, however, the Irish
encountered problems in securing their appropriate allowances and
these difficulties resulted in the appointment of a Welfare Officer,
whose role was similar to that carried out by Learie Constantine on
behalf of the newly-arrived West Indian workers.[228]

Finally, the 1943 Report commented on travel restrictions between
Eire and Britain.[229] Those Irish who wanted to leave employment
and return home could do so at any time even if their employment was
covered by an Essential Work Order.[230] However, if they decided to
return without what the British authorities regarded as good reason,
they faced the prospect of being refused a visa to re-enter Britain.[231]

In the year after this survey was compiled, there were changes in
the method of recruitment. Following the controls in the period
leading up to D-Day, the Irish government placed additional
restrictions on those workers who could leave Southern Ireland; the
recruiting activities of the British had been a source of contention in
Eire since 1941.[232] Moreover, from the British side, all details relating
to recruitment became concentrated in the hands of the Ministry of
Labour.[233] Men and women were no longer recruited for specific jobs
with particular firms but for certain types of work. Once workers had
been selected and recruited the Ministry assumed responsibility for
their delivery, placement and welfare.[234]

In discussing the control that was exercised over Irish workers it
has to be recognised that such control was merely one feature of a
wider wartime mobilisation of labour.[235] The origins of this system
went back to 22 May 1940 when, under the Emergency Powers
(Defence) Act, the government passed Regulation 58A which gave
the Ministry of Labour many of the powers needed to control the
employment and direction of workers. The degree of this control
should not be underestimated.[236] Indeed, it has been suggested that
'one of the most remarkable features of the Second World War was
the extent to which Britain took powers to mobilise and relocate
labour'.[237] None of the other belligerent countries engaged to the
same degree in the conscription of women and in the direction and
allocation of its workers.[238] This policy in turn should be considered
within the context of the wider battery of controls and the increasing
centralisation of power that became evident in Churchill's wartime
government.[239] From the government's point of view it could be

argued that stringent controls over workers were needed to ensure that the most efficient use was made of available resources in a complex situation when the demand for labour could suddenly shift between sectors of the economy. For instance, in 1944 aircraft and civil engineering industries no longer wanted labour to the extent that it was needed in food supply, public transport and hospital work. Then, at the beginning of 1945, as the V2 raids began to wreak their devastation, needs changed once more, when labour shortages developed in the building industry. In this kaleidoscopic situation of shifting challenges, planning and control were at a premium.[240]

In addition to exercising a close control over labour from Southern Ireland the British government engaged in the constant surveillance of nationalist organisations and sympathisers. The IRA bombing campaign, which began in January 1939, and had led to the Prevention of Violence Act, continued into the war in both Northern Ireland and Britain[241] but 'It was poorly prepared and not very effective'.[242] Among those apprehended for such activity was the young Brendan Behan who, as a sixteen year old, was given a three-year Borstal sentence in February 1940, before being deported in October 1941 under the Prevention of Violence Act.[243] Apart from the fear generated by the bombing campaign, the British authorities were concerned about a possible Irish 'Fifth Column', as a result of which the offices of known Republican sympathisers were raided and through the trained eyes of Special Branch, established originally to sniff out Fenian activity, a close watch was generally kept on their activities.[244] There was in fact a more general suspicion of the Southern Irish in British government circles: 'There are plenty of Irish traitors in the Glasgow area . . . .' Churchill wrote in a confidential Admiralty note in 1939.[245] Security fears of this kind prevented the employment of workers from Eire on the sensitive southern coast of England.[246]

But what of attitudes to the Irish that developed outside government circles and the apparatus of the state? Standard histories of the Irish in Britain shed little light on this question, but scattered fragments of information can be gleaned by considering the impressionistic evidence contained in the files of the Ministry of Information.[247] Among other reports the Ministry was informed by a source in Cardiff on 10 June 1940, that there was great discontent over 1,000 Irishmen who were employed in the building of defence works in Anglesey because, it was alleged, they expressed openly anti-

British and anti-royalist sentiment. They were, it was claimed, 'a useful Fifth Column nucleus'.[248] Other reports, many of which had a familiar ring, were critical of various forms of Irish behaviour. It was alleged that the Irish were often drunk and disorderly. A report from the Midlands in 1942, for example, complained that they were 'the terror of law-abiding citizens in the Leicestershire area' and it was emphasised that there was 'much bad feeling locally' towards them.[249] In the previous year the Ministry had also learned that owing to their social mores there was some reluctance to have the Irish in private houses and it was suggested that they should be placed in camps.[250]

These observations heard at the beginning of the war emphasised a mixture of specific political and more general social hostility and these strands of opposition continued to echo through to 1945. In a full report on the Irish prepared in March 1944, for example, it was commented that Irish workers were 'never popular'; indeed, they were 'usually distrusted' and now they were 'bitterly resented'.[251] These perceptions, it was claimed, related partly to the possible implications of Irish neutrality. But other, more fundamental respondents, based their opposition on the ground that the Irish were earning high wages when 'our lads' were in the forces; a reminder, this barbed comment, of earlier hostility towards Jews during the Great War and, likewise, a great distortion.[252] In other cases hostility developed towards the Irish because of their alleged sympathy for Germany as displayed in an alleged predilection for the broadcasts of William Joyce, Lord Haw-Haw, one of their fellow-countrymen.[253] Apart from these fears and antipathies recorded in Ministry of Information files, an analysis of trade union records would underline the persistence of the longstanding perception of the Irish labour as a threat to British workers.[254] Women workers from Eire, it has been suggested, were particularly resistant to industrial work discipline.[255]

Responses during the war towards the longer-established Irish minority remain equally elusive and impressionistic. The evidence from Cardiff of a broadening employment pattern would suggest that in this instance a greater degree of toleration was being exercised.[256] However, responses towards wartime newcomers from Eire suggest that qualifications are needed to any belief that there was a *general* slackening of suspicion and hostility towards the Southern Irish minority. Whatever recognition was accorded to this group for its contribution to the war effort, which was evidenced by its continued recruitment into the economy, whatever camaraderie developed under the stress of the German blitz on British cities,[257] traditional images of the Irish as a troublesome minority, owing no deep-rooted attachment to Britain, feckless and with a passion for brawls, drunkenness and anti-social behaviour, as well as a potential threat to British labour also continued to exist. The neutrality of Eire was important in generating these perceptions which once triggered into being were hardly likely on all occasions to separate the citizen of Ulster from the citizen of Eire. In short, during the war, as in earlier times, attitudes towards the Irish and their treatment were complex.[258]

It might be thought that with Britain engaged between 1939 and 1945 in a fight for freedom and liberty, with support from the Empire and Dominions, benefits would flow from this cooperation for those who had lived under British domination. And over the longer term the war did play an important part in the process by which the Empire was dismantled. The case for change was clearly set out by Reginald Bridgeman, who was indefatigable in the struggle for liberation. 'The colonial peoples of the Empire', he wrote, 'irrespective of race or creed, are called upon to make heavy sacrifices in the war. More than ever before, therefore, have they the right to ask now for at least a substantial extension of democracy and freedom'.[259]

However, it would be erroneous to assume that wartime influences washed away racial intolerance, hatred and discrimination. These tendencies were persistently displayed towards West Indians, whose history during the war, unlike that of the groups from the Indian sub-continent, has been relatively well-reconstructed; such antipathy, moreover, affected the lives not only of newcomers but those Blacks who had been born in Britain.

Intolerance towards the latter was graphically underlined in 1943, in an incident involving Amelia King who was rejected for service in the Women's Land Army. This squalid action, defended by the Ministry of Agriculture on the grounds that it would be difficult to secure employment and a billet for her, encouraged Vicky to draw one of his best-known cartoons, emphasising the contrast between this behaviour and the war aims lauded by the Allies in their fight against Germany.[260] The rebuff of Amelia King was not an isolated incident; there were other instances of roughshod treatment which received less publicity.[261]

In the case of West Indian newcomers, tension soon became

evident.[262] In January 1941 it had been intended to employ 59 Jamaican technicians at Napier's Aero-Engine Factory on Merseyside. However, this intention was thwarted when the firm refused to take the men, 'partly on grounds of colour and partly on the ground of their alleged unsuitability'.[263] But it was not management alone that baulked at the prospect of Black labour. Trade union opinion, to which the government listened, was not always welcoming. On the contrary, the Boilermakers' Society, for example, created problems for those men who were suitable for employment in the shipyards of the north west by opposing the entry of every Jamaican who could not prove that he had served a bona fide apprenticeship. Difficulties also arose at a local level with the Amalgamated Engineering Union.[264]

Overall, however, responses to the technicians and trainees were more varied than these strands of evidence would suggest. Electrical workers incorporated the West Indians into their trade union structure.[265] Furthermore, the reports of the North-West Regional Office to the Ministry of Labour between 1941 and 1943 recorded that employers such as ICI and de Havilland were satisfied with their Black workers and prepared to take more.[266] But the comment of Arnold Watson, a senior Ministry of Labour official concerned with the employment of Black workers, to the effect that, 'Temporarily at least we have found the prerequisite industrial conditions. Negroes and white men can now work in the same shop', requires sharp qualification.[267]

Moreover, once the technicians and trainees had secured work it would be unwise to assume that their problems were over. Complaints from the Royal Ordnance Factories at Kirkby and Fazakerley regarding promotion prospects suggested that discrimination still continued. Difficulties also arose over pay, over expatriation allowances and working conditions.[268] In the case of the British Honduran forestry workers in Scotland it has been suggested that some discrimination was present over pay in the sense that even skilled workers were paid the minimum wage for unskilled labour, but it needs to be recognised that surviving evidence on this issue is hardly plentiful.[269] Furthermore, it has been claimed that the West Indians were often located on precarious terrain in remote areas and in this respect fared more harshly than their fellow-Canadian workers.[270] Among other occupational groups, there were complaints that Black seamen, along with their Chinese contemporaries, also continued to encounter discrimination and disadvantage.[271]

Discrimination also occurred in the housing market. This problem became evident on Merseyside as Black technicians and trainees attempted to secure private accommodation in preference to hostels. 'It was in this process that many of the men began to appreciate, for the first time, the nature of the attitudes of white people on Merseyside . . . .' The problem of finding accommodation was also underlined by the inability of the West Indians to secure housing on factory-owned estates. In other words, the war brought such workers face to face with a problem which for many years had been a source of grievance to students from Africa, the Caribbean and the Indian sub-continent.[272]

Employment and housing were traditionally sensitive areas for relations between immigrants and members of the receiving society. In addition, in common with the historical experience of other male-dominated groups, immigrant or refugee, there was some hostility towards Blacks based on the fear of sexual competition.[273] It has been recalled that relations between the Hondurans and the local Scottish population were 'strong and friendly'.[274] Overall, however, the reception of the foresters was mixed, with some hostility arising over their relationships with White women. 'Does the Colonial Office have any policy about their association with white women'? the Duke of Buccleuch, writing about the foresters, asked Harold Macmillan, who was then Under-Secretary of State for the Colonies. 'There have been a number of marriages and births and much intercourse is allowed in the camp [at Kirkpatrick Fleming] itself. Personally, I dislike this mixture of colour . . . there are already sufficient births of foreign extraction without the added complication of colour'. The responsibility for this unsettling state of affairs was laid primarily on the Hondurans who had 'totally different standards' from 'our simple country girls'. Macmillan replied, somewhat wearily, in terms which were themselves significant, 'It is, of course, obvious that if you bring coloured men to this country for war purposes, there will naturally be the risk of some undesirable results. . . . All we can do is mitigate the evil'.[275] Buccleuch's concern was not unique. It was shared by the Deputy Director of Timber Production.[276] Years later a Scottish woman who married one of the Hondurans also commented that the involvement of local women with the newcomers was frowned upon.[277] Evidence from Merseyside in 1941 would also suggest that the strong arm of the police could be lured into an abuse of power through an objection to interracial relationships and even a celebratory official report on technicians in Bolton recognised that sexual contact between the West Indians and local White women was a sensitive issue.[278]

It was not only the principle of interracial sex that stirred up feelings. The consequences of such activity, God's wrath in the form of venereal disease, which showed a general increase in the war, was also made an issue. In British Honduras VD was widespread and facilities for coping with it were inadequate. Consequently, a number of the Hondurans who landed in Scotland had already contracted the disease and, whereas there was a general lack of concern about the men's welfare during their stay in Britain, considerable interest was taken in the incidence of VD. The presence of disease among the Hondurans was one of the reasons used by the Ministry of Supply, in spite of dissent from within the Colonial Office, to justify the repatriation of an uncertain number of the forestry workers in 1943, leaving a rump of Hondurans to find alternative employment in wartime Britain.[279]

The insecure status of Blacks in British society was further underlined following the arrival of American troops in the spring of 1942.[280] The GIs might have constituted only one among many military groups that swarmed through Britain during the war, but these racially-segregated troops added a dash of glamour to a bleak society and in both the short and long term their presence contributed to 'the Americanization of popular culture'.[281] More specifically, the Americans also exerted an impact on race relations. The well-known internationalist, Gilbert Murray, had warned the Colonial Office as early as June 1942 of a colour bar being operated by White Americans against the Black British[282] and in the following year Learie Constantine, who in 1942 had been placed in charge of the welfare of Black technicians and trainees on Merseyside, found himself at the centre of an incident which was stimulated by the American presence.[283]

On 30 July 1943 Constantine, who had continued his cricketing career, came to London to play for the Dominions against an English XI. Together with his wife, daughter and three other people, including his Ministry of Labour colleague, Arnold Watson, he had reserved accommodation at the Imperial Hotel in Russell Square.

However, although its booking extended over four nights, the party was told it could not stay for more than one. In taking this decision the hotel management emphasised the sensitivities of the 200 or so White Americans in the hotel.[284] Constantine proceeded to sue the hotel for damages. Mr Justice Birkett ruled in his favour and awarded him £5 in damages.[285] As in the King case, some of the sharpest comment came from a cartoon artist, on this occasion David Low, in the *Evening Standard*.[286]

The second incident, which occurred soon afterwards, involved George Roberts. Roberts had come to Britain from the Leeward Islands, as a skilled technician and by 1943 was working in a Liverpool factory. In the course of his stay he had volunteered for the Home Guard and in October 1943 he was refused entry to the Grafton dance rooms, even though at his second attempt he was wearing his uniform. The dance hall did well out of White American servicemen who were generally disconcerted by Black competition for White women and it was in these circumstances that the management began to discriminate against Blacks. Faced with this rebuff Roberts refused to do Home Guard duty at his factory. As a result he was fined £5 at a Liverpool police court. On 1 August 1944 when Roberts's appeal was heard at Liverpool City Quarter Sessions, where Constantine gave evidence on his behalf, the fine was reduced to one farthing. In giving his judgement the Recorder commented: 'I am told that the position of coloured people has somewhat changed since the nationals of another of our allies joined us in this country . . . .' and he went on to emphasise, 'When people come here to risk their lives they are entitled to think they are coming to conditions of decency and order fit for the title of imperial in its best sense . . . .'.[287] This observation, however, was probably little consolation for Roberts.

The incidents involving Constantine and Roberts attracted widespread publicity, but it should be recognised that other Blacks were being treated in similar fashion as a by-product of the American presence in circumstances which did not attract such public interest.[288] In general, however, the results of the presence of American servicemen on British society were more complex than the public incidents of 1943 would suggest. For example, the rare presence of the Black Americans resulted at times in public displays of affection by young White women, a less glamorous consequence of which was evident in the illegitimate children that resulted from some of these unions. These youngsters were of particular concern to the

League of Coloured Peoples which managed to identify 550 such cases. Such children constituted part of a much wider human problem that arose through sexual contact in wartime.[289]

The presence of American troops also posed a specific problem for the wartime government. Should the racially-segregated American army be tolerated? What would be the consequences of such toleration on opinion in Africa and the Caribbean? The need for continued support from these parts of the world, particularly after the fall of Singapore in 1942, gave an importance to such questions.[290] The need for such continued support eventually encouraged a stress that Britain was colour blind and the establishment by the Colonial Office of an Advisory Committee on the Welfare of Coloured People in the UK in September 1942 was one attempt to reflect this position. Some Black observers such as George Padmore were not impressed; they still detected an official paternalism at work.[291]

The complications generated by the American presence were recognised as temporary and it was also believed in Whitehall and Westminster that the arrival of West Indians would also be reversed when the war was over. In line with the wartime involvement of the Colonial Office in the development rather than the supervision of territory, it was envisaged that Africa and the Caribbean, as well as India, would benefit from the experience gained by their workers in Britain.[292] It was also hoped, by at least one official, that this wartime experience would help eventually to relieve 'the great coloured social problem' which he identified in Britain. 'This problem', he wrote, would be 'greatly eased by the resettlement of African Peoples in West Africa where they could obtain proper and adequate employment'.[293]

It should be emphasised, however, that faced with the immediate issues raised by the American presence and the reactions generated in the British public by the arrival of Caribbean workers, government departments did not always line up together.[294] Moreover, at an individual level ministers and civil servants provided a range of opinion in their papers. In some cases there was evidence of enlightened Liberalism. J. L. Keith of the Colonial Office shone through as one particularly bright beacon of light in his refusal to be stampeded into taking restrictive action against the British Hondurans.[295] He was equally level-headed in dealing with the fears and phobias that arose over interracial sexual contact. He also pressed, to no avail, for measures to combat racial discrimination.[296] But the official files reveal less generous sentiments left by a number of cold Mandarin hands. The 'West Indians are not an industrious race' one War Office official pronounced in February 1941 'and I don't much like the idea of billeting them anywhere in the country'.[297] There was, in fact, a fear that control over Black workers could be difficult to maintain. This came through in an unsigned but telling Colonial Office memorandum of 12 September 1941 in which it was emphasised that unskilled workers engaged in civilian work would not easily 'be kept under discipline'.[298]

Ministerial comment could be equally revealing. Faced with the abuse and violence that some colonial subjects experienced from certain White American servicemen, the Colonial Office suggested in 1942 that such British subjects might wear a badge to distinguish them from Black Americans. Harold Macmillan, the Parliamentary Under-Secretary for the Colonies, thought it a good idea and suggested that the Black British should wear a little Union Jack in their buttonholes.[299] At least Macmillan took the problem seriously which is more than can be said of the prime minister. When in the course of a Cabinet discussion Viscount Cranbourne, the Colonial Secretary, indicated that one of his 'coloured' officials had been excluded from a certain restaurant on account of pressure from White Americans, Churchill retorted, 'That's all right; if he takes his banjo with him they'll think he's one of the band'.[300]

There was, therefore, no shortage of racial stereotypes on offer in Whitehall and government circles during the war and, taken together with the stereotypes of Jews that were also in circulation, such images revealed the extent to which historical conditioning had touched the centre of official life in Britain.[301]

General histories of the Second World War have differed in their assessment of the decisive trends in society brought about by the war. For example, did it lead to an increase in state control, paving the way towards '1984'? Did it hasten the process of economic and social reform?[302] In the case of the minorities living and working in Britain during the war, the responses encountered by groups such as the refugees from Nazism, the workers from Ireland and those from the Caribbean, were more complex than is sometimes assumed.[303] But any optimistic picture which suggested that the war was a total solvent of antipathy would require qualification. If, for example, the expansion of the economy as a result of the war helped to cushion the reception of Blacks in the labour market it could not stifle all hostility and discrimination. Furthermore, housing and personal relations

remained sensitive areas.[304] Indeed, surveys of Liverpool and
Stepney revealed, that wartime Britain could offer a particularly
bleak prospect for the Black population. In general, White
antipathies ran too deep to disapppear in the war and outside
influences such as the arrival of American troops helped to galvanise
or reinforce such hostility. None of this antipathy was created through
the presence of large numbers of Blacks.[305] Within a few years after
the end of the war, however, Blacks began to arrive in larger numbers
than ever before, and as they did so a new phase unfurled in the
history of immigration.

PART THREE

PART THREE

V.   The Postwar Yea [1945–71]

'Do not fool yourselves, my brothers,
Study, read and learn
Thoroughly the foreign things –
But do not shun your own . . .'
[T. Shevchenko, 'To My Fellow Countrymen, in Ukraine and Not
in Ukraine, Living, Dead and as yet Unborn, My Friendly Epistle'
(written at V'yunyshch, 14 December, 1845), in V. Rich (trans),
T. Shevchenko, *Song out of Darkness* (London, 1961), p. 79.]

'Since I come 'ere I never met a single English person who 'ad any
colour prejudice. Once I walked the whole length of a street looking
a room, and everyone told me that he or she 'ad no prejudice
against coloured people. It was the neighbour who was stupid. If
we could only find the "neighbour" we could solve the entire
problem. But to find 'im is the trouble! Neighbours are the worst
people to live beside in this country.'
[A. G. Bennett, *Because they know not* (London, n.d. 1959?), p. 22.]

1.

THE works of contemporary history confirm it. A glance at their titles
and themes reveals an overwhelming concentration on the decline of
Britain as a major world power in the twentieth century, which was
finally confirmed in the postwar years.[1] Following the war, when the
modernisation and reconstruction of the economy were required,
there was in fact a relative decline in British economic power; in
comparison with other major countries the British economy grew at
only a modest rate. Moreover, the retreat from Empire, symbolised

ьy the transfer of power in India and the African continent weakened the international status of Britain. Between 1945 and 1971 such economic and political changes were also to influence public policy and debate over immigration. During these years a steady succession of immigrants and refugees came to Britain and important changes occurred in British society through this process of interaction. However, no attempt is made here to write a comprehensive history of these years. The chronological proximity of such developments poses particular problems of perspective for historians. Moreover, many of the crucial documents in official and private papers are not yet available for inspection.[2]

2.

SOME groups which arrived in Britain after 1945 have been totally or almost completely overlooked. Before any significant transference of workers and their dependants took place from the Indian sub-continent, a small group of 2,000 so-called Baghdadi Jews, fearful of the consequences of Indian independence, came to Britain, However, a fragment only of their history has been recovered.[3] An even greater neglect is evident in the case of the refugees who fled westwards in the course of the Hungarian uprising, 14,000 of whom made a permanent home in Britain.[4] By contrast, a mountain of information has accumulated on those immigrants who arrived from the Caribbean and the Indian sub-continent. But this concentration of effort has tended to mask the arrival of other sizeable groups.

In the immediate postwar years it was recognised in Westminster and Whitehall that the reconstruction of the British economy required an injection of additional labour. At this time the extent of the postwar labour shortage and the particular areas of the economy where it was evident soon became identified.[5] It is also significant that when the Royal Commission on Population reported in 1949 it stated that immigration could be welcomed 'without reserve' only if 'the migrants were of good human stock and were not prevented by their religion or race from intermarrying with the host population and becoming merged into it'.[6] It was against this background that the state recruited workers to assist in the reconstruction of the British economy.

Following the war the Free French returned to France and the

American servicemen returned to the rich world across the Atlantic, in some cases with their GI brides. Furthermore, the POWs who had been held in Britain during the war were repatriated. However, not all of these enemy prisoners departed. Some 15,700 Germans and 1,000 Italians remained in Britain to work as civilian employees in agriculture.[7] But the demand for workers stretched beyond this sector. There was a backlog of neglected work from the war years. At the same time, large numbers of married women and elderly persons were leaving employment which they had taken on or kept up only for the duration of the war; furthermore, 'the number of persons of pensionable age was increasing', and it was recognised that 'the raising of the school leaving age planned for 1947 would cut the number of juveniles available for employment'.[8] It was in such circumstances that steps were taken for the resettlement of Poles in Britain.

In July 1945 the British government transferred its allegiance from the Polish government-in-exile to the recently-created provisional government in Warsaw, formed after the arrival of the Red Army in Poland.[9] In these circumstances it was hoped that Poles in Britain would opt for voluntary repatriation. However, many Poles outside Poland were less than enthusiastic about a return to a Communist Poland. In December 1945 there were an estimated 249,000 members of the Polish armed forces who had served under British command, for some of whom any return could have been hazardous. For example, General Anders, who had commanded the Polish 2nd Corps, stood accused of supporting anti-Soviet activity.[10]

In these circumstances the British government began to modify its view on the desirability of the repatriation of the Poles. In 1946 arrangements were made to assist the placement of those ex-servicemen who remained in Britain through the agency of the Polish Resettlement Corps, enrolment into which began on 11 September 1946, and in the following year other specified needs were met in the Polish Resettlement Act.[11] Those Poles unwilling to contemplate enrolment or their voluntary removal from Britain were soon threatened with demobilisation in the British zone of Germany – hardly an alluring prospect. Against this background it was estimated in 1948 that 114,037 Poles had enrolled in the Polish Resettlement Corps.[12] In addition, the British government allowed for the admission of the dependants of these men; as a result, it has been calculated that another 33,000 Poles were admitted to Britain. The majority came from the Middle East and Africa where they had been transferred after their release from Soviet camps once Russia entered into the war against Germany.[13] In addition, an uncertain number of Poles, former inmates of German camps, were to be found among the ranks of the so-called European Volunteer Workers who began to arrive in Britain in the course of 1946.[14]

It might be flattering to the national ego to assume that in resettling these Poles Britain was engaged in a great humanitarian venture. But this assumption would need to be qualified. The fundamental influence over official policy was the economic context in which the government had to operate and the need for additional workers. As a result, 'A policy of severe restriction of immigration . . . was replaced by a positive immigration policy . . . .'[15] It was in these circumstances that the Poles, among whom there was a predominance of men, settled in London, the centre of the wartime Polish government-in-exile and where the cultural props for an émigré community could be found. However, not everyone settled in the capital. The next most important concentration was in Lancashire, particularly in Manchester. In the West Riding a reasonable-sized settlement grew up in Bradford. In Wales there were settlements in Flintshire and Glamorgan. North of the border, where there had been a noticeable Polish presence during the war, the Poles were drawn particularly towards Edinburgh.[16]

These Poles who stayed at the end of the war constitute the core of the present-day Polish community. Over the years their numbers were supplemented by a small number of people from Poland. Some of these later Poles had relatives already living in Britain; others were refugees intent on escaping from Communist rule.[17] Any attempt to quantify the size of this Polish minority is difficult owing to changes in the boundary of the Polish state. But in 1951 it was estimated that there were 162,339 Polish-born people resident in Britain; this number compared with 44,462 in 1931. Such statistics provide an approximate indication of the size of the Polish minority.[18] Since 1951, however, the black-edged notices in Polish-language newspapers have drawn attention to the Polish-born minority being scythed away by death. In 1961 the number of people born in Poland and resident in Britain was estimated at 127,246 and in 1971 at 110,925.[19]

Apart from the Poles, there were other groups, on whose labour the British government was able to draw in the immediate postwar years.

The so-called displaced persons constituted an obvious pool of human resource. It is impossible to say how many such people there were in Europe at the end of the war. 'Included among the various totals were POWs, deserters, wanderers, East Europeans fleeing the Russians and/or accompanying Germans on their retreat westward, forced and voluntary labourers, concentration camp victims, Spanish Republicans driven out of Spain when Franco came to power in 1939 and an assortment of [other] people . . . .'[20] Indeed, 'in the summer of 1945 mainland Europe was a veritable refugee camp with millions of people encamped across the ravaged continent . . . .'[21] For various reasons not all of these DPs, as they soon came to be called, were anxious to be repatriated to their country of origin. As a result, the British government was able to tap the resources of the DP camps. All those who came, and it has been estimated that Britain recruited more than 80,000 workers, were subjected to controls by the Home Office; labour restrictions also loomed large in the EVW schemes.[22]

The Balt Cygnet scheme, which was approved by the Foreign Labour Committee of the cabinet in April 1946, involved the recruitment of single women of Latvian, Lithuanian and Estonian nationality who had been transported to Germany during the war and following the cessation of hostilities were confined in DP camps in the British zone of Germany. These women, who began to arrive in October 1946, took up work in sanatoria and tuberculosis hospitals. This arrangement was followed by the Westward Ho! scheme, which initially recruited men and women of Balt and Ukrainian nationality from camps in the British zone of Germany and Austria and later displaced persons of all nationalities from all three western zones. The bulk of these workers who were directed towards a number of industries where labour was in short supply arrived in 1947 and 1948.[23]

Other groups were also imported to Britain. 'These included 10,000 single German women and widows' (the so-called North Sea scheme), '2,000 single Austrian women and widows' (the Blue Danube scheme) and '5,000 Italians of both sexes'.[24] Such workers were recruited on two-year contracts. Each of these schemes, except that involving Italian women, which continued until 1951, was terminated in 1950. Before 1950 there were also four additional recruiting schemes which brought a small number of alien workers who were not included in the category of European Volunteer Workers. These initiatives involved the recruitment of Belgian building workers, Belgian female domestic workers, Italian foundry workers and German scientists.[25]

There was one additional dimension to the recruitment of European labour. In 1947, in stark contrast to its involvement in the return of Cossacks to the Soviet Union and anti-Tito Yugoslavs to Yugoslavia, to face whatever punishments these states decided to impose,[26] the British government, through the agency of the War Office, imported 8,397 Ukrainian POWs from camps in Italy. This initiative occurred at a time when the Italian government came under pressure from the Soviet authorities for the return of such prisoners. The Russians were intent at this time on punishing those members of the Halychyna Division who had thrown in their lot with the German Fascist enemy.[27] By 1 January 1949 all but 530 of these Ukrainians had been placed in employment and assumed civilian status. The original intention was that these men would replace the returning German POWs who had been employed in agriculture.[28]

At first, except in the case of the Balt Cygnet scheme, it was possible for European workers to bring in their dependants. However, the government soon took fright over the implications of its policy and after 1 July 1947 recruitment was confined to single persons.[29] Even so, there was a sizeable increase in the alien-born population as a result of the recruitment of Poles and other European workers of various nationalities. In 1939 there were 239,000 aliens over the age of sixteen in the United Kingdom; by December 1950 this figure, swelled essentially by postwar immigration, had increased to 429,329.[30] Apart from the Poles who had served in Britain during the war, few had any knowledge of the country to which they came. This lack of information was particularly true of the DPs. A former Ukrainian University student, who found a new home in exile in Bradford, could recall a knowledge of England derived from Shakespeare and Dickens; others, however, knew nothing and most had little influence over the choice of Britain as their destination.[31]

The resettlement of the Poles and the recruitment of EVWs did not exhaust the army of workers drawn from Europe.[32] The Italian-born population of Great Britain, for example, expanded from 38,427 in 1951 to 87,243 in 1961 and 108,985 in 1971. Such detail offers an approximate indication of the size of the Italian minority, but it needs to be recognised that not everyone born in Italy was an Italian.[33] Some of the Italians came as part of official recruitment schemes, but even when these were discontinued Italians still continued to arrive. The 1950s was a particularly important period in this process, with a peak being reached in 1956. During these years the traditional male dominance disappeared as women came to work in various industries and hospitals. In the 1950s private firms placed advertisements in Italian newspapers and sent representatitves to Italy, as a result of which young women whose horizons had been quite limited were transported to a strange land. Even those individuals who had an awareness of the world outside Italy were capable of being shocked by their first impression of England. 'When we arrived at Victoria Station', one later recalled a memory of 1954, 'I expected something beautiful but at the time it was very very dirty and everything seemed so black. We were very distress, very distress . . . .'[34] It was not until the 1960s that the number of women in the postwar immigration was balanced by men who were recruited for heavy industrial work.[35]

Another distinguishing feature of the immigration from Italy in the 1950s was revealed in the large number of Italians from the southern part of the country, from areas such as Sicily, Campania and Calabria, from the worlds of Carlo Levi and Giuseppe di Lampedusa.[36] The prospects for employment in Britain and the problems of poverty, overpopulation and unemployment, prevailing in southern Italy created the broad impersonal context for the movement of such workers, although, as at all times, the transfer of population was influenced by personal considerations and knowledge. Once these workers arrived in Britain they encouraged others to follow; in other words the southern Italian presence resulted from a process of chain migration.[37]

It was through such influences that Italians, who came from a country which since the late nineteenth century had been a heavy exporter of population, could be found after the war in growing numbers in towns such as Bedford, where the first Italian arrived in 1951, and particularly in south-east England.[38] Immigration began to slow down after the early 1960s and from 1969 there was a reversal of the migratory flow. The relative deterioration in British economic prospects, the consequent reduction in employment opportunities, particularly for the unskilled and semi-skilled, exerted some influence over this development. So did the 'maturing' of the immigration stream, in the sense that a number of Italians had been long enough in the country to accumulate sufficient resources with which to establish themselves in Italy. Finally, the availability of work in northern Italy and neighbouring countries such as Switzerland and West Germany also added its influence.[39]

In the past Britain had drawn much of its reserve labour from Ireland and the postwar years witnessed a continuation of this dependence.[40] Indeed, in the 1950s the absolute numbers of Irish coming to Britain, and adding to the already substantial Irish-born population, reached levels which had not been witnessed since the nineteenth century. Owing to the unrestricted movement of population between Ireland and Britain and the continued element of transience among the Irish, the exact size of the Irish-born population remained difficult to calculate. Census data provides a reasonable guide, however, and at the time of the 1951 Census there were 716,028 Irish recorded as living in Britain at the time of the return. In 1961 the figure was returned at 950,978 and in 1971 at 957,830 when the Irish accounted for just under 2 per cent of the total population of Great Britain.[41] In England and Wales but not in Scotland, the Irish from the Republic – Eire became a Republic in 1949 – were in a massive majority and it is upon these Irish that this postwar survey concentrates.[42] In order to put such numbers into perspective it is sufficient to note that, contrary to much popular belief, down to 1971 the Irish constituted the largest immigrant minority in postwar Britain.[43]

During the years after the war the Irish continued to display a noticeable spatial concentration. By 1951 London was the pre-eminent centre of settlement.[44] Furthermore, the expansion of the engineering and car industries resulted in a growing Irish presence in the west Midlands.[45] Within these areas there were particular concentrations and in London an important change was evident in this respect. The old focus of settlement in the riverside areas disappeared and by 1971 it was estimated that 40 per cent of the Irish lived in seven boroughs, Camden, Kensington and Chelsea, Westminster, Islington, Hammersmith, Brent and Ealing. The concentration of Irish was particularly apparent in Brent.[46]

How is it possible to account for this immigration of predominantly young, unmarried, unskilled and semi-skilled workers?[47] In part, until the 1960s it reflected economic pressures in the Republic where a sluggish economy and a high rate of population increase combined to exercise a significant impact on living standards. At the same time, small farmers, adversely affected by the advent of technological change, helped to fuel the exodus from the rural areas. In addition, the demand for labour in Britain in order to rebuild war-damaged cities, for example, and construct the motorways helped to pull labour out of Ireland. These pressures were further intensified by the fact that the differential between skilled and unskilled workers' wages was greater in the Republic than in Britain. Furthermore, the pay of the unskilled in the Republic fell below what could be earned in Britain. There was also in the latter a better social security net. Such attractions were conveniently massaged by British employers.[48]

But fundamental economic influences did not act alone. Young people began to contrast the rigid moral and social code that prevailed in the Republic with the easier, relaxed ambience of postwar Britain, which the geographical proximity of the two countries served to accentuate. Furthermore, the quasi-Oriental attitudes adopted towards women in the rural areas of the Republic was a specific pressure which encouraged some young women to put Ireland behind them. The uncertainty experienced by religious minorities in both north and south also focused attention on what was available elsewhere. But the movement out of Ireland, primarily from the Republic, was basically 'a labour adjustment mechanism'. Immigration increased in response to the demand for labour in Britain and declined either because of increased opportunities in Ireland or on account of a fall in the demand for labour in Britain, or, more likely, it resulted from a combination of the two.[49]

At the end of the day the initiative to move, to uproot, was a personal decision; as always, it required a certain strength of will. But the decision was probably made easier by the fact that in some parts of Ireland emigration had become an established part of social behaviour. Furthermore, traffic between the two countries was less of an adventure, it involved less uncertainty, than movement to distant parts of the world, and in that respect was undertaken more readily, particularly after entry controls which had been established during the Second World War were dismantled in 1946–47.[50] The existence by 1945 of a well-established Irish community and an even larger population of Irish descent, with a well-established infrastructure, also offered the prospect of contact and support for the newcomers. Such influences were reflected to some extent in the fact that following the end of the Second World War 80 per cent of the emigrants from Northern and Southern Ireland combined to make their way across the water to Britain.[51]

So far an emphasis has been placed mainly upon newcomers from Europe. But an important feature in the history of immigration after the war was the number of arrivals from further afield, particularly from the so-called New Commonwealth.[52] As a result of emigration from territories such as Hong Kong, for example, the Chinese population expanded considerably.[53]

The majority of the Chinese who had served on merchant ships during the hostilities were repatriated at the end of the Second World War. However, the small Chinese population was increased by some 500 individuals who were granted conditional permission by the Home Office to remain in Britain.[54] Nevertheless, it is difficult to provide reliable figures on the size of the Chinese minority. It has been emphasised that, 'immigration and census statistics dealing with the Chinese are notoriously difficult to use'.[55] The 1951 Census recorded 2,217 alien Chinese or Chinese of uncertain origin who were living in England and Wales. In Scotland there was a total of 84 aliens. But there were Chinese who had obtained British nationality by marriage, naturalisation or registration.[56] Moreover, there were other Chinese who were included among those originating from Far Eastern territories.[57] Whatever its precise size, it can be stated that the Chinese population, made up of a variety of population strands with a mixture of cultures, was larger than at the beginning of the century but it still constituted only a relatively small minority group.

A few years later the Chinese population had increased considerably in size. In the mid-1960s it was estimated that there were between 30–50,000[58] Chinese in Britain. In the 1971 Census it was estimated that 96,035 people resident in Britain at the time of the count originated from Hong Kong, Malaysia, Singapore and China.[59] Not all of these people were Chinese but a good proportion were. Furthermore, by the 1960s there was for the first time a significant presence of Chinese families; this development marked a departure from the previous settlement pattern in which solitary Chinese men had predominated.[60]

The postwar increase in Chinese derived mainly from Hong Kong and, against a historical background of emigration by the Chinese, resulted from the interaction of two basic influences. 'First, population pressures on Hong Kong caused by the big build-up of refugees from Mainland China since the Communist victory there in 1949 . . . added to economic competition in agriculture and forced out some of the more conservative class who turned to emigration as an alternative to adapting to new techniques.'[61] But developments in British society also exerted an influence. The 'economic prosperity . . . after the war, coupled with the more sophisticated eating habits of the British people led to a demand for Chinese food' and these economic and social changes helped to pull in the Chinese from Hong Kong.[62] In addition to the workers who entered this sector of the economy, the size of the Chinese minority was increased by students and nurses, mainly from Hong Kong and Malaysia, who had their own educational reasons for coming to Britain.[63]

Until the passing of the Commonwealth Immigrants Act in 1962 there were no restrictions on the entry of Chinese from the Commonwealth. Moreover, the effect of the important 1962 Act on Chinese immigration from the Commonwealth was limited in view of the employment that could be guaranteed in Chinese restaurants. A more potent influence over the inflow of such Chinese came in the mid-1960s with the fading of the restaurant boom. In these circumstances some Chinese began to develop their business interests in Europe in countries such as Holland, Belgium and West Germany, as well as in Scandinavian countries. Indeed, by 1971 there was some re-emigration from Britain to the new European frontier.[64]

During the postwar years London became the major centre of Chinese settlement.[65] But whereas until the war the major base of the Chinese was in the East End, the bombing of the Chinese quarter there in Pennyfields E14, brought about a westward movement. The result was that by the 1960s Garrard Street in Soho was the major Chinese business centre in Britain, indeed in western Europe.[66] The Chinese were also to be found in the established centre of Liverpool;[67] in addition, cities such as Manchester and Birmingham attracted Chinese in relatively large numbers.[68] In general, however, the Chinese minority was widely dispersed throughout Britain in the postwar years.[69]

If the number of Chinese increased significantly in postwar Britain; albeit from a low base, public attention became focused mainly on other long-distance newcomers who arrived from the Caribbean and the Indian sub-continent. The postwar process of immigration from these parts of the world has been well covered; even so, its salient features need to be recorded.

Before doing so, it is worth noticing that the Blacks who came from the Caribbean did not constitute the sole Black newcomers in postwar Britain. The longstanding African population also increased after the war; in fact, 'the early colonial migration into the East End in the years after the war was predominantly from West Africa'.[70] A fair number of these men arrived as stowaways lured to England by their vision of it as El Dorado.[71] As a result, Africans could be found in areas such as Stepney and Liverpool.[72] In the 1950s, Africans were also in evidence on Tyneside and by this time there was also a small African group in Sheffield.[73] Furthermore, in the postwar years, as at previous times, some African students still beat a path to British educational institutions.[74]

As for West Indians, some of the contract workers who had come to Britain during the war, decided to stay once the hostilities were over – a reminder in itself that the West Indian population was not purely a postwar creation.[75] However, the symbolic starting-point for the postwar immigration from the Caribbean came on 8 June 1948 when the SS *Empire Windrush* left Kingston, Jamaica with 492 passengers on board, all of whom were intent on starting a new life, of indeterminate duration, in what they perceived as 'the mother country'. These pioneers, some of whom had been in Britain during the war, were soon followed by others who came on board ships such as the *Orbita* and the *Georgic*.[76] These newcomers led the way for an increase in emigration from the West Indies to Britain which became more marked in the 1950s when, in the words of one calypso artist, 'The trek to England' was 'the only craze'.[77] The majority of those involved in this transfer, 'the final passage',[78] came from Jamaica and although men were in a majority at this time there was a high proportion of women among the West Indian immigrants.[79]

Why did this movement from the British West Indies to Britain take place? It was related in part to the underdevelopment of British territories which had been starved of investment. Such prevailing conditions had resulted in a continual process of emigration by 'surplus labour' which took West Indians to Central and Southern America and the United States in search of employment.[80] In the case of postwar Britain the largest concentration of West Indians came from those islands with the lowest per capita national income.[81] However, it is widely accepted that 'The dominant regulator of West Indian migration up to the time of the first Commonwealth Immigrants Act [of 1962] was the demand for labour in Britain'.[82] There was in fact a keen awareness in the Caribbean of the state of the labour market in Britain. The 'mother country' was not a totally unknown part of the world. On the contrary, one West Indian who came to Britain, was to recall later that 'the South London Press could be bought in Hildage's Drug Store near West Parade in downtown Kingston, Jamaica . . . .'[83]

Against this background, a number of specific influences assisted the migration process. Before 1952 a convenient safety-valve for Jamaicans, among whom there was a particularly long tradition of work-migration, had been available in the United States. However, entry into the US was severely curtailed by the 1952 McCarran-Walter Act which limited the number of immigrants from the British West Indies to 800 per year, of whom only 100 could be Jamaicans. This restrictive legislation encouraged Jamaicans to turn towards Britain. Indeed, it was of considerable general significance in directing West Indians to 'the mother country'.[84]

At one decisive stage, movement from the Caribbean into Britain was also influenced by developments in British politics. In the 1950s the West Indians enjoyed a prescriptive right of free entry into Britain; this had been guaranteed most recently by the 1948 British Nationality Act. Hence the preference of many West Indians to be called 'migrants' rather than 'immigrants'.[85] Towards the end of the 1950s, however, it seemed as if this system of free entry might be threatened. In these circumstances there was a concerted move, particularly evident in 1961–62, to beat any impending legislation. The result was an increase in immigration at this time which helped to fuel the campaign against unrestricted entry from the Caribbean and the Indian sub-continent.[86]

In these circumstances West Indians arrived in the hope of 'A better break' through individual initiative.[87] As always the decision to move, even temporarily, involved a major decision. In some cases, however, it was assisted by pressures from British employers. In 1956, for example, London Transport Executive entered into an agreement with the Barbadian Immigrants' Liaison Service, as a result of which several thousand Barbadians were loaned their fare to Britain; this debt was then repaid out of wages.[88] In 1966 London Transport began to recruit workers in Trinidad and Jamaica.[89] Furthermore, the British Hotels and Restaurants Association, symbolised for many people in the Caribbean by Joe Lyons and Company, joined the public sector in recruiting from Barbados.[90] For those West Indians who did decide to move, and the process developed a self-feeding or 'ratchet effect', the transfer from one part of the world to another was well-greased by private steamship companies and airlines, some of which made large profits out of such business.[91]

The other major transfer of population into Britain which came to magnetise public attention involved the arrival of workers and their dependants from the Indian sub-continent. Following the Second World War a number of former POWs were brought from Japanese-occupied territory to Britain and some decided to stay.[92] These former combatants from the Indian sub-continent added to the existing small population from that part of the world who could be found in Britain.[93] However, the majority of people from the Indian sub-continent arrived in the 1950s and 1960s.

In the 1950s the vast majority of the Indian minority were of Sikh origin and came mainly from two districts in the eastern Punjab in the north of the sub-continent. Among other groups were Hindus from Gujarat, in the west of India. A small number of Muslims and Parsees added to the mixture of the Indian population, even if this diversity, evident in serious and sharp differences in religion and custom, was often unappreciated by the White British.[94]

The majority of Muslims from the sub-continent, however, came not from India but Pakistan which had been created specifically in 1947 to satisfy Muslim aspirations.[95] The majority of the Pakistanis who came to Britain originated in the hill districts in the west and east of the country, from Mirpur and Sylhet, respectively. Once again there was a tendency among the White British to lump together all these newcomers. In fact, however, there were differences in spoken language. Indeed, the two groups had little in common beyond their Muslim faith and a sense of belonging to the same nation. Moreover, this sense of national unity was itself a fragile plant which was uprooted by the emergence of Bangladesh as a separate state in East Pakistan in 1972.[96]

Why did individuals leave the 'heat and dust' of the sub-continent for the greyer terrain in Britain?[97] The movement of Sikhs from the Punjab continued a long tradition of Sikh emigration, but in the 1950s and 1960s it was related to a developing pressure on land resources, which followed the partition of the Punjab between India and Pakistan.[98] This pressure was particularly evident in the Jullundur region. The Sikhs who came from the rural areas were mainly of 'middling wealth and status', intent initially on a temporary stay in Britain which it was hoped would allow for the accumulation of sufficient assets to restore the wealth and status of their families in India.[99] The emigration of the smaller number of educated, urban Sikhs and that of the Gujarati Hindus, most of whom possessed business or professional backgrounds, was also related to economic pressures which they faced in India.[100]

Such developments constituted only half the picture. There was a significant inverse correlation between emigration from the Indian sub-continent and unemployment in Britain. The correlation was neither as substantial nor statistically significant as in the case of the West Indians. The range of alternative destinations – there was a far-flung Sikh diaspora – together with the strength of the internal economy among the Indians in Britain, as well as their extensive social networks, helped to insulate their arrival from specific developments in Britain. Even so, a total insulation was impossible.[101]

Against this background a number of other influences assisted the process of movement. There were links established during the long years of colonial and imperial rule, although arguably these were less significant than might be supposed.[102] What is more certain is that reports sent back to India which portrayed Britain as a land of milk and honey and the appearance of 'England houses' in the Punjab, built with remittances of those who had travelled the seas, encouraged other more hesitant individuals to follow.[103] Furthermore, as in the Caribbean, the process of movement was facilitated by business interests, such as travel agencies, which stood to profit from it.[104]

In the case of the migration from Pakistan, which in its early stages was composed overwhelmingly of men from rural backgrounds, with a low level of literacy, a similar intermeshing of influences was at work.[105] The poverty of what was to become Pakistan had resulted in a tradition of external and internal migration which contributed to the earlier development of a small Muslim community in Britain.[106] It had also led to the men selling their services to the British. Among Mirpuris there was a tradition of service in the British army as well as on British vessels at sea.[107] Furthermore, the Campbellporis, also from West Pakistan, had been recruited as 'bearers, cooks, batmen and caterers' to the British army on the North-West Frontier.[108] Finally, the Sylhetis, from the east, were well known on British merchant ships.[109]

After independence the poor quality of the land and the limited industrialisation of the country left Pakistan with a large pool of labour which found it difficult to secure employment. Furthermore, specific developments in Pakistan such as the 1947 partition which resulted in a considerable number of refugees, the so-called *Muhajirs*, crossing from India to Pakistan, added to this pool. So did the government decision in the 1960s to build a dam at Mangla in the course of which 250 villages were submerged in the Mirpur district.[110]

If there were pressures in Pakistan which helped to create a context for emigration, this movement was also influenced by developments in Britain. The opportunities which existed in Britain to gain work and make money pulled the Pakistanis towards their destination.[111] There was also a discernible inverse correlation between the migration of Pakistanis and unemployment trends in Britain, even if it was weaker than the Indian example.[112] Finally, the process of movement was aided not only by the improvement in communications but also by the strength of kinship and friendship. As a result, a pattern of voluntary chain migration developed in the postwar years in which individuals were encouraged to move in order to help their kinsmen in Pakistan with their remittances and were enabled to do so by those of their kinsmen who had already departed from the sub-continent.[113]

In considering the arrival of workers from the Caribbean and the Indian sub-continent, it is necessary to refer to differences as well as similarities. In this respect there was an important divergence in the 1960s. The rush by West Indians to precede any possible ban over entry was less evident in the case of the Indians and Pakistanis, whose initial entry had occurred more recently.[114] When legislation controlling entry did appear on the Statute Book in 1962, however, it exercised an important influence over entry from both the Caribbean and the Indian sub-continent. After the rush of the early 60s the levels of entry from the Caribbean were reduced. By that time West Indian family units, which had been broken by departures to Britain, were essentially repaired and such reunions provided greater prospect of a permanent stay in Britain.[115] Primary immigration from the Caribbean, however, was sharply and adversely affected once the British government introduced controls.[116] In the course of the 1960s entry from the Indian sub-continent was less significantly reduced but it underwent a number of important changes. Unskilled workers tended to be replaced by skilled and professional workers in line with the entry restrictions imposed by the British government.

Furthermore, it was in the course of the 1960s that dependants began to arrive from the Indian sub-continent in increasing numbers. The early male pioneers were not generally intent on a long stay in Britain: the widespread expectation was that earnings which accrued in Britain would provide for a triumphant return to a better life at a later date on the sub-continent. However, as in the case of the West Indians, although at a later chronological stage, the threat of immigration controls resulted in the arrival of women and children from India and Pakistan.[117] This process of family reunion, which through its implications for the re-creation of the cultures from the sub-continent, helped to generate opposition towards the immigration from India and Pakistan, was particularly evident in the case of Indians.[118] The arrival of women from Pakistan was on a less substantial scale and occurred later, with the result that in 1971 the Pakistani minority was still made up predominantly of men.[119]

Apart from direct emigration from the Indian sub-continent to Britain, the 1960s witnessed the arrival of refugees from Kenya, the so-called Kenyan Asians, whose family roots went back to India. The basic pressure behind the movement of the Kenyan Asians, composed mainly of business and professional groups and their families, was political.[120] In other words, it followed from the Africanisation policies of the Kenyan government. At the end of 1967 only 61,000 Asians in Kenya out of a total Asian population of 140,000 were Kenyan citizens. Following the granting of independence to Kenya in 1963 the majority had elected to maintain their connections with Britain and were in possession of passports issued on behalf of the British government either in Britain or through a British High Commission abroad; as such they were known technically as Citizens of the United Kingdom and the Colonies, a category of citizenship created by the 1948 British Nationality Act. For a variety of reasons, this sojourning minority, with its vigorous commercial life, was viewed with suspicion by Africans and the pressures which developed in Kenya in 1967 were to be experienced later in Uganda in 1972 and in Malawi between 1975 and 1977.[121]

If it is possible to outline the major characteristics of the movement undertaken by workers and their families from the British West Indies, India and Pakistan, along with the arrival of refugee families from Africa, it needs to be recognised that the quantification of such movement remains elusive. This difficulty relates partly to deficiencies in official statistics. In the 1960s, for example, entry figures were widely regarded as unreliable.[122] It was on account of the confusion surrounding their collection that the 1977 Select Committee on Race Relations and Immigration delivered a crushing condemnation of such practices.[123] Problems also lurked for the unwary administrator, planner or politician in other official data such as census returns. For example, not everyone born in the British West Indies was of Afro-Caribbean origin. Furthermore, the servicing of the British Empire guaranteed that some of those individuals returned with a birthplace on the Indian sub-continent were White.[124] In view of these and other complicating problems population assessments need to be presented only with caution. However, some indication of the size of the postwar immigration of the so-called 'coloured population', upon whom attention is concentrated, can be gleaned from the fact that in the 1951 census return there were only 138,072 people in Britain who had been born in the Caribbean and the Indian sub-continent (16,188 from the Caribbean, 110,767 from India, and 11,117 from Pakistan). An uncertain number of these people would have been White. By 1971, however, when an analysis of parents' birthplace was included in the census return, the following picture emerged:

Population of Great Britain by own country of birth and parents' countries of birth.

	Own Country of Birth		
	Caribbean	India	Pakistan
(a) Both parents born in the NCWP [New Commonwealth & Pakistan]	264,905	240,630	127,565
(b) One parent born in the NCWP	7,280	25,140	3,070
(c) Neither parent born in the NCWP	7,590	45,220	6,085
(d) One or both parent's birthplaces not stated	24,300	11,000	3,220

Even with the elimination of category (c), most of whom would have been White, there was a substantial increase over the size of the non-White population that could have been present in 1951. However, set against a total population in Great Britain, estimated in round terms at 54 million in 1971, its relative size remained small.[125]

Before the 1950s and 1960s Africans, West Indians and the small minority population from the Indian sub-continent were concentrated mainly in a number of ports, university centres and major cities. As a result Liverpool and Tyneside were important areas of settlement.[126] So too was Cardiff.[127] In London the focus of the 'coloured quarter' was the East End.[128] The Second World War brought about some change in this distribution. There was a marked increase, for example, in the Black population in Manchester in the 1940s.[129] Moreover, Birmingham saw an increase in its Indian population during the war.[130]

The newcomers of the 1950s and 1960s generally avoided settlement in Scotland, Wales and those parts of England where unemployment tended to be high and went mainly to the large conurbations which were losing population and where there was the prospect of work.[131] London attracted relatively large numbers.[132] Outside the south-east, Bristol, an old centre of the slave trade, witnessed the arrival of a new Black population.[133] In addition, discernible concentrations were to be found in the west Midlands, particularly in the area around Birmingham.[134] Other settlements developed in the east Midlands, in Nottingham, Derby and Leicester.[135] In the north, a predominantly Pakistani population developed in Bradford.[136] Elsewhere in Yorkshire, Chapeltown saw the settlement of newcomers who were predominantly West Indian.[137] Over the Pennines, Manchester attracted some postwar settlement and so did Liverpool, another old centre of the slave trade.[138] Finally, Pakistani workers were to be found in the mill towns of Lancashire, such as Rochdale.[139] By 1971, therefore, compared with 1945, the uncertain number of Blacks, Indians and Pakistanis had become visible over a much greater part of Britain.

If, on the basis of the preceding observations, it is recognised that the history of immigrant and refugee minorities in postwar Britain is more diverse than is sometimes emphasised, it should not be assumed that all the constituent elements in this diversity have now been identified. There was an increase in the size of the Maltese minority, particularly of young men who concentrated particularly in London.[140] There was also an increment, of somewhat larger proportions, in the Cypriot population, which was evident in north London and in some provincial cities such as Birmingham and Manchester.[141]

Apart from these minorities from the Mediterranean, there were still other groups that added to the texture of British society after 1945. There was, for example, a small French population.[142] From

the bridge between Europe and Asia Turkish workers arrived in the
1960s and remained largely invisible.[143] From further afield others
came from the Old Commonwealth; for example, the so-called 'Ned
Kellys' from Australia made their distinctive contribution to postwar
British society.[144] And, as in earlier times, there were political
refugees who found it expedient to flee from political persecution or
uncertainty and were able to persuade the British authorities to
tolerate their exile.[145]

3.

BEFORE considering the economic and social history of the postwar
newcomers, it might be noticed that Britain witnessed the continuing
economic and social influence of certain groups who had arrived in
earlier times. For example, business firms such as Marks and
Spencer, Montague Burton and Thorn Electrical Industries, with
their roots in earlier immigrations in the late nineteenth and early
twentieth century, remained prominent features in British business
life, even if in some cases family connections weakened over the
years.[146] Moreover, some of the Jewish refugees of the 1930s came
into prominence after 1945 as 'celebrities, senior professors,
government advisers [and] occasionally political pundits'.[147] In fact,
an emphasis on business and professional success has been a
prominent feature in assessments of Anglo-Jewry since 1945, but it
should be emphasised that not every Jew was a successful capitalist or
firmly and securely established in a professional career. In the East
End of London, for example, a Jewish proletariat, consisting of
descendants of the earlier Russian Polish community, could still be
found.[148] Moreover, it can be re-emphasised that some of the refugees
from Nazism, far from falling into the 'success story' mould, were still
encountering difficulties in their transition to a new life in Britain.[149]
As for the even more recent 'Baghdadi' minority, if many were able to
continue with their trading and business activities, there was,
nevertheless, a working class drawn from this group which was
'employed in factories and menial labour'.[150]

Among the other groups, from Europe and beyond, a number of
discernible features emerged in their relation to the employment
market. At a time when the shortage of labour and its distribution
were greater problems than unemployment, the Poles, the European

Volunteer Workers, the Italians and the Irish tended to be employed, indeed in the case of the EVWs directed initially into those sectors of the labour market where it was difficult to recruit a sufficient number of British workers.[151]

In the case of the Poles, for example, this helped to account for their presence between 1947 and 1950 in agriculture, the building trades and the mines.[152] The European Volunteer Workers engaged in similar work. They were also to be found in the textile mills. In the case of women refugees there was an early involvement in nursing where labour was 'also difficult to recruit'.[153] The presence of Italians in the steelworks of South Wales and the brickyards in Bedford was also a reflection of the labour shortages which affected these industries in the early postwar years.[154] In the case of the Southern Irish, important civil engineering projects such as the Festival of Britain site, opened in 1951, and the motorway construction of the 1960s generated a demand for unskilled workers whose major characteristic was their physical strength, displayed in the serried ranks of Irishmen in 'McAlpine's Fusiliers' and similar building regiments.[155] For their part, Irish women, like women from the DP camps in Europe, were recruited for the nursing profession.[156]

In the case of those groups who came from beyond Europe, the Chinese became well represented in the restaurant sector. Shrewd Chinese businessmen were able to benefit from the postwar fashion of 'dining out' and prevail upon their fellow Chinese, who, partly as a result of discrimination and the lack of necessary skills, had few alternative sources of employment, to work the long, unsocial hours that the trade required. In postwar Britain, in fact, restaurants and related activities, replaced laundries as the major source of employment for the Chinese, even if some laundries continued to operate and, reflecting an even earlier pattern, some Chinese involvement in the merchant navy was still evident after 1945. The restaurant boom began for the Chinese in the East End, with the initiative of Charlie Cheung, but its major centre and manifestation soon moved westwards to Garrard Street where there were rich pickings to be had, particularly from expense accounts. In engaging in this type of work the Chinese were not alone among the immigrant minorities in Britain. Indians, Pakistanis, Cypriots and Italians were all prominently represented.[157]

After 1945 there was a marked expansion in the range of employment undertaken by Blacks and workers from the Indian sub-continent. For example, Black seamen and pedlars from the sub-continent could still be found but by the 1950s such groups were relatively insignificant. It is well known and frequently emphasised that the transfer of workers from the Caribbean and the Indian sub-continent involved their concentration into types of employment where labour was difficult to recruit. As a result, they were to be found initially in unskilled and semi-skilled sectors of the economy rather than in administrative, clerical or supervisory work. In London a high proportion of West Indian men became concentrated in public transport and general labouring work. In the Midlands Pakistanis were evident as labourers. In the same area Indians were disproportionately represented in the furnaces, foundries and rolling mills. Further north, in the textile mills of Lancashire and Yorkshire, by the 1960s the night shifts, which had difficulty in attracting White workers, were staffed almost entirely by work gangs composed entirely of Indians or Pakistanis. Moreover, by the same date hospitals in all the large conurbations were heavily dependent on Caribbean workers, particularly women.[158]

The passing reference to the restrictions which pressed upon Chinese workers,[159] serves as a reminder that other groups also suffered restrictions on the deployment of their labour which in some cases resulted from officially-imposed controls. For example, agreements reached between employers (through the British Employers' Federation) and the trade unions (through the General Council of the TUC), with Ministry of Labour approval, imposed restrictions on those EVW workers who had already been selected according to manpower needs. Most agreements had a common pattern. For example, placings were always subject to the condition that European workers could be employed only when no suitable British labour was available and there was usually a clause in the contracts which stipulated that in cases of redundancy the EVWs would be the first to be dismissed. In the Balt Cygnet and Westward Ho! schemes there were restrictions placed on any switch in employment. Wages, quotas, upgrading and promotion, were among the other sensitive matters that featured in the arrangements. In order to satisfy the Home Office it was also decided that the EVWs should be allowed an extension of their stay only if they had abided by the relevant employment conditions and behaved as worthy members of the British community. Such restrictions were imposed at a time when Britain still retained a strict general control over workers in key

1 The Bucharester Restaurant and Hotel

This eating establishment was noticed by W. Oesterley in his *Walks in Jewry* which appeared in 1901. The restaurant was situated close to St Saviour's Church in the Cheetham district of Manchester. Such restaurants, where the past could be recreated and a life in exile could be shared, tended to become important focal points for immigrants and refugees.

2 An Italian organ-grinder in Bradford, c.1900

Such itinerant Italians were a familiar sight before the First World War. The music provided by these 'buskers' did not receive universal appreciation: John Tenniel, the *Punch* cartoonist, was a particularly sharp critic. This particular photograph was taken

BELGIAN REFUGEES WHO ARE RECEIVING SHEFFIELD HOSPITALITY AT SHIRE HILLS 15

3 Belgian refugees in Sheffield during the First World War

In common with many other cities, Sheffield witnessed the arrival of Belgian refugees during the Great War. The local press reminded Sheffielders of the city's earlier debt to refugee workers and expressed the hope that the refugees would be welcomed. In their own publication, *La Renaissance*, the refugees who came to the city offered up their gratitude for their reception. Many postcards similar to the posed Sheffield group can still be found across the country.

4   Black and white in Cardiff after the First World War

A snapshot, like a still from a film, can be deceptive. This convivial outing suggests a degree of warm fraternisation between Blacks and Whites in Cardiff. But 1919 witnessed collective racial violence, characterised by Whites attacking Blacks and other minorities, on a national scale in Britain, and Cardiff was one major centre of such violence. Liberal historians, protecting the undiluted myth of Britain as a tolerant society, have revealed little interest in such developments.

5   All behind Britain's war effort

An emphasis on pulling together in the war effort constituted the wartime gloss on this photograph, which showed young men from Italian families clearing up bomb rubble. Wartime attitudes in Britain towards Italians and people of Italian descent showed marked shifts of mood. Many of the workers in the photograph had been released from internment on the Isle of Man.

6   A Chinese hostel in Liverpool

Chinese seamen helped to keep open supply lines during the Second World War through their work in the Merchant Navy. George Beardmore, on his first assignment for *Picture Post*, commented that 'Chinese sailors come cheaper than white'. The men were controlled by crimps who kept the men on tap for the shipping companies. The Censor banned the results of the assignment, fearing that the photographs, taken in May 1942, would damage the image of Britain.

7   Polish women workers

This photograph was taken by Bert Hardy in 1955, at a time when the Warsaw Government tried to lure back the Poles who were exiled in Britain. By this time some Polish women had found work on British farms. The woman in the foreground was one of the many Poles deported to Russia in 1940 who finally ended their lives in Britain.

8 A Cardiff scene, 1954

Cardiff, a major shipping centre, was a cosmopolitan city which in the early twentieth century not only witnessed scenes of collective racial violence in 1919 but numerous blatant examples of discrimination by 'the local state'. Instead of focusing upon such problems the popular press, in particular, was more interested in presenting a sensationalist image of Tiger Bay. The tranquil scene in the photograph, shot by Bert Hardy, appeared in a series carried by *Picture Post* on "The Best and Worst of British Cities".

9 A young West Indian arrives in Britain

By 1956 West Indians were arriving in Britain at the rate of 3000 per month. The weary and pensive child caught by photographer Haywood Magee at Victoria Station in London was one of the West Indians involved in this transference of population. Where is she now? Did she and her family find their dreams fulfilled?

10 A Ukrainian protest march in Bradford in the 1950s

East Europeans who came to Britain after 1945 were generally hostile towards the Soviet Union and continued in their political opposition in exile. A strong commitment to the Ukraine persisted within the community, which in some cases extended to the British-born children.

industries which lasted until March 1950. In the following January EVWs who had been in the United Kingdom for three years were freed from their more onerous restrictions and other EVWs qualified for a similar concession after three years' residence. However, until this time such workers were tightly controlled in the interests of British capital.[160]

The occupational structure of the West Indian, Indian and Pakistani communities which in 1971 revealed that, in spite of variations between the groups, the majority of people were still categorised as employees, with few possessing managerial or supervisory roles, was determined by a number of interacting influences.[161] The ultimate intention of most Pakistani men to return to Pakistan resulted in some preparedness to tolerate unskilled work even under adverse conditions. The barrier of literacy also helped to confine some workers from the sub-continent. Moreover, ties of kinship assisted the concentration of workers. But the influence of these determinants should not be overplayed. If there were no official restrictions on employment in the case of workers from the Caribbean and the Indian sub-continent, there were nevertheless unwritten, unseen barriers which resulted from White hostility. In other words, their occupational pattern after the Second World War, which in some cases resulted in a downgrading of talents, skills and qualifications, was significantly influenced by the discrimination they encountered.[162] So too, if perhaps to a lesser extent, was that of some of the Irish minority.[163]

At this stage, however, it should be emphasised that the economic activity of the various groups that came to Britain after the Second World War is more complex than so far suggested. In referring to the Jewish minority it was remarked that not every Jew was a capitalist or a highly-paid professional; there was a Jewish proletariat.[164] Similarly, it would be a mistake to assume that all the Irish minority was working class. Most were, even if there had been a widening in the occupational structure of the Irish as a result of the Second World War. Even so, there was an Irish middle class employed as doctors, dentists and travel agents, for example.[165] Furthermore, the occupational structure of those who came from the Indian sub-continent also reflected a diverse rather than a simple pattern. At the side of the working class there were successful entrepreneurs: these individuals were evident, for example, by 1971 in the restaurant business and the textile trade.[166] Moreover, the internal economy which was strong among such groups, provided other opportunities. The saree shops in Bradford, Huddersfield and Southall were one reflection of such enterprise.[167] The Pakistani banks which had appeared in Bradford by the 1960s, the shops and cafés in Balsall Heath near Birmingham and the wholesale merchants in Glasgow were other signs of a developing involvement in business.[168] For their part, West Indians found it more difficult to establish businesses. But some individuals, like their contemporaries from the sub-continent, were involved in the letting of property in the 1950s in areas such as Brixton, and there was other evidence of entrepreneurship in the 1950s and 1960s.[169] It is important not to become 'dizzy with success' and exaggerate success in business or professional activity. However, such dimensions need to be recognised.[170]

The fact that patterns of employment were able to shift over the course of time also needs to be acknowledged. For example, in the case of some Polish refugees there was a gradual movement away from the unskilled work with which they were initially involved.[171] There was a tendency among Ukrainians and many other EVWs to beat a retreat from agriculture.[172] Furthermore, notwithstanding a continued presence of Italians in the Bedfordshire brick industry, a large number of Italian contract workers were to move away from industry towards the service sector once their contracts had expired.[173] Some of these Italians went into the leisure industry. The coffee bar boom of the 1950s, fuelled by the spending power of the teenage population, offered an opportunity to the Italians.[174] Others, it has been noticed, went into the restaurant business, where in the 1960s their entrepreneurial flair was symbolised by Mario and Franco, whose *trattorie* 'excited fashionable London'.[175] If Mario and Franco represented the new entrepreneurship, the increasing importance of the business empire of Charles Forte, whose company merged with Trust Houses Limited in 1970, in the year of Forte's knighthood, revealed a longer-term success story which came to fruition after the war.[176] Finally, the beginning of immigration control over entry from the Commonwealth in 1962 and 1965, which restricted vouchers to market needs, started a process whereby a greater number of skilled and professional workers began to arrive from the Indian sub-continent to add to the existing preponderance of unskilled labour.[177]

Even so, an emphasis on change, adaptability and success would obscure the fact that some refugees found the transition to new fields of employment incredibly difficult. There were some Poles, for example, who never achieved it.[178] Moreover, once the British economy entered its problem phase in the 1960s, with higher average levels of unemployment, workers from the Caribbean and the Indian sub-continent became disproportionately represented among the unemployed; as in earlier times this resulted in part from the discrimination which such groups encountered.[179]

Against this layered and shifting background, what was the economic influence of the new workers and their dependants who came to Britain after 1945? In the case of most groups, this question has never been asked or answered, except in broad terms. A eulogistic newspaper account of the foreign workers present in Britain after the war claimed that 'The results can be measured in terms of more food for the workers, more coal for vital industries, more cloth for export, more bricks for housing and more hospital beds for the sick'.[180] In similar vein, a recent television documentary pressed the message of 'Ireland's loss' and 'England's gain'.[181] In the case of the workers from the Caribbean and the Indian sub-continent, popular assessments presented a similar message. For example, in a comment on 'The Dark Million' in 1965 it was suggested that, 'Bus services in several of our major cities would suffer badly, important sections of industry in the Midlands would slow down . . . . Lunches would be harder to get in London's cafés; streets in some cities would become filthy'. In short, 'Life in Britain for many people . . . would be harder and more unpleasant . . .'.[182] Other sources, generally sympathetic to workers from abroad, painted a similar picture.[183]

However, professional assessments revealed less certainty. There were suggestions that, in general terms, immigration had unclear or negative consequences for economic growth rates. On the other hand, some commentators laid great emphasis on the role of immigrant labour in generating economic growth in Europe since 1945. In line with this opinion, there was a suggestion that the long hours worked by Indians and Pakistanis, as well as their preparedness to put up with inferior working conditions, provided employers with a degree of economic flexibility they might not otherwise have enjoyed. In this vein, local employers in Rochdale stressed the important role of Pakistani workers in keeping open the town's textile mills. However, in contrary fashion, it was argued that whatever qualities were present among the workers drawn from the Caribbean and the Indian sub-continent, their net addition to population, even if this could not be gauged with a fine accuracy, was hardly of sufficient size to exert a significant impact on the economy. Similar divisions of opinion were present on related issues such as the consequences for inflation and the balance of payments which followed from the increasing presence of such workers and their families. In short, by 1971, there was no clear conclusion on the economic results of the immigration of those groups upon whom so much public attention was directed.[184]

In common with earlier immigrants and refugees, the groups that came to Britain after 1945 often encountered problems and difficulties in their search for accommodation. The destruction of property during the war and the rise in the net birth rate between 1941 and 1947 exacerbated the existing housing shortage and formed an unpromising context in which newcomers had to establish a housing base.[185] Nevertheless, in discussions of the Jewish minority it has been emphasised that in the course of the twentieth century there was an identifiable movement of older-established Jews into suburban areas, into 'better areas', as a result of which concentrations of Anglo-Jewry were to be found in Brent, Barnet and particularly Redbridge in the area around London. This process continued after the Second World War, even if there was not a total retreat from the old settlement in the East End, which had suffered heavily in the wartime blitz and those Jews who did move were still able to maintain business links with East London. A process of suburbanisation was also evident in the north of England. It was apparent, for example, in Cheetham Hill and Alwoodley, around Manchester and Leeds, respectively. Very little is known, however, regarding the settlement of the more recent refugees from Nazi Germany, although it is evident that in London they concentrated – not without some opposition from local residents – in areas such as Hampstead or Hampstead Garden Suburb where, in properties often purchased with compensation money from the German government, they could dream of similarities with the Grunewald or the Tiergarten.[186]

In the case of the Polish refugees the government recognised that competition for housing might generate tension from within British society and consequently involved itself in the provision of hostel accommodation. In most cases, however, the Poles had left their hostels by the 1950s. As they did so, many of these buildings went into decay or, as at Alfreton in Derbyshire, became converted into offices. Once in the private housing sector it has been suggested that there was a general move towards 'better' and 'nicer' houses which in

London, for instance, involved a movement to areas such as Ealing, the so-called 'Polish corridor'. But it is important to qualify this rose-tinted picture. The presence in the late 1960s of Poles in lodging houses in Bedford and the small terraced houses in Handsworth in the 1970s, adds a much-needed degree of perspective.[187]

The EVWs also started life in hostels, such as that at Buckley Hall in Rochdale, but the numbers in hostels, which were administered chiefly by official bodies such as the National Service Hostels Corporation, also fell quickly, with the net effect that by the mid-1950s most had left this form of accommodation. In a number of cases families clubbed together for the purpose of buying property. This process which began in the north, in cities such as Bradford, soon spread to the Midlands. Furthermore, by the 1950s some EVWs were to be found in council properties and others were attracted to the new towns such as Corby, where Development Corporation Houses were easy to acquire.[188] Italian contract workers tended to follow a similar pattern of movement through hostels, lodging-houses and private property on a journey that was not without its difficulties and tension.[189]

In the case of the unskilled Irish their position in the labour market ensured that many were in the lower rungs of the so-called 'housing classes'. Indeed, parallels were drawn between the conditions endured by the East End Irish in the 1880s and the circumstances under which some Irish lived in parts of Paddington in the 1950s. Apart from the Irish who clustered in the working-class areas of Britain's large cities, many single men employed in the building industry in the 1950s and 1960s lived rough or in basic, functional hostels or camps such as that at Stanford-in-the-Vale which belonged to Higgs and Hill, one of the large civil engineering contractors. Moreover, the famous study of Sparkbrook noticed the continued problems of the Irish working class in the housing market of the 1960s. On a more optimistic note, however it was suggested by one source that by the 1970s, in spite of the discrimination they encountered in the housing market, the Irish generally lived 'in better housing' than the West Indians, Indians and Pakistanis. However, considering the circumstances which many people from the Caribbean and the Indian subcontinent had to endure, not too much should be read into this comparison. Evidence from London, in fact, continued to emphasise the problems of multi-occupation and overcrowding with which many of the Irish, whose status did not allow them to escape to the new towns and the suburbs had to contend.[190]

The groups who came from beyond Europe also had to concentrate their energies on securing accommodation and without government assistance. With the establishment of Chinese family life in Britain for the first time on any significant scale, the Chinese were drawn more heavily into the housing market than at any other time during their history in Britain.[191]

Even so, a much greater interest has been taken in the experiences of the West Indians, Indians and Pakistanis. A survey of Stepney, undertaken shortly after the Second World War, noticed that the Black minority occupied 'the poorest housing property'.[192] Surveys of Manchester and Tyneside noticed a similar pattern, although some did manage to break out of such spatial confinement.[193] A few years later, in the 1960s, in a context of a continuing shortage of housing stock which allowed vicious crooks such as Perec Rachman to benefit from the misery of multi-occupation, the housing conditions of many immigrants who came from the West Indies and the Indian sub-continent, by now heavily concentrated in inner city areas, gave grounds for continuing concern.[194] In such circumstances a fertile context continued to exist for lodging-house landlords, some of whom were drawn from the ranks of the minorities whom they serviced.[195]

Council property was one source through which the working class was able to improve its housing circumstances in the twentieth century. However, down to the 1960s the newcomers from the Caribbean and the Indian sub-continent were not prominent in public sector housing.[196] In some cases, and this involved particularly groups from the sub-continent, little interest was shown in such property.[197] But when an interest was revealed, it was noticed in the 1950s that any allocation of council housing to a Black family created resentment,[198] and in the 1960s it was generally the case that the 'subtle gradations of allocation employed by all local authorities' favoured White applicants.[199]

The relationship of the groups from the West Indies, India and Pakistan, to the housing market showed signs of variation between areas and was subject to change over the course of time. But in general the majority of individuals from such groups were to be found by 1971 in the inferior properties of the inner cities. Located there through an interaction of internal and external influences, in other words through a mixture of choice and constraint, the relative weight of which tended to vary, these newcomers soon became associated with the causes of the infrastructural problems of the grey, forbidding inner city regions and, as with the earlier Jews in the East End, this association was to add a further complication to their lives.[200]

In touching upon their relationships to the labour market and the housing market, attention has been focused upon fundamental aspects of the economic and social history of the groups that came to Britain after 1945. Other areas of their history also need to be considered, but before turning to these matters it should be emphasised that some immigrants and refugees who arrived after the war did not stay in Britain. A number of Ukrainians soon departed to North America and other EVWs also left the country.[201] Some Italian contract workers returned to Italy.[202] There was some re-emigration of the Hungarians who arrived after the 1956 uprising.[203] There was continual evidence of people going back to the Caribbean in the 1950s and 1960s and even later; on 21 March 1971, for example, a party of Jamaicans returned home claiming that life in Britain 'was very rough and getting worse daily'.[204]

Many of those who did stay were sustained by their past or the vision of a better future or a combination of both. Jews, recent refugees as well as British-born, with reminders of recent Nazi persecution vivid in their memory, were able to cling to Zionism even if this did not result automatically in *aliyah* (immigration to Israel).[205] In the case of the Poles there was a government-in-exile and a large number of surrounding organisations such as the Polish Red Cross and a flourishing Polish-language press, including the Polish Daily (*Dziennik Polski*), which were already in existence by 1945. These structures gave the Poles a strong sense of Polish consciousness and emphasised their image as a fighting exile community.[206] For many years, in fact, particularly under the influence of General Anders, London was the spiritual centre of émigré resistance to Communism.[207] Memories of tragedies such as the Katyn Forest massacre, the betrayal of Yalta and continuing acts of aggression against the Polish nation served to underline this eagle spirit which was kept alive by associations such as the Association of Polish Ex-Combatants (SPK), whose Dom Kombatanta were to be found in most centres of Polish settlement.[208] It is significant, however, that in the course of the 1960s there was an increase in the naturalisation of Poles, which implies that there was a growing recognition of the permanence of their exile.[209]

An involvement in their past loomed large in the lives of the other groups uprooted by Communism. This element of continuity was evident in the demonstrations which were mounted in 1956 during the visit to Britain of the Soviet leaders, Bulganin and Khruschev, and the formation in Bradford in November, 1963 of the Captive Nations Committee.[210] There was other evidence, too, of experiences from the past spilling over into the present. For example, among Ukrainians a fierce rejection of Communism led to an opposition to trade union activity in Britain.[211] Moreover, the preservation of Ukrainian culture, which was strengthened by their experiences in the DP camps, was tenacious. 'What do you miss most about your homeland?' one exile was asked. 'I miss *everything*', was the poignant reply.[212] In fact, this attachment to a Ukraine of the early twentieth century, a glorified and glamourised homeland, sometimes stretched through the generations, from the first, to the second, to the third generation of Ukrainian descent.[213]

A continuing attachment to earlier roots which influenced attitudes and behaviour was also evident among other groups. It was remarked that among the Italians, such as the 'Abbazzini' in London, there were those who balanced their lives between two countries, living and working in Britain but with a strong attachment to their birthplace.[214] Among many of the Irish in Britain there was a continuing attachment to Ireland.[215] This was revealed in their county associations, their music, their hurling matches and their pubs, and such cultural links were reinforced by visits to Ireland. There was also a strong link between many Hong Kong Chinese and their villages of origin: the transfer of remittances by restaurant workers underlined this attachment. Indeed, in some instances, as in the case of the village of San Tin, it was suggested that such money transfers were the crucial determinant of village life in Hong Kong.[216] Finally, decisions affecting the lives of the Pakistani minority were sometimes taken in their home villages. Moreover, as with their Indian contemporaries, the link of Pakistanis to their homeland was reflected in the transfer of remittances.[217] There was also a continued involvement in political developments on the sub-continent.[218]

Links with a religious past also helped to sustain a life in Britain. The influence of the Roman Catholic Church, a distinctive feature of social life in Poland, remained strong among the Poles in Britain. Religion, whether of the Catholic or Orthodox variety, was also an important element of support to many within the Ukrainian community. The Italians and the Irish were also significantly involved in the Roman Catholic Church which in turn was busy with such communities. Religion, in various forms, was also important to a wide range of West Indians, even if some newcomers fell by the wayside after their arrival. Furthermore, the long-distance transfer from the Indian sub-continent to Britain underlined the resilience of the Muslim and Sikh religions, reflected physically in the growing number of mosques and *gurdwaras*.[219] Any suggestion, in fact, that groups tended to expunge their past on arrival in Britain needs to be challenged.[220]

As part of their strategy to survive in Britain, there was also a participation from among groups such as the Irish and those from the Caribbean and the Indian sub-continent, in the structure of British politics. In the case of many Irish there was a continuing involvement in the Labour Party, and also in the trade union movement, especially among workers in the construction industry, which overshadowed any contribution to nationalist politics.[221] Among the immigrants who arrived from the West Indies and the Indian sub-continent the strongest commitment down to 1971 was to the Labour cause, even though no-one from these communities was successful in entering parliament.[222] But a concentration on such political activity alone, involving those from the Caribbean and the Indian sub-continent, would miss additional layers of their political activity.

In the course of the 1960s at the same time as immigration controls were established over Commonwealth citizens, a number of institutions were established with the intention of improving race relations. Bodies such as the Commonwealth Immigrants Advisory Council and the National Committee for Commonwealth Immigrants (NCCI), formed in 1962 and 1965 respectively,[223] were followed by the creation of other agencies. For example, the Race Relations Board, was established by the 1965 Race Relations Act, and the Community Relations Commission, which effectively replaced the NCCI, by the 1968 Race Relations Act. Through these avenues talented West Indians, Indians and Pakistanis were brought into government service and, it must be said, in doing so, drove a wedge between themselves and some members of their respective communities.[224]

But there was a further dimension of political activity which became evident in postwar Britain among Black minorities and those from the Indian sub-continent. It was ironic that in the postwar years before the *Empire Windrush* docked, political activists such as Kwame Nkrumah, Jomo Kenyatta and Krishna Menon had all departed. Even so, a continuation of earlier political activity was evident in the League of Coloured Peoples which continued under the leadership of Dr Harold Moody until his death in 1947. After Moody's death, the Presidency of the League was assumed by Learie Constantine, who also provided the LCP with a degree of financial support. But sufficient funds were difficult to obtain and the League effectively died in the course of 1951–52.[225] There was also a final flickering of Pan-African activity in the shape of the Pan-African Federation, based upon Black activists in Manchester. This organisation published a short-lived journal, *Pan-Africa*. On one occasion it flew in a barrister from the Caribbean to defend a West Indian against a murder charge and, on another, it took up the fight against 'Colour persecution on Tyneside'.[226] But all such activity also disappeared quickly, even before the demise of the League of Coloured Peoples.

At a later date there were a number of attempts by groups from the Caribbean and the Indian sub-continent to engage in activity for mutual support against White antipathy. In the case of the West Indians the West Indian Standing Conference was founded in 1958, and the *West Indian Gazette* appeared in the same year, under the editorship of Claudia Jones, a Trinidadian who had been expelled from America in 1957 as a political undesirable.[227] However, there was some resistance to organisation beyond the self-help economic groups that were popular in the West Indies.[228] 'The only society I join is Barclay's Bank', said the fictional Jim Russell, 'I don't want to join anything else'.[229] As for those immigrants from the sub-continent, the Indian Workers' Association, first formed in 1938, was revived in a new centralised form in 1958, but it was essentially Punjabi rather than Indian and prone to conflict and schism.[230] Furthermore, conflicts between East and West Pakistan hampered the attempts to organise Pakistanis on a comprehensive basis.[231]

Nevertheless, there was a quickening of political activity in the 1960s which resulted from a combination of internal and external influences. The increasingly harsh ambience reflected in a gathering, sustained hostility towards the presence in Britain of West Indians, Indians and Pakistanis, evident for example in continued racial discrimination, the onset of immigration controls in 1962, the impact of the Smethwick election in 1964, the emergence of the National Front in 1967 and Powellism in 1968, the increasing incidence in the late 1960s of physical violence, directed particularly against those from the sub-continent, as well as a growing sense of police harassment, contributed in part to this raising of political consciousness. But so did the struggle for civil rights that was taking place contemporaneously in the United States and the development generally of Black consciousness in the world, which was significantly influenced by the liberation of Africa from European control.[232]

The establishment in February 1965 of the Campaign against Racial Discrimination (CARD), under the chairmanship of Dr David Pitt, for example, followed a visit to Britain by the American civil rights leader, Dr Martin Luther King. It was based on King's own organisation, the Southern Christian Leadership Conference. However, CARD, a multi-racial organisation, was soon fractionalised and by December 1967 it had disintegrated.[233] By this time in the United States a more radical response to the issue of Black disadvantage than that displayed in the civil rights movement was reflected in the politics of Black Power groups and this development also crossed to Britain.[234] In Britain considerable publicity was lavished on the activities of the Racial Action Adjustment Society (RAAS), which was formed in 1965 and dominated by Michael de Freitas, who had arrived from Trinidad in 1950. Under the influence of the Black Muslim leader, Malcolm X, who visited Britain in 1965, de Freitas converted himself into Michael X. However, there was little similarity between the dignified battle for racial equality fought by Malcom X and the shady self-aggrandisement of de Freitas.[235] Other examples of American influence included the Universal Coloured People's Association formed in London in 1967, by the African writer, Obi Egbuna, following a visit to Britain by Stokeley Carmichael, one of the patron saints of Black Power, after which Carmichael was informed that any future attempt to enter Britain would not be allowed by the British government.[236] Among other organisations which emerged in the 1960s was the Caribbean Workers' Movement.[237] This group, founded in 1965, was concerned primarily with promoting revolution in the Caribbean but it engaged in propaganda work in Britain and was one of the radical groups that led the assault on liberal elements in the break-up of CARD in 1967.[238] Finally, in 1968 the Black People's Alliance (BPA), representing a militant front against racialism, was formed in the shadow of the 1968 Commonwealth Immigrants Act, on the day that London dockers and meat porters marched in support of Powellism, which was then beginning to emerge as a serious force in the immigration debate. In January 1969, it was the BPA, a mixture of 'Afro-Asian-Caribbean' groups, which led the first Black Power march on Downing Street to protest against the immigration controls of the 1960s and Rhodesia's White minority government.[239]

Most of these organisations were short-lived. The creation of a solid, political consciousness was not an easy task. Moreover, the law was quick to act against radical activists.[240] Nevertheless, when considered alongside industrial activity in the 1960s, such as the strike at Rockware Glass Southall in 1965, at Courtauld's Red Scar Mill at Preston in the same year, and at the Woolf Rubber Company in Southall, also in 1965, as well as the strikes at a slightly later date at various engineering firms in the Midlands, such developments pointed to a growing consciousness among workers from the Caribbean and the Indian sub-continent which was to continue and develop in the following decade.[241]

All told, the groups who arrived in Britain after 1945 included larger numbers than ever before who had their origins outside Europe and these newcomers together with the immigrants and refugees from Europe, added to the cultural diversity of British society. This influence was particularly evident in those parts of the cities where they settled. In Glasgow part of Nicholson Street in the Gorbals, with its settlement of Indians and Pakistanis, was known locally in the 1950s as 'Burma Road'.[242] Manningham Lane in Bradford underwent one transformation with the arrival of the Poles, the Ukrainians and other EVWs, and witnessed another with the arrival of groups from the Indian sub-continent.[243] By the 1950s Moss Side, in Manchester, had lost its character as a Victorian bourgeois stronghold and become known locally as the 'Black Belt'.[244] Parts of Bedford bore the marks of an Italian life-style imported from Busso.[245] In London the southern part of the capital, in Brixton, formerly a haunt of theatrical artistes such as Marie Lloyd and Charles Chaplin, was noticeably changed by the arrival of its West Indian minority.[246] In the eastern part of the city, the area of Brick Lane, which formerly echoed to the sound of Jews from the Russian Empire, saw a brilliant colour transformation of some of its houses, as part of a wider cultural change brought about by the presence of a Bengali minority.[247] These various developments were visible consequences which became noticeable after 1945. But it has already been remarked that British society was changed or influenced in other directions. The varied economic contributions of groups such as the Irish and the Chinese provided some evidence of this wider influence.[248] So did the intellectual activity of various groups. If the German refugees from Nazism were important in this respect,[249] it is necessary to break free from a Eurocentric perspective and recall the work of writers such as George Lamming, Shiva Naipaul and Samuel Selvon.[250] Finally, there was a wider cultural influence resulting from the postwar immigration, revealed for instance in the religious life of Britain.[251]

But if the groups that came to Britain after 1945 influenced the shape and tone of British society they were themselves often changed in the process of their interaction with their new environment. There was evidence of Irishmen who despised the shovel in Ireland seizing hold of it in Britain.[252] Some women from the Indian sub-continent, previously shielded from the outside world, found themselves thrust for the first time into the labour market.[253] Once they began their school career, some children had to face a different culture which made little or no concession to their background and indeed might treat it with contempt.[254] In general, a transfer from rural Ireland, from Busso in southern Italy, from a Hong Kong village such as San Tin, from rural Jamaica or the countryside of the Punjab to a complex industrial society, which was compounded in many cases by differences of language and culture, was a major transformation. Indeed, it was sometimes remarked that the upheaval of movement contributed to personal strain and disorientation, although the evidence on such matters was difficult to evaluate and subject to conflicting interpretations.[255] Even so, there were individuals who triumphed over all such difficulties and the postwar years did witness a number of success stories. But it is important to guard against a cosy image and concentrate exclusively on that which glittered.[256] If some individuals could become integrated into a variety of existing structures – the academic world, the business world, the Labour Movement and the so-called 'race relations industry' – by 1971 there had been no penetration of the traditional elites of British society.[257] In some cases there was little interest in penetrating such structures; in general, the Hong Kong Chinese and the Pakistanis, as self-perceived sojourners, preferred to live within their segregated communities.[258] In some cases the past also placed restrictions on the degree to which groups as a whole could identify with British society. The betrayal of the wartime Polish allies at Yalta in 1945,[259] the internment episode of the Second World War which scarred the German and Italian minorities,[260] the troubled history of Anglo-Irish relations[261] and the Colonial-Imperial epoch, with its memories of the slave trade and slavery and its stains of brutal repression, such as the Amritsar massacre in 1919, were not always easily forgotten.[262] Moreover, it was even less possible to ignore the various strands of hostility which emerged from within British society after 1945, from which none of the immigrant and refugee groups was able to escape entirely unscathed.

4.

THERE might be a temptation in writing about recent responses to the various groups brought to Britain by a process of immigration to paint a flattering picture, to engage in an exercise in self-congratulation. But any account which emphasised complete toleration would be wide of the mark. Equally, however, it would be a distortion if an emphasis were laid on a universal hostility. As in earlier times, responses from within British society, which exercised a crucial effect in determining the lives of the immigrants and refugees living in Britain, were complex.

It was unlikely that a centuries-old antipathy towards Jews would disappear, and the Jewish minority, composed of old-established families, the survivors of the immigration from Russian Poland, along with their descendants, the refugees from Nazi Germany, together with their children, and the recent Baghdadi Jews did not escape hostility. For example, following the war there were attempts to expel foreigners, essentially the German-Jewish refugees, in order to 'help ease the housing shortage' in that part of London which many refugees found particularly attractive.[263] Moreover, during the Cold War the trial of Klaus Fuchs, who had been recruited during the war to work on the British atomic research programme, and then proceeded to pass information to the Soviet Union, together with the Rosenberg spy trial in America, put refugee scientists under some suspicion. Fuchs was not a Jew, but the impact of his action focused attention for a time on all refugee scientists, including those who were Jewish. Such developments suggest that the much-emphasised path to ultimate eminence and respectability was not a smooth and unbroken route.[264] As for the Baghdadi Jews, little has been uncovered, but it is known that they also faced problems both from within the Anglo-Jewish community and outside it. 'We are black to the Jews and Jews to the Gentiles', one of them was to remark.[265]

Furthermore, there were specific developments soon after the war which rebounded on the wider Anglo-Jewish community. The explosion at the King David Hotel in Jerusalem in 1946 and the hanging of two British sergeants by Jewish guerrillas at Natanya in 1947 during the final days of the Palestine Mandate unleashed a sharp but passing hostility, which led to anti-Jewish violence in Liverpool and Manchester.[266] Moreover, in 1948, in a grey period of acute scarcity in which 'spivs' and 'wide boys' could flourish, through the flamboyant activities of 'Sidney Stanley' the whiff of anti-Semitism hung over the Lynskey Tribunal and its enquiry into alleged government corruption. There were echoes here of the black market antipathy of the wartime years.[267] Finally, organised anti-Semitism continued to be evident after 1945. In the dark shadow of the Holocaust Oswald Mosley's Union Movement tended to steer away from the issue; indeed, Mosley in his attempt at self-rehabilitation in his autobiography, claimed that he had never tolerated anti-Semitism even in the BUF.[268] But hardliners such as the veteran Fascist, Arnold Leese,[269] and the gaggle of racial nationalists who operated in Britain in the late 1950s and early 1960s, were undeterred and carried on their own tradition of hostility towards Jews, and continued to draw attention to what they categorised as 'Jew-power' and 'the Jewish menace'.[270]

Down to 1971, however, anti-Semitism never became a serious social issue for the older and newer segments of Anglo-Jewry, and a number of factors have been brought forward to account for its limited appeal. These include: the so-called 'recoil effect' of the Holocaust, the favourable image of Jews which derived from the building and defence of Israel, the presence of easier targets, such as Blacks and newcomers from the Indian sub-continent, the relative affluence of postwar Britain and the alignment of interests between successive British governments and Anglo-Jewry.[271] Some of these claims possess greater weight than others. For example, as time passed the impact of the Holocaust became generally fainter and, in particular, the seeds of the so-called Historical Revisionism, which . denied the fact of the Holocaust, had already been planted by 1971.[272] Furthermore, developments relating to Israel did not produce a static, universally positive image of Jews. For example, if the Israeli feat of arms in the first Arab-Israeli war in 1967 was greeted enthusiastically in some quarters, it alienated certain sections of Socialist opinion, already hostile to Zionism, and proceeded to generate a strand of pro-Palestinian sentiment which at times was indistinguishable from anti-Semitism.[273] In addition, the claim that the arrival of newcomers from the Caribbean and the Indian sub-continent shielded Jews from hostility requires qualification. In racial-nationalist circles Jews were often regarded as *responsible* for the arrival of these newcomers. In a reworking of the Jewish conspiracy theory such immigration was viewed as a Trojan horse which would serve to undermine the stable roots of British society and lead to Jewish domination.[274]

But how substantial are the other factors which, it is claimed, helped to keep anti-Semitism in check? There was an historical relationship between economic crisis and anti-Semitism in Britain, even if the link was seldom direct, and it is possible that the relative affluence of the postwar world was influential in restricting anti-Semitism. But presented in a bald and isolated fashion the suggestion is inadequate. A fuller understanding would need to take into consideration the nature of Anglo-Jewish economic activity, as well as other pressures and influences. After all, despite the prevailing relative affluence after 1945 the postwar economic context did contribute to the creation of the antipathy expressed towards other groups such as the European Volunteer Workers and those minorities who came from the Caribbean and the Indian sub-continent.[275] Finally, the emphasis on the alignment of interests betweeen Anglo-Jewry and British governments should recognise the fragility of this relationship which was particularly subject to international influences. If it did prevail until 1971, the common alignment could not be guaranteed into the future.[276] In such circumstances and bearing in mind the long tradition of antipathy towards Jews, which was capable of revival, the Jewish community's sense of organisation and vigilance was not misplaced.[277]

Whereas the Poles and the Italians experienced a mixed reception in wartime Britain,[278] accounts of their postwar history and the experiences of the EVWs, have stressed that after the war such minorities encountered relatively little hostility. Indeed, an impression was sometimes projected in these generally sympathetic studies, of an inexorable march towards toleration or acceptance. But if, for example, it can be claimed that by the 1960s the Poles were perceived as 'good workers, ratepayers, solid citizens and family men', it is important not to overlook 'the passions and misunderstandings' of the early postwar years.[279] Furthermore, the claim that the presence of the EVWs in Bradford 'produced relatively little reaction'[280] should not result in any suppression of what has been delicately called a certain 'lack of effusion' which such groups encountered in their early history in Britain.[281] Greater knowledge than exists at present might also qualify the image of the Italians as 'model' immigrants, as 'invisible' members of British society, remarkable only for 'their hardworking nature, quiet family life, and low crime rate'.[282]

In the case of the Poles, and the EVWs, on whom more information is available, even if it still remains of uneven quality, a number of key pressures from within British society influenced their history in the immediate post-war years. Once the British government had revised its official view that Poles should return to Poland, it began to assist the resettlement of those Poles who remained in Britain and were prepared to cooperate with the British authorities. The Polish Resettlement Corps and the Polish Resettlement Act were the two major agencies through which this programme was attempted. The Poles were regarded as able-bodied recruits who would help to overcome the country's existing labour shortage. It was against this background that the government also brought in other European workers. So much has been noticed. So have the conditions of entry imposed by the Home Office on the EVWs, the various collective arrangements which regulated employment conditions and the government's provision of hostel accommodation. These aspects of official policy relating to employment and housing were designed to reduce any potential conflict with British workers.[283]

Two additional aspects of what might be termed the official response might now be emphasised. First, the Central Office of Information, with a touching belief in rationality and the strength of the printed word, published booklets such as *To Help You Settle in Britain* and *Contemporary Life in Britain*. This literature was part of a wider educational package introduced by the government to assist the EVWs.[284] Initiatives of this type were not restricted to Whitehall alone. Similar activity was undertaken by the National Coal Board. The NCB's concern was evident in its pamphlet *European Labour in British Coalmining*, which was written for the benefit of its Labour and Welfare officials.[285] The lives of the EVWs were also touched by two

refugee organisations, the Central Co-ordinating Committee of
Refugee Welfare Organisations, established in 1948, and the British
Council for Aid to Refugees, which was founded in 1950.[286] In short, a
number of official and public initiatives were undertaken to smooth
the path of the EVWs. But, in the case of government policy, the
response was Janus-faced. Whatever assistance was offered, it needs
to be re-emphasised that during the period of their contracts such
workers were placed at a disadvantage in relation to British
workers.[287]

The necessity for official assistance to smooth the process of
recruitment of foreign workers becomes evident from a consideration
of early postwar public opinion. Employment was one sensitive issue.
The Trades Union Congress in 1946 heard expressions of support for
the Poles who had been allies in the war and would help to rebuild a
postwar Britain.[288] But, in the same debate, there were demands that
Polish labour should be employed only under strictly controlled
conditions.[289] In the same year George Orwell overheard and noted
one indication of such concern, expressed in a conversation between
two Scotsmen, in which it was remarked, 'There was no coal . . .
because the British miners refused to dig it out, but . . . it was
important not to let Poles work in the pits because this would lead to
unemployment'.[290] Politicians might argue that in view of the labour
shortage the employment of Poles was 'commonsense' but others
could perceive the situation differently.[291]

As a result, opposition developed towards the employment of
foreign labour in industries where labour was in short supply and
foreign workers were directed. There was evidence of this opposition,
for example, from within the National Union of Mineworkers and
their supporters in parliament.[292] On 10 March 1947 Harold Neal,
the Labour MP for the raw mining constituency of Bolsover, argued
that because of their previous privations the physique of the DPs was
inadequate for heavy work in the pits.[293] In the same debate the
Labour MP, John McGovern, suggested that language difficulties
were a major impediment to the employment of such workers and put
forward the proposal that special pits should be sunk which would be
staffed completely by foreigners.[294] The concern for employment
prospects was understandable, bearing in mind the persistence of
xenophobia, and also the scarring experience of the interwar years
which remained strongly embedded in the memory of working-class
communities.[295] In view of the hard-fought industrial struggles of the

past, so was the hostility towards foreign workers who did not adhere to established industrial practices and displayed some reluctance to involve themselves in labour disputes.[296]

The initial unease over Polish labour was also strong among agricultural workers and filled the columns of *The Land Worker*, the journal of the National Union of Agricultural Workers. Following the union's fears about the employment of German POWs, the Poles were perceived as a new menace. There was a persistent fear in such circumstances that the recruitment of foreign and casual workers would dilute the agricultural labour force. Such fears were further intensified in 1949 when the government proposed to import Blacks from St Helena, and proceeded to do so. In fact, however, the anxiety was overdone. In view of its unattractive working conditions, few foreign or Black workers intended for British agriculture stayed in that sector.[297]

But if issues relating to employment were important, other tensions were apparent. The postwar housing market was one sensitive area. 'How do the people of Liverpool feel when they see these Poles with their new uniforms, very well be-medalled, strutting about our streets, when our boys from Burma, heroes from Arnhem, pilots from the Battle of Britain, have to take their wives and families and go squatting? How do they feel when accommodation can be found for these people?' Questions such as these were asked at the TUC Conference in 1946, no matter that such comment glossed over the Polish contribution to the Allied war effort which included action in the Battle of Britain and at Arnhem.[298] An awareness of the country's wartime allies showed a startling capacity to evaporate with a change in context. Moreover, once outside their hostels, the EVWs also encountered opposition in the housing market. In their case, for example, a Bradford source accused the government of lending money to the contract workers and thereby endowing them with a privileged position in the pursuit of property.[299]

Apart from fears relating to employment and housing, it was suggested that Poles and EVWs were given preferential treatment at a time of food rationing. This comment was not merely the currency of ordinary conversation; it was also raised in the House of Commons.[300] There was also a related allegation that some EVWs were busy in the black market.[301] In other words, in the stark postwar world where the shortage of consumer goods matched the shortage of labour, the general bleak austerity provided a fertile context for the easy development of anti-foreign sentiment at a basic materialistic level.

Finally, there was a list of other accusations directed against the Poles and the EVWs. There were references to Poles as 'Fascists' who had fought with the Germans – as indeed some had – and now strutted around with 'Hitler decorations'.[302] In Scotland, the predominantly Roman Catholic Poles were portrayed as Papist spies and there was a lingering, projected image, which had been strong in the wartime years, of Polish men as 'a race of Casanovas' who were a menace to the moral integrity of British women.[303] One of Orwell's Scotsmen, in fact, emphasised that the Poles were 'very degraded in their morals'.[304] As for the EVWs, allegations were heard about their collaboration with the Germans during the war. It was claimed that they were generally a 'bad lot' and the cream among their number had gone to America.[305]

It would be unwise, therefore, to assume that there was a universal toleration of Poles and EVWs in the early postwar years. Echoes of wartime antipathies could still be heard and specific issues in the postwar world added to these tensions. In the latter connection there was at times some hostility from other groups of newcomers. It was remarked in 1951 that 'where Poles and West Indian workers lived in the same hostel there were occasional disputes over the relative dignities of British citizenship and the possession of a white skin' which at times resulted in violence.[306] On other occasions hostility was influenced by political considerations. For example, it was noticed that general trade unions such as the Transport and General Workers' Union were more tolerant than the more specialist unions where rank and file members were sympathetic to the Soviet Union.[307] An orchestrated, politically-motivated hostility also came from the two Communist Members of Parliament, Willie Gallacher and Phil Piratin.[308] In a reference to the Poles the former's advocacy was 'Let them get employment in their own country'. Both Gallacher and Piratin were following the CP 'line' and consequently found it irksome that 'anyone should not volunteer to enjoy the rigours of Stalinism in the Russian satellites of East Europe'.[309] For the most part, however, the opposition encountered by the Poles and the EVWs had a more simple core. It was reflected in the view that 'Half the ills we suffer from today are caused by people who have no real love for England but enjoy the blessing of British nationalisation' (sic).[310] England, it is often asserted, should be for the English and

Britain should belong to the British. Indeed, in contrast to the shaky prose just culled from the *Western Morning News*, the students at Liverpool University in rejecting the admission of a DP in 1949 could openly assert 'British Universities should be for Britishers . . .'.[311]

Once the immediate postwar scarcities started to lift the European refugees faced less hostility, and in the case of those sheltering in Britain as exiles from Communism, this relative toleration was possibly assisted by the growing, carefully-nurtured opposition to the USSR, which effectively buried the enthusiastic images of Stalin, the Red Army and the heroic Soviet Union which had developed during the Second World War. However, such changes did not always guarantee a harmonious relationship. With the Poles condemned to an almost certain permanent exile, with little addition to their numbers from Poland, the British government became progressively less interested in a Poland-in-exile. The withdrawal in 1966 of government funding for the Polish Library and the shabby official response in the same year to the funeral of General Tadeusz Bor-Komorowski, an old wartime leader, were indicative of a declining official involvement in the Polish minority. 'Become British' was the official message, a response which provided another example of an intolerance lurking behind an official face of toleration.[312]

The refugees from continental Europe were not the only source of labour tapped by Britain after the Second World War. The need to rebuild Britain and the opportunities it offered drew in other groups of workers. It has been observed, for example, that in the postwar years there was an upsurge in the number of Irish workers who made their own distinctive contribution to postwar British society.[313] In existing accounts of their postwar history it has been suggested that the Irish, the newcomers as well as the longer-established, encountered relatively little hostility. Indeed, it has been claimed that there was a greater toleration of the Irish in postwar Britain than ever before.[314] A number of reasons have been advanced to account for this contrast with the turbulence of earlier years. One source has emphasised that it was related to a decline in Irish nationalist political activity. A trace of this was still detectable in Britain after 1945 but it was confined to a small minority.[315] In addition, another source has suggested that the Irish benefited from the decline in twentieth century Britain of religious hostility towards Roman Catholicism.[316] There was an assumption in such arguments that these political and religious developments rendered the Irish less visible in everyday life and thereby less exposed to hostility. It has also been stressed, finally, that the immigrant newcomers from the Caribbean and the Indian sub-continent helped to shield the Irish from hostility.[317] At the same time, sources have suggested that some of the Irish shared the antipathy expressed towards those groups from the Caribbean and the Indian sub-continent if only in an attempt to achieve a closer identification with British society.[318]

Some of these emphases need to be treated with caution. In discussing responses towards the Jewish minority it was commented that social contexts can change and perceptions can shift.[319] In the case of the Irish, nationalistic political activity in Britain had previously exposed this minority to hostility and in postwar Britain it was to lead to demands for the institution of passport controls – although down to 1971 the entry of the Irish remained uncontrolled – and for the denial of the vote to the Southern Irish in British elections.[320] Such demands were part of a wider antipathy which the struggle in Ireland was to generate from the late 1960s particularly after the dispatch of British troops to Ulster in August 1969.[321] Furthermore, the argument that the Irish were protected by the diversion of hostility towards groups from the Caribbean and the Indian sub-continent, even if it were an accurate assessment, would raise the question of why and under which conditions this took place. After all, the presence of such groups did not automatically protect the Jewish minority.[322]

In fact, the prevailing general emphasis on toleration of the Irish requires qualification. The long-standing reproduction of anti-Irish sentiment was difficult to dislodge. It was evident, for example, in parts of Scotland. To the wider public this strand of antipathy, directed against 'old' and 'new' Irish, was most evident in the 'ritualistic displays of tribal extremism' which surrounded the football clash in Glasgow between Rangers and Celtic.[323] There was also a continuing strand of antipathy in some Scottish nationalist circles, with concern being expressed over the level of Irish Catholic birth rates and the fact that those who remained citizens of the Irish Republic possessed voting rights which could be used in connection with sensitive moral issues.[324]

Other material, even if impressionistic, serves to qualify an overly complacent history of the postwar Irish. There was evidence of discrimination in the labour market which influenced the occupational structure of the Irish and the discriminatory notices of the 1950s which stated 'No coloured. No Irish' influenced their experiences in the housing market.[325] In addition, if Cyril Osborne, who campaigned against 'coloured immigrants' from the 1950s, and extended his hostility towards European aliens, did not widen his antipathy to include the Irish,[326] and if down to 1971 the racial nationalist circles were also restrained,[327] there were nevertheless those MPs who, in the course of the debate over the Commonwealth Immigrants Bill in 1961–62, regarded the Southern Irish as a social liability, and this view was also reflected in opinion in the areas of Irish settlement in England.[328] Furthermore, in the late 1960s there were housing inspectors who accorded compliments to West Indians over Irish in terms of personal cleanliness.[329] There was also evidence of an antipathy in the 1950s and 1960s from within the legal system, which was revealed in the recommendations of deportation for petty offences.[330] Survey evidence would also suggest a need for caution. In a 1967 Gallup Poll the question was asked: 'Do you think that the country has been harmed through immigrants coming to settle here from Ireland?' Only 16 per cent of those interviewed in the survey were prepared to say that the presence of the Irish had been beneficial. By contrast 22 per cent believed that the Irish presence had been detrimental.[331] Finally, a survey in 1971 of the racial and ethnic jokes which featured in the Independent Television series, 'The Comedians', revealed that anti-Pakistani jokes topped the list but those relating to 'the thick Paddies' came a close second.[332] There was a strong element of historical continuity in this degradation through humour.[333] There are those commentators who would regard such evidence as socially insignificant, but humour reflects the basic preoccupations, suppositions and values of society.[334] In this respect at least the continuing anti-Irish jokes possess a social significance.[335]

Even so, the continued free entry of the Irish, their spread through many more occupations than was the case in the years before the Second World War and the absence of any organised opposition to their presence would indicate that the Irish generally fared better than those workers who came from the Caribbean and the Indian sub-continent. However, there still remains a final note of caution. It might be suggested that the Irish who fared best were those who lost their Irishness. Any noticeable deviation from such self-abnegation could have adverse implications, whether an individual was in pursuit of 'a mortgage, promotion, or public office'.[336]

Before turning to those workers and their families who came from the Caribbean and the Indian sub-continent, it should be noticed that the Chinese minority encountered relatively little hostility at a time when it has been emphasised that the number of Chinese in Britain was greater than in any earlier period.[337] Various factors have been advanced to account for this relative immunity from antipathy. One source has stressed that few Chinese competed directly with the British workers in the labour market.[338] Furthermore, the social separation of the Chinese, 'the most unassimilable group'[339] among the immigrant and refugee groups in Britain, has been regarded as a cushion against hostility.[340]

Once again caution and qualification are in order. For example, there is abundant evidence, which is ignored when it is inconvenient, to suggest that self-segregation can promote suspicion, misunderstanding and conflict with the external world. The history of the Jewish minority, in many countries, is testimony to this. So too are the fantasies which developed in the late nineteenth century over Chinese opium dens.[341] In short, self-segregation does not automatically guarantee safety. A better shield for the Chinese was provided by the nature of their economic activity. In fact, 'apart from competition in the sphere of catering generally' and related trades[342] where they had 'protective economic niches'[343] the Chinese possessed a low visibility in the labour market. Moreover, the scattered nature of the restaurant business reduced the prospect of an opposition fuelled by a concentrated spatial visibility.[344]

Furthermore, it might be suggested, speculatively, that a degree of protection existed because some of their number were refugees from Communism.[345] Other commentators were impressed by the diligence displayed by many Chinese; one observer, for example, referred to them favourably in stereotyped terms as 'extremely hard-working', 'self-sufficient' and 'resourceful'.[346] This positive image was further strengthened by the widespread reluctance among the Chinese to have any recourse to the social security system.[347]

Even so, it would be unsafe to assume that there was no evidence of antipathy. In one area of economic activity where they did compete, trade union pressures restricted the employment of Chinese in the merchant navy.[348] Hostility was also encountered in the housing market in spite of the fact that down to 1971 the Chinese entered it in only small numbers.[349] Furthermore, there were a number of long-standing sources of tension which still persisted. In the early postwar years it was noticed on Tyneside that Chinese men who married English women had to face taunts of 'Chink, Chink, Chinaman' when the couple appeared in public.[350] It was only later, with the development of Chinese family life, which came about as women and children arrived from Hong Kong, that the linking of Chinese men with sexual irregularities – a prominent component of earlier anti-Chinese antipathy – began to dissipate.[351] Other longstanding anxieties remained. For example, in a country where gambling occurred on a prodigious scale, there were, nevertheless, expressions of a 'vague uneasiness' about the propensity for gambling among the Chinese which continued to be a distinctive feature of their social life whether the betting was on greyhounds, horses or in games such as mahjong and *pak kap piu*.[352] Furthermore, even if the numbers involved were very small, it was 'undeniable' that some Chinese were connected with 'the British heroin traffic' and in postwar Britain as in earlier years this involvement in drugs was exploited by the sensationalist press.[353]

In short, the Chinese were not totally invisible and completely secure.[354] Indeed, a dispute over service in a Chinese restaurant in St Helen's in May 1963, which led to the death of a customer, soon brought retaliation in the form of a protest march in the course of which damage was inflicted on Chinese property. In fact, protest groups spread as far south as Birmingham.[355] Furthermore, whatever the economic contribution made by the Chinese in the service sector, those who were Commonwealth citizens did not escape the controls over immigration laid down in the 1962 Commonwealth Immigrants Act and it has been remarked that in 1971 a quota was introduced to limit the entry of non-Commonwealth immigrants who intended to work in the catering trade.[356] Such developments also help to place in perspective the reception of the Chinese in postwar Britain.

In contrast to the lack of information on the Irish and Chinese, the amount of detail on responses to the groups that came from the Caribbean and the Indian sub-continent appears in some respects to be overwhelming. Some of it, however, is characterised by polemic rather than scholarship. Moreover, important areas of the debate remain undiscovered, in some cases because evidence, particularly that contained in official records, is not yet available. In such circumstances there are nevertheless certain key developments which deserve attention.

Whatever amelioration had been evident in the Second World War – and even the extent of this needs to be questioned – the early postwar years revealed evidence of continuing White hostility towards Blacks.[357] For example, in the aftermath of the war, before any large-scale immigration occurred, considerable attention was focused upon African stowaways. Before the Second World War permission to land was always refused. In 1942, however, this policy was relaxed 'out of keeping with the circumstances of the times'.[358] In other words, official policy changed when labour was in short supply in the wartime merchant shipping industry. Following the war, however, the National Union of Seamen campaigned against the stowaways.[359] In these circumstances the government decided in 1949 to revert to the pre-1942 policy.[360] The issue of employment for Blacks was of particular significance in Liverpool where trade unions emphasised that the 'direction of labour' had been tolerated in the war only on condition that it would disappear once the war was over.[361] In a city where unemployment was high and memories of the distress of the 1930s remained strong, there was 'undeniable evidence' of racial discrimination against Blacks.[362] The persistence of such discrimination in another traditionally sensitive area was that which students encountered in their attempts to find accommodation in Britain. Racial discrimination over the letting of property was also evident at an early date.[363]

Social-cultural-moral concerns also surfaced in the postwar years. By 1947 Stepney was viewed by some local inhabitants as a centre of vice and in that year a petition about the so-called café society which had developed during the war was sent to the Borough Council. Fuelled by a section of the press which had traditionally found the East End 'good copy' and prominent local figures such as Father Joe Williamson, the emphasis on vice was extended to suggest that Blacks in Stepney constituted a distinct social and moral problem.[364]

At times, moreover, hostility in the early postwar years boiled over into violence. In May 1948, for example, a crowd of 250 White men besieged and stoned a house in Birmingham where a number of Indians had been living.[365] But this incident was overshadowed by the serious violence in Liverpool at August Bank Holiday, 1948, when a group of Whites, mainly Irish, fought against members of the local Black population.[366] This violence was followed by a skirmish over several nights between Whites and Blacks in Deptford Broadway in July 1949 when a crowd of 1,000 Whites besieged a number of Blacks who were staying in a local hostel, Carrington House, in Brookmill Road.[367]

It was in these early postwar years, in June 1948, that the *Empire Windrush* arrived. The arrival received Pathé newsreel coverage[368] and the press generally was full of 'heavily spiced and peppery stories'[369] about the arrival of the 'Windrushers' as they were soon called in Whitehall.[370] Contrary to what might be commonly understood, however, government opinion was not completely enthusiastic about the arrival of such workers. There were no restrictions to prevent the entry of the West Indians. Indeed, in July 1948 the government passed the British Nationality Act which affirmed that Commonwealth citizens could enter the United Kingdom without restriction. This piece of legislation confirmed existing practice. The Act was certainly not a cynical manoeuvre to allow for the importation of labour which alongside workers from Europe and Southern Ireland, would help to rebuild Britain. In the face of barriers to movement elsewhere in the Commonwealth it was an affirmation of responsibility by the centre of that Commonwealth to its constituent population.[371] However, ideal and reality were uneasy partners and with the arrival of the *Windrush* the prime minister, Clement Attlee, wrote with his blunt red pencil across an official document, 'The question is, who organises this incursion?'[372] More openly, George Isaacs, the Minister of Labour, commented in a parliamentary reply to Tom Driberg, the Labour MP for Essex, Maldon: 'I hope no encouragement is given to others to follow their example'.[373] Civil servants also worried over the difficulty of removing such workers from Britain – a problem which did not arise in the case of the EVWs.[374]

This sense of official concern was reflected eventually in the establishment of a Cabinet Committee, GEN 325, in the summer of 1950, under the chairmanship of the Home Secretary, J. Chuter Ede, to inquire into 'whether the time has come to restrict the existing right of any British subject to enter the United Kingdom'.[375] By January 1951 it was concluded that any problem resulting from such entry was localised but that the matter should be kept under scrutiny. In February 1951 the report of the Committee was accepted without any recorded comment in the cabinet.[376] Nevertheless, such official papers reveal that long before 1962 the prospect of the state establishing controls over Commonwealth immigration – a major step – had been put on the agenda. However, the ideal of a multi-racial Commonwealth and the need for labour to help in the task of postwar reconstruction and development, helped to guarantee that the prospect of controls was shelved at this time.[377]

In 1951 the Labour government was voted out of office and the country was governed for the next thirteen years by Conservative administrations. During these years opposition towards Blacks, Indians and Pakistanis did not disappear. Indeed, it has been noticed that in the early 1950s Cyril Osborne, the Tory MP for Louth, and leader of a campaign which was redolent of the earlier activities of Major Evans Gordon and Sir Howard Vincent, began a crusade to preserve England for the English; in the course of this campaign he laid a constant emphasis on the disease and crime which, in his opinion, resulted from unregulated entry.[378] But the government, which in 1953 modified controls over aliens, in revising the 1920 Aliens Order, did not take such opposition on board.[379] Nevertheless, some ministers were sympathetic to control and between 1953 and 1955 the prospect was mooted on a number of occasions.[380] The possibility of other restrictions was also floated. At the instigation of the prime minister, Winston Churchill, who had an obsessive interest in West Indian immigration, the chancellor of the exchequer, R. A. Butler, was instructed to draw up a memorandum on the possible limitation of recruitment of 'coloured candidates' into the Civil Service. Butler's memorandum of 2 February 1954 came out against any such limitation but the pressure for the exercise made its own point.[381]

However, it was not the Conservatives alone who entered the immigration discourse. In 1954 John Hynd, the Labour member for Sheffield Attercliffe, introduced a debate on West Indian immigration in which he made clear his preference for controls.[382] Some trade union disquiet was also evident.[383] However, the other side of the Labour coin was revealed in the unsuccessful efforts of Reginald Sorensen and Fenner Brockway, both of whom were deeply involved in attempts to secure independence for colonial territories, to introduce legislation which would protect those from the Caribbean and the Indian sub-continent against the rigours of racial discrimination in Britain.[384]

Overall, parliamentary opinion was complex rather than simple and complexity was aided by ministers being more revealing when out of public earshot.[385] Moreover, it has been suggested that among the general public an ambiguity was present, at least as regards immigration from the Caribbean.[386] However, by the 1950s a colour bar operated in relation to platform duties on British Rail stations.[387] Tension between disadvantaged Whites and immigrants in the housing market in areas such as Paddington, where abundant opportunities existed for unscrupulous landlords, had also surfaced by this time.[388] In addition, the persistence of discrimination in public places, which brought back memories of earlier incidents, was revealed quite patently in February 1958 when an Indian student, V. K. Das Gupta, was refused admission to the Scala Ballroom in Wolverhampton.[389] Further and more graphic evidence of hostility had already been revealed in 1954 in Camden Town where 'racial warfare' raged for two days.[390] Public concern at such developments was revealed in the Pathé newsreel, 'Our Jamaican Problem', in 1955, and a BBC Panorama programme of 1956 which engaged in a survey of racial discrimination and disadvantage.[391]

The most dramatic development of the 50s came in 1958 with the outbreak of collective violence in Nottingham and what was loosely called Notting Hill. In Nottingham, where clashes between Whites and Blacks had occurred earlier in the year, the violence began on 23 August in the St Ann's area of the city.[392] In London 'nigger hunting' and 'nigger baiting' had been evident in Notting Hill in July and early August but in London, too, it was on 23 August that the major violence began.[393] In Nottingham there were various confrontations in the course of the following week.[394] In London sporadic incidents occurred until September and the simmering tension after this date was revealed in the still unsolved murder on 17 May 1959 of Kelso Cochrane in Kensal New Town.[395]

In 1958 the violence was described in the press as hooliganism. This response was aptly summarised in the caption, 'The Hooligan Age', which proceeded to categorise teddy boys as the villains of the hour.[396] However, the violence reflected a more broadly-based and growing antipathy towards West Indians whose presence was linked particularly to social problems such as shortages in the housing market and prostitution. In these circumstances racial nationalists such as those in Colin Jordan's organisation, the White Defence League, could fish in troubled waters.[397]

Reactions to the events of '58 were mixed. Scars were cut into the West Indian minority.[398] Among Whites, the Reverend Trevor Huddleston, already noted for his opposition to apartheid during his years in South Africa, proclaimed, 'This puts us all on trial'.[399] By contrast, the Eugenics Society warned of the dangers of racial damage that could result from West Indian immigration.[400] The British film industry also made its contribution to the debate in the film *Sapphire*, the first serious postwar production which attempted to analyse 'the Negro's position in contemporary society'. This film went out on general release in 1959.[401]

But what of the major political parties? Late in 1958 Cyril Osborne introduced a bill to control the entry of 'coloured immigrants'.[402] However, there was no immediate shift towards immigration control. In the 1959 General Election, furthermore, with the exception of a few areas, such as North Kensington, where Oswald Mosley hoped to benefit from a White backlash, immigration was not a major issue. Even so, the election did result in the return of a number of MPs from Birmingham constituencies who were in favour of immigration controls for those non-Whites arriving from the Caribbean and the Indian sub-continent. This parliamentary group was instrumental in helping to bring the demand for control towards the centre of British politics in the course of the 1960s.[403]

In fact, although the history of the earlier postwar years possesses a sometimes unrecognised importance, the 1960s was a crucial decade in the history of responses to the immigration from the Caribbean and the Indian sub-continent. In the autumn of 1961 the Conservative government of Harold Macmillan, introduced the Commonwealth Immigrants Bill, which passed through the Commons in July 1962. The entry of all Commonwealth citizens seeking employment in Britain was henceforth controlled through a voucher system. By any standards it was a decisive step.[404] Notwithstanding the short-term increase in entry which the threat of the Act produced, once it was on the Statute Book the Act, with its particular emphasis on the control of unskilled workers (those eligible for Category C vouchers), exercised a drastic impact over entry of non-Whites from the Caribbean and the Indian sub-continent.[405]

Why was this piece of legislation introduced? It has been emphasised that the absence of many official papers and other key sources hamper a discussion of the postwar years, and any analysis beyond 1955, the last date at present for the selective release of official papers, must be particularly tentative.[406] However, it might be suggested that there were a number of developments which helped to build up the pressure for control. For example, a grass roots hostility was evident in centres such as Birmingham, that former fief of the

Chamberlain family and an old centre of Imperialism.[407] A deputation from the city had gone to the Home Office in January 1955 to argue for restriction of West Indians into the city in view of the strain on local resources[408] and such restrictionist sentiment could draw upon the support of the Bishop of Birmingham, John Barnes, a eugenicist, who referred to West Indians as 'aliens' and 'a social burden'.[409] The government displayed little initial interest in these local problems but the parliamentary presence after 1959 of local MPs sympathetic to the cause of immigration control provided a channel for the transmission of hostility towards Westminster. At the same time, local opposition became better organised with the formation on 13 October 1960 of the Birmingham Immigration Control Association, which had the aim of campaigning at both local and national level 'for restrictions on immigration to Birmingham'.[410]

Other local developments also added to the atmosphere in which pressure for controls built up in the late 1950s and early 1960s. In the East End prostitution was stridently associated by some commentators with particular minorities, such as 'Maltese, Somalis, Cypriots, West Indians and other immigrants'.[411] Furthermore, fears relating to the collapse of the social fabric, evoked by the violence of 1958, were further underlined in the now-forgotten events in Middlesbrough in August 1961 'when thousands of whites chanting "Let's get a wog" smashed the windows of black people's houses and set a café on fire while the terrified Pakistani family that owned it took refuge in the cupboards'.[412] The linking of immigration with disease, which had entered the public debate by the early 1960s was further fuelled in Bradford and beyond in late 1961 and early 1962 by the smallpox outbreak in the city which had its origins in the Pakistani community.[413] The outbreak which occurred 'in the middle of intense national discussion about the [Commonwealth Immigrants] Act' provided advocates of control such as Cyril Osborne with powerful ammunition.[414]

There were therefore a number of local pressures in 1961–62 which need to be taken into account. Moreover, it is interesting to note that a Gallup Poll in May 1961 revealed that 73 per cent of those interviewed were in favour of controls.[415] However, local discontent and such evidence on the state of public opinion do not provide the full picture. After all, it is not unknown for governments to defy public opinion and pressures – at least in the short term – and, even if controls had been contemplated in the secrecy of the inner recesses of the cabinet, successive governments had previously rejected the option of immigration control.[416]

However, there were other pressures at work by 1961–62. By this time what one observer called the postwar 'honeymoon with prosperity' faced an uncertain future.[417] In July 1961 the Conservative government had introduced a crisis package. These measures, which included a raising of the bank rate, a check on government expenditure, a credit squeeze and a pay pause, formed the immediate economic background to the Act. By the early 1960s, it was being emphasised that in the future unskilled labour could become an economic and social liability and a catalyst for tension in British society. There was now a need for the movement of labour to be tightly controlled.[418] However, it has been observed that in 1961–62 the threat of controls drew in larger numbers, particularly from the Caribbean, and this influx was assisted by developments elsewhere as controls over emigration which existed in the Caribbean and the Indian sub-continent were relaxed or became ineffective.[419] This exaggerated short-term leap in immigration added further fuel to the flames.[420] In these circumstances there was an additional pressure to act and the government's resolve to do so was doubtless strengthened by its awareness that any action would be politically popular, particularly in those parts of the country where 'considerable social strains' had already resulted from the immigration.[421]

In short, immediate economic, social and political influences need to be considered in any account of why the 1962 Act was introduced. But there was also a pre-existing history of hostility towards Blacks and those from the Indian sub-continent which can hardly be ignored.[422] In particular, a sense of White supremacy nourished over many years as one element in a complex Imperial tradition was still evident after 1945. It was sometimes, but not often, expressed in an overt fashion; it was seldom that it assumed the character of scientific racism; it was more often than not, possessed of a more inchoate character. Nevertheless, a strand of racial opposition was evident at both popular and elite levels of British society by 1962 and it was to increase in the course of the 1960s. In a strident form in the responses of the National Front, in more veiled shape among Powellites, as well as in the successive measures of government immigration control, a sense of racial division was placed at the centre of the debate over immigration from the Caribbean and the Indian sub-continent which spilled over in a variety of ways, into the daily lives of West Indians, Indians and Pakistanis, and their children, some of whom had been born in Britain. This racial antipathy and the persistence of a well-established more general anti-immigration tradition, help to place an important wider rim around the responses in postwar British society in the period leading up the the 1962 Act and beyond.[423] Moreover, another layer of public opinion assumed an importance. By the 1960s Britain was beating a retreat from its Empire. By this time there was an increasing emphasis on a possible British future in Europe; indeed, when the 1962 Act was passed, negotiations were in train for Britain to join the European Economic Community. In this context a sense of obligation by Britain, the centre of the Commonwealth, towards those Commonwealth citizens who wished to come to Britain, evident in the 1948 British Nationality Act, was in the process of being replaced – not without opposition – by a vision of Britain as an integral part of Europe. In these circumstances those Commonwealth citizens who were not White were particularly exposed.[424]

With the 1962 Act on the Statute Book, a mould was broken. It is true that immigration into Britain from Cyprus, a crown colony, had been subjected previously to entry controls.[425] However, nothing on the scale of the 1962 Act had been enacted. Nevertheless, the new legislative toughness, which limited primary immigration, did not mark the end of the campaign for controls. On the contrary, such pressures continued and, in fact, were assisted by the introduction of legislation on immigration control which in fact encouraged restrictionist sentiment.[426] Furthermore, one consequence of the 1962 Act added to such pressures. In place of individual workers, whose entry into Britain had been closely related to trade cycle fluctuations, and regarded in many cases as a temporary stage in their lives, the threat and ultimate imposition of entry controls gradually encouraged the settlement of families. In turn this development implied permanence of settlement and the re-creation of original cultures in Britain. These new tendencies helped to galvanise the anti-immigration campaign, particularly against groups from the Indian sub-continent.[427]

Between 1962 and 1964 there were a number of other significant developments. The Southall Residents' Association, formed in 1963, raised as an issue the impact on the educational system of children from the Indian sub-continent, but it soon extended its campaign beyond this base.[428] The Southall press reflected and added to these local fears.[429] In Birmingham the English Rights Association was active by this time.[430] Furthermore, acts of 'Paki-bashing' came increasingly into the news by the 1960s.[431] But perhaps the most graphic illustration of hostility in the early and mid-1960s came in Smethwick. In the period leading up to the 1964 General Election, at a time when pressure from the Midlands assumed considerable importance in the agitation for immigration control, the Conservative candidate, Peter Griffiths, articulating fears relating to employment and housing at a time when the area was in recession and experiencing pressure on its housing stock, and also drawing from the well of other local problems, ran a strong anti-immigrant campaign in the columns of the *Smethwick Telephone*. In the general election Griffiths won a victory over Patrick Gordon Walker, who had been one of Labour's spokesmen against the 1962 Act, after a campaign in which some Conservative supporters exploited the slogan, 'If you want a nigger neighbour, vote Labour'.[432] This political victory through which 'the issue of immigration completed the journey from the periphery to the centre of the political debate', exercised a reverberating political impact.[433]

Between 1964 and 1969 similar pressures can be detected. In 1964–65 a British version of the Ku Klux Klan made a brief, fiery, reappearance, which followed a spluttering earlier manifestation in 1956.[434] More significantly, the English Rights Association continued its activities and linked up with the Southall Residents' Association and other groups.[435] Moreover, in 1965 the Racial Preservation Society, a group concerned with the maintenance of racial purity, was established.[436] Then, in the late 1960s, two significant developments occurred. Racial-nationalist groups had long exploited the issue of immigration from the Caribbean and the Indian sub-continent. But groups such as the White Defence League attracted few members and other small organisations such as the British National Party, the National Socialist Movement and the Greater Britain Movement, had been prone to in-fighting and fractionalisation.[437] However, on 7 February 1967 an attempt was made to weave together various strands of racial-nationalist sentiment in the shape of the National Front (NF), which soon put immigration control to the centre of its programme.[438] This commitment was revealed in Clause 8 of the programme with its emphasis on the need to preserve 'our British native stock' by 'terminating non-white immigration'.[439] In pursuit of its aims the NF operated at a number of levels. Its ideology was paraded in publications such as *Spearhead*. The movement also organised itself to fight local and parliamentary elections. But some members were also prepared to engage in street politics.[440]

The other important development involved the emergence of Powellism. Shortly after the emergence of the NF, Enoch Powell, the Tory member for Wolverhampton, further raised the temperature of the public debate over immigration.[441] Powell shot to prominence with a series of speeches beginning in Walsall on 9 February 1968, at a time when the arrival of the Kenyan Asian refugees was becoming a focus of public attention. In his Walsall speech Powell emphasised the dangers which, in his view, would result from the 'continuing influx of immigrants'. In the course of this pronouncement, he warned of the dangers of communalism resulting from the presence of communities insistent on preserving their own cultures.[442] In a speech in Birmingham in the following April Powell returned to the issue of population size, thereby continuing what was to become a persistent stress on the importance of numbers. At a time when primary immigration had already been strictly controlled Powell's emphasis turned to dependants and birth rates, and he was to project a future in which 'whole areas, towns and parts of towns across England' would be 'occupied by different sections of the immigrant and immigrant-descended population'.[443] The dangers of communalism were also reiterated, with the Sikhs singled out in this connection. Furthermore, in dramatic fashion, Powell warned in Birmingham of the possibility of racial conflict resulting in bloodshed. Like the Roman he saw 'the River Tiber foaming with much blood'.[444] In conveying such sentiments Powell transcended the previous tenor of the public debate within the major parties.[445] It was a message that carried a political challenge and led to his dismissal from the shadow cabinet.[446] Nevertheless, Powell received widespread support which cut across class and party lines.[447] 'There's a bit of Powellism in every Englishman', one prominent politician remarked.[448] A crucial element in Powell's philosophy was his perception of the ideal nation as a homogeneous whole. Those who came from 'beyond the oceans'[449] were perceived as essentially alien, with a different national character. As a result, they could not be absorbed into the nation where they were 'encamped';[450] indeed, they were a challenge to its existence. It was partly through this political counterpoint that

Powell was engaged in the process of defining national character in an age when Britain no longer in reality possessed 'a special mission to preserve peace, law and stability in the world'.[451]

However, a concentration upon the NF and Powellism alone in the late 1960s would miss other evidence of hostility. In 1966 it was noticed that a colour bar was in operation among workers at both Paddington and St Pancras stations, which suggested that tensions relating to employment in the public sector still remained.[452] It was reported in the same year that discrimination was practised by certain army regiments.[453] Indeed, two major reports issued in the course of 1966–67 drew attention to the practice of widespread discrimination in British society which affected West Indians, Indians and Pakistanis in their search for employment, housing and services, and helped to shape the contours of their lives in these key areas of activity.[454] Moreover, by the late 1960s there was evidence of increasing physical violence directed particularly against people from the Indian sub-continent.[455] In short, by this time racial discrimination and violence had a wide currency.

Against this domestic background, as well as an international situation in which 'disillusionment with the Commonwealth had reached an apogee', and racial conflict in America regularly cast its summer shadows over Britain, entry controls were progressively strengthened.[456] In August 1965 the Labour government's White Paper, through its more stringent, selective emphasis on the restriction of entry to skilled workers or those who could be guaranteed employment, tightened the provisions of entry laid down in 1962.[457] A major influence over this capitulation by Labour after its election victory in 1964 related to the result in Smethwick. The Labour prime minister, Harold Wilson, dubbed the victor of Smethwick 'a parliamentary leper' but the significance of that election was not lost upon the government.[458] In a revealing entry Richard Crossman recorded in his diary, 'Ever since the Smethwick election it has been quite clear that immigration can be the greatest political vote loser for the Labour Party if one seems to be permitting a flood of immigrants to come in and blight the central area of our cities'.[459] The White Paper was a clear concession to such fears. A few years after this capitulation, with control over primary immigration tighter than ever before, entry requirements were further tightened under the influence of the hostility which greeted the arrival of the Kenyan Asians. As Citizens of the UK and the Colonies this group possessed a legal right to enter the country which had not been restricted by the 1962 Act. However, the 1968 Commonwealth Immigrants Act restricted automatic entry in the future to those Citizens of the UK and the Colonies who had patrial ties with the United Kingdom.[460] 'Patrial' was essentially a euphemism for a White Commonwealth citizen.[461] Through this measure and the 1965 White Paper the Labour Party had travelled a fair distance at a quick pace since its principled opposition to the 1962 Commonwealth Immigrants Act.

A few years later, following a Conservative victory in the 1970 General Election, in which Powellism exerted a significant influence,[462] and at a time when Britain was 'happily proposing to end immigration restrictions on all citizens of Common Market countries once Britain's application [to join the European Community] was successful',[463] an Immigration Act, passed in 1971 and operative from 1 January 1973, carried the 1968 legislation to its logical conclusion. Commonwealth citizens with patrial status were allowed unrestricted entry into the United Kingdom. However, entry for those citizens from the Commonwealth who did not have the patrial connection was dependent on the issue of a work permit. A permit did not confer residence rights, and all permits were subject to the possibility of non-renewal. Through this particular piece of legislation Britain placed itself in a position whereby those Commonwealth citizens without patrial links who sought and obtained employment in Britain, were reduced effectively to the status of contract labour. This act marked the culmination of a series of steps taken by successive governments between 1962 and 1971 which exercised a profound impact over the course of immigration from the Caribbean and the Indian sub-continent, as well as other parts of the New Commonwealth.[464] By the early 1970s the continued mobilisation of White hostility particularly by the National Front, at a more respectable level by Powellism, and at a local level by organisations such as the Yorkshire Campaign to Stop Immigration, which was formed in Bradford in June 1970, had reaped a significant harvest as politicians at Westminster, bending with the wind and simultaneously increasing its draught, capitulated to the pressures for control over entry.[465] Those groups affected by such legislation viewed developments differently. The seeds of official policy were to come to fruition in the 1970s and 1980s and it was a bitter harvest.[466]

At the same time as controls over entry were introduced, greater official attention was paid to the persistence of racial disadvantage in Britain. Before the 1960s successive governments had shown little or no interest in this issue. Civil servants were well aware from an early date that employment and housing stood out as sensitive issues which could result in conflict.[467] Indeed, it has been emphasised that a shortage of housing was a major influence in bringing to an end the recruitment of EVWs.[468] However, attempts to introduce anti-discrimination legislation, to protect particularly those groups from the Caribbean and the sub-continent, were cast aside.[469] The official view, mirrored in some liberal circles, was that nothing could be achieved through the processes of law to assist in this situation.[470] Moreover, successive governments distanced themselves from the economic and social consequences resulting from the immigration; these problems were regarded as the province of local authorities and voluntary bodies.[471] However, by the mid-1960s there was a degree of shift in the official outlook, towards an emphasis on the need for 'good race relations'. This new approach was captured in Roy Hattersley's syllogism in 1965 that 'Without integration limitation is inexcusable: without limitation integration is impossible'.[472] This comment also mirrored a shift away from assimilation as the goal of official policy to the virtues of integration which in a speech on 23 May 1966 by Roy Jenkins, then Home Secretary, was defined as 'Not a flattening process of assimilation but as equal opportunity accompanied by cultural diversity, in an atmosphere of mutual tolerance'.[473] In this context, the 1965 Race Relations Act and the 1968 Race Relations Act were important historical steps. For the first time in British history the government intervened through legislation to prevent racial discrimination by establishing the Race Relations Board in the 1965 Act, and by creating the Community Relations Commission in the 1968 Act, it attempted to promote the cause of racial harmony.[474] It has been remarked that such bodies attracted individual representatives from the West Indian, Indian and Pakistani minorities. However, radicals from such groups, whose activities it has also been observed increased significantly in the 1960s, regarded the agencies as sops which soaked up talent and neutralised it in a bye-way off the main political avenue.[475] At the same time, there was some unease among the White population that such legislation constituted an attack on their basic liberties.[476] Two additional observations might be made. The reputation of this aspect of government policy was adversely affected by the lack of fervour and commitment which characterised it; immigration control, with its adverse implications for the image of West Indians, Indians and Pakistanis, continued to be vested with greater significance.[477] Secondly, whatever good intentions it reflected, the new race relations structure represented a narrowly-focused approach to the problems which the West Indian, Indian and Pakistani minorities were facing: important economic and social cores which had nourished hostility since 1945 remained untouched. For example, nothing in the legislation and its surrounding apparatus guaranteed full employment and an adequate supply of housing, two key areas which affected the reception of all groups that came to Britain.[478]

This flurry of race relations legislation in 1965 and 1968 could not disguise the fact that by 1971 immigration from the Commonwealth of those who did not possess patrial status had become tightly controlled by successive governments. Furthermore, by 1971 evidence had accumulated to reveal that the lives of certain groups who had managed to enter Britain were seriously affected by official harassment. From the 1950s, for example, there was a steady increase in the litany of complaints by Blacks against the police. By 1970–71 the Police Task Force in Liverpool had secured a local reputation for its brutality.[479] There was vociferous resentment in Cardiff in 1970.[480] In London, too, Special Branch surveillance of the developing Black Power activity, which was reflected in repeated raids on the Mangrove Restaurant, culminating in the trial of the 'Mangrove Nine' in 1971, generated resentment.[481] Added to the tightening of official control over immigration such activity gave rise to a belief in institutional oppression.[482]

Even so, in some quarters such developments did not go far enough. The threat of repatriation, which brought back memories of the Elizabethan statute of 1569, the Sierra Leone scheme of 1786 and deportations after the racial violence of 1919 had started to gather momentum once again in the 1960s and by 1971 repatriation was being openly advocated by the National Front as well as by Enoch Powell and his supporters.[483] After all, if the groups from the Caribbean and the Indian sub-continent were perceived as alien, culturally incompatible and a threat to the British nation, and such views gathered momentum in the 1960s, particularly through the conduits of the National Front and Powellism, it was not difficult to perceive of an ultimate solution through a process of repatriation.[484]

It is important to recall, however, that throughout the course of the debate over immigration from the Caribbean and the Indian sub-continent, liberal traditions never totally died. The National Council for Civil Liberties continued as in earlier years, to fight cases of racial injustice.[485] In addition, the Institute of Race Relations from the time of its separate foundation in 1958[486] built on the work of early pioneer investigators, many of whom were associated with the 'Edinburgh School', and tried to promote a liberal outlook on all issues relating to race.[487] Furthermore, in the course of the initial debate over the 1962 Commonwealth Immigrants Act lofty sentiments were expressed from the Labour benches. Hugh Gaitskell's speech was regarded as one of his finest.[488] On the Tory benches Nigel Fisher, a spokesman for the ideal of a multi-racial Commonwealth, also excelled, chiding for their inconsistency those who criticised apartheid and yet were prepared to contemplate entry controls in Britain.[489] At a local level individuals from varying backgrounds came together in 1963 to form the Lambeth Inter-Racial Council.[490] In fact, a phalanx of diverse supporters in organisations such as CARD danced to the civil rights tune in the 1960s only to be overwhelmed by a combination of opposing forces.[491] The steps which led to the progressive tightening of control over entry in the 1960s also encountered strong condemnation in certain quarters. For example, at the time of the 1965 White Paper *The Economist* accused the Labour Party of 'pinching the Tories' white trousers'[492] and *The Guardian* referred to Labour's 'indefensible White Paper'.[493] In Liberal circles the 1968 Act was described as 'a concession to racialism'[494] and one critic of the 1971 Act, with his South African experience behind him, referred to the proposal as 'an ultimately racialist measure'.[495]

The persistence of such activity and sentiments, which reflected a variety of political motivations, various ideologies, tinged in some cases with political expediency, and sometimes characterised by their own traits of ambiguity, cannot be overlooked in a rounded picture of the responses to immigration from the Caribbean and the Indian sub-continent.[496]

5.

IN considering immigration into Britain between 1945 and 1971 it is important to recognise the range of groups that arrived during these years. As a result of the overwhelming concentration upon immigration from the Caribbean and the Indian sub-continent, this characteristic has often gone unrecognised. Moreover, it is necessary to bear in mind that at the time of the 1971 Census it was the Irish who constituted the largest single immigrant minority.

Nevertheless, the postwar period was of crucial significance in the history of immigration from the Caribbean and the Indian sub-continent. It was also these postwar years which witnessed the wider occupational and spatial dispersal of groups from these territories. There was also greater evidence of their cultural influence, which was particularly evident in the case of groups from the Indian sub-continent. Existing cultures did not collapse once these people came to Britain. Indeed, there was strong evidence of cultural resilience among other groups such as those from Eastern Europe, Italy, Ireland and Hong Kong. However, between 1945 and 1971 there was also evidence of change, a degree of re-orientation in the pattern of life-styles, which reflected the changing circumstances that impinged upon immigrants and refugees.

Once immigrant and refugee groups arrived in Britain they entered into a complex set of relationships with sections of British society. Such relationships influenced but did not completely determine the lives of the immigrants and refugees. As in earlier years the experiences of postwar immigrants and refugees in the employment and housing markets were two key areas where such relationships assumed an importance. Moreover, the introduction of controls over immigration from the Commonwealth beginning in 1962 exercised a major impact over the lives of West Indians and the various groups from the Indian sub-continent. Taken in conjunction with the official controls exercised at an earlier date over the lives of the Poles and the European Volunteer Workers, such developments served to underline the importance of official responses in influencing the postwar history of immigrants and refugees in Britain.

Even so, the postwar immigrant and refugee groups, along with those earlier newcomers still in the process of working out a series of relationships in Britain, were bound to encounter celebratory accounts which dilated on a tradition of national toleration in Britain. Viewed from the perspective of many such immigrants and refugees, however, postwar Britain did not offer an all-embracing security. Sophisticated, historically-based theories of British superiority over Europeans and an historically-derived, scientific-based racism which postulated a belief in inherent White supremacy, were thin on the ground after 1945. However, less precise antipathies were in constant circulation in Britain and at times combined with perceptions of immediate threats from immigrants or refugees to generate public opposition towards such groups which could be exploited for political advantage. Even so, it is worth reiterating that down to 1971 British society was not characterised by an unremitting hostility, whether at the level of ideas or action. Society as a whole displayed mixed reactions towards the Poles, the EVWs, the Irish, the Blacks and immigrants from the Indian sub-continent, to mention a sample only of the larger groups whose history has been recovered. Furthermore, attitudes and behaviour could vary between situations; for example, toleration of a Black in one role did not guarantee it in others.[497] Moreover, responses could shift over the course of time according to changing circumstances.[498] A recognition of such nuances, and of the fine dividing line between toleration and intolerance endowed the responses from British society with a complexity which usually goes unrecognised.[499] However, those familiar with the responses revealed towards earlier immigrants and refugees, in other words people who possess an historical appreciation of the experiences of such groups in Britain, would hardly be surprised. In essential respects the complexities of the postwar world were an echo of the responses which had surfaced towards immigrants and refugees between 1871 and 1945.

PART FOUR

PART FOUR

Conclusion

'Those who are shut in within one society, one nation, or one religion, tend to imagine that their way of life and their way of thought have absolute and unchangeable validity and that all that contradicts their standards is somehow "unnatural", inferior or evil. Those, on the other hand, who live on the borderlines of various civilizations comprehend more clearly the great movement and the great contradictoriness of nature and society', I. Deutscher, *The Non-Jewish Jew and Other Essays* (London, 1968), p. 35.

'After the Revolution of 1848 M. Blanc who was a refugee from France and who was connected with the '48 Revolution sat in Hyde Park one day, so the story goes, and saw the fine equipages driving up and down the Row and next to him was a down-and-out tramp, eating chipped potatoes. M. Blanc said to him "Look at ze equipages and ze fine horses and ze fat coachmen driving ze fat women! Does it not make your blood boil?". The tramp turned round and said, "You're a foreigner ain't you? You don't see horses like them in Paris".', Colonel J. Wedgwood, in *Parliamentary Debates* (Commons), Vol. 120 (1919), 22 October 1919, col. 153.

1.

A conclusion offers the prospect of ploughing again the three major furrows that have already been explored in considering immigration between 1871 and 1971 but laying them open more neatly to the public view and revealing other parts of the essential terrain. So where might one begin? First of all, in considering the process of immigration and its causes, it might be reiterated that in this respect Britain is a country with its own distinctive history. It might be convenient, an apt political rationalisation of a policy decision, to proclaim that Britain is not 'an immigration country'.[1] However, it is a remark that has no historical substance. Immigrants, refugees and sojourners have been continually present.[2] Hence, the reference made by one observer to the 'ethnically composite' character of the British.[3]

Nevertheless, a degree of perspective is required. During the century between 1871 and 1971 Britain did not experience immigration to the same relative or absolute degree as America. But in comparing the experience of Britain with that of America, the comparison is with the largest immigration reservoir in the world.[4] Apart from this international perspective, the trends in the arrival and departure of population to and from Britain need to be considered. Between 1871 and 1971 there was a tendency for emigration to exceed immigration.[5] However, this fact, even if it were recognised, did not make any impression on many of those opposed to immigration. In such quarters there was an emphasis on a perceived propensity to import the rubbish or refuse of other lands. These dregs were regarded as a bad exchange for those sturdy and enterprising souls who left to start their lives anew in distant lands.[6]

An examination of the movement of population out of Britain would reveal that in the late nineteenth century, and down to the early 1930s, emigration took place in relatively large numbers to countries such as Australia, Canada and New Zealand. America also attracted emigrants from Britain as well as from many other nations to whom it was also a golden land or a golden mountain.[7] By contrast, the new Empire, acquired in the late nineteenth century, when the map became painted red, excercised a very limited appeal to emigrants from Britain. These tropical areas, which made up one third of the British Empire, required the presence of administrators such as Messrs Maxwell and Westfield in George Orwell's *Burmese Days*, backed up, if necessary, by a military presence but few other Whites ventured to such lonely outposts.[8]

In the course of the 1930s this trend in the export of population was reversed. The world crisis and depression which fractured the economies of the capitalist world after 1929 and continued to exert its influence in the form of heavy unemployment in the 1930s, made emigration a less attractive prospect. This disinclination to engage in voluntary emigration, together with a certain amount of returnee movement and the arrival of refugees who were escaping from the consequences of National Socialism and Fascism, helped to reverse the previous trend in population movement. When the recruitment of refugees after the war to assist in the rebuilding of industry was added to these earlier developments, a process of net immigration into Britain was evident between 1931 and 1951.[9]

In the majority of years between 1945 and 1971, however, a net outflow of population occurred. But there were important periods of exception to this. In the late 1950s and early 1960s, for example, when fears developed that controls were about to be placed for the first time on Commonwealth immigration, the upsurge in immigration 'to beat the Act' resulted in relatively large net inward balances between 1958 and 1962.[10] Nevertheless, by the mid-1960s, once this rush was out of the way, the net outward flow of population recommenced at a time when primary immigration was increasingly limited by legislation between 1962 and 1971.[11]

During most of the years between 1871 and 1971 the movement of population into Britain was composed mainly of Europeans. Within this context one major change occurred in the late nineteenth century. The Irish remained the largest minority but by the 1890s the German dominance of the continental European groups was lost, as a result of the gathering arrival of newcomers from the Russian Empire.[12] In the course of the twentieth century another significant change took place. From the end of the Second World War and particularly since the 1950s immigration 'widened dramatically to beyond the oceans'[13] as workers and dependants from the West Indies, India and Pakistan all of whom in some sources have been labelled quite incongruously as 'Blacks', arrived in larger numbers than ever before. Even so, down to 1971 the Irish remained the largest single immigrant group in Britain.[14]

Such details can be painted with a broad brush but it must be recognised that official statistics hardly allow for a continuous, precise measurement of immigration. For example, it is difficult to ascertain the annual increment of Russian Polish immigrants owing to the deficiencies in official statistics. An act of 1836 required the master of every ship arriving in England from abroad to submit a list of the aliens he was carrying. In the 1850s and 1860s, however, this legislation had fallen into almost total disuse outside the port of London and the deficiency remained unremedied throughout the years of immigration from the Russian Empire. There was an attempt to revive the 1836 act in May 1890, but no adequate mechanism was present in the 1890 act for distinguishing between immigrants who were 'en route' to places outside the United Kingdom and those who intended to take up residence. Moreover, the 1905 Aliens Act did nothing to remedy this deficiency. Furthermore, since Jews were not classified as Jews in any of the immigration returns the annual increment of Jewish immigration remained shrouded in a degree of obscurity. Census returns, however, whatever their deficiencies in terms of underenumeration, vagueness of categorisation and inability to measure interdecennial fluctuations, indicated a rising number of Russian Polish aliens from the 1880s, most of whom were Jewish, whose presence became a matter for vigorous public debate.[15]

It was remarked a few years ago that capitalism was necessarily concerned with measurement.[16] But the fact that serious deficiencies remained in immigration statistics was underlined during the immigration from the New Commonwealth and Pakistan.[17] Indeed, the inadequacy of such data attracted strong condemnation.[18] In spite of these difficulties, however, it can be ascertained that the 1950s and 1960s were crucial years in the history of immigration from the Caribbean and the Indian sub-continent. The 1950s and the early 1960s marked the key period for immigration from the Caribbean; that from the Indian sub-continent was essentially a feature of the 1960s, as primary immigrants who arrived before the imposition of controls were joined by their dependants.[19]

What were the influences that resulted in the movement of population into Britain between 1871 and 1971? Attempts to explain why migration takes place have been of continuing interest since Ravenstein's investigations into the subject in 1885 and 1889.[20] But, a century onwards from Ravenstein's day, there are many different emphases and little agreement in this specialist area of analysis.[21] However, few would wish to argue now that the motivation for movement was ever monocausal or homogeneous. On the contrary, it is widely recognised that a range of influences need to be taken into account in any ideal analysis. These include an examination of conditions in the country of origin, and in the place of destination, as well as the mechanism by which movement can be achieved. A consideration of such influences involves an examination of what has been described as the objective level of migration. But normative influences, in other words the way in which communities perceive and evaluate migration as an alternative course of action, are also regarded as important. So are psycho-social influences; in other words, individual motivation also needs to be considered.[22]

None of these influences operates in isolation but in a process of interaction. In an ideal world, with plentiful sources and access to all information, a start could be made from this base on the reasons why individuals, amounting in some instances to a substantial proportion of their respective communities, decided to leave their roots, a society which was known to them, and start new lives elsewhere. In practice, it is less than easy, dealing with the long historical dimension, to clarify behaviour in such neat and precise fashion. Indeed, even recent events can prove troublesome. Did the postwar Caribbean workers come to Britain primarily as a result of being pushed by conditions in the British West Indies? Or were they primarily pulled to Britain by the labour needs of British capital? There have been serious disagreements on this score.[23]

Whatever difficulties exist in unearthing the historical reasons for movement, in some cases it is crucial that the historical relationship between Britain and various other countries should be taken into account. The immigration from Ireland in the late nineteenth, early twentieth centuries, cannot be fully understood without a consideration of the British domination and exploitation of Ireland. Against a background of such basic pressures a tradition of emigration developed, which in turn further assisted the process of movement.[24] The arrival of other groups, from the Caribbean and the Indian sub-continent after the Second World War, as well as from Malta and Cyprus, for example, was also related to the nature of the historical relationship which had grown up between Britain and these countries.[25] In all such cases the movement of labour reflected the uneven development of world capital.[26]

Immigration over the hundred years ending in 1971 was also influenced by another international development in the shape of the improved network of communications which was a feature of the more complex industrial and commercial society that emerged during these years. The extension of the European railway network, the replacing of sail by steam, and the later advent of air travel, were all factors which assisted the movement of population. These changes, together with other improvements in communication, also helped in the dissemination of knowledge of other societies.[27] Even so, the decision to leave one's roots required at all times a certain 'staunchness of soul', the taking of 'a big decision'.[28] Once the pioneers had moved, it was often easier for others to follow, and a number of immigrations into Britain, for example from Ireland,

Russian Poland and Italy in the late nineteenth, early twentieth centuries and from Hong Kong and the Indian sub-continent at a later date, all showed the characteristics of a chain migration in which the pioneers were joined by family, friends, relatives, neighbours, fellow villagers or townspeople.[29]

A consideration of immigrants intending to start a new life in Britain, or sojourners intent on a shorter stay – the Irish and the so-called New Commonwealth immigrants were groups that had large numbers with initial sojourning intentions – would reveal only part of the picture of arrivals in Britain between 1871 and 1971.[30] In spite of an increasingly restrictionist framework of entry controls, there was a continual succession of refugees who sought safety in Britain from religious, political or racial persecution, or a combination of these pressures. The Communards from Paris, who slipped across Burke's 'slender dyke'[31] and stayed in 'pudique Albion'[32] until they were amnestied, émigrés from Russian Poland, the stricken Belgian refugees of the First World War, the refugees from Nazism, the postwar Polish exiles, and the uprooted European Volunteer Workers, as well as the Kenyan Asians, who began to arrive in the late 1960s, were among the most prominent of such groups.[33] And, as if to emphasise the seamless garment worn by Clio, they were followed after 1971 by refugees from authoritarian regimes in Iran and Chile, by Asians from Uganda and Malawi, who were fleeing from policies of Africanisation, and, more recently still, by the so-called 'boat people' from Vietnam.[34]

Some of these groups were 'acute' refugees who left their roots suddenly and in desperation; others were 'anticipatory' refugees who were able to reflect on their situation and take a more measured judgement about their departures.[35] Some of the refugees already possessed a reasonable knowledge of Britain before they arrived on its shores. Moreover, some groups, Jewish and Polish exiles, for example, could be nourished, if not always wholeheartedly, by existing communities in Britain.[36] But others had little idea of the country to which they came. Some of the Russian Jews fleeing from tsarist persecution had wanted to emigrate to America and had little knowledge of Leeds or the East End of London into which they were dumped by unscrupulous agents.[37] Similarly, listening to the tapes of some of those displaced persons who came as European Volunteer Workers after the Second World War, one is struck by the remoteness of their experience from the tremors felt in British society and their own lack of awareness of what to expect.[38] Such difficulties no doubt helped to explain some of the re-emigration that occurred.[39] However, a refugee such as the anarchist, Peter Kropotkin, welcomed the chance of living in what he knew was a more politically liberal society than any to which he had been accustomed.[40] But, even those refugees who had some knowledge of Britain and its carefully cultivated image of a society characterised by 'fair play, justice and liberty',[41] an image which some immigrants and refugees were to modify on the basis of bitter experience, could be confused by its social conventions and the subtle mechanics of conversation and behaviour.[42]

2.

IN considering the economic and social history of immigrants and refugees in Britain between 1871 and 1971, work was the most fundamental if not the most important relationship into which the newcomers entered on arrival in their new environment and the employment patterns which became evident during these years revealed a number of important characteristics. In spite of a degree of occupational variation, there was strong evidence among many immigrant groups of a clustering at particular times in certain occupations. This characteristic was evident, for example, in the case of the Irish, the Russian Poles and also the small Black groups that could be found in Britain in the early twentieth century, as well as among the workers who arrived in increasing numbers from the Caribbean and the Indian sub-continent after the Second World War. A similar concentration was discernible in the case of refugee groups; the Belgians during the First World War and the later EVWs both displayed this characteristic.[43]

It is apparent, though, that if there was a high degree of concentration, newcomers became spread over a wide slab of British industry between 1871 and 1971. Moreover, there was evidence of a marked involvement in different types of work at different times. The majority of Chinese, for example, found employment initially as seamen in the shipping industry, but moved increasingly towards laundry work, and then, particularly after 1945, joined other groups such as Italians, Cypriots, as well as Indians and Pakistanis, in the restaurant niche of the service sector.[44]

The attention devoted to recent immigration from the Caribbean and the Indian sub-continent has resulted in a strong focus upon working-class immigrants, and rightly so since in the immediate aftermath of the Second World War the demand in the market was for wage-labour. But over the hundred years between 1871 and 1971 some immigrants and refugees were able to follow professional careers. Moreover, there were also those who pursued careers in business. Marks and Spencer, as well as Montague Burton, grew out of the entrepreneurial initiative of immigrants from Russian Poland. The later business involvement of refugees from Hitlerite Europe also attracted attention. But the activities of Italian, Chinese, Indian and Pakistani businessmen, for example, revealed that Jews had no monopoly of business activity. There were, by contrast, some groups that had no salience as entrepreneurs, whether in business or in property, a sector where some other immigrant fortunes were made.[45]

In some cases those who came to Britain were able to pursue work with which they were already familiar or with which they were traditionally associated in their country of origin. A number of the refugees from Austria and Germany, for example, were able to continue with their professional careers, even if this was at times achieved only with difficulty. In addition, some Pakistani traders and Kenyan Asian business people were able to pursue similar activity in Britain.[46] But in other cases employment patterns changed through the process of immigration. This change was evident in the case of the Irish, many of whom were baptised into an industrial society as a result of their immigration.[47] There were Irish, too, who secured employment for the first time in many years when they came to Britain during the Second World War.[48] Some Jewish immigrants from Russian Poland went into tailoring and hawking despite having been in different occupations in eastern Europe.[49] Many of the Cypriots who became involved in restaurant work after the Second World War had no prior experience of such work.[50] A significant transformation was also experienced by certain women immigrants – generally hidden in immigration history, as elsewhere – some of whom entered the employment market for the first time.[51]

In considering the question of employment it would be unwise to assume that newcomers were always able to operate without restraint in the labour market. Their occupational structures were often influenced by external pressures from other sections of British society. For example, the government, in consultation with both sides of industry, laid down strict conditions relating to the employment of

European Volunteer Workers.[52] In other cases, throughout the years between 1871 and 1971 unofficial discrimination was at work in the labour market and the workplace. Evidence relating to the post-Second World War workers from the Caribbean and the Indian sub-continent, for example, revealed that persistent discrimination was influential in determining the kind of work which was undertaken. This differential treatment helps to explain why many were employed below their level of skills and qualifications.[53] In the case of some groups, Jews and Pakistanis come to mind, it was the threat and practice of discrimination which assisted a concentration on self-employment.[54]

Whatever the moulding forces over employment patterns, is it possible to provide any indication of the economic effects of immigration? How, if at all, did the immigrants and refugees influence British economic life? In the literature of immigration a persistent emphasis has been placed on the role played by immigrant entrepreneurs.[55] And who could gainsay the success of some individuals? But such emphases have reflected other influences. A concentration on this variant of 'the great man theory of history' flattered the national ego by encouraging the view that during the hundred years ending in 1971 Britain was an open and tolerant society. Furthermore, an emphasis on prominent individuals from within their ranks no doubt provided a psychic uplift to some immigrant and refugee groups.[56] Successful individuals were enabled to bask in such publicity which was often a version of the rags to riches story.[57] But the advertisement of individual or group success exercised a double-edged impact. Sometimes it led to the view that any lack of success was the sole responsibility of the immigrants or refugees.[58] In addition, a concentration on entrepreneurial success provided an unduly restricted and historically inaccurate picture of the economic life of immigrants and refugees in Britain. This kind of emphasis passed too quickly over business failure. Furthermore, it ignored the large persistent working-class component among many prominent groups of newcomers.[59]

But this comment leaves unanswered the question concerning the economic influence of immigration on Britain. For example, did the Irish by filling gaps in the labour market assist the process of economic growth? Opinion has been divided on this question.[60] Did the Jews from Russian Poland exercise any significant influence over the growth of the British economy? The 1903 Royal Commission on

Alien Immigration was interested in this issue but reached no firm conclusions.[61] A more recent examination of the influence of this group was also prudently cautious.[62] Finally, discussions concerning the economic effects of the more recent immigration from the Caribbean and the Indian sub-continent have been more remarkable for illustrating the proverbial disagreement among economists than for reaching widely-accepted conclusions. Questions such as: How did the newcomers affect, if at all, the process of economic growth? What influence, if any, did they exert over the course of inflation? How did their remittances of funds overseas affect the balance of payments? were asked with increasing frequency by the 1960s. But no clear answers emerged.[63]

If attention is switched at this point from employment patterns to the housing market, there was continuing evidence between 1871 and 1971 of a concentration by immigrants, at least initially, in particular parts of the country and also within certain cities. An Irish population was especially evident in Lancashire in the late nineteenth century, in cities such as Liverpool and Manchester, and it was also noticeable in the Glasgow area and London. In addition, during the interwar years and afterwards there was a significant increase in the number of Irish in the Midlands, particularly in Birmingham. It was in such areas and cities, and particularly in parts of these cities that the Irish were visible between 1871 and 1971.[64]

A similar concentration was present among the immigrants from the Russian Empire. Lithuanians were particularly noticeable in Lanarkshire. Russian Polish Jews were drawn to London, as well as to Leeds and Manchester. Within these cities, this largest contingent from the tsar's empire concentrated in specific areas. In London it was the East End, an old immigrant quarter whose pavements had been trodden by many earlier newcomers, and within this part of the city the favoured spot was Stepney. At the time of the 1901 census 80 per cent of the Russian Poles in London lived in that particular locality. In Leeds the newcomers concentrated in the Leylands area of the city. In Manchester they made their initial home in Redbank. A similar characteristic towards concentration was evident among other groups in the late nineteenth, early twentieth centuries. The Chinese were to be found particularly in Liverpool and also in London in Limehouse. Among other groups in the capital, many of the French congregated around Leicester Square; there was a concentration of Italians in Holborn; refugees of many nationalities found a new base in Soho.[65]

In the years after the Second World War Bradford was regarded as a 'good' town by many of the Poles and European Volunteer Workers whose lives were disrupted by the war. Furthermore, the majority of those who arrived from the Caribbean and the Indian sub-continent soon became concentrated in the large conurbations which were losing population. This development significantly altered the spatial distribution of the Afro-Asian population which before the Second World War was to be found almost exclusively in London, a few university centres and particularly in a number of ports. A degree of change was evident in this pattern of distribution before the major immigration from the Caribbean and the Indian sub-continent, as some seamen moved inland from the ports during the Second World War to work in industry and temporary war workers came to areas such as Lancashire. But it took the immigration of the 1950s and 1960s to effect a major change. As a result, immigrant populations grew up in parts of London such as Brixton and across Britain in centres such as Bristol, in the Handsworth and Balsall Heath areas of Birmingham, the Moss Side area of Manchester, the Manningham district of Bradford and the Gorbals area of Glasgow.[66]

Although these areas of postwar settlement were often loosely referred to as 'ghettos', there was no official compulsion restricting place of residence along the lines which had confronted Jews in Venice, or tsarist Russia, or the Polish general-government. The concentration resulted in fact from a number of interacting pressures. On their arrival the majority of newcomers lacked resources and this afforded them little alternative but to gravitate initially towards inferior properties, in those areas 'inclining to shabbiness', which formed part of the cities where they settled.[67] Furthermore, this concentration developed a self-feeding aspect as most immigrants and refugees preferred to live near to those with whom they shared a common culture and similar experiences. In other words, the pattern of settlement was related partly to internal group pressures and signified a degree of choice. But the hostility that immigrant and refugee groups faced, together with the discrimination they encountered, also assisted the development of this pattern. It was through these interacting circumstances, in which the weight of 'choice' and 'constraint' could vary, that the spatial concentration occurred. Any attempt to explain this trend by referring only to choice or constraint would distort a complex development.[68]

Over the course of time the spatial distribution of some groups underwent a change as movement took place towards so-called 'better' areas. But the case of the post-1945 Polish exiles, cited as one such example, was not necessarily typical in its speed and scale.[69] It was only during and after the First World War that some Russian Polish Jews were able to exchange their homes in the East End for property in north London. Even so, a Jewish population remained behind to face the boots and fists of the British Union of Fascists. The movement of Jews in Manchester from Redbank to Cheetham Hill and in Leeds from the Leylands towards Alwoodley, was also a gradual rather than a dramatic event.[70] The comparatively slow rate of residential improvement involving some West Indians, Indians and Pakistanis, with important changes starting to be especially evident in the 1970s, was not therefore unique.[71] In general, a cosy image of a smooth, rapid improvement in the location and quality of the housing of immigrant and refugee groups needs to be treated with caution. Indeed, it is a sobering thought that some Irish immigrants in the 1950s were living in accommodation in Paddington which was little different in its quality from that occupied by earlier Irish newcomers at the time of Charles Booth's surveys of East End life in the 1880s.[72]

The visible signs of the settlement of immigrants and refugees in Britain still lie waiting for detection by the observant eye. In the rural area of Kirkpatrick Fleming in Scotland there are the graves of British Honduran foresters who confronted the German navy to come to Britain in order to assist in the war effort.[73] In the calm of St Giles Cathedral in Edinburgh deaths of an earlier age are recorded in the cold stone plaque, erected in gratitude by the French community in Edinburgh, which reads: 'HOMAGE AUX SOLDATS ECOSSAIS MORTS EN FRANCE 1914–1918 LA COLONIE FRANÇAISE D'EDIMBOURG'.[74] The Charles Wootten community centre in Liverpool is a continuing reminder of the collective violence of 1919.[75] 'Little Germany' in Bradford is a surviving remnant of the German influence on the city, much lauded by J. B. Priestley, one of the city's sons.[76] General Sikorski's grave in Nottinghamshire is a reminder of Polish exiles of the Second World War,[77] and graves in the Jewish cemetery on the Isle of Man serve as monuments to those who died in the war when they were held in British internment camps.[78] Similar artefacts are scattered across London. Marx's grave in Highgate is well known, a symbol of the fact that Britain was a haven for nineteenth-century political refugees.[79] Less well known is the plaque at 2 Beaumont Crescent, Hammersmith, to Marcus Garvey, another political visionary.[80] Other important episodes in exile are recalled by the plaque at 39 Chepstow Villas, Kensington, which was fixed in 1959 following the arrival of Hungarian refugees in order to commemorate the earlier residence of Louis Kossuth,[81] and that notice attached to the wall at what was 99 Frognall, now the Convent of St Dorothy, which marks the wartime residence in exile of Charles de Gaulle.[82] The Church of St Sophia in Bayswater testifies to the devotion of the nineteenth-century Greek community and the Italian Church in Clerkenwell as well as the Italian Hospital in Bloomsbury, survive as continuing reminders of the Italians in London in the nineteenth century.[83]

But it was in the areas of heavy immigrant settlement that the short-term reminders of immigration were pronounced. The face of Stepney was significantly changed by the arrival of Russian Poles; according to some contemporaries, conscious of the Yiddish posters, the proliferation of Jewish workshops, *steibels* (small home-based synagogues), which catered for the Orthodox, Jewish gaming houses, restaurants such as the Warsaw near Brick Lane, and the so-called Yiddish theatre, the Pavilion, it was as if a piece of eastern Europe had been established in the capital of the British Empire. Evidence of other groups lay elsewhere. Bellshill in Lanarkshire, Pitt Street in Liverpool, Pennyfields in Limehouse and Loudoun Square in Cardiff all underwent transformations as a result of immigration and a range of influences were evident in Soho, in the late nineteenth, early twentieth centuries.[84]

The presence of those groups who arrived at a later date from the Caribbean and the Indian sub-continent was also stamped on their areas of settlement. For example, parts of Southall were transformed by Sikhs into a miniature Punjab. By 1971 a traveller from the north, would dip over the bridge into the heart of the town to be met by saree shops, restaurants, sweet shops and record shops, which created an image of northern India. Some areas of settlement, in fact, underwent a process of continual change. In Spitalfields a Huguenot church which became a synagogue for the ultra-orthodox Machzikei Hadath at the time of the immigration from Russian Poland, was converted later into a mosque (the Jamme Masjid) which, with the increase in the Muslim population in the East End after the Second World War, was 'packed to overflowing at Ramadan as it was yesteryear on Yom Kippur'.[85] Further north, in Bradford, it has been observed that the Manningham area underwent an almost continual cultural transfusion in the years after the Second World War.[86] Still in Yorkshire, the Chapeltown area of Leeds, formerly a place of Jewish settlement, traces of which still remain, not only witnessed the development of a West Indian community after the Second World War – Chapeltown burned in the spring of 1981 along with Brixton and Moss Side at the time of 'Di Great Insohreckshan'[87] – but a physical reminder of other postwar influences stands in the shape of an Anglican church, now converted into a Sikh temple. Finally, the Gorbals district of Glasgow, which provided a base for groups from the Indian sub-continent after the Second World War, had previously witnessed the arrival of Russian Poles from the tsar's empire at the time of the great exodus from Russia.[88]

But there was other evidence of cultural influence between 1871 and 1971, ranging from a presence in the world of entertainment to more serious aspects of British life. As regards the former, there was a well-publicised contribution to sporting life. The presence at the crease of those sovereign sojourners, Ranji and Duleep, revealed an involvement in that most English of games, cricket, which was supplemented later by the appearance of other players such as Learie Constantine and Garfield Sobers.[89] In boxing there was a long tradition of involvement by immigrant minorities.[90] Indeed, such groups have made a contribution over many years to the world of popular entertainment.[91]

As regards intellectual activity Joseph Conrad (Konrad Korseniowski) and Henry James were two early exiles who made their distinctive contributions to English literature. Moreover, the obituaries that have begun to appear with alarming frequency in *The Times* underline the contribution of refugee scholars from Austria and Germany of the 1930s, across a wide range of disciplines. There were also contributions from other groups: for example, Alexander Korda and George Mikes, two Hungarians, and two writers from the Caribbean, Samuel Selvon and V. S. Naipaul, were threads in a rich, yet often unrecognised fabric, which was intricately woven over the years.[92]

In some instances the experiences that encouraged movement and the difficulties which immigrants and refugees had to face, paralysed the spirit and resulted in mental breakdown, as a result of which individuals were confined to an existence rather than a life.[93] But in other cases the process of movement proved uplifting. It was not unknown for those from central Europe to experience a sense of relief and excitement once they left their more tightly-controlled nations and came to Britain.[94] Moreover, the founding of the Ben Uri Gallery in London in 1915 bore witness to the outburst of creativity by young Jews once they were freed in the West from the religious sanctions against art which hung heavy in the Pale of Settlement in Russian Poland.[95] In other cases, in more complex fashion, it might be suggested that creativity developed as a compensation for deficiencies in social and personal life and from the tension of being marginal or an outsider.[96] Whatever the social and personal dynamics, a rich, contrasting, intellectual harvest resulted from the historical process of immigration down to 1971.[97]

The religious life of Britain between 1871 and 1971 was also influenced by the process of immigration. The major influx of the Irish in the nineteenth century during the years of the Great Starvation occurred just before the restoration of the Catholic hierarchy in England and the subsequent development of the Roman Church was aided by a supply of priests from Ireland as well as by the pennies of the Irish poor which helped in the construction of Catholic churches. There was evidence of a similar involvement in Scotland. At the same time, however, it needs to be recognised that the brand of Catholicism which developed in Britain was different from that which prevailed in Ireland and, as a result, the religion of many of those Irish who remained in the Church became modified during the course of their stay in Britain. Moreover, although important as agents who helped to restore Catholicism, and who were in turn open to a degree of influence by the Roman Church, it was less evident down to 1971 that the Irish faithful, and indeed individuals of Irish descent, had managed to make a noticeable impression on the hierarchy of the Church in Britain.[98]

The social and cultural history of other groups of newcomers, such as the Poles, Ukrainians and Italians, was also characterised by the presence of strong religious bonds which sometimes drew individuals across their national groups in marriage.[99] But it was not only Christianity which was imported into Britain. The Russian Polish Jews, who began to arrive in increasing numbers in the late nineteenth century, were not uniformly religious, but those who were brought with them a more orthodox brand of Judaism than that which prevailed in Britain. Over the course of time however, the children of the immigrants often blended into the established religious framework of Anglo-Jewry and came to occupy influential roles within the community.[100] Islam was also imported into Britain by immigrants. There were groups of early believers such as African seamen in Cardiff before the Second World War[101] but it was after the war with the increased immigration from the Indian sub-continent that the practice of Islam increased, particularly with the arrival of immigrants from Pakistan. But it was not only Islam that was imported: Sikhism also became more evident. In both cases the arrival of dependants led to the stronger bonding of cultures imported from the sub-continent than was evident when such immigrations were characterised by the presence of single men. By 1971 the presence of such cultures had already generated shafts of sharp hostility from within British society. However, by that date it was still uncertain whether and how the cultures from the sub-continent would maintain their vitality.[102]

There was also a contribution from among immigrants and refugees to the trade union movement. After an initial stage in which they were perceived and exploited by British employers as a source of cheap and docile labour 'Lithuanians were important in the growth and strengthening of the Scottish miners' union'.[103] In Wales, Spanish miners who were imported into Wales before the First World War in order to undercut the wages of local workers, proceeded to inject a syndicalist tinge into the Welsh miners' union.[104] The involvement of Irish and Jewish newcomers would also need to be taken into account in any history of British trade unionism.[105]

Furthermore, some immigrants and refugees touched the political culture of Britain. There was a long tradition of involvement by the Irish in radical politics that went back at least to the days of Chartism.[106] By the late nineteenth century the Irish tended to support the Liberals, or, where possible, the Irish Nationalists; in other words, their votes were given to those parties that were progressive on the question of Irish freedom. This issue and the defence of Catholic interests were the major influences over Irish political activity. After the First World War, however, although groups committed to the Irish national cause continued to attract support, the weight of political involvement among the Irish and particularly the population of Irish descent shifted increasingly behind the Labour Party. Callaghan and Healey were only two names among many that reflected this development which, it has been strongly argued, provided the Irish with a degree of protection against anti-Irish sentiment.[107]

Some of the newcomers from Russian Poland also became involved in a number of political developments. To Chaim Weizmann and others a base was provided for Zionist activity. To men such as G. V. Chicherin and Maxim Litvinov, who had been hardened by the violent politics of the tsar's empire, Britain was perceived as a temporary base from which they continued to plot and work for the overthrow of the tsarist state. However, those refugees who plotted to this end did not always dispense with an interest in British politics. Indeed, at the same time as working for the ultimate overthrow of the tsarist autocracy, some of the newcomers, through their involvement in Socialist groups such as the Social Democratic Federation, and later, the British Socialist Party, contributed to the growth of Socialism in Britain. In this area, in fact, there was a union of Irish and Russian émigré activity, and the formation of the Communist Party of Great Britain in 1920 was aided by the activity of both groups. It is possible to accept this Irish and Jewish influence without claiming that the CPGB was an alien development, unrelated to the main thrust of British political life.[108] Over the longer term a connection was maintained between Jews and Socialism. This link was evident in Stepney where many Jews reacting partly against Irish control of the local Labour Party, worked for the return of Phil Piratin as Communist MP for the Stepney constituency in 1945.[109] Until recently, however, there was a greater involvement by Jews in the Labour Party, even if this support has been obscured over the past few years by the fact that Anglo-Jewry, in common with Jewish communities elsewhere in the world, has tended to become more conservative in its political orientation.[110]

It was not only Russian émigrés and the earlier refugees from Europe who kept alive the politics of their homeland once they were in Britain. The Social-Democratic refugees from Hitlerite tyranny, the later Poles, and the European Volunteer Workers, did the same.[111] Moreover, at a time when some Russian émigrés in Britain were planning for a future without the tsar, there were Africans in Britain, early representatives of Pan-Africanism, who were working for an Africa free from White control.[112] Indian nationalists were also at work. In view of her important colonial-imperial role it is understandable that such agitation should be carried out in Britain. It was a form of political activity that was to increase from the 1930s and to continue until both Africa and India were able to free themselves from British domination.[113]

The majority of these political activists from Africa, the Caribbean and the Indian sub-continent had left Britain by the time that the major phase of postwar immigration began from the Caribbean and the Indian sub-continent. Down to 1971 these postwar newcomers voted mainly for the Labour Party but there was already evidence, which was to increase in the following decade, of disillusionment with the political system. This disillusionment was fed partly by the procession of legislation to control immigration and the continuing awareness of disadvantage. This disadvantage, evident particularly in the employment and housing markets, was also present in the political system. By 1971, none of the so-called 'coloured immigrants' from the British West Indies or the Indian sub-continent had managed to secure a seat in parliament.[114] In this respect the experience of these groups compared unfavourably with the situation in the late nineteenth and early twentieth centuries, when three Parsees were returned at different times to Westminster.[115] This state of affairs in politics was not unique: by 1971, other than in the 'race relations industry', there was little evidence that the newcomers had managed to make much impression on the prevailing elite structures in Britain. They were essentially invisible in this respect.[116] In such circumstances, and also reflecting the interacting influence of African politics and Black struggles in America, Black Power made its appearance in Britain. This radicalisation was the beginning of a process that was to increase in the following decade. Finally, in common with certain refugee groups, some of the recent immigrant minorites continued to involve themselves in the politics of their homeland. This involvement was evident, for example, among groups from the Indian sub-continent.[117]

It is nevertheless fashionable in some quarters to dismiss the influence of the past history of immigrants and in particular to deny the importance of the cultural patterns which surrounded immigrants and refugees, before they came to Britain.[118] An exclusive, exaggerated emphasis on a group being influenced by 'a sense of common origins', its awareness of 'a common and distinctive history and destiny', its possession of 'one or more distinctive characteristics' and its feeling 'of collective uniqueness and solidarity', in other words by its ethnicity, needs to be guarded against. But so does a sharp dismissal of the past and socially-transmitted cultures.[119] 'Ho cambiato il cielo ma non il cuore' [I have moved from home but left my heart behind], a comment in an Italian guide to Britain published in 1939, was an emotion known to other groups.[120] 'People come to a new country, they start a new life; but the past they can't forget. They bring with them memories attitudes and relationships.'[121] This comment by a woman from Lahore, and the haunting remark, 'I miss *everything*', by a Ukrainian refugee reflecting on a distantly-remembered Ukraine, underlined the significance of the past.[122] In short, the past, with its memories and influences, was not brought to Britain only to collapse entirely in the new environment. It did not continue to exist as a mere response to constant rejections from within British society.[123] On the contrary, previous cultures possessed their own sources of vitality and continued to exert an influence of varying strength upon successive generations of groups such as the Irish, Italians, Poles, Lithuanians and Ukrainians.[124] This retention of cultures, aided in some cases by the improvements in communications and travel which occurred between 1871 and 1971, helped to preserve homeland links and carried significant implications for the organisation of immigrant and refugee life in Britain.[125] One consequence of the interaction between the past and the present was that some immigrants and refugees, as individuals, felt stranded as marginal people straddling two cultures and belonging fully to neither.[126]

Nevertheless, at various times between 1871 and 1971 newcomers were faced with suggestions that they should assimilate or integrate, even if it was not always clear in popular or political discourse what these terms were intended to convey.[127] However, in the present history little emphasis has been given to such hazy concepts. To what, for example, were Jewish newcomers in the late nineteenth century expected to assimilate? There was no unitary society that they encountered on arrival but a society divided into important class and associated cultural divisions.[128] The concept of integration, heavily emphasised in the 1960s, was equally uncertain.[129] Did it refer to groups? Did it refer to individuals? After all, 'Institutional and individual integration are not the same thing'.[130]

Apart from the uncertain definition of such concepts, any attempt to identify a common response from immigrant and refugee groups would distort the complexity of responses that were evident between

1871 and 1971. If, at the extremes, there were broad differences between, say, Austrian and German refugees of the 1930s and Pakistani workers who came in the 1950s and 1960s, which arose through a variety of influences, it is also important to recognise that a complex range of strategies was apparent *within* particular groups.[131] Moreover, it should not be assumed that individuals or groups pursued clear, consistent, and unchangeable goals. Evidence from the various groups who arrived from the Indian sub-continent, for example, would suggest that a degree of ambivalence was not unknown.[132] Furthermore, at all times the response patterns of all groups of newcomers were significantly influenced by their reception and treatment once they came to Britain, and it will be argued that public opinion on immigrants and refugees and behaviour towards them were complex. With this realisation, more needs to be said about the responses that were manifested towards immigrants and refugees in Britain between 1871 and 1971.

3.

THERE is a well-worn opinion that one of the peculiarities of British society is its sense of liberty[133] and there is an equally strong opinion that this quality extends to the history of immigrants and refugees. As a result, it is possible to find references to the acceptance of such groups. It is also possible to find more often a pronounced stress on their toleration, in other words on the positive endurance or the 'putting up with' such groups by British society.[134] It was in possession of such beliefs that Victorians prided themselves on their open-door policy towards refugees.[135] Much later, in continuation of this kind of tradition, it was remarked that Britain was 'the very cradle of liberty and tolerance',[136] and a researcher into recent immigration from the New Commonwealth and Pakistan, was led to comment: 'British people take a pride in their national tradition of freedom and justice'.[137] Indeed, on occasions toleration was claimed as a civic virtue. Hence the comment that Manchester had 'absorbed a rare tradition of tolerance towards strangers and foreigners' which was consistent with its 'great liberal traditions on trade and politics'.[138]

Beliefs always benefit from an echoing reinforcement and it is possible to trace a measure of support from immigrants and refugees for these virtues claimed for Britain and the British. Remarks such as, 'I have been able to make friends among the British people whom I have found to be very kind, generous and sympathetic',[139] together with the comment, 'The gentleness of the Englishman, his ideals and love of fair play, make me miss that country very much',[140] and testimony that, '. . . we thought and still think that England and Bradford is a paradise',[141] revealed that Britain was perceived as possessing more than its propensity for fog, a feature of the country which was also persistently emphasised by immigrants and refugees.[142] Sentiments on the virtues of the British were naturally music to the ears of the believers in the tradition of toleration.

Compared with, say, the historical experiences of racial and ethnic minorities in countries such as tsarist Russia and Nazi Germany and indeed the United States, it can be accepted without too much difficulty that immigrant and refugee minorities in Britain were able to achieve greater security and protection between 1871 and 1971. And yet a degree of caution is required. Any reference to a transcendent moral principle beating at the heart of the nation should be questioned. Differences in the level of hostility between Britain and these other countries during the years 1871 to 1971 related more to certain specific contexts than to any ahistorical impulse. Moreover, the fact that the work of British representatives in the Empire was sometimes covered in blood in the century or so before 1971 should lead to further caution in any discussion on the essential tolerant qualities of the British. Morant Bay, Amritsar and Hola Camp do not square easily with a tolerant, gentle ideal.[143]

This degree of caution is also suggested by events closer to home. In 1967 an editorial in *The Observer* called for a greater awareness of the intolerant responses that immigrants had encountered in Britain.[144] Even earlier a student sojourner had commented on what he called 'a prejudice' which existed towards 'coloured people' in England. It was 'more dignified [than lynching]', 'condescending in its kindness [and] patronizing in its influence' and it was a problem for those who had to confront it.[145] In fact, it is possible to trace a wide range of hostile responses towards immigrants and refugees in Britain between 1871 and 1971, which ranged from the subtle to the crude, the overt to the discreet, and embraced both thought and action.

On occasions hostility was expressed through the spoken word. At the so-called 'monster' meeting of the British Brothers' League held in the People's Palace in the East End of London in 1902, the hearty rendition of popular nationalist songs was followed by torrential speeches attacking Jewish immigrants which were characterised by varying degrees of virulence. Such hostility came from the mouths of Conservative MPs and spokesmen of various East End interests and resulted in shouts from the audience of 'Wipe them out'.[146] Further ahead in time, speeches attacking Jewish aliens were heard once again in the East End in the 1930s from the lips of Mosley's men in the BUF. Indeed, sections of an often-quoted speech in 1936 by 'Mick' Clarke, one of Mosley's ablest lieutenants, attacked Jews in terms which were reminiscent, almost word for word, of some of the attacks made at the People's Palace in 1902, which suggests the existence of an oral tradition of anti-Jewish sentiment in the East End.[147] Further ahead still in time, in his series of major public speeches beginning in 1968, Enoch Powell opened up a new phase in the developing hostility towards the groups from the Caribbean and the Indian sub-continent.[148] Apart from public speeches such as these, verbal attacks were continually made in parliament against a wide range of immigrants and refugees, an indication in itself that hostility was not confined to the 'underworld' or fringes of society. The impression should not be given, however, that any kind of attack could be made with impunity. In the late nineteenth century, for example, public figures often went to great pains to disclaim any trace of anti-Semitism and were frequently capable of substituting the word 'alien' as a cover for 'Jew'.[149] Moreover, in the wake of the Holocaust there was an awareness among public figures that overt attacks based upon racial distinctions could result in public disfavour that few were prepared to court.[150] In short, opposition which involved speaking out against newcomers was evident at varying degrees of subtlety and sophistication. Outside the area of the political debate, hostility was widely present, again with varying degrees of sophistication, in the music hall,[151] in jokes,[152] and in casual conversation where it was reflected in references, among others, to 'wogs', 'niggers', 'chinks', 'frogs' and that contentious verb, 'to jew'.[153]

In addition, antipathy was expressed in a wide range of printed and visual material.[154] Throughout the years between 1871 and 1971 there was scarcely an immigrant or refugee minority that escaped hostile attention in one or more of these sources. In such artefacts antipathy once again ranged from the crude and vicious to the more sophisticated and reflected the attitudes of a cross-section of British society. One of the fiercest examples of anti-Semitism produced anywhere came with the appearance in 1901 of Joseph Banister's *England under the Jews*. In this instance there were no inhibitions, as Banister, writing outside the mainstream of British political life, launched into his wide-ranging attack on the Jewish minority. At one social extreme the Jews were categorised as 'Yiddish money pigs' and, at the other, as the 'semitic sewage' which constituted a key component of the 'alien immigration plague'.[155] By contrast, the collection of essays which had appeared a few years earlier under the title *The Destitute Alien* was less hysterical if still hostile in tone.[156] This distinction reflected a difference of approach between conventional and underground sources, between respectable and disreputable agencies, although it should be remembered that some individuals were capable of operating at more than one level.[157] Years later, in discussions of post-Second World War immigration considerable emphasis has been placed on the role of the media in aggravating existing tensions through the nature of its coverage.[158] However, it needs to be emphasised that the influence of the media was not a new development. Tenniel's cartoons of the Irish, Cecil Hepworth's film, *The Aliens' Invasion*, Claude Blake's fantasies of Chinese vice, the rabid anti-Germanism of the *National Review*, before and during the Great War, the virulent press attacks which followed the sinking of the *Lusitania* in that war and the press hysteria calling for internment in the dark days of 1940 push this development further back in time.[159]

There is no automatic connection between such spoken, written and visual expressions of hostility and action.[160] However, there was no shortage of discrimination towards immigrants and refugees between 1871 and 1971. Action of this sort was evident in the employment market, in the housing market, and in the provision of services and in public places.[161] Some of the most dramatic examples resulted from the actions of individuals but an emphasis on personal antipathy alone would be insufficient. Responses from within the trade union movement, for example, and a variety of public organisations, revealed that discrimination possessed deeper roots in British society. Over the years there were in fact a number of *causes célèbres* which exposed the practice of discrimination. Incidents such as the barring of Paul Robeson from the Savoy Hotel in 1930, of George Roberts from the Grafton dance hall in 1943 and the restricted admittance in the same year of Learie Constantine to the Imperial Hotel were among the most prominent of these incidents.[162] At all times, however, discrimination on grounds of racial or ethnic origin was difficult to pin down. Did Lewis Namier realise at the time that he was denied a Fellowship at All Souls because of his Jewish origins? This fact is known to later generations through written evidence,[163] but participants involved in such activity have always been able to justify or rationalise their responses without reference to race or ethnicity. And it is important to recognise that rejection can occur for reasons which are unrelated to an individual's origins. Immigrants and refugees live in a competitive world and encounter and share its common rebuffs, rejections and disappointments. Nevertheless, one wonders whether the distinguished linguist among the Communard exiles was informed that his failure to secure a chair of Sanskrit at University College, London, was because he had served as a general in the Commune. Or was this rejection also susceptible to a sympathetic gloss?[164]

Spoken hostility, written hostility and discrimination were all evident between 1871 and 1971. So too was collective violence, 'the most extreme form of group competition'.[165] The presence of violence chimes discordantly with the view that Britain is a tolerant country and, perhaps as a result of this embarrassment, relatively little attention has been paid to its various manifestations, which were particularly prevalent in the early twentieth century.[166] The attacks on the Chinese community in Cardiff in 1911, the violence directed against Jews in Tredegar in the same year, the attacks on Germans in 1914, and on the same minority in Liverpool and London in 1915 following the sinking of the *Lusitania*, the violence triggered by the conscription issue in Leeds and London in 1917, and the incidents in Britain's ports in 1919, all provided clear evidence that immigrants and refugees were not immune from physical attack once they had come to Britain. The attacks on Indians in Birmingham in 1948, and incidents in Liverpool in the same year, in Deptford Broadway in 1949, in Camden Town in 1954 and, more spectacularly, in Nottingham and Notting Hill in the summer of 1958, revealed the continued evidence of violence towards newcomers in Britain.[167] These incidents rather like certain instances of discrimination, gained an often transient notoriety. But such events should not be allowed to obscure the fact that the perpetration of violence was not confined to its well-known public manifestations. In the Leylands area of Leeds, for example, Jewish immigrants in the late nineteenth, early twentieth centuries became accustomed to regular attacks at weekends after pay day.[168] In addition, the more recent incidents of 'Paki-bashing', and the promiscuous rather than organised violence directed towards Bengalis and others in the East End, reflected another strand of this dark tradition.[169]

In short, antipathy towards immigrants and refugees assumed a variety of forms in Britain between 1871 and 1971. It has been claimed that at most times refugees have fared better than immigrants but a bald statement of this sort carries little substance.[170] It was not unknown for refugees to encounter a swell of public support on arrival; the experience of the Belgian refugees in the First World War and that of the refugees from the Hungarian Revolution in 1956, would support this observation.[171] However, such sentiment was often short-lived; refugees were kittens who could become very easily unwanted cats. Moreover, public opinion was never uniformly supportive. In general, the collective history of the pre-1914 Russian émigrés, the Belgians in the First World War, the Central Europeans who fled from Hitlerite Europe in the 1930s, and, finally, the exiled Poles, EVWs, and Hungarians, who arrived after 1945, offers little comfort to those intent on emphasising the dominance of a tradition of toleration between 1871 and 1971.

In view of the hostility encountered by immigrants and refugees, including interminority, and indeed intraminority hostility,[172] it has been suggested that in place of the much-vaunted and often-trumpeted virtues of liberty and toleration, celebrated by many historians of the nation, an emphasis should be laid upon the expression of hostility towards immigrants and refugees.[173] There is substance in this suggestion; there is also an obligation to explain why such hostility developed.

For some commentators it has been sufficient to assert that hostility, whether expressed in thought or action, arose out of ignorance and malevolence. It was a reflection of individual or social inadequacy or evil.[174] But those commentators who seize hold of this point put themselves in an intellectual cul-de-sac. An understanding of the hostility encountered by immigrants and refugees can be achieved only after this limited and moralising approach has been abandoned.

A close analysis of hostility between 1871 and 1971 would suggest that a key influence over its emergence was the perception of immigrants and refugees as an immediate competitive threat for society's scarce resources. Immigrants and refugees did not operate in totally separate markets and fears of a dilution of the labour market and anxieties relating to the pressure on resources in the housing market, were particularly important in generating hostility from within British society. If employment and housing were sensitive areas, and economic competition was generally important, the fear of losing British women to immigrants and refugees also received a persistent emphasis.[175]

But the grounds for conflict stretched even further, into the realm of secular and religious cultures. In the late nineteenth century, for example, there was a strand of opposition towards aliens which emphasised their connection with what were termed 'undesirable', 'un-English' forms of political activity, in the shape of anarchism or socialism. Allegations which emphasised the divided political loyalties of certain minorities also surfaced at times particularly as war was threatened or once it had broken out. Germans in Britain were especially exposed in this regard between 1914 and 1918 and again between 1939 and 1945. There was also a persistent opposition between 1871 and 1971 towards groups which tended to preserve their own cultural identity, a trait which could itself be strengthened by external hostility, and thereby created what was regarded as a society within a society. Jewish and Chinese minorities were particular targets of such antipathy before 1914 and the emphasis in Powellism, and other less sophisticated sources in the 1960s, on the peril and damage wreaked by strange, alien cultures, was a forceful reminder of the continuity of such concern. Such cultural hostility, in its secular, and religious forms – the Catholic Irish were a persistent target for militant Protestants – also came into sharp critical focus in the educational system.[176]

It is not suggested, however, that hostility was always easily dissolved into categories such as 'economic' or 'cultural'. The experiences of Chinese and Jewish minorities, for example, revealed how opposition combined a number of different strands. In an interconnected world, hostility possessed its own interconnectedness. Economic hostility was sharpened, for example, against groups which valued their own cultural separateness.[177]

In accounting for such hostility towards immigrants and refugees it would be dangerous to claim that it was always nothing more than an exercise in scapegoating. With a due degree of caution it can be suggested 'that scapegoating is important . . . while believing that scapegoating does not itself furnish a sufficient explanation'.[178] To assume, for example, that between 1871 and 1971 there was no evidence of immigrants and refugees raising the threat of competition in the employment and housing markets in the areas where they settled, would be wide of the mark.[179] Similarly, it would be unsafe to write off all the cultural clashes which occurred between 1871 and 1971 as the product of feverish imaginings that emerged from within the receiving society. Specific areas, for example, witnessed a process of significant cultural change which some of the indigenous population found disorientating.[180] In other words, if it is important to take account of the interests present in the receiving society in an attempt to understand expressions of hostility, it is questionable whether, in this exercise, a consideration of the economic, social, political, cultural behaviour of immigrants and refugees can be dismissed arbitrarily and automatically as of no significance.[181] In short, it is important to bear in mind the prospect that conflict can emerge from complex rather than simple circumstances.[182]

But an awareness of an interactionist approach, which concentrates on immediate pressures and 'irreducible irritations',[183] does not mean that all the antipathy encountered by the immigrants and refugees can be contained within this framework. In the words of one earlier observer, if hostility reflects reality it also distorts it.[184] The selective perception and recall of social phenomena is in fact a persistent human trait.[185] As a result, between 1871 and 1971 the need to make sense of a complex world through a process of simplification created a space in which hostility was articulated.[186] For example, it was easier to claim that Jewish immigrants were responsible for the economic and social problems of the area than it was to unearth the complex pressures that were at work in the East End in the late nineteenth, early twentieth centuries.[187] Furthermore, the persistent view that the resources of society, at any time, were sharply fixed and unable to withstand additional pressures, contributed at times to a distorted assessment of the role and influence of immigrants and refugees and in its wildest form resulted in fears of their domination.[188]

Furthermore, perceptions were affected and distorted by historical influences. Self-images develop within all countries in the course of their historical development, and in Britain these images were nurtured through channels such as comics, schooltexts, youth movements, academic research, the Church (the Kirk in Scotland, for example, was influential in the generating of responses towards the Catholic Irish), newspapers, novels, political tracts, pamphlets, illustrative art and other visual sources, including museum displays, throughout the years between 1871 and 1971.[189] The popular cry 'It's our country'[190] was the internally-directed reflection of this nationalist conditioning. This sentiment was well expressed in South Wales in 1919: 'We went out to France and when we came back we find these foreigners have got our jobs, our businesses, and our houses, and we can't get rid of them'.[191] The important defence of 'hearth and home' from alien influences, the need to preserve 'our churches, chapels and mission halls', the importance of 'our ideas', to which aliens did not conform, and, more recently, the defence of 'our schools', also reflected similar perceptions.[192] It was in gathering up such sentiment, which often sketched a golden age, before adversity was felt, when 'good old names' appeared over shop doors, and houses were 'filled by English people leading . . . decent and cleanly English lives',[193] that politicians could stake out a claim for 'Britain for the British, socially and industrially'[194] and the political pamphleteer could claim 'Britain for those who are truly British'.[195] In spoken, written or merely assumed forms, similar sentiments, which transcended class, united classes, and indeed appealed to people who had no personal contact with immigrants or refugees, need to be taken into account in discussing responses towards immigration throughout the years between 1871 and 1971.[196]

At the same time, again in common with other nations, and as a reciprocal of defining the character and interests of the British, images developed in Britain of groups outside its national boundaries which also affected responses towards immigrants and refugees. In the case of Britain important developments in this respect occurred as a result of industrialisation and the nation's leading role in the world economy which had become established by the early nineteenth century. The predominant view of the world which circulated in British society reflected this economic supremacy.[197]

Little is known, however, about the construction of the images of Europeans which emerged against this background; in popular parlance 'the wogs began at Calais' and near at home across the Irish Sea, but the nature and gradations of the stereotypes of European groups, or indeed their durability and influence, still remain largely unknown and little remarked upon.[198] By contrast, ample reference has been made to the historically-derived stereotypes of Colonial and Imperial groups which, reproduced through the educational system and represented in the artefacts of British society, were especially instrumental, it has been claimed, in fashioning responses from the White British.[199] In short, it has been suggested that the Colonial and Imperial minorities did not step into a neutral ideological context on their arrival. Images relating to their capabilities and capacities came with them, and such images, measured against the carefully-cultivated self-images of the British, helped in the direction and rationalisation of the hostility which they encountered. But in spite of confident assertions about the importance of this Colonial-Imperial legacy, little attempt has been made to unravel its precise impact. As yet, for example, much remains unknown of the specific items from the heavy cultural baggage of Imperialism which were important in influencing responses towards immigrants from the Caribbean and the Indian sub-continent.[200] After all, among some British people there was a discernible sense of obligation, whatever nuances of superiority this still contained, 'towards coloured people from Commonwealth countries' which 'they did not feel towards coloured people from non-Commonwealth countries'.[201]

A similar uncertainty surrounds the relative influence of the range of historically-inherited traditions which were present at any one time. How important, for example, in generating hostile responses towards recent immigration from the Caribbean and the Indian sub-continent, were the local strands of xenophobia derived from previous anti-Jewish campaigns, in relation to those images derived from colonial and imperial influences?[202] Furthermore, in the development of hostility in specific situations, little is known about the relative importance of the past in relation to the pressures of the present within the metropolitan society.[203]

In continuation of such cautionary comment, it is also necessary to guard against the categorisation of all the resulting hostility at the level of ideas and action as racism, particularly when that term is offered without any clear definition. Between 1871 and 1971 there was a species of hostility which emphasised the inherent inferiority of certain groups, even if very little of it assumed the form of a sophisticated scientific theory. More often than not, when an emphasis was laid on racial differences it did not make reference to any congenital distinctions. However, the use of racism as a blanket term obscures awareness of whether reference is being made to a scientific, genetic-based hostility, understood in a sophisticated or crude sense, or to other criteria of differentiation. In addition, it is worth reiterating that any reference to racism which is offered without a full sensitivity to a particular historical context between 1871 and 1971 needs to be treated with caution. The label 'racism' might possess a political convenience. Indeed, since 1945 its association with Nazism has made it an effective weapon which can be turned against political opponents. However, there is no reason why historical enquiries should encourage such bald usage.[204]

It might be assumed that hostility towards immigrants and refugees, produced against a background of immediate and historical pressures, would be particularly evident during periods of economic depression or recession. There were times, in fact, such as in 1911, in the years immediately after the Great War, during the 1930s, and in the early 1960s, when responses were sharpened up in periods of economic and social uncertainty.[205] In such circumstances groups of newcomers were perceived as transcending an allocated role and thereby posing a threat. In contrast, the expansion of employment opportunities during the Second World War was reckoned by some commentators to have eased the reception of the West Indian technicians and trainees who arrived after 1941 even if it did not obliterate all hostility.[206] However, a close, persistent correlation between movements in the economy between 1871 and 1971 would be difficult to trace.[207]

What did appear to affect reactions between 1871 and 1971 was a broader, less-easily defined movement in national or group self-awareness and perception which developed at times of important historical change. The sharpening of an already deep-rooted anti-Catholicism after the restoration of the Catholic hierarchy influenced perceptions and treatment of the Irish.[208] The influence in the late nineteenth, early twentieth century of the Irish Question was also significant in this regard.[209] The emergence of the so-called condition of England question in the late nineteenth, early twentieth centuries, the fear of foreign trade competition and the growing military power of a united Germany influenced responses towards the immigration of Russian Poles and other groups: this changing context also helped to assist the retreat of the state from an open-door policy on immigration.[210] Furthermore, it was during the uncertainty which followed the Great War that stringent legislation over alien immigration in the form of the 1919 Aliens Act was introduced, and that the state involved itself in the deportation of various groups.[211] At a later stage, Poles and EVWs encountered opposition particularly during the early difficult years of the transition from war to peace after 1945 and the changing responses towards immigration from the Caribbean and the Indian sub-continent, evident in tougher immigration laws in the course of the 1960s and early 1970s, were affected by the transformation in Britain's role in the postwar world and the search for a new national identity to replace the old Empire or Commonwealth ideal.[212] Moreover, the history of the years between 1914–18 and 1939–45 revealed that war and its associated developments exercised a significant impact on responses towards various groups living in Britain.[213] Enemy aliens were particularly exposed in wartime. However, the strengthening of national bonds meant that it was not such groups alone that encountered the sharp lash of British xenophobia, as 'friendly aliens' found to their cost in the Great War.[214] In short, whether in peace or war, responses towards immigrants and refugees need to be located within their wider context in order to be understood.[215]

So far an attempt has been made to construct the social context, defined in its broadest sense, in which hostility developed towards immigrants and refugees. It is at this point that the importance of two specific variables, the role of individuals and the question of numbers, can be built into the discussion.

There is a sprawling literature originating from psychiatrists and psychologists which discusses the influence of individual personality constructs on the production of prejudice.[216] For historians, however, these concepts are difficult to utilise; it is impossible, for example, even in possession of the appropriate expertise, to psychoanalyse the dead. It is possible that Joseph Banister's persistent and undiluted hatred of Jews was related essentially to his personality. But it is difficult to prove this suggestion.[217] Nevertheless, it is necessary to recognise that between 1871 and 1971 a number of individuals played a prominent role in directing hostility towards immigrants and refugees. The names of Sir Howard Vincent, the Tory MP for Sheffield Central, and Major William Eden Evans-Gordon, the Tory MP for Stepney, will always be associated with the opposition that developed towards newcomers from Russian Poland.[218] Similarly, the names of Sir Cyril Osborne and Enoch Powell will remain linked with the opposition to unrestricted immigration from the Caribbean and the Indian sub-continent.[219] But they constitute four names only in a larger group, consisting of other politicians, whether working on the national or local scene, journalists, academics and trade union officials who expressed their opposition towards one or more of the various groups that came to Britain between 1871 and 1971.

In many cases our understanding of individual motivation is also hindered by the absence or retention of private papers.[220] What can be emphasised, however, is that at all times the influence of such individuals was significantly affected by the economic, social and political context in which they worked.[221] In tsarist Russia and indeed in other European countries, writers similar to Arnold White, a visitor to St Petersburg, were able to exercise a greater appeal. The First World War gave nationalists such as Leo Maxse, and that arch-populist, Horatio Bottomley, a context for anti-Germanism, of which they had previously dared only to dream. The striking contrast between the influence of Cyril Osborne in the 1950s and Enoch Powell in the 1960s, although related in part to the qualities of the respective individuals, also underlines that context was important.[222]

If the activity of individuals needs to be placed within its appropriate historical context – a requirement sometimes forgotten in studies of immigration and race – the quantitative argument derived from the weight of numbers needs to be similarly circumscribed. It is necessary, in fact, to question the often-repeated view that the larger the size of the immigrant or refugee group, the greater the prospect of hostile reactions developing towards it.

Politicians and others opposed to immigration were never slow to emphasise that numbers were of crucial significance and proceeded to lay a stress upon the number of arrivals, or the net birth rate of the immigrants, or indeed upon both.[223] Furthermore, an investigation of the imagery of opposition towards immigration – a theme that still remains largely unexplored – would reveal a constantly reiterated emphasis on a 'flood' of arrivals, and a related image which projected a picture of specific areas, or sometimes British society in general being swamped by the process of immigration.[224] Other imagery, sometimes dramatic in form, hammered home a similar message. 'Ten grains of arsenic in 1000 loaves would be unnoticeable and perfectly harmless', Major Evans-Gordon told the Commons in 1902, 'but the same amount put into one loaf would kill the whole family that partook of it'.[225]

But, in fact, the relationship between numbers and the

development of hostility is less simple than such comments would suggest. Indeed, it has been argued in a comparative study of French and British society that 'there is no clear and necessary relationship between the number of foreigners living in the country and the emergence of negative attitudes. . .'.[226] In fact, evidence from Britain between 1871 and 1971 would strongly suggest that relatively small groups were unable to escape hostility and, more significantly, before 1914, the fiercest hostility was directed towards the smallest group of arrivals, the so-called German gypsies.[227] In comparison, the responses towards Russian Polish Jews and the even larger Irish group were relatively mild even if these groups fared less well than is sometimes supposed.[228]

In addition, the accumulated evidence from 1871–1971 would suggest that hostility was directed towards groups that were growing or stationary; in appropriate contexts both groups came under attack. For instance, the increasing immigrant group from the Caribbean found itself facing hostility in the 1950s and 1960s: the declining Irish immigrant population in the early twentieth century could not escape it.[229] The post-Second World War Chinese encountered less hostility than the much smaller pre-First World War Chinese minority.[230] Rather than retire the debate over numbers at this juncture, it is possible to weave two additional emphases into the discussion. First, although it might be accepted that there is a numerical point beyond which further immigration will encounter resistance there is no historical evidence to suggest that this point can be predicted with any degree of accuracy, whether the focus is upon absolute numbers or on the 'tipping point' in particular localities. 'Past experience of numbers cannot explain how many is too many'.[231] Finally, even if it is true that rate of build-up is important, in the labour market for example, a close refinement of this view, which would add substantial statistical flesh to the claim, cannot be provided.[232]

In this concluding attempt to make sense of the hostility which emerged between 1871 and 1971 the responses by successive governments have received little emphasis other than a passing acknowledgement that the state adopted a progressively tougher line towards alien, and Commonwealth immigration.[233] There can be no doubt, in fact, that between 1871 and 1971 official policy towards the arrival of immigrants and refugees became more restrictive. In 1871 there were no restrictions on entry into Britain. It was not until 1905, in fact, that the tradition of free entry for aliens was broken in significant fashion, even though the Anglo-Jewish elite had for some time exercised a degree of control over the entry of Jews from Russian Poland.[234] The Aliens Act of 1905 was not as rigorous as the anti-immigration lobby would have wished and down to 1914 it was interpreted quite generously by the Liberals who became responsible for its administration in 1906. Even so, it is significant that the Liberals never repealed the Act which did mark a decisive break in policy in the sense that it made the entry of aliens a discretionary rather than an automatic right.[235]

The most decisive rupture with previous practice, however, occurred during and soon after the First World War. The 1914 Aliens Act vested far greater powers in the Home Secretary and this was reaffirmed and extended in the important Aliens Act of 1919. As a result of these measures, the Home Secretary was given considerable powers over the entry, movement, residence and deportation of aliens. It is historically significant that the tough 1919 measure, supplemented by various Orders in Council of 1920 and 1953, for example, remained the basis of official policy on alien immigration down to the 1971 Immigration Act.[236]

The amount of control over immigration vested in the Home Office in the course of the twentieth century, as a consequence of such developments was illustrated in graphic fashion in the case of political refugees. Whereas governments in the Victorian age tolerated the likes of Dr Marx, Peter Kropotkin and a stream of other radicals who wished to tear up society's roots,[237] in the early twentieth century the Home Office jibbed at the prospect of allowing Leon Trotsky to spend any time in Britain.[238] Moreover, a toughness in government policy towards refugees continued to be evident. After 1951, in considering applications for asylum, the British government applied the definition of refugee status drawn up in that year by the United Nations and, later, in that organisation's 1967 Protocols. As a result, refugees were defined as those who had a 'well founded fear of being persecuted for reasons of race, religion, nationality, membership of a particular social group or political opinion' if they stayed in or returned to their own country.[239] However, in practice, there could be great variations in the response to particular groups and between individual cases.[240] For example, it did not prevent the British government refusing admittance in 1963 to General Humberto Delgado, and returning Colonel Amekrane from Gibraltar in 1969 to face a Moroccan firing squad.[241] The telling, opaque statement which announced that an individual's presence in Britain, or British territory, was not 'conducive to the public good', could have chilling consequences.

Once aliens took up residence there were continuing official restrictions on their employment. The old-style religious disabilities which affected nonconformists and Catholics disappeared in the early nineteenth century and Jewish emancipation, symbolised by a series of measures in 1858, 1871 and 1890, was achieved later in the century. But restrictions on all aliens – (as opposed to specific controls established at specific points in time) – still remained in force in the civil service and armed forces, for example, and sometimes extended to the British-born second generation. Evidence would also suggest that aliens were persistently placed at a disadvantage in terms of securing social welfare benefits, a problem which was exacerbated by the difficulties which were put in the path of applications for naturalisation. By contrast, aliens were not subjected to any *numerus clausus* in education and it can be re-emphasised that they were also free from official restrictions on their place of residence.[242]

The imposition of official controls over the entry of Commonwealth citizens was longer delayed. The tradition of *Civis Britannicus sum* which prevailed in the nineteenth century was reaffirmed in the 1914 British Nationality Act, at a time when tighter controls were being placed over the immigration of aliens. This tradition of free movement into Britain from the Commonwealth and Empire was further recognised in the 1948 British Nationality Act.[243] But government measures in 1962, 1965 and 1968, culminating in the 1971 Immigration Act and the significant rules of 1973 that accompanied it, shattered the tradition of free entry and, after 1968 by steadily increasing the emphasis on 'patrial' links as a condition of unrestricted entry, injected a clear as opposed to a discreet racial distinction into official immigration policy.[244] By 1971, in fact, there was a significant blurring in the distinction between aliens and non-patrial Commonwealth citizens as Britain established a legal framework which enabled capital to make use of a migrant labour system which could be utilised when there was an inadequate supply of 'local' labour.[245]

Workers from Commonwealth countries, however, unlike aliens, never encountered official restrictions and limitations on their employment. Nevertheless, *de facto* discrimination did occur. For example, Black workers recruited from the Caribbean during the

Second World War encountered discrimination regarding their expatriation allowances. It was also well recognised that by the 1960s *de facto* discrimination occurred at local authority level in the allocation of public housing resources, as a result of which Black applicants for council properties were disadvantaged.[246]

In discussing these official responses it is insufficient to concentrate solely upon a political or administrative elite operating in an independent and arbitrary fashion. Politicians, for example, responded to certain pressures that emerged between 1871 and 1971 and in turn influenced official responses towards immigrants and refugees. In the late nineteenth, early twentieth centuries those East End Conservative MPs who took a firm stand against Jewish immigration almost certainly had their sights on the personal political advantage they hoped to gain in their East End constituencies. In turn, they were able to exercise an influence at Westminster. It would be a mistake, however, to regard the pressure from the East End in the shape of the British Brothers' League as a mere reflection of the organising activities of such MPs. The East Enders who joined the League were not an inert mass, capable of response only when moulded by outside pressures. The League resulted from an interaction between grass roots opinion and national political figures which in turn heightened the pressure on parliament for immigration control.[247] Similarly, the Birmingham caucus which operated in parliament after the 1959 General Election acted not only as a conduit but also as a pressure group for immigration control which was partially satisfied in 1962. Furthermore, an understanding of the influential current of Powellism cannot be obtained through an exclusive concentration on Powell's personality: it reflected strong opinions surging in sections of British society.[248]

Even if governments did not always respond to such pressures there were a number of other crucial interactions between governments and public opinion between 1871 and 1971. The anti-German campaign during the First World War, and the drive towards the internment of enemy aliens which began in the dark days of 1940, were both developments when governments responded to popular pressures, and, at the same time, through particular policy initiatives assisted in the progress of opposition towards immigrant and refugee groups.[249]

Such accumulated evidence serves to qualify the image of a tolerant state, and in some recent discussions of postwar immigration from the Caribbean and the Indian sub-continent considerable emphasis has been laid on state repression. Indeed, some commentators have referred to 'institutional racism'.[250] On a wider perspective, the increasingly tough restriction of alien immigration,[251] the controls thrown over the employment of all aliens,[252] and the specific controls over the EVWs,[253] when added to the problems posed for groups from the Caribbean and the Indian sub-continent as a result of official policies at both national and local level,[254] certainly revealed a harsh side of official policy. Moreover, there was other evidence of a similar kind. The treatment by police and magistrates of German gypsies between 1904 and 1906, the pressures to repatriate Blacks who had engaged in the collective violence of 1919, the deportation of Jews and Lithuanians which occurred in the course of the same year, the efforts of the 'local state' in Cardiff in the 1920s and early 1930s to deny British citizenship rights to a range of people who could legitimately claim it, the 'transfer' to Germany of Poles who decided against joining the Polish Resettlement Corps, and some of the more grotesque decisions on refuge and asylum, were among the developments which revealed the darker side of Janus's face.[255]

However, a number of specific developments revealed that there was another aspect. Just before the Great War the police helped to dampen complaints about the Chinese as a social problem. The police and the military limited the scale of violence directed against the small immigrant Jewish community in Tredegar in 1911. The Jews in Leeds recognised the value of local police support in 1917 and publicly expressed their appreciation of it. The official records of the collective violence of 1919 in Liverpool also revealed a degree of police protection which has sometimes passed unrecognised. In addition, the state's implementation of stricter Public Order provisions in the 1930s, after the passing of the Public Order Act in 1936, helped to protect the Jewish minority against the BUF. Finally, albeit after a long delay, the state did begin in the 1960s to take the first faltering steps against racial discrimination.[256]

In general, immigrant and refugee groups were more likely to be tolerated if their interests were in alignment with those of the government of the day. It also helped if groups had access to the corridors of power. By contrast, those groups that were perceived to possess interests opposed to the government were more exposed and vulnerable particularly at times of uncertainty resulting from important historical change, and the same applied to those groups that were 'remotest from the nation's centre of political gravity'.[257]

In short, official responses towards immigrants and refugees were more complex than is sometimes acknowledged. It pays to be cautious and particularly when offered the tasty opinion that hostility towards immigrants was promulgated in order to divide the workers along the lines emphasised in 1870 by Marx in a well-known letter on the Irish.[258] If, for example, workers from Ireland, Russian Poland, the Caribbean and the Indian sub-continent often faced hostility from fellow workers in Britain these conflicts can be explained without postulating an official conspiracy.[259] Furthermore, if official policies at times assisted or extended opposition towards immigrants and refugees it was also apparent that among those wielding power between 1871 and 1971 there were significant differences of opinion, between Ministers, between Departments and between central and local government.[260]

Moreover, it was not only official responses towards immigrants and refugees that were complex. There was, more generally in Britain, much evidence of ambiguity and variability. In other words, a clear, constant dividing line between admiration and fear, toleration and intolerance, was not always easily drawn. Moreover, it should be recognised that liberal thought, generally favourable in its disposition towards immigrants and refugees could contain its own, often unrecognised bias against such groups.

In relation to American society it has been observed that, in spite of their function of simplifying a complex world, stereotypes were seldom one-dimensional but contained a mixture of 'positive and negative charges'.[261] There was also evidence of this tendency in Britain in the mixture of admiration and rejection expressed towards German clerks by an English clerical worker in *The Clerks' Journal*.[262] Arnold White's stereotyped representation of 'the Jew' as a social threat to British society but simultaneously someone whose commercial acumen would help to raise Britain's prestige in the world, provided evidence from a better-known source of the complexity of an individual's perceptions.[263] It is possible that some of these mixed perceptions were nothing more than a 'rhetorical ruse',[264] designed to camouflage hostility. But their complexity also reflected the fact that society is seldom perceived in a clear-cut and consistent fashion, but rather in an inchoate and contradictory manner.[265] Apart from such complexity, other evidence would suggest that individuals seldom enjoyed 'an undivided state of mind'.[266] For example, G. D. Kelley, secretary of the Manchester and

Salford Trades Council, 'was cheered as the champion of the sweated Jewish workers in the waterproof industry's strike of 1890 but could slip into anti-Semitic imagery with the failure of the Jewish tailors to maintain their union organisation in that same year'.[267] Such variability was not unique.[268]

The complexity of attitudes was evident not only among individuals, whether clerical workers, publicists, or trade unionists. A consideration of the extensive range of attitudes towards the Irish in the nineteenth century noticed that the Irish stereotype 'had both its good points and its bad'.[269] A recent survey of the nineteenth-century Italian minority came to a similar conclusion.[270] Moreover, the categorisation of Poles in the wartime Mass Observation surveys,[271] and the stereotypes of Asian and African students that circulated in the 1950s,[272] also underlined that perceptions were not easily compartmentalised and congealed into 'good' or 'bad', 'tolerant' or 'intolerant'. Attitudes towards EVWs in Bradford revealed a similar complexity.[273] Moreover, recent work on labour and immigration which has stressed that 'Working class attitudes towards "outsiders" were incredibly complex, combining both positive and negative stereotypes',[274] would serve to underscore this emphasis on the complexity of responses. Finally, it should not be overlooked that a bias was detectable at the heart of the ideology of liberal toleration in the sense that, at the time of the immigration from Russian Poland, for example, 'Jews were validated not on the grounds of their Jewish identity, but on the basis of their conformity to the values and manners of bourgeois English society'.[275] Furthermore, years later, the presence of a 'schoolmasterly' strand of 'egocentricity' within the postwar liberal assimilationist camp, with its emphasis upon the need for adjustment and conformity on the part of immigrants, was not lost upon perceptive observers.[276]

It was not only at the level of ideas that such complexities were revealed. There was a long tradition of tolerating minorities in the worlds of entertainment and sport but denying their full social equality: well-known personalities such as Paul Robeson and Learie Constantine were brought face to face with this distinction.[277] It is ironic, in fact, that when in 1958 an Indian was barred from the Scala Ballroom in Wolverhampton and a spokesman for the management said, 'the rest of the people in the ballroom just don't want to know coloured people', the same ballroom was hiring Black entertainers.[278] In other words, a toleration in certain roles and situations did not

guarantee its general application.[279] Hence the comments of a
Liverpool taxi-driver: '. . . I can take them or leave them the same as
anybody else you know. I don't mind having a drink with a coloured
chap. I've met some very nice coloured people but with regard to
intermarriage I think I'd draw the line there . . .'.[280] Similarly, Sir
Ernest Cassel, the German-born financier, discovered that members
of high society in London might be anxious to draw upon his financial
acumen in order to derive a personal benefit but this surface
camaraderie did not automatically lead to their wider acceptance of
his company. Beyond the world of finance he could be treated as an
outsider. Money did have a smell.[281] This variability was
encountered elsewhere at different times. A survey of Manchester
after the Second World War, for example, noted that '. . . although a
coloured doctor . . . may be treated as an equal of a white doctor by
his white clients, yet it is a known fact that generally in various social
situations he is discriminated against as any other coloured
person'.[282]

In short, at the level of ideas, images of immigrants and refugees
often revealed a complex rather than a simple structure and, as
regards behaviour, individuals could encounter varying treatment
according to the particular situation.[283] In general, it is worth
re-emphasising that they were more likely to be tolerated when
fulfilling a role in which they were not perceived as a threat; hence the
toleration frequently extended to them as entertainers. But the
perception of what constituted a social threat also varied. For
example, those British clerks who feared the competition of German
clerical labour did not view the arrival of German clerks in the same
light as the owners of those City counting houses who wanted to
utilise the skills of these German workers. One group feared for its

employment, the other hoped to benefit from the commercial skills of
the clerical newcomers.[284] Conflicting responses which grew out of a
similar context, were evident on other occasions.[285] Assessments of
the social-cultural influence of immigrants and refugees also varied.
Socialists in Britain were not troubled by the political philosophy
imported by Socialist refugees: conservatives were.[286] If some women
in wartime Britain were attracted to romantic Polish servicemen it
was not uncommon for English and Scottish men to categorise the
Poles as sexual predators.[287] There were no simple hierarchies of
acceptance, toleration or rejection of individuals or groups.[288]

The main thrust of the preceding discussion on the dynamics of hostility has been to warn against the dangers of simplicity in dealing with responses towards immigrants and refugees between 1871 and 1971. This degree of caution has been emphasised both in relation to attitudes and action. If, at the end of it all, the arithmetic of responses emerges as a complex equation, it is better to recognise this complexity than to persist with emphases which, if easier to explain and utilise, have less of substance to recommend them.

4.

DURING the hundred years that ended in 1971 there was a continual if not continuous movement of population across the earth's surface. At times some of this movement occurred in the form of indentured labour. This phenomenon was evident in the transport of Chinese workers to Cuba and the West Indies, and of Indians to Africa and the Caribbean in the late nineteenth century.[289] Other groups such as the Poles who were transported to the Soviet Union between 1939 and 1941, bore witness to the movement of population through a policy of forced deportation.[290] During the late nineteenth century, through a process of less traumatic movement, emigrants departed in increasing numbers to America. Moreover, whereas previously northern Europe had provided America with its labour, soon after the Civil War, there was an increasing number of immigrants from southern and eastern Europe, as well as the Far East, who sought a better future in the New World. In a reaction against such developments and in defiance of the noble sentiments of Emma Lazarus, inscribed on the Statue of Liberty, legislation was erected in America against the entry of the Chinese in 1882, and the Japanese in 1907, and such measures were followed by a further batch of controls in 1917, 1921, 1924 and 1929, which favoured entry from northern Europe at the expense of Oriental, southern and eastern European immigrants.[291] It was not until the 1965 Immigration Act that this policy was changed. This measure was intended principally to ease restrictions on southern and eastern Europeans but, in the event, it resulted in a large leap in arrivals from South and East Asia and began a new pattern in the continuing process of immigration into the United States.[292] During the years following the Second World War significant changes in immigration also occurred in continental Europe. As workers arrived in Britain from the Caribbean and the Indian sub-continent, the advanced economies of continental Europe recruited migrant workers from southern Europe and North Africa. Hence the phenomenon of the Turkish *Gastarbeiter* in countries such as Sweden and West Germany and the presence of North Africans, formerly under French colonial rule, in the *bidonvilles* and *microbidonvilles* of France.[293]

In addition to this kind of migration, the nineteenth and twentieth centuries witnessed a succession of sad-faced yet expectant refugees who had been obliged to lift their roots and move. The political exiles from European states who found their way to Britain in the nineteenth century were not alone. There were contemporaries in exile scattered elsewhere.[294] Moreover, problems in the twentieth century resulted in a continuing refugee presence in a number of countries, which at different times led to the involvement of the League of Nations and the United Nations in refugee work. The 1917 Revolution in Russia drove 'white' Russians to Germany, France and America. The advent of Hitler not only resulted in the arrival of refugees in Britain: some of those escaping from the intended thousand-year rule went to America.[295] The Second World War added other groups to the world's refugee population. Furthermore, the continuation of conflict, generated through change and oppression, guaranteed the persistence of a refugee problem in the postwar years, which became particularly evident in the world beyond Europe.[296]

These international developments formed part of the wider context against which the arrival of immigrants and refugees in Britain needs to be set, not that a national survey can ever be totally insular. On his return from Catalonia and his part in the Spanish Civil War, George Orwell reflected on the remarkable continuity of an England untroubled by 'Earthquakes in Japan, famines in China and revolutions in Mexico'.[297] In some respects there is truth in this comment, but specific events in faraway countries of which the English – and the British – knew little and cared even less exerted an influence over the history of immigration between 1871 and 1971, by generating movement and helping to shape relations between immigrants, refugees and British society. During these years, British society, and a succession of newcomers, sent on their hopeful journey by varying pressures, were influenced or changed through such contact and, since the wheel of history continues to turn, the working-out of that process of interaction is still with us.

Hitherto, however, in spite of a wealth of kaleidoscopic studies, which have constituted specific snapshots in time, the historical dimension of this process has been neglected. In an attempt to remedy this deficiency, a number of questions have been asked. Who were the immigrant and refugee groups that came to Britain between 1871 and 1971, the most significant years in the history of recent immigration, and why did they come? What were the salient features of their economic and social history in Britain? How were such groups received? Those individuals and organisations concerned with current issues relating to immigration need information on such questions. It is only through such knowledge in fact, that a serious public discussion on immigration becomes possible, and polemic is put in its proper place.

Notes

INTRODUCTION

1. V. G. Kiernan, 'Britons Old and New', in C. Holmes (ed.), *Immigrants and Minorities in British Society* (London, 1978), p. 23.
2. J. Geipel, *The Europeans. An Ethnohistorical Survey* (London, 1969), pp. 163–4.
3. D. Defoe, *The True-Born Englishman. A Satyr* (Durham, 1701), on 'that vain ill-natur'd thing, an *Englishman*'.
4. OPCS, *International Migration* (London, 1980), pp. 8, 2.
5. J. Denvir, *The London Irish* (London, 1892), pp. 390, 392, 433–4. See also *The Times*, 5 May 1981 (Letters).
6. See below for references to these groups.
7. Revealed recently, for example, in 'the Papasoiu affair'. This incident was given liberal coverage in *The Times*, March–April 1983.
8. See below pp. 237, 251.
9. Kiernan, op. cit., p. 49.
10. Ibid., pp. 23–4.
11. Ibid., p. 25.
12. See, for example, W. Cunningham, *Alien Immigrants to England* (London, 1897), Ch. 3; P. Dollinger, *The German Hansa* (London, 1970); P. Hyams, 'The Jewish Minority in Medieval England 1066–1290', *Journal of Jewish Studies*, Vol. XXV (1974), pp. 270–93; B. G. Awty, 'French Immigrants and the Iron Industry in Sheffield', *Yorkshire Archaeological Society Journal*, Vol. 52 (1981), pp. 57–62; idem, 'The Continental Origins of Wealden Ironworkers 1451–1544', *Economic History Review*, Vol. XXXIV (1981), pp. 524–39.
13. H. G. Richardson, *The English Jewry Under Angevin Kings* (Oxford, 1960), pp. 227–8.
14. Kiernan, op. cit., p. 30. See also H. Kellenbenz, 'German Immigrants in England', in Holmes, op. cit., pp. 63–4.
15. Dollinger, op. cit., partic. pp. 341–3.
16. There is no entirely satisfactory account but see, for example, B. Vesey-Fitzgerald, *Gypsies of Britain: An Introduction to their History* (London, 1944), pp. 20ff.
17. P. Edwards, 'The History of Blacks in Britain', *History Today*, Vol. 31 (September, 1981), p. 33. See also E. Scobie, 'The Black in Western Europe', *Journal of African Civilisation*, Vol. 3 (1981), pp. 38–50.
18. J. Walvin, *The Black Presence. A Documentary History of the Negro in England 1555–1860* (London, 1971), pp. 64–5.
19. P. Fryer, *Staying Power. The History of Black People in Britain* (London, 1984), pp. 10–12 is good on the activities of the Elizabethan state.
20. M. Rodgers, 'Italiani in Scozzia', in B. Kay (ed.), *Odyssey. The Second Collection* (Edinburgh, 1982), p. 13.

21. C. W. Chitty, 'Aliens in England in the Sixteenth Century', *Race*, Vol. VIII (1966), pp. 129–45; N. Goose, 'The "Dutch" in Colchester: The Economic Influence of an Immigrant Community in the Sixteenth and Seventeenth Centuries', *Immigrants and Minorities*, Vol. 1 (1982), pp. 261–80. See also J. Burns, *The History of the French, Walloon, Dutch and other Foreign Protestant Refugees settled in England from the Reign of Henry VIII to the Revocation of the Edict of Nantes* (London, 1846), for earlier comment.

22. Kiernan, op. cit., p. 33.

23. See H. Pollins, *Economic History of the Jews in England* (East Brunswick, N.J., London and Toronto, 1982), Chapter 1.

24. The phrase is from Kiernan, op. cit., p. 38.

25. Ibid., p. 39.

26. The most recent account is R. Gwynn, *The Huguenot Heritage* (London, 1985), one of the artefacts produced on the 300th anniversary of the Revocation of the Edict of Nantes. Between May and October 1985 an exhibition, 'The Quiet Conquest 1685–1985', was held at the Museum of London, also by way of commemoration. For an earlier, well-known account of the Huguenots see S. Smiles, *The Huguenots; their Settlement, Churches, Industries in England and Ireland* (London, 1867).

27. A Walk Round Guide, *The Cathedral Church of Winchester* (n.p., n.d.), p. 11.

28. Kiernan, op. cit., p. 41.

29. Cunningham, op. cit., pp. 250ff. tells the story.

30. Fryer, op. cit., pp. 77–9.

31. E. Scobie, *Black Britannia* (Chicago, 1972), p. 12 and Ch. 8. On Francis Barber see F. O. Shyllon, *Black People in England 1555–1833* (Oxford, 1977), pp. 179–86, and *The Times*, 23 October 1983 (Sale Room report). There is an illustration of a Black drummer in J. Walvin, *Black and White: The Negro in English Society 1555–1945* (London, 1973), facing p. 179. See also W. Y. Carmian, 'A Trumpeter in the 1st Horse Guards c 1751', *Society for Army History Research Journal*, Vol. 59 (1981), pp. 190–3. On Harriet see I. Bloch, *Sexual Life in England* (London, 1967 edn). On Hogarth's depiction of Blacks see D. Dabydeen, *Hogarth's Blacks* (Kingston-on-Thames, 1985). Richmond is referred to in H. W. Debrunner, *Presence and Prestige. Africans in Europe* (Basel, 1979), pp. 235–6. On Billy Waters see P. Edwards and J. Walvin, *Black Personalities in the Era of the Slave Trade* (London, 1983), pp. 163–70. This book is generally useful on the period.

32. On Bridgewater see P. Edwards, 'Black Personalities in Georgian Britain', *History Today*, Vol. 31 (September, 1981), pp. 48–51.

33. F. O. Shyllon, *Black People in Britain 1555–1833* (London, 1977), pp. 45–66, on 'Princes, Students and Scholars'.

34. For a recent discussion of these individuals see Fryer, op. cit., Ch. 5.

35. Quoted in K. Little, *Negroes in Britain* (London, 1948 edn), p. 168. See ibid., p. 169 and Fryer, op. cit., Ch. 3 for advertisements, as well as F. O. Shyllon, *Black Slaves in Britain* (London, 1974), pp. 5–11.

36. F. O. Shyllon, *Black Slaves*; D. A. Lorimer, 'Black Slaves and English Liberty: A Re-Examination of Racial Slavery in England', *Immigrants and Minorities*, Vol. 3 (1984), pp. 121–50; on slavery in Scotland see N. Wilson, 'Legal Attitudes to Slavery in Eighteenth Century Britain', *Race*, Vol. XI (1970), pp. 463ff.

37. Fryer, op. cit., pp. 196–203. J. Walvin, *Black and White*, Ch. 9; see also C. Fyfe, *A History of Sierra Leone* (Oxford, 1962), pp. 13ff.

38. On political activists see Fryer, op. cit., pp. 214–26, 263.

39. On Aldridge see ibid., pp. 252–6. Molineaux is discussed in ibid., pp. 446–8 and Debrunner, op. cit., pp. 236–8.

320 JOHN BULL'S ISLAND

40. D. George, *London Life in the Eighteenth Century* (Harmondsworth, 1965 edn), p. 143.
41. See below p. 34 for fuller comment.
42. Kiernan, op. cit., pp. 40–42. The Eastern European dimension has been relatively neglected. But see A. G. Cross, *By the Banks of the Thames: Russians in Eighteenth Century Britain* (Newtonville, Mass., 1980).
43. On the Irish there is J. A. Jackson, *The Irish in Britain* (London, 1963). See also B. Collins, 'Proto-Industrialization and pre-Famine Emigration', *Social History*, Vol. 7 (1982), pp. 124–46. For a study of Irish workers see T. Coleman, *The Railway Navvies* (London, 1965). See also M. Hechter, *Internal Colonialism. The Celtic Fringe in British National Development, 1536–1966* (London, 1975).
44. Jackson, op. cit., p. 11. For the Irish in London during these years see L. H. Lees, *Exiles of Erin. Irish Migrants in Victorian London* (Manchester, 1979). See below pp. 20–22 for additional comment.
45. F. D'Arcy's review of Lees, op. cit., in *Saothar. Journal of Irish Labour*, Vol. 8 (1982), p. 59.
46. B. Collins, 'Aspects of Irish Immigration into two Scottish Towns', *Irish Economic and Social History*, Vol. VI (1979), pp. 71–3.
47. Lees, op. cit., p. 51.
48. C. Richardson, 'Irish Settlement in mid-nineteenth century Bradford', *Yorkshire Bulletin of Economic and Social Research*, Vol. XX (1968), p. 42.
49. P. Millward, 'The Stockport Riots of 1852; A Study of Anti-Catholic and Anti-Irish Sentiment', in R. Swift and S. Gilley (eds), *The Irish in the Victorian City* (London, 1985), pp. 207–24.
50. Kiernan, op. cit., p. 45.
51. For other German capitalists in Manchester see B. Williams, *The Making of Manchester Jewry 1740–1875* (Manchester, 1976), pp. 81–4. On Engels in Manchester see W. O. Henderson and W. H. Chaloner, 'Friedrich Engels in Manchester', *Memoirs and Proceedings of the Manchester Literary and Philosophical Society*, Vol. 98 (1956–7), pp. 13–29; see also recent comment in N. Levine, 'Engels, England and the English Working Class', in G. Niedhart (ed.), *Grossbritannien als gast – und exilland für deutsche im 19 und 20 Jahrhundert* (Bochum, 1985), pp. 58–88.
52. J. Goodman, *The Mond Legacy* (London, 1982).
53. On Brunner see S. Koss, *Sir John Brunner, Radical Plutocrat 1842–1919* (Cambridge, 1970); on ICI see W. J. Reader, *Imperial Chemical Industries. A History* (2 vols, London, 1970).
54. See, for example, J. S. Roberts, *Little Germany* (Bradford, 1977).
55. Noted by Pollins, op. cit., p. 48.
56. E. M. Wilkinson, 'French Emigrés in England 1789–1802. Their Reception and Impact on English Life', unpublished B. Litt. Thesis, Oxford University, 1952, p. 25.
57. B. Porter, *The Refugee Question in mid-Victorian England* (Cambridge, 1979), carries information on refugees in general. On Marx in London see A. Briggs, *Marx in London. An Illustrated Guide* (London, 1982). For Panizzi see M. C. W. Wicks, *The Italian Exiles in London, 1816–1848* (Manchester, 1937), Chs 5 and 6.
58. L. MacNeice, 'The British Museum Reading Room', in *Plant and Phantom* (London, 1941), written in July 1939. See also L. Maisky, *Journey into the Past* (London, 1964), pp. 26–34.
59. Porter, op. cit., is generally useful.
60. See below Chapter 5.
61. A point emphasised in H. Joshua and T. Wallace, with H. Booth, *To Ride the Storm* (London, 1983), pp. 7–8. Fryer, op. cit., has gone some way towards remedying this state of affairs.

62. A theme discussed in various publications by G. L. Anderson. See, for example, 'German Clerks in England: Another Aspect of the Great Depression Debate', in K. Lunn (ed.), *Hosts, Immigrants and Minorities. Historical Responses to Newcomers in British Society 1870–1914* (Folkestone, 1980), pp. 201–21.

63. See J. P. May, 'The British Working Class and the Chinese', unpublished MA Dissertation, Warwick University, 1973.

64. See the work of M. Rodgers, most recently found in 'Immigration into Britain: The Lithuanians', *History Today*, Vol. 35 (July, 1985), pp. 15–20 and K. Lunn, 'Reactions to Lithuanians and Polish Immigrants in the Lanarkshire Coalfield', in Lunn, op. cit., pp. 308–42.

65. A point emphasised in B. M. Walter, 'The Geography of Irish Migration to Britain, with special reference to Luton and Bolton', unpublished D. Phil. Thesis, Oxford University, 1978, p. 13. The general paucity of information on the Irish abroad in the late nineteenth century is remarked upon in R. A. Burchell, 'The Historiography of the American Irish', *Immigrants and Minorities*, Vol. 1 (1982), p. 281.

66. Referred to in R. Palmer, 'Immigrants ignored: An Appraisal of the Italians in Britain', unpublished MA Thesis, Sussex University, 1972, p. 5. Since when, apart from Palmer's continuing interest, there has been L. Sponza, 'The Italian Poor in Nineteenth-Century Britain', unpublished Ph. D. Thesis, London University, 1984. Even so, the point remains valid.

67. H. Goiran, *Les français à Londres. Etude historique* (Pornic, 1933) is dated and restricted to the capital. R. Faber, *French and English* (London, 1925), skims only part of the surface.

68. Work is currently under way at the School of Slavonic and East European Studies on the Polish minority. On the neglect of political exiles, see R. C. Williams, 'European Political Emigrations: A Lost Subject', *Comparative Studies in Society and History*, Vol. 12 (1970), pp. 140–8.

69. H. L. Malchow, *Population Pressures and Government in late Nineteenth-Century Britain* (Palo Alto, 1979); J. Parr, *Labouring Children. British Immigrant Apprentices to Canada 1869–1914* (London, 1980); G. Wagner, *Children of the Empire* (London, 1982).

70. C. Erickson (ed.), *Emigration from Europe 1815–1914* (London, 1976).

71. On the movement to North America see, inter alia, R. T. Berthoff, *British Immigrants in Industrial America 1790–1950* (Cambridge, 1953); P. A. M. Taylor, *The Distant Magnet* (London, 1971); T. Coleman, *Passage to America* (Harmondsworth, 1976 edn); M. Jones, *Destination America* (London, 1976).

72. J. D. Gould, 'European Inter-Continental Emigration: The Road Home: Return Emigration from the USA', *Journal of European Economic History*, Vol. IX (1980), pp. 41–112.

73. An emphasis in J. A. Hobson, *Imperialism. A Study* (London, 1902).

74. Noted in R. K. Kelsall, *Population* (London, 1979 edn), p. 32.

75. Ibid., pp. 29–30, 115.

I. IMMIGRATION IN THE AGE OF IMPERIALISM

1. K. O'Connor. *The Irish in Britain* (Dublin, 1974), pp. 1, 15.

2. See J. A. Jackson, *The Irish in Britain* (London, 1963), Ch. 3, for general comment. See also above pp. 10–11.

3. Compiled from: *Census of Great Britain, 1841*, Irish University Press reprint, Vol. 3 (Shannon, 1971), pp. 84–5; *Census of Great Britain, 1851*, Irish University Press

reprint, Vol. 8 (Shannon, 1970), p. cclxxxvii; *Census of England and Wales, 1861*, Irish University Press reprint, Vol. 15 (Shannon, 1970), p. 64; *Census of England and Wales, 1871*, Irish University Press reprint, Vol. 18 (Shannon, 1970), p. 1; *Census of England and Wales. General Report*, 1931 (London, 1950), p. 20.

4. *Census of Great Britain, 1841*, p. 86; *Census of Great Britain, 1851*, p. cclxxxvii; *Census of Scotland, 1931*, Vol. II (Edinburgh, 1933), p. xxxv.

5. T. C. Barker and J. Harris, *A Merseyside Town in the Industrial Revolution. St. Helens 1750–1900* (Liverpool, 1954), p. 453.

6. Jackson, op. cit., p. 10.

7. *Census, England and Wales, 1901.* Summary Tables (London, 1903), p. 258; *Census of England and Wales, 1911*, Vol. IX. *Birthplaces* (London, 1913), p. iv; *Census of England and Wales 1931* etc., p. 20; *Census of Scotland, 1931* etc., pp. vii and xxxv.

8. Commented upon in C. Booth, *Life and Labour of the People of London, Religious Influences*, Vol. VII (London, 1903), p. 243.

9. Jackson, op. cit., p. 10. See also J. V. Hickey, 'The Origins and Growth of the Irish Community in Cardiff', unpublished M.A. thesis, University of Wales, 1959 and F. Finnigan, 'The Irish in York', in R. Swift and S. Gilley (eds), *The Irish in the Victorian City* (London, 1985), pp. 59–84.

10. Comments about levels of Irish emigration need to be treated cautiously; there might have been some underestimation. C. O'Grada, 'A Note on Nineteenth Century Irish Emigration Statistics', *Population Studies*, Vol. 29 (1975), pp. 145–8.

11. Jackson, op. cit., p. 2.

12. L. H. Lees, *Exiles of Erin. Irish Migrants in Victorian London* (Manchester, 1979), p. 40.

13. Ibid., p. 39.

14. Ibid., p. 41. The complex reasons for Irish emigration are emphasised in J. Mokyr, *Why Ireland Starved. A Quantitative and Analytical History of the Irish Economy 1800–1850* (London, 1983), pp. 278ff.

15. Noted in that excellent survey, M. A. G. O'Tuathaigh, 'The Irish in Nineteenth Century Britain: Problems of Integration', *Transactions of the Royal Historical Society*, Vol. 31 (1981), p. 153.

16. D. Fitzpatrick, 'Irish Emigration in the late Nineteenth Century', *Irish Historical Studies*, Vol. 22 (1980), pp. 126–43 is good on the origins, nature and direction of the emigration.

17. Emphasised in Jackson, op. cit., p. 5.

18. See Billy Kay's article on transients from Donegal, 'From Gorbals to Gweedore', in B. Kay (ed.), *Odyssey*, Vol. 1 (Edinburgh, n.d.), pp. 1–9.

19. Derived from: *Census of England and Wales, 1871* etc., p. li; *Census of England and Wales, 1911* etc., p. 114; *Census of England and Wales, 1931* etc., p. 20.

20. On London see H. Dorgeel, *Die Deutsche Colonie im London* (London and Leipzig, 1881). There is a passing reference to Manchester in V. G. Kiernan, 'Britons Old and New', in C. Holmes (ed.), *Immigrants and Minorities in British Society* (London, 1978), p. 46. See also N. J. Frangopulo, 'Foreign Communities in Manchester', *Manchester Review*, Vol. 10 (1965), pp. 197–202 for more extended comment. On Bradford there is: M. Pratt, 'The Influence of the Germans on Bradford', B. A. Dissertation, Margaret MacMillan College, n.d. A general survey of German Jews is contained in C. C. Aronsfeld, 'German Jews in Victorian England', *Leo Baeck Yearbook*, Vol. VI (1962), pp. 312–29.

21. See the discussion in G. Anderson, 'German Clerks in England, 1870–1914: Another Aspect of the Great Depression Debate', in K. Lunn (ed.), *Hosts, Immigrants and Minorities. Historical Responses to Newcomers in British Society*

1870–1914 (Folkestone, 1980), pp. 201–21, partic. p. 205 for the numerical details.

22. Paragraph based on ibid., pp. 208–9.
23. Aronsfeld, op. cit., p. 312.
24. Ibid., passim.
25. E. D. Howard, *The Cause and Extent of the Recent Industrial Progress of Germany* (London, 1907) is an excellent contemporary survey.
26. An emphasis in Aronsfeld, op. cit.
27. E. Jones, *Sigmund Freud. Life and Work*, Vol. 1 (London, 1953), p. 195.
28. B. Vesey Fitzgerald, *Gypsies of Britain: An Introduction to their History* (London, 1944 and 1973). See also J. P. Clébert, *The Gypsies* (London, 1963), pp. 29ff. and D. Kendrick and G. Puxon, *The Destiny of Europe's Gypsies* (London, 1972), pp. 13–56.
29. See my article, 'The German Gypsy Question in Britain 1904–6', *Journal of the Gypsy Lore Society*, Vol. 1 (1978), pp. 248–67 for details.
30. Details are provided in ibid.
31. Bradford Heritage Recording Unit (BHRU), Tape B 0012/01/29–30, Lisandrina Taglione refers to German musicians. Mrs Taglione was born in Bradford in 1896, the daughter of an Italian organ-grinder. On German waiters see *Royal Commission on Alien Immigration*, British Parliamentary Papers, IX, 1903, pp. 450, 615. See also *Census of England and Wales*, 1911, etc., p. xxi. On German miners see *R.C.* 1903, p. 844. For German labourers see M. J. Tebbutt, 'The Evolution of Ethnic Stereotypes. An Examination of Stereotyping, with particular Reference to the Irish (and to a lesser extent the Scots) in Manchester during the late Nineteenth and early Twentieth Centuries', unpublished M.Phil. Thesis, Manchester University, 1982, p. 160. See also B. Didsbury, 'Cheshire Saltworkers', in R. Samuel (ed.), *Miners, Quarrymen and Saltworkers* (London, 1977), pp. 199–200, for Germans in the Cheshire salt works. On the refugees see B. Porter, *The Refugee Question in Mid-Victorian Politics* (Cambridge, 1979).
32. I. Finestein, 'Anglo-Jewish Opinion during the Struggle for Emancipation', *Transactions of the Jewish Historical Society of England* (later *TJHSE*), Vol. XX (1959–61), pp. 113–44. See also M. C. N. Salbstein, *The Emancipation of the Jews in Britain: The Question of the Admission of Jews to Parliament 1828–1860* (London, 1982). On the elite of this community see C. Bermant, *The Cousinhood: The Anglo-Jewish Gentry* (London, 1971). See also T. M. Endelman, 'Communal Solidarity among the Jewish Elite of Victorian London', *Victorian Studies*, Vol. 28 (1985), pp. 491–526.
33. H. Pollins, *Economic History of the Jews in England* (East Brunswick, N.J., London, and Toronto, 1982), Chs 5, 6 and 7.
34. V. D. Lipman, *Social History of the Jews in England 1850–1950* (London, 1954), p. 65.
35. Based on *Census of England and Wales, 1901*, p. 260; *Census of England and Wales, 1911*, p. xviii; *Census of England and Wales, 1931* etc., p. 20; the Scottish figures are derived from N. H. Carrier and J. B. Jeffery (eds), *External Migration. A Study of the Available Statistics* (London, 1953), p. 128.
36. Emphasised in *R.C.*, 1903, p. 14; *Census of England and Wales, 1911*, p. 136.
37. V. D. Lipman, 'The Rise of Jewish Suburbia', *TJHSE*, Vol. 21 (1968), pp. 78–103.
38. *R.C.*, 1903, p. 14. On Jews in the West End see Count E. Armfelt, 'Cosmopolitan London', in G. Sims (ed.), *Living London* (3 vols, London, 1901), Vol. 1, pp. 241–7.
39. E. Krausz, *Leeds Jewry* (Cambridge, 1964); R. O'Brien, 'The Establishment of the Jewish Minority in Leeds', unpublished Ph.D. Thesis, Bristol University,

1975; J. Buckman, *Immigrants and the Class Struggle. The Jewish Immigrant in Leeds 1880–1914* (Manchester, 1983).

40. Frangopulo, op. cit., pp. 189–206; R. D. Livshin, 'Aspects of the Acculturation of Children of Immigrant Jews in Manchester 1890–1930', unpublished M.Ed. thesis, Manchester University, 1982; B. Williams, *The Making of Manchester Jewry* (Manchester, 1976).

41. See, for example, on Scotland, M. Rodgers, 'Glasgow Jewry', in B. Kay (ed.), *Odyssey. The Second Collection* (Edinburgh, 1982), pp. 113–21; A. Gibb, *Glasgow. The Making of a City* (London, 1983), p. 127; and G. Alderman, 'Into the vortex: South Wales Jewry before 1914' in A. Newman (ed.), *Provincial Jewry in Victorian Britain* (London, 1975), n.p., on Wales.

42. J. A. Garrard, *The English and Immigration. A Comparative Study of the Jewish Influx 1880–1910* (London, 1971), Appendix 1.

43. *Universal Jewish Encyclopaedia*, Vol. 13 (Jerusalem, 1971), p. 27.

44. O'Brien, Ph.D. thesis, p. 133; Pollins, op. cit., p. 133: A. Leon, *The Jewish Question. A Marxist Interpretation* (New York, 1970 edn), carries an emphasis in this direction.

45. H. Frederic, *The New Exodus* (London, 1892).

46 L. Schapiro, 'The Russian Background of the Anglo-American Jewish Immigration', *TJHSE*, Vol. XX (1959–61), p. 23. A recent study of the movement to France, hitherto neglected, is N. Green, *The Pletzl of Paris. Jewish Immigrant Workers in the Belle Epoque* (New York, 1985).

47. T. Kemp, *Industrialization in Nineteenth Century Europe* (London, 1969 edn) is useful on the economic background; S. Lambroza, 'The Pogrom Movement in Tsarist Russia 1903–6', unpublished Ph.D. Thesis, Rutgers University, 1981; S. W. Baron, *The Russian Jew under the Tsars and Soviets* (New York, 1964 and 1977); N. Cohn, *Warrant for Genocide* (London, 1967); J. Frankel, *Prophecy and Politics. Socialism, Nationalism and the Russian Jews 1862–1917* (Cambridge, 1981); and S. M. Berk, *Year of Crisis. Year of Hope: Russian Jewry and the Pogroms of 1881–1882* (London, 1985) all help more specifically with this background. For the impact on individual families see S. Brodetsky, *Memoirs: From Ghetto to Israel* (London, 1960) and R. Odle, *Salt of Our Youth* (Penzance, 1972).

48. Rodgers, op. cit., p. 113.

49. For a discussion of 'acute' and 'anticipatory' refugees see E. F. Kunz, 'The Refugee in Flight: Kinetic Models and Forms of Displacement', *International Migration Review*, Vol. 7 (1973), pp. 125–46.

50. Based on L. Gartner, *The Jewish Immigrant in England 1870–1914* (Detroit, 1960 edn), pp. 26–7.

51. Pollins, op. cit., p. 135.

52. Even so, B. Gainer, *The Alien Invasion. The Origins of the Aliens Act of 1905* (London, 1972) consigns other alien arrivals from Eastern Europe into oblivion.

53. J. D. White, 'Scottish Lithuanians and the Russian Revolution', *Journal of Baltic Studies*, Vol. 6 (1975), p. 2.

54. M. Rodgers, 'Political Developments in the Lithuanian Community in Scotland c. 1890–1923', in J. Slatter (ed.), *'From The Other Shore.' Russian Political Emigrants in Britain 1880–1917* (London, 1984), p. 141.

55. Ibid., p. 142.

56. See below pp. 105–6.

57. M. Rodgers, 'Italiani in Scozzia', in Kay, *Odyssey. The Second Collection*, p. 13; see also Kiernan, op. cit., p. 41.

58. All these figures are taken from Carrier and Jeffery, op. cit., pp. 127–8.

59. See L. Sponza, 'The Italian Poor in Nineteenth Century Britain', unpublished

Ph.D. Thesis, London University, 1984, p. 38; A. Wilkin, 'Origins and Destinations of the Early Italo-Scots', *Association of Teachers of Italian, Journal*, No. 29 (1979), p. 53; R. King, 'Italian Migration to Great Britain', *Geography*, Vol. 62 (1977), p. 177; R. Palmer, 'The Italians: Patterns of Emigration to London', in J. L. Watson (ed.), *Between Two Cultures* (Oxford, 1977), p. 245.

60. Sponza, Ph.D. Thesis, pp. 36–7. See also R. F. Foerster, *The Italian Emigration of Our Times* (New York, 1968; first published 1919), pp. 40, 107, 123ff.

61. Foerster, op. cit., p. 417.

62. An emphasis in ibid., p. 164.

63. Rodgers, 'Italiani', p. 13.

64. Count E. Armfelt, 'Italy in London', in Sims, op. cit., Vol. 1, pp. 183–9.

65. These spatial shifts are referred to by L. Sponza, 'Attitudes Towards the Italian Poor in 19th Century Britain', presented at the Warwick University symposium on 'The Italian Diaspora', held on 12 May 1984. The same ground is covered in more detail in his Ph.D. thesis, Ch. 1.

66. King, op. cit., p. 177 and Sponza, Ph.D. Thesis, passim.

67. R. A. Freeman, 'The New Jersey Sphinx', in *Famous Cases of Dr. Thorndyke* (London, 1929), p. 941.

68. Tan Chet-Qua is referred to in Kiernan, op. cit., p. 41. On the Sackville family there is D. A. Lorimer, *Colour, Class and the Victorians* (Leicester, 1978), p. 25. The affray involving sailors is from V. Berridge, 'East End Opium Dens and Narcotic Use in Britain', *The London Journal*, Vol. 4 (1978), p. 3.

69. Derived from *Census of England and Wales, 1871* etc., p. li; *Census of England and Wales, 1921, General Report* (London, 1927) p. 154; *Report on the Twelfth Decennial Census of Scotland*, Vol. III (Edinburgh, 1913), p. xiii.

70. On which see, for example, G. Barth, *Bitter Strength: A History of the Chinese in the United States, 1850–1870* (Cambridge, Mass., 1964) and A. Markus, *Fear and Hatred, Purifying Australia and California 1850–1901* (Sydney, 1979).

71. Ibid. See also Ng Kwee Choo, *The Chinese in London* (London, 1968), p. 9.

72. M. Broady, 'The Chinese in Great Britain' in M. H. Fried (ed.), *Colloquium on Overseas Chinese* (New York, 1958), p. 29. On Suez see D. A. Farnie, *East and West of Suez: The Suez Canal in History* (Oxford, 1969).

73. F. Lindop, 'A History of Seamen's Trade Unionism to 1929', unpublished M.Phil. Thesis, London University, 1979, pp. 21ff.

74. Ng, op. cit., p. 18.

75. See above pp. 8–10.

76. J. Walvin, *Black and White. The Negro and English Soceity 1555–1945* (London, 1973).

77. E. Dixon, 'The American Negro in Nineteenth Century Scotland', unpublished M.Litt. Thesis, Edinburgh University, 1969.

78. H. Mayhew, *London Labour and the London Poor* (4 vols, New York, 1968), Vol. 3, p. 191, and Vol. 4, p. 425. For additional comment on minstrels see G. F. Rehin, 'Blackface Minstrels in Victorian London and its Resorts: Popular Culture and its Racial Connotations as revealed in Polite Opinion', *Journal of Popular Culture*, Vol. 15 (1981) pp. 19–38.

79. Walvin, op. cit., p. 197.

80. Ibid., pp. 199 and 202–3.

81. E. Scobie, *Black Britannia* (Chicago, 1972), pp. 121–2.

82. See W. A. Ferris, *The African Abroad* (2 vols. New York, 1913), Vol. 2, p. 840 on businessmen. A good account of West Africans in Britain, including students, is in R. Jenkins, 'Gold Coasters Overseas 1880–1919: with specific reference to their activities in Britain', *Immigrants and Minorities*, Vol. 4 (1985), pp. 5–42. For a contemporary, fictional account see C. Hayford, *Ethiopia Unbound* (London,

1911). The student Kwamankra is Hayford, questing for 'the golden tree of knowledge'. On the need to cultivate such student opinion see K. Little, *Negroes in Britain* (London, 1948 edn), p. 193.

83. *Report of the Committee on Distressed Colonial and Indian Subjects*, British Parliamentary Papers, Vol. XXII, 1910, Cd. 5133.

84. J. Salter, *The Asiatic in England* (London, 1873), p. 255.

85. *The Times*, 7 February 1984. See also M. Alexander and S. Anand, *Queen Victoria's Maharaja. Duleep Singh 1838–93* (London, 1980) and K. Vadgama, *Indians in Britain* (London, 1984), pp. 53–6.

86. Vadgama, op. cit., p. 20. 'Munshi' is teacher.

87. R. P. Masani, *Dadabhai Naoroji* (London, 1939), p. 71, notes the foundation of Cama and Co in 1855.

88. BPP 1910, pp. 14–16. See also M. K. Gandhi, *An Autobiography or the Story of My Experiments with Truth* (Ahmedabad, 1958; first edition 1927). Additional comment on Indian student life is in K. Chowdray, 'The Indian Students in England', *The Student Movement*, Vol. XII (1910), pp. 86–8 and 'Indian Students in Great Britain', *Edinburgh Review*, Vol. 217 (1913), pp. 138–56.

89. *The Times* 16 October 1982. See the obituary in ibid., 4 November 1985.

90. R. Bowen, *Cricket. A History of its Growth and Development throughout the World* (London, 1970), p. 141.

91. Gandhi, op. cit., pp. 43–4.

92. H. Bolitho, *Jinnah. Creator of Pakistan* (Karachi, 1966), p. 14. Jinnah returned to Britain between 1930 and 1934.

93. S. Gopal, *Jawaharlal Nehru. A Biography*, Vol. 1, 1889–1947 (London, 1975), pp. 19–22.

94. K. Hunter, *History of Pakistanis in Britain* (Norwich, 1962?), p. 33. Iqbal was the author of 'Tarana': 'We are Muslims, the whole world is ours'.

95. P. K. Martinez, 'Paris Communard Refugees in Britain 1871–1880', unpublished D.Phil. Thesis, Sussex University, 1981; S. Hutchins, 'The Communard Exiles in Britain', *Marxism Today* (March, 1971), pp. 90–2; ibid. (April, 1971), pp. 117–20; ibid. (June, 1971), pp. 180–6. See also P. Villars, 'French London', in Sims, op. cit., Vol. 2, pp. 33–8.

96. J. R. Williams, 'The Influence of Foreign Nationalities on the Life of the People of Merthyr Tydfil', *Sociological Review*, Vol. XVIII (1926), pp. 150–1, and see below p. 290.

97. Kiernan, op. cit., p. 51. For the influence of another émigré from Bohemia, Franz Kapir, see N. Todd, *Roses and Revolutionists* (London, 1985).

98. *Select Committee on Emigration and Immigration*, Vol. XI, 1888, pp. 154–65. See also J. Zubrzycki, *Polish Immigrants in Britain. A Study of Adjustment* (The Hague, 1956), pp. 38–41.

99. F. R. Dulles, *Americans Abroad, Two Centuries of European Travel* (Ann Arbor, 1964), p. 19.

100. S. Weintraub, *The London Yankees* (London, 1979).

101. Dulles, op. cit., p. 16.

102. J. Laver, *Whistler* (London, 1930).

103. R. Kenin, *Return to Albion. Americans in England 1760–1940* (New York, 1979), pp. 227–8, 221; E. Banks, 'American London', in Sims, op. cit., Vol. 2, pp. 107–13.

104. C. O'Connor Eccles, 'Scottish, Irish and Welsh London', in Sims, op. cit., Vol. 2, pp. 267, 271.

105. O'Connor, op. cit., p. 39. On Collins see below p. 150.

106. J. Denvir, *The Irish in Britain* (London, 1892), p. 405; V. G. Kiernan, *European Empires from Conquest to Collapse, 1915–1960* (London, 1982), pp. 20–2; J. Walvin, *Passage to Britain* (Harmondsworth, 1984), p. 49; R. Faber, *High Road to England*

(London, 1985), p. 96; K. O. Morgan, *Wales in British Politics 1868–1922* (Cardiff, 1970 edn), p. 69 notes that the Royal Monmouthshire Militia was commonly known as 'The Pope's Own'.

107. C. Andrew, *Secret Service, The Making of the British Intelligence Community* (London, 1985), p. 19.

108. E. D. Steele, 'The Irish Presence in the North of England 1850–1914', *Northern History*, Vol. XII (1976), p. 226 and R. B. O'Brien, *Lord Russell of Killowen* (London, 1901).

109. E. H. Hunt, *British Labour History 1815–1914* (London, 1981), p. 160.

110. J. Handley, *The Irish in Modern Scotland* (Cork, 1947), pp. 173–4.

111. D. H. Morgan, *Harvesters and Harvesting 1840–1910* (London, 1982), p. 77.

112. R. Jefferies, *Nature Near London* (London, 1883), pp. 82–4.

113. Morgan, op. cit., p. 82; Handley, op. cit., p. 164.

114. O'Tuathaigh, op. cit., p. 154. See also Steele, op. cit., p. 224.

115. Lees, op. cit., Ch. 4.

116. Anon, 'The London Irish', *Blackwoods Edinburgh Magazine*, Vol. CLXX (1901), p. 129.

117. Ibid., p. 126.

118. W. W. Walker, *Juteopolis. Dundee and its Textile Workers 1885–1923* (Edinburgh, 1979), p. 120.

119. Handley, op. cit., p. 122.

120. Paddy the Cope, *My Story* (London, 1939), p. 56. On the author see 'Patrick Gallagher', in J. M. Bellamy and J. Saville (eds), *Dictionary of Labour Biography*, Vol. 1 (London, 1972), p. 128.

121. Handley, op. cit., pp. 136–7. R. D. Lobban, 'The Irish Community in Greenock in the Nineteenth Century', *Irish Geography*, Vol. 6 (1961) p. 271 notes the concentration of the Irish in unskilled and semi-skilled work and ibid., pp. 276–7, refers to the continuity of this work among their Scottish-born children.

122. O'Tuathaigh, op. cit., p. 155; N. Kirk, 'Ethnicity, Class and Popular Toryism', in Lunn, op. cit., pp. 83ff. notes the build-up of the Irish in cotton.

123. Jackson, op. cit., p. 94.

124. Steele, op. cit., p. 224.

125. O'Tuathaigh, op. cit., pp. 157–8.

126. Ibid., p. 159.

127. Walker, op. cit., Ch. III, pp. 130, 139.

128. Steele, op. cit., p. 226.

129. E. P. Thompson, *The Making of the English Working Class* (New York, 1963 edn), pp. 473–5.

130. Jackson, op. cit., p. 93.

131. Hunt, op. cit., pp. 172–3.

132. Ibid., pp. 173–4.

133. All based on ibid., p. 175.

134. G. Stedman Jones, *Outcast London* (Oxford, 1971), p. 149; M. J. Daunton, *Coal Metropolis, Cardiff 1870–1914* (Leicester, 1979), p. 144; T. Gallagher, 'A Tale of Two Cities: Communal Strife in Glasgow and London before 1914', in Swift and Gilley, op. cit., p. 106. On the two latter cities see also J. Smith, 'Labour Tradition in Glasgow and Liverpool'. *History Workshop Journal*, Vol. 17 (1984), p. 49.

135. O'Tuathaigh, op. cit., p. 154; Lobban, op. cit., pp. 275–8.

136. Swift and Gilley, op. cit., pp. 5, 185.

137. Lees, op. cit., p. 16.

138. Minimised in ibid.

139. Based on Handley, op. cit., pp. 228–9.

140. O'Conor Eccles, op. cit., pp. 270–1 and Handley, op. cit., pp. 227–34. On the Hibernians see, for example, Hickey, MA Thesis, pp. 135ff. and J. Denvir, *Life Story of an Old Rebel* (Shannon, 1972; first published Dublin, 1910), pp. 16–19. On Celtic see J. E. Handley, *The Celtic Story. A History of the Celtic Football Club* (London, 1960). See also B. Murray, *The Old Firm. Sectarianism, Sport and Society in Scotland* (Edinburgh, 1984), which constructs a social history of the west of Scotland around the story of Rangers and Celtic.

141. W. W. Walker, 'Irish Immigrants in Scotland, their Priests, Politics and Parochial Life', *Historical Journal*, Vol. 15 (1972), pp. 651, 655.

142. O'Tuathaigh, op. cit., p. 168.

143. D. Gwynn, 'The Irish Immigrants', in G. A. Beck (ed.), *The English Catholics 1850–1950* (London, 1950), p. 265. But for a more cautious view see G. Connolly, 'Irish and Catholic: Myth or Reality?', in Swift and Gilley, op. cit., pp. 225–54.

144. Steele, op. cit., p. 221.

145. Lees, op. cit., Ch. 7. See also R. Samuel, 'The Roman Catholic Church and the Irish Poor', in Swift and Gilley, op. cit., p. 285. Among contemporaries, Booth, op. cit., not only commented on the strength of Roman Catholicism within the 'Fenian Barracks' (p. 243) but also on the nature of the Catholicism of the Irish (p. 247).

146. Walker, *Juteopolis*, Ch. 3 and see below pp. 42, 60–2.

147. K. R. M. Short, *The Dynamite War: Irish-American Bombers in Victorian Britain* (Dublin, 1979); P. Quinlivan and P. Rose, *The Fenians in England 1865–1872* (London, 1982).

148. T. Corfe, *The Phoenix Park Murders* (London, 1968) and see below pp. 58, 60.

149. Denvir, *Life Story* and H. Fyfe, *T. P. O'Connor* (London, 1934) carry details on the activities of leading figures. See also the more recent, L. W. Brady, *T. P. O'Connor and the Liverpool Irish* (London, 1983).

150. H. W. Benjamin, 'The London Irish. A Study in Political Activism', unpublished Ph.D. Thesis, Princeton University, 1976, p. 331.

151. Jackson, op. cit., pp. 120–3; Brady, op. cit. and Gallagher, op. cit. outline such developments and provide some of the context. On Liverpool, see also P. J. Waller, *Democracy and Sectarianism. A Political and Social History of Liverpool 1868–1939* (Liverpool, 1981).

152. S. Gilley, 'Catholics and Socialists in Glasgow 1906–1912' in Lunn, op. cit., p. 167.

153. Walker, *Historical Journal*, p. 655.

154. Handley, *Irish*, p. 302.

155. Barker and Harris, op. cit., p. 457.

156. In general see M. McDermott, 'Irish Catholics and the British Labour Movement; A Study with particular reference to London 1918–1970', unpublished MA Thesis, Kent University, 1979, Ch. 1; on Connolly there is C. D. Greaves, *The Life and Times of James Connolly* (London, 1961) and S. Levenson, *James Connolly: a Biography* (London, 1973); on Larkin see E. Larkin, *James Larkin, Irish Labour Leader 1876–1947* (London, 1965).

157. Lees, op. cit., p. 242. But see, J. Lovell, 'The Irish and the London dockers', *Society for the Study of Labour History Bulletin*, No. 35 (1977), pp. 16–19. Tebbutt, M.Phil. Thesis, p. 111 notes that the unionisation of seasonal agricultural workers prevented the Irish being used in Lancashire as blacklegs in the 1913 Agricultural Labourers' strike.

158. J. Lovell, *Stevedores and Dockers: A Study of Trade Unionism in the Port of London 1870–1914* (London, 1969), pp. 57–8, discusses the role of the Irish in the docks. See also Denvir, *The Irish*, p. 394.

159. Noticed in Stedman-Jones, op. cit., pp. 348–9, who like Lovell, in *Labour History*

Bulletin, is cautious on the degree of involvement of the Irish in the Labour movement. For comment on the situation in Scotland, see I. Wood, 'Irish Immigrants and Scottish Radicalism, 1880–1906', in I. MacDougall (ed.), *Essays in Scottish Labour History. A Tribute to W. H. Marwick* (Edinburgh, 1978), pp. 65–90.

160. Hickey, MA Thesis, p. 130 for comment.
161. Steele, op. cit., p. 240.
162. Gilley, 'Catholics and Socialists', p. 195. See also ibid., pp. 163–4. See also Wood, op. cit., pp. 66, 87.
163. Hickey, M.Phil. Thesis, pp. 133–5; R. J. Cooter, 'The Irish in Durham and Newcastle', unpublished MA Thesis, Durham University, 1972, pp. 42–4; F. Lavery, *Irish Heroes in the War* (London, 1917), p. 32; P. Thompson, *Socialists, Liberals and Labour: The Struggle for London 1885–1914* (London, 1960), p. 26.
164. Anderson, op. cit. On Mr Pooter see G. and W. Grossmith, *The Diary of a Nobody* (London, 1892).
165. J. Goodman, *The Mond Legacy* (London, 1982) and Aronsfeld, op. cit., generally. L. Hannah, 'Entrepreneurs and the Social Sciences', LSE Inaugural Lecture, 1983, contains comment on the importance of immigrant entrepreneurship.
166. Aronsfeld, op. cit., p. 316. See also A. R. Rollin, 'The Jewish Contribution to the British Textile Industry: Builders of Bradford', *T.J.H.S.E.*, Vol. XVII (1951–2), pp. 45–51. More generally see J. B. Priestley, *English Journey* (London, 1968 edn; first published 1934), pp. 160–1.
167. Aronsfeld, op. cit., p. 317.
168. S. D. Chapman, 'The Migration of Merchant Enterprise: German Merchant Houses in Britain in the 18th and 19th Centuries', in *Bankhistorisches, Archiv, Zeitschrift zur Bankgeschichte*, Vol. 1 (1980), p. 29 on N. M. Rothschild. On Cassel see B. Connell, *Manifest Destiny* (London, 1953), Ch. 2.
169. Holmes, op. cit., p. 250.
170. Count E. Armfelt, 'German London', in Sims, op. cit., Vol. 3, pp. 57–62.
171. L. Katscher, 'German Life in London', *Nineteenth Century*, Vol. 21 (1887), pp. 726–41.
172. Ibid., pp. 736, 728.
173. Aronsfeld, op. cit., p. 325.
174. On Speyer, see below pp. 99, 342–3. On Japhet there is S. Japhet, *Recollections from My Business Life* (London, 1931), p. 62.
175. See below, pp. 94–9.
176. Aronsfeld, op. cit., p. 315. W. W. S. Adams, *Edwardian Portraits* (London, 1957), pp. 55–7 is useful on Cassel's financial affairs.
177. Aronsfeld, op. cit., p. 320.
178. P. G. J. Pulzer, *The Rise of Political Anti-Semitism in Germany and Austria* (New York, 1964).
179. Aronsfeld, op. cit., p. 319.
180. Ibid., p. 319. See also N. Cardus, *Autobiography* (London, 1947), p. 48.
181. Pollins, op. cit., is the most recently published general survey of the economic life of the immigrants. For more specific detail see J. White, *Rothschild Buildings: Life in an East End Tenement Block, 1887–1920* (London, 1980), Ch. 6, and Buckman, op. cit.
182. *R.C.* 1903, pp. 19–20.
183. Hunt, op. cit., p. 321. See also S. Lerner, 'The Impact of the Jewish Immigration of 1880–1914 on the London Clothing Industry and Trade Unions', *Society for the Study of Labour History Bulletin*, No. 12 (1966), pp. 12–15.
184. An emphasis in Pollins, op. cit.
185. Ibid.

186.   See below pp. 67–8.
187.   See below pp. 87–8.
188.   See below pp. 67–73.
189.   See below p. 68.
190.   Gainer, op. cit., Ch. 4, 'The Englishman's Castle', partic. pp. 36–44. White, op. cit., is a detailed study of housing for the Jewish immigrants in the East End. A good deal of evidence on East End housing is in J. J. Bennett, 'East End Newspaper Opinion and Jewish Immigration 1885–1905', unpublished M.Phil. Thesis, Sheffield University, 1979, partic. Ch. I.B.
191.   *Heder* (plural *Hadarim*) was literally a one-room school, usually the teacher's house.
192.   White, op. cit; D. Feldman, 'Immigrants and Workers: Englishmen and Jews: Jewish Immigration to the East End of London, 1880–1906', unpublished Ph.D. Thesis, Cambridge University, 1985; W. J. Fishman, *The Streets of East London* (London, 1979). M. Shinwell, *Lead with the Left* (London, 1981) Ch. 1 'East End Childhood' notes the distance within the East End between Dutch Jews and Russian Poles.
193.   L. Schapiro, 'Jews in the Revolutionary Movement', *Slavonic and East European Review*, Vol. XL (1961), pp. 148–67.
194.   R. L. Cohen, 'The Influence of Jewish Radical Movements on Adult Education among Jewish Immigrants in the East End of London, 1881–1914', unpublished M.Ed. Thesis, Liverpool University, 1977; R. Rocker, *The London Years* (London, 1956) and W. J. Fishman, *East End Jewish Radicals 1875–1914* (London, 1975).
195.   Slatter, op. cit.; W. Kendall, *The Revolutionary Movement in Britain 1900–1921* (London, 1965); R. Challinor, *The Origins of British Bolshevism* (London, 1977), Chs, 6, 7, 8.
196.   Buckman, op. cit., Ch. 1 carries trenchant comment on this.
197.   Ibid.
198.   B. Williams, 'The Beginnings of Jewish Trade Unionism in Manchester 1889–1891', in Lunn, op. cit., pp. 263–307, carries an emphasis on this theme.
199.   Lipman, *Social History*, p. 93.
200.   R. Burman, 'The Jewish Woman as Breadwinner', ts. and her 'The Jewish Woman as Breadwinner: The Changing Value of Women's Work in a Manchester Immigrant Community', *Oral History*, Vol. 10 (1982), pp. 27–39. These are based on tapes in the Manchester Jewish Museum.
201.   B. A. Kosmin, 'Nuptiality and Fertility Patterns of British Jewry 1850–1950: An Immigrant Transition?', in D. A. Coleman (ed.), *Demography of Immigrants and Minority Groups* (London, 1982), p. 253. See also O'Brien, Ph.D. Thesis, p. 162.
202.   Kosmin, op. cit., pp. 259–60.
203.   Gartner, op. cit., p. 221, Livshin, M.Ed. Thesis and Feldman, Ph.D. Thesis, are useful on the pressures faced by the newcomers. See also B. Williams, 'The Anti-Semitism of Tolerance: Middle Class Manchester and the Jews 1870–1900', in A. J. Kidd and K. Roberts (eds), *City, Class and Culture* (Manchester, 1985), pp. 92ff.
204.   M. Rodgers, 'The Lanarkshire Lithuanians', in Kay, op. cit., Vol. 1, pp. 19–25.
205.   K. Lunn, 'Reactions to Lithuanian and Polish Immigrants in the Lanarkshire Coalfield, 1880–1914', in Lunn, op. cit., p. 310.
206.   *Select Committee on Emigration and Immigration*, Vol. X, 1889, Appendix 8, pp. 94–5.
207.   See below pp. 73–4.
208.   Based on Lunn, 'Reactions to Lithuanians', partic. p. 325. See also below pp. 73–4.
209.   Lunn, 'Reactions to Lithuanians', p. 326.

210. Rodgers, 'Political Developments', pp. 143–6.
211. Discussion based on ibid., pp. 146–7 and Gilley, 'Catholics and Socialists', *passim.*
212. Sponza, Ph.D. Thesis, Ch. 3 discusses occupations.
213. Quoted in W. H. Wilkins, 'The Italian Aspect', in A. White (ed.), *The Destitute Alien in Great Britain* (London, 1892), p. 166.
214. Sponza, ts. p. 4. See also his Ph.D. Thesis Ch. 4.
215. Detail from Sponza, ts. p. 2. See also his Ph.D. Thesis Ch. 2.
216. Foerster, op. cit., p. 204.
217. C. Sardi, 'I Gelatieri italiani nella Scozia', *Revista Coloniale*, Aug 25–Sep 10, 1911, p. 285.
218. Ibid., p. 286.
219. D. D. Johnson, 'Italian Style', *The Guardian*, 26 June 1974; see also Rodgers, 'Italiani in Scozzia', p. 14.
220. Rodgers, 'Italiani in Scozzia', p. 16.
221. King, op. cit., p. 177.
222. Ibid. One of the most prominent was the so-called 'Mazzini-Garibaldi Club'. See R. Palmer, 'The Italians: Patterns of Migration to London', in Watson, op. cit., p. 254.
223. King, op. cit., p. 177.
224. *Royal Commission on the Housing of the Working Classes*, Vol. XXX, 1884–5 First Report, pp. 135–6, for example.
225. See below pp. 76–7.
226. Ng, op. cit., p. 10 on occupations; J. P. May, 'The Chinese in Britain 1860–1914', in Holmes, *Immigrants and Minorities*, p. 111 on the Blue Funnel Line. The history of the Company is covered in F. E. Hyde, *Blue Funnel* (Liverpool, 1964). On the Chinese in Liverpool see S. Craggs, 'A History of the Chinese Communities in Liverpool', unpublished Local History Diploma Dissertation, Liverpool University, 1983. See above p. 32 for earlier comment.
227. D. Jones, 'The Chinese in Britain: Origins and Development of a Community', *New Community*, Vol. 11 (1979), p. 399.
228. Craggs, Diploma Dissertation, pp. 15, 20.
229. Ng, op. cit., p. 10.
230. Craggs, Diploma Dissertation, pp. 26–8.
231. Ng. op. cit., p. 12.
232. May, op. cit., p. 122.
233. Ng, op. cit., p. 18.
234. Berridge, op. cit., p. 3.
235. Ng, op. cit., p. 20; Craggs Diploma Dissertation, Section 3 and pp. 5, 54.
236. Quoted in May, op. cit., p. 119.
237. Letter 8 December 1906 in PRO HO 45/11843/139147/8.
238. See below pp. 79–80 on all these themes.
239. P. Fryer, *Staying Power. The History of Black People in Britain* (London, 1984), p. 295; Little, op. cit., p. 192.
240. BPP 1910, p. 20.
241. See below p. 82.
242. Salter, op. cit., pp. 8–12.
243. BPP 1910, p. 17.
244. Ibid.
245. See above on these groups and Gopal, op. cit., p. 27 for comment on Nehru's finances when in Britain.
246. Fryer, op. cit., pp. 272, 277–9, 280.
247. Ibid., pp. 287–90 gives a recent character sketch. We still await Ian Duffield's biography of Ali, based on his Edinburgh doctorate.

248. Fryer, op. cit., p. 288. See also G. Spiller (ed.), *Papers on Inter-Racial Problems communicated to the first Universal Races Congress held at the University of London* (London, 1911) and P. B. Rich, ' "The Baptism of a New Era": the 1911 Universal Races Congress and the Liberal Ideology of Race', *Ethnic and Racial Studies*, Vol. 7 (1984), pp. 534–50.

249. See below pp. 93, 136–8, 181–3.

250. R. P. Masani, *Dadabhai Naoroji* (London, 1939), p. 71.

251. Fryer, op. cit., p. 263.

252. Ibid., p. 264.

253. M. Cumpston, 'Some Early Indian Nationalists and their Allies in the British Parliament 1851–1906', *English Historical Review*, Vol. 76 (1961), pp. 279–97. Naoroji drew support from Irish voters.

254. Fryer, op. cit., pp. 265, 267–70.

255. The preceding arguments are based upon Jackson, op. cit.; Lees, op. cit.; G. E. Simpson and J. M. Yinger, *Racial and Cultural Minorities* (New York, 1974 edn), Ch. 5; L. P. Curtis, *Anglo-Saxons and Celts* (Bridgeport, Conn., 1968) and his *Apes and Angels. The Irishman in Victorian Caricature* (Newton Abbot, 1971); R. N. Lebow, *White Britain and Black Ireland, the Influence of Stereotypes on Colonial Policy* (Philadelphia, 1976) and the criticism of Curtis and others in S. Gilley, 'English Attitudes to the Irish in England 1789–1900', in Holmes, *Immigrants and Minorities*, pp. 81–100, and the introduction to Swift and Gilley, op. cit., p. 5. See below Ch. 7 for more discussion.

256. The discussion is derived from Handley, *Irish*, pp. 249, 121; O'Tuathaigh, op. cit., p. 162; *1871 Census (Scotland)* Irish University Press reprint (Shannon, 1970), p. 47; R. Miles, *Racism and Migrant Labour* (London, 1982), pp. 121–50. Keir Hardie's remarks are given in D. Howell, *British Workers and the Independent Labour Party, 1886–1906* (Manchester, 1983), p. 142. R. A. Burchell, 'The Historiography of the American Irish', *Immigrants and Minorities*, Vol. 1 (1982), p. 281, refers to the paucity of information on the Irish abroad in the late nineteenth century. The work of Miles, op. cit., is based essentially on earlier years. Swift and Gilley, op. cit., has gone some way – but not very far – towards rectifying the situation.

257. Orange and Green violence is discussed in Handley, *Irish*, pp. 117–19; P. McGeown, *Heat and Furnace Seven Times More* (London, 1968), p. 15, recalling his childhood in Craigneuk, 'a beautiful place before the advent of slag tips and belching stacks'; A. H. Campbell, *The Lanarkshire Miners* (Edinburgh, 1979), pp. 316–19. The violence generated by the issue of Home Rule is referred to in Cooter, MA Thesis, p. 267; Handley, *Irish*, pp. 257–9; Kay, 'From Gorbals', p. 6; Gallagher, op. cit. See also Murray, op. cit., p. 101 for a graphic visual illustration.

258. Morgan, op. cit., p. 69.

259. J. Parry, 'The Tredegar Anti-Irish Riots of 1882', *Llafur*, Vol. III (1983), pp. 20–3 based on HO 144/100/A 18355. On Phoenix Park see Corfe, op. cit.

260. Stedman Jones, op. cit., pp. 148–9. J. Schneer, *Ben Tillett: Portrait of a Labour Leader* (London, 1982), does not develop Tillett's views on the Irish, Jews or Germans. See above for the Irish in trade unions.

261. W. O. Henderson (ed.), *Engels: Selected Writings* (London, 1967), p. 95.

262. Hunt, op. cit., p. 162. See also L. O. Pike, *A History of Crime in England* (2 vols, London, 1876), Vol. 2, pp. 517–22, 527–28, 670–72. There are passing references in K. Chesney, *The Victorian Underworld* (London, 1970).

263. Cooter, MA Thesis, pp. 42–4; Lees, op. cit., pp. 207–11.

264. O'Tuathaigh, op. cit., p. 169.

265. See above p. 40.

266. Jackson, op. cit., p. 137.

267. Ibid., p. 154.

268. PRO HO 45/1138/186474/1 Communication from the Head Constable of Liverpool to the Attorney-General, 24 May 1909. See also Waller, op. cit., Chs 11, 12, 14 partic.; Gallagher, op. cit.; Smith, op. cit.; P. O'Mara, *Autobiography of a Liverpool Irish Slummy* (London, 1934), pp. 86ff and A. Shallice, 'Orange and Green and Militancy: Sectarianism and Working-Class Politics in Liverpool 1900–1914', *North-West Labour History Society, Bulletin*, No. 6 (1979–80), pp. 15–32. The reference to Liverpool Marseilles is from T. H. S. Escott, *England; Its People, Policy and Pursuits* (London, 1985 edn) p. 85.

269. Claimed in Jackson, op. cit., p. 154.

270. E. R. Norman, review of W. L. Arnstein, *Protestant Versus Catholic in mid-Victorian England* (1982) in *The Times Literary Supplement*, 16 July 1982, p. 758. See also E. R. Norman, *Anti-Catholicism in Victorian England* (London, 1968).

271. See above p. 58.

272. Hunt, op. cit., p. 171; Waller, op. cit., pp. 25, 141.

273. Walker, *Juteopolis*, p. 121; T. P. McDermott, 'Irish Workers on Tyneside in the 19th Century', in N. McCord (ed.), *Essays in Tyneside Labour History* '(Newcastle, 1977), pp. 154–75.

274. F. Thompson, *Lark Rise to Candleford* (Harmondsworth, 1976 edn), p. 236. See also S. Barber, 'Irish Migrant Agricultural Labourers in Nineteenth Century Lincolnshire', *Saothar*, Vol. 8 (1982), p. 21.

275. Lees, op. cit., p. 242 moves in this direction. See also O'Tuathaigh, op. cit., pp. 171–3 for details and changes that were taking place.

276. Waller, op. cit.; Gallagher, op. cit.

277. R. Roberts, *The Classic Slum* (Harmondsworth, 1974 edn), pp. 22–3.

278. See above p. 58.

279. O'Tuathaigh, op. cit., pp. 171–2.

280. Gilley, 'The Irish', *passim*. The drawings of John Tenniel, many of which are reproduced in Curtis, *Apes and Angels*, provide some of the most vivid testimony of this alleged inferiority.

281. Swift and Gilley, op. cit., Introduction, p. 9.

282. Roberts, op. cit., p. 22.

283. Swift and Gilley, op. cit., p. 5.

284. Some indication of attitudes towards Germany can be found in Aronsfeld, op. cit., p. 314 and Curtis, *Anglo-Saxons and Celts*, Ch. VI. See also H. A. MacDougall, *Racial Myth in English History* (Montreal, 1982). On Freeman see C. J. W. Parker, 'The Failure of Liberal Racialism: The Racial Ideas of E. A. Freeman', *Historical Journal*, Vol. 24 (1981), pp. 835–46 and J. W. Barrow, *A Liberal Descent. Victorian Historians and the English Past* (Cambridge, 1981) Pt III. For additional comment see Faber, op. cit., p. 162. On Cobbett see D. Green, *Great Cobbett. The Noblest Agitator* (Oxford, 1985), pp. 345ff. On German refugees see Porter, op. cit. A. Hennessy, paper delivered at the International Conference on the History and Ideology of Anglo-Saxon Racial Attitudes c. 1870–1970, Selly Oak, Birmingham, 13 Sept. 1982, referred to British perceptions of Europe and Europeans. Comment is also carried in Lorimer, op. cit., p. 16, and M. D. Biddiss, 'Racial Ideas and the Politics of Prejudice', *Historical Journal*, Vol. XV (1972), pp. 570–82, partic. p. 572.

285. Anderson, op. cit., p. 208.

286. G. Anderson, *Victorian Clerks* (Manchester, 1976), pp. 60–5.

287. G. R. Searle, *The Quest for National Efficiency: A Study in British Politics and Political Thought 1899–1914* (Oxford, 1971); C. Holmes and A. H. Ion, 'Bushidō and the Samurai: Images in British Public Opinion', *Modern Asian Studies*, Vol. 14 (1980), pp. 309–29.

288. First published in 1896.
289. See below on this page.
290. The cartoon appears in M. Beerhohm, *Fifty Caricatures* (London, 1913), No. 47. C. Holmes, *Antisemitism in British Society 1876–1939* (London, 1979) Ch. 5 discusses the anti-Semitic dimension.
291. G. M. Mitchell, 'John Buchan's Fiction: A Hierachy of Race', *Patterns of Prejudice*, Vol. VII (November–December 1973), pp. 24–30. D. H. T. Stafford, 'Conspiracy and Xenophobia. The Popular Spy Novels of William Le Queux, 1893–1914', *Europa*, Vol. 4 (1981), pp. 163–85; idem, 'Spies and Gentlemen: The Birth of the British Spy Novel 1853–1914', *Victorian Studies*, Vol. 24 (1981), pp. 489–509.
292. A good example of the spy scare can be found in J. E. Porteous, *Peaceful Invasion of Great Britain* (London, 1914). For a saner perspective there is Andrew, op. cit., Ch. 2, 'Spies and Spy Scares. The Birth of the Secret Service Bureau'. He notes (pp. 53–4) that German spies were at work in Britain but it was a network of 'poorly paid and clumsy part-time agents'. For a wider sweep of Anglo-Saxon relations see A. J. A. Morris, *The Scaremongers. The Advocacy of Rearmament 1896–1914* (London, 1984), Chs 3 and 8 and P. M. Kennedy, *The Rise of Anglo-German Antagonism 1860–1914* (London, 1980). The radical Right and its opposition to foreigners is discussed in G. R. Searle, 'Critics of Edwardian Society: The Case of the Radical Right', in A. O'Day (ed.), *The Edwardian Age: Conflict and Stability 1900–1914* (London, 1979), pp. 79–96.
293. Taken from PRO HO 45/10313/124855/25.
294. PRO HO 45/10313/124855/77 and 79. See D. Mayall, 'Gypsy Travellers in Nineteenth Century Society', on the hostility of indigenous gypsies. This study will be published by Cambridge University Press in 1987.
295. *Parl. Deb.* (Commons), Vol. 162 (1906), 2 August 1906, col. 1357. See below on the 1905 Aliens Act.
296. See Holmes, 'The German Gypsy Question', for additional details.
297. There is some comment on this in Holmes, *Antisemitism*, Ch. 1. But for a fuller, valuable discussion see A. Lee, 'Aspects of the Working Class Response to the Jews in Britain 1880–1914', in Lunn, *Hosts, Immigrants and Minorities*, pp. 107–33. On the fragility of the emancipation contract see Williams, 'The Anti-Semitism of Tolerance'.
298. Holmes, *Antisemitism*, p. 19.
299. Garrard, op. cit., pp. 42–3, 98–9, 188, 207.
300. Porter, op. cit., Ch. 7 'Aftermath' and Garrard, op. cit., pp. 86ff and Pt III.
301. For factual details see P. D. Colbenson, 'British Socialism and Anti-Semitism 1884–1914', unpublished Ph.D. Thesis, Georgia State University 1977. A distorted view is reflected in E. Silberner, 'British Socialists and the Jews', *Historia Judaica*, Vol. XIV (1952), pp. 27–52 and his *Sozialisten zur Judenfrage* (Berlin, 1962). See Holmes, *Antisemitism*, pp. 21ff. for additional comment. See also above, p. 47, for the involvement by Jews in socialism in Britain.
302. See Bermant, op. cit., on the Anglo-Jewish elite. For a recent discussion of the elite and Jewish immigration see Feldman, Ph.D. Thesis. On the white slavery issue see E. J. Bristow, *Prostitution and Prejudice. The Jewish Fight against White Slavery* (Oxford, 1982).
303. Porter, op. cit., p. 218.
304. J. A. Hobson, *Problems of Poverty* (London, 1891), p. 60.
305. See my argument in 'J. A. Hobson and the Jews', in *Immigrants and Minorities*, pp. 125–57.
306. *East London Advertiser*, 3 March 1888.
307. Ibid., 10 January 1903 is good on landlords and aliens generally.

308. J. W. Carrier, 'The Four Per Cent Industrial Dwellings Company Limited', *East London Papers*, Vol. II (1968), pp. 40–6.

309. *East London Advertiser*, 6 May 1899. See above pp. 46ff. on Jewish culture in the East End.

310. *R.C.*, 1903, pp. 178, 286, 298.

311. *Eastern Post and City Chronicle*, 2 November 1901.

312. Referred to in Gainer, op. cit., p. 113.

313. See J. Banister, *England Under the Jews* (London, 1901) and my article, 'Joseph Banister's Antisemitism', *Patterns of Prejudice*, Vol. 4 (July–August 1970), pp. 29–32.

314. See Stedman Jones, op. cit.; Holmes, *Antisemitism*, Ch. 2; R. T. Shannon, *The Crisis of Imperialism, 1865–1915* (London, 1974), Ch. 5 partic. for this context. See also on the specific link between tariff reform and immigration control, Joseph Chamberlain's Limehouse speech of 15 December 1904 in C. W. Boyd (ed.), *Mr. Chamberlain's Speeches* (2 vols, London, 1914), pp. 262–3. For the eugenics aspect of the 'condition of England' see G. R. Searle, *Eugenics and Politics in Britain 1900–1914* (Leyden, 1976) and R. Solway, 'Counting the Degenerates: The Statistics of Race Deterioration in Edwardian England', *Journal of Contemporary History*, Vol. 17 (1982), pp. 137–64. For specific comment on the urban aspects of the crisis see the speculative unpublished paper by A. Sutcliffe, 'An Urban Crisis in the later Nineteenth Century? The British Case'. For the situation in the East End see Bennett, M.Phil. Thesis and Feldman, Ph.D. Thesis. The reference to the nation and the zenith of its development is from W. E. Evans Gordon, *The Alien Immigrant* (London, 1903), p. 38. See below p. 301 for additional comment on the belief in fixed resources.

315. Simpson and Yinger, op. cit., pp. 28–9.

316. E. E. Burgess, 'The Soul of the Leeds Ghetto', *Yorkshire Evening News*, 19 January 1925.

317. J. Namier, *Lewis Namier. A Biography* (London, 1971), p. 101.

318. *East London Observer*, 18 January 1902.

319. Holmes, *Antisemitism*, pp. 89–97 on the BBL.

320. *East End Argus*, 13 June 1903.

321. E. E. Burgess, 'The Soul of the Leeds Ghetto', *Yorkshire Evening News*, 19 January 1925; see also Roberts, op. cit., p. 171.

322. C. Holmes, 'The Tredegar Riots of 1911: Anti-Jewish Disturbances in South Wales', *Welsh History Review*, Vol. II (1982), pp. 214–25, based on the closed file HO 144/1160/212987.

323. See below p. 73.

324. T. S. Ashton, *An Economic History of England: The 18th Century* (London, 1955), p. 1.

325. Porter, op. cit., is useful on these developments. So is E. Pépin, 'L'Aliens Act de 1905. Causes et Résultats', unpublished DU thesis, Paris University, 1913, livre II, partic. pp. 42ff, 106ff.

326. *R.C.*, 1903, pp. 40–3 for details.

327. See the discussion in Garrard, op. cit., pp. 41–3.

328. Ibid., pp. 44–7. Pépin, Thesis, is an extremly comprehensive survey of the Act.

329. Garrard, op. cit., p. 45.

330. C. Holmes, 'In Search of Sidney Street', *Society for the Study of Labour History Bulletin*, No. 29 (Autumn, 1974), pp. 70–7. D. Rumbelow, *The Hounsditch Murders and the Siege of Sidney Street* (London, 1973) and, more recently, F. G. Clarke, *Will o' the Wisp. Peter the Painter and the Anti-Tsarist Terrorists in Britain and Australia* (Melbourne, 1983). The National Film Archive has 'Hounsditch Murderers: The Great Alien Outrage at Mile End Showing Actual Scenes' (item N354) and

'Sidney Street Siege' (N355). An edited version of the two films is in the Borough of Tower Hamlets Library. For opposition on film to alien immigration see Cecil Hepworth's, *The Aliens' Invasion* (1905), discussed in R. Low and R. Manvell, *The History of the British Film 1896–1906* (London, 1973 edn), p. 58.

331. Lunn, 'Reactions to Lithuanian and Polish Immigrants', pp. 308, 312–14.
332. Ibid., p. 311. See also *S. C. Emigration, Immigration*, 1889, pp. 63–9.
333. Lunn, 'Reactions to Lithuanian and Polish Immigrants', pp. 318ff. See above p. 49–50 for earlier references.
334. *R.C.*, 1903, p. 844.
335. Lunn, 'Reactions to Lithuanian and Polish Immigrants', p. 319.
336. *First Report of the Royal Commission on Mines*, Vol. XIV, 1907, Cd. 3548, Q5022 quoted in Lunn, 'Reactions to Lithuanian and Polish Immigrants', p. 321.
337. Lunn, 'Reactions to Lithuanian and Polish Immigrants', p. 323.
338. See above p. 50. See also K. Lunn, 'Immigrants and Strikes', *Immigrants and Minorities*, Vol. 4 (1985), pp. 38–9 for Lithuanians in the national strike of 1912.
339. *Commonwealth*, 26 November 1887; *Labour Leader*, 12 October 1901.
340. *Bellshill Speaker and North Lanark Gazette*, 21 July 1900.
341. See above p. 49.
342. Lunn, 'Reactions to Lithuanian and Polish Immigrants', pp. 327–8.
343. Ibid., p. 328.
344. See below pp. 105–6.
345. See 'Italy 1785–1985', *The Times*, 30 October 1985. See also Lorimer, op. cit., p. 16 on 'niggers at Calais'; Hennessy, unpublished conference paper and Biddiss, op. cit., refer to European ethnocentrisms. Porter, op. cit. and Kiernan, op. cit., carry information on Italians in Britain. For the definition of toleration which is used throughout the present book see P. King, *Toleration* (London, 1976).
346. Wilkins, op. cit., pp. 158–65 exploits this issue. See Sponza, ts. p. 4, for details. On the urban debate see J. F. C. Harrison, *The Early Victorians 1832–1851* (London, 1971), p. 14ff. On the issue of childhood there is C. J. Sommerville, *The Rise and Fall of Childhood* (London, 1982), partic. Chs 15, 16. See above p. 00 on Italian economic activity.
347. R. Palmer, 'The Italians: Patterns of Migration to London' in Watson, op. cit., pp. 246–7.
348. Quoted by Kiernan, op. cit., p. 41.
349. A theme developed by Wilkins, op. cit.
350. Kiernan, op. cit., p. 51. See Stedman Jones, op. cit., p. 60. See also 'R. Tressell', *The Ragged-Trousered Philanthropists* (London, 1965; first edition 1914), p. 22 on 'Hitalians' and other foreign workers.
351. Sardi, op. cit., p. 288.
352. Ibid. and Rodgers 'Italiani in Scozzia', p. 15.
353. *The Lancet*, 18 October 1979, pp. 590–2.
354. *R.C.*, 1903, p. 515. Evidence of F. H. Birch, one of the receiving officers of the Holborn Union.
355. Sponza, ts. pp. 9–11 and his Ph.D. Thesis, pp. 316ff. See also R. Samuel, *East End Underworld. Chapters in the Life of Arthur Harding* (London, 1984), pp. 134, 182–3, 328–9 on the Sabini gang, based in Clerkenwell.
356. On whom see J. Joll, *The Anarchists* (London, 1964), pp. 174–80. But see Sponza, Ph.D. Thesis, p. 362 for a suggestion that Italians were not deeply involved in anarchist activity.
357. See above p. 73. See generally H. Oliver, *The International Anarchist Movement in Late Victorian London* (London, 1983).
358. Wilkins, op. cit., pp. 146, 149; *R.C.* 1903, pp. 16, 70, 171, 429. On Arnold White

see L. R. Teel, 'The Life and Times of Arnold Henry White, 1848–1925', unpublished Ph.D. Thesis, Georgia State University, 1984.

359. Based on C. Bolt, *Victorian Attitudes to Race* (London, 1971) and P. J. Waller, 'Immigration into Britain: The Chinese', *History Today*, Vol. 35 (Sept., 1985), pp. 8–15.

360. B. Potter, 'East London Labour', *Nineteenth Century*, Vol. XXIV (1888), p. 178.

361. *The Times*, 4 April, 1873.

362. Ibid., 25 August 1877.

363. Ibid., 3 September 1877 and W. M. McArthur, 'The Imperial Aspect', in White, op. cit., pp. 131–45.

364. Lindop, M.Phil. Thesis, pp. 20–1.

365. J. H. Wilson, *My Stormy Voyage Through Life* (London, 1925): see also the entry in J. Bellamy and J. Saville (eds), *Dictionary of Labour Biography* Vol. 4 (London, 1981), pp. 200–8. On Tupper there is *Seamen's Torch. The Life Story of Captain Edward Tupper, National Union of Seamen* (London, 1928) and W. C. Balfour, 'Captain Tupper and the Seamen's Strike at Cardiff', *Morgannwg*, Vol. XIV (1970), pp. 62–80. A good summary of the offical union view on the Chinese is 'Chinese Invasion of Great Britain. A National Danger. A Call to Arms' (n.d. 1913?) MSS 175/3/14/2 Modern Records Centre, Warwick University.

366. *The Maritime Review*, 8 July 1911. See also the manifesto of the Dock, Wharf, Riverside and General Workers' Union of Great Britain and Ireland, dated 21 July 1911 in PRO HO 45/10649/210615/82.

367. PRO HO 45/10649/210615/11. For comment on industrial relations in the shipping industry see B. Mogridge, 'Militancy and Inter-Union Rivalries in British Shipping, 1911–1929', *International Review of Social History*, Vol. VI (1961), pp. 317–42, partic. Pts 1 and 2 and M. J. Daunton, 'Jack Ashore: Seamen in Cardiff before 1914', *Welsh History Review*, Vol. 9 (1978), pp. 176–93. The fullest account of the strike is J. P. May, 'The British Working Class and the Chinese 1870–1911, with particular reference to the Seamen's Strike of 1911', unpublished MA Dissertation, Warwick University, 1973.

368. Craggs, Diploma Dissertation, p. 53.

369. Ibid.

370. *Daily Express*, 18 April 1907.

371. G. Wallas, *Human Nature in Politics* (London, 1908), p. 107. See also Larkin, op. cit., p. 13; J. Sexton, *Sir James Sexton, Agitator. The Life of the Dockers' MP* (London, 1936), p. 203; A. K. Russell, *Liberal Landslide. The General Election of 1906* (Newton Abbot, 1973), pp. 196–8.

372. Based on May, MA Dissertation; Daunton, op. cit.; K. Lunn, 'Race Relations or Industrial Relations?', *Immigrants and Minorities*, Vol. 4 (1985), pp. 10–12.

373. Quoted in May, 'The Chinese', p. 114.

374. Ibid., pp. 117–18.

375. Berridge, op. cit.; see also V. Berridge and G. Edwards, *Opium and the People* (London, 1981), pp. 195–205; T. Parssinen, *Secret Passions. Secret Remedies. Narcotic Drugs in British Society 1820–1930* (Manchester, 1983).

376. *Sunday Chronicle*, 2 December 1906.

377. Tupper, op. cit., p. 51.

378. H. Gollwitzer, *Die Gelbe Gefahr: Geschichte eines Schlagworts. Studien zum imperialistischen Denken* (Göttingen, 1962); C. Blake, 'Should England Welcome the Coloured Man?', *Sunday Chronicle*, 6 December 1906. See also Holmes and Ion, op. cit.; Waller, 'The Chinese', pp. 8–15 and J. M. Winter, 'The Webbs and the Non-White World: a Case of Socialist Racialism', *Journal of Contemporary History*, Vol. 9 (1974), pp. 181–91.

379. Craggs, Diploma Dissertation, pp. 40–1.

380. Ibid., p. 56.
381. PRO HO 45/11843/139147/8 and /18. See above p. 54 for other relevant comment.
382. *Liverpool Courier*, 9 March 1906; see also *The Times*, 25 November 1913.
383. PRO HO 45/11843/139147/8.
384. PRO HO 45/11843/139147/3.
385. Berridge, 'East End Opium Dens', pp. 7–8. See also *The Times*, 25 November 1913.
386. See below pp. 111–12, 254–5.
387. Based on Bolt, op. cit., pp. 144–7; Lorimer, op. cit.; B. Semmel, *The Jamaica Riots of 1865 and the Governor Eyre Controversy* (London, 1962); V. G. Kiernan, *The Lords of Human Kind. European Attitudes to the Outside World in the Imperial Age* (Harmondsworth, 1972 edn), pp. 48–53, 70–1; R. Rainger, 'Race, Politics and Science: The Anthropological Society of London in the 1860s', *Victorian Studies*, Vol. 22 (1978), pp. 51–70; J. M. MacKenzie, *Propaganda and Empire. The Manipulation of British Public Opinion 1880–1960* (Manchester, 1984) and R. Miles and L. Muirhead, 'Racism in Scotland: a matter of further investigation?', in D. McCrone (ed.), *The Scottish Government Yearbook 1986* (Edinburgh, 1986), pp. 108–36.
388. Walvin, op. cit., p. 203.
389. Ibid.
390. Ibid.
391. Little, op. cit., p. 193.
392. Ibid.
393. A. B. C. Merriman-Labor, *Britain through Negro Spectacles or a Negro on Britons* (London, 1909), pp. 175–6.
394. Quoted in Masani, op. cit., p. 263. See Kiernan, *Lords*, p. 210 for another insensitivity by Salisbury in the Kempton case.
395. G. Pillai, *London and Paris Through Indian Spectacles* (Madras, 1893?), p. ii.
396. K. Kriplani, *R. Tagore. A Biography* (London, 1962), p. 220.
397. Masani, op. cit., pp. 264–6.
398. Ibid., p. 264.
399. On the Edalji case see, for example, J. D. Carr, *The Life of Sir Arthur Conan Doyle* (London, 1949), Ch. XV.
400. On Blacks as objects of entertainment see The New Brighton Pier Company Ltd, *The Ashanti Village*, a programme held in the County Museum Department of Merseyside County Council. For earlier evidence see B. Lindfors, 'The Hottentot Venus and other African Attractions in Nineteenth Century England', paper presented at the International Conference on the History of Blacks in Britain, London University, 1981. This paper was concerned primarily with the exploitation of Saartje Baartman.
401. See R. Jenkins, 'Sportsman Extraordinaire', *West Africa*, 3 June 1985, p. 1115 on Arthur Wharton, a runner and footballer from the Gold Coast who became based in the north-east. There is passing comment, too, in E. Cashmore, *Black Sportsmen* (London, 1982), pp. 24, 31. See above p. 35 on Ranji.
402. See *Who Was Who 1920–40* (London, 1941), p. 109 and *The Times*, 15 November 1933.
403. On Archer see B. A. Kosmin, 'J. R. Archer (1863–1932): a Pan-Africanist in the Battersea Labour Movement', *New Community*, Vol. VII (Winter, 1979).
404. S. Allen, *New Minorities. Old Conflicts. Asian and West Indian Immigration in Britain* (New York, 1971), pp. 16–21, advances important critical comments regarding the concept of assimilation (on which see also J. Gould and W. L. Kolb, (eds), *Dictionary of the Social Sciences* (London, 1964), pp. 38–9). Little reference is made

to this unsatisfactory concept in the present survey (see below pp. 293–4 for additional, extended comment). See also below pp. 306–7 for further comment on the role of numbers in generating hostility and on the complexity of attitudes and actions reflected in responses towards immigrants and refugees. See above and below for cautious comment on racism. Note particularly on this Gilley, 'This Irish', M. D. Biddiss, 'Myths of the Blood', *Patterns of Prejudice*, Vol. IX (1975), pp. 11–19 and M. Banton, *Racial and Ethnic Competition* (Cambridge, 1983), introduction.

II. THE STRAINS OF WAR, 1914–19

1. A. D. Smith, 'War and Ethnicity: The Role of Warfare in the Formation, Self-Images and Cohesion of Ethnic Communities', *Ethnic and Racial Studies*, Vol. 4 (1981), pp. 375–97. Mr Britling features in H. G. Wells, *Mr. Britling sees it through* (London, 1916). Two useful general studies of the Home Front, neither of which discusses the history of immigrants and refugees in any detail, are: A Marwick, *The Deluge* (London, 1965) and J. Williams, *The Home Front* (London, 1972). There are also two relevant chapters (3 and 4) in J. Stevenson, *British Society 1914–45* (London, 1984).

2. Details from Ministry of Health, *Report on the Work undertaken by the British Government on the Reception and Care of the Belgian Refugees* (London, 1920), pp. 8–9. Although numbers fluctuated and an accurate calculation is therefore difficult A. J. P. Taylor, *English History 1914–1945* (Harmondsworth, 1979 edn), p. 47, is in error to refer to only 119,000 Belgians. P. Cahalan, *Belgian Refugee Relief in England during the Great War* (New York, 1982), pp. 249ff. discusses clandestine recruitment.

3. T. T. S. de Jastrzebski, 'The Register of Belgian Refugees', *Journal of the Royal Statistical Society*, Vol. 80 (1917), pp. 142–5.

4. Ibid., pp. 146–53.

5. Cahalan, op. cit., is the only detailed study. But his interest is in philanthropy and the middle-class British rather than the refugees.

6. PRO HO 45/11068/374355 and HO 45/19995/419986 are useful on the Russians. See also J. Hope Simpson, *The Refugee Problem* (London, 1939), pp. 339–40. For personal testimony see V. Nabokov, *Speak Memory. An Autobiography revisited* (rev. ed. London, 1967), p. 253. On Pavlova see *The Times* 26 February 1985 for comment prior to the release of *Pavlova*, a film biography.

7. Hope Simpson, op. cit., p. 340; see also F. M. Wilson, *They Came as Strangers* (London, 1959), p. 218.

8. J. Walvin, *Black and White. The Negro and English Society 1555–1945* (London, 1973), p. 205.

9. K. Little, *Negroes in Britain* (London, 1948), p. 56.

10. E. Scobie, *Black Britannia* (Chicago, 1972), p. 153.

11. Little, op. cit., p. 56; on the Chinese see MSS 175/3/16/–1–4, Warwick University Modern Records Centre (NUS archives). In PRO HO 45/11843/139147/125a, there is a reference to Chinese carpenters employed during the war at Bicester aerodrome.

12. Scobie, op. cit., pp. 154–5. V. G. Kiernan, *European Empires from Conquest to Collapse, 1815–1960* (London, 1982), p. 185, notes that the French did make use of Black troops. For continuing fear on this score see R. C. Reinders, 'Racialism on the Left. E. D. Morel and the "Black Horror on the Rhine" ', *International Review of Social History*, Vol. XIII (1968), pp. 1–28.

13. See, for example, Sir H. Johnston, *The Black Man's Part in the War* (London, 1917); C. Lucas; *The Empire at War* (London, 1926), partic. Ch. V; Lt. Col.

Merewether and Sir F. E. Smith, *The Indian Corps in France* (London, 1917); C. Musgrave, *Life in Brighton from the Earliest Times to the Present* (London, 1970), p. 371; J. Greenhut, 'The Imperial Reserve. The Indian Corps on the Western Front, 1914–18', *Journal of Imperial and Commonwealth History*, Vol. XII (1983), pp. 74–93; K. Vadgama, *India in Britain* (London, 1984), pp. 92–106.

14.   Scobie, op. cit., p. 155. On Indian Pedlars see PRO HO 213/242.

15.   Paragraph derived from Little, op. cit., pp. 78, 216; Scobie, op. cit., p. 155; Walvin, op. cit., pp. 204–5. P. Fryer, *Staying Power. The History of Black People in Britain* (London, 1984), p. 296 refers to a Black population of 20,000 in Britain by the end of the war. But the figure needs to be treated with caution.

16.   *Report on Refugees*, p. 29; see also Cahalan, op. cit., pp. 256–9, 262.

17.   *Report on Refugees*, pp. 76–7; Cahalan, op. cit., Ch. 10 discusses the Belgians and alien legislation generally PRO HO 45/10809/311425/1 discusses the Aliens Order of 1916. C. S. Peel, *How We Lived Then 1914–1918* (London, 1929), p. 33 and Mrs R. Henrey, *An Exile in Soho* (London, 1952), refer to Belgians in Soho.

18.   S. Pollard, *The Development of the British Economy* (London, 1967 edn), pp. 76ff discusses changes in wartime occupations in Britain. For specific detail on the Belgians see *Report on Refugees*, pp. 76–7 and Cahalan, op. cit., pp. 286–92. For women in the labour market in Britain see A. Marwick, *Women at War 1914–1918* (London, 1977).

19.   *Report on Refugees*, pp. 76–7.

20.   On Birtley see *History of the Ministry of Munitions*, Vol. V, Part V (London, 1921–2), pp. 58–67. An alternative source is Cahalan, op. cit., pp. 270ff. The Central Library in Newcastle possesses a good collection of photographs. On Twickenham see J. Wallon, *Une cité sur la Tamise* (London and Brussels, 1917). On Kryn and Lahy see *Twenty-Five Years with 600* (Letchworth, 1953), n.p.

21.   Quoted in G. A. Powell, *Four Years in a Refugee Camp* (London, 1920), p. 30.

22.   Taylor, op. cit., p. 47. A qualification to this cosy image is in PRO HO 45/10758/261921/691–3 which contain information on disturbances at Birtley in November and December 1916.

23.   On 'the Belgian houses' in Derby, communication from G. Wood, 29 January 1975. On the Franzoni, communication from the Divisional Librarian, Folkestone, 21 January 1975.

24.   Little, op. cit., p. 57.

25.   Fryer, op. cit., p. 295, does not develop this point. The official history of the Ministry of Munitions does not help.

26.   Walvin, op. cit., p. 205.

27.   Paragraph based on ibid., p. 204 and Little, op. cit., pp. 56–7.

28.   Little, op. cit., pp. 56–7.

29.   The photograph appears on the cover of *Llafur*, Vol. 3 (Spring, 1980).

30.   Based on Fryer, op. cit., pp. 292–4. Archer's speech is given on p. 294. See also I. Geiss, *The Pan-African Movement* (London, 1974), for a number of references to the African Progress Union. See also above pp. 55–6, 84 for the origins of Pan-Africanism and reference to Archer.

31.   J. Jenkinson, 'The Glasgow Race Disturbances of 1919', *Immigrants and Minorities*, Vol. 4 (1985), pp. 62–3.

32.   See above pp. 71–2.

33.   J. C. Bird, 'Control of Enemy Alien Civilians in Great Britain 1914–1918', unpublished Ph.D. Thesis, London University, 1981, pp. 38–43.

34.   DORA, as it became known, is discussed in Marwick, *The Deluge*, pp. 36, 77, 157.

35.   *Parl. Deb.* (Commons), Vol. LXV (1914), 5 August 1914, cols. 1989, 1986.

36.   D. Saunders, 'Aliens in Britain and the Empire during the First World War', in F. Swyripa and J. H. Thompson (eds), *Loyalties in Conflict: Ukrainians in Canada*

during the Great War (Edmonton, 1983), pp. 105–7. On Czechs see H. Hanak, *Great Britain and Austria-Hungary during the First World War: A Study in the Formation of Public Opinion* (Oxford, 1962). And, on the Poles, N. Davies, 'The Poles in Great Britain 1914–1919', *Slavonic and East European Review*, Vol. 50 (1972), pp. 63–89.

37. Saunders, op. cit., p. 103 emphasises this point. See also Cahalan, op. cit., Ch. 10.

38. Bird, Ph.D. Thesis, p. 19.

39. *The Law Reports, The Public General Statutes, 1914* (London, 1914) pp. 32–9; Bird, Ph.D. Thesis, pp. 237–8.

40. P. and L. Gillman, *Collar the Lot!* (London, 1980), Ch. 2. T. Kelly, *For Advancement of Learning. The University of Liverpool* (Liverpool, 1981), pp. 134ff notes that two German-born University Professors who were out of the country decided not to return. One, Kuno Meyer, formerly Professor of Celtic Studies proceeded to conduct a bitter anti-British campaign from Germany. An Englishman, Houston Stewart Chamberlain, author of the *Foundations of the Nineteenth Century* also campaigned against Britain from Germany. His *Kriegsaufsätze* were translated as *The Ravings of a Renegade!* See above pp. 62–4 for the developing prewar hostility.

41. Bird, Ph.D. Thesis, p. 11.

42. C. Andrew, *Secret Service. The Making of the British Intelligence Community* (London, 1985), Ch. 5. See also N. West, *MI5. British Security Service Operations 1909–1945* (London, 1981), pp. 38–40. J. Munson (ed.), *Echoes of the Great War. The Diary of the Reverend Andrew Clark 1914–1919* (Oxford, 1985) provides evidence of continued spy mania (see, for example, pp. 19, 20, 24, 39, 46–7 for the early days of the war).

43. Bird, Ph.D. Thesis traces these developments. See also C. Haste, *Keep the Home Fires Burning. Propaganda in the First World War* (London, 1977), pp. 109ff and also C. Simpson, *Lusitania* (Harmondsworth, 1983).

44. Bird, Ph.D. Thesis, pp. 11–31, 134. For comment by internees there is P. Cohen-Portheim, *Time Stood Still. My Internment in England* 1914–18 (London, 1932). See also 'Alexandra Palace Internment Camp (1914–1918). A Study of the Prisoners by one of them, Rudolf Rocker. Continued by his Son', MSS 233 LSE Library.

45. Based on Bird, Ph.D. Thesis, pp. 175, 178, 199, 13.

46. Ibid., pp. 200, 19–20.

47. Ibid., pp. 147–9.

48. Ibid., p. 136; Munson, op. cit., carries numerous references to German POWs.

49. H. Nicholson, *King George V. His Life and Reign* (London, 1953), pp. 249–50. See also D. Judd, *The Life and Times of George V* (London, 1973), p. 131.

50. *Parl. Deb.* (Commons), Vol. 108 (1918), 11 July 1918, cols. 546–8; *Parl. Deb.* (Lords), Vol. 31 (1918), 2 August 1918, col. 444.

51. Bird, Ph.D. Thesis, pp. 9–10. On atrocity propaganda in the war see Haste, op. cit; A Ponsonby, *Falsehood in Wartime* (London, 1928); J. M. Read, *Atrocity Propaganda 1914–1919* (New Haven, 1941). See below p. 342 for additional comment on German atrocities in Belgium.

52. M. MacDonagh, *In London during the Great War* (London, 1935), p. 6.

53. Williams, op. cit., p. 21. On barbers see the cartoon, 'Shafe Sir?', in *Punch*, 16 September 1914, p. 239. Andrew Clark noted that a thick-smoked wurtz on sale in Chelmsford was no longer a 'German sausage' but a 'Dunmow Sausage' (entry for 10 September 1914 in Munson, op cit., p. 13). Furthermore, Boots was keen to stress that its Eau-de-Cologne was 'of purely British make' (entry for 21 November 1914 in ibid., p. 32).

54. PRO HO 45/10944/257142/2, 4; HO 45/10944/257142/2a; HO 45/10944/257142/19, respectively.

55. Williams, op. cit., p. 33.

56. Marwick, *The Deluge*, p. 31.

57. *John Bull*, 15 May 1915, See also ibid., 22 May 1915, 'The Vendetta Justified'. Note also the reaction of D. H. Lawrence, 'I am mad with rage myself. I would like to kill a million Germans – two million'. Letter to Lady Ottoline Morrell, 14 May 1915 in G. J. Zytaruk and J. T. Boulton (eds), *The Letters of D. H. Lawrence*, Vol. II, *June 1913–October 1916* (Cambridge, 1981), p. 340.

58. Marwick, *The Deluge*, p. 131. See Munson, op cit., pp. 61–2 for perceptive comment by the Rev. Clark. The official Government report on the so-called Belgian atrocities, known as the Bryce Commission, appeared a few days after the sinking of the *Lusitania*. For comment on the report see T. Wilson, 'Lord Bryce's Investigations into alleged German Atrocities', *Journal of Contemporary History*, Vol. 14 (1979), pp. 369–83.

59. P. O'Mara, *The Autobiography of a Liverpool Irish Slummy* (London, 1934), pp. 224ff discusses the attacks on Germans particularly pork butchers – in Liverpool. See also *The Times*, 11 May 1915, 'Ferment in Liverpool'. There is film evidence in *Anti-German Riots in Liverpool. Following Loss of Lusitania*. This is item 183 in the North West Film Archive, Manchester Polytechnic.

60. See *Daily Sketch*, 13 May 1915; *Daily Mail*, 13 May 1915; *Daily News and Leader*, 13 May 1915, which carry photographs of the violence. J. Bush, *Behind the Lines. East London Labour 1914–1919* (London, 1985) discusses life in East London during the war.

61. *East End News*, 18 May 1915.

62. See Williams, op cit., p. 21 and MacDonagh, op. cit., p. 15, on changes of name.

63. J. Bush, 'East London Jews and the First World War', *The London Journal*, Vol. 6 (1980), p. 150 notes the danger posed to Russian Jews. See also M. Cohen and M. and H. Fagan (eds), *Childhood Memories* (n.d., n.p.), pp. 39ff for Hymie Fagan's fears; Jews of Russian origin or descent were not infrequently regarded as German. There is additional useful comment, relating to Manchester, in S. Humphries, *Hooligans or Rebels? An Oral History of Working-Class Childhood and Youth 1889–1939* (Oxford, 1981), pp. 199–200.

64. PRO HO 45/10944/257142/82.

65. Williams op. cit., p. 65.

66. Peel, op. cit., p. 36.

67. Taylor, op. cit., p. 74.

68. S. Koss, *Lord Haldane, Scapegoat for Liberalism* (New York, 1969). On Maxse and White see above pp. 63, 77. For White's obsession with German influence at work in wartime Britain, see his *The Hidden Hand* (London, 1917). Correspondence between White and the Duke of Bedford in the White papers in the National Maritime Museum at Greenwich makes it clear that White had been concerned for some time to remove Haldane. G. Phillips, *The Diehards, Aristocratic Society and Politics in Edwardian England* (Cambridge, Mass., 1979), pp. 92–3 is aware of this connection between White and Bedford.

69. *The Times*, 11 May 1915.

70. *The Englishman*, No. 1, 20 May 1915 was cynical about the move, saying that, if necessary, the 'foxy' German would be willing to express his loyalty in five languages. See also *John Bull*, 22 May 1915 for similar sentiment.

71. C. Holmes, *Antisemitism in British Society 1876–1939* (London, 1979), p. 123. C. C. Aronsfeld, 'Jewish Enemy Aliens in England during the First World War', *Jewish Social Studies*, Vol. XVIII (1956), pp. 275–83, is a good study of German-Jewish difficulties. Speyer was a particular target. See A. Morton

Mandeville, *The House of Speyer* (London, 1915). Mandeville was editor of the *Financial News* and recalled every wretched tip and unsuccessful punt with which Speyer's bank was associated.

72. Holmes, op. cit., Ch. 8.

73. Peel, op. cit., p. 43; Nicolson, op. cit., pp. 307–10.

74. PRO HO 45/10944/257142/186 and 187.

75. The information on Jonas in this paragraph is from my research notes based on local sources.

76. The activities of the BEU are discussed in Haste. op. cit., Ch. 6. F. E. Eddis who was Secretary to the 1903 Royal Commission on Alien Immigration, became involved with the organisation. See his anti-German novel *'That Goldheim': A Spy Story, exposing a Special Danger from Alien Immigration* (London, 1918). The BEU also made a visual attack on Germans in its film *Once a Hun, Always a Hun* which appeared in 1918. See Haste, op. cit., p. 129. On the National Party see W. D. Rubinstein, 'Henry Page Croft and the National Party 1917–22', *Journal of Contemporary History*, Vol. IX (1974), pp. 129–48.

77. See below pp. 112–13.

78. D. Marcombe, *Nottingham during the Great War* (Nottingham, 1984), pp. 39–40.

79. D. Richards and J. W. Hunt, *Modern Britain* (London, 1962 edn), p. 259.

80. Cahalan, op. cit., pp. 13–15. R. C. K. Ensor's *Belgium* (London, 1915) was one of the works which attempted to provide the public with information on Belgium and the Belgians. See particularly Ch. II, 'Several Characteristics of the Country' and Ch. III, 'General Characteristics of the People'. On the Congo agitation which involved E. D. Morel and Roger Casement, among others, see S. J. S. Cookey, *Britain and the Congo Question 1885–1913* (London, 1968).

81. See *Punch*, 12 August 1914, p. 143 and ibid., 26 August 1914, p. 185. There are graphic photographs, guaranteed to generate a sense of outrage, in *Everyman*, Special Belgian Relief Number, November 1914. On the War Refugees Committee see Lady Lugard, 'The Work of the War Refugees Committee', *Journal of the Royal Society of Arts*, 26 March 1915, pp. 429–40.

82. Lugard, op. cit., p. 431.

83. *Nottingham Guardian*, 12 October 1914.

84. *Derby Mercury*, 1 January 1915; *Sheffield Telegraph*, 7 November 1914.

85. Munson, op. cit., pp. 37, 283, for example.

86. K. O. Morgan, *Rebirth of a Nation. Wales 1850–1950* (Oxford, 1981) pp. 159–60, notes the sympathy from within one small nation. For another see also M. Vincentelli, 'The Davies Family and Belgian Refugee Artists and Musicians in Wales', *National Library of Wales Journal*, Vol. XXII (1981), pp. 226–33.

87. *Parl. Deb.* (Commons), Vol. LXVI (1914), 9 September 1914, col. 558.

88. *Minutes of Evidence taken before the Departmental Committee appointed by the President of the Local Government Board to consider and report on questions arising in connection with the reception and employment of the Belgian Refugees in this country*, Cmd. 7779, p. 160.

89. *Report on Refugees*, p. 15; War Refugees Committee, *Third Report*, May 1919, p. 1.

90. *Report on Refugees*, p. 89.

91. *Parl. Deb.* (Commons). Vol. 122 (1919), 3 December 1919, col. 422.

92. *The Times*, 19 March 1919 and 24 March 1919.

93. Figures derived from N. H. Carrier and J. R. Jeffery, *External Migration. A Study of the Available Statistics* (London, 1953), pp. 127–8. These figures exclude Belgians who became naturalised.

94. Marwick, op. cit., p. 31.

95. S. J. Hurwitz, *State Intervention in Great Britain. A Study of Economic Control and Social Response 1914–1919* (New York, 1949), remains useful.

96. Lugard, op. cit., p. 437; E. Hatch, 'Belgian Refugees in the United Kingdom',
     Quarterly Review, Vol. 446 (1916), p. 188.

97. *The Times*, 17 October 1914. See also L. Housman, *The Unexpected Years* (New
     York, 1936), p. 250.

98. See *Minutes of Evidence* for the fears of labour. See ibid. and *Report on Refugees* for
     official policies. See also Cahalan, op. cit., pp. 257ff for responses from British
     labour.

99. *Kölnische Zeitung*, 2 December 1916. See Anonymous, *The Condition of the Belgian
     Workmen Now Refugees in England* (London, 1917), for a reply to the German
     allegations.

100. *A Book of Belgium's Gratitude* (London, 1916).

101. *La Renaissance*, 1 February 1916 (Sheffield City Library).

102. The quotation is from Rupert Brooke's 'Peace' (1914), in B. Gardner, *Up the Line
     to Death. The War Poets 1914–18* (London, 1964), pp. 10–11.

103. On the early recruitment see J. M. Osborne, *The Voluntary Recruiting Movement in
     Britain 1914–1916* (New York, 1982).

104. See above p. 90 on the Belgians and conscription.

105. V. Jabotinsky, *The Story of the Jewish Legion* (New York, 1965 edn), p. 62.

106. Holmes, op. cit., Ch. 3. See also R. Grant, 'G. V. Chicherin and the Russian
     Revolutionary Cause in Great Britain', in J. Slatter (ed.), '*From the Other Shore*'.
     Russian Political Emigrants in Britain, 1880–1917 (London, 1984), pp. 117–38 and
     J. Smyth and M. Rodgers, 'Peter Petroff and the Socialism Movement in
     Britain, 1907–18', in ibid., pp. 100–16.

107. See R. Livshin, 'Aspects of the acculturation of the children of immigrant Jews in
     Manchester 1890–1930', unpublished M.Ed. Thesis, Manchester University,
     1982, pp. 344–5 on pressures and responses at a local level. See Holmes, op. cit.,
     Ch. 8 on the situation in Leeds and the East End.

108. Holmes, op. cit., Ch. 8. Joseph King was also a defender of German aliens.

109. The Chief Constable's comments are in PRO HO 45/10810/311932/40 and HO
     45/10810/311932/43.

110. Holmes, op. cit., p. 135.

111. Ibid., p. 136.

112. We still await Harry Shukman's study of the Convention. Holmes, op. cit.,
     pp. 129–30 assesses the impact of the Convention. See also Grant, op. cit. There
     is additional detail in Grant's 'British Radicals and Socialists and their attitudes
     to Russia c. 1890–1917', unpublished Ph.D. Thesis, Glasgow University, 1985.
     On Russian Jews as profiteers see, for example, Bush, *London Journal*, pp. 150–1,
     155–6, and S. G. Bayme, 'Jewish Leadership and Antisemitism in Britain
     1898–1918', unpublished Ph.D. Thesis, Columbia University, 1977, p. 25. For
     examples of wartime comment see *Clarion*, 20 October 1914 and *Justice*,
     29 October 1914.

113. M. Rodgers, 'Political Developments in the Lithuanian Community in Scotland
     c1890–1923' in Slatter, op. cit., p. 149.

114. Ibid., pp. 149–52. See also his 'The Anglo-Russian Military Convention and
     the Lithuanian Immigrant Community in Lanarkshire, Scotland, 1914–20',
     Immigrants and Minorities, Vol. 1 (1982), pp. 60–88, for additional comment on
     Lithuanians and the Convention.

115. Emphasised in M. Rodgers, 'The Lanarkshire Lithuanians', in B. Kay (ed.),
     Odyssey (Edinburgh n.d.), p. 25.

116. There is an extended discussion of the Irish on p. 132 below. On Irish troops
     in the war, see M. MacDonagh, *The Irish at the Front* (London, 1916), P. Verney,
     The Micks. The Story of the Irish Guards (London, 1970), Chs 3–6 and P. Karsten,

'Irish Soldiers in the British Army, 1792–1922: Suborned or subordinate?', *Journal of Social History*, Vol. 17 (1983), pp. 47ff.

117. See above p. 89.

118. R. Lapiere, 'Race Prejudice: France and England', *Social Forces*, Vol. 7 (1918), p. 111.

119. Fryer, op. cit., p. 297.

120. J. White, 'The Summer Riots of 1919', *New Society*, 13 August 1981, p. 261.

121. See ibid., p. 260 on the general unrest in 1919. On the empire see A. Draper, *Amritsar, The Massacre that ended the Raj* (London, 1981); on the Caribbean there is W. F. Elkins, 'Unrest among Negroes: a British Document of 1919', *Science and Society*, Vol. 1 (Winter, 1968), pp. 66–79. The same year witnessed collective violence in America; see *The Negro in Chicago. A Study of Race Relations and a Race Riot in 1919* (London, 1968, reprint of 1922 edn). See also A. Spear, *Black Chicago The Making of A Negro Ghetto 1890–1920* (Chicago, 1961), Ch. II, partic.

122. Jenkinson, op. cit.

123. D. Byrne, 'The 1930 "Arab Riot" in South Shields: a Race Riot that never was', *Race and Class*, Vol. XV (1977), pp. 263–4; see also Fryer, op. cit., p. 299.

124. *The Times*, 30 April 1919.

125. *Daily Chronicle*, 29 May 1919; *Daily Telegraph*, 17 June 1919; *Daily Express*, 17 June 1919.

126. There are two studies of the events in Liverpool: R. May and R. Cohen, 'The Interaction between Race and Colonialism: A Case Study of the Liverpool Race Riots of 1919', *Race and Class*, Vol. XVI (1974–5), pp. 111–26 and Fryer, op. cit., pp. 299–303. On the Wotten incident the best source is PRO CO 318/352 which contains a CID Report by Inspector Hugh Burgess. Felix Hercules, of the Society of Peoples of African Origin, was particularly concerned to draw the attention of the Colonial Office to the injuries that were sustained during the violence. See PRO CO 323/814 for his letter of 12 June 1919. On Hercules see Fryer, op. cit., partic. pp. 313–16.

127. Noted in N. Evans, 'The South Wales Race Riots of 1919', *Llafur*, Vol. 3 (1980), p. 13. This article, together with the Home Office evidence in the author's 'The South Wales Race Riots of 1919: A Documentary Postscript', ibid., Vol. 3 (1983), pp. 76–87, constitute a comprehensive survey of South Wales. Fryer, op. cit., pp. 305–6 uses an additional useful source, the autobiography of Ibrahim Ismaa'il, a Somali seaman and poet.

128. Evans, *Llafur*, (1980), pp. 14, 17.

129. May and Cohen, op. cit., p. 118; A. Richmond, *The Colour Problem* (Harmondsworth, 1955), p. 235.

130. May and Cohen, op. cit., p. 115; see also PRO HO 45/11017/377969. But Jenkinson, op. cit., whose study of Glasgow reveals a number of important local emphases, is agnostic at times on the importance of sexual competition upon the events in Glasgow (p. 46) but dismissive elsewhere (p. 61).

131. May and Cohen, op. cit., pp. 115–17; see also O'Mara, op. cit., p. 13 on the spatial divisions in Liverpool.

132. It should be said that neither May and Cohen, op. cit., nor Fryer, op. cit., emphasises the impact of hooliganism.

133. A central theme in May and Cohen, op. cit.

134. Evans, *Llafur*, (1980), pp. 14, 22–3, for example. A. Grimshaw, 'Factors relating to Colour Violence in the United States and Britain', *Race*, Vol. III (1962), pp. 3–19, carries useful general comments relevant to this emphasis.

135. PRO HO 45/11017/377969/11.

136. Paragraph based on Evans, *Llafur*, (1980), pp. 21, 23.

137. Ibid., pp. 14, 10, 5 partic. For one graphic illustration of a Black victim of this conflict see the letter from William P. Samuels, born in British Guiana, dated 30 December 1918 and written from Sophia Street, Cardiff. It is in PRO CO 111/621. Most of the letter which is on the need for 'fair play' in employment practices is given in Fryer, op. cit., p. 298.

138. Jenkinson, op. cit., links the strikes and the violence. R. K. Middlemas, *The Clydesiders* (London, 1965), pp. 88–96 provides some indication of the atmosphere in post-war Glasgow. The 'plague spot' reference is from ibid., p. 90.

139. PRO HO 45/11017/377969/11, is the source of the quotations. See above p. 109 for comment on stereotypes.

140. PRO HO 45/11017/377969/20.

141. Walvin, op. cit., p. 208 makes the claim. But see Evans, *Llafur*, (1980), p. 18.

142. PRO HO 45/11017/377969/6.

143. Ibid.

144. PRO HO 45/11017/377969/8.

145. PRO HO 45/11017/377969/6.

146. PRO HO 45/11017/377969/21; HO 45/11017/377969/63; CO 323/814.

147. PRO HO 45/11017/377969 makes this clear. Rufus Fennell, a West Indian, described in official papers as 'an obstreperous coloured man', but who had provided succour to those under attack in Cardiff, was particularly involved in working against the repatriation proposals. See PRO CO 232/814. Fryer, op. cit., pp. 308–10 carries detail on Fennell.

148. See below pp. 154–5.

149. PRO HO 45/11017/377969/6. Evans, *Llafur*, (1980), p. 14, does refer to an attack on the Chinese in Newport.

150. See above pp. 77–82 for prewar hostility. The wartime policy of the NSFU can be gleaned from MSS 175/3/16/1–4, Modern Records Centre, Warwick University. The quotations expressing opposition to the Chinese are from *The Star*, 17 June 1919. Chinese sailors in postwar Britain are referred to in Jenkinson, op. cit., pp. 55–8; see also S. Craggs, 'A History of the Chinese Communities in Liverpool', unpublished Local History Diploma Dissertation, Liverpool University, 1983, p. 59; and M. Broady, 'The Social Adjustment of the Chinese in Liverpool', *Sociological Review*, n.s. Vol. 3 (1955), p. 67. G. Cowan, *Loud Report* (London, 1938), p. 41 refers to the Chinese in labour battalions during the war – a neglected aspect of the history of the Chinese in Britain.

151. See above pp. 80–81 for earlier comment on the Chinese and drugs.

152. PRO HO 45/24683/311604 is useful on the Chinese involvement in drugs during the war. V. Berridge, 'East End Opium Dens and Narcotic Use in Britain', *The London Journal*, Vol. 4 (1978), p. 16 carries comment. See also T. Parssinen, *Secret Passions, Strange Remedies. Narcotic Drugs in British Society 1820–1930* (Manchester, 1983), pp. 121ff., partic. pp. 124–5 and 212–7, on Britain and America.

153. Berridge, op. cit., pp. 21–2; Parssinen, op cit., pp. 21–3. The Home Office file on Chang has been destroyed. The film *Cocaine*, released in 1922, further added to the Chinese association with drugs.

154. Berridge, op. cit., p. 23 provides balance. *East End News*, 1 June 1917 and 12 November 1917 concentrate on the Chinese.

155. *Daily Express*, 1 October 1920.

156. *Evening News*, 4 October 1920.

157. See above pp. 79–81 for earlier comment. See *Evening News*, 4 October 1920 and 6 October 1920 for postwar reactions.

158. *Daily News*, 15 April 1920.

159. See *East End News*, 15 April 1924 on Chang's trial. He was found guilty of possessing cocaine and recommended for deportation. For the continued

association of the Chinese with drugs see *Westminster Gazette*, 24 January 1928, *The Star*, 18 February 1930 and the *Daily Telegraph*, 25 April 1932.

160. The 1918 British Nationality Act is printed in *The Law Reports, The Public General Statutes, 1918* (London, 1919), pp. 119–24.

161. *The Times*, 12 March 1983.

162. *Parl. Deb.* (Commons), Vol. 114 (1919), 15 April 1919, col. 2759.

163. Ibid., cols 2789–92.

164. *John Bull*, 15 May 1915.

165. *Parl. Deb.* (Commons), Vol. 114 (1919), 15 April 1919, col. 2765.

166. Ibid., col. 2782. For patriotic labour in the war see Grant, Ph.D. Thesis, Ch. 8 for the British Workers' League, which was particularly hostile towards Jews. See also J. O. Stubbs, 'Lord Milner and Patriotic Labour 1914–18', *English Historical Review*, Vol. 87 (1972), pp. 717–54, and R. Douglas, 'The National Democratic Party and the British Workers' League', *Historical Journal*, Vol. 15 (1972), pp. 533–52.

167. Ibid., Vol. 120 (1919), 3 November 1919, col. 1262.

168. Ibid., Vol. 114 (1919), 15 April 1919, col. 2799.

169. Ibid., Vol. 120 (1919), 4 November 1919, col. 1355.

170. Ibid., 22 October 1919, col. 58.

171. Saunders, op cit., p. 108. On deportations see *Parl. Deb.* (Commons) Vol. 115 (1919) 11 May 1919, cols. 308–9.

172. On Pemberton-Billing see M. Kettle, *Salome's Last Veil* (London, 1977). The details of this exchange are in *Parl. Deb.* (Commons), Vol. 120 (1919), 22 October 1919, col. 86. An additional impetus to anti-Semitism in the immediate postwar years in Britain came with the formation in July 1919 of The Britons. See G. Lebzelter, 'Henry Hamilton Beamish and The Britons: Champions of Anti-semitism', in K. Lunn and R. C. Thurlow (eds), *British Fascism* (London, 1980), pp. 41–56.

173. On Havelock Wilson see above p. 78. For his case against Chinese aliens see *Parl. Deb.* (Commons), Vol. 120 (1919), 3 November 1919, col. 1196. Cahalan, op. cit., p. 509 emphasises the theme of aliens as Bolsheviks.

174. Details of the act are in *The Law Reports, The Public General Statutes, 1919* (London, 1920), pp. 427–35. The 1919 Act would repay greater attention. There is, however, a useful discussion in P. Foot, *Immigration and Race in British Politics* (Harmondsworth, 1965), pp. 104–7. See also the brief comment in A. Nicol, *Illegal Entrants* (London, n.d.), pp. 11–15.

III. 'THE GLASS IS FALLING HOUR BY HOUR.' IMMIGRATION 1919–39

1. W. A. Lewis, *Economic Survey 1919–1939* (London, 1965 edn), p. 11. The academic achievements of Arthur Lewis were a source of pride to the Black community in Britain. See *The Keys*, Vol. V (July–September 1937), p. 6.

2. W. Adams, 'Refugees in Europe', *Annals of the American Academy of Political and Social Sciences* (May 1939), pp. 37–44 and Sir J. H. Simpson, *The Refugee Problem. Report of a Survey* (London, 1939) are two useful contemporary accounts.

3. M. R. Marrus, *The Unwanted. European Refugees in the Twentieth Century* (Oxford, 1985), pp. 53–61 and see above p. 88.

4. The quotation is from A. J. Sherman, *Island Refuge. Britain and Refugees from the Third Reich 1933–1939* (London, 1973), p. 15. On Nansen and the League see Marrus, op. cit., pp. 86–91.

5. C. F. Delzell, 'The Italian Anti-Fascist Emigration 1922–1943', *Journal of Central European Affairs*, Vol. 12, (1952), pp. 20–55; M. Rodgers, 'Italiani in Scozzia', in

B. Kay (ed.), *Odyssey. The Second Collection* (Edinburgh, 1982), discuss the Italians. N. Bentwich, *They Sought Refuge* (London, 1956), p. 55 notes that Jews were among the refugees from Mussolini. On the Spanish see Y. Cloud, *The Basque Children in England* (London, 1937) and D. Legarreta, *The Guernica Generation, Basque Refugee Children of the Spanish Civil War* (Reno, 1984), Ch. 3.

6. M. Muggeridge, *The Thirties* (London, 1967 edn), p. 261.

7. Imperial War Museum (henceforth IWM) Tape 004483/03, Britain and the Refugee Crisis 1933–1947 Oral History Recordings (F. L. Carsten), and, even more so, IWM Tape 004498/05 (Hans Krebs), IWM Tape 004000/07 (Erna Simion), IWM Tape 004300/06 (Leo Kahn).

8. What this could mean for individuals is well brought out in IWM Tape 004483/03 (F. L. Carsten).

9. L. Dawidowicz, *The War against the Jews 1933–45* (Harmondsworth, 1975), p. 95.

10. M. Berghahn, *German-Jewish Refugees in England* (Leamington Spa, 1984), p. 72; for a personal testimony, see G. Clare, *Last Waltz in Vienna* (London, 1982 edn), p. 228.

11. C. C. Aronsfeld, 'Refugee No. 562 Remembers. . . .', *Jewish Quarterly*, (1973), pp. 24–5.

12. Berghahn, op. cit., p. 72, emphasises the importance of the attacks of 9 and 10 November.

13. Sherman, op. cit. and B. Wasserstein, *Britain and the Jews of Europe 1939–1945* (Oxford, 1979), Ch. I, provide the details. For the degree of receptivity outside Britain see H. L. Feingold, *The Politics of Rescue: The Roosevelt Administration and the Holocaust 1938–1945* (Brunswick, N.J., 1970) and I. Abella and H. Tropez, *None is too many* (Toronto, 1982).

14. Berghahn, op. cit., Ch. 4.

15. L. MacNeice, 'The British Museum Reading Room' (written July 1939) in his *Plant and Phantom* (London, 1941).

16. See below pp. 127–9, 143–4 for more discussion on academics and businessmen.

17. K. Gershon, *We came as Children. A Collective Autobiography of Refugees* (London, 1966); M. Ford, 'The Arrival of Jewish Refugee Children in England, 1938–1939', *Immigrants and Minorities*, Vol. 2 (1983), pp. 135–51. See also the Harris House Diary. This item, which is concerned with the experiences of sixteen teenage girls in Southport in 1939–40, is in the Manchester Jewish Museum.

18. Aronsfeld, op. cit., p. 23 discounts any prescience relating to his own departure.

19. *Census of England and Wales. General Report, 1921* (London, 1927), p. 147; *Census of England and Wales. General Report, 1931* (London, 1950), pp. 20, 168–9; *Census of Scotland, 1931. Report on the Fourteenth Decennial Census of Scotland* (Edinburgh, 1933), p. xxxv. See also above pp. 20–1 for the details of the prewar population.

20. B. Walter, 'Time-Space Patterns of Second Wave Irish Immigration into British Towns', *Transactions of the Institute of British Geographers*, Vol. 5 (1980), p. 300, on the spatial concentration of the Irish.

21. C. Arensberg and S. T. Kimball, *Family and Community in Ireland* (Cambridge, Mass., 1940); D. S. Johnson, 'The Economic History of Ireland between the Wars', *Irish Economic and Social History*, Vol. 1 (1974), pp. 49–61.

22. D. Caradog Jones, *The Social Survey of Merseyside* (2 vols, Liverpool, 1934), Vol. 1, p. 201.

23. The phrase in J. A. Jackson, *The Irish in Britain* (London, 1963), p. 39. See also R. Walshaw, *Migration to and from Merseyside* (Liverpool, 1938), p. 71 on American restrictionism.

24. M. A. Jones, *American Immigration* (Chicago, 1960), p. 276.
25. Based on J. Higham, *Strangers in the Land. Patterns of American Nativism 1860–1925* (New York, 1963 edn), p. 311.
26. Jackson, op. cit., p. 13.
27. Jones, op. cit., pp. 279–80; Jackson, op. cit., p. 13.
28. S. Glynn, 'Irish Immigration to Britain 1911–1951: Patterns and Policy', *Irish Economic and Social History*, Vol. VIII (1981), p. 51.
29. Based on Jackson, op. cit., p. 13 and Appendix XII (p. 194).
30. See above pp. 107–10 on the violence of 1919. On conditions in the Caribbean see *Recommendations of the West India Royal Commission, 1938–39*, 1939–40 Cmd 6174; *Report of the Royal Commission on West India, 1944–45*, Cmd. 6607. For non-official critical comment see W. M. Macmillan, *Warning from the West Indies. A Tract for Africa and the Empire* (London, 1936). For a superb admission of British exploitation see *Parl. Deb.* (Commons), Vol. 180 (1924–5), 11 February 1925, col. 293. The uncertain size of the Black population at this time is noted by, among others, G. A. Smith, 'Jim Crow on the Home Front (1942–1945)', *New Community*, Vol. VIII (1980), p. 317.
31. Caradog-Jones, op. cit., Vol. 1, p. 205 and Vol. 2, pp. 102ff; K. Little, *Negroes in Britain* (London, 1948); J. Walvin, *Black and White: the Negro in English Society 1555–1945* (London, 1973), pp. 209–12; P. Fryer, *Staying Power. The History of Black People in Britain* (London, 1984) and N. Evans, 'Regulating the Reserve Army: Arabs, Blacks and the Local State in Cardiff 1919–1945', *Immigrants and Minorities*, Vol. 4 (1985), pp. 68–115, provide details. See above pp. 107–10 on the collective violence of 1919.
32. C. McKay, *A Long Way from Home* (New York 1937), p. 59. On McKay see W. Cooper and R. C. Reinders, 'A Black Briton comes "Home": Claude McKay in England, 1920', *Race*, Vol. IX (1973), pp. 67–83.
33. Walvin, op. cit., p. 211.
34. J. Murray Brown, *Kenyatta* (London, 1974 edn), pp. 114, 152.
35. C. J. Robinson, *Black Marxism. The Making of the Black Radical Tradition* (London, 1983). Ch. 10 discusses James. Apart from the large body of James's own work, which provides an insight into the man and his world (*Beyond a Boundary* (1963), despite its obvious involvement with cricket, is partly autobiographical), there is a useful vignette in Fryer, op. cit., pp. 336–8. Elsewhere James apears as 'an eminent Trotskyist in Ethel Mannin's novel, *Comrade O Comrade* (London, 1947). On Padmore see J. R. Hooker, *Black Revolutionary* (London, 1967).
36. R. Makonnen, *Pan-Africanism from Within* (Nairobi, 1973).
37. T. J. S. George, *Krishna Menon* (London, 1964), Chs 7 and 8 partic. See below p. 139 for additional comment.
38. E. Scobie, *Black Britannia. A History of Blacks in Britain* (Chicago, 1972), Ch. XII. Adams appeared alongside Paul Robeson in *Song of Freedom* (1936) and *King Soloman's Mines* (1937).
39. Walvin, op. cit., p. 211. See also E. P. Hoyt, *Paul Robeson* (London, 1968).
40. *The Black Man*, Vol. II (November, 1934), p. 3.
41. P. D. Miller, 'Marcus Garvey, Garveyism and Britain 1887–1940', unpublished M.Litt. Thesis, Edinburgh University, 1975.
42. S. Aris, *The Jews in Business* (Harmondsworth, 1973); H. Pollins, *Economic History of the Jews in England* (New Brunswick, N.J., London, Toronto, 1982), discuss economic activity. V. D. Lipman, *Social History of the Jews in England 1850–1950* (London, 1954) carries material on social changes. On the mathematician, Brodetsky, see below p. 324 and the obituary in *The Times*, 18 May 1954. Louis Golding included among his novels *Magnolia Street* (1931) and *Mr. Emmanuel* (1939); see his obituary in *The Times*, 11 August 1958.

43. Based on R. O'Brien, 'The Establishment of the Jewish Minority in Leeds', unpublished Ph.D. Thesis, Bristol University 1975, pp. 162, 174.

44. Ibid., p. 229 and E. Krausz, *Leeds Jewry* (Cambridge, 1964), p. 25.

45. Caradog Jones, op. cit., Vol. 1, p. 73.

46. There is no satisfactory economic and social account of these developments. General comment on the East End can be found in the *New Survey of London Life and Labour* (9 vols, London, 1930–5), produced under the direction of H. Llewellyn Smith. See Pollins, op. cit., Chs. 12 and 13; H. Brotz, 'An Analysis of Social Stratification within Jewish Society in London', unpublished Ph.D. Thesis, London University 1951; J. W. Carrier, 'Working Class Jews in Present Day London. A Sociological Study', unpublished M.Phil. Thesis, London University 1969; A Smith, *Children of Fire* (London, 1934); S. Blumenfeld, *Jew Boy* (London, 1935); H. Fagan in M. Cohen and M. and H. Fagan (eds), *Childhood Memories* (n.d., n.p.) and J. Jacobs, *Out of the Ghetto* (London, 1978), for detail on economic, social, cultural and political trends, respectively. There is a brief appreciation of Blumenfeld in K. Worpole, *Dockers and Detectives* (London, 1983), pp. 97–102.

47. G. Hirschfeld (ed.), *Exile in Great Britain* (Leamington Spa, 1984), pp. 253–4.

48. A. Krausz, *Sheffield Jewry. Commentary on a Community* (Ramat-gan and London, 1980), pp. 7–8.

49. See the obituary in *The Times*, 15 December 1980.

50. Pollins, op. cit., refers to Jews in the entertainment industry. On Korda see K. Kulik, *Alexander Korda. The Man who could work Miracles* (London, 1975).

51. Clare, op. cit., pp. 232–3.

52. See below pp. 128, 142–8.

53. Berghahn, op. cit., p. 121.

54. See above Ch. 2.

55. See below pp. 142–3.

56. Berghahn, op. cit., emphasises this point, noting emigration particularly during and after the Second World War.

57. Bentwich, op. cit., Ch. 6.

58. Berghahn, op. cit., pp. 149–50.

59. H. Loebl, 'Government-Financed Factories and the Establishment of Industries by Refugees in the Special Areas of the North of England 1937–1961', unpublished M.Phil. Thesis, Durham University, 1978, pp. 8, 122.

60. Ibid., p. 147.

61. Pollins, op. cit., p. 206.

62. Loebl, M.Phil. Thesis, pp. 321–6.

63. Ibid., pp. 220–1.

64. *The Times*, 30 July 1985.

65. K. Silk, 'An 80th Birthday Tribute to Walter Fliess', *The Vegetarian* (November–December 1981), p. 4. IWM Tape 003936/06 (W. Fliess); see also G. Spencer, *Beloved Alien: Walter Fliess remembered* (Vancouver and Donhead St Andrew, 1985).

66. Hallgarten and Loeb are referred to in E. Penning-Rowsell, 'A Taste of Germany', *Financial Times*, 6 October 1983. Hallgarten can also be heard on IWM Tape 003967/06 (F. S. S. Hallgarten). See *The Times*, 8 August 1974, for an obituary of Loeb.

67. A main thrust in Loebl, M.Phil. Thesis (see p. 9).

68. Berghahn, op. cit., pp. 83–106.

69. See below p. 144.

70. A common theme in Berghahn, op. cit., Ch. 4 across the refugee spectrum.

71. IWM Tape 004498/05 (Sir Hans Krebs). 'The ugliest town . . .' is George

Orwell's reference to Sheffield in *The Road to Wigan Pier* (Harmondsworth, 1971 edn: first edition 1937), p. 95. On Krebs see the obituary in *The Times*, 23 November 1981 and Sir H. Krebs, *Reminiscences and Reflections* (Oxford, 1981). There is further comment relating to academics and language in K. Popper, *Unended Quest* (Glasgow, 1976), pp. 113ff. Professor Max Perutz made a similar point in 'Britain in the Thirties. Far From Home', BBC2 TV programme, 30 June 1983.

72. P. Hoch, 'The Reception of Central European Refugee Physicists of the 1930's: USSR, UK, USA', *Annals of Science*, Vol. 40 (1983), pp. 217–46, partic. 222–31, and his 'No Utopia: Refugee Scholars in Britain', *History Today*, Vol. 35 (November 1985), pp. 53–6.

73. M. Freedman (ed.), *A Minority in Britain* (London, 1955), p. 132. This is based upon R. N. Salaman, 'The Jewish Fellows of the Royal Society', in *Miscellanies of the Jewish Historical Society of England, part V. Essays in Memory of E. M. Adler* (London, 1948), pp. 146–75.

74. Hirschfeld, op. cit.; Hoch, *History Today*; P. Anderson, 'Components of the National Culture', in A. Cockburn and R. Blackburn (eds), *Student Power* (Harmondsworth, 1970), pp. 214–86 carries critical comment. See *The Times*, 20 August 1983 for a leader on 'The Englishness of Kunstgeschichte', following the death of N. Pevsner, for a celebratory emphasis. Education, as opposed to scholarship, was also influenced. See W. H. G. Armytage, *The German Influence on English Education* (London, 1969), p. 90, which refers to Kurt Hahn and Gordonstoun.

75. F. Lafitee, *The Internment of Aliens* (London, 1940), pp. 57–8.

76. Berghahn, op. cit., pp. 167–9.

77. See the obituary by C. C. Aronsfeld, in *The Wiener Library Bulletin*, Vol. XVIII (April 1964), pp. 13–14; C. Holmes, 'On the Track of Tyranny', *Immigrants and Minorities*, Vol. 3, (1984), pp. 111–13.

78. F. Saxl, 'The History of Warburg's Library', in E. H. Gombrich, *Aby Warburg: An Intellectual Biography* (London, 1970), pp. 337–8.

79. Jackson, op. cit., pp. 97–8; see also Caradog Jones, op. cit., Vol. 1, p. 201.

80. S. Orwell and I. Angus (eds), *The Collected Essays and Letters of George Orwell*, Vol. 1, *An Age Like This 1920–1940* (Harmondsworth, 1979 edn), p. 76.

81. Glynn, op. cit., p. 55; S. Marriner, *The Economic and Social Development of Merseyside* (London, 1982), pp. 98–9.

82. J. V. Hickey, 'The Origins and Growth of the Irish Community in Cardiff', unpublished MA Thesis, University of Wales 1959, p. 148; K. O'Connor, *The Irish In Britain* (Dublin, 1974), p. 45 notes the class split in the Irish community and comments on its consequences.

83. Caradog Jones, op. cit., Vol. 2, p. 202.

84. Based on J. E. Handley, *The Irish in Modern Scotland* (Cork, 1947), pp. 186–8.

85. H. Harris, 'The Other Half-Million. Irish Soldiers of the Great War', in O. D. Edwards and F. Ryle (eds), *1916. The Easter Rising* (London, 1968), pp. 101–15. The half-million included soldiers from Ireland and second and third generation Irish living in Britain.

86. E. R. Norman, *A History of Modern Ireland* (London, 1971), p. 257.

87. On Casement see R. Sawyer, *Casement. The Flawed Hero* (London, 1984), partic. Chs 10 and 11.

88. On aspects of the Rising see Edwards and Ryle, op. cit. See also O'Connor, op. cit., p. 41 for additional comment.

89. Covered, for example, in R. Kee, *The Green Flag. A History of Irish Nationalism* (London, 1972).

90. O'Connor, op. cit., p. 42; G. Brown, *In My Way* (London, 1971), p. 23; S. Cronin, *Irish Nationalism. A History of its Roots and Ideology* (Dublin, 1980), p. 128, all refer to MacSwiney.

91. M. McDermott, 'Irish Catholics and the British Labour Movement: A study with particular reference to London 1918 to 1970', unpublished MA Thesis, Kent University, 1979, pp. 64ff; Jackson, op. cit., p. 125 refers to the Connolly Association. So does Cronin, op. cit., p. 186.

92. Cronin, op. cit., pp. 326–9 has IRA documents on these developments.

93. Ibid., pp. 159–62; L. Fairchild, *The Trial of Peter Barnes and others in the IRA Coventry Explosions of 1939* (London, 1953); T. P. Coogan, *The IRA* (London, 1975); N. West, *MI5. British Security Service Operations 1909–1945* (London, 1981), pp. 309–14.

94. Based on Hickey, MA Thesis, p. 144; McDermott, MA Thesis, pp. 161, 189; W. W. Walker, 'Irish Immigrants in Scotland: Their Priests, Politics and Parochial Life', *Historical Journal*, Vol. XV (1972), pp. 664–5 notes the move towards Labour in Scotland and the role of the *Catholic Herald* under Charles Diamond in this process. See also his *Juteopolis. Dundee and its Textile Workers 1885–1923* (Edinburgh, 1979), p. 468.

95. Based on Jackson, op. cit., p. 125; O'Connor, op. cit., pp. 42, 51; Walker, *Historical Journal*, pp. 649, 665. The involvement of those of Irish descent in the early history of the CPGB is referred to in: H. Pelling, *The British Communist Party: A Historical Profile* (London, 1975 edn), p. 16.

96. S. A. Wa'iz, *Indians Abroad* (Bombay, 1934), pp. 474–6.

97. See below p. 153.

98. Little, op. cit., p. 67.

99. See below pp. 134–5.

100. I. Law and J. Henfrey, *A History of Race and Racism in Liverpool 1660–1950* (Liverpool, 1981), pp. 30–2; see Evans, op. cit., pp. 69–73 on Tiger Bay. See also Little, op. cit., p. 44 and D. Hiro, 'Three Generations of Tiger Bay', *New Society*, 21 September 1967, pp. 385–7. The area was the subject of a 1933 British feature film, called *Tiger Bay*. See *Picturegoer*, 17 March 1934.

101. Little, op. cit., p. 104. See above p. 109 for the significance of territory in the 1919 violence.

102. Based on Little, op. cit., pp. 135–46, 151–9, 110, 113 and Evans, op. cit., pp. 98ff.

103. Fryer, op. cit., is useful.

104. Makonnen, op. cit., pp. 150–1.

105. Fryer, op. cit., pp. 321–3 refers to Congresses held in 1921 and 1923.

106. Ibid., p. 293.

107. Ibid., p. 324. See also R. J. Macdonald, 'Dr. Harold Arundel Moody and the League of Coloured Peoples 1931–1947: A Retrospective View', *Race*, Vol. XIV (1973), p. 291.

108. P. Garigue, 'The West African Students' Union', *Africa*, Vol. XXIII (January, 1953), pp. 55–69. There is a valuable cache of neglected material in Reginald Sorensen's papers in the House of Lords, (see SOR 168 and 174).

109. P. B. Rich, 'Race and Empire in British Politics 1890–1962', ts., p. 87. This was published by Cambridge University Press in 1986.

110. Fryer, op. cit., pp. 329–30, 343.

111. Ibid., p. 325.

112. Ibid., pp. 336–8.

113. Ibid., pp. 342, 346; R. J. Macdonald, ' "The Wisers who are far away . . ." The Role of London's Black Press in the 1930s and '40s', Paper given at the International Conference on the History of Blacks in Britain, 1981; Rich, 'Race and Empire', pp. 94–5. See above p. 123 on Garvey.

114. Macdonald, *Race*, p. 291.

115. Ibid., pp. 292, 307. See also D. Vaughan, *Negro Victory* (London, 1950).

116. *The Keys* Vol. I (January 1934), cover.

117. This aspect is misunderstood by Macdonald, *Race*, p. 295 and underplayed by Fryer, op. cit., pp. 326–8.

118. Vaughan, op. cit., pp. 63ff; Macdonald, *Race*, p. 294; Makonnen, op. cit., p. 126; Fryer, op. cit., p. 328. See also *The Keys*, Vol. I (April–June 1934), p. 70 and ibid., Vol. III (April–June 1936), p. 52.

119. *The Keys*, Vol. II (January–March 1935), p. 55; ibid., Vol. IV (January–March 1937), p. 29; ibid., Vol. IV (April–June 1937), p. 36. I. Geiss, *The Pan-African Movement* (London, 1974), Ch. 17, refers to the League as an example of 'Conservative Pan-Africanism'.

120. Makonnen, op. cit., p. 126.

121. *The Keys*, Vol. II (July–September 1934), p. 16 refers to the split with WASU. For the other perspective see *WASU Protests! Aggrey House – The Truth* (London, 1934). See also Macdonald, *Race*, pp. 295–6 and Fryer, op. cit., p. 325.

122. Macdonald, *Race*, p. 298 recognises the more radical dimension of the League. See *The Keys*, Vol. VI (October–December, 1938), pp. 1–3, for an example of Blackman's work. Blackman is discussed in ' "The Wisers" ', pp. 15–16 and Fryer, op. cit., p. 329.

123. A. J. Mackenzie, 'British Marxists and the Empire', unpublished Ph.D. Thesis, London University, 1978, is a useful source.

124. Padmore is Thomas Lanwood, the totally committed Marxist, in Peter Abrahams' novel, *A Wreath for Udomo* (London, 1956). He edited the *Negro Worker* from Hamburg on behalf of the Communist International.

125. Mackenzie, Ph.D. Thesis, p. 95.

126. LAI, *Report of the International Secretariat for 1934* (Bridgeman Archive, Hull University).

127. Mackenzie, Ph.D. Thesis, pp. 202ff.

128. See the entry in J. M. Bellamy and J. Saville (eds), *Dictionary of Labour Biography* Vol. VI (London, 1982), p. 240. See also W. Gallacher, 'Shapurji Saklatvala 1874–1936', *Labour Monthly* (January 1937), pp. 51–3. On Archer see above p. 84. For Archer's involvement with Saklatvala see B. A. Kosmin, 'J. R. Archer (1863–1932): a Pan-Africanist in the Battersea Labour Movement', *New Community*, Vol. VII (1979), p. 434.

129. D. F. Karaka, *The Pulse of Oxford* (London, 1933), pp. 35–41.

130. On whom see Bellamy and Saville, op. cit., Vol. V. (London, 1979), pp. 132–4. See also V. G. Kiernan, 'Mohan Kumaramangalam in England', *Socialist India*, 23 February 1974, pp. 5–7 and 36 and ibid., 2 March 1974, pp. 13–17, 24. For the quieter life of a prewar student radical see E. C. Brown, *Har Dayal. Hindu Revolutionary and Rationalist* (Tucson, 1975).

131. Based on George, op. cit., pp. 57, 151. On Amritsar see A. Draper, *Amritsar, The Massacre that ended the Raj* (London, 1981).

132. Based on George, op. cit., p. 151. On Meerut see Bellamy and Saville, op. cit., Vol. VI, pp. 84–91.

133. *Parl. Deb.* (Commons), Vol. 160 (1923), 28 February 1923, cols. 2083, 2086, 2105–6, 2117.

134. Ibid., cols 2088, 2097, 2099–2100. See also W. T. Colyer, *The Worker's Passport* (London, 1928). On deportation see PRO HO 45/24675/432156.

135. *Parl. Deb.* (Commons), Vol. 160 (1923), 28 February 1923, col. 2124.

136. Ibid., col. 2123.

137. 'Alien London', in *The Times*, 22, 28 November 1924, 2, 4 and 8 December 1924.

See ibid., 3, 5, 9 and 16 December 1924 for correspondence provoked by these articles.

138. Parl. Deb. (Commons), Vol. 180 (1924–5), 11 February 1925, col. 215. See also C. Andrew, *Secret Service. The Making of the British Intelligence Community* (London, 1985), Ch. 10.

139. On Pearson see E. S. Pearson, *Karl Pearson: An Appreciation of Some Aspects of His Life and Work* (Cambridge, 1938), and D. MacKenzie, 'Karl Pearson and the Professional Middle Classes', *Annals of Science*, Vol. 36 (1979), pp. 125–43.

140. Gartner, op. cit., p. 224.

141. K. Pearson and M. Moul, 'The Problem of Alien Immigration into Great Britain illustrated by an Examination of Russian and Polish Children', *Annals of Eugenics*, Vol. 1 (1925–6), p. 127.

142. On the Britons see G. Lebzelter, 'Henry Hamilton Beamish and the Britons: Champions of Anti-semitism', in K. Lunn and R. C. Thurlow (eds), *British Fascism* (London, 1980), pp. 41–56.

143. *The Hidden Hand or Jewry Ueber Alles* (June 1922), p. 1.

144. G. P. Mudge, *The Menace to the English Race and its Tradition of Present Day Immigration and Emigration* (n.d., n.p., 1919–20?); C. Holmes, *Antisemitism in British Society 1876–1939* (London, 1979), p. 277, FN33 notes the relationship between Mudge and The Britons.

145. See Lt. Col. A. H. Lane, *The Alien Menace* (3rd edn London, 1932), pp. 49–52.

146. See M. Davies and A. G. Hughes, 'An Investigation into the Comparative Intelligence and Attainments of Jewish and Non-Jewish School Children', *British Journal of Psychology*, Vol. XVIII (1927), pp. 134–46, partic. p. 143. On the involvement of the Board see Board of Deputies, *Annual Report* 1927 (London, 1928), p. 40. On Cyril Burt see L. S. Hearnshaw, *Cyril Burt, Psychologist* (London, 1979).

147. L. Kamin, *The Science and Politics of I.Q.* (Harmondsworth, 1977); N. Stepan, *The Idea of Race in Science. Great Britain 1880–1960* (Oxford, 1982).

148. Sherman, op. cit., p. 26 notices Schiff's Belgian Refugee work. See also the obituary in *The Times*, 17 November 1952.

149. Bentwich, op. cit., pp. 14–15.

150. Ibid., pp. 14–49 and Sherman, op. cit., pp. 25, 171–4.

151. Sherman, op. cit., p. 26.

152. Bentwich, op. cit., p. 52; Lafitte, op. cit., p. 43.

153. Bentwich, op. cit., is one example of this response.

154. Aronsfeld, op. cit., p. 26.

155. Berghahn, op. cit., p. 141. There is a copy of the pamphlet in the Board of Deputies.

156. L. Darton, *An Account of the Work of the Friends Committee for Refugees and Aliens, first known as the German Emergency Committee of the Society of Friends 1933–1950* (London, 1954).

157. J. Harris, *William Beveridge. A Biography* (Oxford, 1977), pp. 297–9 and Lord Beveridge, *A Defence of Free Learning* (London, 1959), partic. Ch. I.

158. Sherman, op. cit., pp. 26–7.

159. Ibid., p. 27.

160. Ibid., p. 215; Lafitte, op. cit., pp. 48–50.

161. *British Medical Journal*, supplement, 16 December 1933, p. 311.

162. Ibid., 13 January 1934. See also *Reynolds News*, 11 September 1938 and *Everybody's Weekly*, 17 September 1938. See W. M. Kotschnig, *Unemployment in the Learned Professions* (Oxford, 1937), for an academic assessment.

163. Sherman, op. cit., pp. 123–4; Berghahn, op. cit., pp. 83–7.

164. Berghahn, op. cit., pp. 79 and 80, and Hoch, *Annals of Science* and *History Today*.

165. See the *Sunday Pictorial*, 15 January 1939 for a popular expression of hostility. 'Refugees get jobs. Britons get dole.'

166. P. Foot, *Immigration and Race in British Politics* (Harmondsworth, 1965), p. 111. For an attempt by Ramsay to control alien immigration see *Parl. Deb.* (Commons), Vol. 337 (1937–8), 28 June 1938, cols 1725–8. For other aspects of Ramsay's life see R. Griffiths, *Fellow Travellers of the Right. British Enthusiasts for Nazi Germany 1933–39* (London, 1980), and the obituary in *The Times*, 12 March 1955, which noticed his strong anti-Semitic views. Ramsay's 18B File has still not been released by the government.

167. *Parl. Deb.* (Commons), Vol. 275 (1932–3), 9 March 1933, cols 1351–2 and ibid., Vol. 283 (1933–4), 30 November 1933, cols 1028–30.

168. *Parl. Deb.* (Commons), Vol. 180 (1924–5), 11 February 1925, cols 285–6, and ibid., Vol. 292 (1933–4), 24 July 1934, col. 1645 for an additional contribution by Greene. See below pp. 312–15 for an extended discussion of ambiguity.

169. Muggeridge, op. cit., p. 243.

170. Holmes, *Antisemitism*, Ch. 13.

171. *Sunday Express*, 19 June 1938; *Reynolds News*, 11 September 1938; *Everybody's Weekly*, 17 September 1938.

172. *Action*, 7 January 1939; Holmes, *Antisemitism*, Ch. 10. On the fringe racial nationalists see R. Thurlow, 'Fascism in Britain. A History 1918–1985'. This will be published by Blackwell. [Published, 1987.]

173. F. Brockway, *Inside the Left* (London, 1947), pp. 271–2 gives an eye-witness account by someone hostile to Fascism. See also P. Piratin, *Our Flag stays Red* (London, 1948), pp. 26–48. For a Fascist interpretation see the sources quoted by R. Skidelsky, *Oswald Mosley* (London, 1975), p. 406; for an East Ender's account see Jacobs op. cit., Ch. 12. Joe Jacobs was a CP member. See Skidelsky, op. cit., pp. 416ff on the Public Order Act.

174. Foot, op. cit., pp. 112–14. H. A. Taylor, *Jix, Viscount Brentford* (London, 1933). On the attempted entry of Trotsky, there is C. Holmes, 'Trotsky and Britain: The Closed File', *Society for the Study of Labour History Bulletin*, No. 39 (1979), pp. 33–8. On immigration law and the immigration service during the interwar years see C. F. Fraser, *Control of Aliens in the British Commonwealth of Nations* (London, 1940) and T. W. E. Roche, *The Key in the Lock* (London, 1969), Chs 3, 4.

175. Wasserstein, op. cit., p. 10. See also M. Goldsmith, 'The Refugee Transit Camp at Richborough', *The Nineteenth Century and After*, Vol. 126 (1939), pp. 315–21.

176. Sherman, op. cit., p. 259.

177. See *Palestine*, Royal Commission Report Cmd. 5749 (London, 1937), p. 306.

178. Sherman, op. cit., pp. 260–1.

179. Hope Simpson, op. cit., pp. 337–9 comments favourably on this. But see File 88/1. National Council for Civil Liberties (NCCL) Archives, Hull University, for critical comment.

180. Wasserstein, op. cit., pp. 8–9. See *Encyclopaedia Judaica*, Vol. 15 (Jerusalem, 1951), pp. 1500–2, for a summary.

181. Based on Lafitte, op. cit., pp. 53–4; Sherman, op. cit., pp. 138–55, 220–6, 262–3; A. Calder, *The People's War. Britain 1939–45* (London, 1969), p. 130. Information on the Czech Refugee Trust Fund can be derived from PRO HO 213/292 and 975–986.

182. Sherman, op. cit., p. 264. See also J. H. Simpson, *Refugees. A Review of the Situation since September 1938* (London, 1939), p. 69.

183. Wasserstein, op. cit., p. 19.

184. Ibid., p. 26.

185. Sherman, op. cit., p. 267.

186. Aronsfeld, op. cit., p. 23. For comment on the dangers of 'presentism' in

historical assessment see M. Banton, *Racial and Ethnic Competition* (Cambridge, 1983), pp. 33–4, 76–7. For the role of Shanghai, see PRO HO 213/112 and 113. On restriction in other countries see Feingold, op. cit., and Abella and Troper, op. cit.

187. Handley, op. cit., p. 302.

188. O'Connor, op. cit., p. 74. See above pp. 130–31 for comment on dockers and local authority workers.

189. *The Times*, 10 January and 13 January 1939.

190. P. J. Waller, *Democracy and Sectarianism. A Political and Social History of Liverpool 1868–1939* (Liverpool, 1981), p. 329 and generally. See also above p. 59. See E. Hughes, *Sydney Silverman. Rebel in Parliament* (London, and Edinburgh, 1969), Ch. 5, for evidence of Catholic v Jewish tensions in 1933.

191. G. R. Gair, 'The Irish Immigration Question' in *Liverpool Review*, Vol. XI, 1 January 1934, pp. 11–13, partic. 11–12; in ibid., Vol. IX, 2 February 1934, pp. 47–50, partic. 49–50 and in ibid., Vol. IX, 3 March 1934, pp. 86–8.

192. J. B. Priestley, *English Journey* (London, 1934), p. 248.

193. Handley, op. cit., p. 303; *Glasgow Herald*, 23 March 1922.

194. See above pp. 58–9, 60.

195. Kee, op. cit., p. 693; O'Connor, op. cit., p. 43. On Collins see P. Beasley, *Michael Collins and the Making of a New Ireland* (Dublin, 1926) and M. Forester, *Michael Collins – The Lost Leader* (London, 1971). For Ireland in the 1920s see also C. Townshend, *Political Violence in Ireland – Government and Resistance 1848* (Oxford, 1983), Chs 7, 8.

196. West, op. cit., pp. 309–14; O'Connor, op. cit., pp. 54–5. See above p. 133 for earlier comment.

197. See, for example, J. Brand, *The National Movement in Scotland* (London, 1978), partic. Chs 4, 5.

198. G. M. Thomson, *Caledonia or the Future of the Scots* (London, 1927), p. 10.

199. Ibid., pp. 10–11, 78–9.

200. A. D. Gibb, *Scotland in Eclipse* (London, 1930), pp. 54–5.

201. Ibid., p. 62.

202. J. Torrence, *Scotland's Decline* (London, 1939), p. 17.

203. See above p. 121.

204. Gibb, op. cit., p. 56; Thomson, op. cit., pp. 10–11.

205. Discussed in Handley, op. cit., pp. 322–3. S. Bruce, *No Pope of Rome. Militant Protestantism in Modern Scotland* (Edinburgh, 1985), p. 46 notes that the receipt of the report by the Assembly did not mean that the majority of its members agreed with the report's sentiment.

206. See Bruce, op. cit., Chs 2 and 3 on Ratcliffe and the Scottish Protestant League and John Cormack's Protestant Action Society respectively; B. Murray, *The Old Firm. Sectarianism, Sport and Society in Scotland* (Edinburgh, 1985), pp. 135ff. See also T. Gallagher, 'Protestant Extremism in Urban Scotland 1930–1939: Its Growth and Contraction', *Scottish Historical Review*, Vol. LXIV (1985), pp. 143–67.

207. Handley, op. cit., pp. 309–10.

208. C. M. Grieve, *Albyn or Scotland and the Future* (London, 1927).

209. McDermott, MA Thesis, is useful in this respect.

210. See above p. 148.

211. See above pp. 60–61.

212. J. Wheeler-Bennett, *John Anderson. Viscount Waverley* (London, 1962). See below pp. 173–5, 186–94 on internment during the Second World War.

213. *Parl. Deb.* (Commons), Vol. 321 (1936–7), 2 March 1937, col. 167.

214. Glynn, op cit., pp. 61–8 discusses British public opinion on immigration controls

over the Irish; the paragraph draws heavily from this source. See above pp. 120–21 on American immigration policy.

215. L. Constantine, *Cricket and I* (London, 1942); U. Giuseppi, *A Look at Learie Constantine* (London, 1974), pp. 40–6; the quotation is from *The Keys* Vol. I. (January, 1934), p. 31. There is an obituary in *The Times*, 2 July 1971. See below pp. 196, 202–3, 240, 313 for additional comment.

216. See the obituary in *The Times*, 19 August 1969.

217. A. Jenkins, *The Twenties* (London, 1974), p. 141 and his *The Thirties* (London, 1976), p. 73; see also K. Robbins, *The Eclipse of a Great Power. Modern Britain 1870–1975* (London, 1983), p. 163. PRO HO 45/24778, a recently opened file reveals the problem of one Black entertainer, Sidney Bechet, the clarinettist, who was deported in November 1922 after being found guilty of an assault.

218. P. Noble, *The Negro in Films* (London, 1948), pp. 112–26; M. Seton, *Paul Robeson* (London, 1958), pp. 54–5. See also above p. 123 for reference to Robert Adams.

219. E. Marke, *Old Man Trouble* (London, 1975), p. 99.

220. On Monolulu, the better-known of the two, see *The Tatler*, 5 June 1929.

221. M. Davie (ed.), *The Diaries of Evelyn Waugh* (London, 1976), p. 281, entry for 28 February 1927.

222. N. Cunard, 'Colour Bar', in N. Cunard, *Negro: An Anthology* (New York, 1970 edn), p. 345. The restriction was not lifted until April 1948. Letter, General Secretary of the British Boxing Board of Control to author, 9 September 1985.

223. Scobie, op. cit., p. 115. See below for further discussion of interracial sexual contact.

224. Hoyt, op. cit., p. 49. See Cunard, 'Colour Bar', pp. 342–5 on hotel discrimination generally. Concern was also expressed by sympathetic sources at Westminster. See *Parl. Deb.* (Commons), 1937–8, Vol. 331, 14 February 1938, col. 1544.

225. D. Karaka, 'The Colour Bar in Britain', *The Spectator*, 30 March 1934, p. 456.

226. Scobie, op. cit., pp. 142–4; A. A. Ademola, 'Colour Bar Notoriety in Great Britain', in Cunard, op. cit., pp. 346–7. On WASU see above. For a fictional treatment of the problem see K. Weston, *London Fog* (London, 1934), pp. 84–5.

227. See above pp. 77–82, 111–12 on earlier hostility towards the Chinese.

228. Little, op. cit., and Evans, op. cit. refer to the situation in Cardiff, and to the conditions in the shipping industry. See also Marriner, op. cit., p. 99 and S. G. Sturmey, *British Shipping and World Competition* (London, 1962), Ch. IV.

229. K. Lunn, 'Race Relations or Industrial Relations?', *Immigrants and Minorities*, Vol. 4 (1985), p. 13.

230. Little, op. cit., p. 60.

231. D. Byrne, 'The 1930 "Arab Riot" in South Shields: A Race Riot that never was', *Race and Class*, Vol. XVIII (1977), pp. 261–77. Full details of the situation on Tyneside appear in a neglected source in the Modern Records Centre, Warwick University, 'Durham Assizes. Before Mr. Justice Roche and a Petty Jury. Rex v Ali Said and ors', MSS 175/7/LE/103.

232. Based on F. J. Lindop, 'A History of the Seamen's Trade Unionism to 1929', unpublished M.Phil. Thesis, London University, 1972, Ch. 2 and Evans, op. cit. The 1925 Order was known technically as SR and O (No. 290), 1925. It remained in force until 1943.

233. This discussion is based upon: Little, op. cit., pp. 65, 74–5, 80, and Evans, op. cit., as well as contemporary discussion contained in *Colonial News*, April 1934, p. 4, *The Keys*, Vol. III (October–December 1935), pp. 18ff., and unpublished material in the shape of the Report of a Deputation to the Chief Constable of Cardiff, 8 April 1937, and the letter from the South Wales Association for the Welfare of Coloured People to the Home Office (both in File 92/1, NCCL Archives, Hull University). Finally, the sterotypes contained in a report by the

Chief Constable of Cardiff, dated 7 June 1937 in PRO HO 213/353, revealed a good deal about police attitudes which were of crucial significance in influencing developments in Cardiff. See above pp. 137–8 on the LAI and below on p. 188 the League of Coloured Peoples. See R. Martin, *Communism and the British Trade Unions, 1924–1933. A Study of the National Minority Movement* (Oxford, 1969) on the Minority Movement.

234. For the impact of Morel's pamphlet see R. C. Reinders, 'Racialism on the Left. E. D. Morel and the "Black Horror on the Rhine" ', *International Review of Social History*, Vol. XIII (1968), pp. 1–28. On the Robeson-Ashcroft kiss see above p. 153. On Nancy Cunard, the Lady Tantamount of Aldous Huxley's *Point Counter Point*, see A. Chisholm, *Nancy Cunard* (London, 1979), partic. pp. 118–19. For additional comment by White authors on interracial sexual relationships see the liberal discussion in J. Oldham, *Christianity and the Race Problem* (London, 1924), Ch. X and the negative remarks in J. W. Gregory, *The Menace of Colour* (London, 1925), Ch. XI. For observations by a Black author on these years see J. A. Rogers, *Sex and Race* (3 vols, New York, 1972 edn), Vol. I, partic. pp. 213–15. Caradog Jones, op. cit., Vol. I, pp. 74–5 comments that relations between white women and Chinese men were more favourably regarded. But see above p. 79 for evidence which would qualify this. Note also R. Lee, *The Town that Died* (London, 1975), p. 132 for the difficulties that could arise for the child of a Chinese-Welsh union who was dubbed 'Mr. Chinaman'. The views of the Chief Constable of Cardiff are given in Rich, 'Race and Empire', p. 153.

235. M. E. Fletcher, *Report on an Investigation into the Colour Problem in Liverpool and other Ports* (Liverpool, 1930); P. B. Rich, 'Philanthropic Racism in Britain. The Anti-Slavery Society and "Half-Caste" Children between the Wars', *Immigrants and Minorities*, Vol. 3 (1984), pp. 69–88; Rich (p. 74) comments favourably on the later survey of Merseyside by Caradog Jones. But note that this publication referred to Fletcher's report without criticism. See Caradog Jones, op. cit., Vol. 1, p. 205.

236. Based on Evans, op. cit., F. A. Richardson, *Social Conditions in Ports and Dockland Areas. London, Liverpool and Cardiff* (n.p., n.d.), pp. 14ff., partic. pp. 19–20; M. Banton, *The Coloured Quarter* (London, 1955) p. 37 refers to more accurate but ignored surveys. In this connection see N. Hare, 'The Prospects for Coloured Children in England', *The Keys*, Vol. V No. I (July–September 1937), pp. 11–12 and 25–7.

237. Based on Rich, 'Race and Empire', Ch. 1 and, more partic. Ch. 5, espec. p. 162, and Rich, *Immigrants and Minorities*, pp. 75ff., partic. pp. 76, 80. Additional material, unused by Rich, can be found in PRO HO 213/349, 350, 352, 353. See above pp. 107–10 on the recent interracial violence.

238. See above p. 156 for earlier reference to South Africa. The South African dimension is of particular interest to Rich in his 'Race and Empire', p. 162 and in his *Immigrants and Minorities*, pp. 76–7.

239. Rich, *Immigrants and Minorities*, p. 77.

240. See the entry on Bridgeman in Bellamy and Saville, op. cit., Vol. VII (London, 1984), pp. 26–50. On Meerut see above note 132.

241. For an example of existing comment see, D. S. Wylie, 'Critics of Colonial Policy in Kenya with Special Reference to Norman Leys and W. McGregor Ross', unpublished M.Litt. Thesis, Edinburgh University, 1974. A good deal of additional detail is offered in Rich, 'Race and Empire' and in B. Bush, 'Britain and Black Africa in the Inter-War Years', unpublished Ph.D. Thesis, Sheffield University, 1986.

242. See above pp. 153–4 on students. For comment on working-class groups see

Little, op. cit., pp. 125, 225. For a literary treatment, which traces the problems of 'Caleb Butler' (i.e. the author) see R. Ahmed, *I Rise* (London, 1937), p. 247.

243. Murray-Brown, op. cit., pp. 181–2, 215.

244. See above pp. 154–5.

245. *The Keys*, Vol. II (July–September, 1934), p. 17.

246. See above pp. 154–5.

247. A classic sympathetic study is C. Dover, *Half-Caste* (London, 1937).

248. Rich, 'Race and Empire', Ch. 4 is generally useful and on pp. 157ff., he refers to the academic background and influences relating to the report by M. E. Fletcher (see above p. 156). See also his 'The Long Victorian Sunset. Anthropology, Eugenics and Race in Britain, 1900–48', *Patterns of Prejudice*, Vol. 18 (July 1984), pp. 3–17. See also L. S. Waterman, 'The Eugenics Movement in Britain in the 1930s', unpublished M.Sc. Thesis, Sussex University, 1975, pp. 37–43; G. R. Searle, 'Eugenics and Politics in Britain in the 1930s', *Annals of Science*, Vol. 36 (1979), pp. 159–69; M. Billig, 'The Origins of Race Psychology II', *Patterns of Prejudice*, Vol. 17 (January 1983), pp. 25–31. A certain amount of work has been completed recently on the eugenics movement and not a little controversy has been generated. However, there is still room for a full study of the work of eugenicists on immigrant minorities and indeed on academic perspectives generally.

249. J. S. Huxley, A. C. Haddon, with A. Carr-Saunders, *We Europeans* (London, 1935).

250. See, for example, on popular literature, G. M. Mitchell, 'John Buchan's Fiction: A Hierarchy of Race', *Patterns of Prejudice*, Vol. VII (November–December 1973), pp. 24–30; on film, see Noble, op. cit.; see J. Richards, *Visions of Yesterday* (London, 1973) and his *The Age of the Dream Palace. Cinema and Society in Britain 1930–1939* (London, 1984), partic. Ch. 8; for a detailed study of Blacks in the American cinema see T. Cripps, *Slow Fade to Black. The Negro in American Film 1900–1942* (New York, 1977). Finally, see J. C. Robertson, *The British Board of Film Censors. Film Censorship in Britain, 1896–1950* (London, 1985), pp. 67–70, for useful evidence on cinematic stereotypes of the Chinese.

251. P. B. Rich, 'Doctrines of Racial Segregation in Britain 1900–1944', *New Community*, Vol. XII (1984–5), pp. 75–88, carries useful comment.

IV. IN A CONTEXT OF TOTAL WAR: 1933–45

1. S. Orwell and I. Angus (eds), *The Collected Essays, Journalism and Letters of George Orwell*, Vol. 2. *My Country Right or Left 1940–1943* (Harmondsworth, 1980 edn), p. 389.

2. M. J. Proudfoot, *European Refugees 1939–52* (London, 1957), pp. 71–2. The most recent comment on refugees during the war is in M. Marrus, *The Unwanted. Refugees in the Twentieth Century* (New York, 1985), Ch. 3, 'Last Chance 1939–41' and Ch. 4.

3. B. Wasserstein, *Britain and the Jews of Europe 1939–1945* (Oxford, 1979), p. 82, who notes that there was a degree of re-emigration during the war. This occurred particularly after internment, on which see below pp. 173–5, 186–94.

4. Ibid., pp. 40–2. On the development of Nazi policy see L. Dawidowicz, *The War against the Jews 1933–45* (Harmondsworth, 1977 edn). On Madagascar see J. Tenenbaum, *Race and Reich* (New York, 1956), Ch. 19.

5. Wasserstein, op. cit., p. 45.

6. The obituary of Reuben Ainsztein in *The Times*, 8 December 1981 provides a

graphic account of the determination of one individual to leave Nazi-occupied Europe. Ainsztein managed eventually to escape in 1943.

7. Wasserstein, op. cit., p. 43. See also above pp. 145–48. See N. Shepherd, *Wilfrid Israel: German Jewry's Secret Ambassador* (London, 1984), for wartime attempts to bring Jews out of Europe in the face of Foreign Office inaction. Israel was portrayed as Berhnard Landauer in Christopher Isherwood's *Goodbye to Berlin*. T. W. E. Roche, *The Key in The Lock* (London, 1969), Ch. 5, gives an anodyne account of immigration control during the war.

8. Derived from: S. Cronin, *Irish Nationalism* (Dublin, 1980); N. West, *MI5. British Security Service Operations 1909–1945* (London, 1981), Ch. XII; S. Glynn, 'Irish Immigration to Britain 1911–1951: Patterns and Policy', *Irish Economic and Social History*, Vol. VIII (1981), pp. 68–9; R. Fisk, *In Time of War: Ireland, Ulster and the Price of Nationality 1939–45* (London, 1983). See above pp. 135, 150 for the prewar IRA campaign.

9. Ministry of Labour and National Service, *Report for Years 1939–1946* Cmd. 7225 (London, 1947), p. 54. See also J. W. Blake, *Northern Ireland in the Second World War* (Belfast, 1956), partic. pp. 424–5, 559.

10. H. M. D. Parker, *Manpower. A Study of War-time Policy and Administration* (London, 1957), p. 335.

11. 'The Transfer of Irish Workers to Great Britain', *International Labour Review*, Vol. XLVIII (1943), p. 338.

12. Ibid.

13. Parker, op. cit., p. 341.

14. Ministry of Labour and National Service, *Report* etc., p. 55; J. A. Jackson, *The Irish in Britain* (London, 1963), pp. 99–101. The official documents relating to restrictions on travel in 1944 can be found in PRO HO 213/1284, 1286.

15. Parker, op. cit., p. 339; Jackson, op. cit., p. 99; P. Inman, *Labour in the Munitions Industries* (London, 1957), pp. 167, 173.

16. C. Arensberg and S. T. Kimball, *Family and Community in Ireland* (Cambridge, Mass., 1940) is useful on conditions in Ireland. See also J. Meenan, *The Irish Economy since 1922* (Liverpool, 1970) and F. S. L. Lyons, *Ireland since the Famine* (London, 1973 edn), pp. 599ff. See 'The Transfer of Irish Workers' etc., p. 339 for restrictions that were placed on the emigration of certain classes of workers.

17. Lyons, op. cit., pp. 557, 622–3, and J. O'Donoghue, *In a Strange Land* (London, 1958), p. 43, provide the economic context. On the military involvement of the Irish see J. T. Carroll, *Ireland in the War Years* (Newton Abbot, 1975), pp. 108–9. For a heated correspondence on the military effectiveness of the Southern Irish see *Sunday Telegraph*, 21 July, 28 July, 4 and 11 August 1985.

18. Ministry of Labour and National Service, *Report*, etc., p. 56, refers to the recruitment of British Dominions and Colonial Labour during the war. See above for earlier reference to these groups. See Parker, op. cit., pp. 344–7 on alien workers.

19. M. Gowing, 'The Organization of Manpower during the Second World War', *Journal of Contemporary History*, Vol. VII (1972), p. 151, discusses manpower requirements and shortages.

20. A. Watkinson, 'West Indian Volunteer Technicians', *Time and Tide*, 11 July 1942, p. 556; A. Watson, *West Indian Workers in Great Britain* (London, 1942); A. Richmond, *Colour Prejudice in Britain. A Study of West Indian Workers in Liverpool 1941–1951* (London, 1954); and M. Sherwood, *Many Struggles. West Indian Workers and Service Personnel in Britain (1939–45)*, (London, 1984), pp. 47–92.

21. Watson, op. cit., p. 4 and Sherwood, op. cit., pp. 68, 71.

22. Sherwood, op. cit., pp. 93–130 and the autobiographical recollections in A. A. Ford, *Telling the Truth* (London, 1985), are useful on these workers. Sherwood

revisits the Honduran workers in 'It is not a case of numbers: A Case Study of Institutional Racism in Britain, 1941–43', *Immigrants and Minorities*, Vol. 4 (1985), pp. 116–41.

23. R. Desai, *Indian Immigrants in Britain* (London, 1963), pp. 2–3. For earlier comment see M. Banton, *The Coloured Quarter. Negro Immigrants in an English City* (London, 1955), p. 69.

24. Parker, op. cit., p. 343; A. Bullock, *The Life and Times of Ernest Bevin* Vol. 2 (London, 1967), pp. 206–7.

25. E. Scobie, *Black Britannia* (Chicago, 1972), pp. 186–92 provides a short summary of Blacks in the armed forces. Sherwood, *Many Struggles*, pp. 1–45 has a fuller but unbalanced discussion. More recent comment is contained in D. Reynolds, 'The Churchill Government and the Black American Troops in Britain during World War II', *Transactions of the Royal Historical Society*, Vol. 35 (1985), pp. 113–15. L. C. P. *Newsletter* No. 15 (December 1940), pp. 58–9, carries comment on the first African airman. E. M. Noble, *Jamaica Airman* (London, 1984) is the autobiography of a maintenance man. For the disagreement over numbers, see for example, G. A. Smith, 'Black American Soldiers in Britain 1942–1945', unpublished Ph.D. Thesis, 2 vols, Keele University, 1982, Vol. 2, p. 288 which does not tally with comment in his article, 'Jim Crow on the Home Front (1942–1945)', *New Community*, Vol. VIII (1980), p. 317. Neither of Smith's estimates is the same as that given in Sherwood, *Many Struggles*, p. 45. There is material on Indian troops in K. Vadgama, *India in Britain* (London, 1984), Ch. 9. See above p. 89 for restrictions on the use of Black troops in the First World War. See above p. 137 for Moody.

26. Scobie, op. cit., p. 187; Sherwood, *Many Struggles*, Ch. I, Pt I.

27. Quoted in J. R. Hooker, *Black Revolutionary. George Padmore's Path from Communism to Pan-Africanism* (London, 1967), p. 65.

28. W. Sansom, *Westminster at War* (London, 1947), p. 167 captures this sight in the capital.

29. J. Muir, 'Souvenir, The Tale of a Scottish Eagle', *Scots Magazine* (1941), pp. 273–81; 'A Pole in England. From the Journal of a Polish LAC', *Life and Letters Today* (1942), pp. 99–104; R. McOwan, 'The Friendly Invasion', *Scots Magazine*, n.s. (1982), pp. 482–90, all provide useful detail. See also J. Zubrzycki, *Polish Immigrants in Britain. A Study of Adjustment* (The Hague, 1956), pp. 51–8. For official Polish life see E. Raczynski, *In Allied London* (London, 1962), and G. V. Kacewicz, *Great Britain, the Soviet Union and the Polish Government-in-Exile 1939–1945* (The Hague, 1979). The Poles were the subject of Mass Observation (MO) interest: see, for example, MO File Report, 523B, 'Report on the October Directive. Question C41 . . . Allies', 10 December 1940; MO File Report, 541, 'A Subjective Feeling about various Racial Groups', 9 January 1941; MO File Report, 697, 'Feelings about Foreigners in April 1940 and '41', 14 May 1941; MO File Report, 1669 Q, 'Attitude to Foreigners', April 1943. See also K. Young (ed.), *The Diaries of Sir Robert Bruce Lockhart*, Vol. 2, *1939–1965* (London, 1980), pp. 240–1, 243 for comment in the summer of 1943.

30. B. Porter, *The Refugee Question in mid-Victorian Politics* (Cambridge, 1979), has abundant references to Polish émigrés. See also Zubrzycki, op. cit., pp. 38–47.

31. These figures are taken from the official publication, N. Carrier and J. R. Jeffery, *External Migration. A Study of the Available Statistics 1815–1950* (London, 1950), pp. 127–8.

32. On Poland during the war see N. Davies, *God's Playground. A History of Poland in Two Volumes*, Vol. 2, *1795 to the Present* (Oxford, 1981), Ch. 20. The reference to Poland's 'bitter bread' is from the poet, Cyprian Norwid.

33. Zubrzycki, op. cit., p. 54. On Sikorski see also note 175 below.

34. Zubrzycki, op. cit., p. 54.
35. On Anders and his men see W. Anders, *An Army in Exile* (London, 1949).
36. Ibid., p. 56.
37. See I. M. Maisky, *Journey into the Past* (London, 1964). For the transformation of the Russian image in Britain in the course of 1941 see A. Calder, *The People's War. Britain 1939–45* (London, 1969), pp. 260–3 and P. Addison, *The Road to 1945* (London, 1982 edn), pp. 134–41.
38. Zubrzycki, op. cit., p. 57.
39. On Poles in the Battle of Britain see A. Fiedler, *Squadron 303* (London, 1942); 303 was the Kosciuszko squadron. An acknowledgement was also made in the 'Passage to Britain', Channel 4 TV programme, 16 May 1984. On Poles at Arnhem see McOwan, op. cit., p. 487 and the recent comment in *The Times*, 24 September 1984.
40. BHRU Tape B 0067/01/12, indicates that this action remains a vivid memory.
41. See below pp. 211–12.
42. See Fiedler, op. cit., Ch. XIII, 'A Gallant Czech, Sergeant Frantisek', See also J. V. Polisensky, *Britain and Czechoslovakia* (second rev. edn, Prague, 1968), pp. 76–8.
43. An insight into the offical life of the Free French is given in C. A. J. M. de Gaulle, *War Memoirs* (5 vols, London, 1955–60); there are also references and sources in H. Michel, *The Second World War* (London, 1975). For other comment see MO File Report 523 B, etc., and MO File Report 1669Q, etc. For a Free French voice there is, Jacques, 'A Free Frenchman Speaks', *Nineteenth Century*, Vol. 128 (1940), pp. 500–8, 604–15, and Vol. 129 (1940), pp. 92–104, 276–82.
44. On Germans involved in such activity see L. Kettenocker, 'The Influence of German Refugees on British War Aims', in G. Hirschfeld (ed.), *Exile in Great Britain* (London, 1984), pp. 101–28; Hungarian involvement was referred to in 'Passage to Britain', Channel 4 TV Programme, 30 May 1984. There is also a recent autobiographical memoir, Kellner György, *Magyar antifasiszták Angliában 1940–1945* (Budapest, 1983).
45. On the Americans see Reynolds, op. cit., and N. Longmate, *The GIs. The Americans in Britain 1942–1945* (London, 1975). On Black Americans specifically there is Smith, Ph.D. Thesis and idem, New Community, pp. 317–28. See also C. Thorne, 'Britain and Black GIs. Racial Issues and Anglo-American Relations in 1942', *New Community*, Vol. III (1974), pp. 262–71.
46. There are details on the Chinese in S. Craggs, 'A History of the Chinese Communities in Liverpool', unpublished Local History Diploma Dissertation, Liverpool University, 1983, p. 62 and B. Whittingham-Jones, *China in Britain* (London, 1944) – the title page of which gives *China Fights in Britain*. The *East London Advertiser*, 21 February 1942 carried an article on the hazards faced by the Chinese at sea and referred to their loss of life in the war. For another neglected group of seamen see R. B. Sergeant, 'Yemeni Arabs in Britain', *Geographical Magazine*, Vol. XVII (1944–5), pp. 143–4.
47. SR and O (No. 1133), 1943. See above pp. 154–5 for earlier difficulties.
48. See *Law Reports and Statutes. The Public General Acts and the Church Assembly Measures of 1943* (London, 1944), pp. 27–32.
49. Ministry of Labour and National Service, *Report*, etc., p. 57 notes that in mid-1945 there were 131,800 Italian and 92,600 German, POWs. For later surveys of wartime prisoners see M. B. Sullivan, *Thresholds of Peace* (London, 1979) and M. Kochan, *Prisoners of England* (London, 1980).
50. H. Pollins, *Economic History of the Jews in England* (East Brunswick, N.J., London and Toronto, 1982), p. 222.

51. Munby Papers, S. 610, Tower Hamlets Public Library; N. Barou, *The Jews in Work and Trade* (London, 1946), p. 42.
52. On Wolfson see S. Aris, *The Jews in Business* (Harmondsworth, 1973 edn), Ch. 6. On Berger, see Pollins, op. cit., pp. 229–30.
53. *Anglo-Jewry in Battle and Blitz* (London, 1943), p. 3.
54. A. Levy, *East End Story* (London, 1950), p. 87.
55. Calder, op. cit., p. 185.
56. Levy, op. cit., pp. 14, 19 and D. L. Munby, *Industry and Planning in Stepney* (London, 1951), pp. 4, 35–6.
57. Scobie, op. cit., p. 187 refers to Black children. On Jewish children see J. Grunfeld, *The Story of a Jewish School Community in Evacuation 1939–45* (Tiptree, 1980), and, on evacuation generally, C. Jackson, *Who will take our Children? The Story of the Evacuation in Britain 1939–45* (London, 1985), pp. 44–5, 187–8.
58. A. B. Levy, 'The Jewish Theatre', *East London Papers*, Vol. 6 (1963), pp. 23–32. See also K. Worpole, *Dockers and Detectives* (London, 1983), Ch. 5.
59. See below pp. 184ff on wartime anti-Semitism.
60. On Communist activity in the East End see H. F. Srebrnik, 'The Jewish Communist Movement in Stepney: Ideological Mobilization and Political Victories in an East London Borough, 1933–1945', unpublished Ph.D. thesis, Birmingham University, 1983. On Zionism see P. Goodman, *Zionism in England 1899–1949* (London, 1949), G. Alderman, *The Jewish Community in British Politics* (Oxford, 1983), pp. 125–6, and, more specifically, G. Shimoni, 'Selig Brodetsky and the ascendancy of Zionism in Anglo-Jewry', *Jewish Journal of Sociology* Vol. XXII (1980), pp. 125–61. On Anglo-Jewish relief activity see N. Bentwich, *They Found Refuge* (London, 1956), Ch. 9. The activity of refugees is discussed by A. Glees, in Hirschfeld, op. cit., pp. 83–99 and M. Berghahn, *German-Jewish Refugees in England. The Ambiguities of Assimilation* (London, 1984), pp. 156ff.
61. See above pp. 95–6 for a discussion of internment during the First World War. See below pp. 186–94 for a fuller discussion of the policy pursued in the Second World War. The connecting emphasis is absent from Wasserstein, op. cit., and, more recently, J. Walvin, *Passage to Britain* (Harmondsworth, 1984), pp. 92ff.
62. P. and L. Gillman, *Collar the Lot!* (London, 1980), is useful on the internment episode. The reference to the Isle of Man is from p. 225. *Illustrated* 19 April 1941 carried photographs of internees on the Isle of Man. C. Chappell, *Island of Barbed Wire* (London, 1984), is a study based on Manx sources. E. Koch, *Deemed Suspect. A Wartime Blunder* (Toronto, 1980) discusses the wartime experiences of those internees who were shipped to Canada.
63. R. Stent, *A Bespattered Page? The Internment of 'His Majesty's most Loyal Enemy Aliens* (London, 1980), p. 162.
64. See below p. 187 for the precise categorisation of aliens. The camp near Bury is often referred to, erroneously, as Wharf Mills. F. Lafitte, *The Internment of Aliens* (Harmondsworth, 1941), pp. 101–2, discusses conditions at the camp.
65. Stent, op. cit., p. 153. The camp suffered at one stage from an officer-in-charge with criminal tendencies. IWM Tape 00394/06 (Peter Midgley).
66. Lafitte, op. cit., pp. 104–13.
67. Stent, op. cit., pp. 148–50. The internment files released in February 1986 in categories PRO HO 214 and PRO HO 215, provide fuller details than anything previously available.
68. The designation is from Lafitte, op. cit., p. 102.
69. Stent, op. cit., pp. 87, 189.
70. See SOR 40 in the Sorensen Archives, House of Lords, for the indiscriminate mixing of inmates and PRO HO 215/152, 153, 156, 166, 169 for subsequent

attempts at segregation. See also Gillman and Gillman, op. cit., p. 59 and N. Stammers, *Civil Liberties in Britain during the 2nd World War. A Political Study* (London, 1983), p. 45. E. Spier, *The Protecting Power* (London, 1951), pp. 31–2 and 84–5, carries detail on clashes between Nazis and anti-Nazis.

71. Stent, op. cit., pp. 143, 146. See the editorial in *The Kitchener Camp Review*, No. 7, September 1939, for an emphasis on the Jewish New Year in camp life. The Kitchener camp was at Richborough near Sandwich (see above p. 146).

72. IWM Tape 004304/04 (Hans Gál). *The Camp*, 3 November 1940 carried 'A Hutchinson Camp March' composed by E. E. Verdiers.

73. See the obituary of Walter Landauer in *The Times*, 5 August 1983, for details of their partnership. Marion Rawicz died in 1970.

74. *The Onchan Pioneer*, No. 43, 22 June 1941, p. 5. For similar developments in the First World War see 'Alexandra Palace Internment Camp (1914–1918). A Study of the Life of the Prisoners by one of them, Rudolf Rocker, continued by his son', MSS 233 LSE Library, pp. 12, 18.

75. Stent, op. cit., pp. 194–5

76. The reference is to Kobo Abé, *The Woman in the Dunes* (New York, 1964).

77. See, for example, *The Camp*, 6 October 1940.

78. Stent, op. cit., p. 134.

79. Ibid., p. 167.

80. Ibid., p. 181. Homosexual activity is discussed in ibid., pp. 161, 197.

81. See M. E. Burkett, *Kurt Schwitters. Creator of Merz* (Kendal, n.d. 1964?), p. 6.

82. The young Moser is referred to in Stent, op. cit., pp. 12, 144–5, 150–1.

83. D. Snowman, *The Amadeus String Quartet. The Men and the Music* (London, 1981), p. 11.

84. T. Des Pres, *The Survivor. An Anatomy of Life in the Death Camps* (New York, 1978 edn). A number of the personal files released recently in PRO HO 214, with their evidence of suicide, are a salutary reminder, however, that the potential for survival varies between individuals.

85. Apart from contemporary political critiques, historical works and ensuing memoirs, the internment episode resulted in novels, such as Alex Comfort's *No Such Liberty* (London, 1941) and L. Kahn, *Obliging Fellow* (London, 1946), which traced the experiences of 'Leo J. Raphaelson'.

86. Gillman and Gillman, op. cit., p. 257; 'Judex', *Anderson's Prisoners* (London, 1940), pp. 37ff; A. Perles, *Alien Corn* (London, 1944). There is also information contained on IWM Tape 004483/03 (F. L. Carsten).

87. On refugees and the armed forces generally see Lt. Col. G. W. T. Coles, *Refugees in the British Armed Forces* (London, 1945) and N. Bentwich, *I Understand the Risks. The Story of the Refugees from Nazi Oppression who fought in the British Forces during the War* (London, 1950).

88. R. V. Jones, *Most Secret War* (London, 1978), pp. 83–4.

89. Stent, op. cit., pp. 60–1.

90. P. K. Hoch, 'Gaoling the Victim', *Immigrants and Minorities*, Vol. 4 (1985), pp. 79–83, is insistent on this.

91. P. K. Hoch, 'The Reception of Central European Refugee Physicists of the 1930s: USSR, UK, USA', *Annals of Science*, Vol. 40 (1983), p. 245.

92. A. J. P. Taylor, *English History 1914–1945* (Harmondsworth, 1979 edn), p. 598. M. Gowing, *Britain and Atomic Energy 1939–1945* (London, 1965 edn), pp. 53–4 is useful on aliens, refugees and the bomb. Hoch, *Annals of Science*, p. 245 notes that 'After the war, their work on the successful project at first made them celebrities, senior professors, Government advisers, occasionally political pundits'.

93. See below pp. 195–7 for additional comment.

94. Parker, op. cit; Gowing, *Journal of Contemporary History*.

95. O'Donoghue, op. cit., p. 81.
96. Ibid., Ch. 2.
97. Jackson, op. cit., p. 103.
98. Ibid., pp. 103–4.
99. Inman, op. cit., p. 174.
100. Ibid.
101. Gowing, *Journal of Contemporary History*, notes the shifts in manpower resources during the war.
102. Inman, op. cit., pp. 208–15 discusses preference rulings. See also Gowing, *Journal of Contemporary History*, p. 155 on the allocation of labour.
103. Jackson, op. cit., p. 102.
104. O'Donoghue, op. cit., p. 50.
105. J. V. Hickey, 'The Origin and Growth of the Irish Community in Cardiff', unpublished MA Thesis, University of Wales, 1959, p. 165.
106. Cronin, op. cit., pp. 161–4.
107. I. Law and J. Henfrey, *A History of Race and Racism in Liverpool* (Liverpool, 1981), pp. 31–2.
108. *The Economic Status of Coloured Families in the Port of Liverpool* (Liverpool, 1940), pp. 9–10.
109. Based on ibid., pp. 12, 18, 16, 20. K. Little, *Negroes in Britain* (London, 1948), p. 125 noticed a similar discrimination in the area of rented property. See above Ch. III, note 22 for reference to the 1934 Merseyside survey.
110. *Coloured Families*, etc., p. 11.
111. See above for the various groups of newcomers. On civil defence matters see LCP, *Newsletter*, No. 21, June 1941, pp. 57–9 and E. Ekpenyon, *Some Experiences of an African Air-Raid Warden* (London, 1943). See below p. 200–1 for later comment on merchant seamen.
112. Watson, op. cit., p. 12; Richmond, op. cit., pp. 21, 40–1.
113. See above pp. 166–7 for this group.
114. J. Walvin, *Black and White: The Negro and English Society 1555–1945* (London, 1973), p. 212.
115. The phrase is from Watson, op. cit., p. 5.
116. Sherwood, *Many Struggles*, pp. 63–5 refers to difficulties in hostels.
117. Richmond, op. cit., pp. 71, 74–6. See below p. 201 for additional comment.
118. Sherwood, *Many Struggles*, p. 109. See also Ford, op. cit., p. 60 for a personal recollection and Ch. 7 generally.
119. See above p. 167.
120. Derived from Banton, op. cit., pp. 76–7 and P. Young, *Report on Investigation into Conditions of the Coloured Population in a Stepney area* (London, 1944).
121. Derived from Young, *Report*, pp. 9, 11–12, 18, 24, 26–9; Banton, op. cit., pp. 92–3; N. Deakin, 'The Vitality of a Tradition', in C. Holmes (ed.) *Immigrants and Minorities in British Society* (London, 1978), pp. 171–9.
122. The LCP *Newsletter* faithfully reflected these interests and commitments.
123. See R. J. Macdonald, 'Dr. Harold Arundel Moody and the League of Coloured Peoples, 1931–1947: A Retrospective View', *Race*, Vol. XIV (1973), pp. 302–3 on the fight against official barriers.
124. Ibid., p. 305.
125. Ibid., p. 304.
126. Ibid., pp. 306–7.
127. *Manchester Guardian*, 24 July 1944.
128. Smith, Ph.D. Thesis, Vol. 2, pp. 314–15. There were examples of less wholesome fraternisation. See R. Makonnen, *Pan-Africanism from Within* (Nairobi, 1973), p. 131 for critical reference to the Shangri-la club in Manchester.

129. Makonnen, op. cit., pp. 136–9 is useful on these developments. See above pp. 123, 126, 137 for earlier references to Makonnen.

130. P. Fryer, *Staying Power. The History of Black People in Britain* (London, 1984), pp. 346–7. For an earlier assessment see I. Geiss, *The Pan-African Movement* (London, 1974), pp. 387ff.

131. Geiss, op. cit., p. 408. For contemporary comment see LCP, *Newsletter* No. 72, September 1945, p. 128.

132. *The Autobiography of Kwame Nkrumah* (Edinburgh, 1957), p. 52.

133. H. Marchant, 'Africa speaks in Manchester', *Picture Post*, 10 November 1945, pp. 19–21; G. Padmore (ed.), *History of the Pan-African Congress* (Manchester, 1947 and 1963); see Geiss, op. cit., pp. 385–408, for a later assessment.

134. I. Duffield, 'The Dilemma of Pan-Africanism for Blacks in Britain', Paper presented to the International Conference on the History of Blacks in Britain, 1981, p. 10.

135. V. B. Thompson, *Africa and Unity* (London, 1969), p. 60.

136. For official policy towards 'Friendly Aliens and Allied Nationals' see Parker, op. cit., pp. 344–7. For Ministry of Information on Belgian refugees see Home Intelligence INF 1/264/14, 3 June 1940 (All INF material is taken from the Harvester microfiche edition). For earlier Belgian refugees see above pp. 99–102. MO File Report, 174, Refugees . . . Cricklewood, etc., 6 June 1940 recorded that negative impressions of Belgians in Britain during the First World War were still in existence. For a sample of other evidence relating to allied nationals see MO File Report, 523B, etc.; MO File Report, 541, etc.; MO File Report, 697, etc.; MO File Report, 1669Q, etc.; MO File Report, 238, 'First Report on Refugees', 30 June 1940; MO File Report, 245, 'Second Report on Refugees', 4 July 1940; MO File Report, 262, 'Third and Main Report on Refugees', 11 July 1940. On the Czechs, specifically, there is MO File Report, 1661, 'Feelings about Czechs', first draft, 15 April 1943 and MO File Report, 1664; 'Feelings about Czechs', second draft, 23 April 1943.

137. Wasserstein, op. cit., p. 81.

138. Ibid., pp. 19, 28, 51, 64–7.

139. Ibid., p. 80.

140. See above note 6.

141. See above Chs I, II, III for earlier anti-Germanism.

142. Bentwich, *They Found Refuge*, pp. 117–18.

143. Berghahn, op. cit., p. 139; E. Figes, *Little Eden: A Child at War* (London, 1978).

144. Quoted Berghahn, op. cit., p. 140.

145. A. R. J. Kushner, 'British Antisemitism in the Second World War', unpublished Ph.D. Thesis, Sheffield University, 1986, is the fullest study.

146. L. Thompson, *1940, Year of Legend, Year of History* (London, 1966), p. 40; see also A. J. Trythall, 'The Downfall of Leslie Hore-Belisha', *Journal of Contemporary History*, Vol. 16 (1981), pp. 391–411. For even more recent confirmation see J. Colville, *The Fringes of Power. Downing Street Diaries 1939–55* (London, 1985), pp. 66–9, partic. p. 67.

147. Home Intelligence, INF 1/264/29, 19 June 1940.

148. For hostile comment on the alleged enrichment of alien Jews during the war, see Home Intelligence, INF 1/264/61, 29 July 1940 and Home Intelligence, INF 1/292/122, 26 January–2 February 1943. For comment on Jews in the black market during the war see M. Polanyi's letter, in the *New Statesman*, 27 June 1942, p. 21. The issue also caught the attention of Orwell. See his 'Antisemitism in Britain' in Orwell and Angus, op. cit., Vol. 3, p. 381. The essay was written in 1945. A detailed study and assessment of Jewish involvement in the black market appears in Kushner's Ph.D. Thesis.

149. See above for anti-semitic campaigns in the East End. For criticism of Jews in wartime air raids see the letter from 'Shelter Marshal' in the *New Statesman*, 5 October 1940, p. 331.

150. MO File Report, 1648, March 1943: the report is also available in Board of Deputies of British Jews' Archives, File C6/10/26.

151. A belief reflected in comment in *Civil Liberty*, No. 11 (1943), which was devoted to the campaign against anti-Semitism and Fascism in Britain, and in the *New Statesman*, 25 September 1943, p. 156.

152. *Sunday Dispatch*, 10 January 1943.

153. See File C15/3/20 in the Board of Deputies for details and a discussion of the stance of this paper, and the *Sunday Dispatch*.

154. *New Statesman*, 13 February 1943 and 6, 13, 20 March 1943. (Letters)

155. Home Intelligence, INF 1/292/159, 12–19 October 1943.

156. File C6/9/1/3 F7 in the Board of Deputies.

157. The essay 'Antisemitism in Britain' (see above note 148) first appeared in the *Contemporary Jewish Record* in April 1945.

158. See above pp. 173–5 on earlier references to internment. On Whitehall opinion see Wasserstein, op. cit. For additional comment see my review of Wasserstein, 'Britain and the Jews of Europe', *Jewish Journal of Sociology*, Vol. XXII (1980), partic. pp. 65, 68–9. I. McLaine, *Ministry of Morale. Home Front Morale and the Ministry of Information in World War II* (London, 1979), p. 167 comments that an awareness of anti-Semitic sentiment in Britain was one reason why the British government did not use its intelligence of Jewish suffering at the hands of the Germans. There is more recent comment on official policy in R. Breitman, 'The Allied War Effort and the Jews 1942–1943', *Journal of Contemporary History*, Vol. 20 (1985), pp. 135–56.

159. Wasserstein, op. cit., pp. 83–4. See above pp. 173–5 for earlier comment on internment.

160. Gillman and Gillman, op. cit., p. 30; C. Andrew, *Secret Service. The Making of the British Intelligence Community* (London, 1985), p. 479.

161. *Parl. Deb.* (Commons), Vol. 351 (1938–39), 4 September 1939, col. 367. On Anderson see above p. 152.

162. Wasserstein, op. cit., p. 85. IWM Tape 004483/03 (F. L. Carsten) provides a personal account of an appearance before a tribunal.

163. Wasserstein, op. cit., pp. 83–4.

164. MO File Report, 79, 'Public Feeling about Aliens', 25 April 1940.

165. MO File Report, 107, 'Feeling about Aliens', 14 May 1940. See also MO File Report, 118, 'Internment', 18 May 1940.

166. Wasserstein, op. cit., pp. 86–7; Stammers, op. cit., pp. 39ff.

167. The phrase is from Wasserstein, op. cit., p. 86.

168. Ibid., p. 87.

169. MO File Report 107, etc.; see also M. Panter-Downes, *London War Notes 1939–1945* (London, 1972), p. 60.

170. Wasserstein, op. cit., p. 89.

171. Stent, op. cit., pp. 205–6; Stammers, op. cit., p. 42; *Parl. Deb.* (Commons), Vol. 365 (1939–40), 10 October 1940, col. 488, and Ibid., Vol. 400 (1943–44), 26 May 1944, col. 1064. See below pp. 192–4 for reference to the Italians.

172. See above pp. 67, 142–3 for earlier responses of the Anglo-Jewish elite.

173. Thompson, op. cit., p. 136; Calder, op. cit., p. 132; Wasserstein, op. cit., p. 94. For contemporary comment see MO File Report, 276, 'Supplementary Report on Public Opinion about Aliens', 16 July 1940; MO File Report, 324, 'Attitude to Aliens', 5 August 1940.

174. On Bell see R. Jaspers, *George Bell, Bishop of Chichester* (London, 1967). His

wartime opposition to internment is emphasised in Calder, op. cit., pp. 491–4. On Gilbert Murray see F. West, *Gilbert Murray. A Life* (London, 1984), and, more specifically, Wasserstein, op. cit., pp. 94–5 and Smith, *New Community*, p. 319.

175. See Wasserstein, op. cit., pp. 95–6. Among contemporary sources there is 'Judex', op. cit., pp. 11–12. The NCCL opposition is revealed in File 46/1 (NCCL Archives, Hull University) and NCCL, *The Internment and Treatment of Aliens* (London, n.d. 1941?). It was Cazalet who referred to internment as 'this bespattered page in our history'. See *Parl. Deb.* (Commons), Vol. 364 (1939–40), 22 August 1940, col. 1538. Cazalet was killed along with General Sikorski, the Head of the Polish Government-in-Exile, in an air crash in 1943. On Cazalet see R. R. James, *Victor Cazalet. A Portrait* (London, 1976). The air crash involving Cazalet and Sikorski and Winston Churchill's alleged involvement in it feature in Rolf Hochhuth's play, *Soldaten* (1967). For comment on a Polish request to remove Sikorski's remains from Newark to Poland, see B. Levin, 'Why this hero should be left in peace', *The Times*, 31 March 1981. See also *Parl. Deb.* (Commons), Vol. 7 (1980–81), 30 June 1981, col. 340 (written answers). On Rathbone see M. Stocks, *Eleanor Rathbone* (London, 1949); on Wedgwood there is C. V. Wedgwood, *The Last of the Radicals, Josiah Wedgwood MP* (London, 1951).

176. Wasserstein, op. cit., pp. 96–7. One of the scandals was the *Dunera* incident of 1941. The *Dunera* internees formed the subject of a television play, 'The Dunera Boys', Channel 4 TV Programme, 15 and 16 October 1985. One of the key documents among the recently released internment files is PRO HO 215/263 which contains a diary kept by H. Alexander one of the internees on the *Dunera*. See also PRO HO 215/23.

177. Wasserstein, op. cit., p. 98.

178. Gillman and Gillman, op. cit., p. 209 refers to the incident. A number of files relating to the *Arandora Star* which were transferred to the PRO in February 1986 were apparently soon recalled by the Home Office.

179. Stammers, op. cit., pp. 48ff.

180. Wasserstein, op. cit., pp. 99, 101. For two examples of criticism following the *Arandora Star* tragedy, see H. W. Nevinson, 'To England for Refuge', *Life and Letters Today* (October 1940), pp. 17–28 and 'Behind Barbed Wire', *New Statesman*, 23 November 1940, p. 509. But see Orwell's comments in Orwell and Angus, op. cit., Vol. 2, pp. 71, 195–201, for comment between the spring of 1941 and the autumn of that year.

181. Wasserstein, op. cit., p. 97.

182. Ibid., p. 105.

183. See above p. 187 for the classification of internees.

184. Wasserstein, op. cit., p. 106.

185, Shifts in official policy are noted in Wasserstein, op. cit., Ch. 7. Gillman and Gillman, op. cit., pp. 260–1 refers to Anderson's replacement.

186. Wasserstein, op. cit., p. 107.

187. Gillman and Gillman, op. cit., p. 289.

188. The words are from Addison, op. cit., p. 17.

189. See the graphic account of the family's experiences in Y. Uchida, *Desert Exile: The Uprooting of a Japanese American Family* (Seattle and London, 1982).

190. For particularly tragic cases see NCCL File 46/1, (Hull University), which provides detail on the internment of refugees with many years' residence. These were often people of Central European origin who had been categorised on arrival as Austrian-Polish. IWM Tape 004339/04 (H. M. J. Steinert) refers to one individual, a bookseller, who was interned in the 1914–18 war and again in

the Second World War. For other unfortunate cases see *Morrison's Prisoners. The Story of Czechoslovakian Anti-Fascist Fighters Interned in Britain* (n.d., n.p.).

191. Gillman and Gillman, op. cit., is basically as much an attack on a system of closed government as it is about the history of aliens and internment. The recently released files in PRO HO 214 and PRO HO 215 assist in the explanation of internment policy but do not answer every question.

192. An emphasis of M. Kochan, *Britain's Internees in the Second World War* (London, 1983), Ch. 4.

193. Recognised in an internment camp publication, *The Camp*, 6 October 1940.

194. Stammers, op. cit., pp. 39ff. lays particular emphasis on these influences.

195. Hoch, *Immigrants and Minorities*, p. 82.

196. See C. Holmes, *Antisemitism in British Society 1876–1939* (London, 1979), generally. For specific comment see MO File Report 79, etc.

197. A point emphasised in Kushner's Ph.D. Thesis.

198. Emphasised in Lafitte, op. cit., pp. 168–72. See also MO File Report 332, 'Public Opinion and the Refugee', 7 August 1940.

199. Stammers, op. cit., p. 63.

200. Ibid. See also C. Cross, *The Fascists in Britain* (London, 1961), p. 193 for reference to the early internment of minor Fascists. For general comment see A. Goldman, 'Defence Regulation 18B: Emergency Internment of Aliens and Political Dissenters in Britain during World War Two', *Journal of British Studies*, Vol. XII (1973), pp. 120–37.

201. N. Driver, 'From the Shadows of Exile', unpublished ts, Chs 10–18, provides a Fascist testimony.

202. R. Griffiths, *Fellow Travellers of the Right. British Enthusiasts for Nazi Germany 1933–39* (London, 1980).

203. This began in earnest with O. Mosley, *My Life* (London, 1968). For a recent contribution to the canon see D. Mosley, *Loved Ones* (London, 1985).

204. Stammers, op. cit., p. 65; see also R. Croucher, *Engineers at War* (London, 1982), pp. 92–3.

205. R. Kidd, *Civil Liberties in Danger* (London, 1941) and, later, Stammers, op. cit.

206. Noted, however, in Gillman and Gillman, op. cit., p. 286, and there is now PRO HO 215/28, PRO HO 215/503, as well as a personal file in PRO HO 214/56.

207. This set of figures is derived from Carrier and Jeffrey, op. cit., pp. 127–8. See above pp. 21, 119–20 for the size of the total population of Britain between 1911 and 1931.

208. R. King, 'Italian Migration to Great Britain', *Geography*, Vol. 62 (1977), p. 178.

209. M. Rodgers, 'Italiani in Scozzia', in B. Kay (ed.), *Odyssey, The Second Collection* (Edinburgh, 1982), p. 17.

210. Ibid.

211. D. Mack Smith, *Italy. A Modern History* (London, 1969), p. 399.

212. R. Palmer, 'The Italians: Patterns of Migration to London', in J. L. Watson (ed.), *Between Two Cultures* (Oxford, 1977), p. 255.

213. S. Jackson, *An Indiscreet Guide to Soho* (London, 1946), p. 26. On the north of England see S. J. Rawnsley, 'Fascism and Fascists in Britain in the 1930s. A Case Study of Fascism in the North of England, in a Period of Economic and Social Change', unpublished Ph.D. Thesis, Bradford University, 1981, pp. 91–8. A study with specific reference to the Italians in Manchester is A. Valgimigli, *La Colonia Italiana di Manchester 1794–1932* (Manchester, 1932).

214. V. G. Kiernan, 'Britons Old and New', in Holmes (ed.), *Immigrants and Minorities*, p. 51. *The Scotsman*, 11 June 1940 referred to 'an orgy of window-breaking and looting in different parts of the city' (Edinburgh). See also ibid., 12 June 1940.

There is additional comment in D. Sheridan (ed.), *Among you taking notes. The Wartime Diary of Naomi Mitchison* (London, 1985), p. 65.

215. Orwell and Angus, op. cit., Vol. 2, p. 394. See also Panter-Downes, op. cit., p. 68. MO File Report 184, 'Anti-Italian Riots in Soho', 11 June 1940, thought the reports of attacks on the Italians had been exaggerated in the press.

216. Stammers, op. cit., p. 39.

217. P. G. Leoni, *I shall die on the Carpet* (London, 1966), p. 9. Leoni's personal file was not in the batch of documents transferred to the PRO in February 1986.

218. Calder, op. cit., pp. 130–2. The removal of Italian restaurateurs provided a niche within which Cypriots could squeeze. See Vakis Nearchou (Vic George), 'The Assimiliation of the Cypriot Community in London', unpublished MA Thesis, Nottingham University, 1960, pp. 20–1.

219. See above p. 186 Gillman and Gillman, op. cit., p. 155 says that 300 of these internees were naturalised. But see L. R. Ercolani, *A Furniture Maker* (London, 1975), for the history of a naturalised Italian who was untroubled by the war. Thompson, op. cit., pp. 136–7 says the police used the pretext of internment to deal with Italian criminals on whom there was insufficient evidence to justify an arrest. A full account of an Italian internee which traces his experiences in transit camps and on the Isle of Man, can be found in C. Cavalli, *Ricordi di un emigrato* (n.d., n.p.), Chs 11–16.

220. Noticed in Palmer, op. cit., pp. 256–7.

221. Gillman and Gillman, op. cit., Ch. 14 deals with this.

222. MO File Report, 1669Q, etc. See below for a discussion on shifting responses.

223. See above p. 176 for reference to controls over the Irish. The situation in 1943 is discussed in the *International Labour Review*, etc.

224. Ibid., p. 341.

225. See O'Donoghue, op. cit., pp. 84, 151–6, for the problems this could create.

226. *International Labour Review*, etc., p. 342.

227. Ibid., p. 341.

228. Ibid., p. 342. See also O'Donoghue, op. cit., p. 50 and P. Dooley, *The Irish in Britain* (London, 1943), pp. 5–7. On Constantine see pp. 153, 202–3, 240, 313.

229. *International Labour Review*, etc., p. 341.

230. Parker, op. cit., pp. 137ff.

231. *International Labour Review*, etc., p. 342.

232. Parker, op. cit., pp. 336, 341.

233. Inman, op. cit., p. 172.

234. Parker, op. cit., p. 341.

235. Ministry of Labour and National Service, *Report*, etc., pp. 56–7 refers to controls over aliens, for example. See also Parker, op. cit., pp. 344–7.

236. See Parker, op. cit., and the earlier study, W. Hancock and M. Gowing, *The British War Economy* (London, 1949).

237. Stammers, op. cit., p. 163.

238. Taylor, op. cit., p. 623.

239. An emphasis in Lafitte, op. cit., and Stammers, op. cit.

240. Based on Jackson, op. cit., p. 101. For more general discussions see A. Marwick, *War and Social Change in the Twentieth Century* (London, 1974), p. 12. The impact of bombing is discussed in B. Collier, *The Battle of the V-Weapons 1944–5* (London, 1976) and P. G. Cooksley, *Flying Bomb* (London, 1979).

241. See above for reference to this campaign and the Prevention of Violence Act.

242. Cronin, op. cit., p. 161; see also Lyons, op. cit., pp. 533–6.

243. PRO HO 45/25068 deals with Behan's activities and his contacts with the British government between 1941 and 1954. The file was released in 1984. It is

particularly revealing about the influence of Special Branch over Home Office Policy.

244. M. McDermott, 'Irish Catholics and the British Labour Movement: A Study with particular reference to London 1918–1970', unpublished MA Thesis, Kent University, 1979, p. 195.

245. Quoted in M. Gilbert, *Winston S. Churchill*, Vol. VI, *Finest Hour 1939–1941* (London, 1983), p. 71.

246. Inman, op. cit., p. 139.

247. On this Ministry see McLaine, op. cit., and S. E. R. Watson, 'The Ministry of Information and the Home Front in Britain, 1939–1942', unpublished Ph.D. Thesis, London University, 1980.

248. Home Intelligence, INF 1/264/194, 10 June 1940.

249. Home Intelligence, INF 1/292/82, 16–23 March 1942.

250. Home Intelligence, INF 1/292/308, 3–10 September 1941. See also Inman, op. cit., p. 160 on this.

251. Home Intelligence, INF 1/292/279, 7–14 March 1944.

252. See above p. 105 for the charge against Jews in the First World War. See also above p. 185 for similar accusations during the Second World War.

253. Home Intelligence, INF 1/292/279, 7–14 March 1944. On Joyce see J. A. Cole, *Lord Haw Haw – and William Joyce* (London, 1964).

254. McDermott, MA Thesis, p. 301.

255. Croucher, op. cit., pp. 256, 281. P. Summerfield, *Women Workers in the Second World War* (London, 1984), carries specific comment on the treatment of Irish women workers who have been particularly neglected by historians.

256. See above p. 178.

257. MO File Report, 538, 'Manchester and Liverpool in the Blitz', 6 January 1941.

258. See above pp. 60–1, 152.

259. R. Bridgeman, 'Civil Liberties in the Colonial Empire', *Civil Liberty*, No. 21, January 1941, p. 6.

260. See *News Chronicle*, 24 September 1943 for Vicky's comment; Smith, *New Community*, p. 325 carries details of the case. For contemporary comment see MO File Report, 2021, 1943.

261. See, for example, *Civil Liberty*, No. 12, February 1940, p. 5.

262. Watkinson, op. cit.

263. Quoted in Sherwood, *Many Struggles*, p. 66.

264. Watson, op. cit., p. 8; Sherwood, *Many Struggles*, pp. 73–4.

265. Sherwood, *Many Struggles*, p. 74.

266. Ibid., pp. 70–1.

267. Watson, op. cit., p. 14. A similar claim was made in PRO CO 876/48, a survey of West Indian technicians in Bolton in 1943.

268. Richmond, op. cit., pp. 38–41; Sherwood, *Many Struggles*, pp. 68–71.

269. Sherwood, *Many Struggles*, p. 110.

270. Ibid., p. 110.

271. Letter, Pastor G. D. Ekarte to Ronald Kidd of the NCCL, 11 February 1941 in NCCL Archives (Hull University), refers to problems facing African sailors. Sherwood, *Many Struggles*, pp. 133–7 discusses the difficulties over pay experienced by West Indian seamen. A. J. Mackenzie, 'British Marxists and the Empire', unpublished Ph.D. Thesis, London University, 1978, p. 271, notes support from the Communist Party for Indian seamen over war bonuses. The problems of Chinese seamen are discussed in *News Chronicle*, 20 April 1942 and the *Daily Worker*, 24 September 1942. See also G. Beardmore, *Civilians at War. Journals 1938–1946* (London, 1984), p. 127.

272. See above p. 180 for earlier comment on housing. This paragraph is based on Richmond, op. cit., pp. 73–6. On the difficulties of students see K. Little, 'A Note on Colour Prejudice among the English "Middle Class",' *Man*, Vol. 3 (1943), pp. 104–7. See also A. Richmond, *The Colour Problem* (Harmondsworth, 1955 edn), p. 248.

273. Richmond, *Colour Prejudice*, pp. 77–83.

274. Ford, op. cit., pp. 72, 75.

275. This correspondence is in PRO CO 876/41.

276. Sherwood, *Many Struggles*, pp. 113–16.

277. Sherwood, *Immigrants and Minorities*, pp. 129, 134.

278. Richmond, *Colour Prejudice*, pp. 99–101 discusses the Liverpool incident. Ibid., p. 101 also reports on disputes between West Indians and West Africans, as well as between Blacks and Chinese, and 'Colonials and Liverpool-born groups', in which 'quarrels over women' loomed large. MO File Report, 1885, 'Attitudes to Coloured Races', August 1943, notes the degree of disapproval among whites on the question of inter-racial marriage. For the report on Bolton, see PRO CO 876/48.

279. Sherwood, *Many Struggles*, pp. 106–7, 118–21. For those who remained, see Ford, op. cit., pp. 78–80.

280. See above p. 170.

281. Walvin, *Passage*, p. 95.

282. Smith, Ph.D. Thesis, Vol. 2, pp. 293–4. See above p. 189 and note 174 above on Murray.

283. G. Howat, *Learie Constantine* (London, 1977), p. 21. See above pp. 153, 196 for earlier reference to Constantine.

284. Walvin, *Black and White*, p. 214 simplifies what happened. So does Smith, *New Community*, p. 322. Fryer, op. cit., pp. 364–6 is a better source. See the *Evening Standard*, 3 September 1943 for useful detail. The incident attracted considerable interest. See *Parl. Deb.* (Commons), Vol. 392 (1943), 22 and 23 September 1943, cols 189–91, 370–1, 443–4 and MO File Report, 1944, 'The Colour Bar', 11 October 1943, pp. 2–3. For later comment by Constantine see his *Colour Bar* (London, 1954), pp. 137–8.

285. *The Times*, Law Reports, 4 August 1944.

286. See above p. 199 on King. For Low's cartoon see *Evening Standard*, 23 September 1943.

287. Quoted Richmond, *Colour Prejudice*, p. 90. There is a full report of the case in the *News Chronicle*, 2 August 1944.

288. See, for example, Smith, Ph.D. Thesis, Vol. 2, pp. 302, 305, 321 and Noble, op. cit., p. 54.

289. S. McNeill, *Illegitimate Children born in Britain of English Mothers and Coloured Americans. Report of a Survey* (London, n.d.). For a discussion of sexual mores during during the war see J. Costello, *Love, Sex and War: Changing Values 1939–45* (London, 1985).

290. P. B. Rich, 'Race and Empire in British Politics 1890–1962', ts. p. 184, refers to the significance of this development.

291. Comment which emphasised the problem of maintaining a colour bar appeared in *The Times*, 12 September 1940 ('British Tradition and the Colour Bar') and the *Sunday Express*, 20 September 1942 ('Colour Bar must go' by Brendan Bracken). For a radical criticism of British colonial policy see N. Cunard and G. Padmore, *White Man's Duty* (London, 1942).

292. See J. M. Lee, ' "Forward Thinking" and War: The Colonial Office in the 1940s', *Journal of Imperial and Commonwealth History*, Vol. VI (1977), pp. 64–79 on the CO outlook during the war.

293. Rich, 'Race and Empire,' quoting PRO CO 876/44. The comment came from Ivor Cummings on 23 July 1942.

294. Smith, *New Community*, pp. 320–1. Sherwood, *Many Struggles*, p. 52.

295. See the cameo of Keith in Smith, *New Community*, p. 319.

296. Sherwood, *Many Struggles*, pp. 80, 115 discusses Keith's responses.

297. PRO CO 967/37/12.

298. PRO CO 968/10/4.

299. PRO CO 876/14. See above p. 201 for comment by Macmillan on another matter involving Blacks.

300. Cited in D. Dilks (ed.), *The Diaries of Sir Alexander Cadogan 1938–1945* (London, 1971), p. 483; Reynolds, op. cit., p. 122, somewhat surprisingly, passes this off as an example of Churchill's 'flippancy'.

301. Wasserstein, op. cit., and Holmes, *Jewish Journal of Sociology*. J. Flint, 'Scandal at the Bristol Hotel: Some Thoughts on Racial Discrimination in Britain and West Africa and its Relationship to the Planning of Decolonisation 1939–47', *Journal of Imperial and Commonwealth History*, Vol. XII (1983), p. 79, argues that in the war 'racism' was 'relegated to the sphere of washroom obscurity and was not considered tolerable in polite society'. It is evident, however, this did not prevent its appearance in confidential official papers. At the same time, there were official attempts to educate the British public against racial intolerance. For example, in 1941, the Colonial Film Unit produced *An African in London*, starring Robert Adams (see above p. 123), with this aim in mind. There would seem to be no existing copies of this film.

302. Calder, op. cit., and Addison, op. cit.

303. MO File Report, 1885, etc.

304. See above pp. 199–205.

305. An emphasis in Sherwood, *Many Struggles* and *Immigrants and Minorities*.

V. THE POSTWAR YEARS, 1945–71

1. See, for example, A. Gamble, *Britain in Decline* (London, 1981); K. Robbins, *The Eclipse of a Great Power. Modern Britain 1870–1975* (London, 1983); R. Blake, *The Decline of Power 1915–1964* (London, 1985).

2. P. Fryer, *Staying Power. The History of Black People in Britain* (London, 1984), p. xii carries similar emphases.

3. P. Gottlieb, 'Social Mobility of the Jewish Immigrant', unpublished M.Phil. Thesis, Nottingham University 1970; S. Weil, 'Bene Israel in Britain', *New Community*, Vol. III (1974), pp. 87–91; the Indian background of this group is presented in S. Jackson, *The Sassoons* (London, 1968); S. Ladsky, 'Refugees of the Raj', *Jewish Chronicle*, 17 June 1977.

4. F. M. Wilson, *They Came as Strangers. The Story of Refugees to Great Britain* (London, 1959), pp. 241–5. S. Patterson, *Immigrants in Industry* (London, 1968), has a number of references; M. Levin, *What Welcome?* (London, n.d.) pp. 41ff provides a scattering of information. M. Marrus, *The Unwanted. European Refugees in the Twentieth Century* (New York, 1985), pp. 358–61, carries general comment on the Hungarian exiles.

5. *Economic Survey for 1947*, Cmd. 7046 (1947), pp. 27–8. See also Political and Economic Planning, *Population Policy in Great Britain* (London, 1948) pp. 108–16, for reasons why immigration should be encouraged. For academic comment on the manpower situation see T. Wilson, 'Manpower', in G. D. N. Worswick and P. H. Ady, *The British Economy 1945–1950* (Oxford, 1952), pp. 224–52 and K. O. Morgan, *Labour in Power 1945–1951* (Oxford, 1984), pp. 180–4, partic. p. 184.

6. *Royal Commission on Population, Report*, Cmd. 7695 (1949), p. 124. The Huguenots (see above pp. 7–8) were regarded by the report as an ideal group if only they had been available for recruitment!

7. J. Isaac, *British Post-War Migration* (Cambridge, 1954), pp. 183–5. M. Kochan, *Prisoners of England* (London, 1980), Ch. 9 et seq. discusses POWs in the postwar years.

8. J. A. Tannahill, *European Volunteer Workers in Britain* (Manchester, 1958), p. 3. See also A. Cairncross, *Years of Recovery; British Economic Policy 1945–51* (London, 1985), p. 397.

9. See above p. 169 for the Polish government-in exile.

10. J. Zubrzycki, *Polish Immigrants in Britain. A Study of Adjustment* (The Hague, 1956), pp. 57–8, 81; P. Foot, *Immigration and Race in British Politics* (Harmondsworth, 1965), p. 117. See above p. 169 on Anders.

11. Developments noticed by Zubrzycki, op. cit., p. 81; Foot, op. cit., p. 118. See the important statement by Ernest Bevin, the Foreign Secretary in *Parl. Deb.* (Commons), Vol. 420 (1945–6), 20 March 1946, col. 1876 and following. On the threat of demobilisation in Germany see ibid., Vol. 433 (1946–7), 12 February 1947, cols 471–4 particularly and *The Times*, 13 March 1947 for reference to parties of Polish men leaving each day for Osnabruck in this process.

12. The statistical data here is from Isaac, op. cit., pp. 171–2. On the PRC see Zubrzycki, op. cit., pp. 89–92. Evidence on the PRC made available at a later date can be found on PRO LAB 8/1448–1492 and PRO HO 213/1219–1241.

13. Isaac, op. cit., pp. 153–7; Zubrzycki, op. cit., p. 58. The entry of these dependants was also mentioned in 'Passage to Britain', Channel 4 TV programme, 16 May 1984.

14. Statistical details on the Polish minority are often subject to variation. On the number admitted as EVWs see conflicting calculations in Zubrzycki, op. cit., p. 60, and Tannahill, op. cit., p. 30. The number of Polish troops who came under British command during the war is also in dispute in Isaac, op. cit., p. 171 and Zubrzycki, op. cit., pp. 57–8.

15. Isaac, op. cit., p. 2.

16. Zubrzycki, op. cit., pp. 69–70.

17. BHRU Tape B0081 is concerned with the reunion of families. See also S. Patterson, 'The Poles: An Exile Community in Britain', in J. L. Watson (ed.), *Between Two Cultures* (Oxford, 1977), p. 216 on later arrivals. This essay builds upon a number of earlier sketches by Patterson.

18. See above p. 168 for the 1931 estimate. For 1951 see *Census 1951 England and Wales. General Report* (London, 1958), p. 108; *Census 1951 Scotland. General Volume* (Edinburgh, 1954), p. 55. In 1951 it was estimated that 140,149 of those born in Poland were of Polish nationality. OPCS communication, 3 October 1986. See Patterson, op. cit., p. 217 for the major difficulties attendant on the information on Poles which is provided in official statistics.

19. *Census 1961 England and Wales. Birthplace and Nationality Tables* (London, 1964), p. 5; *Census 1961 Scotland. Birthplace and Nationality* (Edinburgh, 1966), p. 4; *Census 1971 Great Britain. Country of Birth Tables* (London, 1974), p. 26. In 1961 it was estimated that 87,942 of those born in Poland were of Polish nationality. A question on nationality was not asked in 1971. OPCS communication, 3 October 1986.

20. L. Dinnerstein, *America and the Survivors of the Holocaust* (New York, 1982), p. 273.

21. J. Walvin, *Passage to Britain* (Harmondsworth, 1984), p. 102.

22. See the varying numerical assessments in Isaac, op. cit., p. 180; Tannahill, op. cit., pp. 5–6; J. Vernant, *The Refugee in the Post-War World* (London, 1953), p. 343. See below pp. 230–1 for additional comment on the controls over such workers.

23. Isaac, op. cit., p. 177; Tannahill, op. cit., pp. 19–30. There is a useful discussion in E. Stadulis, 'The Resettlement of Displaced Persons in the United Kingdom', *Population Studies*, Vol. V (1951–2), pp. 207–37.

24. Noted by Tannahill, op. cit., p. 6.

25. Noted by Isaac, op. cit., p. 123. On the Belgians see Ministry of Labour and National Service, *Report for the Years 1939–1946*. Cmd. 7225 (London, 1947), p. 191. There is useful information on the latter two categories in PRO LAB 8/1246 and 1501 (Italian Foundry Workers) and PRO LAB 8/1417 and 1449–51 (German Scientists and Technicians).

26. On repatriations to the Soviet Union see N. Bethell, *The Last Secret* (London, 1974) and N. Tolstoy, *Victims of Yalta* (London, 1977). On the return of Yugoslavs see N. Tolstoy, 'The Klagenfurt Affair. The Klagenfurt Conspiracy', *Encounter*, Vol. 60 (May, 1983), pp. 24–37. See also *The Times*, 3, 14, 20 January 1984 and 11 and 15 February 1984. A further study by Tolstoy of these deportations, entitled *The Minister and the Massacres*, appeared in 1986.

27. Tannahill, op. cit., pp. 14–16, 31–3.

28. Isaac, op. cit., p. 184. For references to Ukrainians in Britain at an earlier period see V. Kubijoryc, *Ukraine. A Concise Encyclopaedia* (Toronto, 1971), pp. 1126–7 generally, and, more specifically, D. Saunders, 'Aliens in Britain and the Empire during the First World War', in F. Swyripa and I. H. Thompson (eds.), *Loyalties in Conflict. Ukrainians in Canada during the Great War* (Edmonton, 1983), pp. 99–124.

29. Tannahill, op. cit., p. 46.

30. These figures are from Vernant, op. cit., p. 341 and *Parl. Deb.* (Commons), Vol. 483 (1950–1), 1 February 1951, col. 140 (written answers).

31. BHRU Tape B0046/02/24; BHRU Tape B0031/01/5, 6 and BHRU Tape B0016/01/5, 10.

32. J. Brown, *The Un-Melting Pot. An English Town and its Inhabitants* (London, 1970), pulls together information on a number of these groups in Bedford but the history of the majority of these newcomers has not yet been recovered.

33. *Census 1951 England and Wales*, p. 108; *Census 1951 Scotland*, p. 55; *Census 1961 England and Wales*, p. 5; *Census 1961 Scotland*, p. 4; *Census 1971 Great Britain*, p. 26. In 1951 it was estimated that 23,627 of those born in Italy were of Italian nationality. In 1961 the figure was 70,309. A nationality question was not asked in 1971. OPCS communication, 3 October 1986.

34. BHRU Tape, B0103/01/6, 7. There is similar comment on BHRU Tape, B0069/01/2.

35. Much of the preceding discussion is from R. King, 'Italian Migration to Great Britain', *Geography*, Vol. 62 (1977), partic. pp. 178–80.

36. Ibid., p. 180 notes the southern component. So does Brown, op. cit., p. 82. For the world of the southerners see Carlo Levi, *Christ stopped at Eboli* and Giuseppe di Lampedusa, *The Leopard*.

37. King, op. cit., p. 180 comments on the chain migration. For immigrants from northern Italy see R. Palmer, 'The Italians: Patterns of Migration to London', in Watson, op. cit., pp. 242–68. There is a fuller and wider study in R. C. G. Palmer, 'The Britalians. An Anthropological Investigation', unpublished D.Phil. Thesis, Sussex University, 1981.

38. Brown, op. cit., Ch. 6. discusses the Italian minority in Bedford. See also 'The Promised Land? To Bedford from Busso', Open University Programme, BBC1 TV, 23 and 30 July and 6 August 1983. On the Italian predominance in the south-east see King, op. cit., p. 182. On the previously neglected south-west, there is now B. Bottignolo, *Without a Bell Tower. A Study of the Italian Immigrants in South West England* (Rome, 1985).

39.   King, op. cit., pp. 178–80; Palmer, 'The Italians', p. 242. U. Marin, *Gli Italiani in Gran Bretagna* (Rome, 1975), pp. 95–6 is useful on the maturity of the migrant flow.

40.   See above for earlier references to the Irish minority.

41.   These figures are derived from: *Census 1951 England and Wales*, pp. 104–5; *Census 1951 Scotland*, p. 54; *Census 1961 England and Wales*, p. 1; *Census 1961 Scotland*, p. 1; *Census 1971 Great Britain*, p. 26.

42.   See ibid., on the origins of the Irish minority.

43.   Evident in the census returns and emphasised in C. Peach, 'The Black Population in Britain 1945–1980', in D. A. Coleman (ed.), *Demography of Immigrants and Minority Groups in the United Kingdom* (London, 1982), p. 24.

44.   J. A. Jackson, *The Irish in Britain* (London, 1963), pp. 15–17; S. Glynn, 'Irish Immigration to Britain, 1911–1951: Patterns and Policy', *Irish Economic and Social History*, Vol. VIII (1982), pp. 57–8.

45.   P. Harrison, 'Culture and Migration: The Irish English', *New Society*, 20 September 1973, pp. 699–702.

46.   J. Doherty, 'The Distribution and Concentration of Immigrants in London', *Race Today*, Vol. I (1969), p. 227.

47.   In England and Wales the majority of the Irish immigrants since 1890 have been women. In Scotland there has been a continued predominance of men. See Jackson, op. cit., p. 19. See also S. Markham, *What about the Irish? Irish and Commonwealth Immigration Compared* (London, 1971), p. 5.

48.   B. Walter, 'The Geography of Irish Migration since 1939, with special reference to Luton and Bolton', unpublished D.Phil. Thesis, Oxford University 1978, is useful on the pressures leading to Irish migration. 'The Irish in England', Channel 4 TV Programme, 16 October 1983 carried useful comment on the activities of British employers. The programme also revealed that those who participated in it were convinced that their own departures had been caused essentially by the English exploitation of Ireland. Examples of advertisements placed by British employers are given in Jackson, op. cit., p. 96, with details drawn from the Dublin press. For additional comment on developments in the Irish economy after the war see J. A. Murphy, *Ireland in the Twentieth Century* (Dublin, 1975), pp. 142ff.

49.   Walter, D.Phil. Thesis, partic. pp. 53, 55, 62, 73. For useful comment on the impact and interaction of economic influences on Irish migration to and from Britain, beginning in 1971 see F. X. Kirwin and A. G. Nairn, 'Migrant Employment and the Recession – the Case of the Irish in Britain', *International Migration Review*, Vol. 17 (1983), pp. 672–81; see also J. G. Hughes and B. M. Walsh, 'Migration Flows between Ireland, the United Kingdom and the Rest of the World', *European Demographic Information Bulletin*, Vol. VII (1976), pp. 125–49, which is based on the 1971 Census.

50.   Jackson, op. cit., p. 104 notes the dismantling of controls.

51.   Walter, D.Phil. Thesis, pp. 32, 75, 29.

52.   A term which was used to designate the Commonwealth, with the exception of Australia, Canada and New Zealand. These three countries were designated the Old Commonwealth.

53.   See above Chs I, II for earlier reference to the Chinese.

54.   S. Collins, *Coloured Minorities in Britain* (London, 1957), p. 229; M. Broady, 'The Chinese in Great Britain', in M. H. Fried (ed.), *Colloquium on Overseas Chinese* (New York, 1958), p. 29.

55.   J. L. Watson, 'The Chinese: Hong Kong Villagers in the British Catering Trade', in Watson, op. cit., p. 182.

56.   *Census 1951 England and Wales*, p. 108; *Census 1951 Scotland*, p. 55. In addition,

Broady, op. cit., p. 30 and Ng Kwee Choo, *The Chinese in London* (London, 1968), p. 6 provide disputable figures for England and Wales.

57. The importance of Hong Kong and Malaya in this connection is recognised in Broady, op. cit., p. 30.

58. M. Freeberne, 'Chinese succeed in the UK', *Geographical Magazine* (1981), p. 708.

59. *Census 1971 Great Britain*, p. 26.

60. Watson, 'The Chinese', pp. 202–4.

61. D. Jones, 'The Chinese in Britain: Origins and Development of a Community', *New Community*, Vol. VII (1979), p. 400.

62. Ibid.

63. Watson, 'The Chinese', pp. 182–3.

64. Ibid., pp. 183–4. See below pp. 260–3 for the 1962 Act.

65. Ng, op. cit.

66. Freeberne, op. cit., p. 709. See *Evening Standard*, 31 May 1965 for the destruction by bulldozers of the old Chinese quarter in the East End.

67. There is an impressionistic account in M. Nally, 'The Scouse Chinese', *New Society*, 25 March 1982, pp. 465–6. There are traces of information, too, in S. Craggs, 'A History of the Chinese Communities in Liverpool', unpublished Local History Studies Diploma, Liverpool University, 1983, although Craggs' essay is concerned essentially with the earlier years of settlement.

68. *The Times*, 24 August 1983 carries a discussion of recent developments in Manchester.

69. Watson, 'The Chinese', p. 201.

70. K. Leech, 'The Role of Immigration in Recent East London History', *Cosmos*, No. 4 (1966), p. 12.

71. There is a good fictional account of stowaways in M. Mackay, *Black Argosy* (London, 1954). There is also comment in St C. Drake, 'The "Colour" Problem in Britain: A Study in Social Definitions', *Sociological Review*, n.s., Vol. 3 (1956), pp. 207–8. For stowaways and the British government see below p. 256.

72. On Stepney see M. Banton, *The Coloured Quarter* (London, 1954). On Liverpool see A. Richmond, *Colour Prejudice in Britain. A Study of West Indian Workers in Liverpool, 1941–1951* (London, 1954).

73. On Tyneside see Collins, op. cit. On Sheffield see 'Sheffield's Africa', *New Statesman*, 4 October 1952, pp. 371–2 and the police survey in PRO CO 1028/25.

74. African students are discussed in A. T. Carey, *Colonial Students* (London, 1956).

75. See above p. 166 on these workers. For reference to those who remained after the war, see Richmond, op. cit., pp. 135ff.

76. Ibid., pp. 143–4 notes the arrival of these ships. R. Glass, *Newcomers. West Indians in London* (London, 1960), p. 1 emphasises that many West Indians were intent originally on a short stay. D. Hinds, *Journey to an Illusion. The West Indian in Britain* (London, 1966), partic. Ch. I is useful on perceptions of British society that circulated in the Caribbean.

77. Peach, op. cit., p. 26, notes the importance of the 1950s. Hinds, op. cit., p. 34 cites the Jamaican calypso singer, Count Tasker.

78. C. Phillips, *The Final Passage* (London, 1985) is a recent fictional account of the great emigration of the 1950s.

79. E. J. B. Rose (ed.), *Colour and Citizenship* (London, 1969), pp. 43, 49, 67, carries reference to the importance of Jamaica, and the proportion of women among the West Indians.

80. Hinds, op. cit., p. 30; R. B. Davison, *West Indian Migrants* (London, 1962) p. 1. For official evidence see *Annual Report on Jamaica for the Year 1946* (London, 1949).

81. Glass, op. cit., pp. 6–7; Davison, op. cit., p. 44; D. Lawrence, *Black Migrants: White Natives. A Study of Race Relations in Nottingham* (Cambridge, 1974), p. 17.

82. Peach, op. cit., p. 26. This has been a major theme of Peach's work. See, for example, his *West Indian Migration to Britain. A Social Geography* (London, 1968). See below pp. 260–3 on the 1962 Act.

83. D. Hinds, 'The "Island" of Brixton', *Oral History*, Vol. 8 (1980), p. 49.

84. J. Egginton, *They Seek a Living* (London, 1957), pp. 74–6; J. Wickenden, *Colour in Britain* (London, 1958), p. 5. The importance of the Act was stressed in 'The Promised Land? A Question of Colour', Open University Programme, BBC1 TV, 9 and 16 July 1983 and D. Hiro, *Black British, White British* (London, 1973 edn), p. 6.

85. Glass, op. cit., p. 1 notes the preference for the term 'migrant'. On the 1948 British Nationality Act see N. Deakin, 'The British Nationality Act of 1948: A Brief Study of the Mythology of Race Relations', *Race*, Vol. XI (1969), pp. 77–83. See also V. Bevan, 'The Development of British Immigration Law', [Published, 1986] pp. 112–13.

86. Davison, op. cit., pp. 7–8; Peach, 'The Black Population', p. 29. For a misplaced, optimistic literary treatment of the 'big discussion going on in Parliament', see S. Selvon, *The Lonely Londoners* (Harmondsworth, 1981 edn, first published 1956), p. 8. See below p. 262 for further comment.

87. The phrase is from George Lamming's novel, *The Emigrants* (London, 1980 edn, first published 1954), p. 87. For the pressures and influences on one individual see W. Collins, *Jamaican Migrant* (London, 1965), p. 52.

88. Rose, op. cit., p. 67; Fryer, op. cit., p. 373.

89. D. Brooks, *Race and Labour in London Transport* (London, 1975), Ch. 13.

90. Rose, op. cit., p. 68; Fryer, op. cit., p. 373. Hinds, *Journey*, p. 34 refers to Joe Lyons.

91. Davison, op. cit., pp. 8, 33–6.

92. K. Hunter, *History of Pakistanis in Britain* (Norwich, 1962(?)), pp. 16–17.

93. See above p. 167 for the earlier community.

94. A journalistic guide to the city, H. Davies (ed.), *The New London Spy* (London, 1966), pp. 250–1, refers to the heterogeneity of the Indian minority. The Parsees, individual members of whom had achieved an earlier prominence (see above pp. 56, 84, 138–9), have been generally neglected. For brief comment see G. M. Towler-Mehta, 'Parsees in Britain: The Experience of a Religious Minority Group', *New Community*, Vol. X (1982), pp. 243–50. This article, however, ignores the likes of Saklatvala and generally lacks historical awareness.

95. See P. T. Moon, *Divide and Quit* (London, 1962) and I Stephens, *Pakistan* (3rd edn, London, 1967), partic. Chs 13 and 14 for the background.

96. Rose, op. cit., p. 58 emphasises the differences within the Pakistani minority.

97. The imagery is from Ruth Prawer Jhabvala's novel, *Heat and Dust* (London, 1975).

98. Rose, op. cit., p. 52. H. Tinker, *The Banyan Tree: Overseas Emigrants from India, Pakistan and Bangladesh* (Oxford, 1977), is generally useful on emigration from the sub-continent.

99. Rose, op. cit., p. 453. See also R. Ballard and C. Ballard, 'The Sikhs: The Development of South Asian Settlements in Britain', in Watson, *Between Two Cultures*, pp. 26–7.

100. Rose, op. cit., pp. 52ff.

101. V. Robinson, 'Correlates of Asian Immigration: 1959–1974', *New Community*, Vol. 8 (1980), pp. 115–22.

102. G. S. Aurora, 'Indian Workers in England', unpublished M.Sc. (Econ) Thesis,

London University, 1960, p. 56. This led to *The New Frontiersman. A Sociological Study of Indian Immigrants in the United Kingdom* (Bombay, 1967).

103. Rose, op. cit., p. 54.
104. Ibid., pp. 70–1 notes this form of business activity on the sub-continent.
105. Ibid., pp. 60–1 comments on the characteristics of the Pakistani newcomers.
106. V. S Khan, 'The Pakistanis: Mirpuri Villagers at Home and in Bradford', in Watson, *Between Two Cultures*, p. 64, is among those who have noted this. See also Hunter, op. cit., pp. 8–30.
107. Ibid., p. 65.
108. J. Rex and R. Moore, *Race, Community and Conflict. A Study of Sparkbrook* (Oxford, 1967), p. 115.
109. Hunter, op. cit., pp. 11–14; Rose, op. cit., p. 59. See also M. Banton, 'Social Acceptance and Rejection', in R. Hooper (ed.), *Colour in Britain* (London, 1965), p. 37.
110. Khan, op. cit., pp. 66–8; M. Anwar, *The Myth of Return. Pakistanis in Britain* (London, 1979), p. 24.
111. Anwar, op. cit., p. 25.
112. Robinson, op. cit., pp. 118, 121.
113. Khan, op. cit., p. 58; Anwar, op. cit., p. 22; B. Dahya, 'Pakistanis in Britain; Transients or Settlers?', *Race*, Vol. XIV (1973), pp. 241–77.
114. Robinson, op. cit., p. 118.
115. E. Thomas-Hope, 'Hopes and Reality in the West Indian Migration to Britain', *Oral History*, Vol. 8 (1980), pp. 37, 41, is useful on goals and intentions of the West Indians.
116. Rose, op. cit., p. 84.
117. These developments were noticed in ibid., p. 82.
118. See below pp. 263, 265.
119. Dahya, op. cit., p. 244; Ballard and Ballard, op. cit., pp. 21–2, 34; Anwar, op. cit., pp. 36, 39.
120. The extra-European dimension of the postwar world refugee problem is noticed in Marrus, op. cit., pp. 364ff.
121. BHRU Tape C0006 gives a personal account of the impact of Africanisation and the departure of a Kenyan Asian. On written sources see *Africa Contemporary Record. Annual Survey and Documents 1970–71* (London, 1971), pp. B119–20. On the Ugandan situation see ibid., 1972–3 (London, 1973), pp. A10–1 and ibid., 1976–7 (London, 1977) p. B393. See also Y. Tandon, 'The Asians in East Africa in 1972', in ibid., 1972–3 etc., pp. A3–19. On the origin of developments in Malawi see ibid., 1975–6 (London, 1976), p. B252. The history of the Asians in East Africa can be gleaned from Tinker, op. cit; G. Delf, *Asians in East Africa* (London, 1963) and D. P. Ghai and Y. P. Ghai, *Portrait of a Minority: Asians in East Africa* (Nairobi, 1970). See above and below pp. 221, 257 for the 1948 British Nationality Act. On the Kenyan Asians in Britain see S. Shah, 'Colony to Metropolis: An Analysis of the Cultural Orientation of Kenyan Asians in England', unpublished Ph.D Thesis, London University 1984 and P. Bhachu, *Twice Migrants* (London, 1985).
122. Noticed by R. K. Kelsall, *Population* (London, 1979 edn), p. 32. There is useful general comment in D. A. Coleman, 'Some Problems of Data for the Demographic Study of Immigration and of Immigrant and Minority Populations in Britain', *Ethnic and Racial Studies*, Vol. 6 (1983), pp. 103–10.
123. *Select Committee on Race Relations and Immigration, Report 1977–78* (H.C. 303–1) (London, 1978), pp. xv–xxv.
124. C. Peach and S. Winchester, 'Birthplace, Ethnicity and the Enumeration of West Indians, Indians, and Pakistanis', *New Community*, Vol. 3 (1974), p. 391.

125. OPCS calculations communicated to author, 3 October 1986.
126. Richmond, op. cit., and Collins, op. cit., are useful on Liverpool and Tyneside respectively.
127. K. Little, *Negroes in Britain* (London, 1948) is the classic study. A reprint, with an introduction by Leonard Bloom, appeared in 1972. A popular survey is available in D. Hiro, 'Three Generations of Tiger Bay', *New Society*, 21 September 1967, pp. 385–7.
128. Banton, *The Coloured Quarter* is another classic early study.
129. E. B. Ndem, 'Negro Immigrants in Manchester: An Analysis of Social Relations within and between the various coloured Groups and of their Relation to the White Community', unpublished MA Thesis, London University, 1953. See also J. Reid, 'Employment of Negroes in Manchester', *Sociological Review*, Vol. 4 (1956), pp. 199–211 for a slight addition to Ndem's work.
130. See above p. 167.
131. Peach, 'The Black Population', pp. 30–1, 34.
132. See, for example, on Indians, Aurora, M.Sc. (Econ) Thesis; on Blacks see Glass, op. cit. and S. Patterson, *Dark Strangers* (London, 1963). Patterson's field work was carried out in the 1950s.
133. A. Richmond, *Migration and Race Relations in an English City. A Study in Bristol* (London, 1973).
134. Noted, for instance, in Rex and Moore, op. cit; J. Rex and S. Tomlinson, *Colonial Immigrants in a British City* (London, 1979); P. Ratcliffe, *Racism and Reaction: A Profile of Handsworth* (London, 1981); and, more recently, F. Reeves and G. Holness, *Statistical Data on Racial Minorities in Wolverhampton, with Special Reference to the Afro-Caribbean Population* (Wolverhampton, 1982), pp. 2–3.
135. Nottingham is the most thoroughly studied of these cities down to 1971. See Wickenden, op. cit.; Lawrence, op. cit., and I. Katznelson, *Black Men. White Cities: Race, Politics and Migration in the United States 1900–30 and Britain 1948–68* (London, 1973).
136. B. Dahya, 'The Nature of Pakistani Ethnicity in Industrial Cities in Britain', in A. Cohen (ed.) *Urban Ethnicity* (London, 1974), discusses the early history of Pakistanis in Bradford.
137. For a recent impressionistic account of this area following the violence of 1981 see M. Kettle, 'Why did Chapeltown burn?', *New Society*, 23 July 1981, pp. 145–6.
138. Ndem, MA Thesis; Richmond, op. cit., pp. 143–4. See also I. Law and J. Henfrey, *A History of Race and Racism in Liverpool 1600–1950* (Liverpool, 1981), Ch. 5.
139. Anwar, op. cit., partic. Ch. 6.
140. E. L. Zammit, 'The Behaviour Patterns of Maltese Immigrants in London, with reference to Maltese Social Institutions', unpublished B.Litt. Thesis, Oxford University, 1970; G. Dench, *The Maltese in London: A Case Study in the Erosion of Ethnic Consciousness* (London, 1975).
141. There are three useful theses on the Cypriots. V. Nearchou (V. George), 'The Assimilation of the Cypriot Community in London', unpublished MA Thesis, Nottingham University, 1960; R. Oakley, 'Cypriot Migration and Settlement in Britain', unpublished D.Phil. Thesis, Oxford University, 1972; V. Psarias, 'Greek Cypriot Migration in Greater Manchester', unpublished M.Phil. Thesis, Bradford University, 1979, is a useful study of a provincial community. See also P. Constantinides, 'The Greek Cypriots: Factors in the Maintenance of Ethnic Identity', in Watson, *Between Two Cultures*, pp. 269–300 and S. Ladbury, 'The Turkish Cypriots: Ethnic Relations in London and Cyprus', in ibid., pp. 301–31.

There is also an impressionistic account of Cypriot life in M. Kettle, 'Famagusta N16', *New Society*, 26 March 1981, pp. 533–4.

142. *The Times*, 11 February 1976 carries a discussion.

143. N. Dokur-Gryskiewicz, 'A Study of the Adaptation of Turkish Migrant Workers to living and working in the United Kingdom', unpublished Ph.D. Thesis, London University, 1979.

144. Davies, op. cit., pp. 254–60; A. Garvey, 'Sons of Ned Kelly', *New Society*, 14 August 1975, pp. 357–8; *The Times*, 6 December 1976; *Census 1971 Great Britain*, p. 26 noticed 142,825 people with birthplaces in the Old Commonwealth.

145. See Levin, op. cit. See below p. 280 for a further reference to the admission of refugees.

146. H. Pollins, *Economic History of the Jews in England* (East Brunswick, N.J., London and Toronto, 1982), Ch. 15 carries a useful discussion. See also E. Krausz, 'The Economic and Social Structure of Anglo-Jewry' in J. Gould and S. Esh (eds), *Jewish Life in Modern Britain* (London, 1964), partic. pp. 27–8.

147. P. K. Hoch, 'The Reception of Central European Refugee Physicists of the 1930s: U.S.S.R., U.K., U.S.A.', *Annals of Science*, Vol. 40 (1983), p. 245.

148. See Pollins, op. cit., Ch. 14 on 'Business and the Professions since 1945' and Ch. 14 on working-class Jews. On the Jewish proletariat see also J. W. Carrier, 'Working Class Jews in present-day London: A Sociological Study', unpublished M.Phil. Thesis, London University, 1969 and his 'A Jewish Proletariat', in M. Mindlin and C. Bermant (eds), *Explorations: An Annual on Jewish Themes* (London, 1967), pp. 120–40; *Jewish Chronicle*, 31 March 1978.

149. M. Berghahn, *German-Jewish Refugees in England. The Ambiguities of Assimilation* (London, 1984), p. 121. See above p. 126 for earlier comment.

150. Ladsky, op. cit.

151. See above pp. 211–17.

152. Zubrzycki, op. cit., pp. 66–7.

153. Tannahill, op. cit. is a convenient source. On the recruitment of nurses from Europe see PRO LAB8/90, 1305, 1631, which became generally available at a later date.

154. Brown, op. cit., Ch. 6; King, op. cit., p. 178; J. K. Chadwick-Jones, 'The Acceptance and Socialization of Immigrant Workers in the Steel Industry', *Sociological Review*, Vol. 12 (1964), pp. 169–83 are all useful. So is 'The Promised Land? To Bedford from Busso', Open University Programme, BBC1 TV, 23 and 30 July and 6 August 1983. There are useful oral recollections of Italian women workers who came to Bradford on BHRU Tapes B0089, B0096, B0103 and B0105. Official papers relating to the recruitment of Italians include: PRO LAB 8/47, 104, 1246, 1501, 1741, 1798–9.

155. Jackson, op. cit., p. 106; Davies, op. cit., p. 263; D. MacAmhlaigh, *An Irish Navvy. Diary of an Exile* (London, 1964) are useful written sources. There is visual testimony in 'Passage to Britain', Channel 4 TV Programme, 2 May 1984. There is fascinating oral evidence in BHRU Tape B0161. See also A. J. M. Sykes, 'Navvies: Their Work Attitudes', *Sociology*, Vol. 3 (1969), pp. 21–35 for comment on the Irish involved in heavy labouring work.

156. Oral evidence on the recruitment of nurses was given in 'The Irish in England', Channel 4 TV programme, 16 October 1983. There is also PRO LAB 8/1468.

157. Ng Kwee Choo, 'Some Aspects of the Social Organization of Chinese engaged in the Restaurant Business in London', unpublished MA Thesis, London University, 1965; Chuen-Ling William Cheung, 'The Chinese Way. A Social Study of the Hong Kong Chinese Community in a Yorkshire City', unpublished M.Phil. Thesis, York University, 1975 is a study of the Chinese in York with

considerable comment on the restaurant business. *East London Advertiser* 20 August 1965 and the *Daily Mail*, 15 October 1965, refer to well-known Chinese restaurants in the East End. The latter contains an interview with Charlie Cheung whose East End business spearheaded the postwar boom. Watson, 'The Chinese', is a convenient summary of Watson's views which are reworked in a number of articles. C. Driver, *The British at Table 1940–1980* (London, 1983), provides the context for the postwar restaurant boom. See below p. 232 for additional comment on the Italians in the restaurant business. 'Passage to Britain', Channel 4 TV Programme, 27 June 1984 provided testimony of a lingering Chinese involvement in the laundry trade. Broady, op. cit., p. 30 noticed the involvement of the Chinese in Liverpool in the merchant navy as late as 1957.

158.   Banton, *The Coloured Quarter*; Richmond, *Colour Prejudice*; Rose, op. cit., partic. Ch. 6.; R. Desai, *Indian Immigrants in Britain* (London, 1963); *The Times*, 27 January 1965, 'The Dark Million (9)'; S. Patterson, *Immigrants in Industry* (London, 1968); The Runnymede Trust and Radical Statistics Group, *Britain's Black Population* (London, 1980), Ch. 3; R. Fevre, *Cheap Labour and Racial Discrimination* (London, 1984), Ch. 5, provide evidence and comment on employment patterns from the end of the war down to 1971.

159.   See above p. 229.

160.   Isaac, op. cit., p. 178; Tannahill, op. cit., pp. 20, 50–1, 53–4, 57ff. See also B. Hepple, *Race, Jobs and the Law in Britain* (London, 1968), Appendix II for examples of some 'collective agreements'. Zubrzycki, op. cit., p. 65 and Tannahill, op. cit., p. 5 also refer to restrictions on members of the Polish Resettlement Corps. These restrictions are underlined in Hepple, op. cit., p. 218.

161.   Based on *Census 1971 Great Britain Country of Birth Supplementary Tables. Part II. Migration and Economic Activity* (London, 1978), pp. 71–2ff.

162.   Banton, *Coloured Quarter*, p. 159; Glass, op. cit., p. 31; Rose, op. cit., p. 449; Dahya, *Race*, p. 250; Hiro, *Black British*, p. 144; Fryer, op. cit., p. 374; P. Wright, *The Coloured Worker in British Industry* (London, 1968), p. 215 all carry useful detail. Hepple, op. cit., p. 223 notes that the National Union of Seamen had an agreement which restricted the employment of 'Non-European Seamen'. See below for further reference to discriminatory practices.

163.   'The Irish in England', Channel 4 TV Programme, 16 October 1983 and 'Passage to Britain', Channel 4 TV programme, 2 May 1984, both carried interviews with people who could recall 'No Irish need apply' notices after the war.

164.   See above p. 228.

165.   Markham, op. cit., p. 6; Harrison, op. cit., p. 701; K. O'Connor, *The Irish in Britain* (Dublin, 1974), pp. 98ff; Brent Irish Advisory Service, *Irish People in British Society* (n.d., n.p), p. 3. For the 10 per cent sample of Irish occupations see *Census 1971 Great Britain . . . Migration and Economic Activity*, pp. 67, 104–6. However, O'Connor, op. cit., p. 109 carries some cautionary comment on the degree of Irish business success.

166.   See, for example, Hunter, op. cit., for a number of examples of restaurant entrepreneurship. See also P. Werbner, 'From Rags to Riches: Manchester Pakistanis in the Textile Trade', *New Community*, Vol. VIII (1980), pp. 84–95.

167.   Desai, op. cit., Chs 3 and 4 carries comment on the internal economy.

168.   Rose, op. cit., p. 443. Hiro, *Black British*, p. 117 refers to Pakistani businesses in Bradford and ibid., pp. 162–4 also discusses entrepreneurial activity among Indians.

169.   On Pakistani landlords see Burney, op. cit., p. 167; Rex and Moore, op. cit., p. 165 and Dahya, 'Pakistani Ethnicity', pp. 99–102. On West Indians in

property see, for example, Glass, op. cit., p. 87; Patterson, *Dark Strangers*, and Hinds, *Oral History*, p. 49. For other evidence of Black entrepreneurship see Patterson, *Dark Strangers*. p. 320 and Davies, op. cit., p. 279. For comment on the problems that continued to affect attempts to develop Black capitalism see W. M. Kazuka, *Why so few Black Businessmen?* (London, 1981). F. Reeves and R. Ward, 'West Indian Business in Britain', in R. Ward and R. Jenkins (eds), *Ethnic Communities in Business. Strategies for Economic Survival* (Cambridge, 1984), pp. 125–46 carries later comment.

170.   'Dizzy with success' is a reference to Stalin's famous letter to *Pravda* of 2 March 1930, on collectivisation. See J. Westergaard and H. Resler, *Class in a Capitalist Society. A Study of Contemporary Britain* (London, 1975), partic. p. 357 for pertinent, specific comment on the complex social structure.

171.   Patterson, 'The Poles', p. 221.

172.   Tannahill, op. cit., p. 80.

173.   Marin, op. cit., pp. 100, 183; King, op. cit., p. 178; Palmer, 'The Italians', pp. 258–9.

174.   Palmer, 'The Italians', p. 259.

175.   Driver, op. cit., p. 79. Their significance and the atmosphere of their restaurants is captured in *The Good Food Guide to London* (London, 1968), pp. 31–5. Mario Cassandro was born in Italy. Francesco Lagattola was born in London.

176.   See 'Why there could still be a place for Sir Charles at the Savoy', *The Times*, 18 May 1981. See also the portrait sketch in Palmer, D.Phil. Thesis, pp. 126–9. An autobiography by Sir Charles is promised in 1986. [Published, 1986.]

177.   Rose, op. cit., p. 82. See below pp. 260–7 for immigration controls.

178.   Zubrzycki, op. cit., pp. 172–3; Patterson, 'The Poles', p. 221. *The Times* 21 May 1951, 'Foreign Labour in Britain, (1)', noted the difficulties of 'older officers and former professional workers', at an early stage of their new lives.

179.   See above pp. 154–5 for evidence of earlier Black unemployment. A. Richmond, 'Economic Insecurity and Stereotypes as Factors in Colour Prejudice', *Sociological Review*, Vol. 42 (1950), pp. 18–20 refers to the late 1940s. Banton, *Coloured Quarter*, pp. 127–9 notices the problems faced by Black merchant seamen. For comment on later years see Wright, op. cit., pp. 51–5; Rose, op. cit., p. 180. See also K. Jones and A. D. Smith, *The Economic Impact of Commonwealth Immigration* (London, 1970), pp. 44–5 and S. Castles and G. Kosack, *Immigrant Workers and Class Structure in Western Europe* (London, 1973), pp. 90–3.

180.   *The Times*, 22 May 1951, 'Foreign Workers in Britain (2)'.

181.   'The Irish in England', Channel 4 TV programme, 16 October 1983 took this as one of its themes.

182.   *The Times*, 27 January 1965, 'The Dark Million (9)'. This series is a useful source but needs to be handled carefully.

183.   Counter Information Services, *Racism: Who Profits* (London, n.d.) and the same group's *Hardship Hotel* (London, n.d.).

184.   See, on these matters, Castles and Kosack, op. cit., partic. p. 394; C. P. Kindleberger, *Europe's Post War Growth. The Role of Labor Supply* (Cambridge, Mass., 1961); E. J. Mishan and L. J. Needleman, 'Immigration: Some Economic Effects', *Lloyds Bank Review*, No. 81 (July 1966), pp. 33–46; K. Jones, 'Immigrants and the Social Services', *National Institute Economic Review*, No. 41 (1967); pp. 28–40; R. G. Opie, 'Britain's Immigrants: do they help the Economy?', *New Statesman*, 15 March 1968, p. 324; E. J. Mishan, 'Does Immigration confer Economic Benefits on the Host Country?', Institute of Economic Affairs, *Economic Issues in Immigration* (London, 1970), pp. 91–122.

185.   J. Burnett, *A Social History of Housing, 1850–1970* (Newton Abbot, 1978),

pp. 277–8 carries comment on the postwar context. See also Morgan, op. cit., pp. 163–70 for a perspective from the level of high politics.

186. Based on Pollins, op. cit., p. 210, Berghahn, op. cit., p. 127; H. Brotz, 'An Analysis of the Social Stratification within Jewish Society in London', unpublished Ph.D. Thesis, London University, 1951, pp. 93–4; R. O'Brien, 'The Establishment of the Jewish Minority in Leeds', unpublished Ph.D. Thesis, Bristol University, 1975, pp. 244–5; R. D. Livshin, 'Aspects of the Acculturation of the Children of Immigrant Jews in Manchester 1890–1930', unpublished M.Ed. Thesis, Manchester University 1982, Ch. I (which notes the start of the spatial transformation) and I. Walker, 'The Jews of Cheetham Hill', New Society, 1 October 1981, pp. 7–10. See Berghahn, op. cit., on restitution or compensation money, and see below p. 244 for opposition to the German Jews in Hampstead.

187. Davies, op. cit., p. 274; Brown, op. cit., p. 38; Patterson, 'The Poles', pp. 221, 223; personal information.

188. R. Paraszczak, 'Ukrainians in Rochdale. A study of an Immigrant Community', unpublished Dissertation, Manchester College of Education, 1969, provides local detail. For additional information see Tannahill, op. cit., pp. 86–7; see also M. Bülbring, 'Post-War Refugees in Great Britain', Population Studies, Vol. VIII (1954–5), pp. 103–5.

189. Brown, op. cit., pp. 83, 89; D. Sibley, 'The Italian and Indian Populations of Bedford – A Contrast in Assimilation', Northern Universities Geographical Journal, Vol. 3 (1962), pp. 48–52; J. Barr, 'Napoli Bedfordshire', New Society, 2 April 1964, p. 8; E. Burney, Housing on Trial (London, 1967), pp. 228–9.

190. Jackson, op. cit., p. 57 carries a discussion which compares the 1880s with the 1950s; MacAmhlaigh, op. cit., Ch. 3 refers to the Higgs and Hill camp; Rex and Moore, op. cit., pp. 44, 54–5 carries reference to the Irish in Sparkbrook (for earlier comment on Birmingham see P. N. Jones, The Segregation of Immigrant Communities in the City of Birmingham Occasional Papers in Geography No. 7 (Hull, 1967)); O'Connor, op. cit., p. 153 refers to the Irish in relation to the groups from the Caribbean and the Indian sub-continent; Brent Irish Advisory Service, op. cit., p. 6 refers to continuing problems of the Irish. The Guardian, 17 August 1982 comments on those Irish who have escaped to the suburbs and new towns. 'Passage to Britain', Channel 4 TV programme, 2 May 1984 furnished testimony on the Irish building workers 'living rough'.

191. Watson, 'The Chinese, pp. 202–3.

192. M. Banton, 'Negro Workers in Britain', Twentieth Century, Vol. 151 (1952), pp. 40–54.

193. Ndem, MA Thesis, p. 247; Collins, op. cit., p. 43. See also Hiro, Black British, pp. 22–3.

194. The problems of the postwar housing market were particularly emphasised in the early 1960s. See S. Alderson, Britain in the Sixties, Housing (Harmondsworth, 1962); R. Glass and J. Westergaard, London's Housing Needs (London, 1965); Report of the Committee on Housing in Greater London Cmnd. 2605 (London, 1965), commonly known as the Milner Holland Report, and Cullingworth Committee, Council Housing. Purposes, Procedures and Priorities (London, 1969). On Rachman see S. Green, Rachman (London, 1979). See Rose, op. cit., pp. 120ff, a survey of 'Housing Conditions of Immigrants' in the 1960s. Dahya, 'Pakistani Ethnicity', p. 105 refers to Pakistanis who managed to locate themselves in the suburbs of Bradford and Birmingham. See also P. Werbner, 'Avoiding the Ghetto: Pakistani Migrants and Settlement Shifts in Manchester', New Community, Vol. VII (1979), pp. 376–89 and S. Nowikowski and R. Ward, 'Middle Class and British? An analysis of South Asians in Suburbia', ibid. (1978–9), pp. 1–10.

195. See above note 194 for sources on such landlords. For sharp literary comment on such individuals see Selvon, op. cit., pp. 11–12 and A. G. Bennett, *Because they know not* (London, 1959?), p. 25 for a portrait of Bob Lee, described as 'an ebonied Shylock'.

196. Burney, op. cit.

197. Anwar, op. cit., p. 36; Peach, 'The Black Population', pp. 36–7; S. Patterson, *Immigration and Race Relations in Britain 1960–1967* (London, 1969), p. 211. Recent work by Vaughan Robinson would suggest that in the 1970s the groups from the sub-continent began to modify this lack of interest.

198. Banton, *Twentieth Century*, p. 42.

199. Patterson, *Immigration*, loc. cit., p. 211.

200. See Rose, op. cit. for a recognition of regional differences. Peach, 'The Black Population', p. 36 and T. R. Lee, *Race and Residence. The Concentration and Dispersal of Immigrants in London* (Oxford, 1977), p. 92 refer to changes in concentration; for a statement of the choice versus constraint debate see Dahya, 'Pakistani Ethnicity' and Rex and Moore, op. cit., respectively. See D. Phillips, 'The Social and Spatial Segregation of Asians in Leicester', in P. Jackson and S. J. Smith (eds), *Social Interaction and Ethnic Segregation* (London, 1981), p. 118 for an awareness of the variation in local pressures and R. Sims, 'Spatial Separation between Asian Religious Minorities: An Aid to Explanation or Obfuscation?', in ibid., pp. 123–5. For the tendency for the newcomers to be associated with the cause of decline in the inner cities, see Peach, 'The Black Population', p. 40. See above p. 68 for the linking of Jews with the decline of an area.

201. Paraszcżak, Dissertation, p. 55; Tannahill, op. cit., p. 81.

202. Palmer, 'The Italians', p. 258.

203. *Parl. Deb.* (Commons), Vol. 582 (1957–8), 20 February 1958, col. 172.

204. Quoted in E. Scobie, *Black Britannia. A History of Blacks in Britain* (Chicago, 1972), p. 303. See also, Egginton, op. cit., Ch. XIII 'The Disenchanted'; B. Davison, 'No Place Back Home: A Study of Jamaicans returning to Kingston, Jamaica', *Race*, Vol. IX (1968), pp. 499–509; H. O. Patterson, 'West Indian Migrants returning Home; Some Observations', ibid., Vol. X (1968), pp. 69–77.

205. See, for example, G. Alderman, *The Jewish Community in British Politics* (Oxford, 1983), Ch. 6ff.

206. See Zubrzycki, op cit., p. 139ff on *Dziennik Polski*; see Patterson, 'The Poles', pp. 214, 233–6; J. Mills, 'Britain's Community of Poles', *New Society*, 18 July 1963, p. 13, for more general comment.

207. W. Anders, *An Army in Exile* (London, 1949) is a personal testimony on the exile. For additional comment see B. Wojciechowska, 'Generational Differences in Ethnic Consciousness. A Study based upon Post-Second World War Britain, with Special Reference to Coventry and London', unpublished MA Dissertation, Warwick University, 1976, p. 5.

208. BHRU Tape, B0067/01/12 reveals the bitterness which memories of Yalta continued to evoke and the continuing memory of the Katyn Forest massacre. On Yalta and Katyn see N. Davies, *God's Playground. A History of Poland in Two Volumes*. Vol. II, *1795 to the Present* (Oxford, 1981), pp. 14–15, 488 and 452, respectively. *The Times*, 23 February 1985, noted that Cardinal Josef Glemp's visit to Britain was 'a poignant reminder of exile'.

209. Patterson, 'The Poles', p. 238.

210. On this demonstration see *The Times*, 14 February 1956. See also Latvian National Council, *Be on the alert against Bulganin and Khruschev. Treachery hides behind their smiles* (n.p., 1956), available in the BHRU. On the Captive Nations Committee see its publication *The Captive Nation* (Bradford, 1981).

211. BHRU Tape, B0009/01/21; BHRU Tape, B0016/01/13; BHRU Tape, B0031/

01/14. For a general study of Ukrainian political activity in Britain, see W. Petryshyn, 'Britain's Ukrainian Community: A Study of the Political Dimension in Ethnic Community Development', unpublished Ph.D. Thesis, Bristol University, 1980.

212. BHRU Tape B0016/03/42.

213. R. B. Perks, ' "A Feeling of Not Belonging": Interviewing European Immigrants in Bradford', *Oral History*, Vol. 12 (1984), pp. 64–7. See also Brown, op. cit., Ch. 4 and D. White, 'The Ukes of Halifax', *New Society*, 12 June 1980, pp. 201–2.

214. King, op. cit., pp. 184–5 refers to Italians continuing their links with Italy. On those from 'Abbazzia' see Palmer, 'The Italians', pp. 260–2. For the importance of birthplace in Italian culture see P. Nichols, *Italia, Italia* (London, 1973), p. 58. For additional comment see Marin, op. cit., pp. 131–50 and M. Rodgers, 'Italiani in Scozzia', in B. Kay (ed.), *Odyssey. The Second Collection* (Edinburgh, 1982), p. 21. See, finally, R. Firth (ed.), *Two Studies of Kinship in London* (London, 1956), pp. 69–93 for an argument stressing the importance of kinship in the activities of Italians in London.

215. Rex and Moore, op. cit., p. 153 notices the importance of the County Clare Association in Sparkbrook. See also Harrison, op. cit., p. 701; J. Bugler, 'Ireland in London', *New Society*, 14 March 1968, pp. 769–70; 'The Irish in England', Channel 4 TV Programme, 23 October 1983.

216. On San Tin see Watson, 'The Chinese', pp. 207–11 and his 'Restaurants and Remittances: Chinese Emigrant Workers in London' in G. M. Foster and R. V. Kemper (eds.), *Anthropologists in Cities* (Boston, 1974). For additional comment on remittances see Ng, MA Thesis, p. 166.

217. Dahya, *Race*, is useful on Pakistani remittances, on those to India see Rose, op. cit., p. 54 which notes that remittances provided for *pukka* (brick built) houses in the Punjab. A. Helweg, *Sikhs in England. The Development of a Migrant Community* (Delhi, 1979), pp. 90–1, notices the difficulty of any precise calculation. For additional passing comment by Helweg for the years down to 1971 see 'Emigrant Remittances: Their Nature and Impact on a Punjabi Village', *New Community*, Vol. X (1983), pp. 435–43.

218. Dahya, *Race*, p. 259; Anwar, op. cit., p. 118.

219. On religion and the Poles see Patterson, 'The Poles', pp. 219, 230–3; on the Ukrainians see Paraszczak, Dissertation, p. 62 and Brown, op. cit., pp. 64–5; on the religious affiliation of the Italians see Barr, op. cit., p. 7 and Palmer, 'The Italians', pp. 260–1. On the Irish and the Roman Catholic Church see Rex and Moore, op. cit., pp. 150–3 for the church in Sparkbrook; Brent Irish Advisory Service, op. cit., pp. 3–4; J. C. Heenan, 'The Irish Immigrants: Liability or Asset?', *The Month*, March 1957, p. 42; J. Hickey, *Urban Catholics* (London, 1967). On the West Indians see, Patterson, *Dark Strangers*, p. 304 for an early reference to Ras Tafari, on which see also E. E. Cashmore, *Rastaman* (London, 1983 edn), partic. Ch. 9. Reference to some falling away in religious observance among West Indians in London can be found in C. Hill, *West Indian Migrants and the London Churches* (London, 1963). For other work on West Indian religious activity see M. J. C. Calley, *God's People: West Indian Pentecostal Sects in England* (London, 1965). On Sikhs see Ballard and Ballard, 'The Sikhs', pp. 35–8. On Moslems see Dahya, *Race*, for references to the faith and deviation from it (pp. 272–3) whilst Khan, 'The Pakistanis', pp. 77–8 refers to the strength of ancient customs in a new environment. See also M. M. Ally, 'History of Muslims in Britain', unpublished MA Thesis, Birmingham University 1981, Pt II. Hiro, *Black British*, pp. 127, 133, refers to the number of mosques and *gurdwaras*.

220. G. S. Betts, 'Working Class Asians in Britain: Economic, Social and Political

Changes 1959–1979', unpublished M.Phil. Thesis, London University, 1981 is one crude example in which the past is cast down.

221. M. McDermott, 'Irish Catholics and the British Labour Movement: A Study with Particular Reference to London', unpublished MA Thesis, Kent University, 1979. For an autobiographical account of a trade union activist see B. Behan, *With Breast Expanded* (London, 1964). Jackson, op. cit., pp. 125–6 refers to postwar nationalist activity. See also O'Connor, op. cit., pp. 86ff. Hickey, op. cit., p. 158 notes the decline in nationalist political activity.

222. For general comment see Z. Layton-Henry, *The Politics of Race in Britain* (London, 1984), pp. 170ff. For comment on one specific city, Nottingham, see Lawrence, op. cit., p. 137. The relatively large swing against Dr David Pitt in the 1970 General Election was to result in some hesitancy even in the selection of candidates from these communities; this was known as 'the Pitt factor'. Pitt, who fought Hampstead for Labour as early as 1959, and became the chairman of CARD (see p. 241) in 1964, was never returned to the Commons but now sits in the Lords. On Pitt's experience in Clapham in the 1970 General Election see N. Deakin and J. Bourne, 'Powell, the Minorities, and the 1970 Election', *Political Quarterly*, Vol. 41 (1970), pp. 410–11.

223. The former was established by the 1962 Commonwealth Immigrants Act and the latter following the 1965 White Paper. See below pp. 268–9 on this aspect of official policy.

224. For a critical discussion of these 'buffer' organisations see Katznelson, op. cit. For comment on the involvement of individuals from minority communities see Anwar, op. cit., p. 173 and C. Mullard, *Black Britain* (London, 1973), Chs 7, 8, 9. One of the original members of the Race Relations Board, was Learie Constantine. See above p. 196 for his earlier activity during the war and below p. 240 for his involvement with the LCP. See also S. Morris, 'Leary Constantine', *New Community*, Vol. 1 (1971–2), pp. 68–70 and the obituary in *The Times*, 2 July 1971. See below pp. 268–9 for later, similar comment on these 'buffer' organisations.

225. R. Macdonald, 'Dr. Harold Arundel Moody and the League of Coloured Peoples, 1931–1947; A Retrospective View', *Race*, Vol. XIV (1973), p. 307 catches the dying days of the LCP. See also S. Morris, 'Moody – The Forgotten Visionary', *New Community*, Vol. 1 (1971), pp. 193–6. See above for the earlier LCP and the activities of Nkrumah, Kenyatta and Menon. WASU (see above p. 136) also had a postwar history. See Sorensen Archives, House of Lords (SOR 168 and 174).

226. Ndem, MA Thesis, pp. 123–5; M. Winters and J. Hatch, 'Colour Persecution in Tyneside', *Pan-Africa*, Vol. 1 (1947), pp. 24–30.

227. Rose, op. cit., pp. 500–2 refers to the origins of the Standing Conference which in its origins was a discussion group embracing Blacks and some White sympathisers. Ibid., p. 497 notes the formation of the *West Indian Gazette*. Claudia Jones was later a member of the Lambeth Inter-Racial Council (see below p. 270).

228. Patterson, *Dark Strangers*, pp. 301–2 comments on such schemes in Brixton. See also S. K. Ruck (ed.), *The West Indian comes to London* (London, 1960), pp. 74–5 and S. B. Philpott, 'The Montserratians: Migration Dependency and the Maintenance of Island Ties with England', in Watson, *Between Two Cultures*, pp. 110–11.

229. Bennett, op. cit., p. 21.

230. Patterson, *Immigration and Race Relations*, pp. 316–17; Rose, op. cit., p. 497; D. W. John, *Indian Workers' Association* (London, 1969).

231. Patterson, *Immigration and Race Relations*, pp. 317–22.

232. Derived from Hiro, *Black British*, pp. 76–95, 175–6; Walvin, op. cit., p. 138; The Times News Team, *The Black Man in Search of Power* (London, 1968), p. 143 and Ch. 11; I. Katznelson, 'The Politics of Racial Buffering in Nottingham 1945–1968', *Race*, Vol. XI (1970), p. 437; A. Sivanandan, *A Different Hunger. Writings on Black Resistance* (London, 1983), p. 19. See below p. 266 for further comment on American influences.

233. B. Heineman, Jnr, *The Politics of the Powerless* (London, 1972). On King see his *Why We Can't Wait* (New York, 1954) and two contrasting biographies, C. S. King, *My Life with Martin Luther King jr* (London, 1970) and D. L. Lewis, *Martin Luther King. A Critical Biography* (London, 1970).

234. Noticed in The Times News Team, op. cit., Scobie, op. cit., Ch. XVI.

235. Patterson, *Immigration and Race Relations*, pp. 322–4 and the Times News Team, op. cit., p. 144 provide details of the organisation and its origins. On de Freitas see M. A. Malik, *From Michael de Freitas to Michael X* (London, 1968). For reference to de Freitas as a professional sponger see H. Golbourne, 'Black Workers in Britain', *The African Review*, Vol. 7 (1977), p. 69. For a more complimentary opinion see Sivanandan, op. cit., p. 16. De Freitas was executed for murder in Trinidad in 1975. On Malcolm X, see *The Autobiography of Malcolm X* (London, 1966). The book, written with the assistance of Alex Haley, who was responsible later for 'Roots', was first published in America in 1965, the year of X's murder.

236. G. L. Watson, 'The Sociology of Black Nationalism: Identity, Protest and the Concept of Black Power among West Indian Immigrants in Britain', unpublished D.Phil. Thesis, York University, 1972, pp. 212, 257–8. For Egbuna's politics see his *Destroy This Temple* (London, 1970). For Carmichael's philosophy see S. Carmichael and C. Hamilton, *Black Power. The Politics of Liberation in America* (London, 1968). Carmichael was allowed into Britain in 1983 but was denied entry in 1984. See the report in *The Times*, 23 January 1984, which also refers to the action of the Home Secretary, Roy Jenkins in 1967. On Black Power generally see T. Draper, *The Rediscovery of Black Nationalism* (London, 1971).

237. Watson, D.Phil. Thesis, Ch. X is a reasonably comprehensive listing of such groups.

238. Heineman, op. cit., pp. 187–8, 197, 208. M. Banton, *Racial Minorities* (London, 1972), Ch. 2.

239. Scobie, op. cit., pp. 277–8; Hiro, *Black British*, p. 146; Sivanandan, op. cit., p. 25. See below pp. 265–7 for reference to Powellism and the immigration controls of the 1960s.

240. Cashmore, op. cit., pp. 44–9, who regards the Black Power activists of the 60s as preparing the ground for the Rastafarian movement of the 1970s. See below p. 269 for further reference to police action against Black political activists. B. Lapping, 'The Choice for Immigrants', *The Guardian*, 20 July 1965 emphasises the difficulty in forming militant organisations. See also Hiro, *Black British*, pp. 43–4 on this theme.

241. For comment on these developments see Sivanandan's essay, 'From Resistance to Rebellion', in Sivanandan, op. cit., partic. pp. 15, 22. See also The Race Today collective, *The Struggle of Asian Workers in Britain* (London, 1983), partic. Ch. I. On the Preston strike see J. Torode, 'Race moves in on the Unions', *New Society*, 17 June 1965, pp. 5–7. On the strike at Woolf's see P. Marsh, *The Anatomy of a Strike: Unions, Employers, and Punjabi Workers in a Southall Factory* (London, 1967).

242. Noted in G. W. Kearsley and S. R. Srivastava, 'The Spatial Evolution of Glasgow's Asian Community', *Scottish Geographical Magazine*, Vol. 90 (1974),

p. 112, which traces later changes in the concentration of the small number of Indians and Pakistanis in the city.

243. The tapes in the Bradford Heritage Recording Unit are essential for an appreciation of such changes.

244. Ndem, MA Thesis, p. 25.

245. Barr, op. cit., Brown, op. cit., Ch. 6.

246. Egginton, op. cit.; Patterson, *Dark Strangers*; Hinds, *Oral History*.

247. W. J. Fishman, *The Streets of East London* (London, 1979), captures these changes in text and photograph.

248. See above p. 229.

249. See above pp. 129, 228. See also J. Pascal, 'When I Dream I Dream in English', *New Society*, 31 May 1984, p. 346. P. Anderson, 'Components of the National Culture', in A. Cockburn and R. Blackburn (eds.), *Student Power* (Harmondsworth, 1970 edn), includes such intellectual émigrés in his discussion of an early twentieth-century 'Counter-revolutionary emigration'.

250. For examples of the work of Lamming and Selvon see references on p. 378 below. On S. S. Naipaul, younger brother of V. S. Naipaul, see the obituary in *The Times*, 16 August 1985. See also his collection of essays and stories, *Beyond the Dragon's Mouth* (London, 1984), for his early student life in London, a city of 'dreadful anonymity'.

251. See above pp. 238–9.

252. An observation by D. MacAmhlaigh, in 'The Irish in England', Channel 4 TV programme, 16 October 1983.

253. Dahya, *Race*, pp. 271–2. For additional comment on problems encountered by women from the sub-continent see Anwar, op. cit., p. 123 and A. Wilson, *Finding a Voice* (London, 1981 edn), pp. 7, 48. See also S. Allen, 'Perhaps a Seventh Person?', in C. Husband, *'Race' in Britain. Continuity and Change* (London, 1982), for a critique of the prevailing stereotypical images of women from the sub-continent.

254. Comment on this, in relation to West Indian children and those from the sub-continent was made in the 1960s in Patterson, *Immigration and Race Relations*, p. 261 and Rose, op. cit., pp. 281, 447. For later comment see Walvin, op. cit., pp. 73ff. The issue was to become of increasing importance in relation to the Black children born in Britain who entered the educational system. Children of Irish descent also encountered tension, particularly in history lessons. Comment on this appeared in 'The Irish in England', Channel 4 TV programme, 23 October 1983.

255. On the Poles see Zubrzycki, op. cit., pp. 186ff; on the EVWs see Stadulis, op. cit., pp. 229ff and F. F. Kino, 'Refugee Psychoses in Great Britain. Aliens' Paranoid Reactions', in H. B. M. Murphy (ed.), *Flight and Resettlement* (Paris, 1955), Ch. 3; on the Irish see Jackson, op. cit., pp. 68–70; O'Connor, op. cit., p. 115 and C. Bagley and A. Binitie, 'Alcoholism and Schizophrenia in Irishmen in London', *British Journal of Addiction*, Vol. 65 (1970), pp. 3–7; for West Indians (and others), see R. L. Littlewood and M. Lipsedge, *Aliens and Alienists. Ethnic Minorities and Psychiatry* (Harmondsworth, 1982), Ch. 4. There is specific comment on West Indians in Nottingham in Lawrence, op. cit., pp. 197–8. For a degree of general scepticism see R. Cochrane and M. Stopes Roe, 'The Mental Health of Immigrants', *New Community*, Vol. VIII (1980), pp. 123–8, in which it is argued that there is 'no necessary association between migration and vulnerability to mental illness' (p. 128).

256. See above pp. 126–7 and see below pp. 294–311.

257. The use of the term 'traditional' elites follows the discussion in A. Giddens, 'An Anatomy of the British Ruling Class', *New Society*, 4 October 1979, pp. 8–10. This

powerlessness at a national level is reflected in the thundering silence on such groups in A. Sampson, *Anatomy of Britain* (London, 1962) and the subsequent revised editions. Powerlessness at a local level, in Nottingham, is emphasised in Katznelson, *Race*, p. 444.

258. Watson, 'The Chinese'; Dahya, *Race*.

259. See above p. 208.

260. On the German past see the comment by Marion Berghahn in Pascal, op. cit., p. 348. On the Italian experience see Palmer, 'The Italians', pp. 256–7.

261. Emphasised in 'The Irish in England', Channel 4 TV programme, 23 October 1983.

262. Emphasised in Hiro, *Black British*, p. 16, and two television productions, 'The Promised Land? Colonisin' in Reverse', Open University Programme, BBC1 TV, 13, 20 and 27 August 1983 and 'The Promised Land? Punjab to Britain', Open University programme, BBC 1 TV, 3, 10 and 17 September 1983.

263. *New Statesman*, 20 October 1945, p. 263; ibid., 27 October 1945, p. 277; ibid., 3 November 1945, pp. 298–9. See above p. 234 for the attraction of Hampstead.

264. See above p. 176 for refugee scientists during the war. For comment on their ultimate respectability see below p. 364. For the issue of national loyalty see Hoch, op. cit., p. 245. See also H. M. Hyde, *The Atom Bomb Spies* (London, 1980), Ch. 3. On the Rosenberg affair see, among many sources, R. Radosh and J. Milton, *The Rosenberg File* (New York, 1984).

265. Ladsky, op. cit.

266. On the King David Hotel incident see D. Leitch, 'Explosion at the King David Hotel', in M. Sissons and P. French (eds), *Age of Austerity 1945–1951* (Harmondsworth, 1964 edn). This essay also considers the Netanya incident, on which see also *An Editor on Trial. Rex v. Caunt. Alleged seditious Libel* (n.d., n.p.); the anti-Jewish violence was noticed in the *Manchester Evening News*, 4, 5, 6, 7 August 1947 and the *Jewish Chronicle*, 8 and 15 August 1947. The hanging festered in racial-nationalist sources. See, for example, *Combat*, No. 10 January–February 1961 supplement. This was produced at the time of the Eichmann trial in Jerusalem. The issue was resurrected at a later date in anti-Jewish circles. For an academic analysis of Britain in Palestine in the closing years of the Mandate see M. J. Cohen, *Palestine and the Great Powers 1945–1948* (Princeton N.J., 1982).

267. See J. Gross, 'The Lynskey Tribunal', in Sissons and French, op. cit., pp. 266–86; see also H. F. T. Rhodes, *The Lynskey Tribunal* (Leigh-on-Sea, 1949) and S. W. Baron, *The Contact Man: The Story of Sidney Stanley and the Lynskey Tribunal* (London, 1966). See above p. 185 for reference to black market activity. Finally, see D. Hughes, 'The Spivs', in Sissons and French, op. cit., pp. 86–105 for additional context.

268. O. Mosley, *My Life* (London, 1968), Ch. 18. For Mosley's postwar career see R. Skidelsky, *Oswald Mosley* (London, 1975) Ch. 26, 'The Vision Splendid' and Ch. 27, 'A New Beginning?'

269. J. Morell, 'The Life and Opinions of A. S. Leese. A Study in Extreme Antisemitism', unpublished MA Thesis, Sheffield University, 1974, is the fullest study of Leese.

270. See, for example, M. Walker, *The National Front* (London, 1977), Ch. 2. For a sample of anti-Jewish hostility see particularly the 'Gleanings from the Ghetto' column by Julius in early issues of *Spearhead*, when it was the organ of the Greater Britain Movement.

271. E. J Hobsbawm, 'Are we entering a New Era of Antisemitism?' *New Society*, 11 December 1980, pp. 503–5.

272. A. R. J. Kushner, 'British Antisemitism in the Second World War', unpublished Ph.D. Thesis, Sheffield University, 1986 discusses the early

revisionists. For one specific postwar example, see 'Six Million Jewish Lies', by Julius in *Spearhead*, No. 7, May 1965, p. 5.

273. W. D. Rubinstein, *The Left, the Right and the Jews* (London, 1982), Ch. 3; M. Billig, 'Anti-Jewish Themes and the British Far Left', *Patterns of Prejudice*, Vol. 18 (January 1984), pp. 3–15 and ibid., Vol. 18 (April 1984), pp. 28–34. It should be emphasised that the link between anti-Zionism and anti-Semitism is more complex than is often recognised.

274. A cartoon on this theme called 'Trojan Horse 1980' appeared in *Combat*, No. 8 October–November 1960, p. 8. For similar sentiment see *The National Socialist*, No. 7, 1963?, p. 1. See also *Spearhead*, February 1965, p. 5 for the observation that 'if Britain were Jew-clean she would have no "nigger neighbours" to worry about'. There is a useful discussion of later conspiracy theory in J. F. Douglas, 'Antisemitism and Conspiracy Theory in National Front Propaganda', unpublished M.Sc. Thesis, Bath University, 1983; M. Billig, *Fascists. A Social Psychological View of the National Front* (London, 1978) and N. Fielding, *The National Front* (London, 1981).

275. See below pp. 247–51, 255ff.

276. Rubinstein, op. cit., partic. pp. 93, 96–7.

277. C. Holmes, 'Antisemitism in Britain', *Jewish Chronicle*, 14 September 1979.

278. See above Ch. IV.

279. Patterson, 'The Poles', p. 240.

280. M. Le Lohé, 'Effects of Immigrants in Bradford', in R. Miles and A. Phizacklea (eds), *Racism and Political Action in Britain* (London, 1979), p. 186. See also Paraszczak, Dissertation, p. 65.

281. Tannahill, op. cit., p. 70.

282. The reference to invisibility is derived from J. S. and L. D. MacDonald, *Invisible Immigrants* (London, 1972), which includes data on the Italians in its survey. The other quotation is from King, op. cit., p. 184. Brown, op. cit., Marin, op. cit., pp. 104–5, and Palmer, 'The Italians', p. 250, all write in optimistic vein about Italian life in Britain. So does Barr, op. cit., but he notes (p. 8) that the Italians' demand for housing in Bedford was one factor which generated hostility in the 1950s. H. J. Fyrth and H. Collins, *The Foundry Workers. A Trade Union History* (Manchester, 1959), p. 255 notes shop floor opposition to Italian workers but also comments, significantly, 'when the Government pressed the Union to accept Poles demobilized from General Anders's army the National Council drew the line'. In general the union view was that the injection of European workers was tinkering with an industry which faced serious economic problems. Finally, the need for caution in writing the history of the postwar Italians is suggested by the observation in J. K. Chadwick-Jones, 'The Acceptance and Socialization of Immigrant Workers in the Steel Industry', *Sociological Review*, Vol. 12 (1964), pp. 177ff. that differences developed between Italians and other workers in the steel industry.

283. See above pp. 230, 235. The sensitivity of the employment and housing markets to pressure from foreign workers was recognised in Political and Economic Planning, op. cit., p. 116.

284. Tannahill, op. cit., pp. 68–74.

285. Ibid., p. 69.

286. Ibid.

287. Insufficiently emphasised in ibid. generally.

288. Trades Union Congress, *Conference Report* (London, 1946), pp. 362, 364.

289. Ibid., p. 171.

290. S. Orwell and I. Angus (eds), *The Collected Essays, Journalism and Letters of George Orwell*, Vol. 4 *In Front of Your Nose* (Harmondsworth, 1978 edn), p. 315.

291. *Parl. Deb.* (Commons), Vol. 427 (1945–6), 11 October 1946, col. 947.
292. Stadulis, op. cit., p. 221. I hope to turn on another occasion to the responses of the NUM to foreign labour in the postwar world.
293. *Parl. Deb.* (Commons), Vol. 434 (1946–7), 10 March 1947, col. 1047.
294. Ibid., 11 March 1947, col. 1200.
295. Recognised by Tannahill, op. cit., p. 63.
296. Ibid., pp. 70–1.
297. On disquiet over POW labour see *The Landworker*, Vol. 26 (January 1945), p. 9; ibid., Vol. 26 (August 1945), p. 2; ibid., Vol. 26 (October 1945), p. 4; ibid., Vol. 27 (January 1946), p. 3; ibid., Vol. 27 (March 1946), pp. 5, 10; ibid., Vol. 27 (July 1946), pp. 8, 11; ibid., Vol. 27 (August 1946), p. 4. On the early antipathy towards Polish labour see ibid., Vol. 27 (October 1946), pp. 6, 11; ibid., Vol. 27 (December 1946), p. 9; ibid., Vol. 28 (January 1947), p. 6. Such opposition towards foreign labour was still evident at a later date. See, for example, ibid., Vol. 29 (February 1948), p. 8. The basic fear was that agricultural work would become casualised. B. A. Holderness, *British Agriculture since 1945* (Manchester, 1985), p. 133, notices the POWs, in passing, but is silent on the injection of Polish labour. On the issue of workes from St Helena see PRO LAB 43/12 which contains correspondence between the General Secretary of the National Union of Agricultural Workers and the Ministry of Labour. Alfred Dann, the General Secretary, wrote on 30 October 1947: 'We appreciate of course that these people are human beings, but it would seem evident that to bring coloured labour into the British countryside would be a most unwise and unfortunate act'. On 8 December 1947 he put his cards on the table: 'You will appreciate that our people have already put up with a great deal, we have had COs, POWs, Poles and EVWs thrust upon us, and if coloured labour was imported, it would prove to be the last straw'. See M. Bülbring and E. Nagy, 'The Receiving Community in Great Britain' in Murphy, op. cit., pp. 114–15 for general comment on trade union responses. See above p. 232 for reference to Ukrainians and other EVWs leaving agriculture.
298. TUC, *Annual Report*, 1946, p. 357. The remarks came from L. McGree of the Amalgamated Society of Woodworkers. See above p. 170 for the contribution of Polish forces in the Battle of Britain and Arnhem.
299. Tannahill, op. cit., p. 86. See the *Yorkshire Observer*, 27 July 1951, 'How the EVWs Buy Their Property', which was an attempt to defuse opposition in Bradford. See ibid., 26 July 1951 and 30 July 1951 for the two other articles on the EVWs written in similar vein.
300. *Parl. Deb.* (Commons), Vol. 433 (1947–8), 27 October 1947, col. 497; ibid., Vol. 463 (1948–9), 28 March 1949, col. 816.
301. Tannahill, op. cit., p. 72.
302. TUC, *Annual Report*, 1946, p. 358, comment by C. McKerrow of the TGWU. See Zubrzycki, op. cit., pp. 56–7, on those Poles who fought with the Germans.
303. Zubrzycki, op. cit., p. 82.
304. Orwell and Angus, op. cit., p. 315.
305. Zubrzycki, op. cit., p. 82; Tannahill, op. cit., p. 72.
306. *The Times*, 21 May 1951, 'Foreign Labour in Great Britain (1)'. For later evidence of hostility from Ukrainians towards West Indians, Indians and Pakistanis – as well as Italians – see Brown, op. cit., pp. 66–7. For one example of violence see the reference in A. Thomas, 'Racial Discrimination and the Attlee Government', *New Community*, Vol. X (1982), p. 273, to an incident in Birmingham in August 1949.
307. Stadulis, op. cit., p. 219.

308. *Parl. Deb.* (Commons), Vol. 482 (1946–7), 4 February 1947, col. 1555 and ibid., Vol. 440 (1946–7), 12 July 1947, col. 595.

309. Foot, op. cit., p. 118, who enjoys scoring a political point with this observation. See also *No British Jobs for Fascist Poles* (London, 1946). This Communist Party Folder, a mélange of old and new antipathies, is in the Lazar Zaidman collection, Sheffield University.

310. Quoted in Tannahill, op. cit., pp. 20–1.

311. *Liverpool Daily Post*, 4 March 1949, p. 2.

312. See above p. 77. See *Parl. Deb.* (Lords), Vol. 277 (1966–7), 27 October 1966, cols 381–423 for these issues which were raised in a debate on 'Former Polish Allies in Great Britain'.

313. See above p. 229.

314. O'Connor, op. cit., p. 72.

315. See above p. 239.

316. Hickey, op. cit., pp. 159–60.

317. M. O'Shea, 'We are asserting our Irish nationality', *New Labour and Ireland*, No. 9, October–December 1985, p. 11.

318. For critical comment see ibid. Brooks, op. cit., p. 125 discusses relations between Irish and West Indian workers employed by London Transport.

319. See above pp. 245–6.

320. Reported in the *Sunday Times*, 22 January 1978; *The Guardian*, 18 March 1980; ibid., 18 August 1982; *The Times*, 2 September 1982. See above pp. 58, 60, 150 for evidence of a backlash against the Irish in Britain following events and developments in Ireland.

321. Traced in *Nothing but the same Old Story. The Roots of Anti-Irish Racism* (London, 1984), which is generally alert to such developments and committed to their critical advertisement.

322. See above pp. 244–5.

323. See 'Glasgow goes on the March', *The Times*, 21 February 1981 for the linkage between football, religion and politics. See also *Parl. Deb.* (Commons), Vol. 18 (1981–2), 24 February 1982, cols. 846–7. The reference to 'tribal extremism' is in O'Connor, op. cit., p. 119. See also B. Murray, *The Old Firm. Sectarianism Sport and Society in Scotland* (Edinburgh, 1984), pp. 191–279.

324. H. J. Paton, *The Claim of Scotland* (London, 1968), pp. 178–9. Jackson, op. cit., p. 157 notes evidence of continuing religious antipathy in Liverpool.

325. Cited in Jackson, op. cit., p. 63. See also ibid., pp. 108, 177. Michael Banton tells me that he noticed more 'No Irish' than 'No coloured' notices in Sparkbrook in a survey carried out in July 1952.

326. On Osborne, see *Who Was Who 1961–70* (London, 1972), p. 860. His reference to 'coloured immigrants' is from *Parl. Deb.* (Commons), Vol. 594 (1958–9), 29 October 1958, col. 195. N. Deakin, 'The Politics of the Commonwealth Immigrants Bill', *Political Quarterly*, Vol. 39 (1968), p. 28 notes Osborne's antipathy towards aliens. For Osborne's complimentary, if somewhat double-edged remark on the Irish see *Parl. Deb.* (Commons), Vol. 709 (1964–5), 23 March 1965, col. 402. There is a need for a thorough study of this backwoodsman.

327. *Combat*, No. 14, November–December 1961, p. 7.

328. *Parl. Deb.* (Commons), Vol. 649 (1961–2), 16 November 1961, col. 761 and ibid., Vol. 654 (1961–2), 27 February 1962, col. 1251. See Rex and Moore, op. cit., pp. 62, 70–1 for opinion on Sparkbrook and ibid., p. 155 for comment on Irish tinkers.

329. Burney op. cit., p. 73. Jackson, op. cit., p. 52 has comment of earlier years on

cleanliness among the Irish. There is also revealing comparative comment of a more general nature in a Whip's note of a meeting of the Commonwealth Affairs Committee on 22 January 1955 in PRO PREM 11/824 in which it was reported that one of those present contrasted 'loyal and hard-working Jamaicans' with 'disloyal (sic) Southern Irish (some of them Sinn Feiners)'.

330. Jackson, op. cit., pp. 157, 183–4. On the Irish and crime see ibid., pp. 67–8 and later comment in A. E. Bottoms, 'Delinquency amongst Immigrants', *Race*, Vol. VIII (1967), pp. 358–63.

331. O'Connor, op. cit., p. 121.

332. Referred to in ibid., p. 142. For a satirical rejoinder see the postcard, 'There were these thick Paddies . . .' by Bob Starrett, published by Leeds Postcards (author's possession).

333. S. Gilley, 'English Attitudes to the Irish in England, 1780–1900', in C. Holmes (ed.), *Immigrants and Minorities in British Society* (London, 1978), pp. 81–110.

334. See G. E. Simpson and J. M. Yinger, *Racial and Cultural Minorities* (fourth ed., New York, 1972), pp. 222–4 and C. Davies, 'Ethnic Jokes, Moral Values and Ethnic Boundaries', *British Journal of Sociology*, Vol. XXXIII (1982), pp. 383–403 for the importance of jokes.

335. E. Leach, 'The Official Irish Jokesters', *New Society*, 20/27 December 1979, pp. vii–ix, carries specific evidence.

336. R. Hattersley, 'The Irish: Moving up the Social Pyramid', *The Times*, 16 February 1971. The telling of anti-Irish jokes (see above notes 332, 334) and the expression of hostility towards West Indians, Indians and Pakistanis (see above note 318) were avenues through which some Irish attempted to distance themselves from their Irishness and achieve a closer identification with British society.

337. Watson, 'The Chinese'; M. Broady, 'The Social Adjustment of Chinese Immigrants in Liverpool', *Sociological Review*, Vol. 3 (1955), p. 73.

338. Watson, 'The Chinese', p. 194.

339. Ng, MA Thesis, p. 190.

340. Broady, *Sociological Review*, p. 74.

341. See above p. 80.

342. Jones, op. cit., p. 401.

343. Watson, 'The Chinese', p. 194.

344. Jones, op. cit., p. 401; Freeberne, op. cit., p. 709.

345. Jones, op. cit., p. 400 notes the refugees from Communism.

346. The words are from Freeberne, op. cit., p. 707. See above p. 66 for earlier stereotyped comment on the Russian Polish Jews of the late nineteenth, early twentieth century.

347. Watson, 'The Chinese', pp. 203–4.

348. Ng, MA Thesis, p. 15. Cheung, M. Phil. Thesis, p. 94 refers to the lack of skills among the Chinese which also restricted employment opportunities.

349. Watson, 'Restaurants and Remittances', p. 217 refers to discrimination in the housing market.

350. Collins, op. cit., p. 232.

351. See Watson, 'The Chinese', p. 201, for comment on the creation of Chinese family life. See above pp. 79–80 for hostility towards the Chinese couched in sexual terms.

352. Freeberne, op. cit., p. 706 refers to the unease. *East End News*, 29 December 1946 refers to a police raid on a Chinese betting house in Pennyfields where *fan tan* was played. See Ng, MA Thesis, pp. 129–32 and Cheung M. Phil. Thesis, pp. 119–20 for the importance of gambling among the Chinese.

353. Watson, 'The Chinese', p. 206; Nally, op. cit., p. 406; see *News Chronicle* 16 June

1946 and *East London Advertiser* 2 February 1951 for police action against Chinese involved in drugs. T. Mo, *Sour, Sweet* (London, 1983) weaves the drug theme into a novel of contemporary Chinese life in Britain. See above pp. 80, 111 for earlier references to the Chinese and drugs.

354. A report in *The Times* 19 March 1984 refers to the Chinese as a 'hidden' minority.

355. Ng, MA Thesis, pp. 118–19.

356. Noted in Freeberne, op. cit., p. 708.

357. See above pp. 199–205 for comment on the war years, and also for earlier expressions of hostility. See E. R. Braithwaite, *To Sir With Love* (London, 1959) for an emphasis on the difficult transition from war to peace. This theme was also prominent in the first stages of 'The Promised Land? A Question of Colour', Open University Programme, BBC 1 TV, 9 and 16 July 1983. Thomas, op. cit., is a useful source on early postwar racial discrimination and collective violence.

358. PRO CAB 129/40, 18 May 1950.

359. P. B. Rich, 'The Politics of Surplus Colonial Labour: Black Immigration to Britain and Government Responses 1940–1962', ts. pp. 16–17. PRO MT 9/5463 reveals that the NUS had a policy of enrolling as members only those Blacks who had served during the war.

360. There is a useful discussion in M. R. Risebrow, 'An Analysis of the Responses of the British Government to Coloured Colonial Immigration during the Period 1945–51', unpublished BA Dissertation, East Anglia University, 1983, p. 18.

361. Richmond, *Colour Prejudice*, p. 43.

362. Ibid., p. 47.

363. A. T. Carey, 'London Landladies and Colonial Students', *Fortnightly Review*, Vol. 180 (1953), pp. 235–42; Political and Economic Planning, *Colonial Students in Britain* (London, 1955), pp. 75, 84, 147; *Parl. Deb.* (Commons), Vol. 470 (1948–9), 21 November 1949, cols 2–3 reveals that Phil Piratin, the CP Member for Stepney, drew attention to clauses which restricted the letting of property to 'coloured tenants' and urged official action. This intervention is overlooked by those who concentrate on the later campaigns of Fenner Brockway and Reginald Sorensen (on which see below p. 258).

364. Banton, *Coloured Quarter*, pp. 77–8, 81; N. Deakin, 'The Vitality of a Tradition', in Holmes, *Immigrants and Minorities*, pp. 173ff; J. Williamson, *Father Joe* (London, 1967). For similar issues in Hull, a relatively recent area of settlement, see Drake, op. cit., pp. 209–10 and Winter and Hatch, op. cit., pp. 24–30, for similar tension on Tyneside.

365. Scobie, op. cit., p. 205.

366. Fryer, op. cit., pp. 367–71.

367. Scobie, op. cit., p. 206.

368. Shown in 'The Promised Land? A Question of Colour', Open University Programme, BBC 1 TV, 9 and 16 July 1983.

369. Scobie, op. cit., p. 196.

370. PRO LAB 8/1516.

371. See Deakin, *Race*, pp. 77–83 and Bevan, 'Immigration Law', pp. 112–13. For full details of the Act see *The Public General Acts and the Church Assembly Measures of 1948*, Vol. II (London, 1948), pp. 1241–65.

372. PRO PREM 8/827, 15 June 1948. See also PRO HO 213/715 for similar comment in a letter of 5 July 1948 to J. D. Murrray MP.

373. *Parl. Deb.* (Commons), Vol. 451 (1947–8), 8 June 1948, col. 1851.

374. PRO HO 213/716.

375. PRO CAB 128/37, 19 June 1950.

376. Risebrow, BA Dissertation, pp. 31–2.

377. Deakin, *Political Quarterly*, p. 26.

378. Noticed, among others, by Layton-Henry, op. cit., p. 31. See above p. 253 for an earlier reference to Osborne's activities. See also below pp. 260–6. See above p. 70 on Evans Gordon and Vincent.

379. S. R. and O. (No. 1671), 1953.

380. On these developments see, for example, PRO CO 1028/22 Draft Report of the Working Party on Coloured People seeking Employment in the United Kingdom, 17 December 1953 (this document also appears in PRO CAB 124/1911); PRO PREM 11/824; PRO CAB 129/65, 30 January 1954; PRO CAB 128/29, 21 June 1955; PRO CAB 129/77, 22 August 1955; PRO CAB 128/29, 15 September 1955; and PRO CAB 128/29, 3 November 1955.

381. PRO CAB 129/65, memorandum of 3 February 1954. Churchill's obsession is well illustrated by his memoranda in PRO PREM 11/824.

382. Parl. Deb. (Commons), Vol. 532 (1953–4), 5 November 1954, cols 821–31.

383. Noted in Deakin, Political Quarterly, p. 29. For additional comment see R. Miles and A. Phizacklea, The TUC, Black Workers and New Commonwealth Immigration, 1954–1973, SSRC Research Unit on Ethnic Relations Working Paper No. 6 (Bristol, n.d.) and their Labour and Racism (London, 1980). However, a detailed sensitive, historical analysis of labour responses is still needed along the lines adumbrated in K. Lunn, 'Race Relations or Industrial Relations? Race and Labour in Britain 1880–1950', Immigrants and Minorities, Vol. 4 (July 1985), pp. 1–29.

384. On Sorensen and Brockway see below p. 395 and Parl. Deb. (Commons), Vol. 480 (1950–1), 17 November 1950, col. 2044. There is an unpublished autobiography (SOR 230), left by Sorensen in the House of Lords Library. On Brockway's efforts to introduce legislation see Parl. Deb. (Commons) Vol. 554 (1955–6), 12 June 1956, cols 247–50 for the beginnings of his campaign. Brockway was involved in organisation such as the Congress against Imperialism, founded in 1948 and its successor, the Movement for Colonial Freedom established in 1954.

385. The issue of official public secrecy relating to the immigration from the Caribbean and the Indian sub-continent is discussed in M. Cockerell, P. Hennessy and D. Walker, Sources close to the Prime Minister (London, 1984), pp. 96–100.

386. Patterson, Dark Strangers, p. 125.

387. The Times, 9 February 1954. Brooks, op. cit., pp. 141–6 and 214–17 refers to antipathy among white workers on British Rail. See Daily Herald 19 August 1954 for opposition to the employment of West Indians in the pits. See File 28/4 NCCL Archives (Hull University) for other cases.

388. Daily Telegraph, 29 January 1954; The Times, 8 November 1954, the first of two articles on 'The West Indian Settlers'. For a fictional treatment see G. R. Fazackerley, A Stranger Here (London, 1959), pp. 23–6.

389. File 29/6 NCCL Archives (Hull University). See above pp. 202–3 for earlier incidents.

390. Glass, op. cit., p. 129; Scobie, op. cit., pp. 206–7.

391. Extracts from both programmes were featured in 'The Promised Land? A Question of Colour', Open University Programme, BBC 1 TV, 9 and 16 July 1983.

392. See K. Coates and B. Silburn, Poverty. The Forgotten Englishman (Harmondsworth, 1970), for a survey of this area.

393. Glass, op. cit., pp.. 139–42; Scobie, op. cit., p. 214. C. MacInnes, Absolute Beginners (London, 1953) is a good literary treatment of the atmosphere in Notting Hill. P. Jephcott, A Troubled Area (London, 1964), appeared as a survey of the area shortly after the violence.

394. Glass, op. cit., pp. 130–3; Scobie, op. cit., pp. 210–11; J. Wickenden, Colour in Britain (London, 1958), p. 34.

395. Glass, op. cit., pp. 164–7; Scobie, op. cit., p. 231.
396. *The Times*, 2, 3, 16 September 1958. For the 'Teddy Boy' phenomenon see P. Rock and S. Cohen, 'The Teddy Boy', in V. Bogdanor and R. Skidelsky (eds), *The Age of Affluence, 1951–1964* (London, 1970), pp. 288–320 and, more recently, G. Pearson, *Hooligan. A History of Respectable Fears* (London, 1983), Ch. 2.
397. This was recognised in an account of the violence in Nottingham which appeared in the *Manchester Guardian* 26 August 1958. The two local papers the *Nottingham Guardian Journal* and the *Nottingham Evening Post* noted the intrusion of the teddy-boy element but remarked on other influences. More accessible and relevant comment on Nottingham and London is available in Wickenden, op. cit., pp. 25, 37; Glass, op. cit., pp. 171–9; Hiro. *Black British*, pp. 39–42; Lawrence, op. cit., pp. 1–2; R. Miles, 'The Riots of 1958. Notes on the Ideological Construction of "Race Relations" as a Political Issue in Britain', *Immigrants and Minorities,* Vol. 3 (1984), pp. 252–75.
398. Fryer, op. cit., p. 379.
399. Quoted in the *Daily Mail*, 3 September 1958. Huddleston was the Bishop of Stepney. His South African experiences told in *Naught for Your Comfort* (London, 1956), and Alan Paton's earlier novel, *Cry the Beloved Country. A Study of Comfort in Desolation* (London, 1948), were important influences affecting the image of South Africa in liberal circles in Britain.
400. G. C. L. Bertram, *West Indian Immigration* (London, 1958), partic. pp. 6, 14, 17, 19, 20, 21, 23. See Patterson, *Dark Strangers*, pp. 247ff for a discussion of 'inter-group sexual relations and inter-marriage'.
401. *Monthly Film Bulletin*, Vol. 26 (June 1959), pp. 68–9.
402. *Parl. Deb.* (Commons), Vol. 596 (1958–9), 5 December 1958, col. 1552.
403. See Skidelsky, op. cit., p. 512 for a brief reference to the North Kensington episode. O. M. had sought previously to benefit from the situation in Birmingham. See A. Sutcliffe and R. Smith, *Birmingham 1939–1970* (London, 1974), pp. 371–3. On the influx of Birmingham MPs see Layton-Henry, op. cit., p. 37.
404. *The Public General Acts and Church Assembly Measures of 1962* (London, 1963), pp. 112–34. The Act receives full attention in Bevan, 'Immigration Law', pp. 77–9.
405. See above pp. 224–5.
406. See above p. 210 for an earlier reference to the restriction on access to official records. The published accounts of this time written by the prime minister, Harold Macmillan, and the Home Secretary, R. A. Butler, are not especially revealing. See H. Macmillan, *At the End of the Day 1961–1963* (London, 1973), pp. 73–83 (in which Macmillan draws on his diary) and R. A. Butler, *The Art of the Possible. The Memoirs of Lord Butler* (London, 1971), pp. 205ff.
407. M. D. Blanch, 'Nation, Empire, and the Birmingham Working Class', unpublished Ph.D. Thesis, Birmingham University, 1975, is a useful study of the city in the age of Imperialism.
408. *The Times* 9 November 1954. See Sutcliffe and Smith, op. cit., p. 369 for comment.
409. J. Barnes, *Ahead of his Age. Bishop Barnes of Birmingham* (London, 1979), p. 427.
410. Foot, op. cit., p. 195. There is useful comment on the changing local context in R. Ward, 'Race Relations in Britain', *British Journal of Sociology*, Vol. 29 (1978), pp. 469–72.
411. Williamson, op. cit., pp. 135–6; Deakin, 'Vitality of a Tradition', pp. 178–9. See also Dench, op. cit., p. 91 for reference to the link that was made between immigration and organised prostitution, and the Maltese as a focus of opposition in both debates. On the link between prostitution and 'the colour problem', see PRO CAB 129/65, 30 January 1954. The issue of Blacks and prostitution was

also present in the 1958 violence. See Wickenden, op. cit., p. 25. For later comment and an emphasis on an involvement by West Indians in another social problem, drugs, see Lord Elton, *The Unarmed Invasion. A Survey of Afro-Asian Immigration* (London, 1965), Ch. 8 and Norman Pannell's views in N. Pannell and F. Brockway, *Immigration. What is the Answer?* (London, 1965), pp. 29–31. For a balanced contemporary discussion of these issues see Bottoms, op. cit., pp. 365ff and J. A. G. Griffiths et al., *Coloured Immigrants in Britain* (London, 1960), p. 35.

412. Fryer, op. cit., p. 380. See *The Times*, 21, 22, 23, 24 August 1961 and the *Daily Worker* 21 August 1961 for contemporary newspaper coverage. For a contrary interpretation to both see *Combat*, No. 13, August–October 1961, which carried the headline, 'Middlesborough. Whites Victimised'.

413. E. Butterworth, 'The 1962 Smallpox Outbreak and the British Press', *Race*, Vol. 7 (1966), pp. 347–66. For public concern over disease see Griffiths, op. cit., pp. 33–5 and *The Times*, 20 January 1965, 'The Dark Million (3)'.

414. Foot, op. cit., p. 141.

415. Layton-Henry, op. cit., p. 38.

416. See above pp. 257–8.

417. Foot, op. cit., pp. 13ff, 136; also noticed in Deakin, *Political Quarterly*, p. 41.

418. S. Brittan, *Steering the Economy. The Role of the Treasury* (Harmondsworth, 1970 edn), Ch. 6 is useful on the economic background. Sivanandan, op. cit., pp. 144–5 emphasises the increasing tendency of capital to utilise 'a cheap and plentiful supply of labour in the periphery, in Asia in particular' which reduced the necessity to move labour from the periphery to capital in the advanced countries. The changing economic situation and its significance was emphasised by R. A. Butler when he introduced the Bill. See *Parl. Deb.* (Commons), Vol. 649 (1961–2), 16 November 1961, col. 693. See also the comments of Lt. Col. J. K. Cordeaux, the Tory MP for Nottingham Central in ibid., Vol. 654 (1961–2), 27 February 1962, col. 1256. Z. Layton-Henry's review of Sivanandan's *A Different Hunger* in *Immigrants and Minorities*, Vol. 2 (1983), p. 203, contains pertinent criticism but its assertion that 'political and social reasons alone' lay behind the immigration control of the early 1960s is too restrictive.

419. On controls at source see Rose, op. cit., pp. 70–1 on the Indian sub-continent the less effective controls in the Caribbean. See above pp. 221, 224 for earlier comment.

420. See above p. 221.

421. Layton-Henry, op. cit., p. 40. The reference to 'considerable social strains' is from Denis Healey, in *Parl. Deb.* (Commons, Vol. 654 (1961–2), 27 February 1962, col. 1267. See also A. Marwick, *British Society since 1945* (Harmondsworth, 1982), p. 167.

422. See above.

423. J. Rex, *Race, Colonialism and City* (London, 1973), is one of a number of works by John Rex which stresses the need to take account of the Colonial-Imperial past. But see P. B. Rich, 'Doctrines of Racial Segregation in Britain 1900–1944, *New Community*', Vol. XII (1984–5), pp. 75–88, for an expression of concern about any reference to an amorphous, undifferentiated tradition. See also Rich's unpublished paper, 'History and Theory in British Race Relations: Some General Reflections', ts. p. 15, on the need to take account of an existing 'nativist and anti-immigration tradition . . .'. For expressions of opposition on the grounds of race see Bertram, op. cit.; PRO CAB 129/77, 22 August 1955 in which one voice distinguished between the immigration of the Irish and 'Coloured people' on grounds of race; PRO CAB 128/29, 3 November 1955, in which one voice (that of the Marquis of Salisbury?), expressed concern about 'a

significant change in the racial character of the English people' if immigration 'from the Colonies and for that matter from India and Pakistan were allowed to continue unchecked . . .'. For popular comment see *The Times*, 18 January 1965, 'The Dark Million (1)' and the *Nottingham Evening News*, 25 August 1958 for reference to St Ann's as 'Nottingham's Jungle'. For racial nationalist comment urging a need to defend 'the white race' see *Combat*, No. 6. May/June 1960, pp. 1, 4–5. See below pp. 263–7 for a discussion of the National Front, Powellism and the Immigration legislation of 1962–71. See also below Ch. 6 for a return to the themes raised in this paragraph within a more general context.

424. Noticed, among others, by Patterson, *Immigration and Race Relations*, p. 19. See also Brittan, op. cit., pp. 236–8.

425. Psarias, M.Phil. Thesis, pp. 47–8.

426. G. P. Freeman, *Immigrant Labour and Racial Conflict in Industrial Societies. The French and the British Experience 1945–1975* (Princeton, N.J. 1979), p. 81.

427. Lawrence, op. cit., p. 34. See also R. Miles and A. Phizacklea, *White Man's Country. Racism in British Politics* (London, 1984), p. 22. See above p. 225 for reference to the re-creation of original cultures.

428. Patterson, *Immigration and Race Relations*, p. 229; Walker, op. cit., pp. 51ff.

429. Foot, op. cit., p. 214. On the reporting of issues involving racial minorities see P. Hartmann and C. Husband, *Racism and the Mass Media* (London, 1974; C. Husband (ed.), *White Media and Black Britain* (London, 1975); and B. Troyna, *Public Awareness and the Media. A Study of Reporting on Race* (London, 1981). See below p. 297 for additional comment.

430. Foot, op. cit., p. 214; Patterson, *Immigration and Race Relations*, pp. 379–81.

431. For a study of a 1964 case see G. Pearson, 'Paki-Bashing in a North-East Lancashire Cotton Town: A Case Study and its History', in G. Mungham and G. Pearson (eds), *Working Class Youth Culture* (London, 1976), pp. 48–81.

432. Foot, op. cit., pp. 44ff. For a selection of Griffith's views see his *A Question of Colour?* (London, 1966). At present he is Tory MP for Portsmouth North which he has represented since 1979; he lost Smethwick in 1966. A. Roth, *Parliamentary Profiles* (London, 1984), pp. 313–14 carries an incisive cameo. In the 1964 election Fenner Brockway, the veteran campaigner against racial discrimination, was defeated at Eton and Slough. On the '64 election see N. Deakin (ed.), *Colour and the British Electorate: Six Case Studies* (London, 1965).

433. The words are those of Deakin, *Political Quarterly*, p. 43. See below p. 266 for additional comment.

434. 'Racialists in Britain: The Ku Klux Klan', *Wiener Library Bulletin*, Vol. XIX No. 4 n.s. (1965), pp. 9–11. See *The People*, 30 September 1956 for an earlier manifestation of the KKK which placed the following advertisement in the press and asked for helpers 'KKK Pro-Patria. And with horror we saw coming towards us thousands of black beatles . . .'. See the *Nottingham Guardian Journal*, 28 August 1958 for evidence of other activity which had links with the Klan in the United States.

435. Walker, op. cit., p. 59.

436. Patterson, *Immigration and Race Relations*, pp. 381–2. For a sample of its literature see M. Howarth, *The Great Betrayal. Facts on Immigration* (n.d., n.p.).

437. C. Cross, 'Britain's Racialists', *New Society*, 3 June 1965, pp. 9–12.

438. Emphasised, for example, in S. Taylor, *The National Front in English Politics* (London, 1982), and in his 'The National Front: An Anatomy of a Political Development', in Miles and Phizacklea, *Racism and Political Action*, pp. 141–4.

439. Reprinted in *Patterns of Prejudice*, Vol. 1 (March/April 1967), p. 23.

440. Walker, op. cit., Taylor, *The National Front*; C. Husbands, *Racial Exclusionism and the City. The Urban Support of the National Front* (London, 1983) are generally useful

and accessible sources on the NF. Scobie, op. cit., p. 279 refers to the activities of an NF street gang in Leeds in July 1969. See also Searchlight Special, *The Murderers are amongst us* (London, 1985).

441. For contrasting interpretations see P. Foot, *The Rise of Enoch Powell* (Harmondsworth, 1968) and T. E. Utley, *Enoch Powell. The Man and his Thinking* (London, 1968).

442. See above for the arrival of the Kenyan Asians. Powell's speech is reprinted in B. Smithies and P. Fiddick, *Enoch Powell on Immigration* (London, 1969), pp. 19–22.

443. Ibid., pp. 35–43. The quotation is from p. 36.

444. The reference to Sikh communalism is from ibid., pp. 42–3. The Sikh insistence on the symbolism of the turban was an issue which raised the charge of communalism in Powell's own constituency. See D. Beetham, *Transport and Turbans. A Comparative Study in Local Politics* (London, 1970), Ch. 3. Powell's reference to the prospect of racial violence and his allusion to ancient Rome is in Smithies and Fiddick, op. cit., p. 43.

445. D. Schoen, *Enoch Powell and the Powellites* (London, 1977), pp. 34–44. See R. Crossman, *The Diaries of a Cabinet Minister Vol. 3 Secretary of State for Social Services 1968–70* (London, 1977), p. 29, in a diary entry for 21 April 1968, noted the impact and political importance of the speech.

446. Layton-Henry, op. cit., p. 71.

447. Hiro, *Black British*, pp. 243–4; D. Spearman, 'Enoch Powell's Postbag', *New Society*, 9 May 1968, pp. 667–8.

448. Frank Byers (later Lord Byers), quoted in Scobie, op. cit., p. 291. See also Freeman, op. cit., p. 295. Foot, *Enoch Powell*, pp. 116–17, notices that following the Birmingham speech dockers and meat porters marched through London in support of Powell in a display of populist support reminiscent of that accorded to certain Tory MPs by the BBL. See above p. 70.

449. V. G. Kiernan, 'Britons Old and New', in Holmes, *Immigrants and Minorities*, p. 54.

450. Smithies and Fiddick, op. cit., p. 75, reproducing Powell's speech at Eastbourne on 16 November 1968.

451. R. Skidelsky, 'Suez', in Bogdanor and Skidelsky, op. cit., p. 188. Powell's attempts at the definition of nationality have been noticed particularly by his critics. See A. Gamble, *The Conservative Nation* (London, 1974), pp. 115ff; M. Barker, *The New Racism* (London, 1981), pp. 39–42 and T. Nairn, *The Break-Up of Britain* (London, 1981 edn), p. 274.

452. Patterson, *Immigration and Race Relations*, p. 170; NCCL Archives File 140/4 (Hull University Library) contains material on St Pancras.

453. Noticed in *Nottingham Evening Post* 1 December 1966. This is one press cutting among the voluminous files on allegations of racial discrimination to be found in the NCCL Archives, Hull University Library.

454. 'Political and Economic Planning', *Racial Discrimination* (London, 1966); H. Street, G. Howe, G. Bindman, *Report on Anti-Discrimination Legislation* (London, 1967). See also *Report of the Race Relations Board for 1967–8* (HC 262) (London, 1968), Appendix IV, covering the period from 1 April 1967 to 31 March 1968.

455. Hiro, *Black British*, pp. 175–6, who notices that sometimes White youths were joined by young West Indians in making such attacks. For a personal account of one such racial attack see P. Mohanti, *Through Brown Eyes* (Oxford, 1985), pp. 159–64.

456. Deakin, *Political Quarterly*, p. 43. On the disenchantment with the multi-racial Commonwealth see D. Ingram, *Commonwealth for a Colour Blind World* (London, 1965), Ch. 9. On the American situation, the atmosphere is well caught in contemporary publications such as L. Lomax, *The Negro Revolt* (New York,

1962); C. Silberman, *Crisis in Black and White* (New York, 1964); K. Clark, *Dark Ghetto* (New York, 1965). See above note 236 for additional references. An official publication which captured a good deal of interest in Britain was the *Report of the National Advisory Commission on Civil Disorders* (New York, 1968), commonly known as the *Kerner Report*. See the *Report of the Race Relations Board for 1966–7* (H.C. 437) (London, 1967), p. 21 for an official awareness and influence in Britain of developments in America. This was also evident in parliamentary debates at least from 1958 onwards. The treatment of Stokely Carmichael (see above p. 241) was an official attempt to prevent Black Power spreading to Britain from America.

457. *Immigration from the Commonwealth* Cmnd. 2739 (1965). Roy Hattersley in *Parl. Deb.* (Commons) Vol. 709 (1964–5), 23 March 1965, col. 381, signalled the need for skilled workers only before the publication of the White Paper. For critical comment on the 'one-way technical assistance' involved in the White Paper strategy and a reference to 'a protracted discussion' in Cabinet on the policy see B. Castle, *The Castle Diaries 1964–70* (London, 1984), p. 47.

458. *Parl. Deb.* (Commons), Vol. 701 (1964–5), 3 November 1964, col. 71. For later comment by Wilson see his book, *The Labour Government 1964–70* (Harmondsworth, 1974 edn), p. 55.

459. R. Crossman, *The Diaries of a Cabinet Minister. Vol. 1 Minister of Housing 1964–66* (London, 1975), pp. 149–50. This was a diary entry for 5 February 1965. On the same day Crossman referred to immigration as 'the hottest potato in politics' and commented that the chief responsibility in the matter fell to Sir Frank Soskice, who was 'a disaster as Home Secretary'. See below note 476 for critical comment of a different kind on Soskice.

460. *The Public General Acts and Church Assembly Measures, 1968* (London, 1969), pp. 169–75. Bevan, 'Immigration Law', pp. 80–3, now offers a useful discussion of the Act and the following 'sweetener' in the shape of the 1969 Immigration Appeals Act. For the UKC category of citizenship see ibid., and Deakin, *Race*, and Bevan, op. cit. From a political point of view, R. Crossman, *The Diaries of a Cabinet Minister Vol. 2. Lord President of the Council and Leader of the House of Commons 1966–68* (London, 1976), p. 733, reflected in his diary on 24 March 1968 on 'the lack of preparation and the incompetence of the last-minute rush' which characterised this piece of legislation. Castle, op. cit., p. 381, refers to her 'own remissness' on the Commonwealth Immigrants Bill.

461. Noted in Sivanandan, op. cit., p. 27.

462. Deakin and Bourne, op. cit.

463. Gamble, *The Conservative Nation*, p. 183. See Bevan, 'Immigration Law', pp. 201–3 for the provisions regarding the entry of EEC Nationals, once the United Kingdom became a member of the European Community in 1973.

464. *The Public General Acts and Church Assembly Measures, 1971* Pt II (London, 1972), pp. 1653–1715. Bevan, 'Immigration Law', pp. 83–4, has a careful recent discussion of the Act and its implications, including its provision for family deportations.

465. See Le Lohé, op. cit., pp. 198–202 on the Yorkshire group.

466. Sivanandan, op. cit., p. 28, a source which is generally useful on this perspective.

467. PRO LAB 8/1560 and LAB 8/1571.

468. PRO LAB 8/1571, and noted above p. 257.

469. See above p. 258. The lack of official interest in any such action was emphasised by Kenneth Little in the course of an interview during 'The Promised Land? A Question of Colour', Open University Programme, BBC1 TV, 9 July and 16 July 1983.

470. See, for example, 'Is There a British Colour Bar?', *Picture Post*, 2 July 1949,

pp. 23–8. The author was Robert Kee. The photographs were by Bert Hardy. See also PRO CAB 192/40, 18 May 1950.

471. Deakin, *Political Quarterly*, pp. 25–6. Sutcliffe and Smith, op. cit., pp. 369–70; P. B. Rich, 'Blacks in Britain: Responses and Reaction 1945–62', *History Today* Vol. 36 (January 1986), pp. 14–20.

472. Quoted in Rose, op. cit., p. 229.

473. Cited in ibid., p. 25.

474. See Hepple, op. cit., Ch. 8 for these developments. K. Hindell, 'The Genesis of the Race Relations Bill', *Political Quarterly*, Vol. 36 (1965), pp. 390–403 refers to the origins of the shift in policy. The 1965 and 1968 Acts were followed by another Act in 1976 which, among its provisions, led to the establishment of the Commission for Racial Equality. This organisation effectively assumed the roles of the Race Relations Board and the Community Relations Commission.

475. See above p. 239. For specific comment see Katznelson, *Race*, pp. 441–2; Lawrence, op. cit., pp. 215–16; Mullard, op. cit., pp. 75–88.

476. Layton-Henry, op. cit., p. 71. For an extreme illustration of such sentiment see *Spearhead*, No. 8 July 1965, p. 5, which commented that Soskice (i.e. Sir Frank Soskice, the Home Secretary) was 'the man aptly chosen to introduce alien repressive edicts into Britain and to destroy British Law'. This was written in response to the 1965 Race Relations Bill. The same feature carried a cartoon with the heading 'Harold Wilson – Watchdog of Democracy', which portrayed the prime minister on a leash held by a Jew.

477. C. Jones, *Immigration and Social Policy in Britain* (London, 1967), p. 162.

478. Lawrence, op. cit., p. 219. See above and below generally for the importance of the employment and housing variables.

479. Fryer, op. cit., p. 325.

480. See L. Bloom's introduction to Little, op. cit. (1972 edn), p. 35.

481. Fryer, op. cit., p. 394. For the Mangrove, 'a resting place in Babylon', see Sivanandan, op. cit., pp. 32–3. On the trial see C. MacInnes, 'The Mangrove Trial', *New Society*, 23 December 1971, p. 126. For additional comment on police strategy see Scobie, op. cit., p. 300; D. Sington, 'The Policeman and the Immigrant', *New Society*, 24 February 1966, pp. 13–15; J. Hunte, *Nigger Hunting in England?* (London, 1966); D. Humphrey, *Police Power and Black People* (London, 1972); J. Sandford, *Smiling David. The Story of David Oluwale* (London, 1974), (see Fryer, op. cit., p. 392 on this 1971 case); T. Bunyan, *The History and Practice of the Political Police in Britain* (London, 1978 edn), p. 147.

482. Sivanandan, op. cit., is a statement of this belief.

483. On the Elizabethan statute see Hiro, *Black British*, pp. 3, 5. On the Sierra Leone scheme there is C. Fyfe, *A History of Sierra Leone* (Oxford, 1962), partic. Ch. I. See also Fryer, op. cit., pp. 196–203. See above p. 110 for the deportations in 1919. For opinion in the 60s see Elton, op. cit., p. 91 and Pannell and Brockway, op. cit., p. 55. On the NF and repatriation see *Patterns of Prejudice* (March–April, 1962), loc. cit., p. 23 and Fielding, op. cit., pp. 99–100. On Powell and repatriation there is Schoen, op. cit., pp. 42–50. For general comment see Hiro, *Black British*, pp. 302–11.

484. Barker, op. cit., partic. pp. 39–42.

485. The files of the NCCL at Hull University are a rich, neglected source.

486. On the Institute there is C. Mullard, 'Race, Power and Resistance. A Study of the Institute of Race Relations 1952–1972', unpublished Ph.D. Thesis, Durham University, 1980. A published edition appeared in 1985.

487. On the 'Edinburgh school' see M. Banton, 'The Influence of Colonial Status upon Black-White Relations in England', 1948–58', *Sociology*, Vol. 17 (1983), pp. 546–59.

488. See particularly Hugh Gaitskell's reference to the 'miserable, shameful, shabby Bill', *Parl. Deb.* (Commons), Vol. 649 (1961–2) 16 November 1961, col. 803. See P. M. Williams, *Hugh Gaitskell. A Political Biography* (London, 1979), for an account of Gaitskell's position.

489. For Nigel Fisher's contribution to the debate see *Parl. Deb.* (Commons), Vol. 649 (1961–2) 16 November 1961, cols 778–84, 785–8. Fisher admitted later to an error of judgement in opposing the 1962 Act. See ibid., Vol. 709 (1964–5) 23 March 1965, col. 385.

490. An impression of its activities can be gleaned from the *Lambeth Inter-Racial News.*

491. Heinemann, op. cit., and see above p. 241.

492. *The Economist*, 7 August 1965.

493. *The Guardian*, 25 September 1965.

494. Ibid., 23 February and 6 March 1968. See also D. Steel, 'Respectable Racialism', in ibid., 25 June 1968 and his book, *No Entry* (London, 1969). For biting satirical comment (and a possible strain of anti-Irish antipathy?) see Osbert Lancaster's cartoon in the *Daily Express* 28 February 1968, which contrasted the continuing free entry of the Irish, without British passports, and the controls thrown over Asians who had kept their links with Britain as Citizens of the United Kingdom and Colonies.

495. Peter Hain, quoted in Scobie, op. cit., p. 303.

496. See below p. 313 for the complexity in liberal assimilationist ideology.

497. See Ndem MA Thesis, p. 198; Glass, op. cit., passim. See below p. 314 for additional comment.

498. See the reference to the shift in Nigel Fisher's position over the question of immigration control in note 489 above. Fenner Brockway also came to the view that a measure of immigration control, mutually agreed with Commonwealth governments was needed in order to prevent social problems in Britain, particularly in the housing market. See 'The Colour Problem in Britain', *The Spectator*, 4 December 1964, p. 777.

499. See above pp. 84–5 and below pp. 312–15 for an echo of these arguments.

CONCLUSION

1. R. A. Butler in a debate on the Hungarian refugees in *Parl. Deb.* (Commons) Vol. 565, 21 February 1957, col. 83.

2. See above p. 4 for the definition of these categories.

3. J. Geipel, *The Europeans. An Ethnohistorical Survey* (London, 1969), pp. 163–4.

4. On the immigration into America see J. Higham, *Strangers in the Land. Patterns of American Nativism 1860–1925* (New Brunswick, N.J., 1955); M. A. Jones, *American Immigration* (Chicago, 1960); L. Dinnerstein, R. C. Nichols, D. M. Reimers, *Natives and Strangers. Ethnic Groups and the Building of America* (New York, 1979); N. Glazer (ed.), *Clamor at the Gates. The New American Immigration* (San Francisco, 1985).

5. Noticed in R. K. Kelsall, *Population* (London, 1979 edn), pp. 29–30, 115.

6. See, for example, above p. 146 for the comments of Karl Pearson. See also the remarks uttered at the People's Palace in 1902, reported in the *East London Observer*, 18 January 1902. See also the message of the photographs in P. Griffiths, *A Question of Colour?* (London, 1966).

7. The golden imagery is evident in both European and Asian perceptions of America. To Jews America was the 'goldeneh medina', El Dorado. See L. Rosten, *The Joys of Yiddish* (Harmondsworth, 1978 edn), p. 235. The golden

America of the Chinese is evident in B. L. Sung, *Mountain of Gold* (New York, 1967).

8. Orwell himself was part of the administration in Burma. See B. Crick, *George Orwell: A Life* (Harmondsworth, 1982 edn) Ch. 5 'An Englishman in Burma (1922–7)'. *Burmese Days* was published in New York in 1934. On the direction of emigration, the predominant theme of this paragraph, see Kelsall, op. cit., p. 29.

9. Kesall, op. cit., pp. 29–30; N. H. Carrier and J. R. Jeffery, *External Migration. A Study of the Available Statistics 1815–1950* (London, 1953), p. 114; J. Isaac, *British Post-War Migration* (Cambridge, 1954), p. 217.

10. See above p. 221.

11. Kelsall, op. cit., p. 115.

12. See above p. 22.

13. V. G. Kiernan, 'Britons Old and New', in C. Holmes (ed.), *Immigrants and Minorities in British Society* (London, 1978), p. 54.

14. See above p. 216.

15. See the discussion in J. A. Garrard, *The English and Immigration. A Comparative Study of the Jewish Influx 1880–1910* (London, 1971), pp. 213–14.

16. See T. S. Ashton's reference to this in his *An Economic History of England. The 18th Century* (London, 1955), p. 1. See also O. R. McGregor, 'Social Research and Social Policy in the Nineteenth Century', *British Journal of Sociology*, Vol. 8 (1957), pp. 147ff.

17. See below p. 376 for the definition of New Commonwealth. Pakistan left the Commonwealth in 1972 and Pakistanis ceased to be categorised as New Commonwealth immigrants in the summer of 1973.

18. *Select Committee on Race Relations and Immigration*, Vol. 1, Report 1977–8 (HC 303–11), pp. xv–xxv.

19. See above pp. 221–2, 224–5 for details.

20. E. G. Ravenstein, 'The Laws of Migration', *Journal of the Royal Statistical Society*, Vol. 42 (June 1885), pp. 167–227 and idem, 'The Laws of Migration', in ibid., Vol. 52 (June 1889), pp. 241–301.

21. There is a useful summary of more recent theories in B. M. Walter, 'The Geography of Irish Migration to Britain since 1939, with Special Reference to Luton and Bolton', unpublished D.Phil. Thesis, Oxford University, 1978, Introduction. See also P. White and R. Woods (eds), *The Geographical Impact of Migration* (London, 1980), Ch. 1.

22. Based on G. Germani, 'Migration and Acculturation', in P. Hauser (ed.), *Handbook for Social Research in Urban Areas* (Paris, 1964), pp. 159–78.

23. See above p. 220.

24. See above pp. 21–2. L. H. Lees, *Exiles of Erin. Irish Migrants in Victorian London* (Ithaca, New York, 1979), refers to the significance of this in assisting settlement in Britain.

25. See above pp. 221, 223, 227.

26. R. Miles, *Racism and Migrant Labour* (London, 1982), p. 161 carries this emphasis.

27. L. Gartner, *The Jewish Immigrant in England 1870–1914* (Detroit, 1960), p. 36 and J. A. Jackson, *The Irish in Britain* (London, 1963), pp. 11, 14.

28. The soul's requirement is in R. F. Foerster, *The Italian Emigration of Our Times* (New York, 1968 edn, first published 1919), p. 164. The emphasis of the 'big decision' is in M. Banton, *Racial and Ethnic Competition* (London, 1983), p. 310. The various tensions involved in the decision can be gleaned from Erskine Nicol's painting, 'Irish Immigrants', in the Graves Art Gallery, Sheffield. It is reproduced on the cover of R. Swift and S. Gilley (eds), *The Irish in the Victorian City* (London, 1984).

29. See above pp. 21–2, 28, 30, 218, 224, 225.

30. On the sojourning phenomenon see P. C. P. Siu, 'The Sojourner', *American Journal of Sociology*, Vol. 58 (1952), pp. 34–44. Siu's *The Chinese Laundryman. A Study in Social Isolation*, with its emphasis on the concept of the 'sojourner', was published in America in 1986. See below p. 376 for a definition of New Commonwealth.

31. E. Burke, *Reflections on the Revolution in France*, etc. (London, 1955 edn, first published 1793), p. 82, '. . . we are divided from you but by a slender dyke of about twenty-four miles and . . . the mutual intercourse between the two countries has lately been very great . . .'.

32. H. France, *La pudique Albion. Les nuits de Londres* (London, 1885).

33. See above for these various groups.

34. These groups underline the growing importance of the extra-European context in the production of refugees, emphasised in M. Marrus, *The Unwanted. European Refugees in the Twentieth Century* (New York, 1985), pp. 347, 364–5, 367–71.

35. On the distinction between 'acute' and 'anticipatory' refugees see E. F. Kunz, 'The Refugee in Flight. Kinetic Models and Forms of Displacement', *International Migration Review*, Vol. 7 (1973), pp. 125–46.

36. See above pp. 67, 126, 212.

37. H. Pollins, *Economic History of the Jews in England* (East Brunswick, N.J., London and Toronto, 1982), p. 131, 'Folk stories are common of the migrants who landed in England thinking they had made the complete journey to America'.

38. The reference here is to the tapes in the Bradford Heritage Recording Unit.

39. Noted, for example, in R. Paraszczak, 'Ukrainians in Rochdale. A Study of an Immigrant Community', unpublished Dissertation, Manchester College of Education, 1969, p. 25. See also Isaac, op. cit., pp. 175, 182, and J. A. Tannahill, *European Volunteer Workers in Britain* (Manchester, 1958), p. 97.

40. P. Kropotkin, *Memoirs of a Revolutionist* (Boston, New York, 1899), p. 377, '. . . As I went to the steamer, I asked myself with anxiety, "Under which flag does she sail – Norwegian, German, English?" Then I saw floating above the stern the union jack – the flag under which so many refugees, Russian, Italian, French, Hungarian and of all nations, have found an asylum. I greeted that flag from the depth of my heart'.

41. Colonel J. Wedgwood in *Parl. Deb.* (Commons), Vol. 114 (1919), 15 April 1919, col. 2791.

42. Noticed in that little classic, G. Mikes, *How to be an Alien* (London, 1965, first published 1946). See particularly 'In England everything is the other way round' (p. 14) and '. . . this whole language business is not at all easy' (p. 34). In more serious vein, the difficulties which the English language could pose, and the crucial significance of contact through language, the comments of Professor Max Perutz, in 'Britain in the Thirties. Far From Home', BBC 2 TV Programme, 30 June 1983, are of significance. See also P. Neuberg, 'Born of the Shock', *The Listener*, 2 January 1964, pp. 17–18, for the experiences of someone who arrived from Hungary in 1957.

43. See above.

44. See above Chs I, V.

45. See above for supporting evidence. Banton, op. cit., pp. 385–6 notes the differing experiences of West Indians in America and Great Britain, on which more work might be undertaken.

46. Often within their internal economies.

47. See above. There is also useful comment in J. O'Connor Power, 'The Irish in England', *Fortnightly Review*, Vol. XXVII (1880), p. 411. See also Lees, op. cit.

48. J. O'Donoghue, *In a Strange Land* (London, 1958), p. 43.

49. Pollins, op. cit., p. 145.
50. S. Ladbury, 'Choice, Chance, or No Alternative? Turkish Cypriots in Business in London', in R. Ward and R. Jenkins (eds), *Ethnic Communities in Business. Strategies for Economic Survival* (Cambridge, 1984), p. 112.
51. See p. 243 for a reference to women from the Indian sub-continent. The German governesses who came to Britain before the First World War and the Polish women, former inmates of Soviet camps, who came as dependants of the men in the Polish Resettlement Corps, are among the groups of women who have been neglected. The experiences of the *ayahs* (servants/nannies) brought to Britain by families returning from the sub-continent have also been scarcely investigated. There is useful material on women immigrants in the Manchester Jewish Museum Tapes and in the recordings held by the Bradford Heritage Recording Unit. For contrasting experiences see A. Wilson, *Finding A Voice* (London, 1981 edn), and F. Soloman, *From Baku to Baker Street* (London, 1984).
52. See above p. 230.
53. E. J. B. Rose (ed.), *Colour and Citizenship* (London, 1969), p. 57; S. Allen, *New Minorities, Old Conflicts. Asian and West Indian Immigrants in Britain* (London, 1971), pp. 147ff.
54. S. Aris, *The Jews in Business* (Harmondsworth, 1973 edn), p. 210; M. Anwar, *The Myth of Return. Pakistanis in Britain* (London, 1979); B. Kosmin, 'Exclusion and Opportunity. Traditions of Work amongst British Jews', in S. Wallman (ed.), *Ethnicity at Work* (London, 1979), pp. 37–70. Anwar, op. cit., draws an analogy between the Jewish and Pakistani responses. This was also the theme of a conference 'The Immigration Experience; Jews and Muslims', held at the Whitechapel Methodist Mission on 24 October 1984.
55. L. Hannah, 'Entrepreneurs and Social Change', LSE Inaugural Lecture 1983.
56. Noted in K. O'Connor, *The Irish in Britain* (Dublin, 1974), p. 101.
57. P. Werbner, 'From Rags to Riches – Manchester Pakistanis in the Textile Trade', *New Community*, Vol. 8 (1980), pp. 84–95.
58. Ward and Jenkins, op. cit., p. 234. See also the letter of Alfred Sherman in *The Times*, 4 February 1978, which used the Jews as exemplars and the critical response in ibid., 7 February 1978.
59. For one early twentieth-century stereotype of Jews as capitalists, which often involved a simultaneous stereotyping of Huguenots, see the comments of Charles Rolleston in the *New Liberal Review* (March 1904) pp. 236–7 which categorised Jews as 'sober, self-denying and intelligent' as well as 'very progressive'. For scathing comment on this image and later works which have treated all Jews as capitalists or incipient capitalists see J. Buckman, *Immigrants and the Class Struggle. The Jewish Immigrant in Leeds 1880–1914* (Manchester, 1983). The Chinese have sometimes been treated as the personification of the capitalist ethos. See M. Freeberne, 'Chinese Succeed in the UK', *Geographical Magazine* (1981), p. 707 for references to the minority as extremely 'hard-working', 'law-abiding', 'self-sufficient', 'patient and resourceful'. For a much-needed reminder that the success of Chinese restaurant owners depended upon the sweat of Chinese waiters and cooks, see 'Goodbye Chop Suey', Channel 4 TV Programme, 22 February 1985.
60. See J. A. Jackson, *The Irish in Britain* (London, 1963), p. 106, for one perspective and E. H. Hunt, *British Labour History 1815–1914* (London, 1981) pp. 168, 175 for another.
61. *Royal Commission on Alien Immigration*, British Parliamentary Papers, IX, 1903, pp. 19–20.
62. An emphasis contained in *Pollins*, op. cit.
63. See above pp. 233–4 for details of this debate.

64. See above.
65. See above Ch. I.
66. See above Ch. V.
67. The evocative reference to 'shabbiness' is from K. Little, *Negroes in Britain* (London, 1948), p. 93.
68. See above pp. 236–7 for earlier comment on such matters.
69. S. Patterson, 'The Poles', in J. L. Watson (ed.), *Between Two Cultures* (Oxford, 1977), p. 221 presented as one part of a generally optimistic survey of the Polish minority.
70. See above pp. 124, 125, 234.
71. See below p. 385. For additional comment see Banton, op. cit., p. 357. It is important to guard against those commentators who present a static picture in the housing and employment markets.
72. Jackson, op. cit., p. 57.
73. See the autobiographical account, A. A. Ford, *Telling the Truth. The Life and Times of the British Honduran Forestry Unit in Scotland (1941–44)* (London, 1984), p. 73, for a balanced survey.
74. It can be found in Albany Aisle in the north west of the Kirk.
75. See above pp. 107–9 on the violence. The centre spells the name as Wooton. Other sources give it differently. See, for example, P. Fryer, *Staying Power. The History of Black People in Britain* (London, 1984), pp. 300, 315, where it is given as Wotten.
76. For Priestley's comments on the Germans in Bradford see his *English Journey* (London, 1968 edn, first published 1934), pp. 160–1 and his article in *Civil Liberty*, No. 4 (April 1939), pp. 1–2.
77. Dead bones still live as a reminder of the past and as a hope for the future. Hence the attempt to transfer Sikorski's remains to Poland. See below p. 368 on this. See also *The Times*, 26 January 1982 for a report that the home secretary would not allow the Hungarian government to exhume General Lazar Meszaros. An 1848 émigré, Meszaros, a symbol of 'Hungary's fight for freedom from oppression', died in 1858 in Herefordshire.
78. There is photographic evidence in M. Kochan, *British Internees in the Second World War* (London, 1983), facing p. 83.
79. On Highgate see A. Briggs, *Marx in London. An Illustrated Guide* (London, 1982), pp. 75–81. This book covers other London sites associated with Marx.
80. See above p. 123.
81. *The Times*, 6 June 1959 noted the fixing of the plaque to Kossuth.
82. Ibid., 21 February 1983 noted the unveiling of the plaque to de Gaulle in Hampstead. Another symbol of the wartime resistance in London is the pub, The French House, in Dean Street, Soho, the name of which derives from this association.
83. There is comment on the Italian Hospital in J. Turner, 'Hospital, Italian Style', *New Society*, 21/28 December 1978, pp. 681–2.
84. See above Chs I, II for such developments.
85. W. J. Fishman, *The Streets of East London* (London, 1980 edn), p. 92. This work is an excellent re-creation of immigrant life in the area in text and also in photographs (taken by Nicholas Breach). See above for a first comment on such changes in the East End.
86. BHRU Tape M0006 is a vivid oral testimony to such changes. See above p. 242 for earlier comment.
87. The reference is to the poem, by Linton Kwesi Johnson on '1981' which 'woz a truly an historical okayjan', See J. Berry, *News for Babylon* (London, 1984), pp. 65–6.

88. Noted in M. Rodgers, 'Glasgow Jewry', in B. Kay (ed.), *Odyssey. The Second Collection* (Edinburgh, 1982), p. 120. See above p. 242 for earlier comment.

89. See R. Bowen, *Cricket* (London, 1970), for these cricketers.

90. This involvement still awaits its historian.

91. Kiernan, op. cit., provides numerous examples from different epochs. There is a little relevant comment in E. Cashmore, *Black Sportsmen* (London, 1982) Ch. 2.

92. Conrad became a British subject in 1886. On James see above p. 36. P. Anderson, 'Components of a National Culture', in A. Cockburn and R. Blackburn (eds.), *Student Power* (Harmondsworth, 1970 edn), pp. 229ff. carries critical comment on the 'White Emigration' from Europe; this is in sharp contrast to the usual praise accorded to these intellectual émigrés. See M. Freedman, *A Minority in Britain* (London, 1955), pp. 131–2 for such positive comment. An exhibition of 'Art in Exile in Great Britain 1933–1945' took place in Berlin and London in 1986. On Korda see K. Kulik, *Alexander Korda. The Man who could work Miracles* (London, 1975), Mikes came to Britain to report on the Munich Crisis and stayed; 'Passage to Britain'. Channel 4 TV Programme, 30 May 1984 contained some autobiographical details. Selvon, born in Trinidad, came to England in 1950. V. S. Naipaul, the brother of S. S. Naipaul (see below p. 389) was born in Trinidad in 1932. The Irish contribution to cultural life in Britain is often overlooked. Apart from Wilde, it should not be forgotten that Robert Tressell was born in Ireland. See *The Robert Tressell Papers* by Robert Tressell Workshop (Rochester, 1982), pp. 25–7. The cultural life of British society was also assisted by refugee publishers such as André Deutsch and also Walter Neurath, the founder of Thames and Hudson. See Pollins, op. cit., pp. 223–4. Finally, culture needs money and support, and the Jewish minority was important in both respects. See C. C. Aronsfeld, 'German Jews in Victorian England', *Leo Baeck Yearbook*, Vol. VII (1962), p. 314 who notes the role of Edgar Speyer in financing the Promenade Concerts and other ventures. This financial support should be regarded as one part of a more general charitable endeavour by German Jews, among whom Ernest Cassel's benefactions were colossal. Ibid., p. 325.

93. See above p. 243. See also particularly and specifically Stefan Zweig's difficulties in his *The World of Yesterday* (London, 1943). Zweig committed suicide soon afterwards.

94. E. Jones, *Sigmund Freud. Life and Work*, Vol. 1 (London, 1953), p. 195.

95. See the report in *The Times*, 7 March 1984.

96. For comment on the relationship between marginality and creativity see E. V. Stonequist, *The Marginal Man. A Study in Personality and Culture Conflict* (New York, 1937), p. xvii. See below for further comment on marginality.

97. S. Rushdie, 'The Empire Writes Back with a Vengeance', *The Times*, 3 July 1982, glances into the future, concentrating on literature.

98. See above for comment on the interaction between the Irish and the Church. For additional comment see E. Norman, *Roman Catholicism in England from the Elizabethan Settlement to the Second Vatican Council* (Oxford, 1985), pp. 73–4. G. A. Beck (ed.), *The English Catholics 1850–1950* (London, 1950), pp. 284–5 refers to the importance of the Irish in a number of fields but is silent on the Irish, and those of Irish-descent in official positions in the Church. So are Jackson, op. cit., and O'Connor, op. cit., both of which are generally eager to emphasise Irish contributions to society.

99. See above pp. 238–9 for comment on the religious life of these minorities. There is interesting personal oral evidence on intermarriage on BHRU Tapes B0089/02/28 and B0105/01/7.

100. Gartner, op. cit., Ch. VII. But see also p. 49 above.

101. Noticed in Little, op. cit., pp. 110–12, 149–50. See also M. M. Ally, 'History of Muslims in Britain', unpublished MA Thesis, Birmingham University, 1981.

102. See above pp. 225, 239, 265–6.

103. K. Lunn, 'Race Relations or Industrial Relations?', *Immigrants and Minorities*, Vol. 4 (1985), p. 9. The work of Lunn and Murdoch Rodgers has opened up the history of the Lithuanian minority. See, for example, K. Lunn, 'Reactions to Lithuanian and Polish Immigrants in the Lanarkshire Coalfield' in K. Lunn (ed.), *Hosts, Immigrants and Minorities. Historical Responses to Newcomers in British Society 1870–1914* (Folkestone, 1980), pp. 308–42; M. Rodgers, 'The Lanarkshire Lithuanians', in B. Kay (ed.), *Odyssey*, Vol. 1 (Edinburgh, n.d.), pp. 19–25; idem, 'The Anglo-Russian Military Convention and the Lithuanian Immigrant Community in Scotland, 1914–20', *Immigrants and Minorities*, Vol. 1 (1982), pp. 60–88, his 'Political Developments in the Lithuanian Community in Scotland c.1890–1923', in J. Slatter (ed.), *'From the Other Shore'. Russian Political Emigrants in Britain 1880–1917* (London, 1984), pp. 141–56 and 'Immigration into Britain: The Lithuanians', *History Today*, Vol. 35 (July, 1985), pp. 15–20.

104. H. Francis and D. Smith, *The Fed. A History of the South Wales Miners in the Twentieth Century* (London, 1980), p. 13.

105. See above pp. 42, 47–8, 239.

106. R. O'Higgins, 'The Irish Influence on the Chartist Movement', *Past and Present*, No. 20 (1961), pp. 83–96 and E. P. Thompson, *The Making of the English Working Class* (New York, 1963 edn), both notice this connection.

107. T. Gallagher, 'Scotland, Britain and Conflict in Ireland', in Y. Alexander and A. O'Day, *Terrorism in Ireland* (London, 1984), p. 60.

108. Slatter, op. cit., C. Weizmann, *Trial and Error* (New York, 1950 edn), Ch. VIIff.

109. See H. F. Srebrnik, 'The Jewish Communist Movement in Stepney. Ideological Mobilization and Political Victories in an East End Borough 1933–1945', unpublished Ph.D. Thesis, Birmingham University, 1983 and J. Jacobs, *Out of the Ghetto* (London, 1978) are useful accounts.

110. W. D. Rubinstein, *The Left, The Right and The Jews* (London, 1982) and G. Alderman, *The Jewish Community in British Politics* (Oxford, 1983) are both useful on recent Anglo-Jewish political behaviour.

111. See above pp. 170, 237–8.

112. See Chs I–IV.

113. See above Ch. III.

114. See the letter on this, and its implications, by David Lane, 'Colour Values in the House' in *The Times*, 12 December 1983.

115. See above pp. 56, 84, 138–9.

116. A. Sampson, in *The Anatomy of Britain* (London, 1962) and his later survey *The New Anatomy of Britain* (London, 1971), silently underline such powerlessness.

117. See above pp. 240ff.

118. Seen at its most extreme in G. S. Betts, 'Working Class Asians in Britain; Economic, Social and Political Changes, 1959–1979', unpublished M.Phil. Thesis, London University, 1981, p. 3.

119. The preceding definition of an ethnic group is taken from A. D. Smith, *The Ethnic Revival in the Modern World* (Cambridge, 1981), p. 66. Buckman, op. cit., has been criticised for discounting ethnic influences. See T. M. Endelman, 'Native Jews and Foreign Jews in London 1870–1914', in D. Berger (ed.), *The Legacy of Jewish Migration 1881 and Its Impact* (New York, 1983), pp. 127–8 for critical comment on Joe Buckman's work and also on J. White, *Rothschild Buildings: Life in an East End Tenement Block 1887–1920* (London, 1980). See Miles, op. cit., p. 71 and Lunn, op. cit., p. 3 for attempts to balance the respective influences of class and ethnicity.

120. Quoted in the prefatory section of R. Palmer, 'Immigrants Ignored: An

Appraisal of the Italians in Britain', unpublished MA Thesis, Sussex University, 1972.

121. Wilson, op. cit., p. 1.

122. Oral testimony from BHRU Tape B0016/03/42. For an additional yearning for 'The old familiar ways' see St Clair Drake's introduction to C. McKay, *A Long Way From Home* (London, 1985 edn, first published 1937), p. xvi.

123. See Michael Banton's swift dismissal of this position in his review of E. E. Cashmore and B. Troyna, *Introduction to Race Relations* in *New Society*, 13 October 1983, p. 70.

124. See above pp. 237–80. However, this is not to argue that ethnicity was incapable of modification or suppression. See, for example, S. Ladbury, 'The Turkish Cypriots: Ethnic Relations in London and Cyprus', in Watson, op. cit., pp. 315–16 and G. Dench, *Maltese in London. A Case Study in the Erosion of Ethnic Consciousness* (London, 1975).

125. Emphasised by Banton, *Racial and Ethnic Competition*, p. 306.

126. Apart from the 'confession' by George Mikes in 'Passage to Britain', Channel 4 TV programme, 30 May 1984, there was useful comment in 'To Bedford from Busso', Open University Programme, BBC 1 TV, 23 and 30 July 1983. The theme also appeared in B. Bottignolo, *Without a Bell Tower. A Study of the Italian Immigrants in South West England* (Rome, 1985). A number of Indian students, in Britain for only a short time, were marginalised. See Nehru's comment 'I have become a queer mixture of the East and West, out of my place everywhere and at home nowhere', quoted in F. Moraes, *Jawaharlal Nehru* (New York, 1956), pp. 42–3. See also the comment, 'As he grew up he must have suffered from a sense of isolation, of being stranded between two continents and belonging truly to neither' in V. G. Kiernan, 'Mohan Kumaramangalam in England', *Socialist India*, 23 February 1974, p. 6. For a literary treatment of marginality see K. Markandaya, *The Nowhere Man* (London, 1973).

127. See, for example, the comments of James Johnson before the *R.C.* 1903, p. 286. See also the comments of Colonel J. Wedgwood in *Parl. Deb.* (Commons), Vol. 114 (1919), 15 April 1919, col. 2791.

128. A point emphasised in D. Feldman, 'Immigrants and Workers: Englishmen and Jews: Jewish Immigration to the East End of London', unpublished Ph.D. Thesis, Cambridge University, 1985. For other critical comment on the concept of assimilation see J. Rex and R. Moore, *Race, Community and Conflict. A Study of Sparkbrook* (London, 1967), pp. 13–14.

129. See above p. 268 for reference to this development.

130. Allen, op. cit., p. 21.

131. Anwar, op. cit.; M. Berghahn, *German-Jewish Refugees in England* (London, 1984), Chs 6, 7.

132. Anwar, op. cit., p. 222; see also B. Dahya, 'Pakistanis in Britain. Transients or Settlers?', *Race*, Vol. XIV (1973), pp. 267–8 and R. C. Ballard, 'The Sikhs: The Development of South Asian Settlements in Britain' in Watson, op. cit., p. 41. For a recognition of the difficulties inherent in any attempt to classify the responses of the Irish, see the comprehensive summary article M. A. G. O'Tuathaigh, 'The Irish in Nineteenth Century Britain: Problems of Integration', *Transactions of the Royal Historical Society*, Vol. 31 (1981), pp. 150–1 and elsewhere.

133. A. Bryant, *A History of Britain and the British People* Vol. 1 *Set in a Silver Sea* (London, 1984) is a recent celebratory volume in this tradition.

134. Hence, the amazing statement, 'Nowhere does the Jew receive better treatment than in Great Britain. There is not a single disability. Anti-semitism does not exist', J. F. Fraser, *The Conquering Jew* (London, 1915), pp. 115–16. See also comment in the *Nottingham Guardian Journal*, 25 August 1958, written after the

violence of that year in the city, on the strength of toleration. See P. King, *Toleration* (London, 1976), on the difficult concept of toleration.

135. B. Porter, *The Refugee Question in Mid-Victorian Politics* (Cambridge, 1979), provides evidence of this strand of thought.

136. *Parl. Deb.* (Commons) Vol. 594 (1958–9), 30 October 1958, col. 418. The comment was made by Nigel Fisher.

137. J. Henderson, 'Race Relations in Britain', in J. A. G. Griffiths (ed.), *Coloured Immigrants in Britain* (London, 1960), p. 47.

138. N. Frangopulo, *Rich Inheritance. A Guide to the History of Manchester* (Manchester, 1962), p. 110.

139. R. M. Gatheru, *Child of Two Worlds* (London, 1964), p. 211.

140. W. Collins, *Jamaican Migrant* (London, 1965), p. 122.

141. *Bradford Telegraph and Argus*, 31 October 1984, in a letter entitled 'A Paradise with Shops full of Goods'. It was written by a Ukrainian, Vera Smereka, whose recollections may be heard on BHRU Tape B0046. M. Lang, *The Austrian Cockney* (London, n.d.), carries a dedication in similar vein.

142. See, for example, on this persistent theme, the poem of a Communard exile, ('Je respirais les brouillards noirs') quoted in P. K. Martinez, 'Paris Communard Refugees in Britain 1871–1880', unpublished D.Phil. Thesis, Sussex University, 1981, p. 298. See also K. Weston, *London Fog* (London, 1934); G. R. Fazackerley, *A Stranger Here* (London, 1959), p. 9; Z. Ghose, *Confessions of a Native Alien* (London, 1965), p. 62; L. R. Ercolani, *A Furniture Maker* (London, 1975), p. 28.

143. This is a restatement of my argument in 'Antisemitism and the BUF', in K. Lunn and R. C. Thurlow (eds.), *British Fascism* (London, 1980), pp. 125ff.

144. *The Observer*, 23 April 1967.

145. D. F. Karaka, 'The Colour Bar in Britain', *The Spectator*, 30 March 1934, p. 496. See also the comments by 'Marcus John' to 'Jacob Nelson' in Fazackerley, op. cit., p. 19.

146. *East London Observer*, 18 January 1902 carries an atmospheric report.

147. For an example of Clarke's opposition see, R. Skidelsky, *Oswald Mosley* (London, 1975), pp. 400–1. For reference to a 'very locally based and socially transmiited vigilantist culture' in the East End see C. T. Husbands, 'East End Racism 1900–1980. Geographical Continuities and Extreme Right-Wing Political Behaviour', *The London Journal*, Vol. 8 (1982), p. 21.

148. See above pp. 265–6.

149. Garrard, op. cit., presents this as a main theme.

150. N. Deakin, 'The Politics of the Commonwealth Immigrants Bill', *Political Quarterly*, Vol. 39 (1968), pp. 26–7 refers to the impact of Nazi policy.

151. For comment on the Irish in music hall culture, see M. J. Tebbutt, 'The Evolution of Ethnic Stereotypes: An Examination of Stereotyping, with Particular Reference to the Irish (and to a lesser extent the Scots) in Manchester during the late Nineteenth Century', unpublished M.Phil. Thesis, Manchester University 1982, pp. 26–66. On music hall criticism of foreign financiers, see J. Camplin, *The Rise of the Rich* (New York, 1979), p. 158 for 'I am the rich Mr. Hoggenheimer'. For comment on Jews see *Jewish Chronicle*, 10 January 1913. On the cultural importance of the music hall see G. S. Jones, 'Working-Class Culture and Working-Class Politics in London, 1870–1900: Notes on the Remaking of a Working Class', *Journal of Social History*, Vol. 7 (1973), pp. 477–8.

152. C. Davies, 'Some Ethnic Stereotypes in British Jokes', *Shakti*, Vol. 1 (1982), pp. 29–30.

153. All these terms appear in E. Partridge, *A Dictionary of Historical Slang* (Harmondsworth, 1972 edn).

154. Investigators have dug into some of these quarries, but not all of them. For

example, little attention has been paid at one extreme to graffiti. See S. Patterson, *Dark Strangers* (Harmondsworth, 1965 edn), p. 215 and D. Brooks, *Race and Labour in London Transport* (London, 1975), for evidence of its appearance. See also File A 49301 C/8C (Home Office), for the important scrawling which attempted to incite hostility towards Jews at the time of the Jack the Ripper murders. At the other extreme, the culling of memoirs and diaries, another fruitful source of comment, has not been pursued with much vigour. For an indication of what private thoughts might reveal see B. Webb, Diaries, Vol. 14(2), p. 29 for a reference to the Irish as 'that ramshackle race' (16 August 1892), LSE Archives; M. Davie (ed.), *The Diaries of Evelyn Waugh* (London, 1976), pp. 66 and 281 for revealing comment on two pianists, Solomon and Leslie Hutchinson, 'an appalling little Jew' (8 April 1920) and 'another nigger' (28 February 1927) respectively. See also D. Pryce Jones, *Cyril Connolly. Journal and Memoirs* (London, 1983), pp. 135–6.

155. See J. Banister, *England under the Jews* (London, 1901). For a discussion of Banister see my *Antisemitism in British Society, 1876–1939* (London, 1979), pp. 39–42. Banister was equally virulent in private correspondence. See his blistering letter to David Soskice, written on 25 January 1904, which contained the sentiment, 'It is a pity some kind of vermin exterminator could not be invented by which your vile breed could be eliminated', Soskice Archives, BA/1, House of Lords.

156. A. White (ed.), *The Destitute Alien* (London, 1892).

157. Arnold White, for example, could engage in the discourse of politics at the highest level. Material in PRO HO45/10063/B2840/A35; HO45/10063/B2840/A36; HO45/10063/B2840/A17 reveal his links with government. However, he was equally at home at the BBL meeting in the Peoples' Palace in 1902. See the report of his speech in the *East London Observer*, 18 January 1902. Oswald Mosley was also capable of operating at more than one level. On the one hand his prepared speeches were intended to present a reasoned case against Jewish interests: under pressure from hecklers, however, another rougher persona appeared. See W. F. Mandle, *Antisemitism and the British Union of Fascists* (London, 1968), p. 9 for his retorts at Manchester on 29 September 1934. For more general comment, relating to attitudes towards internment, see S. Orwell and I. Angus (eds), *The Collected Essays, Journalism and Letters of George Orwell*, Vol. 3 *As I Please 1943–1945* (Harmondsworth, 1978 edn), p. 383.

158. See above p. 264 and note 429 above.

159. See above Chs I, II, IV for reference to these matters.

160. Emphasised, for example, in that well-worn classic, G. W. Allport, *The Nature of Prejudice* (Reading, Mass., 1954), p. 14.

161. See above.

162. See above pp. 152, 202–3. For earlier less well-known discrimination see J. P. Green, '*In Dahomey* in London in 1903', *Black Perspectives in Music*, Vol. 11 (Spring 1983), p. 38 which notes the discrimination against Blacks practised by some public houses in Central London at the time of this musical. See also above pp. 230, 236, 266 for official discrimination.

163. For details see Holmes, *Antisemitism*, pp. 110–11. For a suggestion that anti-Semitism was rife in Oxford at this time see A. N. Wilson, *Hilaire Belloc* (London, 1984), p. 82.

164. Referred to in Martinez, D.Phil. Thesis, p. 137.

165. The categorisation is from Banton, *Racial and Ethnic Competition*, p. 120.

166. H. Joshua and T. Wallace with H. Booth, *To Ride the Storm* (London, 1983), pp. 7–55 attempts to remedy this deficiency but it does not dig deep and, in any case, is restricted in its coverage to Blacks and Chinese.

167. See above Ch. V on these episodes.

168. E. E. Burgess, 'The Soul of the Leeds Ghetto', *Yorkshire Evening News*, 19 January 1925. See S. Humphries, *Hooligans or Rebels? An Oral History of Working-Class Childhood and Youth 1889–1939* (Oxford, 1981), p. 198 for similar evidence relating to an attack on Armenians in London.

169. See above p. 266 on 'Paki-bashing'. See Bethnal Green and Stepney Trades Council, *Blood on the Streets* (London, 1978) for additional and more extended comment.

170. The claim was made by Mark Bonham Carter in his review of Bernard Porter's *The Refugee Question in Mid-Victorian Politics* which appeared in *The Times Literary Supplement*, 22 February 1980, p. 200.

171. See above Ch. II for a discussion of the Belgians and their interaction with sections of British society. P. Cahalan, *Belgian Refugee Relief in England during the Great War* (New York and London, 1982) leaves untouched many aspects of the reception accorded to the Belgians. As yet, there is no comprehensive study of responses towards the Hungarian refugees. The official papers for this period remained closed until 1987.

172. For expressions of hostility between minority groups see, for example, Berghahn, op. cit., pp. 187–9 (Jews v Blacks and Asians); E. B. Ndem, 'Negro Immigrants in Manchester', unpublished MA Thesis, London University, 1953, p. 199 (Irish v Blacks); R. O'Brien, 'The Establishment of the Jewish Minority in Leeds', unpublished Ph.D. Thesis, Bristol University, 1975, p. 398 (Irish v Jews); *The Times*, 21 May 1951 'Foreign Labour in Britain (1)' (Poles v EVWs); M. Banton, *The Coloured Quarter* (London, 1955), p. 181 (West African v Jews). For intra-minority tensions see Martinez, D.Phil. Thesis, p. 78 on the French; Feldman, Ph.D. Thesis, carries an emphasis on hostility from within Anglo-Jewry to newcomers from the Russian Pale.

173. C. Holmes and K. Lunn, 'Introduction', in Lunn, *Hosts, Immigrants and Minorities* p. 16. I. G. Cummings of the Colonial Office who addressed the Jamaicans arriving on the *Empire Windrush* in 1948 spoke better than he knew and saner than most other commentators, when he said: 'I am afraid you will have many difficulties. . . . All that remains for me to say is that I wish you the very best of luck'. Few were prepared to be so open in public on the prospect of intolerance. PRO LAB 8/1516.

174. See, for example, A. Watkinson, 'West Indian Technicians', *Time and Tide*, 11 July 1942, p. 556 and G. Alderman's letter in *The Times*, 17 August 1982.

175. See above Chs I, II, III. There are useful insights for understanding the economic background to hostility in E. Bonacich, 'A Theory of Ethnic Antagonism: The Split Labour Market', *American Sociological Review*, Vol. 37 (1972), pp. 547–59. As yet there is no satisfactory historical account of the sexual competition referred to here. There are passing references in J. Walvin, *Passage to Britain* (Harmondsworth, 1984). But see B. J. Bush, 'Britain and Black Africa in the Inter-War Years', unpublished Ph.D. Thesis, Sheffield University, 1986, for evidence of greater complexity, specifically in Black-White relations.

176. See above p. 149.

177. See above Ch. 1. See E. Bonacich, 'A Theory of Middleman Minorities', *American Sociological Review*, Vol. 38 (1973), pp. 583–94 for useful comment. For specific evidence see A. White, *The Problems of a Great City* (London, 1895), pp. 142, 147 and E. Tupper, *Seamen's Torch. The Life Story of Captain Edward Tupper, National Union of Seamen* (London, n.d. 1938?), pp. 23, 25, 51 on the Chinese and Banister, op. cit., and Lt Col. A. H. Lane, *The Alien Menace* (London 1932 edn), on the Jews.

178. M. Banton, 'It's Our Country', in R. Miles and A. Phizacklea (eds), *Racism and Political Action in Britain* (London, 1979), p. 230.

179. See above pp. 58, 62, 73–4, 76, 109, 154, 261 for example. Lunn, *Immigrants and Minorities*, pp. 19–20 makes the important point that impressions relating to competitive pressures in the labour market, drawn from a national perspective, could be contradicted by the conditions prevailing in local labour markets. This observation serves to underline the need for local studies. On the need for local investigations see F. A. D'Arcy's review of *Exiles of Erin* in *Saothar, Journal of the Irish Labour History Society*, Vol. 8 (1982), p. 62.

180. See above pp. 68–9, 81, 149, 256. Immigration restrictionists could draw local support from this context and often proceeded to chide open-door advocates for their isolation from local problems. The activities of Peter Griffiths in Smethwick provided one example of this. See P. Foot, *Immigration and Race in British Politics* (Harmondsworth, 1965), Ch. 2.

181. This constitutes a more complex analysis than that presented for example, in R. Miles and A. Phizacklea, *White Man's Country. Racism in British Politics* (London, 1984), p. 6 and its assertion that 'the problem is not "them" but "us"'.

182. J. Higham, 'Antisemitism in the Gilded Age', *Mississippi Valley Historical Review*, Vol. 43 (1956–7), p. 566.

183. Ibid.

184. Ibid.

185. See Allport, op. cit., on 'selective perception'. See also the poet's testimony in Countee Cullen's poem, 'Incident', in N. Cunard (ed.), *Negro. An Anthology* (New York, 1970 edn), p. 261 which recalls a racial insult and ends on the note 'I saw the whole of Baltimore/From May until December/of all the things that happened there/That's all that I remember'.

186. An argument presented in Holmes, *Antisemitism*, p. 232. See also Husbands, op. cit., p. 21; Miles, op. cit., p. 172.

187. For example, see, *R.C.* 1903, p. 177, Q5235, 'you cannot make land', in a discussion of population pressures in the East End Tannahill, op. cit., p. 64; J. Parry, *The Observer Colour Supplement*, 19 December 1971, p. 33; D. Hiro, *Black British, White British* (London, 1973 edn), p. 279. See above p. 149 for the attribution of economic and social problems in Liverpool to the presence of the Catholic Irish.

188. Hence the reference to the prospect of '. . . the Jew driving the Gentile out of the land . . .', *Eastern Post and City Chronicle*, 19 March 1887. For fears of an alien domination of Britain see Holmes, *Antisemitism*, Ch. 5 'Our New Masters?' In the case of Jews these fears evident in earlier publications such as Englishman, *Britons Awake!* (London, 1909) were brought together in *The Protocols of the Elders of Zion* which was first published in Britain in 1920. For other fears of domination see 'A City Man', *The Bubbles of Finance* (London, 1865) Ch. VIII which predicted a future in which the commercial threat of the Manchester Greeks was emphasised. The threat of Irish Catholic domination was a powerful fear in some Scottish circles. See above pp. 150–1. None of these anxieties matched the message of John Gray's fantastic story, *Park*, published in 1932 which offered a future in which Black Catholics dominated a society in which White Englishmen were consigned to living underground in caverns.

189. The best study, which covers part of this development, is J. M. MacKenzie, *Propaganda and Empire. The manipulation of British Public Opinion 1880–1960* (Manchester, 1985). J. A. Hobson, *The Psychology of Jingoism* (London, 1901) and his *Imperialism. A Study* (London, 1902), can still be read with profit. For those who prefer to see rather than read there is an excellent display of relevant artefacts in the Advertising and Packaging Museum at Gloucester.

190. Banton, 'It's Our Country'; see also J. Oldham, *Christianity and the Race Problem* (London, 1924), pp. 66–7.

191. Quoted in N. Evans, 'The South Wales Riots of 1919', *Llafur*, Vol. 3 (1980), p. 14. See PRO LAB 43/12 for similar sentiment by Alfred Dann, Secretary of the National Union of Agricultural Workers.

192. Taken from evidence in *R.C.* 1903, pp. 286, 287, 69, respectively. See also the novel by Walter Wood, *The Enemy in Our Midst. The Story of a Raid on England* (London, 1906), pp. 7–8 for similar sentiment. See also D. Lawrence, *Black Migrants, White Natives* (Cambridge, 1974), p. 85 which carries Nottingham voices referring to 'our place', 'our right' to council houses and 'our country'. See ibid., p. 114 for similar sentiment relating to employment.

193. *Eastern Post and City Chronicle*, 18 January 1902 (report of the monster meeting of the BBL). See Rex and Moore, op. cit., p. 60 for additional reference to a golden age.

194. The words are Horatio Bottomley's. See *Parl. Deb.* (Commons), Vol. 114 (1919), 15 April 1919, col. 2765.

195. BUF, *Britain and Jewry* (n.d., n.p.), p. 8.

196. See above for examples relating to the BBL and Powellism. See Banton 'It's Our Country', p. 230 for a recognition of hostility in the absence of personal contact. See also Glassman's work cited in Note 226 below.

197. Miles, op. cit., pp. 113–15 lays strong emphasis on this development. But his blunt analysis of industrial capitalism in Britain needs to be read alongside the sensitive treatment, particularly relating to the symbiosis of the bourgeoisie and aristocracy, in M. J. Wiener, *English Culture and the Decline of the Industrial Spirit 1850–1980* (Harmondsworth, 1981 edn), p. 8, etc. See also H. Cunningham, 'The Language of Patriotism, 1750–1914', *History Workshop Journal*, Vol. 12 (1981), pp. 8–33.

198. In this respect, the comments in M. D. Biddiss, 'Racial Ideas and the Politics of Prejudice 1850–1914', *Historical Journal* Vol. XV (1972), pp. 570–82 and A. Lee, 'Working Class Response to Jews in Britain 1880–1914', in Lunn, *Hosts, Immigrants and Minorities*, pp. 107–33 remain relevant and pertinent. The haziness of foreigners is revealed in BHRU Tape M0006/01/22 which notes that in postwar Bradford every foreigner was 'a "bloody Pole" ', irrespective of origin. George Mikes in 'Passage to Britain', Channel 4 TV Programme, 30 May 1984, revealed that one hostess on being told that Mikes was Hungarian, asked, 'Is he white?' For two classic examples of an almost total sense of superiority over foreigners see the account of the attitudes of Aldred Harmonsworth (Lord Northcliffe) in P. Brendon, *Eminent Edwardians* (London, 1979), pp. 38–9 and comment by Sir Horace Rumbold such as 'a nation of apes and cads' (the French); 'about the vainest people in Europe' (the Hungarians); 'a beastly people' (the Persians); 'untruthful, dirty and inclined to idleness' (the Spanish); 'damned fools' (the Austrians); 'thoroughly corrupt' (the Poles). These are culled from M. Gilbert, *Sir Horace Rumbold* (London, 1973), pp. 24, 25, 30, 61, 113, 187. It is refreshing to note that Rumbold, a senior Foreign Office official, could also comment, 'I have become definitely anti-foreign' (ibid., p. 451). For useful general comment see George Orwell's essays, 'Boys' Weeklies' in G. Orwell, *Inside the Whale and Other Essays* (Harmondsworth, 1966 edn), p. 187. L. P. Curtis, *Anglo-Saxons and Celts* (Bridgeport, Conn., 1968) attempted to categorise the English stereotype of the Irish. But see the fundamental critique in S. Gilley, 'English Attitudes to the Irish in England, 1780–1900', in Holmes, *Immigrants and Minorities in British Society*, pp. 81–110. Gilley acknowledges the greater degree of restraint in Curtis's *Apes and Angels. The Irishman in Victorian Caricature* (Newton Abbot, 1971). This is one of the few books which has for its

theme the visual representation of minorities, a potentially fruitful area of research.

199. The work of John Rex has laid particular emphasis on this theme and its significance. C. Bolt, *Victorian Ideas on Race* (London, 1971), touches in part, not always successfully on this issue. See also V. G. Kiernan, *The Lords of Human Kind. European Attitudes to the Outside World in the Age of Imperialism* (London, 1969). Future work will be able to draw upon E. W. Said, *Orientalism* (London, 1978), a provocative account of Europe and the East. There is also important, qualifying comment in S. J. R. Martin, 'British Images of the Zulu c.1820–1879', unpublished Ph.D. Thesis, Cambridge University, 1982. In recent years a good deal of work has been completed on education and Empire. See, for example, F. D. Glendenning, 'The Evolution of History Teaching in British and French Schools in the Nineteenth and Twentieth Centuries, with Special Reference to Attitudes to Race and Colonial History in History Textbooks', unpublished Ph.D. Thesis, Kent University, 1975 and D. W. Hicks, 'Textbook Imperialism, A Study of Ethnocentric Bias in Textbooks with Particular Reference to Geography', unpublished Ph.D. Thesis, Lancaster University, 1980. Such work is in sharp contrast to the lack of interest in Europe, although we have now M. J. Hickman, 'The Problemmatic Irish: An Analysis of the Presentation of Britain's Relationship to Ireland in School Texts', unpublished M.Sc. Thesis, Southbank Polytechnic, 1980. For the moulding impact of compulsory state education, see E. J. Hobsbawm, *The Age of Capital* (London, 1975), pp. 94–7. The generation of stereotypes from literature has also captured attention. See A. J. Hoskin, 'Racism and Popular Consciousness', unpublished MA Thesis, Birmingham University, 1973 (which is particularly useful on the Chinese) and D. Dabydeen (ed.), *The Black Presence in English Literature* (Manchester, 1985). As yet, however, there is no comparative study of immigrants and refugees in literature. A neglected source for fashioning perceptions is museum displays. See J. Jelinek, 'The Fields of Knowledge and Museum', *Journal of World History*, Vol. 14 (1972), pp. 13–23 (the issue as a whole is devoted to museums) and I. Melish, 'Black Man's Burden', *The Guardian*, 9 November 1974.

200. See above p. 160.

201. Banton, *Racial and Ethnic Competition*, p. 290.

202. See Husbands, op. cit., p. 21 and P. B. Rich, 'History and Theory in British Race Relations. Some General Reflections', ts. p. 15.

203. An issue which is discussed in A. Phizacklea and R. Miles, 'Working Class Racist Beliefs is the Inner City', in their *Racism and Political Action*, pp. 120–1. Their emphasis on immediate influences is supported by D. A. Lorimer, *Colour, Class and the Victorians* (Leicester, 1978) which relates ideas on race to an emergent class conflict in Britain.

204. For comment on the issue of racism see, for example, Banton, *Racial and Ethnic Competition*, pp. 33–4, 76–7 and J. Rex, *Race Relations in Sociological Theory* (London, 1970), Ch. 6 for contrasting emphases. See also M. D. Biddiss, 'Myths of the Blood', *Patterns of Prejudice*, Vol. 5 (September–October 1975), pp. 11–19; M. Banton, 'The Idiom of Race: A Critique of Presentism', *Research in Race and Ethnic Relations*, Vol. 2 (1980), pp. 21–42 and Banton's, 'Following the Colour Line', *The Times Literary Supplement*, 20 July 1984, p. 813. There is additional cautionary comment in G. M. Frederickson, *White Supremacy. A Comparative Study in American and South African History* (New York, 1981), p. xii. For examples of scientific racism see above on Pearson (p. 141) and Bertram (pp. 259–60). For somewhat lower-order expressions see Mudge (p. 141) and Gair (p. 149). For elementary-level expressions see above on Joseph Banister (p. 69), and, among more recent nationalists, the thought of Arnold Leese (on which see J. Morell,

'The Life and Opinions of A. S. Leese. A Study in Extreme Anti-Semitism', unpublished MA Thesis, Sheffield University, 1974, Ch. 3). For good examples of antipathy without reference to congenital differences see Gilley, op. cit., which in its study of attitudes towards the Irish is generally useful as an historical critique, of the lax usage of racist terminology. See also Mandle, op. cit., for a discussion of Oswald Mosley and the Jews, and, finally, the sentiments of Cyril Osborne (on whom see below p. 393), in particular his contribution to 'The Colour Problem in Britain', *The Spectator*, 4 December 1964, p. 777.

205. See above.

206. See above pp. 180, 200.

207. The caution expressed in R. Glass, *Newcomers. West Indian Immigrants in London* (London, 1960), pp. 218–19 should be noted. Lunn's emphasis in *Immigrants and Minorities* on local contexts carries an implicit warning on trying to correlate antipathy with macro-economic movements.

208. See above p. 59.

209. See above pp. 59–60.

210. See above pp. 67–72.

211. See above pp. 112–13.

212. See above pp. 263, 265–6.

213. See above Chs II, IV A. Smith 'War and Ethnicity: The Role of Warfare in the Formation, Self-Images and Cohesion of Ethnic Communities', *Ethnic and Racial Studies*, Vol. 4 (1981), pp. 375–97.

214. See above for all these matters.

215. There is useful imagery on this in E. Burney, *Housing on Trial* (London, 1967), p. 4. Lunn, *Immigrants and Minorities* emphasises the need for this approach. So does A. R. J. Kushner, 'British Antisemitism in the Second World War', unpublished Ph.D. Thesis, Sheffield University, 1986.

216. D. W. Bethlehem, *A Social Psychology of Prejudice* (London, 1985), pulls together a good deal of the literature.

217. The concept of prejudice is a problem in itself. See H. J. Ehrlich, *The Social Psychology of Prejudice* (New York, 1973), pp. 3–4. In the present study greater reference is made to antipathy, on which see M. Banton, *Race Relations* (London, 1967), p. 298. Banton's distinction between antipathy and prejudice was similar to the different varieties of prejudices emphasised in J. Dollard, 'Hostility and Fear in Social Life', *Social Forces*, Vol. 17 (1938), pp. 15–26. On Banister, see above p. 69 and note 155. The papers of another leading anti-Semite, Arnold Leese, which are held in the archives of The Britons, are sufficiently full and personal to allow for a speculative study of Leese's essential psychological condition, but the whole exercise would require caution.

218. See above p. 70.

219. See above pp. 253, 258, 260, 265–6.

220. For example, there are no significant surviving private papers relating to Horatio Bottomley, William Evans-Gordon, Howard Vincent or Cyril Osborne. An advertised search for any papers relating to Joseph Banister drew a blank. The numerous studies of Enoch Powell have had to make do without access to private papers. For rueful comment on the absence of information on immigration in papers that have survived see B. Gainer, *The Alien Invasion. The Origins of the Aliens Act of 1905* (London, 1972), p. 268 (Asquith) and p. 272 (Rosebery).

221. Rex and Moore, op. cit., p. 83. See also John Higham's remarks about the need to achieve a balance between the ideas inside men's heads and the world outside. See, Higham, *Strangers in the Land* (New York, 1963 edn), p. 403.

222. See above pp. 253, 258, 260, 265–6 on these individuals.

223. It was a prominent feature of some Scottish nationalist opposition to the Southern Irish and of Powellism. See above pp. 150–1, 265. Similar sentiments were heard at the time of the immigration from Russian Poland. See Holmes, *Antisemitism*, Chs 2, 6. See also the speech beginning 'We're overrun with 'em', in R. Tressell, *The Ragged Trousered Philanthropists* (London, 1965 edn, first published 1914), p. 22. Sidney Webb accepted that it was 'impossible to exclude the alien immigrant' and proceeded to emphasise the number of children 'freely born to the Irish Roman Catholics and the Polish, Russian and German Jews', but, noting that 'these races' were being influenced towards family limitation, commented, 'The ultimate future of these islands may be to the Chinese'. S. Webb, *The Decline in the Birth Rate*, Fabian Tract No. 131 (London, 1907, reprinted 1910), p. 17.

224. There is comment on this imagery in C. Holmes, 'The Impact of Immigration on British Society 1870–1970', in T. Barker and M. Drake (eds), *Population and Society in Britain 1850–1980* (London, 1982), pp. 178–9.

225. *Parl. Deb.* (Commons), Vol. 101 (1902), 29 January 1902, col. 1274.

226. G. P. Freeman, *Immigrant Labor and Racial Conflict in Industrial Societies. The French and British Experience 1945–1975* (Princeton, 1979), p. 275. For supporting comment on British society see the letter of G. Alderman in *The Times*, 17 August 1982 which refers to the anti-Jewish violence in South Wales in 1911. For a generally sceptical view about the importance of the weight of numbers see the letter of Ruth Glass in ibid., 16 February 1978. It should not be forgotten that hostility can exist in the absence – or virtual absence – of a particular group, see, B. Glassman, *Anti-Semitic Stereotypes Without Jews. The Images of Jews in England 1290–1700* (Detroit, 1975). See also Hiro, op. cit., p. 36, for additional comment on numbers.

227. See above pp. 64–8.

228. See above pp. 57–61, 65–73.

229. See above pp. 120, 148–52, 226, 257–69.

230. See above pp. 32, 77–82, 218, 253–5. This reverses the argument presented in Ng Kwee Choo, 'Some Aspects of the Social Organization of Chinese engaged in the Restaurant Business in London', unpublished MA Thesis, London University, 1965, p. 5.

231. Parry, op. cit., p. 28.

232. Allen, op. cit., pp. 59–60; Brooks, op. cit., p. 333.

233. See above pp. 277–8.

234. Porter, op. cit., notes the increasingly tough policy on alien immigration. Feldman, Ph.D. Thesis, discusses the activities of Anglo-Jewry. A useful summary of the actions of the Anglo-Jewish elite was available years ago in V. D. Lipman, *A Century of Social Service 1859–1959. The History of the Jewish Board of Guardians* (London, 1959), pp. 94–7. See also *Select Committee on Emigration and Immigration*, British Parliamentary Papers, XI (1888), p. 166, for early reference to such activity by the Board of Guardians for the Relief of the Jewish Poor.

235. Porter, op. cit., p. 218 notes the nature of the Act. Garrard, op. cit., Ch. VII is useful on Liberal responses to the Act. For the place of the Act in British immigration control see V. Bevan, 'The Development of British Immigration Law' (forthcoming), pp. 67–72. [Published, 1986.]

236. See above pp. 112–14 for the developments. Of these the 1919 Act would repay greater attention than has so far been focused upon it.

237. Porter, op. cit., is the best source.

238. C. Holmes, 'Trotsky and Britain. The Closed File', *Society for the Study of Labour History Bulletin*, No. 39 (1979), pp. 33–8.

239. Quoted in Marrus, op. cit., p. 11.

240. Noted, cynically, by Sydney Silverman when Hungarian refugees were arriving

in Britain. See *Parl. Deb.* (Commons), Vol. 560 (1956–7), 20 November 1956, col. 1627. For later comment see A. Wilson, 'Hardly a Safe Sanctuary', *New Statesman*, 19 October 1984, pp. 16–17.

241. On Delgado, a leader of opposition to Salazar's rule in Portugal, see *Parl. Deb.* (Commons), Vol. 685 (1963–4), 26 November 1963, col. 43 (written answers); ibid., Vol. 705 (1964–5), 21 January 1965, col. 112 (written answers); ibid., 4 February 1965, cols 308–9 (written answers); ibid., Vol. 707 (1964–5), 4 March 1965, cols 295–6 (written answers). On Amekrane see *The Times*, 14 August 1974. There is a full discussion in Bevan, 'Immigration Law'.

242. See, above on Jewish Emancipation. The continuing restrictions on aliens are noted in B. Hepple, *Race, Jobs and the Law* (London, 1968), pp. 49–50. See above p. 230 for specific comment on the restrictions on EVWs. S. Cohen, 'Anti-Semitism, Immigration Controls and the Welfare State', *Critical Social Policy*, Vol. 5 (1985), pp. 73–92 carries some untidy reflections on welfare discriminations.

243. See above p. 257 on the 1914 and 1948 legislation.

244. See above pp. 260–9 on this legislation.

245. A. Phizacklea and R. Miles, *Labour and Racism* (London, 1980), pp. 10ff carries this emphasis.

246. See above p. 236.

247. See my discussion of the BBL in *Antisemitism*, pp. 89–96. A good insight into the exploitation of alien immigration for personal political gain can be gained from an examination of the press cuttings and political ephemera in the David Hope Kyd collection at the LSE.

248. See above pp. 260, 265–7 on both the Birmingham caucus and Powellism.

249. See above Chs II, IV.

250. For a recent discussion see, J. Williams, 'Redefining Institutional Racism', *Ethnic and Racial Studies*, Vol. 8 (1985), pp. 323–48.

251. See above pp. 71–3, 112–14.

252. See above p. 309.

253. See above p. 230.

254. See above pp. 256–69.

255. See above.

256. See above. See also Holmes, *Antisemitism*, pp. 101, 132, 197. For comment on the importance of the role of the central authorities in influencing such tensions, see A. D. Grimshaw, 'Relationships among Prejudice, Discrimination, Social Tension and Social Violence', *Journal of Intergroup Relations*, Vol. 2 (1961), p. 303.

257. The quotation is from a perceptive aperçu by Michael Dummett in *The Sunday Times*, 30 November 1980. For additional comment see my 'Antisemitism and the BUF', pp. 126–7. For one useful case study see my article, 'The German Gypsy Question in Britain 1904–06', *Journal of the Gypsy Lore Society*, 4s Vol. 1 (1978), pp. 248–67. See also above p. 256 for changing official attitudes to African stowaways and above pp. 211–13 for the official recruitment of European refugee labour after the Second World War.

258. K. Marx to S. Meyer and A. Vogt, 9 April 1870 in *Marx-Engels. Selected Correspondence* (London, 1956), pp. 286–7.

259. See above for such hostility. There are some useful comments on this issue in Miles, op. cit., pp. 85, 119, 146–7, 174.

260. Evident, for example, during the internment episode of the Second World War and the postwar immigration from the Caribbean and the Indian sub-continent.

261. Higham, *Mississippi Valley Historical Review*, p. 563.

262. Noted in G. Anderson, *Victorian Clerks* (Manchester, 1976), p. 62.

263. A. White, *The English Democracy* (London, 1894), pp. 154, 165. It is interesting to

note that in 1922 when his contact with anti-Semitic circles was still evident he could state in a letter to Sir Isodore Spielmann, that he was compelled 'to do my little in endeavouring to make an alliance of friendship between the Jewish race and the English race'. This was predicated on the view that English society required to benefit from Jewish power and influence. WHI/113 A. White to I. Spielmann, National Maritime Museum Archives, Greenwich. In common with many others, White's opposition towards Jews blended fear and admiration. See particularly his book, *The Modern Jew* (London, 1899).

264. The reference to a 'rhetorical ruse' is from L. R. Teel, 'The Life and Times of Arnold Henry White: The Fusion of Pre-Modern Politics and Journalism in Victorian and Edwardian Britain', unpublished Ph.D. Thesis, Georgia State University, 1984, p. 273.

265. For particular evidence of such hedging see V. Grayson, 'Among the Foreign Aliens. A Russian Ghetto', *Clarion*, 27 June 1911 which juxtaposes pro-Jewish and anti-Jewish sentiments. However, Higham, *Mississippi Valley Historical Review*, pp. 562–6 writes of more than a ruse. See also Lee, op. cit., pp. 110–11; Phizacklea and Miles, *Labour and Racism*, pp. 131–2; R. E. Lane, *Political Ideology* (New York, 1962), p. 377.

266. Higham, *Mississippi Valley Historical Review*, p. 562.

267. Quoted in Lunn, *Immigrants and Minorities*, p. 5.

268. See Foot, op. cit., pp. 51–2 for the post-election pronouncements of Peter Griffiths.

269. Gilley, op. cit., p. 85.

270. L. Sponza, 'The Italian Poor in Nineteenth Century Britain', unpublished Ph.D. Thesis, London University, 1984, p. 165.

271. MO Report, 523 B, 10 December 1940. The wartime Mass Observation Surveys are generally useful for illustrating the complexity of attitudes. See, for example, MO Report 541, 9 January 1941 and MO Report 1669Q, April 1943.

272. A. T. Carey, *Colonial Students* (London, 1956), p. 143.

273. See the comment by M. Le Lohé, 'The Effects of the Presence of Immigrants upon the Local Political Situation in Bradford, 1945–77', in Miles and Phizacklea, op. cit., p. 186.

274. Lunn, *Immigrants and Minorities*, pp. 2, 23–4. This essay is much more sophisticated than 'The Socialist Attitude', in Garrard, op. cit., Ch. 10.

275. B. Williams, 'The Anti-Semitism of Tolerance: Middle Class Manchester and the Jews, 1870–1900', in A. J. Kidd and K. W. Roberts (eds), *City, Class and Culture* (Manchester, 1873), p. 94. See also above p. 143. See J. Salter, *The Asiatic in England* (London, 1873), p. 12 for evidence of mixed motives in the treatment of Muslims stranded in Britain and succoured by the Strangers' Home for Asiatics. See also above p. 77 for Arnold White's comment on the Italians in Britain.

276. Hiro, op. cit., p. 321. See above pp. 251, 253 for similar attitudes towards Polish and Irish minorities, respectively. Much work remains to be done on tensions within the liberal assimilationist tradition. There is some additional, sobering comment on liberal thought in S. Kitzinger, 'Conditional Philanthropy towards Coloured Students in Britain', *Phylon*, Vol. 21 (1960), pp. 167–72.

277. See above for references to gypsies and Blacks as entertainers. Moreover, full equality did not prevail within the sporting world. See above pp. 153, 202–3 for evidence of restrictions on Black boxers, even those born in Britain and for the incidents involving Robeson and Constantine. For continuing evidence of discrimination in sport see D. Miller, 'First Class Athletes. Second Class Citizens', *The Times*, 16 August 1985.

278. H. Jetson, 'The Responses of People in Wolverhampton to New Commonwealth and Pakistani Immigration in the Years 1958 and 1968', unpublished BA Dissertation, Sheffield University (Department of Economic and Social History), 1985, pp. 17–19.

279. Patterson, *Dark Strangers*, p. 241, underlines this.

280. Quoted in M. Banton, 'Social Acceptance and Rejection', in R. Hooper (ed.), *Colour in Britain* (London, 1965), p. 115.

281. For Cassel's essential loneliness see B. Connell, *Manifest Destiny* (London, 1953), p. 82.

282. Ndem, MA Thesis, p. 198. See also B. A. Kosmin, 'J. R. Archer (1863–1932): A Pan-Africanist in the Battersea Labour Movement', *New Community*, Vol. VII (1979), p. 430 for comment of general significance.

283. Banton, *Racial and Ethnic Competition*, p. 132 carries comment on this, based on American society.

284. See above p. 61.

285. If British sailors worried about competition from the Chinese, Charles Dilke could welcome their replacement by the Chinese, 'the Irish of Asia', since 'Anglo-Saxons were too valuable to be used as ordinary seamen'. C. Dilke, *Greater Britain. A Record of Travel* (London, 1885), pp. 187–8. See above pp. 78–9 for the fears of those who encountered Chinese competition at sea.

286. See above pp. 74, 76–7.

287. See above p. 303.

288. The social distance theory is traditionally associated with E. S. Bogardus, *Immigration and Race Attitudes* (Boston, 1928). For a comment on the perception of 'virtues' (to one source) or 'vices' (to another) see J. A. Hobson, *Problems of Poverty* (London, 1891), pp. 58–60 which contains important comment on Jewish immigrants. See also the Civil Servant's comment in 1906 that '. . . the real objection to Chinese consists in their virtues rather than their vices' in PRO HO 45/11843/139147/8.

289. P. C. Campbell, *Chinese Coolie Emigration to Countries within the British Empire* (London, 1923) and P. Richardson, *Chinese Mine Labour in the Transvaal* (London, 1982), are useful on the Chinese. For the Indians see H. Tinker, *A New System of Slavery. The Export of Indian Labour Overseas, 1830–1920* (London, 1974). See also K. Saunders, *Indentured Labour in the British Empire* (London, 1983).

290. See J. Zubrzycki, *Polish Immigrants in Britain. A Study of Adjustment* (The Hague, 1956), pp. 51–3 and N. Davies, *God's Playground. A History of Poland in Two Volumes, Vol. II 1795 to the Present* (Oxford, 1981), Ch. 20 'Golgota'.

291. Dinnerstein, et al., op. cit., pp. 233–6, 240–2. The early development of such controls was of interest to the British government at a time of alien immigration from Europe. See, *S. C. Emigration and Immigration*, 1888, *Select Committee on Emigration and Immigration*, British Parliamentary Papers, Vol. X (1889) and *Reports to the Board of Trade on Alien Immigration to the United States*, British Parliamentary Papers, Vol. LXXI (1893–4).

292. See Glazer, op. cit., and D. Reimers, 'South and East Asian Immigration into the United States: From Exclusion to Inclusion', *Immigrants and Minorities*, Vol. 3 (1984), pp. 30–48.

293. Freeman, op. cit.; C. Kindleberger, *Europe's Post-War Growth. The Role of Labour Supply* (Cambridge, Mass., 1967); S. Castles and G. Kosack, *Immigrant Workers and Class Structure in Western Europe* (London, 1973); M. Castells, 'Immigrant Workers and Class Struggle in Advanced Capitalism: The Western European Experience', *Politics and Society*, Vol. 5 (1975), pp. 33–66; M. Nikolinakos, 'Notes towards a General Theory of Migration in Late Capitalism', *Race and Class*,

Vol. 17 (1975), pp. 5–18 provide information from varying perspectives. The loneliness attaching to the lives of migrant workers is well captured in R. W. Fassbinder's film, *Fear Eats the Soul* which was released in Britain in 1974.

294. Marrus, op. cit., pp. 27–39.

295. See, for example, H. S. Hughes, *The Sea Change. The Migration of Social Thought 1930–1965* (New York, 1975); H. A. Strauss, *Jewish Immigrants of the Nazi Period in the U.S.A.* (4 vols, New York, 1979–82); J. C. Jackman, *The Muses Flee Hitler. Cultural Transfer and Adaptation 1930–1945* (Washington DC, 1983); M. Jay, *Permanent Exiles. Essays on the Intellectual Migration to America* (New York, 1985).

296. Noted in Marrus, op. cit., pp. 369–71.

297. G. Orwell, *Homage to Catalonia* (London, 1970 edn, first published 1938), p. 211.

Select Bibliography

In view of the documentation already provided, a full bibliography is hardly required. What follows, therefore, is a list of printed items, which had appeared by February 1986 and from which I derived particular academic benefit. It should be stressed that the inclusion of an item in this bibliography does not necessarily mean that I agree with the arguments it puts forward.

M. Anwar, *The Myth of Return. Pakistanis in Britain* (London, 1979).

C. C. Aronsfeld, 'German Jews in Victorian England', *Leo Baeck Yearbook*, Vol. VII (1962).

M. Banton, *The Coloured Quarter* (London, 1954).

A. G. Bennett, *Because they know not* (London, 1959?).

J. C. Bird, 'Control of Enemy Alien Civilians in Great Britain, 1914–1918', Ph.D. Thesis, London University, 1981.

J. Buckman, *Immigrants and the Class Struggle. The Jewish Immigrant in Leeds 1880–1914* (Manchester, 1983).

L. P. Curtis, *Apes and Angels. The Irishman in Victorian Caricature* (Newton Abbot, 1971).

G. Dench, *The Maltese in London. A Case Study in the Erosion of Ethnic Consciousness* (London, 1975).

N. Evans, 'The South Wales Race Riots of 1919', *Llafur*, Vol. 3 (1980).

D. Feldman, 'Immigrants and Workers: Englishmen and Jews: Jewish Immigration to the East End of London, 1880–1906', Ph.D. Thesis, Cambridge University, 1985.

W. J. Fishman, *The Streets of East London* (London, 1979) particularly its photographic evidence.

P. Foot, *Immigration and Race in British Politics* (Harmondsworth, 1965).

P. Fryer, *Staying Power. The History of Black People in Britain* (London, 1984).

L. Gartner, *The Jewish Immigrant in England 1870–1914* (Detroit, 1960).

R. Glass, *Newcomers. West Indians in London* (London, 1960).

D. Hinds, *Journey to an Illusion. The West Indian in Britain* (London, 1966).

G. Hirschfeld (ed.), *Exile in Great Britain* (London, 1984).

C. Holmes, *Antisemitism in British Society 1876–1939* (London, 1979).

C. Holmes (ed.), *Immigrants and Minorities in British Society* (London, 1978).

J. A. Jackson, *The Irish in Britain* (London, 1963).

L. H. Lees, *Exiles of Erin. Irish Migrants in Victorian London* (Manchester, 1979).

D. Lawrence, *Black Migrants White Natives. A Study of Race Relations in Nottingham* (Cambridge, 1974).

K. Little, *Negroes in Britain* (London, 1948 and 1972).

D. Lorimer, *Colour, Class and the Victorians* (Leicester, 1978).

K. Lunn (ed.), *Hosts, Immigrants and Minorities. Historical Responses to Newcomers in British Society 1870–1914* (Folkestone, 1980).

D. MacAmhlaigh, *An Irish Navvy. Diary of an Exile* (London, 1964).

M. Marrus, *The Unwanted. European Refugees in the Twentieth Century* (New York, 1985).

P. K. Martinez, 'Paris Communard Refugees in Britain 1871–1880', D.Phil. Thesis, Sussex University, 1981.

R. Miles, *Racism and Migrant Labour* (London, 1982).

R. B. Perks, '"A Feeling of Not Belonging". Interviewing European Immigrants in Bradford', *Oral History*, Vol. 12 (1984).

H. Pollins, *Economic History of the Jews in England* (East Brunswick, N.J., London and Toronto, 1982).

J. Rex and R. Moore, *Race, Community and Conflict. A Study of Sparkbrook* (London, 1967).

P. B. Rich, 'Philanthropic Racism in Britain: The Liverpool University Settlement, the Anti-Slavery Society and the Issue of 'Half-Caste' Children, 1919–51'. *Immigrants and Minorities*, Vol. 3 (1984).

M. Rodgers, 'The Anglo-Russian Military Convention and the Lithuanian Immigrant Community in Lanarkshire, Scotland, 1914–20', *Immigrants and Minorities*, Vol. 1 (1982).

E. J. B. Rose (ed.), *Colour and Citizenship* (London, 1969).

A. Sivanandan, *A Different Hunger. Writings on Black Resistance* (London, 1983).

J. Slatter (ed.), *'From the Other Shore'. Russian Political Emigrants in Britain 1880–1917* (London, 1984).

L. Sponza, 'The Italian Poor in Nineteenth-Century Britain', Ph.D. Thesis, London University, 1984.

H. F. Srebrnik, 'The Jewish Communist Movement in Stepney. Ideological Mobilization and Political Victories in an East London Borough, 1933–1945', Ph.D. Thesis, Birmingham University, 1983.

J. A. Tannahill, *European Volunteer Workers in Britain* (Manchester, 1958).

M. A. G. O'Tuathaigh, 'The Irish in Nineteenth Century Britain: Problems of Integration', *Transactions of the Royal Historical Society*, Vol. 31 (1981).

J. Walvin, *Black and White. The Negro in English Society 1555–1945* (London, 1973).

B. Wasserstein, *Britain and the Jews of Europe 1939–1945* (Oxford, 1979).

J. Watson (ed.), *Between Two Cultures* (Oxford, 1977).

J. Zubrzycki, *Polish Immigrants in Britain. A Study of Adjustment* (The Hague, 1956).

The tastes of those interested in immigration are generally catered for in journals such as *Ethnic and Racial Studies*, *Immigrants and Minorities* and *Race and Class*. A weather eye should also be cocked towards more specialised journals such as *Jewish Social Studies*, the *Journal of the Gypsy Lore Society*, *Llafur* and *Saothar*. Finally, there is an excellent guide to theses in the shape of V. F. Gilbert and D. Tatla (eds), *Immigrants, Minorities and Race Relations. A Bibliography of Theses presented at British and Irish Universities 1900–1981* (London, 1984). This compilation is updated at intervals in the journal *Immigrants and Minorities*.

Index

PERSONS

PLACES

SUBJECTS